Empowering Women in Higher
Education and Student Affairs

Empowering Women in Higher Education and Student Affairs

Theory, Research, Narratives, and Practice From Feminist Perspectives

Edited by

PENNY A. PASQUE
SHELLEY ERRINGTON NICHOLSON

Foreword by

LINDA J. SAX

ACPA
College Student
Educators International

1996–2011 15ᵀᴴ ANNIVERSARY
Stylus
PUBLISHING, LLC.

Published by Stylus Publishing, LLC
22883 Quicksilver Drive
Sterling, Virginia 20166-2102

Library of Congress Cataloging-in-Publication-Data
Empowering women in higher education and student affairs : theory,
research, narratives, and practice from feminist perspectives / edited
by Penny A. Pasque and Shelley Errington Nicholson ; foreword by
Linda J. Sax.
     p.   cm.
  Includes bibliographical references and index.
  ISBN 978-1-57922-350-2 (pbk. : alk. paper)
  1. Women in higher education.   2. Women college teachers.
3. Women college students.   4. Feminism and higher education.
I. Pasque, Penny A.   II. Nicholson, Shelley Errington.
  LC1567.E47   2011
  378.0082–dc22

                                                        2010018756

13-digit ISBN: 978-1-57922-350-2 (paper)

Printed in the United States of America

All first editions printed on acid free paper
that meets the American National Standards Institute
Z39-48 Standard.

Bulk Purchases

Quantity discounts are available for use in workshops
and for staff development.
Call 1-800-232-0223

First Edition, 2011

10   9   8   7   6   5

We would like to dedicate this book to all the people who intentionally empower women on a daily basis.

In addition, Shelley would like to thank Sue and Tim Errington for never setting boundaries based on gender and to Scott Nicholson for being a feminist husband and husband to a feminist. Penny would like to thank her mom, Suzanne Haberstroh, for her perseverance as a single mother and her partner, Frank Kaminsky, for endless love and support.

Materials for Course and/or Professional Development Using This Book

A slideshow presentation and annotated bibliography are available to download for courses and professional development opportunities using this text at: http://www.styluspub.com/resrcs/other/1579223508_otherlink.pdf

The materials were funded by a grant through the American College Personnel Association (ACPA) Commission for Professional Preparation.

They have been developed for use in courses such as: gender in higher education and student affairs, diversity in higher education, and intergroup dialogue courses that focus on gender. The slideshow is also suitable for a class session or workshop on women and leadership, mentoring between women, intersectionality, or other related topics.

Contents

Acknowledgments   xi

Foreword   xiii
    Linda J. Sax

Preface   xv
    Penny A. Pasque and Shelley Errington Nicholson

Section One
SETTING THE CONTEXT
A Contemporary (Re)Examination of Women in Higher Education and Student Affairs   **1**

1   AN INTRODUCTION TO FEMINISM AND FEMINIST PERSPECTIVES IN HIGHER EDUCATION
AND STUDENT AFFAIRS   3
    Shelley Errington Nicholson and Penny A. Pasque

2   REFLECTIONS FROM "PROFESSIONAL FEMINISTS" IN HIGHER EDUCATION
    Women's and Gender Centers at the Start of the Twenty-First Century   15
    Susan Marine

3   "EACH GENERATION OF WOMEN HAD TO START ANEW"
    A Historical Analysis of Title IX Policy and Women Leaders in the Cocurriculum   32
    Jennifer Lee Hoffman

4   THE POWERFUL COLLABORATIONS BETWEEN DEANS OF WOMEN AND DIRECTORS OF
PHYSICAL EDUCATION
    Syracuse University's Contributions to the History of Student Affairs, 1930s–1950s   47
    Thalia Mulvihill

    Narratives on Gender and Feminism
    From Disembodied to Whole: Carving Out Space for My Race and Gender Identities   60
      Rosemary J. Perez
    She's Just a Girl   62
      Cindy Clark
    Storied Institutions: The Complexity of Catholic Women's Colleges   63
      Kelly T. Winters

Section Two
CONSIDERING EXPERIENCES OF WOMEN
THROUGHOUT THE ACADEMY
An Exploration of Undergraduates, Graduate Students, and Administrators   67

5 FEMALE GRADUATE STUDENTS' WORK–LIFE BALANCE AND THE STUDENT
   AFFAIRS PROFESSIONAL   69
   Racheal L. Stimpson and Kimberly L. Filer

6 HIGH-ACHIEVING WOMEN
   Navigating Multiple Roles and Environments in Academic and Student Affairs   85
   Monica Marcelis Fochtman

7 TOWARD SELF-INVESTMENT
   **Using Feminist and Critical Race Lenses to Analyze Motivation, Self-Esteem, and
   Empowerment of Women's College Students**   104
   Annemarie Vaccaro

8 THE INFLUENCE OF GENDER
   A Conceptual Model From Women Doctoral Students in Computer Science   121
   Jennifer Sader

   Narratives on Gender and Feminism
   The Story of One *YAO* Woman   138
   Dorothy B. Nkhata
   Growing Up at Douglass   139
   Jennifer Dudeck-Lenis
   Intercultural Contexts When Traveling Abroad   141
   Kristie Atkinson
   Inconsistency as Constant: One's Story of Reclaiming Gender   143
   Robbie

Section Three
EXPLORING IDENTITY CONTEXTS
**The Intersections of Class, Gender, Race, and Sexual Orientation
for Faculty, Administrators, and Students**   145

9 HOW RACE MATTERS
   **Race as an Instrument for Institutional Transformation: A Study of Tenured Black
   Female Faculty**   147
   Venice Thandi Sulé

10 LIFE STORIES OF THE DAUGHTER OF FIRST-GENERATION ITALIAN IMMIGRANTS
   **Gender, Ethnicity, Culture, and Class Intertwine to Form an Italian
   American Feminist**   163
   Florence M. Guido

11   ECONOMICALLY DISADVANTAGED WOMEN IN HIGHER EDUCATION
       Hearing Their Stories and Striving for Social Justice   178
       Penny J. Rice

12   SISTER CIRCLES
       A Dialogue on the Intersections of Gender, Race, and Student Affairs   194
       Amanda Suniti Niskodé-Dossett, Mariama Boney,
       Linda Contreras Bullock, Cynthia Cochran, and Irene Kao

13   USING QUEER THEORY TO EXPLORE LESBIAN COLLEGE STUDENTS' MULTIPLE
       DIMENSIONS OF IDENTITY   213
       Elisa S. Abes and David Kasch

14   IDENTITY DEVELOPMENT IN COLLEGE WOMEN   231
       Amy Stalzer Sengupta and Yvette Loury Upton

       Narratives on Gender and Feminism
       The Story of Maya   246
           Xyanthe Neider
       Intersection of Identities: One Woman's Journey   248
           Kimberley Fernandes
       Is Your Profundity a Trammel or a Treasure? Lessons in Ability and Identity   250
           Rachel Wagner

                                      Section Four
                                ADVANCING THE FUTURE
                        Strategies for Changing Dominant Paradigms   **253**

15   THE CAMPUS WOMEN'S CENTER AS CLASSROOM
       A Model for Thinking and Action   255
       Jennifer R. Wies

16   IN (RE)SEARCH OF WOMEN IN STUDENT AFFAIRS ADMINISTRATION   270
       Tamara Yakaboski and Saran Donahoo

17   CAMPUS-BASED SEXUAL ASSAULT PREVENTION
       Perspectives and Recommendations From Program Facilitators   287
       Lindsay M. Orchowski, Eric Zimak, Troy Robison,
       Justin Reeder, Ryan Rhoades, Christine A. Gidycz, and Alan Berkowitz

18   LEARNING AND LEADING TOGETHER
       A Cohort-Based Model for Women's Advancement   306
       Lee S. Hawthorne Calizo

       Narratives on Gender and Feminism
       Testimonial and Future Thinking   317
           Kelly E. Maxwell

On Love, and Its Place in the Academy   319
    Cayden Mak
Change a Life   322
    Vanidy Bailey

Section Five
ENVISIONING AND ACTING ON A FEMINIST FUTURE   **323**

19   ENVISIONING A NEW FUTURE WITH FEMINIST VOICES
       Research and Practice From Feminist Perspectives   325
       Amanda Suniti Niskodé-Dossett, Penny A. Pasque, and Shelley Errington Nicholson

About the Contributors   335

Index   343

Acknowledgments

WE THANK THE MANY authors who contributed to this book for their willingness to embark on this iterative and collaborative process. You were willing to read the work from the other authors and reflect upon connections between your feminist research and the research offered throughout this manuscript at various stages in the publication process. Subsequently, the book we offer is threaded together in a unique manner and makes for a more intentional and powerful contribution to the field. Thank you.

In addition, the editorial board was instrumental in providing its unique perspectives and insights to the manuscript. The board offered thoughtful feedback to the editors and chapter authors. This special group of women ensured that this book was approached with multigenerational, multidisciplinary, and multiple feminist perspectives in mind.

We also thank Dorothy Nkhata, graduate assistant for this project through the Educational Leadership and Policy Studies Department at the University of Oklahoma, whose efforts helped us tremendously during the 2008–2009 academic year. Dorothy, we wish you well in your academic pursuits and know you will make a strong contribution to higher education in the United States and Malawi. In addition, we thank Pam Harjo and Brenton Wimmer, graduate assistants through the same department, whose efforts helped us with the final stages of completion during the 2009–2010 academic year. Thank you for your willingness to come late to the project and work on the final details. We also wish you well and know you will both make a strong contribution to the field of student affairs.

Kara Morgan, graduate assistant from The Center for Educational Development and Research, University of Oklahoma, was helpful in transcribing the Sister Circle dialogue between women about gender, race, and student affairs (chapter 12). This transcript was a useful starting point for the chapter included in this book. Thank you, Kara.

Importantly, thank you to the American College Personnel Association (ACPA) Books and Media Board, and Stylus Publication, including Holley Belch and Ellen Broido; we appreciate your advice, counsel, and support throughout this process. Holley, we sincerely believe this book is stronger because of your willingness to work collaboratively with us to fine-tune the manuscript. On the basis of these changes, we believe it has the potential to have a sustaining impact on the field of higher education and student affairs.

Finally, we thank ACPA's Standing Committee for Women (past, present, and future) for providing opportunities for women to come together in order to further strengthen the field in terms of feminist research, scholarship, and practice. The intergenerational and supportive nature of the committee encourages voices to be heard and dreams to be realized.

Editorial Review Board

Linda Contreras Bullock, Assistant Dean of Student Diversity/Director of Intercultural and International Student Services, University of Houston—Clear Lake

Cynthia Cochran, Coordinator of Student Organizations and Leadership Programs, Northwestern University

Sarah E. Hoffert, Community Service Programs Coordinator, University of Vermont

Janelle Perron Jennings, Director of New Student Programs, Fairfield University

Melissa McDonald, Area Coordinator, University of Illinois at Urbana Champagne

Amanda Suniti Niskode-Dossett, Project Associate/Graduate Student, Indiana University

Graduate Student Assistants

Dorothy B. Nkhata, University of Oklahoma

Pam Harjo, University of Oklahoma

Brenton Wimmer, University of Oklahoma

Special thanks to Matthew King and Mikale Pilgrim, graduate assistants at the Center for Educational Development and Research, Jeannine Rainbolt College of Education at the University of Oklahoma for assistance with the index.

Foreword

"YOU MEAN, THAT STILL HAPPENS?" This was the response I received from a campus administrator when I commented, over lunch, on the subtle and overt barriers that hinder women's achievement and advancement in higher education. As I described the persistent challenges faced by women in higher education and the need for more research on gender equity issues, the administrator—a woman with a wealth of knowledge and experience in higher education—seemed astonished that such work was still necessary.

Students may be skeptical as well. In my experience teaching students about gender issues in higher education, I find that they too are often surprised by the extent to which gender remains such a potent force in shaping the experiences of students in higher education. Many of them assume that the Women's Movement brought an end to sex discrimination and that the academic successes of today's college women are a testament to our having already achieved gender equity. Today's students encounter so many women professionals in higher education—faculty, staff, and administrators—that they are frequently unaware of the persistent gender inequities that exist within each of those populations, whether in terms of salary, resources, power, or prestige.

And yet, if you have picked up this book, you are probably part of another group—one that is either long aware of or perhaps newly curious about the role that gender plays across multiple sectors in higher education. You might be a student enrolled in a women's studies or education course, a student affairs professional aiming to improve the experiences of college women, or a researcher or faculty member thirsting for fresh perspectives on gender in higher education.

The contents of this book, carefully chosen and organized by Penny Pasque and Shelley Errington Nicholson, have the potential to both enlighten the skeptics and satisfy the needs of those seeking evidence and allies in the movement for gender equity. This book does much more than simply document persistent gender inequities (though such evidence is provided). What distinguishes this book is its intimacy. The editors have assembled a diverse collection of research papers, historical essays, personal narratives, and quotes that add texture and flavor to the topic of women in higher education. As readers, we are invited into the lives of the authors and, in many cases, the lives of their research subjects.

Distinctively feminist in approach, this book tackles a wide range of issues central to women in higher education and student affairs. Although the perspectives represented in this collection are unique, they are universal. Who among us does not struggle with creating a work–life balance? Who does not question his or her multiple identities? Who has not striven for resilience in an oppressive environment? Readers will forge connections with the text in a way that should inform their work, their studies, and their self-exploration.

Also noteworthy about this collection is its ability to blend feminist theoretical/research perspectives with contemporary issues in student affairs. Too often, the theoretical world of feminist theory is divorced from the practical world of campus practice. In this book, readers will find diverse feminist perspectives and approaches used to discuss a wide range of campus services and programs, such as women's centers, health centers, leadership programs, Lesbian, Gay, Bisexual, Transgender (LGBT) centers, and athletics. The fact that this book emerged out of a student affairs professional conference is further testament to the value placed on the profession and the potential to forge stronger alliances between scholars and practitioners.

The notion of "intersectionality" is woven beautifully throughout this book, not as a special case, but as a representation of *all* women's multiple identities that are shaped by race, ethnicity, class, culture, sexual orientation, age, national origin, motherhood, and innumerable other forces that construct our lives as undergraduates, graduate students, faculty, practitioners, and administrators.

Further, the book provides important historical perspectives on the experiences of women in higher education and the evolution of student affairs programs designed to serve them. The majority of us who work in higher education are probably unaware of the unique history that has shaped our particular corner of campus life, and this book provides a glimpse into how the Women's Movement and societal shifts altered the trajectory of campus programming for women and the nature of women's leadership in student affairs. This is not the sort of historical backdrop one would normally encounter in a class on the history of higher education or a women's studies course. This fascinating history will help readers reflect both on the nature of the profession and on their "place" in the history of women in higher education.

Consistent with feminist scholarship, the content of this book is intertwined with the backgrounds of its authors. Collectively, the book's 50 contributors reflect the diversity of higher education in terms of gender, race, class, sexual orientation, and age. They also represent the range of work within student affairs, including advising, athletics, multicultural affairs, women's centers, admissions, residential life, and leadership programming. Variety is reflected in the authors' disciplinary backgrounds, including anthropology, biology, English, education, history, journalism, law, management, math, physical education, physical science, psychology, sociology, theater, and women's studies. The authors also represent a range of feminist perspectives, evidenced by the varying theoretical lenses and approaches used to approach gender equity in higher education. Diversity among the authors is no accident, as the editors intentionally created a community of scholars and practitioners with varied perspectives and experiences and then capitalized on this diversity by facilitating communication between various chapter authors during the writing process, thereby enhancing the connections across chapters.

Their approach appears to have been a success. *Empowering Women in Higher Education and Student Affairs: Theory, Research, Narratives, and Practice From Feminist Perspectives* is a welcome addition to the scholarship on gender and education. It invites readers in, provides them with a mix of personal connections and intellectual substance, and then challenges them to use their positions as students, educators, practitioners, and researchers in order to advance the cause of gender equity in higher education.

Linda J. Sax
University of California, Los Angeles

Preface

Penny A. Pasque and Shelley Errington Nicholson

IN THEIR IMPORTANT RESEARCH ON women's leadership, Helen Astin and Carol Leland (1991) describe a feminist conceptual model of leadership that "rests on the assumption that leadership manifests itself when there is an action to bring about change in an organization, an institution, or the social system—in other words, an action to make a positive difference in people's lives. Leadership, then, is conceived as a creative process that results in change" (Astin & Leland, 1991, p. 116). In this spirit of feminist leadership and social change, we offer *Empowering Women in Higher Education and Student Affairs: Theory, Research, Narratives, and Practice From Feminist Perspectives*, a collaborative book of scholarship from an intergenerational group of women, men, and transgender people with different social identities, feminist perspectives, and professional identities who work at various institutional types. This edited book updates our knowledge of women in higher education and student affairs, as it builds upon and extends research on women students, faculty, and administrators through various feminist lenses and feminist methodological approaches.

The initial idea for this writing project began at the American College Personnel Association (ACPA) convention's 2007 annual meeting of the Standing Committee for Women (SCW) where members were planning for the following convention and SCW's 35th anniversary. In conjunction with the 35th anniversary in 2008, SCW was

pleased to announce a "call for chapters" for this book. At this same convention, Carol Gilligan (2008) delivered the insightful closing address and asked all members of the association to consider a new and inclusive gender paradigm that resists the dominant values of the patriarchy (see Guido-DiBrito [2008] for a description of the intimate luncheon after the address). Gilligan also shared a part of her personal story as a mother, scholar, theorist, and activist. She illustrated the ways in which human nature *resists* false dualities often urged under a patriarchy, such as the forced choice between men versus women and nature versus nurture. It is not a woman's or man's problem, she discussed; "we have all been captivated by this false story" and it's time for change.

The manifestations of this false story are actualized in the inequities lived by members of our educational communities. For example, women and people of color do not reach the position of Chief Student Affairs Officer at similar rates as do White males (Reason, Walker, & Robinson, 2002). Further, women are more likely to be chief diversity officers (56% are women) than chief academic officers or provosts (38% women; King & Gomez, 2008), where only 7% of all senior administrators are women of color and only 3% of chief academic officers are women of color (King & Gomez, 2008). Importantly, the percentage of degrees conferred to women has increased over the years (Ropers-Huilman, 2002), yet the disparities across institution type (e.g., community colleges, regional institutions, Ivy League universities) are not often addressed.

The wage gap also continues where women who work full time earn approximately 78 cents for every dollar men earn (U.S. Census Bureau and the Bureau of Labor Statistics, 2008). Moreover, African American women make approximately 67 cents and Hispanic women approximately 58 cents on the dollar as compared with White men. Numbers for Native American women, Middle Eastern American women, and transgender persons were not available, signifying another gap—a gap in research. After their review of pay inequities for recently hired faculty, Porter, Toutkoushian, and Moore (2008) state that "pay equity by gender and race remains an important, and unresolved issue in academe" (p. 482) and "there are fewer gender differences in pay for recently hired faculty than is true for the entire academic labor market" (p. 483). As a resource to further explore these statistics, the American Association for University Women (2008) provides a pay gap table, where people may click on a state and see the gender earnings gap for that specific state.

These disparities are far-reaching and reify patriarchal trends found throughout history. Matilda Joslyn Gage (1826–1898) and Elizabeth Cady Stanton (1815–1902) called this inequity the "four-fold oppression" of women's lives as women had no say in government, religion, economics, or social life (cited in Wagner, 1996). A century later, issues of inequity have not been completely addressed. In our review of the archival materials[1] of SCW in anticipation of this publication, we found that the national association continued to struggle with issues of gender inequity in 1970, and some of these same issues continue today. For example, ACPA President Charles L. Lewis wrote,

> the changing patterns of administrative organization[s] have unquestionably lessened the impact and involvement of women in central student personnel decisions. The topic and concerns are bantered about frequently in little conclave, but no one

gets the problem out on the board in open discussion. The current women's liberation moves on the college campus indicates some of the frustration.

On February 5, 1970, President Lewis requested a temporary committee on the role of women in the profession to be chaired by Elizabeth A. Greenleaf, which led to the establishment of the Women's Task Force and later to the Standing Committee for Women, where the standing committee continues to address the complex lives of women on college campuses.

As these perspectives and statistics reflect, the lived and systemic nature of sexism continues to prevail. The goal of this book is to add to the current body of knowledge about women and higher education by considering the past experiences of women in a contemporary context and exploring the present experiences of women students, faculty, and administrators in detail through various feminist perspectives. We also address the intersections of gender and other social identities (i.e., race, ethnicity, sexual orientation, class, ability). Specifically, we consider this book a welcomed complement to the National Association for Student Personnel Administrator's *Journal About Women in Higher Education* (we actively encouraged, and continue to encourage, authors to submit to this important journal), the Association for the Study of Higher Education's *Women in Higher Education: A Feminist Perspective* (Glazer-Raymo, Townsend, & Ropers-Huilman, 2000), and Hesse-Biber & Leavy's (2007) *Handbook of Feminist Research: Theory and Praxis*. Our hope is that this book contributes to, not competes with, the scholarship about and by women in higher education and student affairs. We anticipate that the implications garnered from this book are instructive for higher education leaders, researchers, administrators, faculty, and graduate students interested in the most up-to-date research on women in student affairs and higher education and, together, we push against the barriers of sexism and oppression in higher education.

Importantly, we have taken an innovative approach to the writing and revising process, one that mirrors the collaborative nature found in feminist theories. The chapter revision process was unique in that (as outlined in the call for chapters) after selection chapter authors were asked to read other chapters selected for the book that related to their original research and build upon each other's work. This process reflects feminist ideals for learning that are holistic and relational (Ropers-Huilman, 2002). In this manner, the chapters are less siloed (as is typical in an edited book) and instead "talk with each other" at various points. We hope this strengthens the book and more readily advances the current knowledge in the field. For example, during the revision process, the author of the chapter on women's and gender centers (Susan Marine, Harvard University, chapter 2) read the strategies for change chapter on campus women's centers as classrooms (Jennifer Wies, Xavier University, chapter 15) and vice versa. Authors cite each other in an informal manner (utilizing first and last names and the chapter number), as is reflective of our e-mail communication during the editorial process where primarily first names were used. Authors were also able to request any chapter in the table of contents, and in some cases they did request to read additional chapters.

This book includes historical, qualitative, quantitative, narrative, and dialogic chapters, each of which provides a different feminist perspective on the state of women in higher education and student affairs. Each section begins with a quote from seminal scholars in the field who have furthered a feminist and inclusive agenda through their research and/or practice. We offer these quotes to signal that the following chapters build upon the scholarship of people who have come before us and to encourage readers to seek out the original sources.

Section one of this book is titled "Setting the Context: A Contemporary Re/Examination of Women in Higher Education and Student Affairs." In the introductory chapter, we provide a context for the book by distinguishing between various feminist perspectives (i.e., liberal, radical, multicultural, womanist, eco, and global feminism) and explore various feminist methodologies. This chapter discusses the implications of the feminist theories and methodological approaches for higher education and student affairs. In chapter 2, Susan Marine qualitatively explores the role of women's centers as lively, evolving hubs of feminist engagement within the academy. Through interviews with over 20 women from centers across the country, she discusses the importance of more institutional support in terms of resources and human capital to enable women's centers to reach their full potential in pursuit of gender equity. Susan effectively argues for continued use of the word *feminism*, with its myriad definitions and complex history, and discusses the word's importance as we usher in the next generation of leadership for women's and gender centers. Chapter 3 by Jennifer Lee Hoffman provides an intriguing historical analysis of the rise and fall of women leaders in the academy. Subsequently, the effect of various approaches to educating women students both in single-sex and coeducational settings is examined. Jennifer puts forth a strong case for the challenges women still face as educators and administrators in the academy. In chapter 4's unique and historical look at the "powerful collaborations between deans of women and directors of physical education," Thalia Mulvihill explores the organizational and professional experiences of the women who developed this initiative, the first of its kind. Their innovative perspective about how to develop the whole student is one of the foundational principles of student affairs and provides information about current-day leadership toward institutional change. Thalia's chapter provides further historical context through the examination of feminist approaches that were groundbreaking for the field and are relevant today.

This section is (as all sections are) followed by a few short and meaningful narratives on gender and feminism by students, administrators, and faculty throughout the field. These reflections provide an array of diverse perspectives and lived experiences on gender and higher education through various feminist lenses. In addition, the depth of these experiences reminds us of the human faces impacted by the research, policies, and procedures enacted throughout institutions and the field of higher education. In this way, we hope to highlight how theoretical frameworks, research questions, methodological approaches, policies, and procedures *remain political* and have direct implications on people's daily lives. In this specific section, Rosemary Perez reflects on her struggles with internal racism and microaggressions as a "model minority," Cindy Clark discusses the judgment she faced as a stay-at-home mom, a student, and "just a girl," and Kelly Winters describes the collective energy and possibility of women space at women's colleges.

Section two, "Considering Experiences of Women Throughout the Academy: An Exploration of Undergraduates, Graduate Students, and Administrators," explores in depth the qualitative experiences of various women across the country who are educated in and/or are employed by our colleges and universities. In chapter 5, written by Racheal Stimpson and Kimberly Filer, the authors focus on an often-marginalized population of women in higher education, graduate students. Specifically, Racheal and Kim explore the work–life balance for over 800 women graduate students. They offer us personal stories and solid research that illustrates what is already known anecdotally: Women have less confidence in their ability to complete a terminal degree while successfully balancing school and home. The chapter concludes with practical advice for both students and student affairs professionals. In chapter 6, Monica Marcelis Fochtman explores the experiences of "high-achieving women" and how they survive in administrative positions in higher education. Importantly, she found that participant(s) had "different mentoring needs at different times in her career, indicating that the necessity and de-

sire for mentors never goes away, but shifts as her career progresses." Monica's study highlights the need for various mentoring opportunities at different points in a woman's career, which is an underlying principle of this book's editorial and revision process. In chapter 7, Annemarie Vaccaro continues to explore the experience of women in college through her interviews with 58 nontraditional-aged students. She uses feminist, critical race, and racial identity theories to analyze women's educational experiences and introduces a new and important term, *self-investment*. Jennifer Sader, in chapter 8, also explores the experiences of women students, this time women in a predominantly male field, computer science. This chapter serves as an exemplar for graduate students considering feminist qualitative research, as Jennifer intentionally lays out her feminist theoretical framework and methods of inquiry. In addition, her chapter is instructive in terms of the implications for institutional practice such as advising and programming support for women in a male-dominated field.

The narratives round out our exploration of the experiences of women in this section. Dorothy Nkhata shares her lived experiences growing up in Malawi, Africa, and how this motivates her to excel academically; Jennifer Dudeck-Lenis shares her life's journey from an undergraduate at a women's college to student affairs practitioner; Kristie Atkinson considers the complexities of gender in intercultural contexts when studying abroad; and Robbie offers reflections on reclaiming gender and gender construction.

Section three, "Exploring Identity Contexts: The Intersections of Class, Gender, Race, and Sexual Orientation for Faculty, Administrators, and Students," considers the intersections of multiple identities through qualitative research, narrative, and dialogic discussions. In chapter 9, Venice Thandi Sulé employs Black Feminist Thought and Political Race theoretical perspectives to examine how race matters in the lives of tenured Black female faculty at predominately White research institutions. Thandi discusses the important role of institutions to serve as sites of collective action and transformation in order to intentionally address gender and racial inequities. Through storytelling in chapter 10, Florence Guido describes her experience as a first-generation Italian American growing up in the Southwest. Flo explores the complexities of identity across the generations in her family as she addresses the intersections of her own gender, race, nationality, and class and how these constructions influence her research and practice in higher education and student affairs. In chapter 11, Penny Rice examines the economically underprivileged women on our college campuses. Through the lens of social justice work, she provides insight into the lives of three women who share their struggles and triumphs in college. The chapter concludes with an inspiring call to action for all higher education practitioners. Chapter 12 is modeled after the ACPA SCW's Sister Circle discussions held at the convention each year. This roundtable provides a space and opportunity for women of color to dialogue about various professional and personal challenges in the field of student affairs and provides a supportive environment in order to work toward action strategies for change. In this chapter, we have an opportunity to read the verbal dialogue between the women as they reflect on their professional journeys and their own multiple social identities. Elisa Abes and David Kasch use Queer Theory to explore lesbian college students' multiple dimensions of identity in chapter 13, reprinted with permission from the *Journal of College Student Development*. Elisa and David employ constructivist narrative inquiry as they uncover how identities are constantly forming and reforming. The implications are far-reaching for researchers and administrators as they/we challenge heteronormative assumptions underlying student development theory. In chapter 14, Amy Stalzer Sengupta and Yvette Loury Upton discuss a familiar concept, student identity development theory, with a focus on the development of college women and, in a unique manner, explore their findings against the

backdrop of existing feminist theoretical perspectives. More specifically, Amy and Yvette utilize a combination of theoretical and personal narratives that explore women's identity development and its intersection with other forms of identity development (i.e., women of color). This original research advances feminist theories of women student development.

The narratives in this section also exhibit the intersections of multiple identities. Xyanthe Neider reflects upon the legacies from which she grew and discusses the intersections of her own identities as a biracial, nontraditional, first-generation college student who is a single parent. Kimberley Fernandes shares the complexities of skin and gender as she learns how to "break out" of silence to share her story as an Indian woman (from South Asia). Rachel Wagner explores the intersections of dis/ability and gender as she relays her journey toward profundity reaped from her "loss."

Section four, "Advancing the Future: Strategies for Changing Dominant Paradigms," encourages an innovative and strategic look at the future of higher education and student affairs, one that interrupts dominant patriarchal paradigms. In chapter 15, Jennifer Wies explores the connection between Women's Centers and a commitment to education and learning through both quantitative and qualitative methods. Examination of the Women's Center as Classroom model at Xavier University imparts practical information about how to replicate such a program on other campuses. In addition, assessment guidelines and suggestions are put forth in an effort to encourage practitioners to examine the effectiveness of their current programs. Chapter 16 assesses the current state of research on women student affairs administrators. Tamara Yakaboski and Saran Donahoo examine different perspectives of women in student affairs administration including the unique experiences of African American women, Asian and Asian American women, and women with children and families. This chapter concludes with an

examination of some of the gender-based assumptions in student affairs. In chapter 17, Lindsay Orchowski, Eric Zimak, Troy Robison, Justin
Reeder, Ryan Rhoades, Christine Gidycz, and
Alan Berkowitz provide a look inside a sexual
assault prevention program at a midsized Midwestern university. Through an examination of
current issues associated with creating and implementing a sexual assault prevention program,
Lindsay and colleagues encourage readers to identify challenges present on their campuses and provide useful tips on overcoming those challenges.
Lee Hawthorne Calizo, in chapter 18, tells the
inspiring story of how six female administrators
at the University of Maryland, Baltimore, created
a cohort-based model for women's advancement
within the academy. A discussion of the activities of the first two years, in addition to the
significant learning that occurred, is shared in an
effort to inspire the replication of this program
throughout the field. Similar to Monica Marcelis
Fochtman (chapter 6), Lee's focus on high-level
female administrators fills a sizable gap in the
current higher education literature, which often
ignores full-time administrators.

Kelly Maxwell discusses how the personal is
political as she describes how her personal life
and professional work in higher education are
inextricably linked. Cayden Mak reflects on the
antitransgender bias faced as an undergraduate
minority student on campus and love's place in
the academy. Vanidy Bailey grapples with heterosexual norms as she encourages administrators to
recognize the power they/we have to change a life
or destroy a dream, encouraging administrators
to be good stewards of this power.

Together with Amanda Suniti Niskodé-
Dossett, we conclude the book with a unique cap-
stone that reviews the various chapters through
different feminist lenses and methodological approaches that we outlined in chapter 1. In addition, we make a deliberate call for women, men,
and transgender scholars and educators to work
toward centering feminist perspectives (and other
marginalized perspectives) in research and prac-

tice as the complexities of college and university
life continue to evolve. In issuing this call, we
highlight (1) feminist inquiry: uncovering lenses
and assumptions; (2) feminist inquiry: influencing research and scholarship; and (3) questions
and implications for future feminist research and
practice. Finally, we discuss the challenges and
opportunities we face as we look to advance the
role of women who hold multiple identities in
student affairs and higher education.

The ACPA SCW's mission is "to transform
the culture of higher education and student affairs to empower women" (ACPA, 2008). The
vision states that "as a committee of ACPA, the
Standing Committee for Women works to create
an environment that supports the lifelong holistic development of women. We accomplish this
through coalition building, education, and advocacy for women." The process of this book, from
inception to publication, was a collaborative process that, we hope, continues to build coalitions
between scholars and practitioners throughout
the field. We also hope the research and programs
described in this book inspire the next generation
of research, scholarship, and practice about (and
with) women in higher education and student
affairs in order to reduce patriarchal paradigms
and foster an educational climate of equity and
social justice.

NOTE

1. We would like to share a special "thank you" to
Ann Bowers, the ACPA national archivist at Bowling
Green State University, for such convenient and useful
access to the archives.

REFERENCES

American College Personnel Association. (2008). *Mission, vision and statement of inclusion*. Retrieved January 28, 2009, from http://www.myacpa.org/sc/
scw/mission-vision-goals.html

Astin, H. S. & Leland, C. (1991). *Women of influence, women of vision: A cross-generational study*

of leaders and social change. San Francisco, CA: Jossey-Bass.

Gilligan, C. (2008, April 2). "Professionalism with Purpose: Advancing Inclusion and Expertise" Closing Address as presented at the American College Personnel Association National Convention, Atlanta, GA.

Glazer-Raymo, J., Townsend, B. K., & Ropers-Huilman, B. (Eds.). (2000). *Women in higher education: A feminist perspective.* Boston, MA: Pearson.

Guido-DiBrito, F. (2008, Summer). Our intimate lunch with a feminist icon. In *Developments.* Washington, DC: American College Personnel Association.

Hesse-Biber, S. N., & Leavy, P. L. (Eds.) (2007). *Feminist research practice: A primer.* Thousand Oaks, CA: Sage.

King, J. & Gomez, G. G. (2008). *On the pathway to the presidency: Characteristics of higher education's senior leaders.* Washington DC: American Council on Education.

Lewis, C. (1970). Professional letter. Bowling Green, OH: American College Personnel Association national archives.

Porter, S. R., Toutkoushian, R. K., & Moore, J.V., III. (2008). Pay inequities for recently hired faculty, 1988–2004. *The Review of Higher Education, 31*(4), 465–487.

Reason, R. D., Walker, D. A., & Robinson, D. C. (2002). Gender, ethnicity, and highest degree earned as salary determinants for senior student affairs officers at public institutions. *NASPA Journal, 39*(3), 251–265.

Ropers-Huilman, R. (2002). Feminism in the academy: Overview. In A. M. M. Alemán & K. A. Renn (Eds.), *Women in higher education: An encyclopedia* (pp. 109–118). Santa Barbara, CA: ABC-Clio.

U.S. Census Bureau and the Bureau of Labor Statistics. (2008, August). *Annual demographic survey.* Washington, DC: Author. Retrieved January 14, 2009, from http://pubdb3.census.gov/macro/032008/perinc/new05_000.htm

Wagner, S. R. (1996, Winter). The untold story of the Iroquois influence on early feminists. *On the Issues.* Retrieved December 21, 2008, from http://www.feminist.com/resources/artspeech/genwom/iroquoisinfluence.html

Section One

SETTING THE CONTEXT

A Contemporary (Re)Examination of Women in Higher Education and Student Affairs

The intersection between feminist theory and the historical, social, professional, and institutional contexts of higher education sheds light on the educational process and how it frequently tracks, underserves, or discriminates against women.

Judith S. Glazer, Estela M. Bensimon, and Barbara K. Townsend

Glazer, J. S., Bensimon, E. A. & Townsend, B. K. (Eds.). (1993). *Women in higher education: A feminist perspective.* Needham Heights, MA: Ginn Press.

1

An Introduction to Feminism and Feminist Perspectives in Higher Education and Student Affairs

Shelley Errington Nicholson and Penny A. Pasque

Abstract: *Though not all-inclusive by far, this chapter provides an introduction to the three waves of the feminist movement, including the important role that the Native American women played in shaping the ideals for the first wave. In addition, we expand on the three waves by briefly describing the differences between a few different conceptualizations of feminism, including liberal, radical, womanist, Marxist, socialist, multicultural, psychoanalytic, gender, existentialist, postmodern, global, and eco feminism. Next, we share some concepts about feminist methodologies that inform some of the research in this book. Finally, this chapter offers cursory examples from the field that are expanded upon in the feminist perspectives, research, and practical implications provided by the women, men, and transgender authors throughout this text.*

FEMINISM IS A COMPLEX NOTION that has vast differences in meaning and connotation for people spanning generations, ethnic identities, sexual orientations, social classes, nationality, and myriad identities. Feminism is not a static notion; rather, it evolves with us throughout our lives and is shaped by the various lenses we use to view the world at large and, most importantly, ourselves. As the topic of this text hinges on feminism, we designed this first chapter to briefly introduce a few different conceptualizations of feminism as they relate to

research and practice in higher education and student affairs.

In their groundbreaking work, Glazer, Bensimon, and Townsend (1993) provided the context for three forms of feminist thought and perspective: leftist feminism, radical feminism, and liberal feminism. It is our intention to expand upon this seminal work, drawing from scholars within and beyond higher education and student affairs. Eighteen years later, we endeavor to describe definitions of feminism and feminist methodologies, while we further research from feminist perspectives with the addition of this book to the existing literature. In doing so, we draw from the work of many feminists who have come before us and hope this book inspires the next generation of feminists.

In *Feminism Is for Everybody: Passionate Politics*, hooks (2000a) shared her "simple definition of feminism":

> "Feminism is a movement to end sexism, sexist exploitation, and oppression." I love this definition . . . I love it because it so clearly states that the movement is not about being anti-male. It makes it clear that the problem is sexism. (p. viii)

Dr. hooks's simple definition provided us with a common understanding through which to begin the conversation on feminism. From here, we branch off and consider multiple definitions of feminism. It is important to note that many of the definitions of feminism are anything but simple in the ways in which they inform our work with students, programs, policies, and our perceptions of ourselves and others; the implications of our actions based on our perspectives have a direct impact on the lives of the people in our communities.

Though not all inclusive by far, this chapter provides a basic introduction to the three waves of the feminist movement including the important role Native American women played in shaping the ideals for the first wave. In addition, we expand on the three waves by describing the differences between some conceptualizations of feminism including liberal, radical, womanist, Marxist, socialist, multicultural, psychoanalytic, gender, existentialist, postmodern, global, and eco feminism. Some of these perspectives are congruent with each other, some build off of each other, and some are in strict opposition to each other; in other words, they are not all mutually exclusive. We encourage you to read about these and additional feminist perspectives beyond this introductory chapter, both within and outside of the field of higher education, and form your own perspective.

In addition, we share some concepts about feminist methodologies that inform our higher education research. Finally, this chapter offers examples from the field that are expanded upon in the feminist perspectives, research, and practical implications provided by the women, men, and transgender authors throughout this text.

FEMINIST PERSPECTIVES

Three Waves of Feminism

The history of feminism is often described in three temporal waves. The first wave was during the nineteenth and early twentieth centuries, the second was during the 1960s and 1990s, and the third wave extends from the 1990s to the present (Krolokke & Sorensen, 2005). When examining the history of the women's rights movement and foremothers of feminism during the first wave, we see the strong influence of the Native American women with whom they shared the land. For example, Elizabeth Cady Stanton in advocating for divorce laws to protect the rights of women cited Iroquois laws that ensured a man provided for his family on pain of banishment. Countless other examples exist of the pioneers of the women's movement taking their cues from Native American ancestors such as in the Iroquois system of election, whereby the women choose their governmental representative from among eligible men. To remain eligible, these men must not have committed theft, murder, or sexual assault upon a woman.

According to Wagner (1996),

> It is difficult for White Americans today to picture the extended period in history when—before the United States government's Indian-reservation system, like apartheid, concretized a separation of the races in the last half of the nineteenth century— regular trade, cultural sharing, even friendship between Native Americans and Euro-Americans was common. Perhaps nowhere was this now-lost social ease more evident than in the towns and

villages in upstate New York where Elizabeth Cady Stanton and Matilda Joslyn Gage lived, and Lucretia Mott visited. All three suffragists personally knew Iroquois women, citizens of the six-nation confederacy (Seneca, Cayuga, Onondaga, Oneida, Mohawk, and later Tuscarora) that had established peace among themselves before Columbus came to this "old" world. (¶ 6)

Jennifer Lee Hoffman (chapter 3) and Thalia Mulvihill (chapter 4) journey us through the end of the first wave to the beginning of the second wave of feminism with their historical analyses of deans of women, athletic directors, and physical education directors. The innovative ways in which these women worked within their roles to create change in higher education is an example of the strength of this second wave.

The second wave unfolded in the context of the antiwar and civil rights movements and the growing self-consciousness of a variety of marginalized groups around the world. For example, there were several major characteristics of this wave: the publication of *The Feminine Mystique* by Betty Friedan, the passage of Title VII of the Civil Rights Act of 1964, the formation of the National Organization for Women, the passage of Title IX in the Education Amendments of 1972, and the *Roe v. Wade* decision, among other changes that impacted the cultural milieu. The New Left was on the rise, and the voice of the second wave was increasingly radical. Rampton (2008) described the following:

> Whereas the first wave of feminism was generally propelled by middle class white women, the second phase drew in women of color and developing nations, seeking sisterhood and solidarity and claiming "Women's struggle is class struggle." Feminists spoke of women as a social class and coined phrases such as "the personal is political" and "identity politics" in an effort to demonstrate that race, class, and gender oppression are all related. They initiated a concentrated effort to rid society top-to-bottom of sexism, from children's cartoons to the highest levels of government. (¶ 8)

The third wave began in the 1990s, continues today, and is informed by postcolonial and postmodern thinking. This wave often mystifies earlier feminists as many third wavers have reclaimed lipstick, high heels, and cleavage (Rampton, 2008). The third wave breaks constraining boundaries of gender, including what it deems as essentialist boundaries set by the earlier waves. Controversy and disagreement around identity politics between feminists in the third wave have escalated (Whelehan, 2000).

As one dives deeper into the various waves of feminism, there are numerous feminist perspectives to consider, some of which are distinct and some of which overlap. A *few* of these perspectives are outlined below.

Liberal Feminism

The first feminist perspective to consider is liberal feminism, which was established as a part of the first wave of feminism. This is the traditional conceptualization of feminism and often the root of comparison when deconstructing contemporary conceptualizations of feminism. Liberal feminism adheres to the simple definition offered above by hooks but can be broadened to include "female subordination" as the root cause of social injustices against women. This perspective argues that "society has a false belief that women are by nature less intellectually and physically capable than men" (Tong, 2009). Furthermore, Tong goes on to state that this false belief "excludes women from the academy, the forum, and the marketplace" (p. 2). The result of this exclusion is that the true potential of women's contribution to society is unfulfilled. The liberal feminist perspective expounds upon the merits of a level playing field that would allow women to seek the same opportunities as men, especially the opportunity to excel in various fields.

Modern liberal feminists argue that patriarchal society fuses sex and gender together, making only those jobs that are associated with the traditionally feminine appropriate for women to pursue. As such, society pressures women into jobs such as teaching and childcare and subsequently steers women away from jobs in business, technology, engineering, and mathematics. Higher education programs such as the Women in Science and Engineering living learning community at the University of Michigan (WiSE, www.wiserp.umich.edu) and Women in Engineering that reaches out to high school students at Michigan State University (WIE, www.egr.msu.edu/future-engineer/) are opportunities that try to combat such traditional perspectives. Another example is the national chapter of the Society of Women Engineers, an organization that provides career mentoring for women engineers as well as pipeline programs aimed at young women interested in engineering and science.

Liberal feminism can be further deconstructed into two forms—classic/libertarian feminism with a focus on freedom from coercive interference and egalitarian liberalism with its focus on personal autonomy. Classic liberal feminism focuses on equity through political and legal reform, whereas egalitarian feminism focuses on the notion that the physical demands of reproduction and motherhood are a drain on women and their natural potential, and woman therefore should be afforded the freedom of birth control and other technologies to limit pregnancy, if they so choose. It is beyond the scope of this text to further deconstruct these foci, but the reader is encouraged to further explore expanded definitions.

As it relates to our work in higher education and student affairs, liberal feminism has served as the backbone of the feminist approach to our field and can be reflected in the discussions by women in the field as far back as the early 1900s. For example, in the minutes of the Conference of Deans of Women of the Middle West (1903), the leaders discussed the complexities of life for women students in the residence halls including issues of mental health, academics, mentorship, and coeducational spaces (also see information

from the Student Affairs History Project, 2006). However, some have found this definition of liberal feminism to be too broad, too limiting, or too exclusive of people other than White middle- and upper-middle-class women.

Radical Feminism

Radical feminism is probably the second most notable form of feminism. However, this too is more complex than is reflected in this brief overview. Radical feminists think liberal feminist perspectives are not drastic enough to address the centuries of systemic, institutional, and individual oppression that have ensued. Radical feminism is further deconstructed into libertarian radical feminism and cultural radical feminism. Similar to the definition above, libertarian radical feminism focuses on personal freedom of expression but also turns to androgyny as an option. Libertarian radical feminists' ideal is to allow for genders to exhibit a full range of masculine and feminine qualities, stating that "No human being should be forbidden the sense of wholeness that comes from combining his or her masculine and feminine dimensions" (Tong, 2009, p. 3). As this informs our work in higher education, we need look no further than our work with students of all genders, gender identities, and forms of gender expression. For example, our work with lesbian, gay, bisexual, and transgender communities are particularly affected by this thinking which has laid the foundation—or served as a converse catalyst—for the development of some queer identity theories. Stated another way, some perspectives emerged from a push against the notion of androgyny, while others embraced it as a part of gender identity and expression.

Cultural radical feminism, however, expressly argues against the radical libertarian movement by arguing that the root cause of the problem is not femininity, but the low value that patriarchy assigns to feminine qualities. If society placed a higher value on feminine qualities, then there would be less gender oppression. One additional way in which these two different forms of radical feminism are distinct is the cultural feminist argument that our femininity has its roots in nature and true freedom can only be found by one embracing her true or naturally feminine self, whereas radical liberation feminists resist this notion.

Black Feminism and Womanist

Wheeler (2002) defined a Black feminist as

a person, historically an African American woman academic, who believes that female descendents of American slavery share a unique set of life experiences distinct from those of black men and white women . . . the lives of African American women are oppressed by combinations of racism, sexism, classism, and heterosexism. (p. 118)

Having its roots in the writings of Alice Walker, the term *womanist* is often used to describe the experiences of a woman of color, including the intersections of race and gender. In her narrative in section three of this book, Kimberly Fernandes includes a poignant quote by Walker, where she discusses the intersection of her various identities, to make just this point. Fernandes states, "Alice Walker (1983) coined the phrase, 'A womanist is to feminist as purple is to lavender' and its relevance is one I live every day. As women, we all bring a complex set of identities with us, and our gender is only a piece of that puzzle."

The Black Womanist feminism (or Black Feminist Thought) movement comes out of the feminist movement in the 1970s and is a direct interface with the civil rights movement, as it recognizes that women of African descent in the United States faced a unique set of issues that were not being addressed by the predominantly White feminist movement. The *womanist* term has also been used frequently to denote any difference between the White feminist perspective and perspectives of all women of color, as the

first and second waves of the feminist movement were often constructed by and for White women of the middle and upper-middle class.

As we place multiple layers of our identity over our gender identity, we see opportunities for their intersection. Black Feminist Thought enables people to resist a unilateral approach and work through the interconnections of gender, racial, ethnic, and class identity development simultaneously (Collins, 2000). In addition, Black Feminist Thought encourages African American women to create self-definitions and self-valuations that support positive and repel negative images (Wheeler, 2002). Third, Black Feminist Thought connects academic intellectual thought and political activism (Wheeler, 2002).

In student affairs, we may observe students focusing their identity development on one single aspect of their identity such as gender or race, without the ability to consider multiple identities simultaneously. A womanist perspective provides the opportunity to consider many layers of oppression at once and engage the personal, intellectual, and activist parts of the self. Importantly, author Venice Thandi Sulé utilizes Black Feminist Thought to consider the experiences of African American faculty members in her analysis in chapter 9 of this book.

Marxist and Socialist Feminism

Marxist and socialist feminism take their cues from the perspectives of social justice as well, with a focus on socioeconomic differences. Marxist feminists argue that the path to gender equality is led by the destruction of our capitalist society (Tong, 2009). This is an interesting concept when framed with the knowledge that, for many centuries, women were considered the property of men and a key cog in the capitalist machine from a commodities perspective and now, as this perspective argues, contribute to their own oppression through participation as a consumer. These systemic perspectives also speak to some of the many issues plaguing women in the academy including unequal pay, obstacles to achieving tenure or excelling in certain fields, and the frequent lack of family-friendly policies at many of our institutions.

Socialist feminists purport that women can only achieve true freedom when working to end both economic and cultural oppression and that these two forms of oppression are not mutually exclusive; rather, they are dependent on each other. This form of feminism has its roots in the Marxist feminist perspective as well as the radical feminist perspectives and its focus on the role of gender in a patriarchal society.

While author Penny Rice (chapter 11) does not specifically identify herself as a Marxist or socialist feminist in her chapter, she does address economically disadvantaged women in higher education through a feminist lens. Penny offers a call for higher education and the U.S. government to address the needs of economically disadvantaged women and the opportunity education brings to all of our futures.

Psychoanalytic Feminism

Psychoanalytic feminism is that body of writing that uses psychoanalysis to further feminist theory and, in principle, feminist practice (Jaggar & Young, 2000). This particular theory developed in part because of the negative influence of Freud and his treatment of women through psychoanalysis. This conceptualization aids us in deciphering why, as feminists, we still often engage in nonfeminist or patriarchal behavior. For example, it is believed that gender inequity originates in our childhood experiences where we are labeled as feminine or masculine and then adopt gendered characteristics, only to find that there is a value judgment placed on being feminine and/or masculine that is clearly in favor of masculinity. In essence, psychoanalytic feminists argue that people are socialized from a young age to believe in the inferiority of the female gender experience and therefore women may undermine their own confidence in such things as the pursuit

of careers. This is illustrated in Jennifer Sader's chapter on women doctoral students in computer science (see chapter 8). From this perspective and from the perspective many student affairs professionals impart upon students, one first needs to identify and become fully aware of the problem in order to change it.

Much of the field of student affairs has its roots in this type of psychoanalytic identity development, and many of us work with students on a daily basis as they (and we) move through developmental stages (Evans, Forney, Guido, Renn, & Patton, 2009). Through many of the different psychosocial and identity development theories, we see intermediary stages at the time when there is dissonance and the students move toward independence in thought and action. As student affairs professionals guide students through these awareness stages, whether it is awareness of their gender, race, or another issue, administrators often employ the tools of psychoanalysis, and in the case of gender oppression, specifically psychoanalytic feminism.

A final perspective of note is a care-focused feminist perspective, such as is found in the work of Carol Gilligan (1982) and as utilized by Florence Guido (chapter 10) in her stories from a daughter of first-generation Italian immigrants. Care-focused feminists "are interested in understanding why, to a greater or lesser degree, women are usually associated with the emotions and the body, and men with reason and the mind . . . [they] seek to understand why women as a group are usually linked with interdependence, community, and connection, whereas men as a group are usually linked with independence, selfhood, and autonomy" (Tong, 2009, p. 7).

Gender Feminism and Equity Feminism

Christina Hoff Sommers (1995), in her book *Who Stole Feminism? How Women Have Betrayed Women,* coined the phrases *gender feminism* and *equity feminism.* Gender feminism's main use is in the criticism of contemporary gender roles, whereas equality feminism takes this concept to another level demanding full equity for all gender roles. Gender feminists also advocate for women from a legal perspective—they argue preference be given to women in cases such as domestic violence, sexual harassment, child custody, divorce, and pay equity, to name a few, because of the historical and contemporary lack of gender equity in society and the social disadvantage of women.

This conceptualization is closely tied to principles of social justice (Adams, Bell, & Griffin, 2007) and focuses on some of the most basic elements essential for success and prosperity both in and outside the academy. For women to excel, there are certain inherent rights and equalities that must be recognized and mechanisms must be in place in order to fight inequalities should they arise.

Some examples in higher education that could address these concerns from a gender and equity feminist perspective include seminars on pay equity and negotiation skills, legal consultation and support in cases of sexual harassment or sexual assault, and recruitment *and* retention strategies so that our faculty (including tenured faculty) and administrative staff reflect the demographic breakdown of our students.

Existential Feminism

Simone de Beauvoir (1952) brought us another conceptualization of feminism—existentialist feminism. Existential feminism puts forth the admittedly controversial idea that prostitution empowers women both financially and within the general hierarchy of society. When compared to Marxist and socialist feminism, the contrast with this type of entrepreneurial spirit is clear: Whereas Marxist and socialist feminism work outside of the current patriarchal structure to tackle feminism from an economic and political perspective, existential feminism subverts the current patriarchy from within. Existential feminism, however, is often overshadowed by the ex-

ample of prostitution but actually encompasses much more.

Central to this perspective is the concept that one is not born a woman but becomes a woman. In this conceptualization, de Beauvoir emphasized that women must transcend their natural position and choose economic, personal, and social freedom. This is in direct contrast to the cultural radical feminist notion that women must embrace their natural femininity. Whereas cultural radical feminists make a case for the "nature" side of the nature versus nurture argument, de Beauvoir argued for the "nurture" side of the argument. Jennifer Sader (chapter 8) draws from Simone de Beauvoir as she develops a conceptual model from women doctoral students in science and technology.

Multicultural Feminism and Global Feminism

Multicultural feminists "focus on the basic insight that even in one nation—the United States, for instance—all women are not created or constructed equal. Depending on her race and ethnicity but also on her sexual identity, gender identity, age, religion, level of education, occupation or profession, marital status, health condition, and so on, each U.S. woman will experience her identity and status as a woman differently" (Tong, 2009, p. 200). As multicultural feminism takes into account a number of different interconnected identities and influences, it is sometimes utilized as an umbrella feminist perspective, of which womanist (as described above), Chicana feminist, Asian American feminist, Native American feminist, and multiple race- or ethnicity-based feminist perspectives can be considered. Some argue that if people across race, gender, gender expression, socioeconomic status, age, ability, and other social identities could unify under a multicultural feminist perspective, then it would provide added strength to this perspective, which is concerned with the intersections of multiple identities.

Others argue that it is not a useful umbrella for myriad feminist perspectives that are historically and culturally distinct, as it collapses groups and divorces itself from a focus on a specific race, geographic region, and/or unifying language.

As we began this chapter with an example of Native American women and the connection with the first wave of feminists, we will expand on contemporary Native American feminists as an example for this section. We encourage readers to explore Chicana Feminist, Asian American feminist, womanist, and other perspectives, and a number of examples may be found throughout this book including a multiracial feminist perspective in the Sister Circle dialogic chapter on the intersections of race and gender (chapter 12).

The Native American feminist experience is unique and brings in elements of postcolonial feminism, which relies heavily on a historical and dialectic approach to understand women's lives (Kim, 2007). In addition to racial issues informing feminism, Native American women also have the history of colonization: genocide via the "Trail of Tears," smallpox and other illnesses, and the lasting effects of historical oppression with which to contend (Foreman, 1932/1995; Reese, 1997). Although the same could be said for various other cultures that have been colonized and/or enslaved by a patriarchy, the Native American experience has a uniquely lingering affect in the United States due, in part, to the loss of land and sovereignty issues associated with colonization. When coupled with the environmental concerns and injustices such as lack of funding for basic necessities on many reservations, we see woman carrying a significant burden in Native American communities (Reese, 1997).

It should be noted that another common definition of Native American feminism places a great focus on the preservation of cultural identity and the role women play within the tribe as the keepers of that identity, thus ensuring that the culture is subsequently passed on to the future generations. According to Waters (2003),

Native women have a unique role to play in feminist politics. Native women struggle against resource wars, gaming economics, and biocolonialism. It is Native women's sacred obligation and responsibility to lead the way, through traditional women's leadership and authority, to reclaiming the earth, humanity, and all our relations via an ecoethics of reciprocity. (p. xii)

One of the concepts introduced in Native American feminist theory is the recognition that all our relations are indigenous to some place and as women we must struggle as the traditional keepers of the earth—a concept that will be further explored below, in reference to eco feminism.

As an example of multicultural feminist research, Amy Stalzer Sengupta and Yvette Loury Upton (chapter 14) draw from womanist, Asian American feminist perspectives, and Chicana feminism as they discuss college women's identity development. Amy and Yvette address multiple social identities as interconnected, such as gender, race, class, sexual orientation, ability, religion, and age.

Global feminists take a slightly different viewpoint when it comes to equal treatment of women. Whereas multicultural feminists "focus on the differences that exist among women who live within the boundaries of one nation-state or geographical area" (Tong, 2009, p. 8), global feminists "challenge women in developed nations to acknowledge that many of their privileges are bought at the expense of the well-being of women in developing nations" (Tong, 2009, p. 8). In this manner, global feminists argue that the personal and political are one and the same. In her narrative in section two, Dorothy Nkhata talks about her experiences as a woman in both Malawi and the United States. In this way, she connects the global and local through her reflections.

Eco Feminism

In its most basic definition, eco feminism is the recognition of the common ground in both feminism and environmentalism. Again, we see that two areas of identity overlap and inform each other. This is a natural pairing as eco feminists argue that there is a correlation between the destruction of the planet and the exploitation of women worldwide by the patriarchy. This particular area of feminism intersects with issues of socioeconomic privilege, speciesism, and racism. Eco feminists contend that both the destruction of the planet and its inhabitants are at stake, and the only way to avert these disasters is through taking a feminist perspective of the world.

Postmodern Feminism

Postmodern feminism is one that has slowly permeated our culture throughout the recent years, often in the guise of other forms of feminism, and is connected most closely with the third wave of feminism. Olson (1996) stated that postmodern feminists

> see female as having been cast into the role of the Other. They criticize the structure of society and the dominant order, especially in its patriarchal aspects. Many Postmodern feminists, however, reject the feminist label, because anything that ends with an "ism" reflects an essentialist conception. Postmodern Feminism is the ultimate acceptor of diversity. Multiple truths, multiple roles, multiple realities are part of its focus. There is a rejectance of an essential nature of women, of one-way to be a woman. (p. 19)

Multiple truths, multiple roles, and multiple realities reflect the ways in which postmodern feminists are open to a multiplicity of identities, lived experiences, and definitions of gender roles.

One of the most obvious ways in which postmodern feminism has permeated society is through our use of language (Butler, 1990). Postmodern feminists maintain that our gender is constructed through language and language constructs gender. An example of this type of feminism includes the urging of the use of the word *women* in place of *girls* when talking about all

college-going females, including 17- to 21-year-olds. Postmodern feminists also question the use of words such as *lady, woman,* or *female,* as they have their roots in the patriarchy and therefore imply a second gender and "other" (i.e., a derivative of gentleman, man, or male). However, one should be careful to note that postmodern feminism argues that women's subordination has no single cause or single solution, and language is merely an everyday applicable example of lived oppression.

FEMINIST APPROACHES TO RESEARCH

Another important concept to raise is the complex way in which the chapters in this book present various feminist approaches to research. Notions of epistemology, theory, methodology, and methods are often confused in both higher education and student affairs; therefore, we offer several descriptions for the sake of clarity, but not with the intention of encouraging rigidity. (Also see Broido & Manning, 2002; Harding, 1987; Hesse-Biber, 2007, Jones, Torres, & Arminio, 2006; Ramazanoğlu, 2002).

Feminist theory is founded on three main principles (Ropers-Huilman, 2002). First, women have something valuable to contribute to every aspect of the world. Second, as an oppressed group, women have been unable to achieve their potential, receive rewards, or gain full participation in society. Third, feminist research should do more than critique, but should work toward social transformation. As you will notice, some authors in this book make explicit their perspective on feminist theory, and for others, their perspective is more implicit.

Feminist methodology emerged in order to allow women's experiences—as lived, shared, and (re)interrupted by women themselves—to be the subject of social research (Better, 2006). As Ramazanoğlu (2002) clearly pointed out in her book *Feminist Methodology,*

A methodology in social research comprises rules that specify how social investigation should be approached. Each methodology links a particular *ontology* (for example, a belief that gender is social rather than natural) and a particular *epistemology* (a set of procedures for establishing what counts as knowledge) in providing *rules* that specify how to produce *valid knowledge of social reality* (for example, the real nature of particular gender relations). (p. 11)

More specifically, feminist epistemology—the philosophical grounding for deciding what kinds of knowledge are possible—addresses the connections between knowledge and its social uses and how patriarchal values have shaped the content and structure of that knowledge.

Further, taking a feminist methodological perspective requires "examining how knowledge and power are connected, and so making visible both the hidden power relations of knowledge production and the underpinnings of gender" (Ramazanoğlu, 2002, p. 63). The researchers in this book have engaged in many different methodological approaches to feminist research including narrative analysis, discourse analysis, historical analysis, phenomenology, and thematic analysis. Feminist research, in a similar manner to critical race theory, shares four main assumptions,

(a) Research fundamentally involves issues of *power*; (b) the research report is not transparent, but rather it is *authored* by a raced, gendered, classed, and politically oriented individual; (c) race, class and gender [among other social identities] are crucial for understanding experience; and (d) historically, *traditional research has silenced* members of oppressed and marginalized groups. (Rossman & Rallis, 2003, p. 93)

We add queer theory to this list, as it includes the ways in which research is authored by sexual orientation. This concept is explored further by Elise Abes and David Kasch in chapter 13.

The authors in this book have used different methods for their feminist research including the use of interviews (semi-structured and open-ended), focus groups, storytelling, questionnaires, document analysis, participant photography, journaling, and qualitative software. Simply put, one may mix and match a feminist theory with a methodological approach and specific methods, as long as the connections between the choices remain congruent (Jones, Torres, & Arminio, 2006) and the researcher is able to argue for/describe said congruence. In this way, we hope the chapters in this book, both independently and taken together, advance conceptualizations of feminist research. We would like to highlight Jennifer Sader's (chapter 8) and Thandi Sulé's (chapter 9) chapters for readers looking for strong examples of congruent feminist research.

CONCLUSION

In conclusion, as you read this chapter, you may have inevitably thought about a feminist author who was not included in our brief introduction, or have a different understanding of feminism than was portrayed in this chapter. Some see this as a problem for feminists: the inability to agree upon a sound definition and, "without agreed upon definition(s), we lack a sound foundation on which to construct theory or engage in overall meaningful praxis" (Vasquez, as cited in hooks, 2000b, p. 238). For example, in the essay "Towards a Revolutionary Ethics," Carmen Vasquez expressed her frustration by stating

We can't even agree on what a "feminist" is, never mind what she would believe in and how she defines the principles that constitute honor among us. In key with the American capitalist obsession for individualism and anything goes as long as it gets you what you want. Feminism in America has come to mean anything you like, honey. There are as many definitions of feminism as there are feminists, some of my sisters say, with a chuckle. I don't think it's funny. (as cited in hooks, 2000b, p. 238)

Many agree with Vasquez's description of the problem, whereas many feminists disagree with

Vasquez: the lack of definition *is* its strength, as reflected by bell hooks (2000a) in the title of her book, *Feminism Is for Everybody: Passionate Politics*. From here, you get to decide your own perspective on this argument, and we invite you to consider the multiple feminist perspectives, methodologies, methods, research findings, and practical implications from the women, men, and transgender authors in this book who hope to further feminist research and praxis in higher education and student affairs.

REFERENCES

Adams, M., Bell, L. A., & Griffin, P. (2007). *Teaching for diversity and social justice* (2nd ed.). New York: Routledge.

Better, A. S. (2006). *Feminist methods without boundaries*. Paper presented at the annual meeting of the American Sociological Association, Montreal Convention Center, Montreal, Quebec, Canada.

Broido, E., & Manning, K. (2002). Philosophical foundations and current theoretical perspectives in qualitative research. *Journal of College Student Development, 43*(4), 434–445.

Butler, J. (1990). *Gender trouble*. New York: Routledge Classics.

Collins, P. H. (2000). *Black feminist thought*. New York: Routledge.

Deans of women of the middle west. (1903). Minutes of the conference of deans of women of the middle west. Retrieved on September 12, 2009, from http://www.bgsu.edu/colleges/library/cac/sahp/word/1903ConferenceofDOW.pdf

de Beauvoir, S. (1952). *The second sex*. New York: Vintage Books.

Evans, N. J., Forney, D. S., Guido, F. M., Patton, L. & Renn, K. A. (2009). *Student development in college: Theory, research, and practice* (2nd ed.). San Francisco, CA: Jossey-Bass.

Foreman, G. (1932/1995). *Indian removal: The emigration of the five civilized tribes of Indians* (Vol. 2). Norman, OK: University of Oklahoma Press.

Gilligan, C. (1982). *In a different voice: Psychological theory and women's development*. Cambridge, MA: Harvard University Press.

Glazer, J. S., Bensimon, E. M., & Townsend, B. K. (1993). *Women in higher education: A feminist perspective*. Needham Heights, MA: Ginn Press.

Harding, S. (Ed). (1987). *Feminism and methodology: Social science issues*. Bloomington, IN: Indiana University Press.

Hesse-Biber, S. N. (Ed.). (2007). *Handbook of feminist research: Theory and praxis*. Thousand Oaks, CA: Sage.

Hoff Sommers, C. (1995). *Who stole feminism: How women have betrayed women*. New York, NY: Touchstone.

hooks, b. (2000a). *Feminism is for everybody: Passionate politics*. Cambridge, MA: South End Press.

hooks, b. (2000b). Feminism: A movement to end sexist oppression. In M. Adam, W. J. Blumenfeld, R. Castaneda, H. W. Hackman, M. L. Peters, & Z. Zúñiga (Eds.), *Readings for diversity and social justice: An anthology on racism, anti-semitism, sexism, heterosexism, ableism, and classism* (pp. 238–240). New York: Routledge.

Jaggar, A. M., & Young, I. M. (2000). *A companion to feminist philosophy*. Malden, MA: Blackwell.

Jones, S. R., Torres, V. & Arminio, J. (2006). *Negotiating the Complexities of Qualitative Research in Higher Education: Fundamental Elements and Issues*. New York, NY: Routledge.

Kim, H. S. (2007). The politics of border crossings: Black, postcolonial and transnational feminist perspectives. In S. N. Hesse-Biber (Ed.), *Handbook of feminist research: Theory and praxis* (pp. 107–122). Thousand Oaks, CA: Sage.

Krolokke, C., & Sorensen, A. S. (2005). *Gender communication theories and analyses: From silence to performance*. Thousand Oaks, CA: Sage.

Olson, H. (1996). *The power to name: Marginalizations and exclusions of subject representation in library catalogues*. Unpublished dissertation. University of Wisconsin–Madison.

Ramazanoğlu, C. (with Holland, J.). (2002). *Feminist methodology: Challenges and choices*. Thousand Oaks, CA: Sage.

Rampton, M. (2008). Three waves of feminism. The magazine of Pacific University. Retrieved September 12, 2009, from http://www.pacificu.edu/magazine/2008/fall/echoes/feminism.cfm

Reese, L. W. (1997). *Women of Oklahoma, 1890–1920*. Norman, OK: University of Oklahoma Press.

Ropers-Huilman, B. (Ed.). (2003). *Gendered futures in higher education: Critical perspectives for change*. Albany, NY: SUNY.

Rossman, G. B., & Rallis, S. F. (2003). *Learning in the field: An introduction to qualitative research* (2nd ed.). Thousand Oaks, CA: Sage.

Student Affairs History Project. (2006). Home. Retrieved September 12, 2009, from http://www.bgsu.edu/colleges/library/cac/sahp/index.htm

Tong, R. (2009). *Feminist thought: A more comprehensive introduction.* Philadelphia, PA: Westview Press.

Wagner, S. R. (1996). The untold story of the Iroquois influence on early feminists. *On the Issues.* Retrieved December 21, 2008, from http://www.feminist.com/resources/artspeech/genwom/iroquoisinfluence.html

Walker, A. (1983). *In Search of Our Mothers Gardens: Womanist Prose* (pp. xi–xii).

Waters, A. (2003). Introduction: Indigenous women in the Americas. *Hypatia*, 18(2), ix–xx.

Wheeler, E. (2002). Black feminism and womanism. In A. M. Martínez Alemán & K. A. Renn (eds.), *Women in higher education: An encyclopedia* (pp. 118–120). Santa Barbara, CA: ABC Clio.

Whelehan, I. (2000). Feminism, postmodernism, and theoretical developments. In J. Glazer-Raymo, B. K. Townsend, & B. Ropers-Huilman (eds.), *Women in higher education: A feminist perspective* (2nd ed., pp. 72–84). Boston, MA: Pearson.

2

Reflections From "Professional Feminists" in Higher Education

Women's and Gender Centers at the Start of the Twenty-First Century

Susan Marine

Abstract: *Many women's centers were founded in the 1970s and 1980s in response to second wave feminism within the academy. Although women's centers today have a prominent place on many campuses, little is known about the work, including challenges and successes, done by women's center staff in the current political and fiscal climate. A qualitative descriptive study of the experiences of 21 women's center staff from a diverse array of institutions revealed that women's centers are vibrant, evolving hubs of feminist engagement with the academy. Challenges dictate that more resources, visibility, and social capital are needed to enable women's centers to reach their full potential in pursuit of gender equity.*

IN THE THREE DECADES since the beginning of the second wave of the feminist movement,[1] activism in higher education has resulted in an increased number of women participating as students, faculty members, and administrators. Women's voices and perspectives now infuse the everyday decision making on every campus in America. Title IX of the education amendments of 1972 enabled women to take on inequities in campus athletics and to see necessary changes made to policies and practices both in the classroom and on the playing field. An extensive body of research about women's lives, perspectives, and experiences has been conducted in this era, result-ing in the emergence of the interdisciplinary field of women's studies. Though women are still underrepresented in positions of power relative to their numbers in the general populace, tenured faculty and senior administrators are now far more likely to be "she" than at any other time in history.

On the twentieth-century college campus, evidence suggests that women have mobilized to draw attention to many diverse aspects of feminist struggle, such as creating responses to sexual violence, breaking silence on issues of gendered racial inequity, and instituting affirmative action in hiring and admissions (Collins, 2000; Dziech

& Weiner, 1990; Komarovsky, 1989; Miller-Bernal & Poulson, 2004; Peril, 2006). Progress, both hard won and precarious, has been made, and higher education has been transformed by the work and persistence of women activists and their allies.

Women's centers on American college campuses are a natural home for the work of campus activism for gender equity. Those who lead women's centers—and I am fortunate to count myself among them—work to advance awareness of women's issues on campus, and to support the promotion of women's visibility. Mostly founded in the 1970s and 1980s in direct response to the emergent ideologies of second wave feminism, there are now approximately 460 women's and/or gender centers existing on college campuses in America[2] (Gribi, 2008). Diverse in their missions and founding precepts, these centers typically focus on provision of services and programs that enable women to achieve equality on the coeducational campus as students, employees, and scholars (Willinger, 2002). Campus women's centers serve as spaces for women's free expression and as clearinghouses for research on women and gender. In addition, women's and gender centers enhance women's sense of belonging to the institution and its mission and seek to address the ongoing disparities experienced by women in competitive higher education environments (Davie, 2002). Many women's and gender centers today also incorporate broader issues of gender exploration into their work, including attention to men and masculinities, as well as transgender identities.

Although the purposes and initiative of each center vary, symbolically women's centers represent the very heart of feminist engagement with the academy. As a microcosm of women's leadership, this engagement is vitally shaped by the commitments of those who lead and support women's centers, whose values in turn direct the work yet to be done. At the same time, women's centers are living, dynamic communities that seek to be highly responsive to and reflective

of the needs and concerns of those who utilize their services.

Despite the impact that women's centers have had on the contemporary American campus, little is known about the ways that those of us who hold leadership roles within women's centers create and enact a vision to amplify women's voices toward the goal of gender equity on campus. Further, little is known about the collective challenges faced by women's center staff and the ways we creatively address these challenges in tandem with allies on our respective campuses and with support from each other. An edited anthology (Davie, 2002) exploring the contours of women's center work established a baseline of information as the twenty-first century dawned, which included data from a 1994 survey of women's centers; yet, little additional commentary has been added to the conversation since that time. In the continued spirit of demystifying the less-than-visible yet essential work of women's centers, my intention in this study is to provide firsthand perspectives on the ways that women's center directors conduct the work of change on campus. As part of the effort to address the paucity of research on women's center work, the findings described in this chapter provide a (avowedly preliminary) point of departure for continued research on feminist student affairs practice in the twenty-first century.

METHODOLOGY

The approach used in this study is qualitative descriptive research. According to Sandelowski (2000), qualitative descriptive research aims to both faithfully represent and make meaning of experiences, events, or processes that humans take part in, and particularly, to describe the commonalities of those processes across participants.

The particular paradigmatic stance adopted in the analysis of this research is avowedly feminist in nature. According to Olesen (2006), feminist research "centers and makes problematic women's diverse situations, as well as those institutions that frame those situations" (p. 216). Feminist research seeks to locate the truths of women's experiences in their own words and acts and to use this truth to scrutinize the features of institutions that deter, or promote, women's agency. Feminist research approaches emerged from the postmodern shift toward interpretive, participatory, and dialectical forms of knowledge production and thus are always concerned with accurate representation of the socially located realities of research participants, including naming and deconstructing their multiple and intersecting identities (Hesse-Biber, Gilmartin, & Lyderberg, 1999).

McCracken (1988) proposed that in order to conduct qualitative research effectively, the researcher must "use the self as instrument of inquiry" (p. 32). In conducting this study, I affirm that my dual subjectivity as both a researcher and a director of a campus-based women's center matters to the outcomes of the data collection and analysis that I have conducted. In seeking to better understand the nature of the work of my women's center colleagues, I have inevitably viewed and analyzed their perspectives through the lens of my own work and values. The conflagration of researcher as participant in the topic, which I have sought to understand through this study, invites both richness and potential for bias in the topics that were explored with participants in this study and in the analysis that I have employed to interpret them. Through member checking with study participants, I have sought to determine the validity of the findings in this study, as well as verify the contextual placement of these findings.

Methods

The purpose of this study was to better understand the perceptions, experiences, and challenges faced by women's center directors and related staff at this current moment in history. The data presented in this study were gathered through a series of focus group conversations that took place in July 2008. Participants in these focus groups were self-identified staff of campus women's centers, including directors and assistant directors as well as coordinators of initiatives to address violence against women.

Recruitment was conducted using purposive sampling (Patton, 1990), adhering to predetermined criteria that all participants must have direct professional experience in a leadership role at a campus-based women's center. Participants were recruited through a listserv for staff at women's centers known as WRAC-L (the women's resources and action centers listserv), which is moderated by the Director of the Center for Women and Gender at Dartmouth College. Currently, more than 400 staff and supporters of women's centers subscribe to WRAC-L. A recruitment e-mail seeking interest in participation from staff of women's centers was sent on three different occasions to the WRAC-L list to ensure that all who might be interested in the study were aware of the opportunity. In addition, I recruited interested participants for the study in person by announcing the study at a workshop for women's center staff at the National Women's Studies Association annual conference in Cincinnati, Ohio (June 18–23, 2008).

Twenty-four participants, all women, answered the call for participation; of those 24, 17 responded to a survey sent to select a time to participate in one of three conference calls. Each call was conducted in a conference call format, with between 4 and 7 participants calling in to voluntarily participate in a session. Each participant who dialed in completed the call, lasting approximately one hour, and each received a gift card voucher as compensation for her time. One participant was not able to complete the call at one of three designated times and agreed to an individual interview at another time to provide answers. Three additional participants mailed written responses to the questions discussed in the call.

Of the 21 total participants, 13 are staff at women's centers on public university campuses (including one at a community college), and 8 hold positions at women's centers in a private college or university setting. Of those 8 participants, 4 work in women's centers located at private institutions that are religiously affiliated.

The average length of time each participant has worked in a women's center is 4.5 years; 5 participants have held multiple positions within a women's center, whereas the remaining 16 were in their first and only women's center professional position. Three of the women in the study identified as women of color, including 1 who identified as biracial, and 18 identified as White/Anglo American. All of the participants have earned a master's degree in women's studies, higher education, student affairs, public administration, or a related human services field. Four participants have also earned a PhD or other doctoral equivalent.

Women's centers represented in the study are on campuses ranging in size from 1,300 students to 50,000 students, with the average enrollment being 21,000. The average operating budget for women's centers in this study was $43,000; the range of budgets given was $5,000 to $293,000. In some cases, these budgets included salary and benefit allocations, information that was provided by some, but not all, participants.

Although the participant pool in this study represented a broad cross section of women's centers in the United States, it is important to note that this study does not purport to provide a comprehensive picture of *all* women's centers in the United States. Rather, the data provide a glimpse of some women's centers' staff experiences from the perspective of a relatively diverse sample of directors, coordinators, and other staff.

Analysis

Once data were collected, the focus group recordings were transcribed and analyzed for thematic patterns. The six-step rubric outlined by Miles and Huberman (1994) as a means for analysis of qualitative research data was employed to analyze the data as follows:

1. Line-by-line coding of data from focus group interviews
2. Recording of first impressions and insights from the data
3. Sorting through data to note recurring themes in responses, including themes in content, context, and sequence
4. Noting the frequency of recurring themes as well as differently recounted perspectives in the data
5. Arriving at a subset of generalizations in the data
6. Examining these generalizations with reference to existing information about this population

In this study, I asked participants five specific questions:

1. What characterizes the work of your women's center, and drives your goals and priorities?
2. What are the challenges you face in your work, and what can you claim as your most meaningful accomplishments?
3. Who are allies in the work that you do?
4. What should inform the work of women's centers in the twenty-first century?
5. What stirs you to continue the work?

In the answers provided, the richness of perspective of those who lead women's centers (and, by extension, those who often lead feminist change on campus in the current era) emerged as complicated, colorful tapestries of both the joys and challenges of this work in student affairs. Of course, many other aspects of the work are important to explore and understand—including how women's centers assess the outcomes of the work that we do, and how we seek and integrate community input into the focus of our work. These questions, although essential for future inquiry, are beyond the scope of this current study, which sought principally to document the foci of women's centers' work as the twenty-first century begins and to invite reflection on the demands inherent in the work in varying institutional contexts.

FINDINGS

In both individual consideration of these questions and in dialogue with each other, women's center staff participating in these focus groups spoke openly and enthusiastically of the unique alchemy of their work. The women endeavored to strike a balance between inviting dissonance, extending support, and creating spaces for quiet comfort and fortitude for boundary pushing. They also expressed hopeful optimism for the growth of women's centers' impact as the twenty-first century continues, thoughtfully interrogating the ways they might better and more creatively engage their communities in forging a better campus for people of all genders.

In this section, I describe the thematic findings that emerged from the voices of women's center leaders. These include foci of women's centers' work today, challenges of women's center work, allies in doing the work, success stories of women's centers, and the future of women's centers.

Foci of Women's Centers' Work Today

Not surprisingly, the results of this study suggest that the scope and tenor of work being conducted by women's center staff varies widely across institutional context. This affirmed what Bonnie Clevenger (1988) noted in a similar study of women's center staff 20 years ago when stating that "there are no universally applicable models for how women's centers express their mission" (p. 4). Women's center staff participating in this study noted that they derive their mission, accompanying activities, and programs from three particular influences: their specific institutional context, the attendant political milieu, and the relative weight/importance of student, faculty, and staff needs and concerns, which tended to be mutually reinforcing, rather than distinct, categories. Participants frequently pointed to long-standing mission statements to explain and codify the driving ethos of their work; others noted that their work tends to evolve year to year, based on the changing needs and demographics of their respective target communities.

The five primary activities that supported the missions described by women's center staff included advocacy, outreach, educational programming, service provision (including services for pregnant and parenting students, faculty, and staff, as well as services for survivors of sexual and domestic violence), and policy development. Each participant in this study described some or all of these activities as a primary feature of their daily work and provided concrete examples of the ways in which these five categories formed the epicenter of their work around gender equity on campus.

Advocacy for equity included activities such as supporting student efforts to adopt a safety escort service; creation of funding, facilities, and positions for support of mothers on campus; development of resources for international women who are spouses of graduate students; and promotion of mentoring among junior and senior women faculty. A willingness to take a stand on behalf of a needed change on campus was cited as an essential part of the role of many women's center staff. One director at a midsized university in the western United States noted, "without my being an advocate, certain things here just won't get done for women."

Several participants talked about the importance of outreach on their campuses and the ways that they generate community among women. As one director at a small private college in the Midwest noted,

> Outreach, to me, is figuring out how to sell the idea of community to women . . . to help other women, especially students, to realize the benefits of just being together, sharing experiences and knowledge.

My college doesn't offer many chances to know the value of this, so this is where my work comes in, making this happen for women, and helping them to see the worth of it.

Outreach involves both actual travel to alumni gatherings, athletic events, health fairs, and faculty meetings and a willingness to extend one's self (and one's mission) beyond the limitations of one's designated space. Several participants talked both literally and metaphorically about "taking the message out to the masses" and "spreading the word beyond our center's space" as crucial to their current successes, moving beyond the familiarity of the women's center to engage students, staff, and faculty in understanding the work of women's centers. For many, this message felt essential to the success of their work in developing educational opportunities for their communities on issues relating to women and gender.

More than half of the participants in the study described educational programs and awareness raising as a central focus of their women's center work. Contemporary women's centers are especially focused on programming that engages students, faculty, and staff in exploration of social justice issues, typically featuring an angle that encourages the deconstruction of socially inscribed gender roles that serve to oppress.

One assistant director of a small public university in the South noted,

Programming which takes a look at the ways that women live, and the ways that men and women live in relation to each other that continues to impede women's full equality, would never happen if it weren't for us at the women's center. Not having a women's studies program, it's truly up to us to make sure these ideas reach students and that they are called to question certain things, certain notions of what makes a woman and what makes a man.

Sharon Davie (2002) noted that these experiences are germane to the healthy operation of a campus women's center and, to paraphrase Johnson's (1987) notion of "encounters with otherness" (p. 19), she proposed that they invite both risk and growth. In creating opportunities for reflection upon one's gendered self and the gendered realities of others, we at women's centers forge understanding across differences and new avenues for the transformation of future possibilities.

Commitments to reducing the occurrence of sexual and domestic violence, and educating communities and individuals regarding their role in this effort, continues to be a priority for most of the women's center staff interviewed in this study. As noted by Kaplan, Hindus, Mejia, Olsen, and La Due (2002), "women's centers play such a central role in sexual assault intervention prevention work on college campuses that at times it seems that is all we do" (p. 198). Operation of crisis lines, employment of professionally trained advocates, accompaniment to legal and medical services, and assistance with navigating the ins and outs of the campus disciplinary process and local judicial system are some of the regularly described features that participants in this study acknowledged as part of their quotidian response to gender violence. Several participants also remarked upon the tremendous visibility inherent in being the designated "campus voice" for antiviolence activism. One director of a women's center at a midsized Midwestern university described as one of her center's proudest accomplishments the coordination of the annual Take Back the Night March, routinely the largest in her state, averaging 600 participants.

Notably, the lone participant in the study representing community colleges offered a markedly different perspective from the other women in the study. For her, pragmatic issues such as childcare, financial aid, health insurance coverage, domestic violence advocacy, and even the most basic issues such as securing transportation to the campus were the priorities of her center. At the end of the day, she explained, these alone were the issues that determine the difference between retention and disengagement for women in her community, and thus was the defining mission of her women's center's work.

Challenges of Women's Center Work

The challenges faced by women's center staff participating in this study were described as both ideological and material in nature. Many staff of women's centers participating in this study acknowledged struggling with students' (and others') perception that the work of the women's movement is complete and, therefore, the relevancy of feminism in the twenty-first century is moot. Ambivalence about adopting a feminist identity, especially among young women of all races and women of color of all ages, has been documented widely in both the academic literature and the popular press of the last decade (see Baumgardner & Richards, 2000; Hogeland, 1994; Hymowitz, 2002; Rudman & Fairchild, 2007; Zucker, 2004). According to participants in this study, those who lead women's centers often find themselves stymied by the decision to adopt, or not adopt, an avowedly feminist stance in our explicitly stated missions, but there is little to no ambivalence about adopting work that is feminist in nature.

When asked about the use or avoidance of the term *feminism* to describe the explicit or implicit aims of their work, responses from participants were mixed and appeared to be dependent on the extent to which the institution, as a whole, enabled pursuit of an explicitly progressive mission. Encountering resistance to the word in her campus community, one director at a midsized public university in the Midwest explained her perspective as follows:

> We do use the word feminism, but we use it strategically. It depends on who our audience is, but it's in the long version of our mission statement. It's just got such negative connotations now that it becomes difficult to put it out in certain venues. We've had pushback for doing things that are similarly feminist, such as certain kinds of advertising for the Vagina Monologues.

While the term *feminist* was not universally embraced by participants in the study, the infusion of symbiotically feminist values, particularly women's empowerment, safety, and enhanced access to educational equity, into the work of women's centers was noted as unambiguously crucial. One director of a women's center at a large public university in the Southwest noted,

> In terms of the work we do at our center, the word "feminist" is consistently in our verbal rhetoric when we introduce programs, but it's not featured in our written materials . . . there's a choice being made there, but I am not sure what that choice means. I'll have to think about it more.

Other participants endorsed a more fluid and evolving manner of identifying their center's core values through a process that aims to be responsive to the needs and political climate of the institution and the individuals invested in women's center work. Walking this line was described as particularly delicate in the context of the women's centers located in religiously affiliated institutions. As noted by a director in one such women's center in the Midwest,

> Our mission is about learning the lay of the land and inventing a different future, while honoring the past, which is delicate . . . We didn't create a mission until we did a needs assessment, and in the needs assessment, we were able to identify phrases, words, and philosophies that wouldn't work for our community. Our mission, therefore, does not include the word "feminism," which seems to be too polarizing.

Some noted that an explicit emphasis on the values of feminism could serve to deter productive alliances with other campus constituencies concerned with identity. This concern is described by one director of a women's center at a private college in the Mid-Atlantic, when she noted,

> The staff of centers for students of color, and for LGBT students on my campus seem more inclined to work with me if we keep the "happy friendly"

language of social justice in play. If I get too focused on the whole notion of women's empowerment, they sometimes tune me out for being insensitive to what they see as their purpose . . . and it's not really all about women, as they say.

The challenge inherent in this effort to redefine and reassert the values of feminism (both on campuses and in national associations) was echoed by one assistant director of a midsized private university on the East Coast.

> One of my greatest challenges is educating people about "feminism". What goes hand in hand about that is dispelling stereotypes about feminists, and what the women's center is and does . . . there's a prevailing belief that we don't need feminism anymore.

Challenges faced by women's center staff who are working to raise awareness about women's issues have not been limited to the resistance expressed by students; indeed, some of the greatest challenges appeared to emanate from efforts to build alliances with colleagues in student affairs around issues of concern to women. As noted by one director at a midsized Catholic university on the East Coast,

> I have also struggled with colleagues; survey data has revealed that body image and eating disorders are a big concern on our campus. When I have tried to initiate, in a collaborative way, some changes so that [my university] is better equipped to serve students who have clinical eating issues, I have been surprised by reticence and confusion about the nature of these illnesses, and absolute resistance from colleagues, who should know there's mental and physical health and safety at risk, and who should be willing to support students differently.

Collegiality typically requires playing nicely within a system. In contrast, Ng (2000) asserted that activist stances are crucial for the transformation of the contemporary university, imploring women to act "against the grain" in "recognizing that, and how, routinized courses of action

and interactions within the university are imbued with unequal power distributions which produce and reinforce various forms of marginalization and exclusion" (p. 366). Bumping up against hierarchical structures within the college and university setting sometimes served to call into question the consistency of a center's feminist ethos. In the experience of one director of a women's center at a midsized university on the West Coast,

> Working in a hierarchical institution while trying to promote feminism feels like it is at odds . . . the system is set up in such a way that you can only hit certain heights, you can't go as far as you want to go, and that's due to gatekeepers. Trying to be more "bottom up" in terms of leadership style is challenging.

In addition to the persistent complexity of negotiating feminism in centers' work, resource allocation, an issue also faced by many women's organizations throughout history, continues to be a challenge for many women's centers. This appears to be particularly true for women's centers located in public institutions where state funding has been sharply cut or in some cases eliminated. Virtually all participants in this study employed at public institutions were expected to operate on less-than-adequate funding and function in conditions that they acknowledge inevitably limited the effectiveness of programs and initiatives. As lamented by the director of a women's center at a midsized public university in the Midwest,

> This is my tenth year, and my operating budget is less now than when I started, yet we're expected to do more and more. How you continue to do more with less funding is challenging, but we do the best we can with what we have and seek creative funding options while continuing to seek support for increased operational dollars.

Women's center staff frequently noted the inherent tension arising from finding themselves in competition for resources with other offices and initiatives that they recognized as offering an otherwise natural (and meaningful) alliance. As noted by a seasoned director of a public university women's center in the western United States,

> We're often compared to the multicultural centers, and students sometimes ask, "why does the women's center get so much [funding and staff]?" . . . I hate to be compared to them, when we're all dealing with issues of social justice and identities, and we should all be working together to get the best resources for all of us.

Another director at a public university in the Southwest described the recent trend in state funding that resulted in a 40% shortfall for programs and initiatives and the disappointing publicity that followed.

> What killed me most about getting this [negative budget] news was that it wasn't just the fact that we wouldn't be able to offer pizza anymore at our lectures. We wouldn't be able to subsidize diapers for student mothers, or to ensure 24-hour coverage for our rape crisis hotline. That's where the cuts hurt the most, but the student newspaper depicted the issue as "no more cookies at the faculty brown bags."

Finally, an additional challenge echoed by several staff participating in the study was the ongoing issue of creating an environment that is inclusive of the needs and concerns of women of diverse backgrounds, as opposed to functioning as a women's center that continues to be disproportionately responsive to the values and priorities of White, middle-class feminists. One director at a midsized private institution in the Midwest noted,

> At this predominantly white institution, addressing the needs of minority women and especially women of color is an ongoing struggle, which we all know is a historical issue for women's centers in general. We're making inroads but we have a lot of work left to do.

Effective engagement with multiple identities is another area of challenge for many women's center leaders. Another director at a midsized private university on the East Coast noted that

> [t]here's a lot of work being done on my campus with race, class, and other [individual] identities, and we are not doing everything we could be or should be around intersectionality.

In summary, two particular trends—resource limitations and ideological fissures—emerged as the primary challenges faced by staff of women's centers taking part in this study. Fiscal constraints appear to be a continuing challenge for many, particularly those who operate women's centers in public institutions, contributing to both unmet need and unrealized visions. The extent to which many women's center communities, and their leaders, feel they can productively take up the banner of feminism appears to be a point of contention, while most acknowledged that the heart of their work remains essentially feminist in nature. Other less frequently mentioned challenges include marginalization of the work, tensions between academic and student affairs' missions, and the inevitable burnout that arises from making futile efforts to address all the needs, all the time.

Allies in Doing the Work

Participants in this study enthusiastically acknowledged the many gifts inherent in connections they forged with supportive allies. According to Lisker (2002),

> Allies [of women's centers] . . . perform multiple tasks: they volunteer to help with the work, they refer people to the center's services, they speak positively of the center to their friends and colleagues, and they help convince university administrators that the women's center has broad-based support. (p. 365)

The vast majority of participants in this study declared that two specific sources of support were

crucial in their day-to-day operations. These included other offices devoted to student identity exploration and affirmation, such as LGBT
and multicultural/ethnic student services, and
the faculty and staff of the affiliated (or independent) department of women's and gender studies.
One director at a midsized public university in
the Midwest noted,

> I simply cannot imagine where I'd be without the
> ability to plan, collaborate with, and commiserate
> with the two other directors in my unit, one of
> whom conducts programs for black student com-
> munity and the other, for Hispanic students. It
> would be unfathomable that I would create a pro-
> gram or initiative without running it by this brain
> trust for input and support . . . and really, if they
> said it wasn't going to fly, I'd move on, since I
> trust their investment in what I am trying to do
> implicitly.

Although most spoke of bridge-building
among students, staff, and faculty of their own
institutions, invaluable women's center alliances
sometimes extend beyond the confines of the
campus itself and take surprisingly robust forms
in the way of advocacy from women leaders in
the surrounding community. As noted by one
director of a midsized public university women's
center in the Midwest,

> We're really fortunate to have an amazing local
> women's community. We have a lot of strong and
> wealthy women who support the work of the
> women's center, the women's council, and gender
> studies, so they have been wonderful allies for us
> because they have the ear of the movers and shakers
> in the community and in the administration . . . as
> a result, the women's center is very protected.

While the contours of steadfast alliance appeared to emanate from relationship building,
making one's women's center relevant to the mission of the institution is not something that a
women's center can afford to be casual about.
In the eyes of one director of a women's center
at a different midsized public university in the
Midwest,

If your university has a strategic plan, look at where
you might fit into that plan, and ask yourself, "how
can we best contribute to the academic mission
of the institution?" . . . [This requires] making sure
that everything you do is part of the broader spectrum of what the university is trying to accomplish
in educating students for the future.

One women's center director at a relatively
new center located in a community college concurred that making alliances was not simply ap-
pealing, it was in fact crucial to the successful
establishment of her center in its early years.

> When I got here, and this is just my style, I built
> coalitions. I did not come to the college saying,
> "we're going to have a women's center, and here's
> how it is going to be." I met with many constituen-
> cies on campus, as many people as I could, to figure
> out what the women's center should be, I developed
> buy-in for the women's center. Had I come in say-
> ing, "here's how the women's center is going to be"
> I would have faced really serious challenges.

No woman is an island, and this is clearly
never more true than when listening to women's
center staff describe the numerous and innovative ways they have forged alliances on and off
campus.

Success Stories of Women's Centers

Although acknowledgment of challenges in the
narratives of women's center staff flowed abun-
dantly as dialogue unfolded in the focus groups,
participants were equally able to name the
achievements of their centers and describe both
the energy and strategies required to bring
these accomplishments to fruition. Acting in
concert with members of their communities,
these women's center leaders had made satisfying strides toward full involvement and inclusion
of women's voices and perspectives on campus.

Bridge building among women of different
generations on campus was regularly noted as an
accomplishment by participants in this study. In
the words of one director of a midsized public
university in the Midwest,

We had a reunion last year of the 10th anniversary of our women's center and the 30th anniversary of women's studies—inviting back everyone who was ever part of one of these places and was involved in activism, the community, or scholarship. We had panels featuring alumnae from the 70s, 80s and 90s and early 00s, talking about how feminism has informed their lives and work, and what kind of activism they have done . . . and how what they have learned through women's studies or from the women's center have colored the choices they made in their life. It was so empowering!

In addition to creating community among women across generations, women's center staff are making strides to infuse the cocurriculum of their institutions with perspectives that are uniquely women centered. As one director of a women's center at a midsized Catholic institution in the Northeast describes,

We've done some work with an initiative looking at the future of the church on campus. Before we got involved with it, the issues addressed did not include a feminist perspective, leaving male clergy and male leaders with the central voice. Not only have we been able to bring more women into the conversation, but [we] are also bringing a feminist perspective to this program.

Development of initiatives for childcare and support of women who are pregnant or parenting had provided several participants with the emotional fuel to feel energized about working for change. One director of a private, small college in the Midwest notes,

Gone are the days [at my institution] when trying to manage being a parent, and a student are impossible. I spent three whole years making sure we had access to changing rooms, safe areas for breastfeeding, and affordable, on-campus child care, and it was worth every minute. I see students and even faculty pushing their babies in a stroller across campus, and I know that I have been part of that reality.

Time and collaborative effort were the most frequently mentioned features of successful change on campus. Additional areas of success included measurable improvement in the provision of services for women after experiencing sexual or domestic violence. As one assistant director of a women's center at a large public university in the South described,

There was a time when saying the words "rape" or "sexual assault" on our campus was met with skepticism, if not downright hostility. Thanks to what we've created here, there's now real ownership of the problem, and a sense that the university is no longer trying to keep its head in the sand about violence. I think we made that happen, though it was not an easy path. I can sleep better knowing that women are being helped and that the help is professionally trained.

Additional areas of satisfying growth were encountered in the forging of intellectual domains with women's and gender studies, in the development of policies and procedures for response to sexual harassment and other forms of bias, in the support of women faculty and staff in their efforts to achieve tenure and to enable work/life balance, and in the promotion of awareness of LGBT issues and concerns. While the work feels constant and sometimes urgent to participants in this study, the rewards are regular and immensely gratifying, leading one director at a small private college on the East Coast to comment that "she simply cannot imagine a better position for herself than what this job allows her to be—a professional feminist."

Looking Ahead to the Future of Women's Centers

When pressed to describe what should be the most meaningful goals of the campus women's center in the twenty-first century, some prefaced their answer by saying, "this may only be true for my center, but. . . . " This tendency toward relativity was balanced by other equally passionate responses that signified a clear and urgent need for the unification of women's causes and concerns, transcending the barriers of institutional type, size, and prevailing political sense. One frequently mentioned future need was the importance of inviting others into the work remaining to be done around gender equity in American society. As noted by the sexual assault program coordinator of a women's center at a small college on the West Coast,

> I feel strongly that we should include men in our work. I want to make the shift of inclusion that works. It's this whole idea that women have been doing this work for years and years, the same issues are coming up. Where do we need to focus our energy that feminism benefits the entire society?

Others mentioned that in addition to extending the possibilities for men to be involved in the work of gender equity, the work of gender equity must be continually responsive to, and in dialogue with, other forms of antioppression work and that the symbiosis between antiracism, antihomophobia, and antipoverty work must be paid more than simple lip service in its realization within women's centers. Specifically, the interests and concerns of women of color were repeatedly acknowledged as ongoing, and glacially slow, areas of improvement for many of the centers in this study. As described by DiLapi and Gay (2002),

> Feminism and the women's movement hold the promise of addressing the needs and concerns of all women. This promise, however, has not always translated into reality . . . this dynamic is reflected on white-majority campuses, where women's centers are too often utilized by, and perceived to be a space for white women only. (p. 204)

One women's center director, a White woman at a small rural college in the South, stated that she felt that her center's primary calling was to be the leader in taking on the institutional racism which, she said, "continued to poison the basic premise of the place." Others described that they were committed to broadening dialogue on the integration of social justice issues and sim-

ply needed to continue building strategies to get others on board, as noted by a director of a women's center at a midsized Mountain States university:

> Right now we're experiencing the challenge of some of the philosophical shifts in what feminism means, and to whom, and it feels somewhat intergenerational in nature . . . there are some people who are really ready to move forward with a feminist agenda that is anti-oppression oriented, and some who aren't ready to go that far yet, and want to concentrate on gender as the primary oppression.

Clearly, the integration of women's issues with other forms of social justice work will continue to be a focus of the twenty-first century women's center, for at least some participants in this study.

In closing, some staff of women's centers chose to represent the impact of their work as more than simply *other*-directed, adopting a positive stance toward the value of *inner* transformation. As noted by one director at a midsized religiously affiliated university on the East Coast,

> Women's centers are uniquely poised to help people make a connection between creating an external environment that promotes peace and justice, and helps people to do the inner work that has to happen to bring that [change] about in the world . . . how to look internally at ourselves in a loving, honest way and to be clear about who we are . . . and to let that authenticity be a guide for that external work. Women's centers can be an opening for the new wave of consciousness in the world.

Fuel for the Road: What Keeps Women's Center Staff Moving Forward

It is the individual, personal rewards of women's center work, as well as the collective spirit that drives the work in new and expansive directions, that was excitedly recounted by all participants in this study, many of whom described their positions as "their dream jobs" or "the best possible avenue for me in higher education." Many admitted, usually with mirth, that the positions they hold in women's centers are far from being lucrative, and thus the rewards of the work must come from other kinds of internal and external compensation. For some, being a link in the chain of success for individual women visiting their center was the key to feeling energized for the work's challenges. In the words of the director of a large community college women's center,

> Knowing that I play a role in empowering women, that's what motivates me . . . Just being an excellent listener, and being there for the journey. My goal in every conversation is to say, "what are your options?" . . . the local paper did an article on me and referred to me as a "helper by nature" and that makes me feel really good.

Other directors noted the importance of watching students undergo personal transformation, and then watching with even greater satisfaction as that frequently led to efforts to transform the institution on behalf of other women, or even more optimally, in concert with other women. Through deliberative processes of determining potential courses of action, and then engaging students in self-directed choice making, women's center staff experienced the satisfaction of enabling younger women to gain confidence in their abilities to decide, and to act, for their own benefit. One director of a private, religiously affiliated college on the East Coast noted,

> This job reminds me that once I thought I couldn't do things for myself that I now help other women to do . . . getting to see their faces when that excruciatingly difficult decision comes to pass in a really good way, when they realize they won't pass out or die if they stand up for themselves . . . that's worth a lot of money to me, really more money than this job could ever afford to pay me!

Participants expressed the importance of invested mentorship for bringing generations of women behind them into the professional practice of feminism on the college campus, noting that the possibilities of working in a women's center had not occurred to them until a mentor

in a center took an interest in their potential. As noted in Monica Fochtman's (chapter 6) study in this volume, mentorship, support networks, and sharing of work/life balance strategies are vitally important to the advancement of women in the field of postsecondary student affairs administration. Directors and other staff in women's centers in this study often spoke of offering this type of mentorship and group support to students and faculty; we can and should extend this investment in the potential of other women in student affairs. Many participants in this study concurred that making this investment in ourselves, and each other, at "home" where it can benefit emerging feminist leaders is a natural progression for us and should be encouraged.

Along with creation of networks for professional development and cultivation of future women's center leaders, a continued commitment to conducting research—such as this study—on women's center staff experiences was echoed by participants in this study. In the words of one women's center director at a private college in the East Coast,

> It's my personal mission to spread the word that you don't have to become an investment banker if you feel like social change is really your calling. I want to make sure that the students who work with me know what this kind of work has to offer and that figuring out a way to integrate your personal values into your job is really pretty amazing! And yet, not something that I feel I can ever take for granted.

For some participants, relationships are the key. Getting to know, and work with, an endlessly interesting and diverse array of people and communities on one's campus and in one's local community is enormously beneficial. For others, being able to create, innovate, and lead is truly the draw of the work. In the words of one director,

> The one thing that keeps me excited about this job is the autonomy . . . I don't have to go to the dean and say, can I do this? As long as what I do is in

line with the mission of the institution and what our students need, I have support to get things done . . . to be innovative, and to move forward.

ANALYSIS AND IMPLICATIONS

Thirty-five years ago, in her landmark essay *Toward a Women-Centered University*, Adrienne Rich (2000) invited readers to consider the costs of passive participation in the current system and to "choose what we will accept and what we will reject of institutions already structured and defined by patriarchal values" (p. 4). As evidenced in the findings of this study, women's center leaders today face these quandaries in real time each day. Making decisions about political positioning, allegiances, and priorities, women's center staff navigate the always changing terrain of their particular campus milieus, relying mostly on experience and instinct to guide them through. In what ways does this study suggest that the work of professional feminism has been helped or hindered by the gains of the last 30 years, and where might our collective compass be leading us in the next 30 years?

Arguably, the voices in this study resoundingly reflect the progress of the last three decades in the myriad ways they resist marginality on campus. Creation and expansion of services (such as child-care assistance, sexual assault response hotlines, career development centers, and counseling) for women students, faculty, and staff— many of which have easily demonstrable, quantifiable outcomes—ensure that women's center work remains relevant in the academy, particularly as long as women, especially those who are mothers, bear the lion's share of responsibility for managing work and family balance. Our challenge, echoed in this study, is to find better and more transparent ways to document and disseminate the findings that this work yields about women's experience on campus.

A hallmark of feminist organizing, the initiation and cultivation of personal relationships,

typifies successful women's centers' operations and creates channels for amplification of the work and values that drive feminist change on campus. Women's center directors in this study exhibit remarkable savvy in negotiating substantial collaborations and forging better and stronger avenues for shared concerns. To the extent that relationship-building energies are expended toward connecting with institutional power brokers, campus policy and practices have been transformed. Women's center leaders invariably locate both purpose and power in the facility with which they are able to connect with the priorities of others, and to significant effect.

In spite of the stereotype of the humorless, crusading feminist activist, ideological flexibility and sincere openness to varieties of identity and experience more accurately characterizes the work of today's women's center director. Aptly defined by bell hooks (2000), this mindset expands the boundaries of what is properly considered feminist, engendering

> a movement to end sexism, sexist exploitation, *and oppression* [emphasis mine] . . . I liked this definition because it did not imply that men were the enemy. By naming sexism as the problem it went directly to the heart of the matter . . . it is a definition which implies that all sexist thinking and action is the problem, whether those who perpetuate it are female or male, child or adult. It is also broad enough to include an understanding of systemic institutionalized sexism. (p. 1)

Resolve to address the issues that continue to plague women and other gender minorities is now mostly accomplished through inclusive language and action, as well as a commitment to continually expanding the circles of engagement in solving gendered dilemmas. Men, transfolks of all genders, and faculty, staff, and students' families now participate in the driving ethos and activities of the twenty-first century women's center; each has a role in self-exploration and transformation, as well as participation in collective catalysis. Simultaneously, creativity devoid of subterfuge is employed in ensuring that many women's centers remain committed to offering the elusive "safe space" for women-identified individuals to explore self in relation to others, faithful to the values promised in their founding.

Despite these harmonizing tendencies, participants' commentary about ongoing challenges conveyed that not all is rosy in the world of feminist educational advancement. Marginality is mightily resisted, but the ongoing struggle to make feminist aims and symbolism relevant to today's millennial student is very real, consuming significant amounts of energy and time. Coeducation in terms of sheer numbers is now a quaint, archaic concept: As the twenty-first century dawns, women outnumber men among undergraduates nationally, as well as in many graduate fields and professional programs. But coeducation as a reality—the standard operating procedure of the university—remains elusive in many environments. As generally well-informed foot soldiers of social change needed on our campuses, we who lead women's centers bear a crucial responsibility for making our case, for defining and articulating the terms of the ongoing challenges to gender justice and other forms of social inequity on campus. We sometimes relinquish this responsibility in favor of the more gratifying, less tendentious "daily win" of supporting individuals. Expressing a coherent, steady vision—regularly, confidently, and consistently in the "public sphere" of hurdles yet to be crossed—is more needed than ever among women's center leadership. We may quietly or loudly assert our rightful place at the table in conversations on our campuses about the nature and purpose of higher education in the twenty-first century, but we must assert it nonetheless, using our considerable skills of outreach, collaboration, and participatory action to model the way. Through establishing and maintaining a visible public presence on our campuses, we will be better able to marshal resources and support for our programs and services, enlisting more diverse constituencies in the work of feminist

change in the academy as the twenty-first century unfolds.

Finally, what of that complicated little concept, *feminism*? Where are we bound to end up as we actively distance ourselves from it, with our own ambivalence and that of our campus communities in tow? We collectively cannot afford to withdraw from this trend or indulge in the current view of fashionable apathy to cultural transformation. The time is ripe to reengage, both in dialogue and in action, with the word and its myriad meanings and to formulate each unique women's center setting, so that it may realize its potential of what Jennifer Wies (chapter 15) describes as the classroom of the women's center—that which is simultaneously dedicated to fomenting action and critical thinking. Inviting students, faculty, and staff into these efforts, and making room to "expose individuals to new bodies of research, programs, practices and policies in the United States and beyond that center on situations of women, girls, and/or gender" (see Jennifer Wies, chapter 15) is arguably critical to the work of building an ongoing commitment to feminist change.

Reaching beyond the purely educational, our calling is to determine the ways in which our leadership styles and modes of practice can serve as a formidable, inspirational platform for broad, inclusive, and truly radical social change on campus. Such centers include the creation of environments of inclusion, attention to issues of voice and agency, a focus on empowerment of others, and a penchant for adopting activist stances emblematic of what Virginia Rosser (2003) and others have named "feminist student affairs practice." We needn't insist on a false comfort level with the word *feminism* that is often belied by its complicated and exclusionary history. Our actions and the ways we attempt to model a unique variety of leadership in higher education and student affairs will continue to speak volumes about the meaning and value of "feminisms" writ large if we are not afraid to claim and defend the multiplicity of meanings of the word.

Though it is not without risk, leading with heart, vision, integrity, and connection is a strategy women's center innovators can actively employ to resist the patriarchal traditions that subsume much of higher education student affairs, even today, 35 years after the second wave of feminism ushered in the beginnings of change once again.

CONCLUSION

Forward movement for change, for growth, and for the continued advancement of women and the concerns of women surfaced time and again in these lively conversations. The theme of persistently moving ahead, while often encountering a step or two backwards, yet remaining undaunted was the tenor and spirit of discussions that ensued when I began to ask my colleagues, "What are women's and gender centers about in the start of the twenty-first century?" The women, who openly shared their stories, successes, and challenges, imagined a bright, if tentative, future for women's center work in the twenty-first century. This group, although not representative of all women leading women's centers in all states across the nation, nonetheless had many insights about where we have been and where we are going. Women of color, women working in centers affiliated with women's studies research institutes, and women in campus women's centers with a strong community outreach component were not adequately represented in this study despite efforts to invite and expand participation among these constituencies and amplify their voices. This is a significant limitation that begs correction in future research efforts.

The representatives in this study offered invaluable insights into what will be required of the next generation of leadership of campus women's centers. In listening to their words, and offering the themes therein for reflection and consideration, I have never been more proud—and more humbled—to be part of this fearless, faithful sisterhood of leaders and visionaries working steadily for change and for good in the world, on campus and beyond.

NOTES

1. The "waves" of contemporary American feminism are typically defined as follows: the First Wave, comprising the suffragist and abolitionist movements of the late nineteenth and early twentieth centuries; the Second Wave, encompassing the consciousness-raising and civil rights movements of the 1960s and 1970s; and the Third Wave, emerging with riot grrl, a focus on the intersectionality of race, class, gender, and other identities, and other forms of youth-centered feminist activism of the 1990s to the present day (Siegel, 2007).

2. As of the writing of this article, approximately 25% of centers that were originally designated as "women's centers" in the United States now include the term *gender* or *men* in their centers' titles (Gribi, 2008).

REFERENCES

Baumgardner, J., & Richards, A. (2000). *Manifesta: Young women, feminism and the future*. New York: Farrar, Straus, & Giroux.

Clevenger, B. M. (1988). Women's centers on campus: A profile. *Initiatives, 51*, 3–9.

Collins, P. H. (2000). *Black feminist thought: Knowledge, consciousness, and the politics of empowerment*. New York: Routledge.

Davie, S. (2002). *University and college women's centers: A journey toward equity*. Westport, CT: Greenwood Press.

DiLapi, E., & Gay, G. (2002). Women's centers responding to racism. In S. L. Davie (Ed.), *University and college women's centers: A journey toward equity* (pp. 203–224). Westport, CT: Greenwood Educators Reference Collection.

Dziech, B. W., & Weiner, L. (1990). *The lecherous professor: Sexual harassment on campus* (2nd ed.). Urbana, IL: University of Illinois Press.

Gribi, G. (2008). *Campus women's centers postal mailing list*. Retrieved July 8, 2008, from http://www.creativefolk.com/wc.html

Hesse-Biber, S., Gilmartin, C., & Lyderberg, R. (1999). *Feminist approaches to theory and methodology: An interdisciplinary reader*. New York: Oxford University Press.

Hogeland, L. M. (1994). Fear of feminism: Why young women get the willies. *Ms Magazine, 4*, 13–14.

hooks, b. (2000). *Feminist theory: From margin to center* (2nd ed.). Boston, MA: South End Press.

Hymowitz, K. S. (2002, Summer). The end of herstory. *City Journal: A quarterly magazine of urban affairs*. Retrieved July 2, 2008, from http://www.cityjournal.org/html/12_3_the_end_of.html

Johnson, B. (1987). Nothing fails like success. In B. Johnson (Ed.), *A world of difference* (pp. 11–16). Baltimore, MD: Johns Hopkins Press.

Kaplan, C., Hindus, M., Mejia, E., Olsen, J., & La Due, L. (2002). Violence against women: Women's centers' responses to sexual assault. In S. L. Davie (Ed.), *University and college women's centers: A journey toward equity* (pp. 149–202). Westport, CT: Greenwood Educators Reference Collection.

Komarovsky, M. (1989). *Women in college: Shaping new feminine identities.* New York: Basic Books.

Lisker, D. (2002). Forging unlikely alliances—The women's center and the locker room: A case study. In S. L. Davie (Ed.), *University and college women's centers: A journey toward equity* (pp. 362–370). Westport, CT: Greenwood Educators Reference Collection.

McCracken, G. (1988). *The long interview.* Newbury Park, CA: Sage.

Miles, M. B., & Huberman, A. M. (1994). *Qualitative data analysis: An expanded sourcebook* (2nd ed.). Thousand Oaks, CA: Sage.

Miller-Bernal, L., & Poulson, S. L. (2004). *Going coed: Women's experiences in formerly men's colleges and universities, 1950–2000.* Nashville, TN: Vanderbilt University Press.

Ng, R. (2000). A woman out of control: Deconstructing sexism and racism in the university. In J. Glazer-Raymo, B. K. Townsend, & B. Ropers-Huilman (Eds.), *Women in higher education: A feminist perspective* (2nd ed., pp. 360–370). Boston, MA: Pearson Publishing.

Olesen, V. (2006). Early millenial feminist qualitative research: Challenges and contours. In N. K. Lincoln & Y. S. Denzin (Eds.), *The Sage handbook of qualitative research* (pp. 235–278). Thousand Oaks, CA: Sage.

Patton, M. Q. (1990). *Qualitative evaluation and research methods* (2nd ed.). Newbury Park, CA: Sage Publications.

Peril, L. (2006). College girls: Bluestockings, sex kittens, and coeds, then and now. New York: Norton and Co.

Rich, A. (2000). Toward a women-centered university. In J. Glazer-Raymo, B. Townsend, & B. Ropers-Huilman (Eds.), *Women in higher education: A feminist perspective* (2nd ed., pp. 3–15). Boston, MA: Pearson Publishing.

Rosser, V. J. (2003). Feminists in student affairs: Negotiating the process of change. *Dissertation Abstracts International, 64*(6), (UMI No. 3095324).

Rudman, L. A., & Fairchild, K. (2007). The F word: Is feminism incompatible with beauty and romance? *Psychology of Women Quarterly, 31*(2), 125–136.

Sandelowski, M. (2000). What ever happened to qualitative description? *Research in Nursing and Health, 23*, 334–340.

Siegel, D. (2007). *Sisterhood, interrupted: From radical women to girls gone wild.* New York, NY: Palgrave Macmillan.

Willinger, B. (2002). Women's centers: Their mission and the process of change. In S. Davie (Ed.), *University and college women's centers: A journey toward equity* (pp. 47–65). Westport, CT: Greenwood Press.

Zucker, A. (2004). Disavowing social identities: What it means when women say "I'm not a feminist, but . . . " *Psychology of Women Quarterly, 28*, 423–435.

3

"Each Generation of Women Had to Start Anew"

A Historical Analysis of Title IX Policy and Women Leaders in the Cocurriculum

Jennifer Lee Hoffman

Abstract: *Deans of Women and Women's Athletic Directors have a rich history. These women focused on leading women-specific aspects of the cocurriculum on coeducational campuses. Yet, women remain underrepresented in leadership of student affairs and intercollegiate athletics. Despite their legacy, why do so few women hold leadership roles in these areas? In the coeducational period from 1890 to 1972, the purpose of educating women students in coeducational institutions was highly differentiated by gender. Women leaders leveraged four strategies to maintain leadership positions but each generation had to start anew. After the emergence of gender equity policy, symbolized by the passing of Title IX in 1972, only one strategy for women leaders remained. Even after the gender equity era, women leaders today still start anew.*

TITLE IX OF THE EDUCATION AMENDMENTS ACT of 1972 is widely credited for providing equity in access and educational opportunity for women students in 10 educational program areas and for promoting and retaining women in positions of leadership. Yet, women leaders are underrepresented among the leadership of student affairs and intercollegiate athletics today. It was not always this way. Deans of women and women's athletic directors have a rich history in campus administrative po-

sitions and their commensurate professional associations.

With a legacy of women in leadership roles before this policy, why do women remain underrepresented today? The elimination of deans of women, women's athletic directors, and their professional associations marks significant changes in how women have ascended to leadership roles in higher education in the years following Title IX. This chapter examines the purpose of educating women before and after Title

IX and the role of women's leadership in the cocurriculum. Changes in the purpose of educating women students brought on by gender equity policy help explain the lack of women leaders in student affairs and intercollegiate athletics today.

This chapter begins by describing the decline of women leaders in the cocurriculum, specifically deans of women and women's athletic directors. Then the chapter turns to explaining the period from 1890 to 1972, when the purpose of educating women students in coeducational institutions was highly differentiated by gender. Next, the strategies leveraged by women leaders in the cocurriculum are situated in the pattern of women's leadership throughout coeducation. The decline of women leaders in the gender equity era from 1972 to the present, symbolized by the passage of this policy, is described. The chapter concludes by explaining how, even after the gender equity era, women leaders in higher education still must *start anew* (Glazer & Slater, 1987, p. 231).

This chapter on women leaders in the cocurriculum is further contextualized by Thalia Mulvihill's (chapter 4) account of the alliance between Eunice Hilton, Dean of Women, and Katherine Sibley, Director of Physical Education (PE), at Syracuse University. My focus on Title IX policy and women leaders compliments Mulvihill's work by adding Title IX's impact on women athletic leaders in education after the decline of deans of women.

WOMEN LEADERS IN THE COCURRICULUM

The significance of deans of women and women's athletic directors[1] has been well described (Carpenter & Acosta, 2001; Nidiffer, 2000, 2003; Paul, 2001) and critiqued (Schwartz, 1997b). Prior to the passage of Title IX, 90% of women's athletics programs were led by Women's Athletic Directors in a separate women's department (Acosta & Carpenter, 2008). Today women lead only 21.3% of all National Collegiate Athletic Association (NCAA) programs under a combined model. At the NCAA's most visible, Division I level, women make up only 8.4% of all Athletic Directors.

Deans of women, once in a prominent leadership position, lost their leadership roles as men's and women's student service programs combined in the generation before Title IX. In the immediate post–World War II years, deans of women were increasingly threatened, "both in numbers and as a symbol" (Schwartz, 1997a, p. 433). As early as the mid-1940s, deans of women were reporting to a coordinated office of student services rather than the university president in the name of administrative efficiency (Nidiffer, 2000; Schwarta, 1997). As the student personnel movement grew, universities eliminated deans of men and deans of women, replacing them with a coordinated dean of students, who oversaw services such as admissions, counseling, and advising. Men assumed the dean of students role and women were assigned positions with lower status and salary. In 1956, the National Association of Deans of Women (NADW) added the role of counselors into their national association and became the National Association of Deans of Women and Counselors (NAWDAC), but deans of women faced elimination at the institutional level by the late 1960s. Later NAWDAC changed its name once again to the National Association for Women in Education (NAWE) in 1991, before discontinuing operations in 2002.

In 1991, Touchton and Davis (1991) reported that women held 31% of Senior Student Affairs Officer (SSAO) positions at four-year private institutions but only 18% in four-year public institutions. Among women of color, only 3.6% held SSAO roles in all two- and four-year institutions (Touchton & Davis). By 1996, a College and University Professional Association for Human Resources (CUPA-HR) survey of all two-year and four-year public and private institutions found that women held 32.7% of the Chief of SSAOs (Glazer-Raymo, 1999). In 1997, women held 27.3% of SSAO roles at doctoral universities, 33.4% at comprehensive universities, 40.5% at general baccalaureate-degree-granting schools, and 35.6% of two-year colleges (Jones & Komives, 2001). Today SSAOs are still overwhelmingly White (79.7%), and women continue to be underrepresented in this role except at associate's-degree-granting institutions (King & Gomez, 2008). At doctorate-granting institutions, women make up only 38.5% of SSAOs. At master's- and baccalaureate-degree-granting schools women are 36.7% and 38.5%, respectively.

Women have historically faced significant limits on access to leadership roles since male and female students started being educated together. However, when stratified by class, aristocratic women had more access to education, property, and political power throughout both the coeducation and gender equity era than White middle- and working-class women and women of color (Macralid & Taylor, 2004; McCandless, 1999). Regional differences and institutional type further disaggregate access across gender and ethnicity. Women of color in historically Black colleges and universities (HBCUs) and predominantly White institutions (PWIs) faced even greater barriers to the curriculum and cocurriculum. Black women often lacked access to the political and social movements that propelled White women into higher education. For example, in the south, Black women had to overcome significant obstacles to higher education (McCandless, 1999). As coeducation emerged and grew, these African American students became the "forgotten women" of this region's higher education history (McCandless, 1999, p. 19). When race and gender are considered together, not all women enjoyed the same preparation for leadership roles in the cocurriculum.

COEDUCATION AND THE CHANGING PURPOSE OF EDUCATING WOMEN

Today, arguments for Title IX policy often credit its powerful impact in giving women greater access to higher education. However, the formal entrance of women into higher education actually began much earlier, with the creation of several all-female academies from 1790 to 1850 (Solomon, 1985). The purpose of education for women in these schools focused on religious and social preparation for their work as wives and mothers. The role of women preparing their children to be engaged citizens in the new nation characterized by "Republican Motherhood" after the Revolutionary War was paired with the "ideal of the Christian wife, mother, and teacher" (Solomon, 1985, p. 16). Emma Willard is most notable for her role in promoting education for women in preparation for their duty as teachers—"both at home with their own children and in the schools" (Newcomer, 1959, p. 11). The initial purpose of formal education at all-women institutions focused on these Republican and Christian rationales (Solomon, 1985).

The emergence of coeducation—educating women and men in the same institution—was marked soon thereafter when Oberlin College of Ohio opened as the first coeducational institution in 1833. Over the next 60 years, women attended normal schools, women's colleges, coordinate colleges, and coeducational institutions (Clifford, 1989; Solomon, 1985). The late nineteenth century was also a time of tremendous change in higher education, in which "a number of historical forces occurred simultaneously and independently" (Gerda, 2006, p. 149). On campus, the Morrill Land Grant Act of 1862 expanded both the purpose and the system of higher education, adding state-sponsored education. The Morrill Land Grant Acts of 1862 and 1890 set aside land and money to establish agricultural and mechanical education. The Morrill

Act of 1862 set aside 30,000 acres of land and established 69 land grant institutions.

By the 1890s, the majority of women college students were attending coeducational institutions (Newcomer, 1959). Opportunities for women expanded both in the new public land grants and in private women's colleges, including opportunities to study subjects such as mathematics and science, which were considered the domain of men. In the earliest coeducation years "men's and women's student lives proceeded along separate, although parallel, paths" (Gordon, 1990, p. 3). As women students entered coeducational institutions in greater numbers at the turn of the century, some feared the effects women would have. In particular, "top-level administrators, male, began to fear that these new women students would drive men out of the College of Letters and Liberal Arts" (Nerad, 1999, p. 10). Coeducational institutions responded to the arrival of women students at the turn of the century, initiating specialized roles for women leaders to oversee women students.

The earliest women leaders in the coeducation period were deans of women, appointed to counter fears that enrolling women would feminize male students or the institution. Regarding the job of these early deans, Thalia Mulvihill (chapter 4) notes, "Deans of Women were given responsibility for guiding (some would say controlling) the lives of all women students at their institution." Women in these administrative roles responded to concerns over educating women students and the changing purpose of educating women students during coeducation.

A *separate spheres* ideology common to this early coeducation period created opportunities for women leaders to supervise women students (Gordon, 1990, p. 1). Institutions created separate departments led by women administrators to oversee the "woman problem" (Nidiffer, 2000, pp. 31–32; see also Clifford, 1983). Women graduates with advanced degrees found positions within these departments, whereas outside the academy there was little use for them or

their advanced expertise. These women leaders in higher education developed a set of strategies that "served a 'client' (women students) largely ignored by men," established parallel professions within higher education for women, and created options for women students with advanced degrees that the first generation of women students lacked (Nidiffer, 2000, p. 8).

Hiring women as "deans, physicians, hygiene, and PE instructors" coincided with other strategies that university presidents used to respond to changes occurring during this era in coeducation (Gordon, 1997, p. 489). Concurrently, intercollegiate competition in debate and athletics was replacing interclass activities (Gordon, 1997). Women students participated in intercollegiate athletic competition, mainly in basketball, during the earliest years of coeducation. In Thalia Mulvihill's (chapter 4) chapter, she also notes the interest and participation by women students in organized basketball games and athletics such as the Women's Basketball Association and the Women's Athletics Association. As women students were not welcome in many aspects of academic and student life, women leaders helped promote and build separate but parallel departments and activities for women students. Meanwhile, men's presence on campus was underscored, particularly in the cocurriculum, with the attention given to men's intercollegiate athletics (Gordon, 1997).

Despite the significant proportion of women's enrollment, women's success in the classroom, and women leaders building professions for women, the Progressive Era brought a backlash against women in higher education (Clifford, 1983; Gordon, 1990, 1997; Nidiffer, 2000). The high numbers of women students and their success in parallel programs challenged previously all-male institutions and renewed questions about the purpose of higher education for women. Although university presidents of the Progressive Era "included women in their vision of a new democratic society, their vision was of a traditional woman, simply more cultured, more emotionally mature, and better educated than average" (Nerad, 1999, p. 28). In the 1920s, women made up almost half the enrollment of students at coeducational institutions, but institutions implemented tactics to curtail their impact. Some limited women in admissions and created segregated classes; others built separate coordinate colleges (Gordon, 1990).

Institutions feared feminization, and the purpose of higher education for women began to reverse back to its original purpose: emphasis on preparing women for their duties as wives and mothers. This pushed women students and faculty out of fields such as medicine and science, closing parallel women's medical colleges and limiting fields of study (Cott, 1987; Gordon, 1990; Rossiter, 1982). The purpose of educating women became specific to "exclusively 'female' interests of students" (Fass, 1997, p. 701). During this change in the purpose of education for women students, women faculty responded by using separatist strategies to create separate communities and fields, as had once been the norm. The advances in women's education were taking a giant step backward. The women's PE movement and home economics movement created separate departments led by women faculty (Nerad, 1999; Paul, 2001). These women-specific departments prepared women students for their newly defined roles and became the "women's work" within higher education (Rossiter, 1982, p. 239). Women leaders also promoted separate programs for women students in the cocurriculum by building strong, women-led professional associations within feminized fields. This was particularly true for deans of women and women physical educators who used the gender-differentiated purpose of women's education to create NADW and CWA (Committee on Women's Athletics) in the late 1920s.

In the 1930s, the *separate spheres* approach to educating men and women declined some, but the purpose of educating women continued to be different than that of educating men. Men and women students began to enjoy a more "gender-integrated model" in classroom and social activities, but even until the late 1950s, the purpose of higher education for women was still highly differentiated by gender (Horowitz, 1987). With integration came less resistance to women students on campus, but women and men students "shared few intellectual or practical interests and did not participate in the same groups and clubs" (Nidiffer, 2000, p. 139). Women leaders such as Syracuse University's Dean of Women Eunice Hilton and Katherine Sibley, Director of PE (see chapter 4 of this book), continued to oversee separate communities for women students even as higher education became less hostile to women and more gender integrated in many aspects of campus life (Horowitz, 1987).

During World War II, women continued to attend college, "where during the war they outnumbered men for the first and only time" during the coeducational period (Fass, 1997, pp. 704–705). Women earned approximately 56% of all degrees awarded between 1944 and 1946 (p. 705). After World War II, women's enrollment and degrees earned continued to increase, but their proportion decreased sharply (Eisenmann, 2006). The GI Bill promoted enrollment for returning veterans—who were mostly men—further solidifying the emphasis on educating men and reducing the visibility of women (Eisenmann, 2006). Women students remained educated in separate women-specific fields and activities, but the purpose of educating women broadened.

After the war, and by the 1950s, women leaders saw their roles decline in status and frequency as coeducational institutions focused their attention on the returning GIs and new models of higher education leadership (Eisenmann, 2006). Women leaders continued to rely on models that proved effective for serving women students. This included the monitoring of student social lives, hygiene, and academic pursuits, but their initial success was followed by a "period of stasis and/or decline not reversed until the 1960s and 1970s," after the coeducational model for educating women students gave way to gender equity in higher education (Cott, 1987, p. 220).

Coeducation shifted to a gender-combined model of higher education inside and outside the classroom. Institutions combined separate departments of deans of women and deans of men into new deans of students units, with women leaders losing their administrative positions or relegated again to a secondary role. Separate women's and men's athletic departments combined into one department. Under these mergers, the men's athletic director was named to oversee the department and women's athletic director moved into an assistant role.

On June 23, 1972, Title IX of the Education Amendments Act of 1972 was signed into law. Widely known as "Title IX," this legislation simply states, "No person in the United States shall on the basis of sex, be excluded from participation in, be denied the benefits of, or be subjected to discrimination under any educational program or activity receiving Federal financial assistance." When Title IX went into effect in 1972, it created both a change in policy and a symbolic shift in the purpose of educating women. Changes in higher education, the feminist movement in the 1960s and 1970s, and the passage of Title IX challenged the women-specific, gender-separate role of deans of women and women's athletic directors. This *gender-combined gender equity* era, marked by the passage of Title IX in 1972, further mandated equity for women in all educational programs, including the cocurriculum. At this time, women-designated administrative and faculty leadership roles were rare in both role and purpose.

WOMEN LEADERS IN COEDUCATION: FOUR STRATEGIES

Early women leaders in higher education responded to a changing purpose of educating women and contended with intense barriers to leadership roles on campus. One way they ad-

dressed both was by creating new professions for themselves and their students. The notion of a profession and the criteria on which to determine a profession first gained renewed popularity with Abraham Flexner's 1910 report, "Is Social Work a Profession?" (Nidiffer, 2000). Belief in the ideals of professionalism, such as public trust given to doctors, lawyers, and clergy, was already common. In the Progressive Era, "a renewed interest in professionalism and the drive for professionalization for all sorts of occupations" developed the idea of expertise derived from university training; "self-regulation and control over entry became important criteria for professions" (Nidiffer, 2000, p. 7). The training of experts in university-based programs was not enough. Professions had to develop a "coherent body of literature" that was "scientific rather than journalistic in character" (Bashaw, 1999, p. 162; see also Glazer & Slater, 1987; Flexner as cited in Nidiffer, 2000). Women leaders were influenced by this Progressive Era ideal and professionalized their positions by developing self-regulating degree-based training programs, peer-reviewed research literature, and governing associations. Regardless of the path chosen by individual women leaders, four strategies and combinations of strategies are integral to understanding the success of women during a coeducation model and their decline during the gender equity era. First described by Glazer and Slater (1987), these four strategies are further developed by Nidiffer (2000, p. 8):

1. **Superperformance**—seeking status with extraordinary efforts and a willingness to sacrifice traditional relationships
2. **Subordination**—accepting a subordinate position within a male-dominated profession
3. **Innovation**—establishing a new professional field. Often, this allowed women to remove themselves from direct competition with male professionals, especially if

they took up work or served clients typically neglected by men

4. **Separatism**—working in environments, such as women's colleges, where women were senior administrators and faculty members, even in traditionally male disciplines

Nidiffer (2000) cited the "separatism as strategy" of early feminists (p. 136). With this strategy, women leveraged the social and political "separate spheres" to create opportunities for leadership and advancement in women's organizations and within male-dominated institutions. For example, in Thalia Mulvill's (chapter 4) description of Eunice Hilton and Katherine Sibley at Syracuse University, she describes how early women leaders throughout the East were "organizing to have their work seen as essential to the overall curriculum."

Although women leaders such as Hilton and Sibley were initially successful in developing women-led professions, many women experienced a backlash in the Progressive Era. Feminized professions such as home economics, education, library science, nursing, and social welfare (Nerad, 1999) represent the ways in which

> [w]omen often shifted from one strategy to another, depending on the particular circumstances they were facing. Although the strategies are not totally separable and they often overlap, they offer a way of looking at the texture, the range, and the limits of the possible in these women's lives. (Glazer & Slater, 1987, p. 14)

The separate domains for women faculty and limited opportunities for women students after graduating led to separatism as a strategy, integral to bringing the first group of women deans together, later creating the foundation of the NADW. In later years, the rise of deans of men, the emerging student affairs profession, as well as social and political trends altered the perception and function of deans of women. at first, deans of women relied on a combination of strategies to adjust to this backlash and didn't experience

a decline until after World War II, when many institutions combined men's and women's programs or did away with women-only or women-led departments (Eisenmann, 2006).

Reorganization into student personnel units often eliminated the position of dean of women or reassigned women to the "Director of Women's Education," with less responsibility (Nidiffer, 2000, p. 150). During the shift toward gender equity, deans of women were not passive bystanders in these changes, as there was debate for and against the dean of women role in which they were engaged. Opponents of the position maintained that it set women apart and prevented their full integration into the life of the campus. Those in favor cited the evidence that "women students still continued to avail themselves of the services of the dean" (Nidiffer, 2000, p. 150).

The role of women's athletic director did not emerge on campus until the 1960s, well into the end of coeducation. However, this role on campus can be traced back to the rise of intercollegiate sport competition that also coincided with the emergence of coeducation and women's physical educators at the turn of the century. As "guardians of women's health," early women's physical educators challenged deans of women for authority over women's sports (Paul, 2001, p. 196). Through their strong professional network, a body of research, and degree training programs, women's physical educators were successful in placing graduates in high school and college women's PE programs that promoted a noncompetitive, women-specific athletic model (Costa & Guthrie, 1994). Through interclass games and play days, women's physical educators promoted what was deemed as the "right" kind of athletic program philosophy for women (Festle, 1986). Even as the deans of women positions were declining, women physical educators with their faculty status, separate campus programs, and professional associations continued to lead women-specific athletic activities.

During the postwar years, women's PE programs expanded to include extramural competitions. With the increased interest and demand from undergraduates to compete in extramural competition, women's physical educators promoted women-specific extramural events and competitions. Still maintaining a women-specific competition model, the American Intercollegiate Athletics Association for Women (AIAW) was formed by leaders in women's PE in 1971. Institutions often appointed a women's athletic director from among women faculty in the women's PE department or recent graduates from the women's PE department.

In the changes brought on by gender equity, women's athletic directors and AIAW leaders leveraged strategies from the coeducational period, such as separatism, innovation, and superperformance, that initially proved successful in serving women student athletes. Initially, women's athletic directors maintained their women-specific, gender-separate role in the gender equity era. There are several reasons for this, including disagreement over what the law actually required. The women's athletic director role in a feminized subspecialty of intercollegiate athletics provided some shelter from the reorganizations in athletic departments even after the passage of Title IX. The first generation of women's athletic directors also maintained their role in separate women's athletic departments using innovation strategies. Like women in education after World War II described by Solomon (1985), women leaders in athletics were "still pioneering in men's territory" of intercollegiate athletics (p. 187).

However, for women's athletic directors who reestablished intercollegiate athletics for women students, Title IX proved to be a "double-edged sword" (Hult, 1999, p. 27). The policy did not require a merging of departments; yet, just as the deans of women a generation earlier, women's athletic directors were not able to leverage the strategies of the past to maintain their position. As institutions merged separate men's and women's departments, the strategies of subordination, separatism, and innovation were ineffective in stemming the move toward combining men's and women's programs.

The combining of athletic departments had the same impact as the combining of deans of women and deans of men. The change from a separate women's athletic department to a combined department meant women's athletic directors were relegated to secondary positions (Hult, 1999). That women's athletic directors chose a feminized subspecialty within intercollegiate athletics is significant in explaining the shifts in women's athletic leadership roles instigated by Title IX (Nidiffer, 2000; see also Cott, 1987). Analyzing the strategies women leaders developed in coeducation and the history of their implementation is helpful in contextualizing the erosion of deans of women and parallels to women's athletic directors after the passage of Title IX.

WINNING FOR TITLE IX, LOSING CONTROL OF WOMEN'S SPORT

In the 1950s and 1960s, a new generation of women students and women's PE faculty prompted the reemergence of competition in schools and colleges. "A new host of women athletic leaders came into power and demanded policies to encourage elite competition" (Hult, 1999, p. 25). These women wanted to create opportunities for women's athletics beyond the play days and sports days. The governance of women's athletics was under the jurisdiction of Division of Girls and Women in Sport (DGWS), the national women's PE organization. The DGWS began to soften its stance against competition and developed a competition model specific to women's athletics. According to Katherine Ley of DWGS, "we must chart a course for all levels, including the stars and Olympic hopefuls" (Hult, 1999, p. 26). In 1965, the DGWS formed the Commission on Intercollegiate Athletics for Women (CIAW) to offer women's championship events based on a vision of school-based sports that featured women-led competition that was fundamentally different than men's competition. By 1969 "the alternative model of women's intercollegiate athletics was ready" (Hult, 1999, p. 27). In 1971, the original CIAW broke away from the DGWS and formed the Association of Intercollegiate Athletics for Women (AIAW), completing the establishment of an independent, women-specific governance model for women's intercollegiate athletics.

The shift from the CIAW within DGWS to the independent, separate AIAW marked both the first women's competitive governance model and an alternative to the men's NCAA competitive model. The vision of the AIAW was for a "student-centered, educationally oriented model with built-in safeguards designed to avoid abuses observed in male athletics (e.g., athlete exploitation and recruiting violations)" (Hult, 1999, p. 29). Similar to the vision for educating the whole student from a student personnel perspective (National Association of Student Personnel Administrators & American College Personnel Association, 2004), the women who founded the AIAW wanted to create change in the new era of women's sports and "did not want to follow the men's athletic trails or men's athletic summit" (Hult, 1999, p. 25).

Leaders of the AIAW maintained their goal of developing an education-based philosophy and leadership model for women students emphasizing four guiding principles:

1. Voting representatives were to be faculty members
2. Elected student athletes participated in the decision-making process
3. Minority representation was mandated at all levels of AIAW governance
4. No distinction was made between major and minor sports (Carpenter & Acosta, 2001, p. 212)

Women leaders of the AIAW based their four principles on a commitment to women's control of women's athletics, continuing to distinguish

the mission of women's intercollegiate athletics from the mission of men's intercollegiate athletics. This mission also included four points:

1. Fostering broad programs consistent with educational objectives
2. Assisting member institutions in program extension and enrichment
3. Stimulating the development of quality leadership
4. Encouraging excellence in performance (Wushanley, 2004, p. 16)

These principles created a clear distinction in philosophy between women's intercollegiate competition and men's intercollegiate competition. This gender-specific governance of women's athletics and the women-led governance model were intended to maintain women's control of women's college athletics. New organizational ties, both through educational networks and institutional affiliation, coupled with a commitment to fostering and cultivating leadership among women, characterized women's intercollegiate sports after the passage of Title IX.

When Title IX came into law in 1972, it created controversy by "[forcing] educational institutions to make room" for women to participate in college athletics (Boutillier & San Giovanni, 1994, p. 103). The AIAW and the NCAA battled each other over the passage of Title IX. When Title IX became law, women leaders in PE and the AIAW achieved a huge victory. Women would be treated equally under the law in education, including K–12 and college-based athletics. Yet, when Title IX went into effect, the details of compliance at the institutional level were far from finalized. Institutions were slow to meet or even acknowledge the obligations of Title IX. Women leaders of athletics continued to make sure athletics would be addressed in the guidelines. According to Hult (1999),

Title IX was truly an uphill battle. The AIAW actually suspended, in part, their focus on an alternative athletic model as they fought and won the battle for implementation of Title IX guidelines. At the same time, they lost the war and their decision-making power. (p. 29)

The war Hult (1999) is referring to is the fight for who would control women's athletics. Although there is some differing opinion in the literature about the conflict between the AIAW and the NCAA over the governance of women's athletics, it can only be characterized as a hostile and unwelcome "takeover" of the AIAW by the NCAA (Festle, 1986; Wushanley, 2004). The loss of women's control of the less commercialized, more educational sports model can only be blamed on the men's competitive, spectator-oriented leadership model within the NCAA (Festle, 1986). At the time when women were charting a women-specific model of women's sports, Title IX, ironically, created a situation where difference based on gender left the AIAW vulnerable to the NCAA's takeover of women's athletics (Suggs, 2005). Despite lobbying hard to prevent Title IX from becoming law, the NCAA "carefully worded their opposition to Title IX" and continued to promote itself as interested in creating opportunities for women athletes (Festle, 1986, p. 130).

After Title IX, institutional leaders first opted to combine women's and men's programs into one athletic department, rather than leave women's athletics under the control of women's PE departments (Suggs, 2005). The AIAW continued to try charting a different course for women's competitive athletics, even as departments merged but maintained different standards for women's athletics. Specifically, this meant no scholarships for students or recruiting women students to participate in sports. Women students were part of the governance of their sport and women leaders maintained appointments in PE. But women students and coaches of women's teams also wanted what the men's programs had—scholarships, recruiting, notoriety, and resources. Men's programs became the standard

from which equity was judged. The AIAW continued to fight two battles—fighting for equity through Title IX and shaping the AIAW into "a fair, democratic organization that governed lightly" such as including student athletes in governance, institutional self-policing, and women's leadership of women's athletics (Festle, 1986). Women maintaining control of women's sports programs at the institutional level would quickly change.

In December 1980, the NCAA voted to begin offering championships for women's athletics. This decision forced institutions to choose between membership in the AIAW or the NCAA. Most schools chose the NCAA. Grundy and Shackelford (2005) explain, "the NCAA had two things the AIAW could not hope to match: money and status" (p. 179). Not only would more resources benefit women's programs across the country, but the prestige and status that men's athletics garnered was also thought to be available to women only through the men's organization, not the women's organization. According to the University of Tennessee's women's basketball coach, Pat Summit, the NCAA gave "instant credibility to women's athletics." She felt that without the NCAA and its "championships in a first-class arena," women "may never have the opportunities to make the strides that are necessary for women to have what they have today" (Grundy & Shackelford, 2005, p. 180). Not only did the NCAA takeover of the AIAW lead to the end of women's leadership of women's athletics, it also marked the shift from athletics based on gender-specific notions of participation to a male-gendered model of intercollegiate athletics.

WOMEN LEADERS IN THE GENDER EQUITY ERA: STRATEGIES BREAKDOWN

The gender equity era represents a major shift in the purpose and role of higher education for women students. It also represents a distinct change in how women leaders advance in leadership positions. Without specific differences in the actual purpose of higher education for women, and separate programs for women students, the women-led organizations and institutional departments that had once created a relative power base for the advancement of women leaders dissolved.

The change in sentiment about educating women and men that eroded the position of dean of women and the NADW presents several parallels to the rise and fall of women athletic directors and the AIAW. The historical examination of deans of women and women's athletic directors is situated in a longer pattern of women's leadership in higher education. The "sex-separate" conditions and philosophy useful in the coeducation period were ineffective during the shift toward gender equity. When Title IX mandated equity for women students, the separate infrastructure and philosophy of earlier eras that built and strengthened women's leadership on campus and women's professional organizations such as the NADW and the AIAW quickly deteriorated. This left women leaders without the strength of women-led professions to prepare and sustain them in leadership roles on their own campus.

Women leaders in the cocurriculum now must rely on individual strategies to attain leadership in positions, and these efforts have largely failed. The pipeline created by professional associations and degree-granting programs specific for women dissolved, and the leadership opportunities for women students in the NADW and AIAW are gone. Gender equity era legislation that created tremendous opportunity for women students does little to provide women leaders in athletics or student affairs with a pathway to leadership roles.

When examined from the perspective of the strategies that women leaders have taken, deans of women "chose the path of a male-dominated profession in an established field (e.g., medicine or academia)" and women in PE chose "a feminized subspecialty (pediatrics or home economics)" (Nidiffer, 2000, p. 8). When the strategies of women to professionalize in both of these examples are taken in the context of coeducation, deans of women persisted in their positions and professions, within their limited status, after the backlash of the Progressive Era. The persistence of their professional roles is evident in the strength of their professional associations, success in implementing policy that created the "right kind" of cocurricular activities for women, and for deans of women reporting to presidents. Deans of women such as Eunice Hilton at Syracuse University gained legitimacy and maintained status in their roles, as the purpose of educating women remained distinct during the coeducational period. However, in the 1960s, deans of women saw the separatist strategies used by early women leaders start to breakdown. These women met the same fate as women who chose superperformance in a male-dominated profession during the Progressive Era, such as women's medical schools. As the purpose of education for women shifted from being parallel to men to separate and distinct from men, women had to *start anew*, creating new leadership roles. This pattern was repeated later as institutions combined the roles of dean of men and dean of women often in the name of efficiency. Women found themselves dismissed or demoted as "secondary officers" in reorganized offices of Student Affairs (Nidiffer, 2000, p. 149; see also Eisenmann, 2006).

Finally, even though women's athletic directors fought for a woman-specific athletic model during the shifts toward gender equity, their association with athletics further distanced them from emerging feminist perspectives and organizations within higher education. Women's athletic directors were further "isolated from the support of academic feminists because of the perceived institutional sexism associated with intercollegiate sports" (Estler & Nelson, 2005, p. 62).

ANOTHER GENERATION STARTING ANEW

The history of deans of women and women's athletic directors in the cocurriculum helps explain how women's opportunity for leadership roles shifted within higher education since the advent of women's access to coeducation from 1890 to 1972. Specifically, women in the professions initially enjoyed success in gaining access to higher education, but in the 1920s women experienced a backlash in higher education (Gordon, 1990). Women responded using a variety of strategies, but the progress made by women in the first generation of women leaders "did not continue to ascend steadily through the twentieth century" (Cott, 1987, p. 217).

Deans of women and women physical educators who promoted a women-specific athletic model achieved greater success in withstanding this backlash. However, they too met a similar fate when women-led programs and organizations disappeared as institutions combined men's and women's programs during the onset of gender equity. Despite their efforts and early pioneering work, women leaders continued to face barriers throughout coeducation. As a result, each generation had to *start anew* (Glazer & Slater, 1987).

This important pattern of repioneering or starting anew distinguishes this analysis from others. Schwartz (1997b) took a different perspective that assessments by earlier scholars dismissed the pioneering efforts of early deans of women. For instance, Schwartz (1997b) critiqued the analysis by Solomon that Lois Matthews of the University of Wisconsin "ended up" a dean of women rather than a historian, her field of study. Schwartz contended that Solomon's description of the significant contribution Matthews made to the profession of dean of women is overlooked (1997b). However, it was *because* of many forces, including the changing purpose of educating women, that barriers were created to the professoriate and

women were kept out of faculty roles in their field of study.

This pattern was repeated when women physical educators in coeducational institutions promoted a women-specific form of athletics. Markels (2000) described the early role of women's physical educators as more complex than simply leading the changes in women's athletics from competition to recreation. In addition, "the history of women's basketball . . . is a much more tangled story than that of simple suppression initiated by women physical educators" (Markels, 2000, p. 44). Like deans of women, the philosophy and role of women physical educators and later women's athletic directors grew out of a separate purpose of educating women students.

The influx of women students, the response of higher education, and the subsequent pioneering and repioneering efforts of women leaders throughout the rise of coeducation presents an important historical significance to understanding the decisions of women leaders throughout coeducation. It also helps clarify the limits women faced after the gender equity era in achieving leadership roles in student affairs and intercollegiate athletics today.

The decline of deans of women and women's athletic directors in higher education after the gender equity era is also influenced by other factors. The demands of balancing family responsibilities, fears surrounding the sexual orientation of the deans and directors and the influence that may exert on their students, and socially constructed barriers such as the "old boy's network" also offer important explanations for the underrepresentation of women leaders in higher education today. Yet, the dramatic decline of women leaders since the passage of Title IX is troubling. This chapter situates this decline in a historical pattern of women's leadership in higher education since the rise of coeducation. This perspective contributes to the argument that although challenged throughout coeducation, women leaders were sustained by a set of strategies consistent with differentiating the purpose of education by gender. Once the purpose of educating women separately from men was replaced with a purpose less differentiated by gender, the strategies women leaders had relied on in earlier generations were less effective.

Thirty-seven years since the passage of Title IX, new generations of women leaders have had time to ascend to the top of the leadership structure but have failed to make significant progress. An examination of the biographies of the five women serving as athletic directors among 119 Division IA institutions in 2007 showed that "first" is included in their background, often several times. All were the "first" woman athletic directors of a combined program at their institution. Two had been the "first" woman athletic directors at more than one institution and within the athletic conference. Even today, women are still repioneering, still starting anew. The combining of men's and women's student services and intercollegiate athletics has been an important and significant contribution of Title IX policy. However, the impact of this policy will not be fully realized until women leaders of future generations are no longer the "first," when women leaders no longer have to start anew.

CONCLUSION

This chapter situates the decline of women leaders in the cocurriculum after Title IX in a historical pattern since the rise of coeducation. This perspective contributes the argument that although challenged throughout coeducation, women leaders were sustained by a set of strategies consistent with differentiating the purpose of education by gender. As the purpose of educating women separately from men was replaced with a purpose less differentiated by gender, the strategies women leaders relied on in earlier generations were less effective. Dismantling of separate purposes for educating women students also meant dismantling the infrastructure to promote

women leaders. Instead of a combination of four strategies, only one remains: superperformance. Using the case of women leaders in the cocurriculum, this chapter presents an argument that helps explain the pattern of each generation of women having to *start anew* and the reliance on superperformance as a strategy to advance the generation of women leaders after the passage of Title IX.

NOTE

1. Women's PE faculty preceded the women's athletic director position. Women faculty often served dual roles and became the coaches and administrators in women's intercollegiate athletics. Thus, the role of women's PE faculty in the cocurriculum is discussed.

REFERENCES

Acosta, R. V., & Carpenter, L. J. (2008). *Women in intercollegiate sport: A longitudinal, national study thirty-one year update 1977–2006*. New York: Brooklyn College.

Bashaw, C. T. (1999). *"Stalwart women": A historical analysis of deans of women in the south*. New York: Teachers College Press.

Bouttilier, M., & San Giovanni, L. (1994). Politics, public policy, and Title IX: Some limitations of liberal feminism. In S. Birrell & C. L. Cole (Eds.), *Women, sport, and culture* (pp. 97–118). Champaign, IL: Human Kinetics.

Carpenter, L. J., & Acosta, R. V. (2001). Let her swim, climb mountain peaks: Self-sacrifice, and success in expanding athletic programs for women. In J. Nidiffer & C. T. Bashaw (Eds.), *Women administrators in higher education* (pp. 207–229). Albany, NY: State University of New York Press.

Clifford, G. J. (1983). "Shaking dangerous questions from the crease": Gender and American higher education. *Feminist Issues, 3*(2), 3–62.

Clifford, G. J. (1989). *Lone voyagers: Academic women in coeducational universities 1870–1937*. New York: The Feminist Press.

Costa, M., & Guthrie, S. (1994). *Women and sport: Interdisciplinary perspectives*. Champaign, IL: Human Kinetics.

Cott, N. F. (1987). *The grounding of modern feminism*. New Haven, CT: Yale University Press.

Eisenmann, L. (2006). *Higher education for women in postwar American, 1945–1965*. Baltimore, MD: The Johns Hopkins University Press.

Estler, S., & Nelson, L. J. (2005). *Who calls the shots?: Sports and university leadership, culture, and decision making*. San Francisco, CA: Wiley Subscription Services.

Fass, P. S. (1997). The female paradox: Higher education for women, 1945–1963. In L. F. Goodchild & H. S. Wechsler (Eds.), *The history of higher education* (2nd ed., pp. 699–723). Boston, MA: Simon & Schuster Custom Publishing.

Festle, M. J. (1986). *Playing nice: Politics and apologies in women's sports*. New York: Columbia University Press.

Gerda, J. J. (2006). Gathering together: A view of the earliest student affairs professional organizations. *NASPA Journal*, 43(4), 147–163.

Glazer, P. M., & Slater, M. (1987). *Unequal colleagues: The entrance of women into the professions, 1890–1940*. New Brunswick, NJ: Rutgers University Press.

Glazer-Raymo, J. (1999). *Shattering the myths: Women in academe*. Baltimore, MD: The Johns Hopkins University Press.

Gordon, L. D. (1990). *Gender and higher education in the progressive era*. New Haven, CT: Yale University Press.

Gordon, L. D. (1997). From seminary to University: An overview of women's higher education, 1870–1920. In L. F. Goodchild & H. S. Wechsler (Eds.), *The history of higher education* (2nd ed., pp. 473–498). Boston: Simon and Schuster Custom Publishing.

Grundy, P., & Shackelford, S. (2005). *Shattering the glass: The remarkable history of women's basketball*. New York: The New Press.

Horowitz, H. L. (1987). *Campus life: Undergraduate cultures from the end of the eighteenth century to the present*. New York: Knopf.

Hult, J. S. (1999). NAGWS and AIAW: The strange and wondrous journey to the athletic summit, 1950–90. *Journal of Physical Education, Recreation & Dance*, 70(4), 24–31.

Jones, S. R., & Komives, S. R. (2001). Contemporary issues of women as senior student affairs officers. In J. Nidiffer & C. T. Bashaw (Eds.), *Women administrators in higher education: Historical and contemporary perspectives* (pp. 231–248). Albany, NY: State University of New York Press.

King, J., & Gomez, G. (2008). *On the pathway to the presidency: Characteristics of higher education's senior leadership*. Washington, DC: American Council on Education.

Macraild, D., & Taylor, A. (2004). *Social theory and social history*. New York: Palgrave Macmillan.

Markels, R. (2000). Bloomer basketball and its suspender suppression: Women's intercollegiate competition at Ohio State, 1904–1907. *Journal of Sport History*, 27(1), 31–49.

McCandless, A. T. (1999). *The past in the present: Women's higher education in the twentieth-century American south*. Tuscaloosa, AL: The University of Alabama Press.

National Association of Student Personnel Administrators & American College Personnel Association. (2004). *Learning reconsidered: A campus-wide focus on the student experience*. Washington, DC: Authors.

Nerad, M. (1999). *The academic kitchen: A social history of gender stratification at the University of California, Berkeley*. Albany, NY: State University of New York Press.

Newcomer, M. (1959). *A century of higher education for American women*. New York: Harper and Row.

Nidiffer, J. (2000). *Pioneering deans of women: More than wise and pious matrons*. New York: Teachers College Press.

Nidiffer, J. (2003). From whence they came: The contexts, challenges, and courage of early faculty women administrators in higher education. In R. Ropers-Huilman (Ed.), *Gendered futures in higher education* (pp. 15–34). Albany, NY: State University of New York Press.

Paul, J. (2001). Agents of social control: The role of physical educators as guardians of women's health, 1860–1960. In J. Nidiffer & C. T. Bashaw (Eds.), *Women administrators in higher education: Historical and contemporary perspectives* (pp. 183–206). Albany, NY: State University of New York Press.

Rossiter, M. W. (1982). *Women scientists in America: Struggles and strategies to 1940*. Baltimore, MD: The Johns Hopkins University Press.

Rossiter, M. W. (1995). *Women scientists in America: Before affirmative action, 1940–1972*. Baltimore, MD: The Johns Hopkins University Press.

Rudolf, F. (1990). *The American college and university: A history*. Athens, GA: University of Georgia Press.

Schwartz, R. A. (1997a). How deans of women became deans of men. *Review of Higher Education*, 20(4), 419–436.

Schwartz, R. A. (1997b). Reconceptualizing the leadership roles of women in higher education: A brief history on the importance of deans of women. *The Journal of Higher Education, 68*(5), 502–522.

Solomon, B. M. (1985). *In the company of educated women: A history of women and higher education in America*. New Haven, CT: Yale University Press.

Suggs, W. (2005). *A place on the team: The triumph and tradedy of Title IX*. Princeton, NJ: Princeton University Press.

Title IX of the Education Amendments Act of 1972, 38, 20 U.S.C., 1681 (1972).

Touchton, J. G., & Davis, L. (1991). *Factbook on women in higher education*. New York: American Council on Education.

Wushanley, Y. (2004). *Playing nice and losing: The struggle for control of women's intercollegiate athletics, 1960–2000*. Syracuse, NY: Syracuse University Press.

4

The Powerful Collaborations Between Deans of Women and Directors of Physical Education

Syracuse University's Contributions to the History of Student Affairs, 1930s–1950s

Thalia Mulvihill

Abstract: Dean M. Eunice Hilton (1899–1975) led the heralded Student Dean Program for women at Syracuse University from 1935 to 1949. This graduate program was among the first of its kind and prepared women to administer comprehensive services, give instruction, and provide guidance and counsel to women students through positions in higher education. Hilton's vision for how educational communities for women students, faculty members, and administrators should be created and maintained included a new organizational model that she put to work at Syracuse University. This included specific instructions for bringing women academics (faculty and administrators) into the center of the conversations regarding an institution's mission, which she believed must be about developing the whole student. This notion of educating the whole student was articulated in depth in 1937 by the American Council on Education, which developed the Student Personnel Point of View *commonly referred to as the SPPV. This chapter explores Hilton's leadership at this critical time and how it fostered sustained institutional change.*

DEAN M. EUNICE HILTON (1899–1975) led the heralded Student Dean Program for women at Syracuse University from 1935 to 1949. This graduate program, which was among the first of its kind, prepared women to administer comprehensive services, give instruction, and provide guidance and counsel to women students through positions in higher education. Hilton's vision for how educational communities for women students, faculty members, and administrators should be created and maintained included a new organizational model that she put to work at Syracuse University. Hilton insisted that institutions of higher education needed the input of deans of women on all aspects of curriculum issues, not just student service issues. This included specific instructions for bringing women academics (faculty and administrators) into the center of the conversations regarding an institution's mission, which she believed must be about developing the *whole student*. This notion of educating the whole student was articulated in depth in 1937 by the American Council on Education, which developed the *Student Personnel Point of View* commonly referred to as the SPPV (affectionately known by some as the PPV). The SPPV stated that educators ought to focus on the physical, social, emotional, spiritual, and intellectual development of students. This articulation was the first systematic philosophical statement put forth by the growing profession of student personnel professionals.

Hilton's pervasive influence helped create and develop new positions for women in academe, new collegial relationships between women academics, and new ways to frame conversations about the role and responsibilities of women in higher education through regional and national organizations. One of the most noteworthy examples of Hilton's philosophy, beyond her more commonly known work as a dean of women and director of the student dean program, was the impact she had on integrating the physical education program into an accepted, and essential, component of the education of every female college student. She accomplished this by developing a strong collegial relationship with Katherine Sibley, the director of physical education at Syracuse University in the 1930s and 1940s. They worked together to eliminate the artificial boundaries placed between their programs, and Hilton used their success at Syracuse as a model for other colleges and universities.

During the middle decades of this century, women physical educators at Syracuse University, and at other institutions throughout the east, were organizing to have their work recognized as essential to the overall curriculum. Hilton's leadership at this critical time epitomized the particular form of collegial advocacy Hilton believed was necessary in order for lasting institutional change to occur. By focusing on the intersections

between Hilton's Student Dean Program and the women's physical education program at Syracuse University, we can learn more about how professions for women in higher education were shaped and how curricular changes were made to reflect the needs of women students. This information is important as we consider strategies for change in student affairs and higher education that support women.

BACKGROUND

Hilton's leadership resulted in a coordination of women's roles as faculty and administrators, as they worked together to provide a comprehensive curriculum for women students. Hilton's influence on the development of a form of professional collegiality between student personnel professionals and physical educators spread throughout the eastern part of the United States. Hilton's personal background made this connection a natural one for her. Hilton was born and raised in Lincoln, Nebraska, attended Cotner College (1917–1918), received a Bachelor of Arts degree (1922) in physical education, a master's degree (1926) in physical education from the University of Nebraska, and taught English and history while serving as dean of women at McCook Junior College in Lincoln, Nebraska (1926–1931). These early professional experiences brought her an insider's knowledge about the promises and problems that existed for women college students in the classroom, in physical education programs, and in higher education environments. Hilton believed that all of these environments constituted the "curriculum" and she worked to integrate the learning experiences for women students.

Historical Beginnings of the Syracuse Student Dean Program

In 1926, Dr. Iva Peters, a faculty member at Syracuse University's School of Citizenship, was asked to take on additional responsibilities as the dean of women at Syracuse University, a post she held until 1931. As Clifford (1989) reported in *Lone Voyagers*, this arrangement was not unusual. The first generation of deans of women were, by and large, women faculty members at coeducation institutions who were asked to care for and guide women students in all aspects of their collegiate experience. Very often, these women were one of a few women faculty members at the institution, and it was commonly believed by the male university presidents of the time that they would be the best qualified to understand and work with the women students. While taking on this assignment, Dr. Iva Peters envisioned a graduate academic program that she referred to as "Personnel Work for Women," designed to prepare women for these administrative positions. Dr. Eugenie Leonard, a professor of education, became the next dean of women (1931–1935), and she brought Peters's vision to fruition. In 1931, she initiated the Student Dean Program, a master's degree program designed to prepare women for personnel positions in higher and secondary education. It included a seminar called "Student Personnel Administration" and offered a practicum to discuss and solve practical problems encountered by the "student deans" (women graduate students admitted to this new master's program) who headed small residential cottages. The cottages were boarding houses for women students, maintained and staffed by the dean of women's office. The responsibilities of the student deans included guiding undergraduate women students as they struggled with personal concerns, assisting them with research and study skills, helping to construct appropriate social activities, assisting with vocational plans, and providing a general orientation to the university. This residency requirement, in the form of an "assistanceship [sic],[1]" was unique to the Syracuse program at the time and was an essential component of the student dean program, for it served as a professional laboratory in their training.

Between 1931 and 1960, some 800 women went through the program to become deans of women, residence hall directors, and high school guidance counselors. Graduates in later years held more specific titles such as director of activities, director of housing for women, and director of placement. Some became senior vice presidents of student services and directors of institutional research, and at least one became president of a college. These women were known as the "Hilton Elite," perhaps because Dean M. Eunice Hilton had such high aspirations for the women (see Mulvihill, 1994).

Eunice Hilton arrived in Syracuse in 1931 as a graduate student pursuing a doctorate in education. In 1932, after she had completed the one-year student dean program, she became the assistant dean of women under Eugenie Leonard. While maintaining this position as assistant dean, Hilton worked on her doctorate and in April of 1934 became the first woman to receive a PhD from the School of Education's Student Dean Program. Hilton's dissertation was entitled *The Dean of Women in the Public Co-ed Junior College* (Olds, 1991). With that credential, she was encouraged by Leonard, in 1935, to take on the position of dean of women at Syracuse University, with a faculty appointment within the School of Education. She remained in that position until 1949 and during those 14 years she strategically added scope of responsibility, national recognition, and additional status not only to her own position but to other developing professions for women in higher education as well.[2]

Hilton and Sibley Converge the Developing Fields of Student Personnel and Physical Education

Establishing the context for the history of student personnel and physical education is important to understand the significance of Hilton's contributions to merge the two areas. "Dean of women" first came into existence in 1892 with Alice Freeman Palmer's dual appointment at the University of Chicago as professor of history and dean of women. Deans of women were given responsibility for guiding (some would say controlling) the lives of all the women students of their institution. Their particular duties varied, yet soon the title *dean of women* was commonly understood to mean the woman on campus in charge of all the women students. A study conducted in 1911 found that out of 55 coeducational institutions surveyed, 44 had deans of women. By 1928, deans of women were present in 93% of coeducational institutions and of these 75% also held faculty appointments (Clifford, 1989, p. 13). Physical education, as a field, was also bringing more women into professional positions within colleges and universities. For example, Hult (1985) identified some of the earliest developments in the history of physical education for women and found that they were initiated by those in higher education institutions. In the 1870s and 1880s "several colleges appointed female physical education instructors to teach gymnastics and calisthenics to the increasing numbers of young women who had begun to enter institutions of higher learning" (Hult, p. 64). As early as 1885, a physical education curriculum was present in all women's colleges in the east and "sports for women" were organized in many colleges and universities in the Midwest (Clark, 1873, p. 40).[3]

At Syracuse University, Katherine Sibley was appointed as the first instructor of physical education for women in 1903. She helped create the Women's Athletic Association (WAA) and was named the organization's first president in 1904.[4] The WAA "directed all athletic activities relating to women and staged the 'field day' events that featured Women's Day each spring" (Galpin, 1960, p. 265). Syracuse University saw its first organized basketball game between women teams in 1898. The teams were divided by class standing with the class of 1900 playing the class of 1901. Also, in 1898, the Syracuse women's team, captained by senior Mary L. Storm, defeated the Normal School in Cortland by a score of 6 to 2.

Dressed in suits of regulation specifications, the girls from Syracuse must have attracted much attention as they appeared in "white broadcloth trimmed lavishly with orange, orange sashes, and long white capes lined with orange"...The University Athletic Association contributed $25 for these suits, which were cut and tailored by the members of the team and their friends. (Galpin, 1960, p. 264)

On March 31, 1898, Miss Mattie Goodrich from the Syracuse class of 1899 formed the Women's Basketball Association and became the association's first president. "A constitution and bylaws were adopted and plans were made for outdoor games on a 'grass court'" (Galpin, 1960, p. 265). The Women's Athletics Association was the next organization of this kind at Syracuse University, and it held its first meeting on October 19, 1904. These Syracuse University organizations had their counterparts on most coeducational campuses and they all encountered the tensions that existed between advocates for health improvement and advocates for competitive sports.

Dorothy S. Ainsworth, the director of physical education at Smith College in the 1940s, articulated some of the tensions that existed as she contextualized the development of physical education for college women.

Once we thought health of the body the end all of our program and in pursuit of this aim we sought first muscular and then organic strength.... In the late 1890s and 1900s games crept into the program but not as a part of "the serious work" of the department. That still consisted of gymnastic exercises. Physical Education had been put upon a scientific basis and such was the fear of being considered unscientific that in my own college that Dance, when first introduced, was called aesthetic gymnastics.... With the changes brought in by the modern education method between 1910 and 1920 physical educators now are concerned with not merely the physical (muscular and organic well being) but all sides of the human being. No longer have we done our duty if we produce a muscular and organic marvel. In fact, the fear that we may produce muscles is rather against us. (EADPECW, 1940, p. 5)

These conditions led to expanded roles for women hired to direct women's physical education on college campuses. Clifford (1989), in *Lone Voyagers*, reminded us that "a woman hired to direct women's use of a college gymnasium or to take charge of physical training was often one of the earliest faculty women [at coeducational institutions]; she would be asked to instruct in physical culture, hygiene, or physiology, as well as to administer the gymnastics program or coach women's team sports" (p. 12). This accurately described Katherine Sibley's role at Syracuse University with her dual appointment as professor of physical education and hygiene and president of the Women's Athletic Association. In 1918, the physical education department at Syracuse University was created under the direction of Sibley, who remained in the director's position until her retirement in 1950. In 1919, the first class of women "phys-ed majors" graduated (*Post Standard*, 1950). By 1922, the degree of Bachelor of Science was awarded to those completing a four-year course in physical education and certificates were given to students completing a two-year sequence in physical education (Galpin, 1960). At this time, the Teacher's College (later in 1934 to be renamed the School of Education) at Syracuse University was filled predominately with women students. In 1922, 2,779 students out of 3,108 enrolled in Teachers College, or 89.4%, were women. In that year, the bachelor's degree was awarded to 92 in Pedagogy, 79 in Music, 36 in Art, 19 in Physical Education, and 39 in Science (Galpin, 1960).

On the national level, professional organizations were gaining strength and started building agendas for how college and university physical education programs ought to be focused. For example, the slogans "A sport for every girl" and "Every girl in a sport" were the representing ideals that guided the Committee on Women's Athletics and the National Section of Women's Athletics (Hult, 1985, p. 69). In the 1920s and 1930s, the argument made by members of both organizations was that athletic opportunities needed to

be available for all the girls and women, not just a select few who would be competing against another select few. Competition was not disdained but rather criticism was directed at the type of organizational structures that eliminated the vast majority of females from participation in the name of improved competition (*The Daily Orange*, 1923).[5]

Understanding the power of organization, women physical educators knew that they would need to be a stronger entity in the American Physical Education Association if they were to effectively fight the "elitism and exploitation" that had come to characterize men's athletics and was beginning to creep into women's athletics (Hult, 1985, p. 66). In 1923, the *Official Handbook of the National Committee on Women's Athletics*, edited by Elizabeth Burchenal, was published. This document was in fact the first publication to set forth the standards concerning "athletic activities for girls and women [and how they differed from] a set of rules and standards designed primarily for men" (Burchenal, 1923, p. 14).

The *Sport Guides*, published by the National Section of Women's Athletics in the 1930s, were meant to help create quality standards that would be embraced by the larger profession. The *Guides* "included skill development, coaching strategies, techniques of officiating, and direct and implied statements of belief regarding what values should occur from sports, as well as problems to be avoided" (p. 66). Hult (1985) understood the *Guides* as powerful tools to educate and to persuade readers to accept a new authoritative organization whose purpose was to guide and direct all activities related to each women's sport. The *Guides*, indeed, became widely used and relied-on documents.[6]

Integration of Programs for Women as a National Focus in Professional Organizations

Although women academics were organizing on the national scene, Hilton was called on by women physical educators both at Syracuse and at other campuses to instruct them on how to best operate as a collective. For example, in 1940, Hilton was invited by the Eastern Association of the Directors of Physical Education for College Women (EADPECW) to be a guest speaker at a symposium whose topic was "Integration of the Student Program from the Points of View of the Dean, the Personnel Officer, and the Director of Physical Education." The symposium attendees were from 35 colleges and universities, totaling 41 women physical education staff and 22 deans of women staff. Seventeen institutions sent both the physical education director and the dean of women (and/or their assistant dean or representative). Of these 17 institutions, 5 sent more than 1 person in the category of dean of women. Eighteen institutions sent only directors of physical education and no representatives for the dean of women. Barnard sent 5 physical education staff members in addition to the director of physical education and Colby sent 2 physical education representatives. These numbers symbolize the commitment of deans of women and directors of physical education to integrating programs for women on their campuses in 1940.

Representing Syracuse University were Katherine Sibley, the director of physical education, and M. Eunice Hilton, the dean of women. Special guests attending the symposium included the esteemed Dr. Esther Lloyd Jones, professor of education and director of Guidance Clinic at Teachers College of Columbia University.[7]

The symposium report provided the transcript of the opening remarks made by Julia R. Grout, the president of the Eastern Association of the Directors of Physical Education for College Women and the director of physical education at Duke.[8] She explained the reasons why these women had been called together:

> I can say with certainty that the opportunity to meet our deans, to hear their opinions on problems which concern us, to have a day of discussion,

formal and informal, was most satisfying. We hope that our deans likewise found much of value in these meetings. Such combined conferences should lead to a better understanding of each other's work as it applies to problems of mutual concern. (EADPECW, 1940, p. 6)

Esther Lloyd Jones's address pointed to one of the conditions that made the Symposium necessary:

> One very obvious reason why directors of physical education have not been able to coordinate their work with the personnel program is because on most college campuses the various elements of the personnel program are themselves so poorly coordinated. To try to articulate with something that is itself but loosely hung together is always difficult. (EADPECW, 1940, p. 7)

The significance of Jones's overall contribution to the symposium is twofold. First, she represented tradition for those in attendance—she was a prominent woman within higher education representing Teachers College of Columbia, one of the first institutions to create a graduate program for women preparing for university administration, and she was considered a pioneer researcher in the area of student personnel work.

Additional significance can also be found in her willingness to identify the problem of disjointed efforts on campuses to provide services and to create educational environments for women students. This was, more than anything else, an evaluation of the power dynamics that existed on most campuses. Institutional arrangements were not conducive to coalition building by women, for women. Because of the respect that Jones and her work commanded nationally, many believed that if Jones said it, it must be so. The women this symposium brought together were given greater latitude, and permission of sorts, to create a new agenda for women students and to garner the strength and fortitude they would need to go back to their campuses to start the task of realizing the agenda. While Jones announced the need for the agenda, two other notable women academics became the architects of the strategy.

Dorothy S. Ainsworth and Eunice Hilton were selected as the keynote speakers for physical education and deans of women, respectively, and they each set the stage for the organizational and curricular changes that would follow the symposium. "The Physical Education Point of View" was the title of the address given by Ainsworth, the director of physical education from Smith College. This title purposely imitated the well-known *Student Personnel Point of View* (1937). The SPPV became the manifesto of all student personnel professionals. It stated that each student should be treated as a unique individual and that a quality liberal education demanded that the whole student be taken into account. This approach was predicated on the central idea that intellectual development is inextricably connected to emotional, social, physical, and spiritual development. By making the decision to borrow the rhetoric of the SPPV as she described the philosophical orientation to her field, she accomplished two things. First, she provided a clear demonstration that these two groups of professionals can use and understand each other's professional discourse. Second, an integral part of the collegiate experience for all women ought to include physical education in equal proportion to the other areas of their developing lives.

Hilton, within her address entitled "Integration of the Student Personnel Program from the Standpoint of the Dean of Women," presented her philosophy of how the services for women on college campuses should be organized. Hilton's arguments were compelling as she explained the complexities of her vision. Hilton's remarks included the basic principles she employed at Syracuse University and offered them as instruction on how to build a comprehensive, integrated program for women students on other campuses. For example, she recommended to the members of the symposium that academic status and formal classroom teaching responsibilities are goals for both deans of women and physical educators of women. This assertion was necessary given the progressively diminishing status deans of women experienced throughout the twentieth century. Very often faculty status was withheld from the dean of women or given only as a concession after a potential employee made it a condition of hire. Hilton was indicating that the problem, historically, was shared by both professional groups.

The second point Hilton emphasized was that physical educators needed deans of women because the dean is often the "only woman executive on a campus entitled to meet with the administrators to determine [institutional] policies" (EADPECW, 1940, p. 4). Hilton was advocating for a professional alliance between deans of women and physical educators that would position them as a united front working for the best in curriculum, services, and policies for women students as well as for the best working conditions for women faculty and administrators. This alliance would prepare deans of women to speak on behalf of the physical educators of women when matters of policy were being discussed. This suggestion implies that policies influencing physical educators of women and their programs could be shaped by deans of women who were often consulted with regarding what other women employees at the institution should be doing. Hilton called the director of physical education the "chief ally of the dean of women" (EADPECW, 1940, p. 4), indicating that she perceived the relationship as mutual but recognized the political reality that on most campuses deans of women carried more clout with the administration than physical educators.

Hilton cautioned that unless all the professionals concerned with counseling the whole student "work out some means of defining areas of responsibility and of cooperating with one another, we are likely to do real harm where we are seeking to do only good" (EADPECW, 1940, p. 4). Hilton was attempting to order the form and function of counseling relationships that may informally or formally develop between students and female academics. By counseling, Hilton does not mean clinical counseling. The use of the term as it relates to student personnel services meant at that time a relationship of influence, whereby the faculty member or dean would make it a priority to know each student not only by personal experience but also by way of survey and interview material; by using professional guidance techniques, they take responsibility for advising and influencing female students. According to the SPPV, the success of this form of counseling was highly dependent on the students' ability to perceive the genuine care and concern the faculty and/or dean had for them as individuals.

Hilton's concern was that, within such a system of influence, colleagues must always know what their counterparts are doing and work cooperatively to nurture the student. A student may easily be confused, bored, or disenchanted if disunion is detected among the advice givers. According to Hilton, this must be avoided at all costs. This "right relationship" between women academics is indeed one of the prime motivators for Hilton as she developed ways to integrate the educational experience for college women, while maintaining that the dean of women is always ultimately responsible for the quality of the educational community.

Hilton warned against having physical educators attempt to accomplish all of these goals alone.

> Even in doing just its part in attaining this aim [physical education] runs a great chance of working toward the same aim or at a chance of working at cross purposes with [other departments] . . . The expanding aims and functions of the physical education department for women on most campuses demand cooperation with many divisions of the college or university. (EADPECW, 1940, p. 7)

Hilton recommended that physical education faculty receive some specific training in guidance and counseling techniques and encouraged them

to see this function as essential to the role of all faculty (EADPECW, 1940).

These remarks had particular relevance for Hilton, four years later, on her own campus. Correspondence between Dean Hilton and Professor Katherine Sibley, dated May 15, 1944, documented the ongoing struggle with role confusion among women academics when it came to specific responsibilities for women students. Within this letter, Hilton is documenting a conversation she had with Sibley regarding a Miss Penfield, the director of social activities and social education, under Hilton's supervision, and a Mr. Andreas, the recreational activities director, under the supervision of Sibley. Hilton says the relationship between Penfield and Andreas

> should be defined carefully in the interest of understanding and cooperation. Since recreational activities are social and social activities are recreational a twilight zone always will exist between the two areas of responsibility even after we do this; therefore in addition to a careful definition we should plan the organization so that lines of communication and cooperation are easy. (Hilton, 1954, May 15)

At the 1940 symposium, Dorothy S. Ainsworth, director of physical education at Smith, concurred with Hilton that the student program for women must be one of integration:

> The place of physical education [belongs] in the Teaching Service of the College. . . . Curriculum revision[s] concern us because we can and wish to contribute to the liberal arts background of the student. . . . Since all our work is planned to meet individual needs and problems, we are most grateful and hopeful of advice and help [from deans of women]. . . . We are more than willing to undertake faculty responsibility and social responsibility whenever it may fall, and . . . one of the objects of this meeting was to offer our full cooperation in the furthering of the general college program and the education of our undergraduates. (Hilton, 1944, May 15, pp. 9–11)

At the conclusion of the symposium, the members of the Eastern Association of Directors of Physical Education for College Women developed a document entitled "The Aims and Objectives of the Physical Education Program" that specified the means by which they hoped to coordinate their programs with the overall student personnel programs. In addition, this association adopted resolutions, which in effect represent a philosophical position related to the education of their female students. Katherine Sibley, of Syracuse University, was one of four educators who signed this document, which emphasized that the strength of America, with its democratic ideals, was dependent "not only upon its military preparedness but upon its moral, spiritual, and physical preparedness as well" (Hilton, 1944, May 15, p.19).[9] Linking educational reforms for women to the larger national, democratic agenda was considered an effective strategy in the 1940s (see Mulvihill, 1994).[10]

THE ROLE OF ACADEMIC WOMEN IN THE DEVELOPMENT OF THE GENERAL EDUCATION CURRICULUM AND THE NECESSITY OF RELATIONSHIPS BETWEEN WOMEN COLLEAGUES

Eight years after the symposium, in March 1948, the dialogue about integrating programs for women students continued to be prioritized by the Eastern Association, and once again they called on Hilton to serve as a keynote speaker on the topic of general education (Hilton, 1948). Hilton identified herself as a "general educator" and indicated that she had "a little more contact with physical education than most deans of women" because she had a minor in physical education and was the "head of a department of physical education in a secondary school for one year" (Hilton, 1948, p. 1). This may, in part, account for her relative ease with envisioning the role of physical education as integral to the overall program for women students. The other key can

be found in her understanding of what it meant to be colleagues.

Hilton used her relationship with Sibley as an example of what colleagueship between women academics can accomplish within higher education. In the 1948 keynote address she said,

> Actually my best contact with the field of physical education . . . has been some fifteen years of happy and stimulating association with Katherine Sibley and her fine staff in the women's physical education department at Syracuse. Under her patient and competent tutelage it has been my privilege to keep pace with developments in the field, to cooperate in planning help for individual students and groups of students through their participation in physical education classes and activities, and to look ahead to really adequate facilities for a proper program of physical education on our campus. (Hilton, 1948, p. 2)

Hilton pointed out that

> general education has not paid much attention to physical education which has suffered a long time from the departmentalization in modern colleges and universities. Set off by itself, often without devices for integrating the various courses properly with the total academic program, frequent difficulties have arisen. (Hilton, 1948, p. 3)

There were additional problems within the university community with status and image issues related to women's programs. Hilton described these problems as they impacted physical educators:

> The idea that physical activity is not respectable *academically* results in the treatment of the program of the physical education department as an appendage to, rather than a force in, the total educational experience of the individual student and the life of the campus. This fact results in other difficulties. The physical education faculty sometimes is not held in the same esteem as the philosophy, mathematics, or even the psychology faculties are. From time to time moves are made to make all physical education courses optional and/or without credit. Most unhappy of all difficulties . . . is that of finding the budget of the women's physical

education department held down more drastically on a comparative basis than that of other departments and the salaries of faculty members lower than those of their fellows in other departments. (Hilton, 1948, p. 6)

This pattern of neglect by the central administration and the tendency to be viewed as a satellite of the central mission of the institution are conditions that deans of women contended with as well. Hilton met these challenges head-on and became very successful at reorganizing her campus. She accomplished this by securing faculty appointments for herself and certain members of her staff. She also maintained a direct line of communication to Chancellor Tolley and forged an enduring reputation as an expert on all issues concerning women college students. Therefore, Hilton was not perceived by physical educators as an outsider giving advice but rather an insider sharing strategy and wisdom about carrying out an effective plan for change.

Hilton outlined a political action plan for physical educators that mirrored her own actions with regard to the development of the student dean program. For example, Hilton (1948) suggested that

[o]ur whole faculties and communities should be made aware of what is going on in the physical education through planned publicity. Deans and presidents who understand and value the contributions of physical education to all education should be availed upon to carry the good word.... Public relations devices of all kinds should be known and used daily by staff members. Results of research and evaluation studies should be widely circulated. Only careful planning and good evaluation in these ways can win for physical education and the educators in that field the esteem and influence which they deserve.... This is the time to strike for adequate facilities, conference rooms and records space as well as sports equipment and room for activities. This is a time for bold experimentation and for making plans to "win friends and influence people" in other departments on our campuses. (p. 4)

At Syracuse University, Hilton had developed a remarkable relationship with Chancellor Tolley who did indeed understand and value the contributions of Dean Hilton and her staff. Hilton always insisted that she report directly to the chancellor and whenever the arrangement was questioned, Chancellor Tolley always defended her point of view. Hilton's campuswide influence was also connected to the institutional data she and her staff collected about the women students. For example, she was in the business of conducting and distributing research and evaluation studies regarding women students and their educational needs. She sparked lively conversation about the findings among her colleagues across campus. She often used these forums as opportunities to secure more resources, such as physical space, for female students.

One significant project that represented coordination of efforts between the physical education program and the student dean program at Syracuse University was the Women's Building project. This project required extensive effort by many women to secure a special facility for women on a coeducational campus. The Women's Building was dedicated on November 15, 1953, and was marked by a moving speech given by Katherine Sibley. She began with a review of her early years at Syracuse when she was greeted with no proper facilities for women at all. Sibley found the students "eager for a change from formal Swedish gymnastics, heavy apparatus work, rope climbing on old splintery hemp ropes, and other big muscle activities." Sibley recalled that "Giving a course in social dancing posed [another] problem, when I made a request for an accompanist. Eyebrows were lifted— dancing taught in a Methodist institution? So I changed the course to singing games which necessarily included dance steps" (Sibley, 1953, p. 2). Sibley recounted the efforts it took to raise money for the building:

It was during 1907–1908 that money began to flow into the alumnae treasury from the graduates and the students for a building. The alumnae organized many paying social affairs which were financially successful. The students sold candy, pencils, cookies, in the living centers. Each week they sold in the Hall of Languages, popular but awful ginger cakes with thick chocolate frostings. The physical education staff cooperating with the students, gave a large dance known as the Annual Military Ball. The attendance grew so great—over 500 girls—we had to move it into the Archbold Gymnasium. The admission fee was $.25 which included refreshments presented by friends from neighborhood stores. The proceeds were deposited in the Alumnae treasury. It was truly amazing the way this fund grew each year—well over a hundred dollars a year. During the First World War all our energies and time were devoted to war projects. For the most part money raising by students was for war kits for our soldiers. By 1920 the building fund again gained impetus. (p. 4)

As early as 1923, Sibley met with the university architect, Mr. Dwight Baum, regarding a building design, yet it took several more decades of fund-raising activity before the project moved forward. Sibley's description of these events years later reveals the persistence and dedication required by many to shepherd this project to its completion. She recounted the events:

> In the late thirties...Mrs. Graham called a few influential Syracuse graduate women together to form a committee for the purposes of asking permission of the Board of Trustees to conduct a nationwide drive for funds for the Women's Building. [In November 1940, a] fund raising committee was organized in each state, but again all plans were canceled and the drive came to an end with the Pearl Harbor catastrophe. In the fall of 1948 the University Department campaign was organized and set in motion in 1949. The drive for the Women's Building was absorbed into this larger campaign but the alumnae and friends were privileged to earmark their donations for our building. The University engaged Mr. Lorimer Rich, as the architect for the building. We spent nearly two years in the study of exterior and interior design.... The building also includes the offices of the Dean of Women and her staff. (p. 5)

This was no afterthought! Housing the dean of women's office and the physical education department together was part of the intentional plan of Hilton and Sibley. Being in such close proximity would help guarantee a more integrated program for women.

In her building dedication speech, Sibley gave special thanks to Dean Hilton, who was then the dean of the School of Home Economics. Dean Marjorie Smith, the dean of women at the time, and Lucille Verhulst, the director of physical education for women since Sibley's retirement in 1950, were also honored for their advice and guidance in making the Women's Building "highly functional" (p. 6). There was a proud recognition of a new generation of professionals, from both programs, working together under Hilton's plan.

The Women's Building was dedicated eight years after Sibley was decorated with the George Arents Pioneer Medal in 1945 for excellence in her field. The citation read,

> Upon thousands of young women you have left the impress of your integrity, your unfailing standards, your characteristic disdain for the superficial or tawdry. Among the first to rebel against the formal exercise and routine drill that made gymnastics a distasteful requirement for many college women, you led the movement to make physical education an integral and zestful part of their general development. (Wilson, 1984, p. 374)

And with a fitting touch, the pool in the Women's Building was named the Katherine Sibley Pool in honor of the woman who had worked so long for its establishment (*Post Standard*, 1955). These events took place many years before the passage of Title IX of the Educational Amendments of 1972; yet, they represent an example of how the discourse was being shaped by deans of women and directors of physical education leading up to the passage of Title IX.

A significant part of the history of physical education can be located in the tensions that emerged between the Association of Intercollegiate Athletics for Women (AIAW) and the National Collegiate Athletic Association (NCAA). When the NCAA subsumed the AIAW, many women leaders within higher education were directly affected. Mergers almost always resulted in women losing authority as they were demoted from director positions to assistant director positions reporting to a male director. (Mulvihill, 2002, p. 188)

Jennifer Lee Hoffman's chapter (chapter 3) provided a rich context to further understand the impact of these organizational changes.

CONCLUSION

During the M. Eunice Hilton and Katherine Sibley years, many breakthroughs were made for women students at Syracuse University. The strength of Hilton's organizational model and educational philosophies attracted other women in higher education to study her methods of bringing about change. The pervasive influence Hilton had on creating and developing new positions for women in academe was extended to physical educators in the eastern part of the United States as evidenced by the conferences and symposiums, where Hilton was called on to guide them in the next phase of their professional development on college and university campuses. While this case study documents just one of the partnerships between academic women that resulted in significant gains for women between 1930 and 1950, it is clear that Hilton and Sibley recognized that successful programs for women students were built primarily through successful collegial relationships. Hilton and Sibley dedicated themselves to defining what a successful collegial relationship ought to be and developed a model that many other academic women adopted as their own.

Lee Hawthorne Calizo's chapter (chapter 18) tells another, more contemporary, story of collaboration between six women administrators on a single campus (UMBC), who intentionally and conscientiously worked together at a single institution to explore common themes of interest to them as women in higher education. Hilton and Sibley perhaps represented a more politically conscious partnership, while the UMBC group represented a more support group arrangement whereby self-directed professional development was paramount. In both cases, these collaborations are powerful representations of women's associations that were motivated by women reading their institutional environments and building action plans for change. The forms and functions of colleagueship will no doubt continue to be rewritten by women in higher education today as they adapt to the current demands and build even more innovative ways to work collaboratively.

NOTES

1. I wish to thank Dr. Joan N. Burstyn, Dr. Timothy Chandler, and Marion Waterman Meyer for reading earlier drafts of this manuscript. And a special thank you to Dr. Claire M. Olds, former Syracuse student dean and dean of students at Skidmore College (1964–1983), who introduced me to Margaret Paulding (1907–1999), the late professor of physical education at Skidmore College. In the early stages of this research, Claire and Margaret were very generous with their insights about the historical development of physical education for women and the connections that existed within collegiate programs designed for women.

2. Dr. Claire M. Olds, a member of the student dean Class of 1955, prepared a brief history of the Student Dean Program in which she summarized Hilton's vitae: "[Hilton's] leadership positions included presidencies of the National Association of Women Deans (NAWDAC), the National Personnel and Guidance Association (APGA), and the New York State Deans, AAUW, BPW, and ZONTA. [Hilton] was also appointed to New York's Women's Council (later, the Equal pay Committee) and Governor Dewey's Educational Commission. She attended two White House conferences on children. She was also active in New York State extension programs in home economics for rural women." *Syracuse University Student Dean Commemorative Seminar: 60th Anniversary Reunion Student Dean Program, June 27–30, 1991*, pp. 11–12.

3. These physical education programs were developing in the aftermath of the damaging effects of medical and academic writers such as Edward Clarke. For example, in *Sex in Education; or, A Fair Chance for the Girls* (Boston: Osgood and Co., 1873), he argued that "The system never does two things well at the same time. A girl upon whom Nature, for a limited period and for a definite purpose, imposes so great a physiological task, will not have as much power left for the tasks of school, as the boy whom Nature requires less at the corresponding epoch" (p. 40).

4. Reported in various newspaper articles found in the George Arents Research Library, Syracuse University, Faculty and Staff Clippings file. Katherine Sibley, in addition to graduating from Syracuse University, studied at the Posse Normal School of Gymnastics in Boston; she was involved in advanced study at Wellesley College, New York University, Stanford University, and at Syracuse University's College of Medicine for three years specializing in anatomy.

5. This argument against elitism carried over into organizational leadership issues as well. For example, page 1 of the December 19, 1923, edition of *The Daily Orange*, Syracuse University's student newspaper, reported that the Women's Athletic Association was being taken over by sorority sisters who wanted to have control of all the offices of the organization and be assured of the recognition and/or honors these leadership positions brought with them. This criticism of the elitism that was being fostered by reserving positions of authority and recognition within the association for members of the Greek system at Syracuse University was reflective of the concerns and conversations happening at the national level.

6. The Student Dean Program at Syracuse University developed *Guides to Guidance*, which served as professional annotated bibliographies. These guides, like those produced for women physical educators, were very influential. They were prepared by the women graduate students in the Student Dean Program and were read by a large national audience as a way to keep current in the profession.

7. Hilton was very influenced by Dr. Esther Lloyd Jones and Ruth Strang and often cited their research within her public addresses, correspondence, and classroom instruction.

8. *Report,* 3. Julia R. Grout (1898–1984) received her BA from Mount Holyoke in 1920 and her MS from Wellesley in 1924. She was a professor of physical education at Duke University from 1924 to 1964.

9. The other three who signed the document were Helen McKinstry, from Russell Sage College, Louise Gray, from Wells College, and Agnes R. Wayman, from Barnard College.

10. For example, see Mulvihill, T. (1994). Hats, heels and high ideals: The Student Dean Program at Syracuse University, 1931–1960. *Courier, XXVI* (2), 141–150, for the connections between Hilton, Mary Beard (the historian), and Eleanor Roosevelt.

REFERENCES

American Council on Education. (1937). *Student personnel point of view*. Washington, DC: Author.

Burchenal, E. (Ed.). (1923). *Official handbook of the national committee on women's athletics and the official rules for swimming, track and field, and soccer, 1923–24,14*. New York: American Sports Publishing Co.

Clark, E. (1873). *Sex in education; or, a fair chance for the girls*. Boston, MA: Osgood and Company.

Clifford, G. (1989). *Lone voyagers: Academic women in coeducational institutions, 1870–1937*. New York: The Feminist Press.

Eastern Association of the Directors of Physical Education for College Women. (1940, October 11 and 12). Integration of the student program from the points of view of the dean, the personnel officer, and the director of physical education. *Symposium for Deans of Women and Directors of Physical Education*. American Women's Club. In M. Eunice Hilton Collection: Box 17 (p. 8). New York: George Arents Research Library.

Galpin, W. F. (1960). *Syracuse University: The growing years*. (Vol. 2). New York: Syracuse University Press.

Hilton, M. E. (1948, March 12). *The place of physical education for women in the college program*. Paper delivered to the Eastern Association for Physical Education, Vassar College. George Arents Research Library, Syracuse University, M. Eunice Hilton collection, Box 17, folder Speeches and Book Reviews.

Hilton, M. E. (1944, May). *Letter to Katherine Sibley*. Katherine Sibley Collection, Box 1. George Arents Research Library, Syracuse University.

Hult, J. S. (1985). The governance of athletics for girls and women: Leadership by women physical educators, 1899–1949. *Research Quarterly for Exercise and Sport, 64, centennial issue*, 64–77.

Mulvihill, T. (1994). Hats, heels and high ideals: The Student Dean Program at Syracuse University, 1931–1960. *Courier, XXVI* (2), 141–150.

Mulvihill, T. (2002). Physical education and women in higher education. In A. M. M. Alemán & K. A. Renn (Eds.), *Women in higher education: An encyclopedia* (pp. 184–188). Santa Barbara: CA: ABC-Clio.

Olds, C. M. (1991, June 27–30). *Syracuse University Student Dean Commemorative Seminar: 60th Anniversary Reunion Student Dean Program.* Syracuse, NY: Syracuse University.

Sibley, K. (1953, November 15). *Dedication of the women's building address.* Katherine Sibley Collec-

tion, Box 1. George Arents Research Library, Syracuse University. Syracuse University. (1923, December 19). Women's athletic association taken over by sorority sisters. *The Daily Orange*, p. 1.

Syracuse University's physical educator retiring after 47 years. (1950, March 19). *Post Standard*, p. 3.

Syracuse University pool named after Miss Sibley. (1955, June 5). *Post Standard,* p. 7.

Wilson, R. (Ed.). (1984). *Syracuse University: The critical years* (Vol. 3). New York: Syracuse University Press.

NARRATIVES ON GENDER AND FEMINISM

From Disembodied to Whole: Carving Out Space for My Race and Gender Identities

Rosemary J. Perez

Have you ever had an "ah-ha" moment? I'm referring to that glorious, split second where something suddenly "clicks" and you have a mind-altering thought about an issue or problem that has always been right in front of you. No matter what you did or how you approached the topic previously, it continuously baffled and befuddled you. But today, something was fundamentally different and, if only for a few flickering seconds, you experienced complete and total clarity. In that moment, your world is completely changed and you are left to wonder how you lived before your intellectual or emotional epiphany.

While writing my master's comprehensive exam, I was fortunate enough to have one of these moments. I had spent months writing a personal scholarly narrative about my experiences with internalized racism and my role as a model minority, when I came across the following quotation:

> I have heard too many community activists explain the intersection of gender and race by referring to disembodied entities, fractions of human experience: "First I am a person of color, then I am a woman. That makes me doubly

oppressed." According to this way of adding, a white man has the most whole identity; his experience is treated as the norm.
>
> (Aguilar-San Juan, 1997, p. x)

The statement on the page sounded strangely familiar, and I realized I had uttered these same words, thus compartmentalizing my identity. In my efforts to fight racism, I had neglected my identity as a woman and the paternalism that occurs within my own culture. At that moment, I started to more fully embrace my identity as a Filipina and as an Asian American woman by widening my comprehension of the intricacies of power and privilege.

Since my "ah-ha" moment, I've struggled at times to accommodate my entire identity rather than placing race in the foreground and gender in the background. In retrospect, this is not surprising given my professional experiences. I did my graduate training at a predominantly White institution and found myself consistently coping with racial microaggressions. In order to cope, I targeted my energy toward nurturing my racial and ethnic identities. Moreover, I have directly reported to men in each of my student affairs positions. Knowing the demographic composition of our field, it's almost shocking to be in the field for more than eight years and to never work for a woman. But, that near improbability was my reality. Although these men were strong mentors and identified as feminists, positional authority and male privilege always separated us.

Today, I am proud to say that I work for a female faculty member as a graduate research assistant. She has served as an example of how to craft a strong academic career while making time for family and friends. Although I appreciate her kindness and constant support, I find myself gravitating back toward two men in the department, one of whom serves as my faculty academic advisor. Our connection is rooted in our shared philosophical orientations and identities as people of color. I have also sought out mentoring from a male professor who has nurtured my burgeoning research interests in organizational behavior and has pushed me to develop my work as a scholar. While my academic interests and career aspirations have primarily driven my selection of counsel, I cannot help but wonder if it also reflects placing gender behind other aspects of my identity. This is not to say that my choice of mentors and advisors should be solely dictated by my gender identity. However, I believe that it is healthy to question my motivation in order to understand how I enact my claimed and assigned identities on a daily basis.

Extending my thinking beyond the workplace, I've often struggled with feelings of invisibility as an Asian American woman. Despite their statistical overrepresentation among college students relative to the general population, Asian Americans seem invisible within the field of higher education and student affairs. As a community, we consistently struggle with carving out a space in a race dialectic that predominantly operates using a Black–White dichotomy. Similarly, feminism was widely perceived as a White woman's movement prior to scholarly contributions from Black feminist scholars such as Patricia Hill-Collins and Angela Davis. Though feminist thinking expanded to consider the meaning of race, the dominant racial paradigm continues to manifest itself within this reconceptualized version of feminism.

With this in mind, I have wondered what space exists for Asian American feminist thought. Where do we belong in the struggle for both gender and racial equity in higher education? There have been good faith efforts to provide space for both gender and race within feminist dialogues, such as the American College Personnel Association's Standing Committee for Women's Sister Circles. And although I have found that environment to be an enriching one, I crave that same sense of connection on more than an annual basis. Furthermore, I long to see the involvement of more Asian American women because I often found myself in isolation during the program. Although I felt supported by my sisters of color, none of them shared my cultural experience as a Filipina.

Since that initial "ah-ha" moment years ago, a flood of questions has overwhelmed me. They have evolved over time, and I now find myself asking, "What would it mean to carve out an experience that allowed for my race and gender identities to coexist in ways that were not in competition? What would that space look like? What would it allow me to become?" My exploration of these questions and constant struggle to live an integrated identity has brought me to where I am today. I have translated those feelings of tension into my academic work and research interests in professional and organizational socialization. I am intrigued by how student affairs administrators are taught the explicit and tacit rules of the profession and of specific work environments. Perhaps more importantly, I want to extend the line of research that examines the alignment of organizational rules and cultures with the larger social constructs of racial and gender identity. My desire is to help us understand what helps professionals survive and what helps them thrive within organizations, knowing that social inequalities and oppression persist in our society and on our campuses. I also have an interest in exploring issues of attribution during the socialization process and want to understand how people make meaning of socialization processes using the various cultural lenses that inform their worldview.

Throughout my doctoral training, I have spent a great deal of time thinking about what I need to thrive as an Asian American woman who aspires to be a tenure-track professor in a higher education and student affairs program. Again, I find myself asking a litany of questions: Where does my identity fit into my work? How will I mentor students and provide space for the multiple dimensions of their identities? To what degree will I be expected to do race- and gender-focused scholarship based on my social identities rather than my own interest? If I do this type of work, is it valued in the academy? Does this particular focus limit the perceptions of my interests and capabilities as a scholar? While these questions lack clear answers, they do reflect my continuing quest to live holistically rather than as disembodied identities. I long to find a

place where my identities or perhaps my oppressions are not in competition for acknowledgment both internally and within the larger society. If I make peace with who I am and who I want to be in this world, I must consider the implications within a society where inequalities are pervasive and oppressed groups are often placed in competition with each other. For now, carving out my space is a step in reclaiming what is mine—my full humanity. Along my journey, I believe I can make a contribution to the larger dialogue on navigating the intersections of race and gender identities and oppressions.

REFERENCES

Aguilar-San Juan, K. (1997). Foreword: Breathing fire, confronting power, and other necessary acts of resistance. In S. Shaw (Ed.), *Dragon ladies: Asian American feminists breathe fire* (pp. ix–xi). Boston, MA: South End Press.

She's Just a Girl

Cindy Clark

As children, students, and mothers, women must confront omnipresent gender issues that affect our ideas of who we are and who we should become. My story is only special because it is mine; it is the same story told by many mature women as they recount their own life experiences as connected to education.

Gender has been an issue in my life for as long as I can remember. I was the only girl in a family of three children. Growing up in a small, southern town during the 1960s, I saw and experienced the expectations placed on girls, and although gender roles may have been unfair, they were quite clear.

The boys at my elementary school were allowed to wear jeans, but as a girl, I was at the mercy of the weather when it came to wearing pants to school. Only if the temperature dipped below a certain level were we allowed to wear

pants. The girls were also expected to sit still, listen, and do well in their studies. However, boys were allowed more lenience when they misbehaved or did not complete their work. I became well aware of the phrase *boys will be boys* and what it meant. Responsibilities and privileges for my brothers and me were doled out by my parents, not always equal but in a way they deemed fair. My chores were inside the house, and I was never asked to take out the garbage or mow the lawn. Those jobs belonged to the *boys*, and because I did not want to take out the garbage or mow the lawn, I did not complain.

My first clear memory of being truly angry about being "just a girl" is when one of my brothers was being taught to drive a tractor in the fields on my grandfather's farm. Although I was physically able to drive that tractor and was older than both of my brothers, I was never allowed to drive it. When I complained to my mother about the unfairness of the situation, she told me that my grandfather was from another time and that it was "just his way." Until that very moment, I never felt like a subordinate, nor did I think I was missing out on anything simply because of my gender.

As a young adult, I knew my parents believed that my education was important because when I decided to get married after my sophomore year in college, my mother tried to talk me into waiting. Her objection was not to my impending marriage; it was to my decision to become a part-time student and enter the workforce full time. As a part of the "Me Generation," my peers and I believed we could do anything and everything. However, I did not understand the unique challenges I would face as a woman student with a family. Because of family obligations and the guilt of spending more time on my studies than with my family, education began to slip to the bottom of my priority list. Even though my husband offered to stay with my daughter so I could attend classes, I felt like a failure as a mother every time I left my house. By then, women had come a long way. We had the choice to work in almost every profession, but I was still unable to consider my own desires and aspirations as equal to—or as important as—those of my family. Although I, as a woman, had more choices than ever before, my decisions were still being influenced by society's idea of a woman.

When my daughter started elementary school, my husband and I made the conscious and unanimous decision that I would become a stay-at-home mom, which was not a trendy decision at the time. It was then that I began to experience another kind of gender discrimination, not from men, but from other women. The same educated, enlightened women with whom I had worked began to treat me differently. Introductions included phrases such as *she doesn't work* and *she's just a stay-at-home mom*. Others assumed that because I did not work outside the home, I was somehow less intelligent, less educated, and less motivated than my employed counterparts. This concept was completely at odds with my ideas of feminism. I believed that feminist philosophy was about women having choices and opportunities.

Over the decades, I have seen changes in society's idea of what women should be and changes in my ideas of who I want to be in society. Every day, I strive to encourage my daughter to develop her own view of who she is, without concern for how others may perceive her. She may have inherited all the rights and privileges that many women fought for, but she will also have her own battles to fight. Women have come a long way. We may not be considered by society as "just girls" anymore, but we still have many struggles to fight and win before gender is no longer a barrier.

Storied Institutions: The Complexity of Catholic Women's Colleges

Kelly T. Winters

The richness of the lives of nuns who, throughout two millennia, have been teachers, scholars, artists, mystics, and writers has not been well documented. Some of that mystery about nuns is because these women's lives were subject to strictures imposed by a male church hierarchy. But even more, their story, like the untold stories of women everywhere, was simply not considered to be important.

(Knoerle & Schier, 2002, p. 338)

Those with limited experience with Catholic women's college often ask me what attending and working at such an institution was like, and I am always both amused and mortified by their questions: Did you have to wear a uniform? Were you locked in at night? Were men allowed on campus and in the residence halls? Did nuns and priests teach all the classes? Was everyone there Catholic or planning to become a nun? Was it weird to live, take classes, and work at an environment that was composed mainly of women? Did such an environment prepare you for life in the "real world"? Can you be a feminist at a Catholic women's college?

I have been asked these sorts of questions in settings as varied as casual dinner parties, graduate school classrooms, and job interviews. These stereotyped stories of the cloistered, Catholic "all-girls school" hinge on beliefs that such institutions operate by enforcing rigid, monolithic definitions of "woman" and that contemporary discussions of feminism are all but barred from campus.

I am a graduate of the College of St. Catherine (now St. Catherine University), a Catholic women's college in St. Paul, Minnesota. In addition to attaining my undergraduate degree from St. Catherine's, I also worked there for eight years in roles as varied as adjunct instructor, academic adviser, admission counselor, and writing center coordinator. My identity as a feminist was developed, strengthened, and sometimes challenged throughout my time at St. Catherine's. I valued how the campus' programs, services, and curriculum were women centered and informed by feminist pedagogies and practices. However, there were also times and circumstances in which women-centered and feminist pedagogies and practices were complicated by the institution's Catholic identity. St. Catherine's sought to educate women to lead and influence; yet, the sisters who founded the institution and continued to serve in senior administrative capacities were exempt from holding many leadership positions within the larger Church. It was in this often-contradictory, and sometimes paradoxical, environment that I learned that being a feminist and taking feminist action

required attention to power, contexts, and identities.

As a White, heterosexual woman who was raised Catholic, I am aware of the ways in which my identities constitute a narrative of privilege that continues to shape how I understand my own experiences as both a scholar of and practitioner in the field of higher education. I am, therefore, hesitant to take on a posture of authority when it comes to writing about my experiences at St. Catherine's. Because this sort of institution has been largely ignored by scholars on women's colleges, Catholic institutions, and higher education (Schier and Russett, 2003), the stories and experiences of a wide range of people have yet to be heard. I choose then to situate my experiences within an exploration of a larger institutional context, one that is represented by bits and pieces of a story. Such a presentation requires that the reader take on an active and critical role in composing meaning from the various pieces that constitute a "whole" story (Barone, 2007; Ely, 2007; Lather, 2007; LeCompte, 1993).

It is the first day of The Reflective Woman (TRW) class, and I have asked the students, who are all in their first term at the College of St. Catherine, to come prepared with questions and observations for our discussion of the excerpts from *More Than a Dream: Eighty-Five Years at the College of St. Catherine* (Ryan & Wolkerstorfer, 1992) that have been reprinted in the course's reader. In order to enhance the discussion, I prepared a slide show of archival photographs of the campus and the people who had a hand in building it. The printed and visual documents retell the story of the college's founding in 1905, detailing how a relatively small group of women, the Sisters of St. Joseph of Carondelet, St. Paul Province, worked to establish and build a women's college; the women's college that the early Sisters supported from activities as varied as serving as faculty and administrators to selling books door-to-door now enrolls more than 5,100 students in associate, baccalaureate, and graduate degree programs.

All undergraduate students take TRW during their first term, and the women enrolled in my section of the course have chosen to complete their degree in St. Catherine's Weekend College. I have asked each of the students to create an artistic representation of their lives and sense of self that could be shared with their classmates and have reserved the better part of our time together for storytelling, listening, and reflection on what aspects of our lives brought all of us to be in this shared space.

The stories of the students are powerful. They created poems, drawings, collages, and sculptures that told stories of immigration and citizenship, self-owned businesses that had succeeded and failed, experiences of college throughout their lives, jobs and social situations in which they encountered sexism, racism, and homophobia, social activism, faith and spiritual development, changing careers, moving across the country and around the world, living in transitional housing, learning English, and of their families, friends, children, grandchildren, and partners. Many spoke of their desire to attend a women's college, and of the financial and personal negotiations that they were making to attain a baccalaureate degree.

The image that flashes on the screen is undated, grainy, and fading, a sepia-toned photograph of a nun in full habit, black veil and white wimple framing her face in such a way that her nose, wire-rimmed glasses, and cheeks stand out for their roundness. Sister Antonia McHugh, CSJ (1873–1944), is seated on a plain, wooden chair that had been carried outdoors, placed on a picturesque patch of grass, and turned in such a way so as to appear natural to the landscape. Her left arm is slung casually on one of the rests, body shifted slightly to the right, and gaze directed to the camera. She conveys the intelligence, composure, and confidence of a college president. The image complements one of the passages from the day's assigned reading:

The Sisters had started from scratch in furnishing the new school [the College of St. Catherine], and they sometimes came up short.

According to Sister Bridget [Bonhan]: "We had about ninety boarders, and when their trunks came out with everything, we had sheets enough for about forty-eight or fifty beds . . . Sister Hyacinth [Werden] said, 'I don't know what to do.' 'Well,' I said, 'give us some money, and we'll do the buying.' Sister Edith [Hogan] and I went over to Minneapolis, and you couldn't get sheets ready-made. You had to buy the bolt of unbleached muslin . . . We rented [sewing] machines and Sister Antonia [McHugh] and I sat at those machines from dawn to dark."

(Sister Bridget Bonhan, CSJ, as quoted in Ryan & Wolkerstorfer, 1992, p. 2)

These partial remembrances of Sister Antonia, first president and dean of the College of St. Catherine, complicate some of the popular culture images of Catholic women religious as cloistered contemplatives, silent servants, tragic figures, comedic fools, or singing governesses. She was among the first decade of graduates of the University of Chicago, one of the first women to serve as a college or university president, and is one of the first women religious to have helped found a Catholic women's college (McHugh, 1933; Ryan & Wolkerstorfer, 1992). She also, on at least one documented occasion, stayed up until the wee hours of the morning sewing bed sheets for St. Catherine's students.

It is my hope that the in-class experience of placing personal, lived stories into conversation with the historical documents related to the college's founding will help the students see that women are, and have always been, complex and multifaceted, even if larger institutions and social structures have not recognized it. I see this as part of the continued contribution that women's colleges make to the larger higher education landscape. Many women's colleges have been faced with the challenges of declining enrollments, financial instability, and renewed cultural critiques that question their relevance. As a result, women's college faculty, students, staff, and administrators are marginalized and placed in the footnotes of higher education as though their experiences are quaint, antiquated remnants of a bygone era in which women did not have access to higher education. At present, many scholars, including those represented in this book, have argued that women still continue to face gendered challenges and negotiations in higher education. Recent scholarship has also suggested that the environment at women's colleges warrants further study because of their continued successes in taking women seriously (Kinzie, Thomas, Palmer, Umbach & Kuh, 2007; Wolf-Wendel, 2003). In this respect, Catholic women's colleges are in the complex, and seemingly contradictory, place of being representative of both the historical context of women in higher education, and also a part of the possibility of shifting its dominant paradigms.

REFERENCES

Barone, T. (2007). A return to the gold standard? Questioning the future of narrative construction as educational research. *Qualitative Inquiry, 13*(2), 1–17.

Ely, M. (2007). In-forming re-presentations. In D. Jean Clandinin (Ed.), *Handbook of narrative inquiry* (pp. 567–599). Thousand Oaks, CA: Sage.

Kinzie, J., Thomas, A. D., Palmer, M. M., Umbach, P. D., & Kuh, G. D. (2007). Women students at coeducational and women's colleges: How do their experiences compare? *Journal of College Student Development, 48*(2), 145–165.

Knoerle, J., & Schier, T. (2002). Into the future. In T. Schier & C. Russett (Eds.), *Catholic women's colleges in America* (pp. 325–341). Baltimore, MD: Johns Hopkins University Press.

Lather, P. (2007). *Getting lost: Feminist efforts toward a double(d) science.* Albany, NY: SUNY Press.

LeCompte, M. (1993). A framework for hearing silence: What does telling stories mean when we are supposed to be doing science? In D. McLaughlin & W. G. Tierney (Eds.), *Naming silenced lives* (pp. 9–27). New York: Routledge.

McHugh, A. (December, 1933). What makes Chicago great? *University of Chicago Magazine,* 64–67.

Ryan, R., & Wolkerstorfer, J. C. (1992). *More than a dream: Eighty-five years at the College of St. Catherine.* St. Paul, MN: The College of St. Catherine.

Schier, T. & Russett, C. (2002). *Catholic Women's Colleges in America.* Baltimore, MD: Johns Hopkins University Press.

Wolf-Wendel, L. (2003). Gender and higher education: What should we learn from women's colleges? In B. Ropers-Huilman (Ed.), *Gendered futures in higher education: Critical perspectives for change* (pp. 35–52). Albany, NY: SUNY Press.

Section Two

CONSIDERING EXPERIENCES OF WOMEN THROUGHOUT THE ACADEMY

An Exploration of Undergraduates, Graduate Students, and Administrators

A feminist conceptual model of leadership "rests on the assumption that leadership manifests itself when there is an action to bring about change in an organization, an institution, or the social system—in other words, an action to make a positive difference in people's lives. Leadership, then, is conceived as a creative process that results in change."

Helen Astin and Carol Leland

Astin, H. S., & Leland, C. (1991). *Women of influence, women of vision: A cross-generational study of leaders and social change.* San Francisco: Jossey-Bass (quote from page 116).

5

Female Graduate Students' Work–Life Balance and the Student Affairs Professional

Racheal L. Stimpson and Kimberly L. Filer

Abstract: *This chapter discusses the issue of work–life balance for female graduate students. Understanding how this issue affects female graduate students is necessary in assisting female graduates in degree completion. The authors provide results from a study of over 800 doctoral students at a large research university in regard to satisfaction with work–life balance and confidence in degree completion. Also discussed are the implications of these findings for student affairs professionals and suggestions for practice.*

I take it one day at a time—it's crazy and I've had to learn how to be more flexible when a child is sick or I have a deadline. Definitely my personal/social/fun life has fallen by the wayside. I think I'm happy, but I'm not sure I can even relax anymore; I don't know if I remember how. Am I really happy or just too busy to notice that I'm not?

—Married female graduate student

THE ABOVE QUOTE EMBODIES a married female graduate student's difficulty in balancing her academic workload and personal life responsibilities. Female graduate students earned 59% of all master's degrees and 49% of all doctoral degrees in 2005 (National Center for Education Statistics [NCES], 2007b). With the average age of a doctoral student being 33 years (Syverson, 1996) and the average age (in 2003) for women in the United States to marry being 25 years and for men being 27 years

(Johnson & Dye, 2005), many graduate students come to campus with families in tow. Single graduate students or those married or with a partner may be contemplating a change in status or an addition to their family. As a result, balancing work and life is an issue many graduate students encounter (Brus, 2006). Balancing work and life is a particularly difficult issue for female graduate students as they face more difficulty balancing family commitments, academics, work, and personal lives as well as have less satisfaction in their ability to balance work and life (Brus, 2006). The inability to balance work and life successfully for female graduate students may be a result of the lack of support they receive institutionally whether from their academic department or from other institutional offices. Specifically, female graduate students receive little to no attention from student affairs professionals across the nation (Bair, Haworth, & Sandfort, 2004; Gansemer-Topf, Ross, & Johnson, 2006).

Work–life balance is a topic discussed more frequently in the literature concerning faculty than graduate students in higher education. In fact, the literature addressing graduate students, and particularly female graduate students' work–life balance, is sparse. Full-time employment and commitments to family and home are the traditional definitions of work–life balance. However, when we discuss graduate students, the definition is slightly altered. Because of the nature of their employment and academic work, the work–life aspect for graduate students is unique. The work aspect for graduate students may include an assistantship, academic workload, research, internships, and/or part-time employment. Because the graduate student populace is composed of full- and part-time students, work may also be defined as a full-time job, academic work, and research. Life outside of work for graduate students may include friends, families, organizations, religion, or hobbies. Ultimately then, when discussing graduate students, work–life balance includes academics, assistantships, and personal life commitments such as significant others, parents, and children.

At first glance, the work–life issues for graduate students may seem identical to those of faculty. However, there are differences. Graduate students often lack the policy protection or opportunity that faculty have found in recent years, such as stop-the-clock policies and policies that allow tenure-track faculty to take time away from their research for childbearing and child rearing without affecting the timeline for achieving tenure. Other differences include financial stability, as graduate students often work several jobs, seek student loans or other financial assistance, as well as seek out their own professional identity. Most faculty members have established their professional identity and seek to expand on it while graduate students are just starting to clarify and build their professional identity.

The current study of over 800 female graduate students' satisfaction with balancing work and life and their confidence in completing their degrees is valuable in understanding their specific needs and stress, and ultimately aiding them in their degree completion. Although student affairs professionals predominately interact with undergraduate students and have "traditionally ignored the graduate student population" (Globetti, 1991, p. 42), student affairs professionals should be concerned with graduate students' needs and retention, as the field of student affairs is committed to "educating the whole student and integrating student life and learning" (NASPA online, ¶ 3). This chapter discusses the topic of work–life balance for female graduate students and describes the specific methods for this study, the findings, and the implications for student affairs professionals and higher education in general.

THE IMPORTANCE OF WORK–LIFE BALANCE FOR WOMEN GRADUATE STUDENTS

The most important reason to foster positive work–life balancing skills for women graduate students is to increase their likelihood of completing a graduate degree. With graduate student retention rates ranging from 40% to 60%, depending on the institution and department or program, there is room for improvement (Bair & Haworth, 1999). Many see attrition at the doctoral level as inevitable, where only the most dedicated, brightest, and hardest working will remain. For example, one study of graduate students found that "Students leave less because of what they bring with them to the university than because of what happens to them after they arrive" (Lovitts & Nelson, 2000, p. 50). The conclusion of Lovitts and Nelson's study begins to dispel the thought that students leave without finishing only because of their inability or lack of intellect. Lovitts and Nelson further suggest that graduate students, particularly women and minority students, leave because they are not welcomed, assisted, or socialized into the culture of the program, graduate school, or institution—in essence, a lack of support. This support is relevant and necessary to the successful navigation of balancing work and life (Nesheim, Guentzel, Gansemer-Topf, Ross, & Turrentine, 2006).

Lack of support as it relates to balancing work and life is detrimental to the overall effort to further increase the number of women receiving degrees. When women and minorities leave graduate programs, the result is fewer women and minorities earning terminal degrees and entering the workforce with the credentials to earn more money and attain higher positions. The lack of women entering and graduating from graduate programs is at odds with enrollment and graduation trends witnessed at the undergraduate level. Women are earning baccalaureate degrees in record numbers; yet, fewer women make a successful transition to graduate programs. Some estimates of enrollment in Doctor of Philosophy (PhD) programs place the male enrollment rates at twice those of women (Mullen, Goyette, & Soares, 2003), and we hypothesize that this is in direct relation to the challenges in work–life balance that we will be addressing in this chapter. Men still outnumber women in terms of numbers receiving doctorates; however, the number of women has risen in the past several years. In 2005, 49% of doctoral students receiving degrees were women (NCES, 2007b).

Science research is usually conducted in a structured laboratory-based setting, typically with more than one individual, whereas arts and humanities research is often conducted with fewer resources and often by one individual. These structural differences between disciplines are related to graduate student outcomes including time to degree, completion rates, and career aspirations (Bowen & Rudenstine, 1992); however, these structural differences may not be the only cause of the variation in male and female experiences in the science fields. The tradi-tional male culture, which prides itself on competition and "weeding out" students, is experienced as impersonal and hostile by female students (Rayman & Brett, 1993; Tobias, 1990). These are but a few ways women experience their minority status in a masculine arena; therefore, the issue of academic discipline further complicates male and female experiences and attrition rates. This relates to Jennifer Sader's (chapter 8) study of women doctoral students in computer science.

Women enter doctoral programs in equal numbers as men but take longer to complete their degrees and are more likely to leave their program altogether (particularly in the sciences). Because women have higher grade point averages, score higher on the verbal section of the Graduate Record Examination (GRE), and score comparable to men in other measurements, it is cause for alarm that their attrition rate is higher (Smith, 1995).

One possible reason for women having higher attrition rates may be the issue of children. While children are not the sole responsibility of women, women are still seen as the primary caregivers, which complicates their professional life (Coltrane, 2000). Because of the expectation to care for family and pursue work, women tend to face a conflict in their roles and priorities (Kurtz-Costes, Helmke, & Ülkü-Steiner, 2006). Thus, women are pulled in two directions simultaneously and have to choose one over the other: work or life.

The issue of balancing work and life is not new to academe, but it has not been discussed as extensively concerning graduate students as it has been with faculty. Similar to faculty, balancing work and life is an issue for many female graduate students within the sciences (Smith, 1995). The largest graduate student enrollment differences between the genders lies in the larger number of male graduate students in the physical sciences, engineering, and business and the larger number of female graduate students in the arts and humanities (Redd, 2006). Female graduate students' unique graduate experience (whether married, single, with or without children) and struggle with work–life balance affect attrition rates.

One cause of attrition for women in the science, technology, engineering, and mathematics (STEM) fields is the high demands of their field and their attempt to balance family life with work (Smith, 1995). Women are leaving the sciences before achieving their degrees, causing what many refer to as the "leaking pipeline" in the sciences (Smith, 1995, p. 12). The issue of work–life balance for female graduate students is not being addressed by the disciplines and has an impact on the retention of female graduate students. Jennifer Lee Hoffman's chapter (chapter 3) discusses women being pushed out of the science fields in the 1920s for various reasons, and these continue to plague female graduate students in those fields today.

With fewer women than men in many departments, previous research suggests conditions are not as conducive to the success of female students in fields with predominately male faculty and students (Konrad & Pfeffer, 1991). Female students have fewer mentors to model the role of a successful researcher balancing personal and professional life, with the natural sciences lacking more female role models than other fields of study (Raddon, 2002). Kurtz-Costes et al. (2006) found differences in male and female students' descriptions of an ideal mentor. Women appreciated a female mentor who modeled a balanced lifestyle, whereas men defined an ideal mentor as one with power who could "open doors" with his or her reputation.

The issue of mentors and their relationships with students is an issue impacting graduate student attrition (Workman & Bodner, 1996). Mentors are shown to predict career commitment for students and affect student attrition (Ülkü-Steiner, Kurtz-Costes, & Kinlaw, 2000). This career commitment can be affected positively or negatively by faculty relationships and mentors. Some students are pressured to with-

draw from classes or school by their mentors (Workman & Bodner, 1996). Although faculty members may be the obvious choice as a mentor for graduate students, other individuals on campus can play a positive role. Student affairs professionals may fill the void for female graduate students who are uncomfortable discussing personal responsibilities with their faculty mentor (Gansemer-Topf et al., 2006).

Monica Marcelis Fochtman's chapter (chapter 6) in this book highlights the importance of mentors for women even beyond graduate school. She also discusses how academe favors male tendencies and time lines, which reflect the organizational culture. Many of the issues previously discussed are part of the existing academic culture. Higher education's preference for all things masculine plays a role for female graduate students and their experiences and should not be overlooked when discussing graduate education; solutions for organizational culture change are needed.

STUDENT AFFAIRS AND GRADUATE STUDENTS

Historically, graduate students are not a population of focus for student affairs professionals (Bair et al., 2004). Student affairs professionals encourage and initiate development of the student through various services and programs but have traditionally concentrated these efforts on the undergraduate student (Gansemer-Topf et al., 2006). However, just as with undergraduates, graduate students benefit from cocurricular involvement and experiences such as leadership, athletics, programs, and services (Pontius & Harper, 2006). Why then are student affairs professionals meeting the needs of only undergraduate students?

Several reasons may contribute to student affairs professionals spending the majority of their time with undergraduates and less time with graduate students, including the smaller size of the graduate student population, graduate students requiring fewer resources because of their needs, the belief that graduate students are experienced students who need no assistance, and graduate faculty meeting the needs of graduate students (Pontius & Harper, 2006). This rationale aids in perpetuating student affairs professionals' focus on undergraduate students with the needs of all graduate students, specifically female graduate students, often overlooked.

Graduate Population Size

It is estimated that in the 2007–2008 academic year earned graduate degrees will comprise approximately 25% of the total college degrees conferred for that year (NCES, 2007a), making graduate students a significant population warranting student affairs professionals' time and expertise. However, between campuses, the number of graduate students varies. Despite the number of graduate students, even if they represent a vast majority of the campus population, graduate students' needs and services are often ignored to serve the undergraduate population (Pontius & Harper, 2006).

In recent years, there has been an outcry to meet the needs of older student populations, including graduate students (Bair et al., 2004), but the demand to meet nontraditional populations' needs has caught on only marginally. According to the NCES (2007a), the number of students ages 25 years and older has risen steadily since 1990 but not as much as traditional-aged students. This projection is about to change, as NCES projects the number of nontraditional-aged students to grow faster between 2005 and 2016 than the number of traditional-aged students (2007a). Although not all nontraditional-aged students are graduate students, they may experience some of the same issues, including work–life balance. By having student affairs professionals addressing the needs of female graduate students, they may also be able to serve a different undergrad-

uate population, namely, nontraditional-aged students.

The number of females in higher education is steadily rising, with 57% of undergraduate degrees earned by women in 2005. Women have slowly become the majority of undergraduates and have slowly risen in numbers in graduate school as well. As stated in the Introduction, female graduate students earned 59% of all master's degrees and 49% of all doctoral degrees in 2005 (NCES, 2007b). Although the number of graduate students, and therefore the number of female graduate students, may be numerically low in comparison with the number of undergraduates, they are still a significant population. Even if undergraduate students comprise the majority of the campus population, student affairs should be attending to the needs of graduate students.

Graduate Students' Needs and Experience

Many higher education professionals assume that undergraduate students need more assistance in their growth, development, and cocurricular experience than graduate students. However, this is not the case. Graduate students possess similar needs to those of undergraduate students in areas such as career and professional development (McCaffrey, Miller, & Winston, 1984); however, graduate and undergraduate students differ in their needs in a variety of ways with the largest differences occurring within the subpopulations, such as gender, race, and nationality.

Similar to undergraduates, graduate students need assistance in career planning, job placement, resume writing, and financial resources (Globetti, 1991; Rimmer, Lammert, & McClain, 1982). In a study of 24 graduate students, several stressors were identified, including risks to their health, risks to financial security, risks to personal relationships, and pressure to put their academic life above all else (Wolniewicz, 1996). In general, graduate students need assistance with health habits, balancing personal lives, academics, social activities, meeting deadlines, and making future professional decisions (Caple, 1995). Some research also reports common stressors experienced by doctoral students, including finances, time constraints, family relationships, expectations, evaluation, and amount of work (Kurtz-Costes et al., 2006; Williams, Gallas, & Quiriconi, 1984). However, male and female graduate students have differing experiences, even if attending the same institution or program (Hite, 1985). Areas where male and female graduate students differ are conflict in personal and professional roles, support from faculty, lack of mentors and/or support groups (Hite, 1985), and effects of marriage (McLaughlin, 1985).

The effects of marriage on degree completion and the graduate student experience seem to favor men. Marriage has a negative impact on women's graduate work but not on men's (McLaughlin, 1985). The negative impact of marriage on women's graduate work may coincide with their struggle to balance their work and home lives. Although balance was an issue reported by all graduate students (Caple, 1995), it is overwhelmingly reported by women as a primary concern. "The multiple role demands of employment, academics, and family may result in increased stress for a female graduate student, particularly when coupled with expectations that she fulfill all these roles perfectly" (p. 44). The issue of navigating multiple roles is not new for women working outside the home, but this topic is just beginning to be discussed for graduate women. Because women are still the primary caregivers, whatever other responsibilities they take on, whether it is work or graduate school (or both), they are "more likely than men to face the demands of their competing roles simultaneously" (Dublon, 1983, p. 22). The topic of female graduate students struggling with various life roles is repeated in the few studies conducted on the topic (Dublon, 1983; Hite, 1985; McCaffrey et al., 1984; Sharf & Bishop, 1995); yet, little has been done to aid these women in the pursuit of their degrees and in coping with the balancing of their personal and work lives.

As indicated, the fact that graduate students have previously navigated the higher education system successfully does not mean that they will not need assistance as they pursue their graduate degrees. Graduate students are often left to their own devices on college campuses regardless of the fact that graduate students possess specific needs to enable them to persist (Caple, 1995; Rimmer et al., 1982). With these unique needs, graduate students, specifically female graduate students, are a population that student affairs professionals should and can assist (Rimmer et al., 1982).

Support From Graduate Faculty

In graduate education, the responsibility of retention and degree completion of students often belongs to faculty. Each faculty member is responsible for his or her advisees or students within the department (Weidman, Twale, & Stein, 2001). In a recent study, Bair et al. (2004) found that faculty, administrators, and students perceive the faculty role to include four parts: research and scholarly work, advising and/or mentoring, admission and retention, and maintaining the culture of the program. It is apparent that the faculty role extends beyond the classroom; however, faculty members are not typically trained in issues of student development, programs, or services. Faculty members also tend to be isolated from the services offered on campuses.

Student affairs professionals are trained in student development theory and other areas in higher education, specifically the cocurricular (Evans, Forney, Guido, Renn, & Patton, 2009). With student affairs professionals' knowledge base and expertise in student development, working in collaboration with graduate faculty may aid graduate students beyond the support they receive from their departmental faculty. Professionals in the field of student affairs are poised to aid graduate students in their degree completion because of their knowledge of student development, programming, services, and the cocurricular, thus assisting in improving graduate student persistence. At the undergraduate level, there are institutional-level programs and services to assist multiple undergraduate student populations. Student affairs should be willing and able to offer such services and programs to graduate students, particularly female graduate students. Part of the benefit of the programs and services student affairs professionals offer is the increased student engagement, learning, development, and retention (Pascarella & Terenzini, 2005). Although the effects of student affairs work have not been measured for graduate students, it is possible that student affairs professionals could have the same effect, thus increasing graduate student retention. The issue of retention and work–life balance for female graduate students is closely connected and of concern for student affairs professionals.

THE STUDY

On the basis of the literature, we wanted to examine the satisfaction of male and female graduate students in balancing their work and life. In addition, we wanted to investigate their level of confidence in completing the degrees they were pursuing. We feel this study is pertinent to the field of higher education and student affairs in several ways. First, we believe that understanding the issues graduate students face can aid in meeting graduate students' needs and increasing their retention and graduation rates. Understanding the specific needs of subpopulations within the graduate student population will aid in increasing diversity and graduation rates for those diverse populations. Second, many of the other studies that examined similar issues are either dated or did not investigate this topic through quantitative measures. By surveying a large sample size of students in various doctoral degree programs, we are viewing this issue through a different lens. Lastly, there have been several calls to student affairs professionals to work with graduate stu-

dent populations. By offering current data on the needs of graduate students, specifically female graduate students, we are enabling student affairs professionals to pinpoint areas in which they may be of assistance.

The questions for this study focused only on the satisfaction of graduate students, both men and women, in balancing work and life and their confidence in completing their degrees.

The research questions examined were the following:

♦ Do satisfaction levels with balancing personal and professional lives vary for men and women?
♦ What are the effects of being married, living with a significant other, and/or having children on satisfaction for men and women?
♦ Does confidence in earning a PhD vary for men and women?
♦ Does confidence in earning a PhD vary by satisfaction in balancing personal and professional lives for men and women?

We believe that these findings, in addition to the current literature, paint a picture of the academic work–life issues that female graduate students encounter today and will enable student affairs professionals to better assist these students in their goal of degree completion and successful work–life balance.

METHODS

We surveyed full-time doctoral students at a research university in the southeast. A total of 1,780 surveys were sent out via a graduate school listserv to those individuals not having a privacy restriction. The survey was sent out a total of three times, and 806 usable surveys were obtained for a response rate of 45%. The demographics of the sample (see Table 5.1) were representative of the population of doctoral students at the university.

Table 5.1 Population and Sample Demographics

Group	Population (%)	Sample (%)
Males	62.0	56.3
Females	38.0	43.7
International	—	39.0
Domestic	—	61.0
Caucasian	88.0	59.2
African American	5.5	7.4
Asian	3.8	26.4
Hispanic	1.7	4.3
Native American	0.2	0.8
Multiracial	—	2.0

The questionnaire included a variety of questions investigating graduate students' balance, satisfaction, stress, home responsibilities, school responsibilities, and confidence in degree completion. Items were based on the existing literature in the field and then sampled on a few test participants. Based on the test participants' experience and feedback, the survey questions were reviewed and modified as needed. The topics of home responsibilities, school responsibilities, balancing, emotions and support, and goals were explored in this questionnaire. The test blueprint specifying the subgroups and the items in each subgroup is displayed in Table 5.2.

Measures combined a Likert five-point scale, multiple choice, and open-ended questions. This study offers a mixed-method approach in order to understand the problem of balancing work and life for graduate students, specifically, female graduate students. Mixed-methods research allows researchers to use both qualitative and quantitative methods, in this case simultaneously, to understand a research problem further (Creswell, 2003).

This study used questions asking students to rate their satisfaction with balancing their personal and professional lives and their confidence in degree completion as outcome measures. Quantitatively, a factorial analysis of variance (two-way ANOVA) was conducted to include all combinations of gender and marital status, as well as gender and children in the home, to explain differences in mean scores on the measures of satisfaction with work–life balance and confidence in degree completion. Qualitatively, open-ended responses to satisfaction and

Table 5.2 Questionnaire Blueprint for Measuring the Balance of Work and Life

Subgroup	Question Category	Questions	Question Type
Home Responsibilities	Task responsibilities	8	Five-point scale
	Child-care type	1	Multiple choices
	Child-care satisfaction	1	Five-point scale
	Childcare–financial stress	1	Five-point scale
	Overall satisfaction	1	Five-point scale
School Responsibilities	Workload	5	Open-ended/five-point scale
	Expectations	1	Five-point scale
	Overall satisfaction	1	Five-point scale
Balancing	Frequency of balancing issues	4	Five-point scale
	Strategies	2	Multiple choice/open-ended
	Overall satisfaction	1	Five-point scale
Emotions and Support	Stress frequency	2	Five-point scale
	Coping strategies	1	Multiple choice
	Support received	8	Five-point scale
Goals	Completion confidence	2	Multiple choice/five-point scale
	Career path	5	Multiple choice/five-point scale

confidence questions were examined for trends between and among male and female students, married/living with a partner and single students, as well as students with and without children.

Limitations

Prior to reporting our results, it is important to note several limitations of this study. For this study, participants were asked to respond to a questionnaire consisting of 41 items. These items were designed to measure various aspects of the graduate experience, specifically focusing on experiences related to balancing work and life responsibilities. However, there are limitations of self-reported instruments, including question wording affecting participant answer, participant recall, and potentially objectionable questions to some participants (Dillman, 2007).

With our instrument, students' reports of work and life are contextual and subjective, affecting the response consistency. Although there are limitations of a self-report questionnaire, the questionnaire can be completed in less than 10 minutes at a convenient time for participants chosen at their discretion. In addition, self-report instruments allow participants to share their thoughts and experiences in order to understand better an issue or problem.

Another limitation of this study is that it was conducted at one institution. It is possible that the results reflect the thoughts and opinions of doctoral students situated at this institution based on institutional culture, programs, and services. Although survey respondents reflected multiple programs and departments, the results may be different if this survey were conducted across multiple disciplines in multiple institutions.

A third limitation of the study is that survey participants were all at different phases of doctoral study. Thus, someone in the first year is not differentiated from someone about to have the degree conferred. This is important to note as the satisfaction with balance as well as confidence in degree completion may vary on the basis of how far in the program a student has reached.

A fourth limitation of this study is that we did not examine the work–life issues of graduate students caring for other relatives, such as parents. Expanding the research questions to include this group of graduate students could alter the issues of work–life balance for graduate students.

RESULTS

The results of this study are described in the following sections that address balancing work and life and confidence in ability to complete the degree. We then discuss the implications of these results for student affairs professionals.

Balancing Work and Life

The overall trends in students' ratings of their satisfaction with balancing their personal and professional lives are displayed in Figures 5.1 and 5.2. Overall, the findings reveal that men feel significantly more satisfied than women ($F = 7.863$, $df = 1$, $p < .01$) in their ability to balance work and life. There was no significant interaction between satisfaction ratings and marital status. However, there was a significant interaction effect ($F = 4.746$, $df = 1$, $p < .05$) between being male or female and having a child on satisfaction with balancing personal and professional life.

A single female commented:

> My workload is too much. As a single graduate student, I find myself isolated, consumed with work, taken advantage of (married students or those with families get slack in my department, while the single students are expected to pick up that slack) and unsatisfied personally.

Her comment broaches a subject not discussed in the literature—single graduate students compensating for the workload of their married peers. This was not a theme presented in the open-ended questions of our survey, but we feel it may warrant further attention.

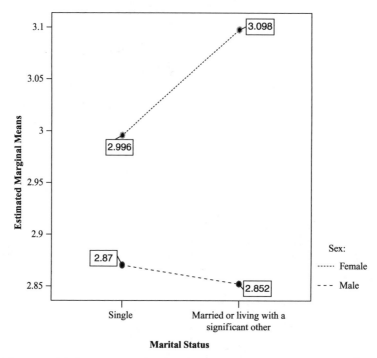

Figure 5.1 Satisfaction with balancing personal and professional life as a function of marital status.

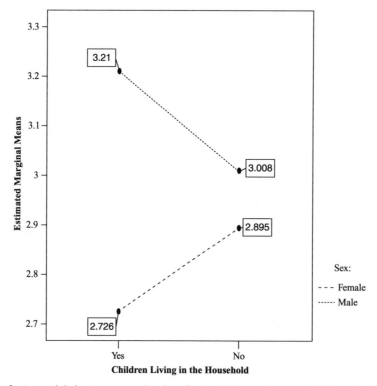

Figure 5.2 Satisfaction with balancing personal and professional life as a function of children in the household.

Another single female stated, "As a PhD student I am extremely busy and barely have time to breathe. Free moments involve trying to visit family and friends. I don't have a balance and I continually try to work on that." This female clearly understands that she does not have a balance and her comments contrast greatly to this statement from a single male graduate student: "I try to give my full attention while I am at work. I try to avoid too much work over the weekends unless there is an upcoming deadline." These two individuals' statements represent the themes we found present in the open-ended data, which also correspond with the quantitative analysis. The male seems more satisfied with his balance while the female does not. This is further exemplified for married females by the following statement:

> I try to set aside time each day for some of everything—personal, full-time job, and my dissertation. On the weekends, Sundays after church are for the dissertation. Saturdays are for errands, cleaning the house, etc. There just isn't time for hobbies, leisure, etc. right now.

This female student finds no time for anything other than work and therefore is not satisfied with her work–life balance as there is none.

These quotes illustrate the point that women do not feel as satisfied with their ability to balance work and life. We next examined the issue of satisfaction with balancing work and life and the interaction effect for male and female graduate students with children versus those without. Again, men were more likely to feel satisfied than women in their ability to balance work and life. In addition, men with children felt more satisfied than anyone else whereas women with children felt the least satisfied in comparison to the other groups.

A married male student with a child commented: "My wife and I schedule school time and family time every week and try very hard to stick to it. It alleviates a lot of stress when you have the week all planned out." Meanwhile, a married female student with a child stated in regard to how she balances work and life that "I don't. It is a mess. I am a new mother and I'm having major difficulties balancing all the demands on my time. I'm going nuts." The first observation one can make about these statements is the issue of time and scheduling. Demands on time are consistent with the juggling of multiple roles and may explain the difference in dealing with balancing work and life between men and women. There were many comments from participants in our study referencing the lack of time or the demands placed on them.

Female graduate students, particularly those married and with children, face large demands on their time and numerous responsibilities. This study confirms that female doctoral students feel less satisfied than males in their ability to balance their academic/work and family life obligations.

Confidence in Ability to Complete Degree

Confidence in completing a degree may certainly affect the retention and attrition rates of graduate students. We asked doctoral students how confident they were in completing their degrees. There was no significant interaction effect between the two variables. And, unlike the satisfaction question, male students were not significantly more confident in earning their PhDs than female students. However, being married/living with a significant other was significant ($F = 11.270$, $df = 1$, $p < .01$), with students who were married or living with a significant other reporting more confidence in earning their PhDs than single students.

Similar to the satisfaction findings, men with children and men without children had higher confidence in degree completion than women with and without children ($F = 3.830$, $df = 1$, $p = .051$). However, there was no significant interaction between the variables in confidence in earning a PhD, and students with children do not show significantly different confidence levels than those without children.

Confidence in degree completion can give us some insight into how certain graduate students are in their ability to complete their degrees. It was not asked in this questionnaire as to why the graduate students felt the confidence level they indicated. To further understand this problem, we investigated our last research question: Does confidence in earning a PhD vary by satisfaction in balancing personal and professional lives for men and women? The results to this question were yes, confidence in earning a PhD varied by level of satisfaction in balancing work and life for women ($F = 21.27$, $df = 1$, $p < .01$) and men ($F = 35.30$, $df = 1$, $p < .01$). On the basis of our findings, men appear more satisfied with their ability to balance work and life. And, as illustrated in women's lack of satisfaction with work–life balance, it stands to reason that women's difficulty in balancing their personal and professional lives may prove detrimental to their degree completion.

IMPLICATIONS FOR STUDENT AFFAIRS PROFESSIONALS

As university administrators hope to retain students until degree completion, it is important to gain a deeper understanding of the lives of female doctoral students and their feelings of stress and satisfaction. The results of this study are relevant to student affairs professionals in a number of ways. First, it is important for student affairs professionals to recognize that graduate students are too often being overlooked. Student affairs professionals strive to meet the needs of all students, but for so long student affairs professionals have concentrated solely on undergraduate students (Bair et al., 2004; Gansemer-Topf et al., 2006), with some exceptions including ACPA's Commission for Commuter Students and Adult Learners and ACPA's Commission for Professional Preparation. Student affairs professionals

should reexamine the scope of their programs and services to ensure they are meeting the needs of both undergraduate and graduate students.

Second, the results of this study concur with previous research on the issue of work and life balance. The results of this study support the notion that female graduate students struggle with balancing work and life more than men. This study also found that exhibiting less confidence in degree completion is not always correlated with student satisfaction with work–life balance. Our findings show that a graduate student more satisfied with work–life balance will be more confident in the ability to complete the degree. If female graduate students are lagging behind in both of these areas, then perhaps assisting them in increasing their work–life balance satisfaction will also increase their confidence in degree completion.

There are a number of ways in which student affairs professionals can assist female graduate students in their balance of work and life and thus in improving their rate of degree completion. These methods include collaborating with faculty and graduate school administrators, assessment, and student development.

Collaborations With Faculty and Graduate School Administrators

By working with faculty and graduate school administrators, the retention and student experience can be enhanced for female graduate students. As described previously in our study, female graduate students are not satisfied with their balance of work and life.

As discussed, graduate students' needs are often considered issues for the faculty within their department (Weidman, Twale, & Stein, 2001). However, there are many roles student affairs professionals can and should play (Gansemer-Topf et al., 2006; Pontius & Harper, 2006). Working together with academic affairs, student affairs administrators can provide expertise on developmental theories that pertain to graduate students (Gansemer-Topf et al., 2006). Student affairs professionals can also offer other campus services, which they currently administer to undergraduates, to aid graduate students in their degree completion. Student affairs professionals have already laid the groundwork for these programs and services and now need to extend these opportunities for growth and development to graduate students.

Student affairs professionals can work with faculty and graduate school administrators in offering programs such as disability services, orientation, childcare, networking opportunities, and career development opportunities and workshops to female graduate students (Polson, 2003). Graduate orientations are useful to all graduate students but can go beyond the basic academic year and assistantship information and can incorporate community information, child-care options, and support services. Because these services are currently being offered, there should not be a strain on finances or personnel.

Some institutions may have childcare on campus that is available to graduate students. These services, as well as other child-care opportunities in the area, should be advertised to all graduate students. It is important that male and female graduate students are aware of their child-care options and that these options are affordable. Some institutions may offer free childcare during special programs and, again, this service needs to be advertised adequately to graduate students. Student affairs professionals and faculty can work together to let graduate students know that there are options in terms of childcare and services as well as assist in obtaining childcare and potential funding.

Finally, career development and professional assistance would be particularly helpful to female graduate students. Aiding female graduates with guidance and mentors in their respective fields may allow them to prepare fully for the demands of their field. In addition, finding mentors in their field who successfully negotiate work and life roles would be beneficial, as is pointed out in Lee Hawthorne Calizo's (chapter 18) findings. This is not always covered in student affairs, but perhaps there is room for collaboration between academic and student affairs with this venture.

As discussed earlier, men and women view networking and mentors very differently. In order to better assist female graduates, creating a formal opportunity to network and/or be matched with mentors may aid them in their professional endeavors as well as in learning effective strategies for balancing work and life. In addition, as it pertains to graduate students in student affairs, it must be considered that this is a field in which women outnumber men in graduate preparation programs and eventually the professional field (Jones & Komives, 2001), however, not in the top positions (see the Preface of this volume for more statistics). These numbers provide an opportunity for female student affairs personnel to serve as role models and mentors for female graduate students. In addition to student affairs professionals, mentors should come from all aspects of higher education. Unfortunately, as Jennifer Lee Hoffman (chapter 3) discusses in her chapter of this book, the integration of men's and women's educational purposes caused a shift in the organizational system, thereby allowing for fewer women in leadership positions. There has been a feminization of student affairs, thus more women available to act as mentors, but this is not the case for other departments and units within higher education.

Assessment

Assessing the needs and satisfaction of female graduate students is the first step in creating programs and services to meet their needs (Bair et al., 2004; Nesheim et al., 2006; Pontius & Harper, 2006). The study we conducted revealed that graduate women are not satisfied with their work and life. Furthermore, this study concluded that married women and women with children were less satisfied than single or married men. The survey given to these doctoral students examined various facets of their lives in order to determine their needs better.

Studies such as this one are needed in order to determine the areas in which graduate students need assistance; however, the assessment can be conducted in a variety of ways, including focus groups, surveys, and interviews. Student affairs professionals cannot offer the proper programs, service, or assistance to female graduate students, or collaborate effectively, without first understanding the population with which they are working (Bair et al., 2004).

In addition, assessing graduate students' learning and development may aid students as well as faculty and administrators in understanding graduate students better. Research shows that undergraduates see gains in areas such as moral and ethical development, psychosocial development, and persistence (Pontius & Harper, 2006). Assessment will allow student affairs professionals to document whether previously established services and programs have similar effects on graduate students.

Student Development

Student development is a realm that student affairs professionals are very familiar with and they should be the experts on their respective campus (Bair et al., 2004). Student affairs professionals are trained to interact, assess, and handle student development issues ranging from identity conflict to moral development. As such, student affairs professionals are once again uniquely situated to offer expertise and guidance to graduate students. As discussed earlier, graduate students and undergraduate students struggle with many similar issues, including identity development, career and professional development, and financial concerns (McCaffrey et al., 1984; Rimmer et al., 1982). Understanding the various developmental theories aids student affairs professionals in working with graduate students and comprehending their problems and concerns. This level

of expertise, in terms of student development theory, also aids student affairs professionals in gauging the individual needs of the student. Cognitive, epistemological, and transition theories can all be applied to graduate students in one form or another. Certainly, these theories can provide insight and understanding into the role conflict and struggles female graduate students experience in the drive to achieve work–life balance. Understanding these issues allows student affairs professionals a glimpse into the world of graduate students' lives and may help in creating solutions to graduate students' issues and needs.

One area of student development theory that student affairs professionals may turn to for more guidance in working with graduate students is adult development and/or development through the life span. Traditionally, student affairs preparation programs focus on student development theory focusing on the traditional 18–22-year-old population. Expanding the theories used would be extremely beneficial to student affairs professionals understanding and dealing with graduate students.

Because student affairs professionals should be the experts in student development at their institution, it is important that they collaborate with other constituencies to educate and inform about the student development process. This means that student affairs professionals need to be current and informed about these theories in order to maintain professionalism and exhibit expertise in this area.

CONCLUSION

Balancing work and life is not an easy task for anyone, especially women. Female graduate students are no exception and, according to our findings, female graduate students are less satisfied with their ability to balance work and life. Student affairs professionals possess the skills and ability to work with faculty and graduate schools in aiding female graduate students to successfully navigate the work–life conflict and achieve degree completion.

Our findings as well as previous research informs us that female graduate students need more support in order to successfully navigate balancing work and life and to complete their degrees. Increasing female graduate retention rates will not only benefit women but also benefit institutions and the workplace. As we see the number of women in higher education continually rise, it remains important that we understand their issues and seek to aid them wherever possible.

REFERENCES

Bair, C. R., & Haworth, J. G. (1999, November). *Doctoral student attrition and persistence: A meta-synthesis of research.* Paper presented at the annual meeting of the Association for the Study of Higher Education, San Antonio, TX.

Bair, C. R., Haworth, J. G., & Sandfort, M. (2004). Doctoral student learning and development: A shared responsibility. *NASPA Journal, 41*(3), 709–727.

Bowen, W. G., & Rudenstine, N. L. (1992). *In pursuit of the Ph.D.* Princeton, NJ: Princeton University Press.

Brus, C. P. (2006). Seeking balance in graduate school: A realistic expectation or a dangerous dilemma? In M. J. Guentzel & B. E. Nesheim (Eds.), *Supporting graduate and professional students: The role of student affairs* (pp. 31–45). *New directions for student services: Vol. 115.* San Francisco, CA: Jossey-Bass.

Caple, R. B. (1995). Counseling graduate students. In A. S. Pruitt-Logan & P. D. Isaac (Eds.), *Student services for the changing graduate student population* (pp. 43–50). *New directions for student services: Vol. 72.* San Francisco, CA: Jossey-Bass.

Coltrane, S. (2000). Research on household labor: Modeling and measuring the social embeddedness of routine family work. *Journal of Marriage and Family, 62*(4), 1208–1233.

Creswell, J. W. (2003). *Research design: Qualitative, quantitative, and mixed methods approaches* (2nd ed.). Thousand Oaks, CA: Sage.

Dillman, D. A. (2007). *Mail and Internet surveys: The tailored design method* (2nd ed.). Hoboken, NJ: John Wiley & Sons, Inc.

Dublon, F. J. (1983). Women doctoral student in higher education administration: Life-style aspirations and multiple role commitments. *Journal of NAWDAC, 47*(1), 20–25.

Evans, N. J., Forney, D. S., Guido, F. M., Renn, K. A., & Patton, L. (2009). *Student development in college: Theory, research, and practice* (2nd ed.). San Francisco, CA: Jossey-Bass.

Gansemer-Topf, A. M., Ross, L. E., & Johnson, R. M. (2006). Graduate and professional student development and student affairs. In M. J. Guentzel & B. E. Nesheim (Eds.), *Supporting graduate and professional students: The role of student affairs* (pp. 19–30). *New directions for student services: Vol. 115.* San Francisco, CA: Jossey-Bass.

Globetti, E. (1991). An assessment of goals and needs of graduate students—Some implications for student affairs and higher education. *College Student Affairs Journal, 10*(3), 41–53.

Hite, L. M. (1985). Female doctoral students: Their perceptions and concerns. *Journal of College Student Personnel, 26*(1), 18–22.

Johnson, T., & Dye, J. (2005). *Indicators of marriage and fertility in the United States from the American community survey: 2000 to 2003 (U.S. Bureau of the Census Population Division).* Retrieved July 7, 2008, from http://www.census.gov/population/www/socdemo/fertility/mar-fert-slides.html

Jones, S. R., & Komives, S. R. (2001). Contemporary issues of women as senior student affairs officers. In J. Niddifer & C. Bashaw (Eds.), *Women administrators in higher education: Historical and contemporary perspectives.* Albany, NY: SUNY Press.

Konrad, A. M., & Pfeffer, J. (1991). Understanding the hiring of women and minorities in educational institutions. *Sociology of Education, 64,* 141–157.

Kurtz-Costes, B., Helmke, L. A., & Ülkü-Steiner, B. (2006). Gender and doctoral studies: The perceptions of Ph.D. students in an American university. *Gender and Education, 18*(2), 137–155.

Lovitts, B. E., & Nelson, C. (2000). The hidden crisis in graduate education: Attrition from Ph.D. programs. *Academe, 86*(6), 44–50.

McCaffrey, S. S., Miller, T. K., & Winston, R. B. (1984). Comparison of career maturity among graduate students and undergraduates. *Journal of College Student Personnel, 25*(2), 127–132.

McLaughlin, M. C. (1985). Graduate school and families: Issues for academic departments and university mental health professionals. *Journal of College Student Personnel, 26*(6), 488–491.

Mullen, A. L., Goyette, K. A., & Soares, J. A. (2003). Who goes to graduate school? Social and academic correlates of educational continuation after college. *Sociology of Education, 76*(2), 143169.

NASPA online. (2008). *Vision.* Retrieved July 7, 2008, from http://www.naspa.org/about/default.cfm

National Center for Education Statistics. (2007a). *Digest of education statistics: 2007.* Retrieved July 8, 2008, from http://nces.ed.gov/programs/digest/d07/

National Center for Education Statistics. (2007b). *Fast facts.* Retrieved July 2, 2008, from http://nces.ed.gov/fastfacts/display.asp?id=93

Nesheim, B. E., Guentzel, M. J., Gansemer-Topf, A. M., Ross, L. E., & Turrentine, C. G. (2006). If you want to know, ask: Assessing the needs and experiences of graduate students. In M. J. Guentzel & B. E. Nesheim (Eds.), *Supporting graduate and professional students: The role of student affairs* (pp. 5–19). *New directions for student services: Vol. 115.* San Francisco, CA: Jossey-Bass.

Pascarella, E. T., & Terenzini, P. T. (2005). *How college affects students: A third decade of research.* San Francisco, CA: Jossey-Bass.

Polson, C. J. (2003). Adult graduate students challenge institutions to change. In D. Kilgore & P. J. Rice (Eds.), *Meeting the needs of adult students* (pp. 59–680). *New directions for student services:Vol. 102.* San Francisco, CA: Jossey-Bass.

Pontius, J. L., & Harper, S. R. (2006). Principles for good practice in graduate and professional engagement. In M. J. Guentzel & B. E. Nesheim (Eds.), *Supporting graduate and professional students: The role of student affairs* (pp. 47–58). *New directions for student services: Vol. 115.* San Francisco, CA: Jossey-Bass.

Raddon, A. (2002). Mothers in the academy: Positioned and positioning within discourses of the "successful academic" and the "good mother." *Studies in Higher Education, 27,* 387–403.

Rayman, P., & Brett, B. (1993). *Pathways for women in the sciences: The Wellesley report, part 1.* Wellesley, MA: Wellesley College Center for Research on Women.

Redd, K. E. (2006). *Graduate enrollment and degrees: 1996–2006.* Retrieved June 20, 2008, from http://www.cgsnet.org/Default.aspx?tabid=168

Rimmer, S. M., Lammert, M., & McClain, P. (1982). An assessment of graduate student needs. *College Student Journal, 16*(2), 187–192.

Sharf, R. S., & Bishop, J. B. (1995). Graduate students, gender differences and the university counseling center. *College Student Affairs Journal, 14*(2), 24–29.

Smith, B. (1995, April). *Hidden rules, secret agendas: Challenges facing contemporary women doctoral students.* Paper presented at the annual meeting of the American Educational Research Association, San Francisco, CA.

Syverson, P. D. (1996). The new American graduate students—Challenge or opportunity? *Council on Graduate Schools Communicator, 29,* 7–11.

Tobias, S. (1990). *They're not dumb, they're different: Stalking the second tier.* Tucson, AZ: Research Corp.

Ülkü-Steiner, B., Kurtz-Costes, B., & Kinlaw, C. R. (2000). Doctoral student experiences in gender-balanced and male-dominated graduate programs. *Journal of Educational Psychology, 92*(2), 296–307.

Weidman, J. C., Twale, D. J., & Stein, E. L. (2001). *Socialization of graduate and professional students in higher education* (ASHE-ERIC Higher Education Report, Vol. 28, No. 3). San Francisco, CA: Jossey-Bass.

Williams, E. E., Gallas, J. A., & Quiriconi, S. (1984). Addressing the problem of dropouts among graduate students. *Journal of College Student Personnel, 25,* 173–174.

Wolniewicz, R. (1996, November). *The psychology of the graduate student: A preliminary study.* Paper presented at the annual meeting of the Speech Communication Association, San Diego, CA.

Workman, M. A., & Bodner, G. M. (1996). *Qualitative analysis of the graduate student experience.* Paper presented at the annual meeting of the National Association for Research in Science Training, St. Louis, MO.

6

High-Achieving Women
Navigating Multiple Roles and Environments in Academic and Student Affairs

Monica Marcelis Fochtman

Abstract: To better understand the lived experience of high-achieving women and address the gaps present in the literature, this study explored the experiences of 10 high-achieving women representing a variety of administrative positions and institutional types. These inspirational stories demonstrate the tenacity and resilience required to persist in the academy and the joys and rewards of a career in academic or student affairs.

MOST OF THE RESEARCH ON HIGH-ACHIEVING WOMEN in education is focused on the disparities between the educational preparation and actual work environments and experiences of K–12 administrators (Dunlap & Schmuck, 1995; Funk, 2004; Gupton & Slick, 1996; Matthews, 1995). Although some of the findings carry over to higher education, caution should be used in making any direct comparisons. The literature most relevant to high-achieving women in postsecondary education is Astin and Leland's (1991) landmark study, *Women of Influence, Women of Vision*. In their cross-generational study, the authors investigated three cohorts of women: predecessors, instigators, and inheritors. Predecessors were women who served in leadership roles, usually as campus administrators, during the 1940s and 1950s. Instigators were active leaders and members of the women's movement from the mid-1960s to mid-1980s. Inheritors were women who began to take over leadership roles in the second decade (1970s) of the women's movement. Findings from my own study conducted in summer 2007 suggest that the generation of women who were identified as inheritors are becoming the new generation of instigators; these women are breaking barriers, challenging the male-dominated academic culture, and actively mentoring their successors.

Current research on high-achieving women in postsecondary education is focused primarily on faculty, with little study about high-achieving academic or student affairs administrators. The research on academic-motherhood–tenure-track women faculty with children conducted by Ward and Wolf-Wendel (2004a) suggested that while both men and women struggle with work–life balance related to parenthood and academe, this burden is borne more heavily by women. Armenti's (2004a, 2004b, 2004c) work with women professors in Canada revealed similar findings. Her studies showed that in order to accommodate their roles as mothers, women significantly altered their childbearing and child-rearing plans to fit their academic lives rather than rearrange their academic plans to fit their hopes of creating a family (Armenti, 2004b). When adjustments needed to be made, it was women, not men, who did so and at great personal and professional cost. These findings suggested that academic culture is based on the male life trajectory and favors male timelines and priorities (Armenti, 2004a).

Ward and Wolf-Wendel's (2004a) findings are particularly important as they were the first to talk about the unanticipated benefits of dual roles and found that having multiple roles allowed women to gain perspective about each role. Although study participants articulated struggle and sacrifice associated with their dual roles, they also stated that they would not change any part of their lives and that their children and families provided a needed perspective about their academic work.

As with the literature on academic motherhood, the existing work–life balance literature covered important ground but stops short of making a needed contribution regarding higher education administrators. Ward and Wolf-Wendel (2004b) suggested that the literature about work–life issues has three foci: examination of policies, analysis of how those policies are used, and prescriptions for future policies. Drago, Colbeck, Stauffer, and Pirretti (2005) found that those faculty with the fewest family concerns and commitments were the most successful, indicating a systemic bias against care giving. Consistent with other work–life balance studies (Curtis, 2004; Mason & Goulden, 2002, 2004; Quinn, Lange, & Olswang, 2004; Ward & Wolf-Wendel, 2004a; Williams, 2004), the authors also found that faculty do not ask for family-friendly policies such as extended tenure clocks or reduced

teaching loads, for fear that it would adversely affect their careers. The literature concluded that merely having family-friendly or work–life balance policies is not enough to change academic culture.

The majority of the work–life balance literature is focused on tenure-track faculty, with little attention given to the challenges facing non-tenure-track faculty, part-time faculty, administrative or student affairs professionals. Overall, the leadership, academic motherhood, and work–life balance literature provides a solid first step in understanding the experiences of women in higher education. However, more research that explores how and why women higher education administrators negotiate their multiple roles is needed. In this chapter, I address this need and explore areas for future research. Specifically, this study explored the questions: How did high-achieving women in academic and student affairs get to where they are, and why do they stay?

BACKGROUND FOR THE STUDY

My personal interest in high-achieving women stems from my own experiences as a student affairs professional, doctoral student, and mother of two young children. During the last three years, I have immersed myself in the literature related to women leaders in the academy, particularly mothers. While this has certainly been an engaging scholarly endeavor, I have been discouraged by the findings: The road for high-achieving women is long and difficult and offers little encouragement about the rewards of such work. Through my experiences as a student affairs professional at several different institutions, I have had the good fortune of working with and for several high-achieving academic women, so I knew these women existed. Yet, I wondered *why* women continued to persist in the academy.

In summer 2007, I conducted an exploratory study in the hopes of understanding the navigational tools and strategies used by high-achieving women. This study was guided by the research question: What navigational tools and strategies do high-achieving academic women in academic and student affairs utilize that help them persist? Exploring this question served two purposes. First, I hope to contribute to the growing body of literature about women leaders. Merely knowing that academic culture is challenging for women is not enough; we must continue to advance our understanding of why this is so. The next generation of women will succeed only if we learn from the current generation of women leaders. My second motivation for conducting this study was more personal; I wondered how I could navigate my own life as a professional and mother. I needed to know that it was possible. I was seeking inspiration and found it in the stories of the 10 women I interviewed. I was struck by their commitment to their families *and* their careers. Every one of them was a selfless leader who served her students, staff, department, and university. They were simultaneously humble and ambitious, decisive yet reflective, confident and self-aware. These are women trying to live lives of convergence and integration—inspiring indeed. I hope that I listened well and that I have given honor to their stories. Any discrepancies, inconsistencies, or other omissions are mine alone.

METHODOLOGY AND METHODS

The purpose of the current study was to better understand the lived experiences of high-achieving academic women; therefore, I utilized the principles of phenomenological inquiry (Patton, 2002; Rossman & Rallis, 2003) to guide the study I identified as a feminist qualitative researcher, and therefore, methodologies that honor and validate women's stories and experiences were employed throughout the current study. Feminist methodologies are distinctive in their intent, methods, and applications; yet, they are also without clear definitions or boundaries (DeVault, 1996). By identifying as a feminist

researcher I do not align myself with a singular methodology or method; instead, I intentionally rely on several different methodologies, which support the notion that meaning is both constructed and contextual.

Ten high-achieving women participated in this study, where all of the participants served as academic or student affairs administrative leaders, ranging from Interim Associate Provost to Vice President for Student Affairs. The women represent a variety of institutional types, including two-year community colleges, career colleges, regional universities, and research universities, all located within the Midwest. Participants' ages ranged from 39 to 56; four of the women were under age 50, six were 50 and older. Eight of the participants had earned terminal degrees, either Doctor of Philosophy (PhD) or Doctor of Education (EdD); one was currently a doctoral student; and one participant had earned a master's degree and did not intend to pursue a terminal degree. Nine of the participants were married and one partnered. Seven participants were mothers; four of them had children still at home. Two participants were childless by choice; a third participant was also childless, but not by choice.

Purposeful sampling strategies were used to solicit participants from a list of attendees at an American Council on Education State Network conference, as the women who attended this conference often matched the parameters identified for this study. I directly emailed all participants who were listed as being presidents, vice presidents/provosts, assistant vice presidents/provosts, deans, and directors. Follow-up e-mails and phone conversations occurred to coordinate interview times and locations. In-depth, one-on-one interviews were conducted with all participants, half of which were face-to-face and half were via phone.

To honor the women and to convey the power of their stories, I utilized a feminist methodological framework identified by Campbell and Wasco (2000) throughout the data collection and analysis procedures. "Feminist research seeks to respect, understand, and empower women. Therefore, feminist epistemologies accept women's stories of their lives as legitimate sources of knowledge, and feminist methodologies embody an ethic of caring through the process of sharing those stories" (p. 778). I perceive feminist epistemology and phenomenological methodology as congruent. Specifically, phenomenology asks us to consider the lived experience of participants. In the case of this study, I examined the lived experience of high-achieving women through their self-described narratives. These narratives are viewed as a source of knowledge and truth for these particular women. In addition, I utilized a semistructured interview protocol guided by my conceptual framework, which included questions about personal history, education, leadership experiences, mentors and support networks, work–life balance, and motherhood, where applicable. Participants were asked a set of predetermined questions but were also given ample opportunity to reflect on their own experiences.

Limitations of the current study include its grounding in positional leadership and the homogenous participant pool. First, leadership was defined as positional: vice president, dean, director, etc. This parameter was set to ease participant solicitation and to distinguish high achievers from entry level or new professionals. I respectfully acknowledge that not all women in formal positions are leaders and that one may certainly lead without formal positions. A second limitation of the study is its lack of participant diversity. Although solicitation messages were sent to a broad audience of women, only one of the participants self-identified as a woman of color. One of the women was identified as lesbian and the rest were married to men, with children. Thus, the findings discussed here reflect the experiences of primarily White women. I did achieve redundancy and saturation (Rossman & Rallis, 2003) in data collection; however, member checks (Lincoln & Guba, 1985) of the interview transcripts and peer review of the coding (Rossman &

Rallis, 2003) are ongoing. I acknowledge that my own thoughts and experiences with leadership, work–life balance, and motherhood have influenced my interpretation of the findings presented here.

The Participants

Analysis of the data uncovered several unexpected generational differences among the participants. Fifty years seemed to be the dividing line between the two generations of women. Thus, for my purposes here, "older" participants are those who are currently 50 years and older; "younger" participants are under age 50. I describe each person in the following section utilizing biographical information from participants and my fieldnotes as a researcher. Pseudonyms are also used for both individuals and institutions.

Younger participants. Abagail is 39 years old, married, with two school-aged children. She currently works as the dean of technology at Baldwin College, a career college with ten satellite campuses across the state, and burgeoning enrollment at each campus. She is the youngest participant and the only African American woman in the study. She is currently pursuing a doctorate degree and expects to graduate in two years. She was recently named as one of the state's most outstanding business leaders under the age of 40. Abagail seems careful and thoughtful, yet strong and confident. She projected an aura of being at peace with herself and her decisions.

Sally is 45 years old, and like Abagail, is married and has two children ages 11 and 7. She serves as the executive director of continuing education at Fenton University, a regional university with expanding enrollment, a recently opened satellite campus in a metropolitan area, and an increased focus on adult education. She earned a doctorate degree in community, agriculture, recreation and resource studies a few months prior to being interviewed for this study. Sally is deeply passionate about international and continuing education. She is honest, funny, and self-deprecating.

Sylvia is 47 years old, married with three children; two of them are in college and one still lives at home. She is a tenured professor and the program director for the educational leadership program at Central Mountain University, a regional comprehensive university. Sylvia is busy. Even the way she speaks is fast paced. She is an extraverted connector; she likes to meet new people and try new things. She is a prolific writer and researcher and is actively involved in various regional and national professional organizations.

Theresa is also 47 years old and has one son who is 15 years old. Although she is married, she functions as a single parent due to her husband's intense work schedule overseas. Theresa currently serves as interim associate provost at Augusta College, a regional comprehensive university. She has a doctorate degree in early twentieth-century Russian Art, one of only about 20 people in the entire country with that particular specialty. Theresa's career followed a traditional faculty career trajectory, and she recently moved into administration. She is thoughtful and pensive and openly admitted that she is struggling with her role as an administrator because it has meant less time for scholarship.

Older participants. *Abby* was married and divorced at a young age. She has since remarried and has three grown children. She currently works as the dean of student services at Blue Lake College, a community college that serves two of the poorest counties in the state. In the last decade, enrollment at Blue Lake has expanded significantly. Abby earned a master's degree in social work; she does not have a terminal degree and has no desire or intent to pursue one. Abby is the shyest of the participants. She seems more comfortable speaking about her work and leadership in the community than her work on campus. Abby is 53 years old.

Anne was also married and divorced at young age and then remarried. By choice, Anne does not have children; she does, however, have two children and two grandchildren through her husband. She is an active and involved grandmother. She currently works as the dean of general education at one of Baldwin College's satellite campuses. She earned her doctorate degree in 2005 through an online program. Anne is down-to-earth and practical. She is passionate about general education and her students. She has varied out-of-work interests, including Habitat for Humanity and soap making. She is 55 years old.

Jill is a passionate, driven, "hot-blooded Italian" who works as the assistant vice president for academic affairs at Fenton University. She has an EdD in curriculum and instruction and prior to becoming an administrator, she was a faculty member in teacher preparation, motor learning, and physical education. Jill is a lesbian, currently in a long-term relationship. Like Anne, she has no children of her own, but has two children from her partner's previous marriage. Jill is also a two-time cancer survivor; she is 56 years old.

Karyn is married and has three grown children and two grandchildren. She currently works as dean of general education at a satellite campus of Baldwin College. She has a doctorate in educational leadership. Karyn seems honest and realistic, yet never negative. Like Jill, she also survived a significant health scare that gave her a sense of perspective about family, life, and work. She is 52 years old.

Suzanne is married and has two grown children. She serves as the vice president for institutional service and technology at Blue Lake College. She earned her doctorate in educational leadership in 2000. Suzanne is careful, wise, and reflective. She spoke at length about her current mission to get to know herself better. She is actively involved in the Higher Learning Commission and has varied out-of-work interests as well. She is truly a lifelong learner. Suzanne is 56 years old.

Tatami currently serves as the vice president for student affairs at Western Mountain University, a regional comprehensive university. She married four years ago and is childless but not by choice. Tatami reflected that if she had her career to do over again, she would have made time to find a partner and start a family. She is actively involved in national professional organizations. She and her husband are in the process of building their dream home and are avid exercisers. Tatami is 50 years old.

FINDINGS AND ANALYSIS

I employed a feminist interpretation of the data and sought to analyze women's experiences and present their voices accurately (Armenti, 2004a). The following themes are presented with the intent of highlighting critical moments and turning points in these women's lives and careers. I believe these themes demonstrate the participants' leadership, strength, commitment, integrity, and resilience—the skills necessary to navigate multiple environments. I hope the following analysis shows each participant's unique story while also highlighting the common struggles and challenges faced by today's women academic leaders.

Thematic analysis of the interview transcripts uncovered five major themes. Three of the themes were related to specific tools and strategies for leadership, or "how" these high-achieving women achieved. These themes uncover (1) the significance of being mentored or "tapped" for leadership, (2) leaning on mentors and support networks, and (3) finding an individual work–life balance strategy. In addition, there were two themes that talked about "why" these women achieved, or more specifically, they explored the broader concept of motivation. These two themes include the following:

(1) A desire to pay it forward
(2) Perspective gained from a "crucible" event (Bennis & Thomas, 2002)

More specifically, Bennis and Thomas (2002) defined the crucible as a life-altering experience

"where essential questions are asked: Who am I? Who could I be? Who should I be?" (p. 99) and is discussed later in this chapter. Each of these five themes will be discussed in the following pages.

This chapter connects the research uncovered about graduate students in Racheal Stimpson and Kimberly Filer's chapter (chapter 5) and Jennifer Sader's chapter (chapter 8) with the findings from Lee Hawthorne Calizo's chapter (chapter 18) as it explores a different aspect of the same problem. The women in this study are "sandwiched" between the women in these other studies, and investigation of the temporal process of women in the academy is an important contribution of this volume. Moreover, researchers have identified that there is not a pipeline problem (Belch & Strange, 1995), however there is something happening within the institutional culture or system of academia that is causing a bottle neck where women are not advancing at the same percentage rate as men. I argue that the higher education system still operates on the male patriarchal model, as discussed in Susan Marine's chapter (chapter 2), and—as researchers—we need to uncover what is going on within the culture of the academy and help to break this cycle.

Tools and Strategies: The "How" to Become a Leader

> I know she is grooming me to be her potential successor. She is gently guiding my career.
> —Abagail

In this study, I sought to answer two important questions:

♦ How did high-achieving women in academic and student affairs get to where they are?
♦ Why do they stay?

In asking questions about experiences with leadership, I expected participants to talk about their current leadership positions. Although they all did discuss their current positions eventually, many of them indicated that their leadership beginnings were significant to their development. For the participants, being recognized by others was a crucial first step, an entrée to the academy, which set the course for their leadership journeys. Someone the participants trusted and respected saw something in her that she did not necessarily know about herself. This gave her confidence to join a professional organization, pursue an advanced degree, or apply for a position she thought was out of reach.

For example, Jill, Karyn, Sally, Sylvia, and Theresa talked about the support they received from their graduate school mentors and doctoral committee advisers. Mentors and advisers often served as gatekeepers to the academy by introducing participants to professional organizations, guiding them through professional job searches, and encouraging them to take personal and professional risks. One of Sylvia's mentors is a faculty member in the doctoral program where she earned her degree. Sylvia's mentor guided her through the decision to quit her job and enroll in the doctoral program full time. She stated, "I just had this dream that I could quit my job and do this. And she [mentor] said, 'Well you can. We have assistantships.'" Upon graduation, her mentor also encouraged Sylvia to pursue faculty positions. "I never thought I could do faculty. So I rode the line all the way to the end. I remember her saying, 'Yeah you can.'"

Theresa's mentor also helped her prepare for the job search upon graduation. She states, "Well, like every other newly mentored PhD, I was on the job market. I had wonderful support from my adviser at [university] and I actually felt good going on the job market." This support helped turn the often difficult job search process into a positive experience for Theresa. In a similar manner, Jill's former master's program adviser introduced her to the national organization for health educators and exposed her to the various professional and research opportunities that such organizations can provide. She reflected,

> In terms of my professional association work, as a doctoral student, getting brought into the research component of AAHPED (American Alliance for Health) and to help pull together the research programming for that conference, that was kind of an exposure to the leadership role of working within the professional association conference guidelines, being on the conference council. I think that was a key first exposure to leadership. My Master's mentor from [university] who was very active in the region pulled me into that.

Tatami was also "tapped" in a way and at a time that she did not expect.

> The man that was my direct supervisor had just finished his PhD from the University of Maryland. He was also the president elect of one of the largest professional associations in the student affairs field. Because I was able to work with him, I made all kinds of connections and met lots of people that were pretty well known in the field. So that was an incredible entrée that I didn't even seek out, it just kind of happened.

Tatami went on to serve in administrative positions in various student affairs functional areas: activities, orientation, and judicial affairs. She currently serves as the senior student affairs officer on her campus.

Being recognized by others was not limited to leadership potential; it included potential as a student and scholar as well. For example, Anne would not have even attended college had it not been for the prodding of her high school guidance counselor. "Fortunately, I had a counselor in high school who—I was not planning on going to college—called me in to her office and said, 'I don't care where you apply, but you're going to apply to college.'" Anne's baccalaureate degree served as an entrée into education in general; she went on to earn a master's in business administration in an accelerated program at Simmons College in Boston, and completed her doctoral degree in 2005.

Abagail's and Jill's stories demonstrate that although being groomed for leadership is certainly important at the beginning of one's career, it is crucial throughout the career process. Jill related her similar experiences by stating,

> I would have to say that right now I don't formally have a mentor. Informally, the person who has opened a lot of doors for me is the dean here who also had been an associate VP here, so has held numerous leadership roles. This person was also the person that provided the opportunity for me to go to the [institute at a university]. It was because of her reaching out to me that I've been able to do these things. I think that my leadership skills were noticed by other women in leadership roles here at this institution and that in a sense I was sort of groomed to be able to be a dean or vice president or assistant vice president.

In a related example, Abagail's potential was recognized by a senior woman leader on campus. "The chief academic officer here at [university], without her telling me, I know she is grooming me to be her potential successor. She is gently guiding my career. She pulls me aside and says, 'this is another way to do this.'" In this manner, she is providing alternatives for Abagail so she may become a stronger leader.

As reflected in the comments from these participants, the impact of a mentor's guidance is critical to future success as women leaders, particularly when that mentor is identifying you for future involvement in the field. This finding is particularly significant for academic advisors and faculty working with undergraduate and graduate students in higher education; advisors and faculty should be mindful of the fact that mentoring, especially in the early stages of one's career, greatly impacts the lifelong contributions of women. In addition, this finding is important information for young scholars and administrators coming up in the field. The identification of a mentor, be it self-identified or provided through a formal mentoring program, is an important relationship that may strengthen leadership throughout one's career.

Mentors and Support Networks

> It's always that give and take, and if you're open to it, it's all there.
>
> —Suzanne

Analysis of the interviews uncovered varied findings related to current-day mentors and support networks. Only Sylvia and Sally currently have mentors. In fact, Sylvia has several different mentors whom she calls on for various reasons—parenting advice, scholarly questions, professional or supervisory challenges, etc. Jill and Tatami do not currently have mentors, yet did not feel that this was a void in their professional development; they are both at a point in their careers where they are being nurtured in other ways. Conversely, Abby and Theresa expressed sadness and frustration at their lack of a mentor. Anne, Karyn, Suzanne, and Tatami take great pride that as older professionals, they are serving as mentors to younger professionals.

The participants articulated different mentoring needs at different times in her career, indicating that the necessity and desire for mentors never goes away, but shifts as her career progresses. For example, when she first entered the faculty ranks, Theresa wanted a mentor to help her navigate work–life balance.

> I don't have a mentor. Now new faculty are, they kind of have this mentoring in place. I never had that. I had a department chair...I used to call it our semester lunch where I would go cry on her shoulder. I was new. And that was about it. Yes, I would have (wanted a mentor) particularly one who would go beyond just all the professional issues, but also dealing with the work family thing. That's what I always had struggles with and never found support for.

Theresa is able to articulate what she is missing, however, articulation is not necessarily enough for her. In another example, at 38 years old, Sally was pregnant with her second child and building her career in the continuing education field. She related that nonverbal messages from her coworkers made her feel that she could not balance both her roles. "I didn't tell anyone. I just didn't feel comfortable with that. I thought I was going to somehow . . . it was all wrong. That was before (a woman became dean) and it was more of a male world. I was six months pregnant and felt like it was not going to work." When I asked if anyone had mentored her through that process, she said, "No. Not at all."

Abby also shared feelings of isolation in her current position; she believed that this was a result of her not fitting the mold of some of the other women on her campus. By her own admission, Abby has no plans to pursue a terminal degree or to leave Blue Lake College. This certainly does not make her any less committed to her students, her position, or the institution. Rather, she has carved a life for herself and her family and is content to stay where she is and eventually retire from Blue Lake. She reflected,

> I really don't think that we as women support each other. I think we're more out to, "How can I move up faster than you?" . . . If I have a mentor it would probably be my husband. I don't have a female mentor I feel comfortable with. You know, it would be something I think would be missing. It would be nice to have somebody that you can talk to, yeah. So I think that's something that's missing. I think that there are mentors there; I just don't think I've connected with one. And I guess some of that, some of the women I see I don't want to connect with them. Because I'm not, like I said, I'm not as aggressive as some people would want to be, and I don't want to be president.

Abby's story raises questions about the experience of older professionals who are toward the end of their careers. Abby is no less committed or motivated than any other woman professional. Yet, she does not necessarily feel supported by other women. Where do women like Abby go to find support and validation? What messages do our own institutions send to and about older professionals who are at the end of their journeys?

If Abby feels isolated, Tatami and Suzanne described thriving in their newfound places of connection. Tatami spoke animatedly about her out-of-work activities: her and her husband's involvement in the local gym, the building of their dream home, and their local church. As a senior level student affairs administrator, Tatami distinguished between networking and mentoring, articulating that networking, rather than mentoring, is more helpful to her and her position.

> I'm at a point in my professional life where I'm not sure that I would feel like that was necessary (having a mentor). And, I don't want that to come across as I don't believe in lifelong learning because I do. But, I just don't feel a need to be mentored at this particular point. . . . Smaller meetings with other vice presidents (from the same athletic conference) right now, truthfully, actually that would be the closest thing I would say to mentoring, but it's really the collaborations and getting ideas from other VPs at this point, that networking is what has become more important than the mentoring piece.

The distinction between networking and mentoring is relevant in the case of Tatami and other women in this study. The distinctions between the two, and relevance at various stages of a woman's career, should continue to be explored.

In another example, Suzanne shared that because of the nature of her current position (vice president of institutional services and technology), she has dropped out of all professional organizations—except the local American Council on Education network—because they no longer align with her current position. "I have a job now that doesn't fit, so organizations I've been involved with in the past, I'm no longer involved with. I basically dropped out of them." Suzanne has found other forms of support and colleagueship because formal organizations no longer provide the support she is looking for as a leader. She supervises and mentors male and female professionals ranging in age from 25 to 52 years; is actively involved in a major construction project on campus; serves as a reader and mentor for the Academic Quality Improvement Program (AQIP) through the Higher Learning Commission; is a member of a younger professional's doctoral committee. "I'm actually on a dissertation committee with just an outstanding young woman. She is also my mentor. I've learned so much from that young lady. She's just an amazing person. So it's always that give and take, and if you're open to it, it's all there." Suzanne's willingness to find other forms of mentoring and support is inspiring. Her story also reflects how mentoring does not necessarily need to be from "older" women to "younger" women, but can be intergenerational and multidirectional. Upon analysis, Suzanne has a youthful eagerness to learn that Bennis and Thomas (2002) call neoteny. "Neoteny is the retention of all those wonderful qualities that we associate with youth: curiosity, playfulness, eagerness, fearlessness, warmth, energy" (Bennis & Thomas, 2002, p. 20). This neoteny keeps Suzanne current and motivates her to stay in the academy.

Ironically, support "networks" were not defined by participants as existing networks or groups of people, but rather consisted of *individual* people: colleagues, friends, fellow church members, or fellow parents known through their children's school activities. These relationships were formed independent of any formal organizations. In addition, participants did not identify national professional organizations as personal support networks. By way of example, Jill distinguished between professional and personal support networks: "As far as my professional and my leadership role, the [institution] experience . . . I've got one friendship there in particular and I wouldn't call her a mentor, but we developed a very close friendship. Pam is just a tremendous support for me. In terms of my personal support, it's my partner and my sister, and my parents are still alive."

Sally also viewed professional and personal support differently. Involvement in professional organizations keeps her up to date on issues, but does not offer personal support. "I guess I'm not looking for any support in that. I look at those as being informational. They support my work. They inform my work." Sally's personal support

came from individual colleagues at her university. "The dean, some people on my own staff who work very, very closely with me. I think I have a very strong support network here, ranging from personal to professional."

It is worth noting that, for the women in this study, their own institutions played little or no role in their search for mentors and/or support networks. Rather, these important relationships were forged on their own time, and sometimes with their own money. This similar finding is discussed further by Lee Hawthorne Calizo (chapter 18). Although academic culture did not directly discourage these relationships, it did little to actively *encourage* them. In this way, higher education is not necessarily fostering relationships beneficial to women leaders. Further, institutions and institutional leaders have the opportunity to learn more about, and offer, multiple relationships. As these findings show, leaders should offer networking and mentoring opportunities for women at various stages of their career and harness the strength of intergenerational and multidirectional mentoring relationships.

Work–Life (Im)Balance Strategies

> If I had a wife, I'm sure my book would have been published years ago.
>
> —Theresa

The older generation of women seemed to draw clear boundaries between work and home, while younger participants utilized a blended approach, without clear demarcations between the two. For example, Karyn said, "[University] gets 40 hours per week and my family gets everything else. I don't answer e-mail or do work at home." Similarly, Tatami said she feels much more balanced now that she is married because she and her husband have agreed not to talk about work while at home. "When I go home, we really don't spend time talking about work. We'll check in with each other and find out how each other's days were, but other than that, we don't talk about work."

This balance has made Tatami healthier and more productive at work. She describes, "When I'm at work, I'm at work. I'm definitely here and focused on being here. And when I'm at home, I'm home. I can be more balanced and take things in stride and keep things in perspective probably a little better than I might have been doing before." In another example, Abby balances her work and home commitments by staying organized and limiting the number of work-related nighttime commitments. "I feel like I have to be very organized and I try to balance it, I try and limit it so I am only out two to three nights a week."

Theresa, Sally, and Sylvia articulated that they could not draw clear-cut boundaries or lines between their personal and professional lives. For Theresa, her identity as a professional and scholar seemed so interwoven with her personal identity that she struggled to separate the two. Specifically, Sylvia was challenged by her workaholic tendencies, whereas Sally felt constrained by lack of time, for work, her children, or herself. This mirrors the findings from Amy Stalzer Sengupta and Yvette Loury Upton (chapter 14), who concentrate on the interconnections between gender and race and found that relationships play an important role in identity development for all women. This is further explored through Theresa's comments about dueling identities. Theresa's competing yet equally important identities are evident as she describes the experiences of women juxtaposed to men.

When we think about our professional careers, our pursuit in our academic lives, so much that it's bound up, I think for women especially, with their personal lives. I can't separate the two very well. I think in my case anyway, the joys and all of that, I can't imagine life without having had a child. And I think it has made my life richer, and my professional life richer. I don't know. I think in some ways I have had to compromise my academic life, but that doesn't mean a whole heck of a lot in the long run. So I think the family stuff for women is so much more part of the fabric of their professional life. I don't think that's true for men, at least in most cases. There's just something so enveloping about both parts of your life. I can't imagine one without the other.

Thus, for Theresa, a manageable work–life balance seems out of reach because of the all-consuming nature of both academia and motherhood.

When asked about how she spends her time outside of work, Sylvia replied, "At work I guess. I don't really have a good work–life balance. I work every night. I probably work 10 or 12 hours a day. We [she and her husband] continually have the conversation of how we need to cut back on work." Sylvia does have one outlet that she fiercely protects, running. She also enjoys writing, which she does to advance her own scholarship; yet, there are times when her personal interests and work overlap, so it becomes difficult to distinguish between writing for herself and "work." She readily admits that she struggles with the concept of work–life balance and feels this is an obstacle in and of itself. "Well, I think there's this assumption that a work-life balance is actually something that's out there. Everybody has different choices about what they like to do." This struggle for a balance between work and home life continues to be an issue for women, as is reflected in the national and regional conference sessions offered every year by the American College Personnel Association, National Association for Student Personnel Administrators, and others.

Sally relayed similar struggles in trying to carve out time for herself. When I asked about work–life balance, she immediately said, "I don't have any." Upon further exploration she said, "I think about it all the time, but do I actually go ahead and do it? No. I'm not as attentive to it as I think I should be." These are common phrases also, found by Racheal Stimpson and Kimberly Filer (chapter 5) in their research on work–life balance for graduate students. Their chapter and research provides an in-depth analysis to this subtheme found in this study and echoes the intergenerational nature of this deep-seeded issue.

Some of the "high-achieving" professional women in this study had clearly defined strategies for navigating their multiple roles whereas others utilized a more fluid approach. Regardless of work–life balance strategy employed, all of the women strive to live lives of convergence and integration; they try to bring their whole selves to their various roles. Communication of approaches and strategies across generations, various social identities (e.g., gender, race, sexual orientation, class), and professional roles (e.g., graduate students, administrators, faculty), as defined in various chapters throughout this book, is an important action strategy to be furthered across institutions.

Motivation for Persisting: "Why" Pay It Forward

> I think at this point, I **am** the mentor.
>
> —Karyn

All of the women talked of the important role they play as mentors to the next generation of professionals, both men and women. Participants expressed a desire to "pay it forward" and help the next generation of professionals because they were either mentored or tapped for leadership, or because they did not have a mentor when they needed one. For example, as Karyn described, "I'm not a quitter and I keep hoping that I can make some change. At this point, I think I *am* the mentor." Anne mirrors Karyn when she stated, "I think I'm at a point where a lot of people come to me, they want me to mentor them. And I'm feeling, it's kind of a new feeling for me." This state of transition—from mentee to mentor—is one not often discussed in the higher education feminist literature.

> In another example, Suzanne is constantly encouraging the next generation of professionals to not downplay their own accomplishments, something she struggles with in her own development.

> For a lot of women that have some success in the workplace, I think, often, we believe that all of our success is kind of luck, that we didn't really deserve it, that it was just "you're in the right place at the right time," and I still feel that way. I know that I have accomplishments, but if I ever have thoughts about it, it's always, "Boy, I was fortunate," and "I was in the right place at the right time" and "fooled them" sort of thing. I see that in others and I try to—because I know it is so strong for me—I try to work with others to say, "No you have real accomplishments, and you have real talents, and you are an incredible asset for this organization. If this is your goal—this is where you want to go— I'll do what I can to try to help you move along to that goal."

Suzanne's comments reflect a keen awareness of her own limitations, yet a burning commitment to help others. A mentor, indeed!

Sylvia devoted her time to students in the PhD program where she is a faculty member and is currently mentoring a number of students. This commitment to the next generation of professionals and the passion with which it was conveyed is reminiscent of the instigators profiled by Astin and Leland (1991). Abagail also articulated a passion for mentoring. She stated, "Leadership is sacrifice. We as leaders have to make ourselves uncomfortable for the greater good. We must adopt an attitude of service; serving others that is what we do in academe. As a result of my leadership, other leaders emerge. I am not at all intimidated, I am entirely comfortable that people I work with and may not have even met yet, will some day be my colleagues or even replace me."

The women in this study consistently mentioned a profound sense of duty, as a woman in the student affairs profession, to mentor the next generation. They shared that this was their calling, higher purpose, and/or obligation. This "pay it forward" perception reflects the cyclical nature of mentoring. Such a strong mentoring process across generations may help reduce the barriers to advancement in the field and break the bottleneck experienced as women advance through student affairs (Belch & Strange, 1995; Nobbe & Manning, 1997).

Perspective From the Crucible

> When you're 17 years old and you're being told that your arm is going to be amputated and by the way, you may not live, it gives you a whole different perspective on life.
>
> —Jill

Bennis and Thomas (2002) defined the crucible as a life-altering experience

> where essential questions are asked: Who am I? Who could I be? Who should I be? They are often places where one becomes increasingly aware of his or her connectedness. They are also places of choice. Crucibles are, above all, places or experiences from which one extracts meaning, meaning that leads to new definitions of self and new competencies that better prepare one for the next crucible. (p. 99)

Women leaders learn from the crucible and incorporate those lessons into their newfound definition of self and their future leadership practices. Participants in the current study reflected that their crucibles provided a sense of perspective about academia, leadership, and motherhood.

For example, Karyn's near-death experience helped her realize what is really important in life.

> I think there are other things that have changed my leadership style, like when I was sick and almost died five years ago, it changed my view of how important something is and what it is like to lose that . . . It was an allergic reaction to sulfur and it shut my liver down. Yeah, I should've died within three days. My records are at U of M and they got taken for study, because it's a real rare occurrence. Yep, I've been told; I'm a miracle, health wise.

Like Karyn, Jill's sense of perspective about work has been influenced by her health; as a two-time cancer survivor, Jill knows the value and meaning of life outside of academe.

I do have a history of cancer and you want to know what's framed my entire life and framed my entire way. I work with people—life is too damn short for some of the crap that happens in the workplace among people. So I have bone [cancer]—well it wasn't really bone. I don't know what to call it. I had cancer in my left arm when I was a senior in high school and then I just had a mastectomy in 2001. So when you're 17 years old and you're being told that your arm is going to be amputated and by the way, you may not live, it gives you a whole different perspective on life.

In a different manner, Sally's crucible involved a deeply painful betrayal by a former mentor. She shared her story.

> Upon his retirement—this is really an ugly story. I don't know how to frame it. Upon his retirement and the bringing in of a new dean; he promoted someone. A male. And gave them a position which I firmly believe should have been mine because I had felt very, that I was paying my dues, doing the work. And I was so angry about it and hurt at the same time. And I don't see myself as being a person who holds a grudge or carries a chip or anything. But this was the very first time ever in my life that I could not shake it. If nothing—I'm not saying that position should have been given to me, but I should have had an opportunity to apply. But it was just given. And that really bothered me. And when I talked to him about it he said, "Well, you know those things kind of happen. And those things will happen to you in your career. We've all gone through it." That, of course, didn't help. But so I was angry. And I did, I felt like I was going to leave my job because I was so angry by the way that that was handled. And the personal side of it was, and this was probably more of the "ah ha" for me, is that I was deeply, deeply, deeply saddened by it because I felt that I had trusted in this individual. And that I felt that my hard work and my loyalty would somehow pay off in an appropriate way. And I felt like I had lost my that I lost something. I lost maybe my naivety. And it was very painful for me to think that I could be—I was just side swiped. And I never expected it. And it was, it was more than kind of the pushing me aside. That didn't bother me as much as the broken trust. Because I had given so much of my loyalty on that side. And there was no even, "this is what I'm going to do."

There was no conversation. It was just kind of told to me over the phone. And there was a really deep sadness.

A crucible such as Sally's, and ones the others mentioned, has a profound impact on one's sense of self and professional—and sometimes personal—perspectives.

Anne's crucible involved her husband's midlife crisis and subsequent divorce.

About halfway through that program (accelerated MBA), unfortunately, my husband at the time decided to have a midlife crisis and run off with a woman who was 20 years younger than him. So I was going through a divorce at the time and that was pretty traumatic. My original intent when I went for the MBA was to continue on in Corporate America, and frankly, the divorce really just made me rethink everything, and I realized that that's not how I wanted to spend my life.

Each of these life experiences of health scares, loss and betrayal, divorce, could have been paralyzing. Yet, all of these women survived their crucibles through their own resilience and emerged on the other side better and stronger for it. Each of the women talked about how their situation was devastating, but it was only devastating at the time. More specifically, it was the lesson that was important, rather than wallowing or "living in" the crucible without further growth and development. The lesson served its purpose and, while a defining moment, it did not define their entire being. The crucible became an important part of—but not all of—their story. Further, the crucibles carried on across generations in two ways. As communicated through the narratives, the students and administrators who surrounded the women during these difficult times became more understanding of the "life" outside of the profession. In addition, the students and administrators were also witness to this sense of resiliency projected by the women, and hence, learned from watching others experience a difficult time. In both cases, learning from watching the experi-

ences of others becomes an important way to communicate and mentor across generations.

SECONDARY FINDINGS

Mothering and Working: Blessing and Burden

It isn't guilt, it's envy. I see all these moms with their kids in the grocery store, and think "That looks good." It just seems so normal.

—Sally

Seven of the ten participants were mothers; parenthood greatly influenced their experiences as women in the academy and how they thought of themselves as leaders. Analysis of the data uncovered generational differences in how mothers balanced their dual roles of academic/administrator and mother. For the purposes of this study, "older" and "younger" refer to the participants' current ages, not how old they were when their children were born. Consistent with the literature on academic motherhood (Armenti, 2004b), "older mothers" put aside their own career to attend the family first. After their children were school aged, the mothers then attempted a new career in another field. For example, Karyn worked as an aide at a daycare facility so she could bring her children with her to work. Once the children were old enough to attend school, she went back to school and earned a master's degree and began her career in higher education administration. Suzanne was able to take six years off from work in order to stay home with her children. Importantly, the older mothers in this study (Abby and Suzanne) currently work at a two-year community college and have spent their careers there, at regional comprehensive universities, or in service fields outside of education. Neither one was employed at research institutions. This finding is consistent with the literature and suggested that the climate of research-intensive universities is not necessarily conducive to integrating parenthood and academia (Drago et al., 2005; Quinn et al., 2004; Ward & Wolf-Wendel, 2004b).

"Younger mothers" managed their dual roles in a different way. Unlike the older mothers who stepped out of their professional lives while having children, all of the younger mothers continued to work outside the home in some capacity. Each woman received significant childcare assistance from a spouse and/or immediate family member (Sally and Theresa) and in some cases were able to bring their children to work for extended periods of time (Sylvia). Unfortunate side effects of this juggling act are feelings of loneliness and isolation.

Sally related a story of how she waited six months before she announced her second pregnancy because she was so afraid that she would not be taken seriously as a professional. Armenti (2004b) referred to this as the *hidden pregnancy phenomenon* (p. 212).

This form of discrimination was felt by most of the women in this study. Nobbe and Manning (1997) also talked about this expectation that new mothers will not come back to the office and, if they do, the women report feeling watched upon returning from maternity leave. Further, all of the mothers in this study articulated obstacles to being both a mother and academic professional including others' perceptions about what a "working mother" looks like; dealing with the expectations of male supervisors who have older children or female supervisors without children; and lack of access to quality, affordable childcare. Abagail had this to say about obstacles.

> An obstacle for me has been other people's expectations of what "good mothers" are. Mothers have a certain profile; they are not in high ranks in an organization. And it surfaces everywhere—my parents, friends, workplace, church, and my children's teachers. Earlier, when they were little, I wasn't at every popsicle sale, on every field trip. Getting past the guilt others try to put on you about what a working mom looks like.

When identifying obstacles, Abby stated, "I think as women we put pressure on ourselves to be the perfect mom, wife, as well as an employee, and I do think, as far as obstacles it might be more perceived obstacles as far as making sure that we got done everything that we needed to get done. So, yeah, I think there are obstacles. You know, it's not easy to attend all the events and I had to learn that it's okay if I didn't attend everything."

In a different description of obstacles, Theresa related that she is having a difficult time dealing with the expectations of her supervisor who is an older male with grown children. "It's a little bit different here, because I'm, I'm experiencing something I never really had to before and that is, hide the child. I don't feel 100 percent comfortable here in that respect." Unfortunately, Theresa's experience is consistent with the literature that suggests there is generational bias from older faculty, both men and women, toward younger faculty (Ward & Wolf-Wendel, 2004). Older faculty who did not have access to family-friendly policies believe that younger faculty should have to endure the same tests that they experienced without policies that support families, which could also be described as a type of hazing process.

Abby related a different set of struggles, that of finding reliable daycare in a small town. "The hardest thing that I found was finding reliable babysitters, and this being a small rural area, there was no organized daycare. Not being from the area, finding women or finding people who would baby-sit was very difficult. Reliable—it seems like every six months I was trying to find somebody. It was a nightmare." Theresa also expressed great frustration at the lack of childcare available, not just for herself but also for the greater campus community.

> I think it's so backward. There are corporations in this world that are far more forward thinking than that, and I think the academic model is so antiquated in many ways for being perceived as progressive thinkers. I think it's one of the most backwards kinds of institutions that exist. For example, we have no daycare on our campus. None. Zip. And I find that just unconscionable. And much

of our demographic is mature women. We do not have traditional, a traditional residential campus. And yet we have no daycare.

Regardless of generational status, all of the mothers admitted that parenthood "slowed their career paths," yet they all expressed great joy with decision and would do it again. As Theresa related,

> Well, it certainly, in some ways slowed it down. I think that's fair to say, because your time is divided. Unlike someone without children, it's just a very different pace. But on the other side of that, I would say that I think I know my students better. I don't know how tangible that is or how to quantify that, but I think it's made me just a different person. I view my life as B.C., and as A.C., before child and after child. That's a huge divide in your life and I think that you become a different person. And I think I have developed over time a greater openness, maybe sensitivity to students' needs. So maybe that's a good side of parenthood in a way. But it, it, I think generally speaking it slows your path.

Suzanne admitted that her decision not to pursue the college presidency was related to her role as a mother. "I'm guessing that my decision not to apply for a presidency somewhere might have been different that I would have gone up the ladder faster. Certainly, in the early years when you're still in the child-rearing age, or the possibility that you could have another child, I think that probably both men and women treat you differently, and it may impede your progress if your goal is to move up." Consistent with Ward and Wolf-Wendel's (2004a) findings about the benefits of motherhood, participants articulated that motherhood has made them better leaders: more confident, flexible, stronger problem solvers, and more adept at handling conflict. In this sense, leadership skills may be interpreted as transferable across roles. In particular, Theresa and Sylvia equated dealing with difficult colleagues to addressing toddler temper tantrums. Theresa said, "I think it all goes back to that people skills thing.

Conflict resolution, sometimes people act like children. Really, it's the same psychology you use. Let them talk it out, propose a rationale solution. It's strikingly similar, and I think it helps. I really do." Sylvia related it this way: "I think of a two year old. I'm like okay, this is what I need to do to deal with him and his tantrum. So what I have as a tactic is just talking very calmly. I can remember when the kids were little it was constantly, 'I'm sorry. That's not appropriate. We're going to need to do something else.' Or 'Here, you're in the time out.'"

Suzanne often works with men and women who are the same age as her own children. She articulated that her role as a mother has helped her better understand and appreciate the unique gifts and talents of the current generation of professionals.

> There are actually people that are in my groups that are my children's age, where I think, "Boy, this reminds me of something." They're so much like the different stages or different times of my children, and I think, "Well sure." Young people learn differently now, they live in a more chaotic and complex world, they multi-task in a way that I just cannot do, and their values are quite different. Instead of being critical, and saying, "Well, what's wrong with you? You're not behaving like me," I think, "Yeah, I wish I had some of those skills to be able to learn in that way, or multi-task in that way, or just have a better work balance, work-life balance than I did."

While parenthood slowed career paths, too much focus on one's career can be equally detrimental. For example, Tatami was childless, but not by choice.

> I got married just four years ago. And I'm 50 now, so I got married a bit later, and truthfully, I think that part of the reason for the delay was I was so focused on getting my degree and getting some professional experience that I really didn't pay a whole lot of attention to my personal life. I do have regrets about that. Oh, absolutely. Actually, my college classmates all thought I was going to be the first one married with a whole slew of kids and that didn't work out that way.

When asked about the environmental messages she received regarding balancing family and career, she stated, "Well, I received messages that said—well truthfully, I was looking around and was looking ahead of me to the position that I wanted, and my reference point at that point was the men that were Dean of Students, they were married and had children. The women that were Dean of Students were single and did not have children." As Tatami expressed, the role models that were before her had an important impact on the professional path she created for herself. Had she witnessed role models who were mothers, or had chosen nontraditional pathways, then her choices may have been different. Again, the importance of role models and mentors is not to be underemphasized.

In a glimmer of hope, all three of the participants who did not have children of their own currently supervise staff members who are parents. They articulated strong sentiments of support for working mothers and families. It was encouraging to find that being childless did not preclude women from acting as supportive supervisors. All of the women in this study, regardless of their own status as parents, talked about being committed to developing, nurturing, and challenging their supervisees, men and women, parent or nonparent. There is certainly reason to be hopeful that change is on the horizon.

For example, Jill does not have children of her own; in fact, she never wanted them. When asked if supervising staff who are parents was a challenge, she stated, "No, not really because I think again because of my commitment to family even though I've never wanted to have children. I understand the dynamics of family and what that takes. So, someone being pregnant, someone having the kid that's got a cold or whatever, it's take care of the family first and we'll make due. We'll deal with whatever has to be done at work."

Although Tatami's own career followed a traditionally direct trajectory, she remains adamant that her staff make decisions that are good and right for them, even if this means a career path that is vastly different from her own. "I think that people need to not get locked into thinking that is has to look one way. I think people need to feel free to follow their hearts. There's no reason why people can't step out to have a family and/or be in jobs that could contribute in meaningful ways and find fulfillment and have a family. Those things can be combined."

SUMMARY

The literature on high-achieving women, academic motherhood, and work–life balance raises awareness about some of the issues facing academic women, but it does not address issues of persistence (how they do it) or motivation (why they do it). In this study, I sought to address this gap by investigating the tools and strategies high-achieving academic women employ to succeed in the academy. Findings from this study uncovered five major themes, three related to *how* women persist and two related to *why* women persist. The three tools and strategies for how women persist included the significance of being mentored or "tapped" for leadership; the importance of mentors and support networks across the career span; and finding an individual work–life balance strategy that worked. Some important findings come in the nuances or distinctions uncovered. For example, there was a clear distinction between mentoring and networking for some of the women. Further, said mentoring could not only be defined as intergenerational but multidirectional as well.

Within the broader concept of motivation, analysis uncovered two themes for why women persist: a desire to pay it forward and perspective gained from the crucible (Bennis & Thomas, 2002). These two themes coincided with a strong sense of duty and resilience, respectively. If institutional cultures do not support these concepts of motivation for women, the implications may include a reduction in job satisfaction, or attrition of high-achieving women. Institutional programs such as the cohort model discussed by Lee Hawthorne Calizo (chapter 18) and support through women's centers as discussed by Jennifer Wies (chapter 15) are examples of such models and should be read in conjunction with this chapter, as they provide important action strategies that might help further an institutional culture that supports efforts of high-achieving women.

Overall findings indicate that professional and personal life as a high-achieving woman is indeed difficult, but not impossible. The inspirational stories of the ten women in this study demonstrate the tenacity and resilience required to persist, and the joys and rewards in doing so. However, the current study also demonstrates that women are persisting in the academy with help from *outside* the academy as well as inside it. Unfortunately, the academy is still rife with barriers for women and especially for women professionals with children. There is still work to be done; no doubt the women profiled here will have a hand in that change.

REFERENCES

Armenti, C. (2004a). Gender as a barrier for women with children in academe. *The Canadian Journal of Higher Education, 34*(1), 1–26.

Armenti, C. (2004b). May babies and post tenure babies: Maternal decisions of women professors. *Review of Higher Education, 27*(2), 211–231.

Armenti, C. (2004c). Women faculty seeking tenure and parenthood: Lessons from previous generations. *Cambridge Journal of Education, 34*(1), 65–83.

Astin, H.S., & Leland, C. (1991). *Women of influence, women of vision: A cross-generational study of leaders and social change.* San Francisco, CA: Jossey-Bass.

Belch, H. A., & Strange, C. C. (1995). Views from the bottleneck: Middle managers in student affairs. *NASPA Journal, 32*(3), 208–222.

Bennis, W. G., & Thomas, R. J. (2002). *Geeks and geezers: How era, values, and defining moments shape leaders* (pp. 87–119). Cambridge, MA: Harvard Business School Press.

Campbell, R., & Wasco, S. M. (2000). Feminist approaches to social science: Epistemological and methodological tenets. *American Journal of Community Psychology, 28*(6), 773–791.

Curtis, J. W. (2004). Balancing work and family for faculty: Why it's important. *Academe, 90*(6), 21–23. Retrieved November 30, 2005, from www.aaup.org

DeVault, M. L. (1996). Talking back to sociology: Distinctive contributions of feminist methodology. *Annual Review of Sociology, 22,* 29–50.

Drago, R., Colbeck, C., Stauffer, K. D., & Pirretti, A. (2005). Bias against caregiving. *Academe, 91*(5), 22–26.

Dunlap, D. M., & Schmuck, P. A. (1995). (Eds.). *Women leading in education.* Albany, NY: SUNY Press.

Funk, C. (2004). Female leaders in educational administration: Sabotage within our ranks. *Advancing Women in Leadership Journal.* Retrieved June 22, 2007, from www.advancingwomen.com

Gupton, S. L., & Slick, G. A. (1996). *Highly successful women administrators: The inside stories of how they got there.* Thousand Oaks, CA: Corwin, Press, Inc.

Lincoln, Y. S., & Guba, E. G. (1985). *Naturalistic inquiry.* Beverly Hills, CA: Sage.

Mason, M. A., & Goulden, M. (2002). Do babies matter? The effect of family formation on the lifelong careers of academic men and women. *Academe, 88*(6), 21–27. Retrieved November 30, 2005, from www.aaup.org

Mason, M. A., & Goulden, M. (2004). Do babies matter (Part II)? Closing the baby gap. *Academe, 90* (6), 11–15. Retrieved November 30, 2005, from www.aaup.org

Matthews, E. N. (1995). Women in educational administration: Views of equity. In D. M. Dunlap & P. A. Schmuck (Eds.), *Women leading in education* (pp. 247–274). Albany, NY: SUNY Press.

Nobbe, J., & Manning, S. (1997) Issues for women in student affairs with children. *NASPA Journal, 34,* 101–111.

Patton, M. Q. (2002). *Qualitative evaluation and research methods* (3rd ed.). Newbury Park, CA: Sage Publications.

Quinn, K., Lange, S., & Olswang, S. G. (2004). Family-friendly policies and the research university. *Academe, 90*(6), 32–34. Retrieved November 30, 2005, from www.aaup.org

Rossman, G. B., & Rallis, S. F. (2003). *Learning in the field* (2nd ed.). Thousand Oaks, CA: Sage.

Ward, K., & Wolf-Wendel, L. (2004a). Academic motherhood: Managing complex roles in research universities. *Review of Higher Education, 27*(2), 233–257.

Ward, K., & Wolf-Wendel, L. (2004b). Fear factor: How safe is it to make time for family? *Academe,* *90*(6), 28–31. Retrieved November 30, 2005, from www.aaup.org

Williams, J. C. (2004). Hitting the maternal wall. *Academe, 90*(6), 16–20. Retrieved November 30, 2005, from www.aaup.org

7

Toward Self-Investment

Using Feminist and Critical Race Lenses to Analyze Motivation, Self-Esteem, and Empowerment of Women's College Students

Annemarie Vaccaro

Abstract: This chapter shares the findings from a three-year qualitative study of 59 nontraditional-age women at one women's college in the West. Feminist, critical race, and racial identity theories were used as tools to analyze women's educational experiences. Diverse patterns of initial motivations to attend school, levels of self-esteem, and sense of empowerment emerged from women's stories. This chapter summarizes these patterns and also introduces a new concept called self-investment (Vaccaro, 2005)—the valuing of oneself enough to believe that personal growth, learning, and development are not merely needed but deserved. It includes an investment of time, energy, and funding to oneself as a person, not merely toward a degree. The chapter concludes with implications and suggestions for practitioners who work in any institution of higher education with female students.

HIGHER EDUCATION LITERATURE is replete with information on the chilly climate, which is synonymous with a culture of hostility, outsiderness, and invisibility that many women experience at coeducational institutions (Hall & Sandler, 1984; Pascarella et al., 1997). It is believed that such unwelcoming environments are virtually absent, or much reduced, at women's colleges (Sadnovik & Semel, 2002). Other documented benefits of attending women's colleges include high social and academic involvement (Smith, 1990; Smith, Wolf, & Morrison, 1995; Whitt, 1994); high

career aspirations and achievement (Bressler & Wendell, 1980; Tidball, 1974, 1980, 1985; Tidball & Kistiakowsky, 1976); and high satisfaction with overall academic experience (Astin, 1993; Smith, 1990).

However, Smith et al. (1995) noted that "missing from the majority of studies on women's colleges is information about the differential experiences of women of color" (p. 248). The environment of a woman's college, or any institution for that matter, may be experienced differently by women from different racial backgrounds (Kinzie, Thomas, Palmer, Umbach, &

Kuh, 2007). Jackson (1998) found that although women's colleges provide a safe space for women's identity to grow, they "fail to support these women's efforts to experience the connection between their race and gender" (p. 371). Women of color are often confronted with compounded effects of both sexism and racism, which may make their experiences at any type of predominantly White institution (PWI) different from those experienced by White women and men of color (Jackson, 1998; Smith & Stewart, 1983; Solórzano, 1998). In short, many women of color experience campus climates that are unsupportive, hostile, or alienating (Ellis, 2001; Fleming, 1983; Jackson, 1998).

These conflicting bodies of literature lead readers in two very different directions. First, women's colleges have a warm and welcoming environment. Second, PWIs (including predominately White women's colleges) may be hostile and have unwelcoming environments for women of color. These contradictory perspectives, combined with a lack of research about racially diverse, adult learners at women's colleges, inspired this three-year qualitative study. This research project explored the intersections of gender, race, and the educational experiences of nontraditional-age, female undergraduates.

THEORETICAL FRAMEWORK

This research was completed with the use of two theoretical lenses. First, feminist methodology was used as a framework for this study, as it uses gender as a basic category of analysis, values the experiences of women, and recognizes women's behavior in the context of social settings (Hesse-Biber, Leavy, & Yaiser, 2004; Reinharz, 1992). It also challenges assumptions that lead researchers to view women from a nonnormative or deficit perspective. A feminist perspective acknowledges women's success in spite of the sexism. In general, feminist theories are based on a number of assumptions that Flax (1993) highlighted as follows:

(1) men and women have different experiences, (2) women's oppression is not a subset of some other social relationship, (3) oppression is part of the way the structure of the world is organized . . . and . . . this historical force . . . is patriarchy. (p. 81)

In addition, this research was informed by critical race theory (CRT), which is also rooted in ideas of social inequality but with a focus on race (Bernal, 2002; Love, 2004; Lynn & Adams, 2002; Solórzano, 1998; Solórzano & Yasso, 2002; Villapando, 2003). There are a number of tenets of CRT. First, CRT consciously places race and racism at the center of analysis. As Thandi Sulé argues elsewhere in chapter 9, race matters. Racism is recognized by critical race theorists as a pervasive factor that impacts the lives of people of color in profound ways. Racial identity theories provide context for these effects and are used as a foundation for the analysis of women's stories. The second tenet of CRT is that race is socially constructed, and thus can be deconstructed. Finally, CRT places the lives of people of color at the center of analysis. By using a combination of feminist and critical race perspectives, unique experiences of women of color and White women were uncovered. More specifically, when women's stories were analyzed through the lens of racial identity, connections to motivation for enrollment, self-esteem, and sense of empowerment emerged.

In this chapter, I share the overall picture of women's lived experiences and the intersections of their racial identities, motivations, self-esteem, and sense of empowerment. Because of space limitations, I have sacrificed a deep analysis to offer a snapshot of the breadth of women's educational experiences. I hope that this chapter serves as a starting point for conversations about diverse women learners and the various ways they experience education.

Before reading on, it is important for readers to consider the role of the researcher in this study. In qualitative research, the researcher herself is often referred to as the instrument. As a feminist scholar, I am keenly aware of the ways not only my theoretical lenses but also my own social identities influence my research. More specifically, I take to heart Helms's (1993) warning that "if a researcher is unable to examine the effects of her or his own racial development . . . then the researcher risks contributing to the existing body of racially oppressive literature rather than offering illuminating scholarship" (p. 242). Hence, the creation of this chapter is the result of three years of academic analysis and deep personal reflection on my roles and assumptions as a White, feminist researcher.

METHODS

Grounded theory methods were used in this qualitative study where "new theories is their purposeful systematic generation from the data of social research" (Glaser & Strauss, 1967, p. 28). Data were collected in three phases over a span of three years. A total of 59 nontraditional-aged, women learners participated in this study.

The setting for the study was a small, all women's college that catered to an older population of students. Participants in this study ranged in age from 23 to 65. The total college enrollment for this four-year bachelor's-granting institution was fewer than 500 women. In the first phase of the study, 28 women participated in one, in-depth, face-to-face interview that lasted from 60 to 90 minutes. The sample mirrored the overall population by class year, major, and racial group.

Data were coded and analyzed using the grounded theory constant comparative process (Glaser & Strauss, 1967; Strauss & Corbin, 1998). This process has been described as a zigzag (Creswell, 1998), whereby researchers gather information, analyze it, and use the analysis to shape further questions and gather more information. This back and forth movement between data collection and analysis occurs throughout the grounded theory process. As connections between racial identity and the educational expe-

riences of participants emerged, additional questions about racial identity, motivation, and empowerment were added to the latter two phases of the study.

Phase two of the research project included two mixed-race focus groups with a total of 12 women. In these groups, initial themes and analyses about women's racial and educational experiences were explored further. The third phase of the study included five focus groups. These groups were limited to women of color so that differences between the three racial identity stages for women of color (as opposed to two stages for White women) could be analyzed more deeply. Nineteen women participated in this last phase of the study.

Racial and other demographics were obtained through official university records. Unfortunately, university forms did not allow women to select more than one race. The lack of options for biracial and multiracial women certainly limited the forthcoming analysis. See Table 7.1 for a summary of race of the participants in each phase of the study.

FINDINGS

This chapter contains three main findings sections. First, since racial identity provides a foundation for the chapter, a brief overview of participant's identities is provided. The second section presents findings on women's initial motivations, self-esteem, and sense of empowerment. These phenomena are analyzed by, and divided into, racial identity stages to highlight the differences and similarities between women. The chapter concludes with a single phenomenon that all women shared: self-investment (Vaccaro, 2005).

Racial Identity

The use of a critical race perspective inspired me to use racial identity as a primary tool to understand women's experiences. Racial identity

Table 7.1 Summary of Participants by Race

Research Phase and Method	Number of Participants	Race
Phase 1—Individual Interviews	28	American Indian (3%) Asian/Pacific Islander (2%) Black (14%) Hispanic/Latina (18%) White (61%) Unknown (2%)
Phase 2—Focus Group Interviews	12	White (75%) Black (8.4%) Hispanic/Latina (16.6%)
Phase 3—Focus Group Interviews	19	American Indian (5.6%) Asian/Pacific Islander (11.1%) Black (33.3%) Hispanic/Latina (50%)

relates to "the sense of group or collective identity based on one's perception that he or she shares a common racial heritage with a particular reference group" (Helms, 1990, p. 3). Some studies suggest that racial identity is a significant factor that shapes student experiences (Cokley, 2001; Jones, 1997; Shorter-Gooden & Washington, 1996). Further, racial identity development has been tied to various developmental measures such as self-esteem (Goodstein & Ponterotto, 1997; Munford, 1994), moral development (Moreland & Leach, 2001), career development (Jackson & Neville, 1998), and coping strategies (Neville & Heppner, 1997).

Racial identity development happens for all people, yet the process is experienced differently by people of color and White people, as they have differing access to power and privilege. Although a host of racial identity development models are available, Hardiman and Jackson's (1992) model is used as a tool for analysis in this chapter. This model is sometimes used to compare people from all races (Adams, Bell, & Griffin, 1997), yet the original research for this theory was completed with African American (Jackson, 1975) and White (Hardiman, 1979) participants. Table 7.2 presents a brief interpretation of the stages of Hardiman and Jackson's (1992) combined model.

Table 7.2 Stages of Racial Identity Development

Stage of Racial Identity	Hallmarks of the Stage of Racial Identity Development
Naive	Little or no awareness of race.
Acceptance	Active or passive acceptance of dominant White culture. Whiteness is valued and normalized.
Resistance	Increasing awareness and understanding of oppression, including both individual and institutional factors involved in racism.
Redefinition	Creation of an identity not rooted in an oppressive system. Connection to like-minded and like-experienced others.
Internalization	Incorporation of new identity. Attention to and work on multiple social justice issues.

Note. Adapted by A. Vaccaro from Hardiman and Jackson's (1992) Racial identity development: Understanding racial dynamics in college classrooms and on campus.

No racial or ethnic identity development model is a perfect tool for analyzing the complexity of human life. Choosing Hardiman and Jackson's (1992) model of racial identity development limited the analysis to one rooted in power and privilege. While this model illuminates important similarities and differences among women, it does not recognize cultural difference, especially between women of color. Nor does this research explain the experiences of biracial, or multiracial women. By using more culturally specific, biracial, or multiracial identity models, future researchers may uncover nuances that went unnoticed in this study. In addition, it should be noted that race is one of many lenses through which women's stories can be analyzed. As Elisa Abes and David Kasch (chapter 13) and Amy Staltzer Sengupta and Yvette Loury Upton (chapter 14) discuss elsewhere in this book, individuals have multiple and sometimes fluid identities. Issues of social class, age, sexual orientation, and ability emerged only slightly in this study.

Not all of the study participants were easily placed into a racial identity category. Through an etic process, women's stories were analyzed within the framework of existing theoretical stages. In short, the stages were placed on top of the narratives of women, rather than emerging from the narratives as in an emic process (Johnstone, 2002). Hence, I encourage readers to see the forthcoming racial identity categories loosely. The categorization was not meant to place women into finite and unchanging categories. Instead, it was one way in which critical race theory allowed me to best comprehend the patterns and trends in women's lived experiences.

To assess the racial identity of women in this study, I relied on my expertise as a professor who teaches developmental theory and categorized women by indicators of basic tenets of each identity stage. I shaped the interview and focus group questions around the hallmarks of racial identity theory. Research questions included the following:

1. What does your race mean to you? How have your perspectives changed over your lifetime?
2. How are your interactions with family, friends, and peers shaped by race?
3. What are your opinions about a student group exclusively for women of color?

4. Have you ever experienced racism? Would you share some examples?
5. What are your thoughts on a student group for women of color?

Participants showed signs of belonging to only some of the five potential stages of racial identity. The women of color involved in the study reflected the identity stages of acceptance, resistance, redefinition, and internalization. White women displayed hallmarks of two stages: acceptance and resistance.

The lack of White women's voices at later stages may be the result of three things. First, it is possible that a small sample size excluded White women at the later two stages. Second, there may be very few White women at advanced stages, as resistance and redefinition require a vast amount of time and self-work. These stages include recognizing White privilege, acknowledging racist assumptions, and questioning our entire worldview. During the time of this study, the women at this particular college reported no structured experiences where they could explore their own White privilege and create an antiracist identity. Third, administrators at this institution lived the mantra of "we are all women here." This call for women to band together as women, despite their racial differences, may have stifled White women's exploration of their race privilege. Hence, it is not likely that many White women in this college were in later stages of racial identity development. Lack of White women at later stages is also consistent with Hardiman and Jackson's (1992) finding that most White undergraduates are in the stage of acceptance.

White women in acceptance. A majority of the White women in this study would fall within the acceptance stage (Hardiman & Jackson, 1992). A hallmark of this stage of identity includes an unquestioning acceptance of one's whiteness. At the extreme of this stage, Whites believe that they are superior to people of color. Other thoughts related to acceptance include consciously or unconsciously believing stereotypes about other races.

Inability (or unwillingness) to see racism is a hallmark of this stage of racial identity. Many White people at this stage claim that they do not see color, nor can they see themselves as racist beings. Further, Whites may argue that an incident is not racial, because they do not believe that racism exists. To illustrate, when a Latina peer made a claim of racism during a class session, one White participant, Marnie, had this reaction:

> In . . . class she suggested that the teacher gave her a lower grade because of her race. It was so out of line, totally not true. There were other Hispanics in this class. It was that this person had not done what the teacher had asked her to do. I felt bad for the teacher.

Without knowing the details of the situation and without reading her peer's paper, Marnie automatically decided that racism could not be at play.

White women in acceptance also tend to believe that anything "racial" is either exclusionary or reverse discrimination toward them. Whitney harbored such thoughts. She said, "Women's studies courses . . . I really hated every one of them . . . Professors tend to focus on ethnic and minority issues, and I'm not. I think there is a certain amount of discounting that goes on to non-ethnic women."

Finally, nonrecognition of the significance of race, or one's White privilege, is also a hallmark of acceptance. At the time of the study, initial talks began on campus about the possibility of creating a student group solely for women of color. White women at this stage of racial identity development did not believe racism or White privilege were pervasive in society. Thus, they did not understand the need for women of color to have a space away from racism (and away from White peers). They viewed the group as a form of reverse racism.

White women in resistance. White women who showed signs of the racial identity stage of resistance began to recognize that oppression existed. Even though White women at this stage began to see racism, they still viewed the world through a set of White-normed eyes. They intellectually understood that life for women of color was different because they experienced racism in addition to sexism. Further, White women in resistance also realized that they could not completely comprehend the experiences of women of color. Finally, White women in resistance intellectually understood the need for a group for women of color. Unlike their White sisters in acceptance, they did not view the group as a form of reverse racism.

White women were unsure of how to verbalize their reactions when they realized that women of color had vastly different experiences with the same life phenomena. Instead of dismissing others' experiences as bad or deficient (which would happen in a previous stage of identity development), White women at this stage attempted to grapple with the concept that everyone was not treated equally. On her journey of resistance, Laura realized "things that I had never considered" affected women of color differently than White women like herself. Gretta also explained that for "women of color and there was an added level [of racism]."

Women of color in acceptance. In the stage of acceptance, people of color (consciously or unconsciously) assimilate into the dominant White culture. Sometimes, internalized racism takes hold. Shame associated with not being able to assimilate into a White crowd was something some women constantly battled. Pilar described herself to me as White but admitted that her Mexican American family, especially those with much darker skin, would be very upset to hear her call herself White. Since she reported her race as "Hispanic/Latina" on official university records, she is included in this section. However, the diversity of descriptors that she used to describe herself calls attention to the complexity of race, racial identity, and the limitations of any study findings that claim to offer definitive findings related to race and racism.

Like Pilar, other women at this stage of racial identity either downplayed or were ashamed of their race. For Sharon it was her language proficiency that made her self-conscious. Since English was not her first language, she said she was "afraid that I'm destroying the English language." Further, Frieda's normalizing and valuing of White culture is apparent in her perspective that Spanish, as spoken by Whites, was somehow more pure and perfect than the "slang" spoken by those with brown skin (including herself). She said, "I want to learn how to speak Spanish the way the Spaniards do. I don't want to learn how the Mexicans use their slang and everything because that's the way I speak now."

Three decades after Cross's (1971) original writing on racial identity development, Cross and Fhagan-Smith (2001) added the concept of race salience to Cross's earlier model of racial identity. They suggested that people of color in this stage are "not necessarily self-hating persons.... Rather they are people who, though nominally Black, operate with a self-concept built upon an assimilationist-American base(and) a hunger for individualism" (p. 255). At times, people of color at this stage are not taught their heritage as children. Adults may choose not to pass on their heritage to future generations, especially if they think that their children's lives will benefit. Some women in this study described having such parents.

Women of color in resistance/redefinition. Some women of color showed signs of belonging to the resistance/redefinition stage. In this stage, people of color refuse to accept the dominant White worldview and begin to question why things are "the way they are." The pain and frustration of constantly challenging dominant White paradigms eventually forces people of color to move into a place where they can re-

define their identity. Since these stages may be so intertwined for women of color, I do not separate resistance and redefinition here.

Women in these stages resisted conforming to White, dominant norms. For example, Carmelita stated, "You have to assimilate [to] ... succeed ... I noticed when I started. I have a difficult time with that assimilation because it just doesn't feel right to me. I know that some women can but then you do lose a part of you!" Reclaiming and appreciating one's culture, ethnicity, and race were crucial to these women. In the struggle to redefine their lives, people of color often seek refuge in communities of color and are thus often labeled "separatists" by Whites who do not understand the need for in-group support (Tatum, 1992). In fact, one of the women in this stage was the student who fought to create the student group for women of color.

Women in resistance/redefinition were frustrated not only by racist peers but also by an entire educational system that allowed racism to be perpetuated. Hence, women in this stage of identity were especially sensitive to underrepresentation of people of color in the faculty, staff, and student body. Many women such as Latifa viewed racism as societal and structural. She lamented,

> There are not a lot of minority faculty [here] nor anywhere. And I don't think that that is merely that there are not a lot of educated minorities ... [Education] shuts out minorities.

Women at this place of racial identity all felt that the college was merely another place where they were "the other." In spite of this fact, each of them cherished their heritage and refused to assimilate.

Women of color in internalization. At this late stage of racial identity development, people of color incorporate racial identity into their positive self-concept. People are proud of their ethnicity and race. Mahla stated, "I love my heritage and I love my roots.... No one has to remind me of the color of my skin. The only thing I remind myself of is where I'm going."

Developing compassion for other forms of oppression, such as classism, sexism, and heterosexism, is a hallmark of this stage. People at this stage are likely to see the struggles of other oppressed groups and want to serve as an ally for change. Lisa said of her race, "It's everything I am. I'm very proud of who I am. . . . It brings a uniqueness to me. I feel more compassion towards other minorities." Similarly, Abby shared, "I don't care if you're gay, it doesn't matter with me. I'm a lover of people and I know no boundaries."

Women of color at this stage possessed resilience in the face of individual and institutional racism (O'Conner, 2002). At this point in their lives, they had refined tactics for combating racism: tactics that did not harm their inner being. They did not let racism take their energy and passion for life or school away. Women like Tallie said this of racism, "You grow up with it. . . . You expect it. . . . You just don't let it bother you." Similarly, Fatima said, "you live around it . . . you just tune it out."

Motivation, Self-Esteem, and Empowerment Through the Lens of Racial Identity

In this section, racial identity is used as a framework through which women's educational experiences are analyzed. Specifically, women's motivations to attend school, levels of self-esteem, and sense of empowerment are viewed through the lens of racial identity.

Motivation. Differences between women's initial motivation to earn an undergraduate degree were uncovered when women's experiences were analyzed via racial identity. Women who entered college for career-related reasons generally progressed to deeper, internally driven reasons to stay. Other women's motivations never changed, as they entered college with existing noncareer-related or intrinsic motivations.

Motivation for all white women and women of color in acceptance. White women in both stages of identity and women of color in the acceptance stage shared the same type of initial motivations. Thus, they are discussed together in this section. All White women and women of color in the acceptance stage were more likely than others to list practical reasons for initially attending the college. Even when women did not have their sights set on particular promotion, their aspirations were initially rooted in career and financial success. Donna shared, "I want to see (my) progress . . . I want to put myself in a place where I can't see that next level."

While women at these stages may have described initial motivations as purely fiscal or career related, they all talked of changing motivations as they spent more time at school. Practical and work-related motivations often turned into deeper reasons for persistence. None of the White women or women of color in acceptance were initially in search of deeply meaningful, internal growth experiences, even though that is what many women experienced. Mae described how school "became less about what it could do for me financially or career wise . . . and just more about what I was getting out of it personally."

Motivation for women of color in resistance/ redefinition. For women of color in resistance/ redefinition, career-related motivations were barely mentioned. Far deeper and more intrinsic motivations emerged during our conversations. These women described their initial motivation as a personal challenge or self-test. They came to the college to fulfill a life goal of achieving education. This dream was often connected to their sense of life accomplishments and self-worth. Lani recalled, "All my friends had degrees. I didn't. It was twenty something years by the time I decided to come back . . . I wanted to see if I could actually do it. It was a personal goal." Others, like Angel, felt a personal obligation to earn a degree to combat ethnic stereotypes.

She refused to be another "statistic" or a Latina "failure." She was determined to show the world that Latinas could be successful.

> My culture . . . and my race has created some stereotypes, even for myself. . . . You are afraid. I heard someone, say . . . that failure is so much easier because you get so used to it. Success is so much more difficult because it is new. And so, I think that my culture is a big part of what drives me.

Overall, women of color in resistance/redefinition arrived at the college with personal hopes and dreams, not simply economic motivations. Earning a degree was a deeply personal achievement, instead of a career-based one. Graduation was their ultimate self-test of strength, persistence, and character.

Motivation for women of color in internalization. Similar to the women discussed in the previous section, women of color in internalization were internally motivated to get their degree. However, while women discussed in the previous section felt that they had to prove their worth by succeeding, women in internalization already believed they were worthy. They did not have to prove anything to anyone, but merely wanted the self-satisfaction of accomplishing their life-long dream of earning a degree.

Ginger talked about grades not mattering. Instead, it was personal growth and development that motivated her to seek a degree at the age of 64. Francie, who was also near retirement age, expressed similar motives. "This degree is not for me to get promoted within my company. I'm ready to retire. This is something personal to me . . . this is my number one priority." Even Tallie, a small-business owner, steered clear of specific career motivations. For her, the motivation was twofold. First, she was motivated to achieve an internal goal. Second, she was motivated by her family. She recognized that as she grew, her family was inspired to grow, too. She said, "they see Momma goes to college (and) they

pay more attention to school!" For Inez, instability in her personal life inspired her to finish. After her recent divorce, she was able to focus on her life and her dreams. Inez explained, "I'm giving 100%, I have always wanted to do this. . . . It is part of my dream, my goals." Like her peers in this stage of racial identity, Inez was motivated by intrinsic rewards.

Self-esteem and empowerment. As part of the study, the women were asked to talk about their self-esteem and sense of empowerment. Women with differing racial identities responded in two distinct ways about their levels of self-esteem upon entry to college. Women in early stages of racial identity experienced a transformation at college. Other women, however, reported consistent levels of self-esteem and empowerment throughout their tenure at the institution.

Self-esteem and empowerment for all White women and women of color in acceptance. White women at both stages of development and women of color in acceptance described a transformation from starting school with low self-esteem to achieving self-confidence and empowerment. Building self-esteem and becoming empowered to take control of their lives became the two driving forces behind these women's educational experiences. Women described changing in positive and sometimes surprising ways. At the college, many women felt their self-esteem and sense of empowerment grow for the first time in their lives. Nola described,

> I found myself doing things that I didn't know I could do. . . . In many ways it has made me fearless. I definitely found that I could handle more than I thought I could. I don't know if I always was or I just realized it now, but I definitely feel stronger after this experience.

Women who lived lives where they were silenced found new ways to express themselves. They learned that they actually had something valuable to say. Women began to feel that both their academic work and their entire being were of value. Venus shared,

> Every morning when I wake up, I have something to look forward to. I see myself as a different person. I am not to take what is left over, but I can go and get the big thing. I am worth more. I do have value.

Finally, women at these stages of racial identity also talked about finding role models in their peers and empowerment in the environment. Rhonda shared, "I think it's empowering just to be with all these women who . . . have all the same obstacles that you have, that you're encountering when you come back to school."

Self-esteem and empowerment for women of color in resistance/redefinition. Unlike their peers, women of color in resistance/redefinition talked about arriving at the college with high levels of self-esteem and empowerment. Some even suggested that the reason they chose to go to school was because they felt empowered enough to make a better life for themselves.

Women of color in resistance/redefinition talked about having to rely on their high self-esteem and sense of empowerment to deal with an unwelcoming racial climate at the college. Latoya was determined to succeed in spite of the racist environment. As long as racism was not physical, she had the esteem and courage to persist. She said, "I really want that degree. . . . It is what I've fought for . . . I'm not going to quit, as long as nobody is spitting on me, and putting their hands on me. I can stand a few hours of people not talking to me."

Julietta was similarly frustrated by her experience. She had confidence in herself as a strong Latina, but when she reported her experiences with racism to the administration, her complaints were brushed aside. In the following quote, she explains how she tried to maintain her self-esteem and pride in spite of rejection from the university administration.

> It's frustrating that I am a single mom, raising three men and I am trying to teach them that women are strong and can come together. Yet . . . I've cried and repeatedly brought it [racism] up. I haven't heard one thing that says "we hear you and we're working towards this." It's kinda like it's brushed away.

Julietta was determined to show her children how strong she was, even in the face of racism.

Self-esteem and empowerment for women of color in internalization. Unlike their peers discussed in the previous section, women of color in this stage described the environment in a relatively neutral manner. They "lived around" racism and persisted to achieve their dreams. Women of color in internalization also arrived at the college with high self-esteem and a sense of empowerment. Many of the women at this stage of racial identity laughed at the thought that they somehow gained strength and self-esteem in college. None of these women believed they would be enrolled if they had not already been empowered to change their lives. Tallie shared,

> Having no motivation, I mean, why would you say, "Oh yeah, I'll go to school now? And NOW I'm empowered? Now I have all this power! Now I can do this! Now I can do that!" . . . If it wasn't there before, why do you think it's in you now?

Nani described being empowered as a young girl by her grandmother who told her that she could accomplish anything. Her self-esteem and empowerment can be seen in her dedication to making a better life for herself and her boys. She was determined to earn her degree, "get off of welfare, and make a life for myself and my sons. I was not going to become the norm . . . and I chose to make a change."

In sum, while women in earlier stages of racial identity believed that their college experience gave them the self-esteem and sense of empowerment to achieve their dreams, women of color in later stages of development described how they decided to enroll in the college because they *already* possessed high self-esteem and a sense of empowerment. In short, while some women arrived at the doors of the college believing that they deserved the gift of knowledge and the accompanying degree, others needed to attend school to learn how to believe and invest in themselves.

Self-Investment: A New Educational Concept

Critical race theory helped me to see differences in women's racial identity and corresponding motivations, self-esteem, and sense of empowerment. A feminist lens helped me see one significant similarity among all women. No matter what initially inspired the women to enroll, eventually all of the women exhibited a desire to continue their studies not for career, but for deeply personal reasons. Women shared a common desire to invest in themselves, whether or not they began with high self-esteem or a sense of empowerment.

A new educational concept emerged from this study, which I call self-investment (Vaccaro, 2005). Self-investment is the valuing of oneself enough to believe that personal growth, learning, and development is not merely needed but deserved. It includes an investment of time, energy, and funding to oneself as a person, not merely toward a degree on a piece of paper.

The idea of investing in oneself is significant as we live in a society where women, and the roles they play, are devalued. Feminist researchers have argued that women have been historically (and inappropriately) viewed from an andocentric or deficit perspective (Hayes, 1992; Stalker, 1996). Similarly, nontraditional-age, female students have been described as distracted by family (Home, 1997, 1998) and thus less engaged than their younger student counterparts (Astin, 1993; Pascarella & Terenzini, 1980; Yair, 2000). Findings from this study show women not from a deficit but instead through an inspirational perspective.

Self-investment was related to women's self-esteem and sense of empowerment in that the women often described these phenomena in the same sentence. Unfortunately, we still live in a world where women are socialized to believe that they have a moral obligation to put care for others before self-care (Gilligan, 1982/1993). Yet, the women in this study recognized that care for self was equally important as care for others. Students like Yvette became empowered to care for and invest in themselves.

> Women start to do something entirely for themselves, unlike being caregivers. . . . So when this is something just for them, it's so valuable for them as an affirmation of something for ME, nobody else! I want that grade to be the best, because [it is] an affirmation of self-importance.

In this study, women's commitment to bettering themselves was a desire all women shared, no matter what their initial motivations, levels of self-esteem, or empowerment. Despite other differences, all of the women, regardless of their racial identity, came to invest in themselves. Rarely did the desire for a promotion propel women to endure years of evening classes. Instead, they realized a host of reasons why going to school was good for their soul. By doing what was good for their soul, in turn, they were practicing self-care in general and self-investment in particular.

While all of the women came to invest in themselves, it is important to note that only the women in later stages of racial identity development began school with the desire and readiness to invest in themselves. Women of color in resistance/redefinition arrived with self-investment but had a few fleeting doubts. For this group, graduation was a test whereby they could prove to themselves that they were the strong women they believed themselves to be. Conversely, all White women and women of color in acceptance entered the college with low levels of self-esteem and empowerment. Yet, they grew into

Table 7.3 Summary of Key Findings

Racial Identity	Initial Motivation	Self-Esteem and Empowerment	Self-Investment
White women in acceptance	Career/Financial	Transformed from low to high at college	Learned through college experience
White women in resistance	Career/Financial	Transformed from low to high at college	Learned through college experience
Women of color in acceptance	Career/Financial	Transformed from low to high at college	Learned through college experience
Women of color in resistance/redefinition	Personal challenge or self-test	Arrived with high levels and relied on it to fight racism	Arrived with the desire to invest in self
Women of color in internalization	Life-long dream	Arrived with high levels	Arrived with ability to invest in self

women who were ready to invest in themselves. They learned to believe that once they invested in themselves, they could do amazing things. For example, Fern stated, "When you feel empowered to speak out . . . you begin to make that statement and that commitment to yourself. I matter. I have an opinion. I can influence my environment and my surroundings." Ultimately, all of the women in this study invested in themselves, not merely to gain a new job but to be strong and powerful women. Women shared things, for example, "It means a lot to me that I do this for myself" and "I am proud of me." In short, the study participants did not just invest in their education; they invested in their own growth and development.

DISCUSSION

A number of significant conclusions can be drawn from this research. First, inspired by feminist perspectives, this study documented a new educational concept called self-investment (Vaccaro, 2005). It is similar to self-esteem and empowerment; however, it is distinctly an educational concept. While it is likely that women's self-esteem and sense of empowerment affected their behavior in other realms of life (such as work), self-investment was tied directly to their educational growth and personal development.

Second, through the use of racial identity theory, important patterns and trends in women's educational experiences were uncovered. As is shown in Table 7.3, all the White women and women of color in acceptance have nearly identical patterns of initial motivations, levels of self-esteem, and sense of empowerment. Their patterns of growth in three of these areas were also similar.

While there were differences between White women and women of color, especially at later stages of identity, there were more differences *between* women of color at different stages of racial identity. Research about the unique experiences of women of color (Ellis, 2001; Fleming, 1983; Jackson, 1998) is incredibly important to our field, yet it is not sufficient in explaining the diversity of experiences between women of color at various racial identity stages. Nor does contemporary student affairs literature sufficiently explain the similarities between White women and women of color in acceptance.

The similarities and differences uncovered in this study remind us that we should not make sweeping conclusions about ways that women of color and White women's experiences may differ within the same college environment. A category (or even the term) "women of color" seems insufficient in describing the vastly different educational experiences of the women in this study. Not all women learners are the same and should not be treated as such by educators. I would like to echo the sentiments of Hayes (2001) who warned that "a 'generic' category of women . . . renders invisible the considerable diversity among women" (p. 36). In this chapter, the use of two identity categories for White women and three categories for women of color uncovered important educational differences that would have remained invisible if I had viewed participants through single (all women) or binary (women of color and White women) lenses.

One of the most intriguing differences explored by this study was that women of color in the two later stages of racial identity were the only ones who reported arriving at college with high self-esteem, a sense of empowerment, and readiness to invest in themselves. Sadly, this study does not ascertain why. One possibility is that women of color in internalization had higher levels of self-esteem because the racial identity stage of resistance is built upon a positive self-concept, one not rooted in oppressive notions. Further, the strength they used to fight a lifetime of racism (and sexism) may have been derived from the same inner fire that inspired women to invest in themselves.

Similarly, this study does not tell us how White women and women of color in acceptance grew to invest in themselves once they arrived at college. As Rhonda shared, many women found strength and role models in their peers. It is quite possible that women of color in internalization served as role models for their peers as they exhibited self-investment in the classroom. This may especially be true for women of color in later stages of racial identity development, who, like Jackie, saw it as their responsibility to support women who had "less strength" than themselves. Many feminists have written about the importance and power of female role models (Walker, 1983). Further, critical race educators have shown that positive mentoring relationships influence the ways students experience their educational environment (Luna & Cullen, 1998). More research is needed to explore the connections between racial identity, self-esteem, role models, and self-investment.

Implications for Higher Education and Student Affairs Practitioners

This chapter began with the concept of the chilly climate. Research has shown that a chilly climate has a negative effect on women's cognitive growth (Pascarella et al., 1997) and self-confidence (Duncan, Wentworth, Owens-Smith & LaFavor, 2002). All White women and women of color in acceptance described a positive college environment in which their self-esteem grew and where they felt empowered. This finding partially supports research that shows women's colleges to be positive spaces for women (Kim, 2002; Miller-Bernal, 1993, 2002). Yet, women of color in resistance/redefinition stages did not find the environment to be empowering. In fact, they had to rely on their self-esteem to persist in an unwelcoming environment. Thus, findings from this study also mirror those by Kinzie, Thomas, Palmer, Umbach, and Kuh (2007) who found that women of color at women's institutions had less positive experiences than did their White peers. However, findings from this study go even deeper and describe differences not merely between women of color and White women but *between* women of color at different stages of racial identity. The intersections of other identities, such as age and socioeconomic status, should be explored in future studies.

Those of us who work in all women's colleges, or any type of women's environment (such as athletics or residence halls), should be concerned with how the environment (climate, policies, structures, etc.) may be experienced in vastly different ways by women at different stages of racial identity development. Just because an environment is an all-female space, it does not necessarily mean it is a "warm" space, free from racism. As higher education practitioners, we cannot be satisfied with a positive climate for *some* of our students. It is our ethical obligation to create campus environments free from racism (American College Personnel Association, 2006). This study shows that even though some students of color said they were able to navigate ("live around") racism, other students of color were profoundly affected.

Previous studies have shown that students of color develop coping mechanisms for racism, which include withdrawal, separation, or assimilation (McEwen, Roper, Bryant, & Lang, 1990). Study participants, especially women of color in resistance/redefinition and internalization, developed effective coping strategies. Yet, it is quite possible that others dropped out of the college because they experienced an unwelcoming environment. Missing from this study are the voices of women who left the institution. Their experiences would have added important data to the development of the concept of self-investment.

Study findings suggest that racial identity is intricately tied to a host of variables, including women's intrinsic and extrinsic motivations to earn a degree. While previous research has documented various adult student motivations (Douglas, 2000; Houle, 1961), none have made connections to racial identity. Further, these findings only partially support those of Douglas who found that women's motivation was associated with connected knowing, noncompetitive peer relationships, active learning, and an environment where expression of inner voice is supported. While the women in this study arrived at the institution with different motivations, they all eventually began to see a larger reason to persist. In short, they were worth investing in as women. More research is needed to determine how and why this transformation in motivations took place. As student affairs professionals who work in various functional areas with adult women, we should not assume that their initial motivations to apply are the same motivation that keep women enrolled.

This study supports earlier research (albeit completed with very different student populations), which suggests that there may be con-

nections between racial identity and self-esteem (Goodstein & Ponterotto, 1997; Munford, 1994). Increased self-esteem and empowerment is of utmost importance to me as a feminist practitioner. More research needs to be conducted to understand how some women were inspired to become empowered and to invest in themselves and why others arrived at college having already done so. A best practice of our field is that we strive to meet students where they are developmentally (Sanford, 1966). This study reminds us how important it is to accurately gauge, support, and inspire women who arrive at school with vastly different levels of self-esteem, empowerment, and self-investment.

REFERENCES

Adams, M., Bell, L. A., & Griffin, P. (Eds.). (1997). *Teaching for diversity and social justice: A sourcebook.* New York: Routledge.

American College Personnel Association. (2006). *ACPA statement of ethical principles and standards.* Washington, DC: Author.

Astin, A. W. (1993). *What matters in college: Four critical years revisited.* San Francisco, CA: Jossey-Bass.

Bernal, D. D. (2002). Critical race theory, and critical race-gendered epistemologies: Recognizing students of color as holders and creators of knowledge. *Qualitative Inquiry, 8*(1), 105–127.

Bressler, M., & Wendell, P. (1980, November/December). The sex composition of selective colleges and gender differences in career aspirations. *Journal of Higher Education, 51*(6), 650–663.

Cokley, K. O. (2001). Gender differences among African American students and the impact of racial identity on academic psychosocial development. *Journal of College Student Development, 42*(5), 480–487.

Creswell, J. W. (1998). *Qualitative inquiry and research design: Choosing among five traditions.* Thousand Oaks, CA: Sage.

Cross, W. E., Jr. (1971). The negro-to-black conversion experience: Toward a psychology of black liberation. *Black World, 20*(9), 13–27.

Cross, W. E., Jr., & Fhagen-Smith, P. (2001). Patterns of African American identity development: A life span perspective. In C. L. Wijeyesinghe & B. W. Jackson III (Eds.), *New perspectives on racial identity development: A theoretical and practical anthology* (pp. 243–270). New York: University Press.

Douglas, K. A. (2000). *Becoming veterinarians: A relational account of the experiences of ten women. Dissertation Abstracts International*, 60 (8-A).

Duncan, L. E., Wentworth, P. A., Owens-Smith, A., & LaFavor, T. (2002). Midlife educational, career, and family outcomes of women educated at two single-sex colleges. *Sex Roles, 47*(5/6), 237–247.

Ellis, E. M. (2001). The impact of race and gender on graduate school socialization, satisfaction with doctoral study, and commitment to degree completion. *The Western Journal of Black Studies, 25*(1), 30–46.

Flax, J. (1993). Women do theory. In A. M. Jaggar & P. S. Rotehenberg (Eds.), *Feminist frameworks: Alternative theoretical accounts of relations between men and women* (3rd ed.). Boston, MA: McGraw-Hill.

Fleming, J. (1983). Black women in black and white college environments: The making of a matriarch. *Journal of Social Issues, 39*(3), 41–54.

Gilligan, C. (1982/1993). *In a different voice.* Cambridge, MA: Harvard University Press.

Glaser, B. G., & Strauss, A. L. (1967). *The discovery of grounded theory: Strategies for qualitative research.* Chicago, IL: Aldine.

Goodstein, R., & Ponterotto, J. G. (1997). Racial and ethnic identity: Their relationship and their contribution to self-esteem. *Journal of Black Psychology, 23,* 275–292.

Hall, R. M., & Sandler, B. R. (1984). *Out of the classroom: A chilly climate for women?* Washington, DC: Association of American Colleges, Project on the Status and Education of Women.

Hardiman, R. (1979). *White identity development theory.* Unpublished doctoral dissertation. University of Massachusetts, Amherst.

Hardiman, R., & Jackson, B. (1992). Racial identity development: Understanding racial dynamics in college classrooms and on campus. In M. Adams (Ed.), *Promoting diversity in college classrooms: Innovative responses for the curriculum, faculty, and institutions* (pp. 21–37). San Francisco, CA: Jossey-Bass.

Hayes, E. R. (1992). The impact of feminist on adult education publications: An analysis of British and American journals. *International Journal of Lifelong Education, 2*(2), 125–138.

Hayes, E. R. (2001). A new look at women's learning. In S. B. Merriam (Ed.), *The new update on adult learning theory* (pp. 3–11). San Francisco, CA: Jossey-Bass.

Helms, J. E. (1990). *Black and White racial identity: Theory, research, and practice.* Westport, CT: Praeger.

Helms, J. E. (1993). I also said, "White racial identity influences White researchers." *The Counseling Psychologist, 21,* 240–243.

Hesse-Biber, S. N, Leavy, P., & Yaiser, M. L. (2004). Feminist approaches to research as a process. In S. N. Hesse-Biber & M. L. Yasser (Eds.), *Feminist perspectives on social research* (pp. 3–26). Oxford, England: Oxford University Press.

Home, A. M. (1997). Learning the hard way: Role strain, stress, role demands, and support in multiple-role women students. *Journal of Social Work Education, 33*(2), 335–346.

Home, A. M. (1998). Predicting role conflict, overload, and contagion in adult women university students with families and jobs. *Adult Education Quarterly, 48*(2), 85–97.

Houle, C. O. (1961). *The inquiring mind.* Madison, WI: University of Wisconsin Press.

Jackson, B. (1975). Black identity development. In L. Golubschick & B. Persky (Eds.), *Urban social and educational issues* (pp. 158–174). Dubuque, IA: Kendall Hall.

Jackson, C. C., & Neville, H. A. (1998). Influence of racial identity attitudes on African American college students' vocational identity and hope. *Journal of Vocational Behavior, 53*(1), 97–113.

Jackson, L. R. (1998). The influence of both race and gender on the experiences of African American college women. *The Review of Higher Education, 21*(4), 359–375.

Johnstone, B. (2002). *Discourse analysis.* Malden, MA: Blackwell.

Jones, S. R. (1997). Voices of identity and difference: A qualitative exploration of the multiple dimensions of identity development in women college students. *Journal of College Student Development, 38,* 376–386.

Kim, M. M. (2002). Cultivating intellectual development: Comparing women only colleges and co-educational colleges for educational effectiveness. *Research in Higher Education, 43*(4), 447–481.

Kinzie, J. K., Thomas, A. D, Palmer, M. M., Umbach, P. D., & Kuh, G. D. (2007). Women students at women's colleges: How do their experiences compare? *Journal of College Student Development, 48*(2), 145–165.

Love, B. J. (2004). Brown plus 50 counter storytelling: A critical race theory analysis of the Majoritarian

Achievement Gap Story. *Equality and Excellence, 37,* 227–246.

Luna, G., & Cullen, D. (1998). Do graduate students need mentoring? *College Student Journal, 32*(3), 322–330.

Lynn, M., & Adams, M. (2002). Introductory overview to the special issue—Critical race theory and education: Recent developments in the field. *Equality and Excellence, 35*(2), 87–92.

McEwen, M. K., Roper, L., Bryant, D., & Lang, M. (1990). Incorporating the development of African-American students into psychosocial theories of student development. *Journal of College Student Development, 31*(5), 429–436.

Miller-Bernal, L. (1993, November). Single-sex versus coeducational environments: A comparison of women students' experiences at four colleges. *American Journal of Education, 102,* 23–54.

Miller-Bernal, L. (2002). Conservative intent, liberating outcomes: The history of coordinate colleges for women. In A. Datnow & L. Hubbard (Eds.), *Gender in policy and practice: Perspectives on single-sex and coeducational schooling.* New York: Routledge.

Moreland, C., & Leach, M. (2001). The relationship between black racial identity and moral development. *Journal of Black Psychology, 27*(3), 255–271.

Munford, M. B. (1994). Relationship of gender, self-esteem, social class, and racial identity to depression in blacks. *Journal of Black Psychology, 20*(2), 157–174.

Neville, H. A., & Heppner, P. P. (1997). Relations among racial attitudes, perceived stressors, and coping styles among African American college students. *Journal of Counseling and Development, 75,* 303–311.

O'Conner, C. (2002, Winter). Black women beating the odds from one generation to the next: How changing dynamics of constraint and opportunity affect the process of educational resilience. *American Educational Research Journal, 39*(4), 855–903.

Pascarella, E. T., & Terenzini, P. T. (1980). Predicting freshman persistence and voluntary dropout decisions from a theoretical model. *Journal of Higher Education, 51*(1), 60–75.

Pascarella, E. T., Whitt, E. J., Edison, M. I., Nora, A., Hagedorn, L. S., Yeager, P. M., et al. (1997). Women's perceptions of a "chilly climate" and their cognitive outcomes during the first year of college. *Journal of College Student Development, 38*(2), 109–124.

Reinharz, S. (1992). *Feminist methods in social research.* New York: Oxford University Press.

Sadovnik, A. R., & Semel, S. F. (2002). The transition to coeducation at Wheaton College: Conscious coeducation and gender equity in higher education. In A. Datnow & L. Hubbard (Eds.), *Gender in policy and practice: Perspectives on single-sex and co-educational schooling.* New York: Routledge.

Sanford, N. (1966). *Self & society: Social change and individual development.* New York: Atherton Press.

Shorter-Gooden, K., & Washington, C. N. (1996). Young, black, and female: The challenge of weaving an identity. *Journal of Adolescence, 19*(5), 465–475.

Smith, A., & Stewart, A. (1983). Approaches to studying racism and sexism in black women's lives. *Journal of Social Issues, 39*(3), 1–15.

Smith, D. G. (1990). Women's colleges and coed colleges: Is there a difference for women? *Journal of Higher Education, 61(2),* 181–197.

Smith, D. G., Wolf, L. E., & Morrison, D. E. (1995). Paths to success: Factors related to the impact of women's colleges. *Journal of Higher Education, 66*(3), 245–266.

Solórzano, D. G. (1998). Critical race theory, race, and gender microaggressions, and the experience of Chicana and Chicano scholars. *Qualitative Studies in Education, 11*(1), 121–136.

Solórzano, D. G., & Yosso, T. J. (2002). Critical race methodology: Counter-storytelling as an analytic framework for education research. *Qualitative Inquiry, 8*(1), 23–44.

Stalker, J. (1996). Women and adult education: Rethinking andocentric research. *Adult Education Quarterly, 46*(2), 98–113.

Strauss, A. L., & Corbin, J. (1998). *Basics of qualitative research: Techniques and procedures for developing grounded theory* (2nd ed.). Thousand Oaks, CA: Sage.

Tatum, B. D. (1992). Talking about race, learning about racism: The application of racial identity development in the classroom. *Harvard Educational Review, 62*(1), 1–24.

Tidball, E. M. (1974). The search for talented women. *Change, 6*(4), 51–52.

Tidball, E. M. (1980). Women's colleges and women achievers revisited. *Signs, 5,* 692–712.

Tidball, E. M. (1985). Baccalaureate origins of entrants into American medical schools. *Journal of Higher Education, 56,* 385–402.

Tidball, E. M., & Kistiakowsky, V. (1976). Baccalaureate origins of American scientists and scholars. *Science, 193,* 646–652.

Vaccaro, A. (2005). *Self-investment and engagement of older women students: Uncovering connections to racial identity, gender, support, and motivation.* Unpublished doctoral dissertation, University of Denver, Colorado.

Villapando, O. (2003). Self-segregation or self-preservation? A critical race theory and Latina/o critical theory analysis of a study of Chicana/o college students. *International Journal of Qualitative Studies in Education, 16*(5), 619–646.

Walker, A. (1983). *In search of our mothers' gardens: Womanist prose.* San Diego, CA: Harcourt.

Whitt, E. J. (1994). I can be anything: Student leadership in three women's colleges. *Journal of College Student Development, 35*(3), 198–207.

Yair, G. (2000). Educational battlefields in America: The tug of war over students' engagement with instruction. *Sociology of Education, 73*, 247–269.

8

The Influence of Gender

A Conceptual Model From Women Doctoral Students in Computer Science

Jennifer Sader

Abstract: This chapter explores the ways that constructions of gender shaped the choices and expectations of women doctoral students in computer science. Women who engage in graduate work in computer science still operate in an environment where they are in the minority. Ten women from four different institutions of higher education were recruited to participate in this qualitative study. The goal was to examine what constructions of computer science and of gender—including participants' own understanding of what it meant to be a woman, as well as the messages they received from their environment—contributed to their success as graduate students in a field where women are still greatly outnumbered by men.

PARTICIPANTS VARIED in demographic characteristics such as age, race, and ethnicity. Still, there were many common threads in their experiences. For example, their construction of womanhood did not limit their career prospects to traditionally female jobs. Most had positive constructions of programming as something that was "fun," rewarding, and intellectually stimulating. The biggest obstacles for most were feelings of isolation and a resulting loss of confidence. The implications for practice are included, particularly the recommendation that institutions provide more support, including academic advising throughout the pipeline, for all of their students. The importance of women faculty in these students' success also suggests that schools that wish to counteract gender imbalances should more actively recruit women faculty to teach in male-dominated fields.

"It just 'clicked' for me," said one of the participants in this study about her first programming class. She loved it immediately. In the process of my interviews for this project, most of the women involved said that computer science was an engaging, creative, and rewarding field, though several said they found it uncomfortable to be the only woman in the room when they took upper-level computing classes.

The National Science Foundation (NSF, 2004) found that women "made up 74 percent of the graduate students in psychology, 54 percent in biological sciences, and 52 percent in social sciences" but represented only "20 percent of graduate students in engineering and 30 percent of graduate students in computer sciences in 2001" (p. 21). Graduate school seems to be a turning point where women leave academic computer science. Statistics from Damarin (1992) and the U.S. Department of Education (1994) showed that "although the proportion of women in the U.S. who take MAs in computer science is similar to the proportion taking BAs, females still account for only 10–14% of doctoral candidates in this field" (as cited in Woodfield, 2000, p. 5). It would follow, then, that a qualitative study of the experiences of doctoral students in computer science may be able to provide some insight about what experiences may contribute to this phenomenon. It can also suggest some ways that institutions of higher education could better recruit women to the sciences, through academic advising and other initiatives, and support them as they study their chosen field.

Women doctoral students in computer science still operate in an environment where they encounter few other women as faculty members or fellow graduate students. Similar to the Black women participants in Thandi Sulé's study (chapter 9), these women stood out as different in "institutions and departments that were unused to difference." As graduate students, most had already successfully navigated similar territory as undergraduate computer science students. The aim of this research was to study how constructions of gender—including participants' own understanding of what it means to be a woman and the messages they receive from their environment—shape the choices these women make and their career goals and expectations. The experiences of these participants suggest the various constructions of gender and computer science that contributed to their decisions to ac-

cept the challenges of studying in this kind of environment.

THEORETICAL FRAMEWORK

A key assumption of this study is that gender is socially constructed. Lincoln and Guba (1985), in their description of the naturalist paradigm, cited Schutz's (1967) description of reality as "rooted in the meanings that are constructed and attached to everyday life by individuals" (p. 77). There is no single objective meaning to being a man or a woman, but there are plenty of social meanings attached to gender, most of which are subconscious.

Johnson (2001) said that when we deal with a social construction of a category such as race or gender, "we forget the social process that created it and start treating it as 'real' in and of itself," making the construction all the more powerful because of its invisibility (p. 23). Valian (1999) used the term "gender schemas" to explain how even though we are not aware of it, "implicit ideas about men and women as a whole condition our reactions to men and women as individuals" (p. 3). These ideas shape our lives, including what we imagine as possibilities for ourselves, what our relationships are like, and what others expect of us.

In higher education in general, and the sciences in particular, the mythology of the academy as a meritocracy, combined with women's relative lack of success in reaching the upper levels of the academic hierarchy, has led some to believe that women lack drive, talent, or ability. This is reflected in former Harvard President Summers's (2005) notorious speculation that "in the special case of science and engineering, there are issues of intrinsic aptitude, and particularly of the variability of aptitude, and these considerations are reinforced by what are in fact lesser factors involving socialization and continuing discrimination" (p. 4). Many of these assumptions about differences in abilities between men and women are unchallenged beliefs that have little basis in fact.

For example, Zuckerman (2000/2001) found that "To the extent that [ability or competence] can be measured by intelligence tests or academic performance, abilities of women scientists equal or surpass those of men" (p. 70). Hyde, Fennema, and Lamon (1990) debunked the widely held belief that men outperform women in math. They found "the gender difference was close to zero (favoring females slightly) for general samples; a larger gender difference favoring males was found for each successive level of selection for higher ability," but they speculated that this was because lower skilled men were less likely to pursue higher education (p. 148).

Other researchers focused on stylistic differences between men and women. Cuny and Aspray (2001) suggested that women "are often less aggressive than male students in promoting themselves, attempting new or challenging activities, and pursuing awards and fellowships" (p. 2). Margolis and Fisher (2003) stated that many of the women in their study were intimidated by the single-mindedness of men in their computer science programs. "I'm just not like that at all," one informant told them, "I don't dream in code like they do" (p. 5). Whether any such differences in style are a result of natural tendency, socialization, or the result of women's experiences in science is difficult to untangle.

Some researchers suggested that the desire for a family may discourage women from considering a science major. Xie and Shauman (2003) speculated that because of a perceived conflict between family life and a science or engineering career, women may be less likely to choose to study these fields. Women may have different priorities or may expect to shoulder a heavier load at home in addition to their career responsibilities. Pattatucci (1998) disagreed with the assessment that women scientists with families necessarily left because of conflicts with family, "although this has sometimes been expressed as an afterthought" (p. 6). Instead, she said, women left the field "because they had finally reached their level of tolerance for what I call the *extra stuff*" (p. 6). "Extra stuff" reflects her assertion that science, including computer science, is not attractive to women because women within the field are not treated fairly, or because the culture is not friendly to women.

Feminist theory gives us an alternate way of looking at these issues using the lens of social expectations associated with gender. In her introduction to *The Second Sex* (1949/2003), de Beauvoir introduced the idea of the second sex when she wrote that the invisibility of men's gender sets women up as not only inferior to men but also defined by inferiority. "Man represents both the positive and the neutral, as is indicated by the common use of *man* to designate human beings in general; whereas, woman represents only the negative, defined by limiting criteria, without reciprocity" (p. 33). In higher education, as in other arenas, "women are everywhere within civilization the second sex, but everywhere differently so" (Mitchell [1975], quoted in Thornham, 2000, p. 75). Because of the "maleness" of gender neutrality, attempts at gender-blindness may contribute to continuing inequality between the sexes. To reach out to women might take multiple targeted efforts.

Bias can happen even without a conscious attempt to exclude women because of an unconscious tendency to underestimate women's accomplishments and abilities. Kolodny (2000) wrote that "even in our supposedly most 'advanced' societies, women's capacities are still judged as somehow inherently inferior to the capacities of men; and women's work, however necessary or innovative, is assessed as less valuable than men's work" (p. 133). Woodfield (2000) found in her study of a software company that "no woman was described as ever having sufficient 'flair' or as demonstrating the right kind of 'style' for really fitting in." Even women that men in the company singled out as exceptionally gifted could not meet "the additional tacit criterion of actually being male" (p. 161). The influence of these intangibles is subtle and often unconscious, but powerful.

METHODS OF INQUIRY AND
SOURCES OF DATA

In search of a better understanding of how doctoral students in computer science construct gender, I conducted face-to-face interviews with 10 women students selected from four schools with varying structures and missions. All 10 participants were enrolled in doctoral programs in computer science at the time of the first interview. Three of these participants were in a Direct PhD program and had not yet earned a separate master's degree. Because of the small number of women in computer science graduate programs, I have used pseudonyms for both the participants and their schools to help maintain confidentiality.

The participants ranged in age from their early 20s to their late 50s and included two students from Asia, two who had been born in the Caribbean and came to the United States at an early age, and six American students. Two participants were Asian, three were Black, and five were White. Participants were at various points in the degree process, from their first semester of graduate school to late in the dissertation stage. Two students were attending school part time while working full time. The rest were full-time students.

An interview protocol was used to give structure to the interview. This interview protocol was piloted with a volunteer who had studied in the sciences as an undergraduate. Her responses helped me refine the protocol and anticipate what kinds of probing questions might be required for follow-up.

Interviews lasted approximately 60–90 minutes and focused on participants' experiences as women doctoral students in computer science. All interviews were digitally recorded. Conducting the interviews in person also allowed for participant observation to be used as another source for information. These observations included descriptions of the physical characteristics of the participant, the campuses under study, and the surroundings for the interview. These descriptions were recorded in my research log after each interview to provide additional contextual information. I also recorded my impressions of what major themes seemed to emerge from the interview.

I transcribed each interview personally and sent transcripts to participants by e-mail to verify accuracy and to clarify their meanings where necessary. For some of the participants, I conducted follow-up interviews and exchanged additional e-mails to check details or sharpen the focus on their experiences.

Coding was used to reduce the collected data into manageable sets. NVivo, a qualitative research software package, was used to aid in coding the data collected. This data coding was an iterative process. Once all the data were coded, a data model emerged that helped to suggest the themes that were most important to the participants' experiences.

The primary measure of credibility was the study participants' approval and confirmation of the results, a process known as "member checking" (Lincoln & Guba, 1985; Patton, 2002). During the interview, I made every attempt to verify that I correctly understood that participant's meaning. I also provided transcripts of the interview to each research participant to allow her to check for accuracy and delete any material she did not want included in the study results. I created an online community to share my preliminary findings with the participants. Although I received only a few comments on the items I posted there, the comments I did receive helped me guide my further analysis. I sent each participant her profile and refined the profiles according to their responses. Once I had completed drafts of the results, findings, and conclusion sections, those were also sent to the participants for review. I received only a few responses, but they were thoughtful. The final product reflects this input.

Peer debriefing, described by Lincoln and Guba (1985) as a process by which the researcher's "biases are probed, meanings explored, the basis for interpretations clarified" by a peer who is not involved in the study, was also used in the data analysis (p. 308). This helped to ensure that I had not unduly imposed my own preconceptions and values on the participants' words. Two of my colleagues in the higher education administration program served as peer debriefers and their contributions during these sessions were valuable to my evolving constructions and final text.

Triangulation (Lincoln & Guba, 1985) requires that the information gathered "be verified by at least one other source (for example a second interview) and/or a second method (for example, an observation in addition to an interview)" (p. 283). Themes were created only around those ideas that fit this criterion. Sharing my preliminary findings with computer science faculty and students at two regional conferences also helped to verify the trustworthiness of my themes. I conducted a "Birds of a Feather" discussion session at one of these conferences and, though most of the participants were undergraduates, their comments also helped to provide confirmation of some of the themes that emerged from interview data.

I maintained a research log to provide an audit trail of the research process and the decisions made over the course of the study (Ely, 1991; Lincoln & Guba, 1985). It also helped to provide raw material for the final text. Documents and related materials collected during the study, including transcripts, tapes, and personal observations, were maintained in this log. This served both as a record of the decisions made during the research process and helped me in analysis and reflection as I was working through the data.

FINDINGS AND ANALYSIS

Within the framework of the theory of gender constructions, the participants' constructions of what it meant to be a computer scientist, and their constructions of what it meant to be a woman, must fit together. If a participant held constructions of her gender and computer science that were mutually exclusive, then she would not have been likely to choose this field; the constructions have to fit together.

The participants I interviewed seemed to have gender constructions for women, or at least for themselves, that were less restrictive than traditional gender roles and norms. They have also defined computer science in ways that are compatible with their views of themselves. When asked to define a successful computer scientist and then to describe themselves, most said they were close to their definition and were working to bring themselves closer. These constructions of themselves and the field seemed to grow from similar experiences and environments. The data model described now highlights these common elements.

A Conceptual Model of the Experiences of Women Graduate Students in Computer Science

The following model is intended to give an overview of the essential elements of the participants' experiences. Although each of the participants was obviously an individual, there were common experiences that give a sense of what inspired the first "click" of interest, and what sustained these women as they studied in a field where women are still in the minority.

Family influences are the root. Family influences seemed to be critical in shaping the expectations and aspirations of these women. One important thing that a family could contribute was a sense of possibility and a freedom from confining gender roles. Most of these participants were encouraged by their families to pursue education and were taught that women could do anything they wanted to do. More specifically, most participants were not limited to imagining typically "female" careers or expected to fulfill only a domestic role as wife and mother. The participants' mothers may have been stay-at-home moms or may have worked outside the home. In all cases, they valued education. Most encouraged their daughters to think about careers from an early age. Family expectations and values helped shape participants' career goals. Family members also provided role models and support, both financial and emotional. Family circumstances such as health crises, divorce, and financial pressures affected some participants' choices.

Family influences and gender constructions. Seven of the participants said their parents and other family members gave them the message that gender did not limit their possible career choices. As Becky said, "Maybe it's just my background or even how I was brought up by my parents, as far as being told that I could do whatever, and it didn't matter whether I was male or female." The participants had the freedom to consider all possibilities and explore all their interests.

Camille, Ginger, Olivia, Ishvani, and Linn all reported that at least some members of their family were "chauvinistic" or "gave priorities to the guys instead of the girls." In Camille's case, her father, even though he was a "chauvinist," raised his daughters to be independent and strong. "I kind of grew up thinking that I could do and be anything that I wanted to, in one sense, and then thought that I had a role that I had to play in another sense." Other than Camille, the participants who talked about male chauvinism were born outside the United States and some saw these messages simply as a function of their parents' culture. The participants rejected sexist ideas when they were countered by other examples and experiences. Ginger said that her father told her he would never vote for a woman prime minister. "As I grew up, I kind of realized that he's just a representative of the culture that he's from, and there is all that ignorance there." Olivia said that even though her family talked about traditional gender roles, "my family is, just a lot of strong women."

A focus on education. All the participants' families valued education for their daughters. The participants were pushed to focus on academic success from an early age and this prepared them for the challenges of graduate school. Linn said that her family left her mostly on her own and school was her primary focus. Adelaide, whose mother did not work outside the home, said, "Homework always came first, no matter what." Becky's parents were both professors and she described, "It had always kind of been assumed that I would go on for graduate school." Ishvani's very traditional family believed that she should get an education, even if it was just considered something to keep her busy until marriage. This education gave her a good start toward her future career.

Financial motivation. Although most of the participants enjoyed computer science for its own sake, a few said that family influences led them to consider the potential salary when making career decisions. This was one of the things that helped push them toward a technology career. When Camille's father "didn't want to pay any more money" for her schooling, she got her first job at a telecommunications company that trained her as a programmer and opened up a high-paying career. Susan's father, who supported her through most of her schooling, was not willing to pay for a master's degree in social work because "you get paid peanuts," so Susan decided to study computer science. Olivia relayed that part of the reason she was interested in computing was to be able to contribute to her family's income. Valerie's mother suggested that she consider earning potential when planning her career; "What are you going to be able to do that you'll be able to have some secure job where you can support yourself?"

Even if participants were initially interested in computer science because it seemed to be a lucrative field, their motivations could change. Ishvani originally just wanted a job when she started working in computing in Australia.

Although she already had some interest in computers, the chance to work in a technical field was also a good financial opportunity for her. When she started working on her doctorate she said, "I hadn't planned a lot on how I was going to use my qualification." She was studying to help her through grieving her husband's death and chose to study computer science because she had experience in that field and it interested her.

Creating and Sustaining Factors

Family influences were important in shaping participants' expectations for their careers and shaping them into women who knew that they could succeed. For them to choose to enter the field of computer science, participants also had to have experiences that promoted an interest in technology. Once they made the choice to study computer science, there were also common experiences that helped sustain their interest and provided support as they continued their studies.

The first "click" of interest. When Valerie described programming as something that "clicked" for her, she said it was because it immediately made sense and seemed to fit the way she thought. What made this initial click of interest turn into a career for her and for the other women in this study?

Participants had their interest sparked during a required general education course, work experience, or through the influence of someone they admire. Early experience with computers helped, the earlier the better. Another part of the click seems to be an analytical mind and an interest in problem-solving. Programming is a problem-solving tool, and these participants saw what computing could do. For example, Ishvani was interested in computing because her friend and her father were in technical fields and she looked up to them. As an adult, she got a chance to pursue computer science education through a Technical Jobs for Women program.

Olivia was in a technical track already but then switched to computer science as a major because she was struggling in electrical engineering and because a woman faculty member at her on-campus job suggested that she take a computer science course and see if she liked it. There was a required computer science course for her major anyway, and she found that it was "a perfect match." Hazel had been "programming since she was ten" and then took a computer course as part of her undergraduate education. She did not switch majors at that time, because "they made you take random engineering courses," but the interest was there.

Chance. Once they became interested in computing, chance seemed to play a role in some participants' career choices. Adelaide said that when she was starting out as an undergraduate, she decided to take a computer science class instead of a chemistry course because she was put off by the students who administered the chemistry placement exam and because "the books were cheaper for computer science." She already had an interest in both subjects, but chance tipped the balance and started her off on a career path in computer science. When applying for graduate programs, Becky was interested in both biology and computer science but opted for computer science partially because she was a "nervous test-taker," and "the exams to get in for computer science were usually less hectic than the biology ones."

Ginger had initially ruled out Rosary University because she thought the program there focused on older programming languages such as COBOL but happened to run into a woman on the train reading a Java textbook and struck up a conversation. "She said she went to Rosary. I thought, Rosary? She's learning Java at Rosary? Well, maybe they've done some different things . . . that's when I decided to maybe give them another try."

Early academic success. All of the women in this group were academically successful, but several of them specifically mentioned their earlier academic success. They seem to draw confidence from these earlier successes, especially Olivia, who said she was determined to do well as an undergraduate even when she found school to be tougher than she expected. "Everybody thought I was so smart, there was no way I was going to let them down."

Valerie was in a similar situation, struggling with her early experiences in graduate school but able to reflect on the undergraduate professors who suggested she apply to top graduate programs, "I suppose because they thought I had the potential to do something great at a big name university." When Camille's GRE scores proved to be an obstacle to getting into a PhD program, she knew that if she did some work at the school, she could get in. She was confident that once the faculty members got to know her, they would be impressed with her abilities. "I'm going to meet faculty. I'm going to show them that I can do this, regardless of my test scores." She performed well in her master's program, graduating with distinction and winning two scholarships for her doctoral program.

Peer support. Participants reported seeking out and benefiting from peer support. Some participants naturally gravitated toward seeking support from women, but some were comfortable seeking support from other women and men in the program. Linn said that the upper-class men who shared an office with her helped her out a lot, even though they teased her that having a woman around meant they had to be more careful with their jokes around the office. Camille had found a group of several women that she worked with closely and speculated that women might be more likely to seek out peer support than men. "I need that support group. I don't know if men do or don't need—but I think they do." Without her support network, Camille said, "it could be lonely and it could be discouraging, because there are a lot of men out there and not a lot of women."

Valerie said that working with another woman in her program helped in navigating an otherwise large and anonymous graduate school experience. "You have all these things to do and you're kind of left on your own to figure things out. . . . Especially lately, in the last couple of weeks, we realized, if we're going to make it through here, we need to stick together and help each other out."

Feeling comfortable with themselves. Several participants said that an important part of their success was being comfortable with themselves. It seems only logical that women would be better equipped for success in the computer science field if they were secure in themselves and were not trying to fit into someone else's idea of who they should be. This includes comfort with nontraditional gender roles but also extends to a general sense of confidence and competency. Most described themselves as independent and comfortable being different from other people around them.

Students who were newer to graduate study were more likely to mention anxiety, self-doubt, and fear that they did not fit in with the other students in their program. They still said that they wanted to be more confident, and knew that they were being too hard on themselves. Camille, Adelaide, and Olivia were all further along in their graduate programs and said they have made peace with who they were over the years and had become more comfortable with themselves. It could be that successfully navigating a difficult field gave them that confidence, or it could be that those without it would be more likely to leave graduate school and/or the field of computer science.

Fitting together relationships and computer science. Three participants, Hazel, Ginger, and Olivia, were married when the interviews were conducted. Two, Adelaide and Linn, mentioned serious dating relationships. All said that their partners were supportive of their career aspirations. Ginger said that her husband is "open to letting me do whatever I want to do," especially since she takes care of the household expenses. Olivia said her husband was supportive and joked that she was getting her doctorate just so she would have the upper hand in arguments. Olivia did seem to feel some obligation to fulfill certain expectations but suggested that the pressure came from her and her family and not from her husband. "I do think, I feel, I'm the wife. So I should do some things." Hazel wrote, in a follow-up e-mail exchange, that her husband was in the military, and she did not get to see him much because he was stationed in another state. She said that because he is a computer programmer, she sometimes talks about her work with him, "but it's a lot more common for him to talk problems through with me." Ishvani was widowed, but she said her husband had helped her and encouraged her when she was starting a technical career. "We always had pretty much of an equal relationship, so that was OK."

Several participants mentioned motherhood, whether or not they were mothers, as a factor that they considered when making career plans. Some, like Becky, said that they saw a family as optional. Women like her, she said, wanted to have an intellectually challenging career and then "maybe later on we decide to do the family thing." Valerie said that she was more attracted to the idea of working at a small college because her professors were able to have families and successful careers.

In only a very few cases did I ask the women whether they had children. The fact that childless women, and even unmarried childless women, had considered the demands of parenting when making their career goals underscores an important difference in the upbringing of men and women. Women are encouraged to think of themselves as wives and mothers first, not only in a traditional culture like Ishvani's but also here in the United States. Women like Valerie are encouraged to consider careers that have flexibility and security, criteria more suitable for women with families who still bear the majority of the

housekeeping and childrearing responsibilities at home.

Smaller undergraduate institutions. Several of the participants in this study attended smaller colleges and universities and a couple suggested that their experiences there were part of what helped create or sustain their interest in computer science. Adelaide went to a small school where two of the three computer science faculty members were women. She got an early teaching experience as an undergraduate because her school did not have a master's or PhD program from which to draw teaching assistants. She also said that attending a program where most of the instructors were women meant that "there was no question whether or not you could be successful as a woman." Linn said that even though she was shy and did not speak a lot of English when she first got to her selective women's college, "all the professors knew me because of the small-sized classes." Most of her classes had fewer than 10 students in them. Valerie also suggested that the small size of her undergraduate program was important, and her relationship with her advisor there, who was also the department chair, was critical in shaping her career aspirations.

Teaching experience. Several participants had already done some teaching as adjuncts and many of the rest had teaching assistantships. Many of the participants had taught or co-taught courses. They seemed to find the experience empowering, and for many, teaching experiences helped shape their career aspirations.

Linn was in her first year of graduate school when she participated in this study, and she said it was sometimes hard to balance her teaching responsibilities with her classes. She enjoyed the helping aspect of teaching. "I like explaining stuff to students, and if they don't understand, they come and ask me and I explain it to them, and I have satisfaction, and I think that's good." Valerie echoed the idea of getting satisfaction from helping students. "I love teaching, because you can see the results. You can see how you help people." Olivia said that she liked having an opportunity to help make a difference for women and minorities "just by doing something I enjoy, just by sharing the knowledge I have, just by being there."

Teaching experiences seemed to help reinforce and strengthen participants' commitment to computer science. Adelaide found that there were a lot of opportunities for teaching as a computer science student. "I did some lab assisting and teaching assisting all throughout my undergraduate [years], and then by the time I got to graduate school I got to run my own class. All because I got into computer science." It was easy to tell that teaching was one of the primary things that motivated her. Her face lit up every time she talked about being in the classroom. "I love it." Valerie's dream of being a professor helped maintain her determination at school when things got tough. "That's really been the one thing I'm holding onto as things have gotten a little shaky. I want to be a professor. So I'm still here and I'm trying to stick things out."

Faculty (especially women faculty). Like Valerie, most participants said that faculty members served as important role models and mentors when they were making their career decisions. Although the National Science Foundation (2004) found that women are only a small minority of computer science professors, almost all the participants named a woman computer science faculty member as someone who had helped or encouraged her. One woman faculty member in particular was the advisor to one participant, had encouraged a second to change her major to computer science from electrical engineering, and was mentioned as a role model by a third participant; every one of the participants who had come into contact with her had been influenced or touched by her in some way. The few women who are faculty in this field are having a disproportionately powerful influence on women students.

Role models were important to most of these women. Seeing someone with whom they could identify, often a woman, pursuing computing as a career and seeming to enjoy it made a big difference. It seemed especially important to Ginger that she saw women being treated as leaders in the field, possibly because she also aspired to be a leader. "These aren't just women that are sort of relegated to the back."

Becky and Ishvani both mentioned that they felt more comfortable approaching their advisors, who were women faculty members, than they would have been about approaching a man. Ishvani said, "I think it comes from my side. I guess I'm much more comfortable having female advisors." Valerie, who had not yet chosen an advisor, suggested that she might give preference to women when making her selection.

Love of the field. It is hard to overstate the importance of a love for the field, which several participants cited as an important characteristic of a successful computer scientist. The women who were feeling less sure of their love for the field were also feeling most unsure about their chances for success. These feelings of doubt may just be a temporary response to the stresses of graduate school. Their interest could always be sparked again by a new idea or project. If a student truly loses interest in computer science, she is going to find it more difficult to overcome obstacles and challenges that could put her at risk of leaving the graduate programs and the field. "If I didn't love it, I wouldn't be here," says Becky. Love of the field, and the related attitude that computing is "fun," can help sustain women in the field even as they encounter challenges or feelings of isolation. Loving the field makes it worth it to swim against the current and be the only woman in the class and one of the few in the field.

Obstacles and Challenges

Participants encountered similar obstacles and challenges on their path to becoming computer scientists. Depending on the quality of support and other sustaining factors in their lives, these obstacles could be minor problems for them or could be major setbacks that could challenge their commitment to the field or their confidence that they could succeed.

Graduate admissions. One of these challenges was the graduate admissions process. Although the conventional wisdom is that graduate programs are competing to lure the few interested women applicants, the experiences of this group of academically successful women suggests otherwise. Just getting into graduate school was difficult for many of the participants. Some applied to only two or three schools. A few were rejected on their first try and did some coursework at the school they wanted to attend to introduce themselves to faculty and prove they could handle the work. A couple said the reason they chose their graduate school was because it was the only place where they were offered funding. One student wanted to go to a master's program to explore computing as a field, but the only school that accepted her with funding accepted her on the condition that she enter the Direct PhD program.

It was striking that so many of the women had trouble with graduate admissions. This could suggest that they were not getting good advice about how many applications they should submit or what schools they should target. It could also be an example of admissions committee members consciously or subconsciously choosing people like themselves. This may be a bigger influence in programs where graduate admission is a "matchmaking" process in which faculty members choose students with whom they would like to work. It was interesting that so many of the participants mentioned having women advisors, when women are such a minority of graduate computer science faculty. Women may be more likely than men to choose to work with women students.

Advisor issues. In the programs these women attended, where the student's dissertation project is often determined more by their advisor's research agenda than by their own, choosing an advisor is probably the most important decision that a graduate student makes. Changing advisors because of personality conflicts or because of a change of direction in research interests means slower progress through the program. In this study, 3 out of 10 participants had changed advisors and each said that doing so meant at least an extra year of work. Sometimes this process was painful and involved hurt feelings on both sides. One participant seriously considered changing schools in the aftermath of an advisor change, which would have undoubtedly meant even more of a delay.

Participants who had not yet chosen their advisors were understandably nervous about the process. Linn said she wanted to make the right choice because "I have to work with him or her for another five or six years." Valerie was feeling anxious about looking for an advisor when we spoke. "How do I get to know these people and find out what they're like before I commit to doing a project with somebody?" She felt that being in the Direct PhD program put her under pressure to commit to a project when she would rather be exploring the field of computer science as a master's student.

Losing confidence. Graduate school can be challenging even for students who have always been academically successful. Adelaide said that teaching on her own for the first time terrified her and she seriously thought about turning down her assistantship because the idea of teaching scared her. Other participants said that they worried that they would not make it through their coursework. Linn said, "I'm afraid that if I don't pass the qualifying exam, I'll get kicked out of school. You have two chances. But there are people who got kicked out, so I'm really nervous about it." Valerie said that feeling lost and not knowing how to navigate the program made her wonder if she was motivated enough to make it through a doctoral program. The newer a participant was to graduate school, the more likely she seemed to worry that she was not smart enough or determined enough to make it through.

"I don't spend my free time programming!" Some participants in this study reported doubts about themselves or the computer science field because, as Linn said, "even though I claim I like computers and I like programming, I don't think I want to do it 24 hours [a day]." Linn preferred to spend her free time playing video games, shopping, or cooking. This made her anxious about her choice of field. She said, "The guys are all into it so much that sometimes I'm scared. If I don't like it that much, will I be able to make it?" Valerie said she had the same doubts, but had worked through them.

> I had a little revelation, you might call it, which is pretty obvious, but it hadn't crossed my mind. If you go to some accounting major, do you think they do accounting in their free time? I realized this all of a sudden. You know what? There's nothing wrong with that. There's nothing saying that I'm any less of a computer science major because I don't spend my free time programming! And that just made me feel so much better once I realized that.

This revelation helped her to see that it did not mean that she was not devoted to her field if she chose to pursue other interests. She said that she preferred to read a novel or reconnect with her first love, music.

Ginger explained that she was initially turned off from computer science because it seemed computer science majors at her undergraduate institution "lived in the computer lab" and were "so intensely into [computers] and seemingly interested in absolutely nothing else." She said that one of the reasons she chose the doctoral program at Rosary was because it was friendly to part-time students and, as a married woman with a job and a love of travel, this appealed to her. "This program takes five years even as a full-time student. I

just was not keen on putting everything on hold for five years until it was over."

Olivia said that the nerdy image of computer science did not bother her because she had always been sort of brainy.

> When I first got started in it, people who were in computer science weren't very social. I know, that sounds like a bad thing. But, I was kind of, being a bookworm, you were kind of to yourself. Nerds have nerdy friends, right? So we weren't big on the social skills, but this was something that we could do, this was something that I enjoyed.

Adelaide and Hazel also indicated that they did not mind, and even embraced, computer science's image as a "geeky" field.

Hopes and Dreams

Participants' hopes and dreams often helped sustain them in the face of obstacles they encountered, but they seem to be more than just another sustaining factor. Hopes and dreams tell us what these participants wanted to become, both as computer scientists and as women. When participants talked about future plans, they talked about more than what jobs they wanted to hold. They talked about the things that they wanted to accomplish with their careers *and* with their lives. These hopes and dreams seemed to be grounded in their constructions of computer science; they saw careers in computer science as a way to achieve the things they wanted for themselves, not just for their careers. Participants wanted to engage in activities that were intellectually challenging. Most participants also said that they wanted to have a chance to help others. Finally, they also wanted a balanced life.

Intellectual challenges. Most of the participants said that they found computer science, and especially programming, to be "fun." Participants said they enjoyed mental challenges, from debugging a program to solving crossword puzzles. They wanted careers that would be mentally stimulating and let them put their analytical skills to good use. Becky said, "I definitely like solving problems. I definitely like figuring out what's wrong, in certain cases, just, there's that challenge aspect." Ishvani looked forward to a career in computing because she would always be learning. "Technology fascinates me, especially electronics. It's been changing all the time, so it's a challenge to keep ahead of it." Most participants said that what made computer science so exciting was the fact that computer science is such a challenge and would continue to challenge them throughout their careers.

Making a difference in the world. When asked what she saw when she thought about a happy or satisfied woman, Valerie said that women feel rewarded when they have the ability to help people. During the member checking process, Hazel read this comment and rejected the idea that women had an inherent need to help others in order to feel fulfilled. She said that her family's values, and not her gender, were the biggest influence on her goals and expectations. She said, "I'm getting the very subtle impression that we are attempting to justify or excuse or explain or motivate our career choices within the stereotypically feminine framework." It is possible, and probably more accurate, to frame these women's career goals as a desire to make a difference in the world through their lives and work.

Most participants did seem to want to make a difference in the world. Some wanted to serve as role models and mentors, like Camille and Olivia. Others looked forward to the rewards of teaching and sharing their knowledge, like Valerie and Adelaide. Ginger saw research and technology development as another way to make an impact.

> I think what I want to do is focus on those areas that help people who are in the greatest need, where there's a lot at stake, to use technology as a partner to create tools that they can actually use, either to make important decisions or do better things with their lives.

"Not only was computer science challenging, it was practical and you could see the results right away," Hazel said. "Whereas if I was in physics, maybe I would get something that worked, but mostly I'd probably be studying for the rest of my life before I made any real impact on the world."

Work-life balance. Most participants said that they wanted a balanced, well-rounded life, whether or not they wanted to have children and a family. Camille left a high-powered career as a manager to pursue an academic career, a move that was a conscious choice to put her quality of life over salary concerns. Participants wanted a challenging career, but they also wanted to have time for family and leisure. Linn wanted to emulate her undergraduate advisor, who taught during the school year and spent his summers traveling. A career in academia, or at least one at a small four-year college, was perceived as a career where there was an opportunity to have a fulfilling personal and home life. Valerie saw that her professors were able to have the flexibility to spend time with their families and pursue other interests, and that made the career more attractive to her. Ginger, who had many ambitious career plans, said, "I do, very much, want to have a balanced life."

The participants were an impressive group of women—bright, ambitious, and enthusiastic about their field. It was encouraging to see these women succeeding and thriving in graduate programs in computer science. Although they faced some challenges, most, especially those who had been in their graduate programs the longest, found their graduate school experiences generally positive and rewarding.

IMPLICATIONS FOR PRACTICE

Examples of outright sexism in graduate programs were rare. Only a few of the participants had encountered individual faculty members who seemed hostile to the women and/or minorities in their classes. More common were "microinequities," small slights or subtle differences in treatment that can create a "chilly climate" for women (Hall & Sandler, 1982; Rowe, 1990). For example, one of the participants in Thandi Sulé's study (chapter 9), Nia, said that she felt like her race was like a scar on her face that everyone saw, but no one would talk about. It affected her interaction with people even though they never mentioned it. Similarly, Camille, one of the participants in this research study, said that although no one said anything explicitly, "as soon as they see me, they question whether I 'have it' in order to be a PhD student or not. But like I said, I don't know if that's the woman part or the minority part." She seemed to take constantly proving herself as a challenge. Some of the same participants who said that gender did not seem to be important to their experiences also talked about confronting the expectation that women did not belong in science. And, while there are undeniably sociopolitical and cultural differences between race, gender, and choosing the field of computer science, there are important intersections across multiple identities held simultaneously (e.g., race, gender, women in computer science) as well as important parallels that can be made between people with targeted identities. These messages can be discouraging if they are not negated by more positive messages.

For women in computer science, these microinequities can be compounded by a sense of isolation and a lack of peer support. Because women are such an extreme minority of most doctoral programs in computer science, they may see these incidents as a reflection of a lack of ability on their part and may not be able to compare their experiences with those of other women. If women already feel that faculty members or other students in their program question their competence, they may not want to ask questions about program requirements or about other issues with which they are struggling.

Some of the participants seemed to see themselves as different from other women and spent more time with men. This could be a survival strategy in a world where men generally do have some advantages. Women, like it or not, may internalize some of the messages that women are less respected than men. Rather than trying to reject gender roles outright, many successful women may see themselves as the exceptions to the rule, more independent and brave than other women.

The findings from this study suggest ways that computer science programs could better recruit and support women students. Overcoming the remaining barriers to women's full participation in computer science would give departments a richer, more varied talent pool from which to draw. The following are some suggestions for ways that schools can help.

Give Undergraduates the Big Picture

Providing undergraduates more exposure to and experience with research may help students see themselves as potential researchers. This may be provided through discussions with academic advisors, faculty, and peers. Discussions about current research with undergraduate students could show these students "the big picture" and give them a sense of a career in computer science. Participants who had already worked in industry or who had previous research experience were more interested in pursuing opportunities in research. But even in a teaching-focused environment, aspiring faculty members will be expected to do some research.

These participants' feelings about teaching show that experience can help students feel less intimidated by challenging activities. Participants were able to overcome their fears about teaching after gaining classroom experience. Similarly, earlier exposure could demystify the research process for students and help build their confidence. Faculty members who involve undergraduates in research and encourage them to attend local conferences could also help students see the "big picture" of computing. Students might not think to attend a conference unless computer science departments actively encourage them to attend. If undergraduate computer science majors and even interested nonmajors attended conferences and were exposed to faculty research projects, they may be more likely to aspire to be researchers themselves.

Recruit the Right Women

At one school I visited, I met a woman who worked in multicultural affairs and also worked with women. She said that, among other recruitment efforts, she was conducting programs that emphasized the more feminine aspects of technology. Two examples she mentioned were the technology of fashion and the technology of cosmetics. This kind of program may reach out to a different audience than the current group of computer scientists. However, the strategy could also backfire and make the program less attractive to women who "could [not] care less about that stuff," like many of the women I interviewed.

Women students may be more attracted to computing if promotional efforts emphasized the creative and problem-solving aspects of programming. Some participants were attracted to computing's connection to language and logic. Efforts to promote computing in this way might attract women with strong analytical skills who might otherwise major in English, math, or music. It may also be wise to recruit women who are interested in other sciences such as biology, in which computers are used for cutting-edge research.

If graduate programs in computer science are going to reach out to these groups, faculty on admissions committees and academic advisors would also need to be receptive to qualified students from all backgrounds. Departments should

consider their admissions policies carefully. If highly qualified and successful students would be excluded because of standardized test scores that do not provide a fair assessment of their abilities, admission committees should consider whether a strong emphasis on these exams serves the best interests of their programs.

Take Advantage of Chance

Several participants mentioned chance occurrences as an influence in their entry into computer science majors. Schools cannot plan for chance events to occur, but they can take advantage of them. Many participants said that their interest in computer science increased as they learned more about it. If low-level and general education courses are challenging and engaging, students may consider computer science as a major. Computer science department chairs might also consider publicizing the interesting research that their faculty members are doing or announcing interesting speakers and events to the campus at large. Departments should not ignore the importance of word-of-mouth recruitment or the power of undergraduate academic advising conversations to encourage women to consider the computer science pipeline.

Further, students who are excited about their studies could be an effective conduit for recruiting efforts. This should be added incentive for departments to provide support and encouragement to their graduate students.

Actively Recruit Women Faculty

The participants saw women faculty as especially good role models for their own careers. Women faculty members were also more likely to reach out to women students and take a special interest in mentoring them. Departments with few or no women faculty should realize that they will have a hard time recruiting and supporting women students in their program. This is not to say that men could not, and should not, be mentors and role models for women. Many of the participants, however, expressed a preference for women as advisors and found it easier to approach a woman for help. Departments that are serious about increasing the number of women students in their programs should actively recruit women faculty to their programs.

Facilitate Faculty-to-Student and Peer-to-Peer Support

Most students could name at least one or two faculty members who took a personal interest in them during their college or graduate school years. These faculty members served as important mentors and role models; they not only supported women in computer science, they showed what a successful computer scientist looked like. Creating opportunities for faculty and students to interact may help students meet role models and mentors they might not otherwise encounter.

Peer support was also critical to help students feel connected and supported. Many participants said that they found it difficult to connect with other students and their schools did not do enough to encourage collaboration among students. Especially when they are new to graduate school, students may appreciate it if departments facilitated opportunities for students to socialize and work together. Leaving it completely up to students to find peer support makes it more likely that women and other minority groups are left out. Computer science departments might consider partnering with other departments, the graduate college, and student affairs offices on their campus to develop appropriate programming and facilitate other support services for all their graduate students. As Racheal Stimpson and Kimberly Filer (chapter 5) suggested, though student affairs offices are usually focused on the needs of undergraduates, extending services to graduate students could play a valuable role in engagement and retention.

Share Information Through Official Channels

Relying on the "grapevine" to distribute information may leave computer science students, especially women and minorities, without the knowledge of processes and procedures necessary to successfully navigate graduate school. Departments could easily provide detailed information about program requirements, announcements of upcoming events and deadlines, and models of successful research projects available on their web pages. They could offer workshops and other informational sessions for their students to make sure they know where to find these resources. Student groups could also be encouraged to post the kinds of unofficial information that incoming students need on organization websites and discussion boards, such as where to find quiet places to study, how students connect with advisors, or how to study for comprehensive exams.

One university that created more official channels for information and socialization of doctoral students found that their students graduated "at a rate substantially higher than the national average" (Ali & Kohun, 2006, p. 32). Doctoral students who fail to complete their degrees represent a significant waste of resources to their departments. In light of this fact, why leave something so essential to student retention to chance? Providing official channels of communication would be a cost-effective way to protect departments' investment in their students.

CONCLUSION

There are many reasons for the continued underrepresentation of women in computer science, especially at higher levels of the academic hierarchy. The messages they receive from their environment shape the choices these women make and their career goals and expectations. By emphasizing gender constructions through a feminist theoretical framework, I do not mean to discount the other influences in this complex situation. I just want to focus on one important influence as a starting point.

The implications that emerged from the women in this study include giving undergraduates the full picture, recruiting the right women, taking advantage of chance, recruiting women faculty, facilitating faculty-to-student and peer-to-peer support, and sharing information through official channels. This starting point connects theory to practice and may be useful for faculty and student affairs practitioners as we further develop curricular programs and cocurricular efforts that support women students.

What we imagine for ourselves helps to determine our reality. Our constructions of ourselves are not something we assemble consciously like a model airplane. They are more organic and grow out of our experiences. Computer science departments that wish to encourage healthy development of their students can act more thoughtfully to provide the right conditions and support for that growth.

REFERENCES

Ali, A., & Kohun, F. (2006). Dealing with isolation feelings in IS doctoral programs. *International Journal of Doctoral Studies, 1,* 21–23.

Cuny, J., & Aspray, W. (2001). *Recruitment and retention of women graduate students in computer science and engineering: Report of a workshop June 20–21, 2000.* Washington, DC: Computing Research Association.

de Beauvoir, S. (2003). Introduction. In C. R. McCann & S. K. Kim (Eds.), *Feminist theory reader: Local and global perspectives* (pp. 32–40). New York: Routledge. (Reprinted from *The second sex,* pp. xv–xxxiv, H.M. Parshley, Trans., 1952, Random House, original work published 1949)

Ely, M. (1991). *Doing qualitative research: Circles within circles.* London, England: Falmer.

Hall, R. M., & Sandler, B. (1982). *The classroom climate: A chilly one for women?* Washington, DC: Project on the Education and Status of Women.

Hyde, J. S., Fennema, E., & Lamon, S. J. (1990). Gender differences in mathematics performance: A

meta-analysis. *Psychological Bulletin, 107*(2), 139–155.

Johnson, A. G. (2001). *Privilege, power, and difference.* Boston, MA: McGraw-Hill.

Kolodny, A. (2000). Women and higher education in the twenty-first century: Some feminist and global perspectives. *National Women's Studies Association Journal, 12*(2), 130–147.

Lincoln, Y. S., & Guba, E. G. (1985). *Naturalistic inquiry.* Newbury Park, CA: Sage.

Margolis, J., & Fisher, A. (2003). *Unlocking the clubhouse: Women in computing.* Cambridge, MA: MIT.

National Science Foundation, Division of Science Resources Statistics. (2004). *Women, minorities, and persons with disabilities in science and engineering* (NSF Publication no. 04-317). Arlington, VA: Author.

Pattatucci, A. M. (Ed.). (1998). *Women in science: Meeting career challenges.* Thousand Oaks, CA: Sage.

Patton, M. Q. (2002). *Qualitative research methods & evaluation methods* (3rd ed.). Thousand Oaks, CA: Sage.

Rowe, M. (1990). Barriers to equality: The power of subtle discrimination to maintain unequal opportunity. *Employee Responsibilities and Rights Journal, 3,* 153–163.

Summers, L. H. (2005, January 14). Remarks at NBER conference on diversifying the science and engineering workforce. Retrieved February 18, 2005, from http://www.president.harvard.edu/speeches/2005/nber.html

Thornham, S. (2000). *Feminist theory and cultural studies: Stories of unsettled relations.* New York: Oxford University.

Valian, V. (1999). *Why so slow? The advancement of women.* Cambridge, MA: Massachusetts Institute of Technology.

Woodfield, R. (2000). *Women, work, and computing.* Cambridge, MA: Cambridge University.

Xie, Y., & Shauman, K. (2003). *Women in science: Career processes and outcomes.* Cambridge, MA: Harvard University.

Zuckerman, H. (2001). The careers of men and women scientists: A review of current research. In M. Wyer, M. Barbercheck, D. Geisman, & M. Wayne (Eds.), *Women, science, and technology: A reader in feminist science studies* (pp. 69–78). New York: Routledge. (Reprinted from *The outer circle: Women in the scientific community,* pp. 27–56, H. Zuckerman, J. Cole, & J. Bruer, Eds., 2000, Washington, DC: National Academy)

NARRATIVES ON GENDER AND FEMINISM

The Story of One *YAO* Woman

Dorothy B. Nkhata

At a young age, I once overheard my aunt telling her friends that my own mother could not conceive soon after her marriage to my father, so they sought the help of an herbalist. That is how she started bearing children—eight of us. Her first baby was my sister, followed by three girls—*four* girls in total, no boy. This was not good enough, for she had to have a boy. It is still common for most couples in Malawi, Africa, to prefer boys to girls. If the first child is a girl, chances that a couple will want another child in the hope that it will be a boy are high. If the first child is a boy and the couple wants just one child, they may quit having babies. Therefore, when my mother could not conceive a boy, she was taken to another herbalist, again. Indeed, the next baby was a boy whom they named after my grandfather. After all the excitement, I was the next baby, another girl. I am not sure whether they went to a herbalist again, but the next child after me was my brother, after whom my mother had another girl that died soon after birth.

Although I did not ask my mother the truth of this matter, it has been the driving force all my life. I have many unanswered questions: Did my parents want me? Why did my parents allow their friend to name me? Since childhood, my life has been to prove that I am just as important as my brothers—maybe even smarter. I resolved to work harder to succeed academically. I have always wanted to attain the highest educational qualification. Majoring in physics was not out of interest, but I wanted to take on the most challenging degree on campus, to compete with boys.

Because I come from a country where gender is mainly male or female, I seek to broaden my views on gender. Nevertheless, I believe that everyone should be free. My battle

against sexism has been like many other married women, a silent one. I refused to succumb to the pressures of male-dominated society. The only way for me was to rise through higher education and maybe teach the next generation by example. In my life, I have come to understand the rationale behind many painful rituals *Yao* women and girls go through to enhance their sex life, to please men. Yao women, like other African women, have to bear children until they have a boy just to stay in a marriage, and where there are no modern conveniences (electricity, running water, and electric stove), women and girls suffer. When I see a girl, I want to say to her "work hard in school so you can come out of this maze."

Although I have respect for the rich *Yao* culture, I feel that certain customs are very oppressive to women and that they need to be challenged. As a married *Yao* (African) woman, I was inspired by other women. One inspiring woman was my physics professor's wife who was studying toward her master's degree. She said, "You can do it." Thus, I have continued learning from other women and from my own experience. This is only part of my story. In the next paragraphs, I present a transformational experience that made me change my attitude toward older, nontraditional students who enroll in colleges and made me reevaluate my career goals.

It was in July 1992 that I had to leave college because I was pregnant with my first child. During that time, you were either a "normal entry" or "mature entry" student depending on how you enrolled in college. The younger students, straight from secondary school, were considered "normal" whereas adult (and all returning) students were called "mature entry" students. I remember making fun of "mature entry" undergraduate students, thinking they were not smart enough to be in college. We used to call them "chuwa" (short for "mature entry students"). When I left college, I knew that I would have to come back as "chuwa" in order to get my degree. I struggled with the idea of going back to college as one of the mature entry students. What I feared most was the lack of accommodation for adult students. I could only pray that the normal entry students would be kind and respectful toward me, especially when it came to sharing a room. I hoped that the administrator would spare a room for me in the Kamuzu Hall, which had a few single rooms for graduate students.

When my daughter was born, I was still hesitant to go back to college. However, reflecting on earlier conversations with friends and the wife of one of my physics professors helped me realize that I needed to change my way of thinking. My husband challenged me to go back as soon as possible. He did not think that I was being fair with myself when I told him that I was anxious about going back because of the way that normal entry students thought about mature entry students. I then understood that going back to college was the only opportunity for me to contribute to the higher education system, to address some of the issues and hardships that adult students face in college. I had to go back to Chancellor College this time as a "mature entry" student who was still an undergraduate. It was a very humiliating experience, which taught me many valuable lessons about college life for adult students. I shared a room with a first-year

student for several months before I became eligible for a room in the prestigious Kamuzu Hall!

After college, I taught in high schools where I took great interest in female students who were older, helped them to maintain good grades, and encouraged them with my story. Eight years later, I started teaching at the Malawi College of Health Sciences where most of my students were at least 18 years old. A few that were older and married were not given any special attention. I felt empathetic toward one male student who had just married but his wife could not spend a night with him while in college. Because I believe that helping a woman means helping more than one person, I found work for his wife and helped this couple find an apartment in the same area. This proved to be a life-changing decision for this couple and it increased my joy of serving students. However, I realized that I needed to enroll in graduate school to gain the necessary skills in order to help improve the Malawian higher education system and make life better for nontraditional students.

I feel that I am still formulating a plan of action, which includes acquiring knowledge and skills on my transformative journey to development. I am glad that I made that brave choice to go back to college, because I have been able to help students in some smaller ways while working toward my long-term goals to improve the lives of nontraditional students in college. I look forward to serving older students in college.

Growing Up at Douglass

Jennifer Dudeck-Lenis

I always had high hopes for college, and I always had high hopes for myself. Having accompanied my older sister on a campus visit when I was in the eighth grade, I became excited about college at an early age and wished to fast-forward through my

high school years so that I could get to the "good stuff." To me, higher education represented the opportunity and freedom to explore all of the possibilities of the world and all of the possibilities of myself. As a high school student, I excelled academically, was very involved in cocurricular activities, and read books about positive thinking in my spare time, fascinated by the idea of human potential. In spite of my many successes in high school, I still struggled with confidence issues. It was not that I was unaware of my potential; rather, I was unaware of how to actualize it in the face of my internal struggles with self-esteem and personal identity. As I searched for a college during my junior and senior years in high school, I began to take a serious look at women's colleges, recognizing their excellent track record of graduating strong, confident women leaders—the type of woman whom I aspired to be in life.

My search led me to Douglass College of Rutgers, The State University of New Jersey. At first, I was accepted to a traditional private women's college that was too expensive for my family. I was a bit skeptical that the unique design of Douglass—a public women's college where women take most of their classes with men—would really provide me with the type of single-sex experience that I was seeking. I am happy to say that I was completely wrong and that Douglass surpassed my expectations of what a women's college could offer. Upon enrolling in Douglass, I eagerly took advantage of many opportunities that helped me explore my academic, personal, and professional potential. I enjoyed my *Shaping a Life* course, where I read about issues that impact women's lives and listened to accomplished women share their personal stories about their various roads to success. I also enrolled in honors seminars that helped me explore academic disciplines through the context of women's experiences. My learning expanded beyond the classroom into the realm of cocurricular involvement. I joined the Emerging Leaders program as a first-year student and became active on campus, eventually assuming Executive Board positions of the Red Pine Ambassador tour guide association within the Douglass Recruitment Office. I also participated in the Extern program, where I shadowed Douglass alumnae in their jobs and learned about opportunities available in the professional world.

At Douglass, women role models surrounded me. On a daily basis, I was inspired by the Douglass deans, staff, and most importantly, my fellow Douglass students. The supportive atmosphere of Douglass provided me with a safe space to explore and form my emerging adult identity and to grow in both my intellectual and leadership abilities. My involvement in the Red Pine Ambassador Executive Board was the most life-changing experience for me. Through Red Pine, I discovered new strengths that I had, developed a stronger self-concept, and slightly altered my career path. Although my original goal was to become an English professor, my work with Red Pine revealed to me that I truly enjoyed the more interpersonal and action-oriented nature of higher education administration.

After graduating from Douglass, I moved forward in my career by working at a few other institutions of higher education and completing my master's degree in College Student Personnel from the University of Maryland, College Park. I had always hoped to return to Douglass in a professional capacity, and about five years after graduating from Douglass, I had the opportunity to do so. I joined the staff of the Douglass Recruitment Office, which was the same office where I had worked as a Red Pine Ambassador. My growth was not limited to the professional realm. Within the time span of my first five years working at Douglass, I met my future husband, got engaged, married, gave birth to my first child, and bought my first home. I also assumed greater levels of responsibility within the Recruitment Office and in my former supervisor's words, returned from my maternity leave "at a whole new level." I am more confident professionally and personally, both because of and in spite of my efforts to balance a career with family life.

As an undergraduate and then as a young professional, I had always worried about how I would someday combine a rewarding career with a fulfilling family life, not wanting to sacrifice either. While Douglass had prepared me to be successful in whatever career I chose, the question of work/life balance had always lingered and had created great anxiety for me.

A refrigerator magnet that I bought while in graduate school provided me with some practical, though not specific, advice. It reads, "you have to live your questions, live your way to the answers"; this is what I have been doing for the past five years while working at Douglass.

Juggling all of the items on my personal and professional "to do" lists can be challenging at times and from this experience I have learned to set boundaries and prioritize. While I try to be as involved as possible in campus life, there are limits to my involvement, which is a good thing for both me and the students. By making time for my family and personal commitments, I am serving as a role model to women students, showing them that work/life balance is possible, though it is not easy. I know that someday the students themselves will face similar challenges and need to make their own difficult decisions, based not upon what others expect of them, but upon what they expect of and want for themselves. Society still sends women mixed messages, and I have learned that you need to know what you want, why it is important to you, and to make peace with yourself. Only then will you have the courage, confidence, and strength to live the life that you desire, not the life someone else wants you to live.

Intercultural Contexts When Traveling Abroad

Kristie Atkinson

Growing up in small-town Mississippi, I was exposed to an expectation that most women have to be prim and proper at all times. We were expected to always be "put together." My grandmother was, and still is, the best example of this today. She dressed in her nicest clothes when simply cleaning the house, and before she left the bathroom in the morning her hair was fixed and makeup applied. I have never seen my grandmother look just "thrown together." Not only did she manage to always be made up but she also managed to be hospitable and ready for every occasion. The home was cleaned to perfection, and a meal could be ready in minutes. The women in my family carry these characteristics with pride. It is a part of our southern heritage.

Growing up with my father, I never really had women in my life to enforce this expectation of what it means to be a successful woman. My father did not hold me to the traditional gender roles practiced by many southern women and, though I did not practice these traditional gender roles, my father still respected me. In my father's household, I was given the ability to choose which traditional roles I wanted to emulate as an adult. Others may see my southern heritage as a limitation, but I have never felt limited by my culture or my upbringing.

Once I moved to college, I certainly did not follow the norms of most of the women in my family, even though some of the cultural upbringing is still a part of who I am today. (I still have the table set perfectly for a guest to come over and the house must be clean!) In college, I was afforded the opportunity to become involved with international students. This involvement with international students on campus exposed me to a new world outside of the southern culture that I would later embrace. Through relationships with the students, I learned of new cultures and languages. College gave me the opportunity to explore life outside of the United States. It helped me acquire an infatuation with traveling and other cultures. This infatuation with travel and culture influenced my decision to move to Indonesia, which ultimately created a shift in what I would consider my normal gender role in the United States.

After the first several months of living in Indonesia, I realized that my rights as a woman had changed. My southern heritage did not affect me in a negative way, though my new role as a woman in Indonesia had many negative effects. I quickly learned after arriving in the country that as a single White female, traveling alone was seen as promiscuous. It is also probably one of the reasons I experienced so many challenges in my time there. Indonesians often trust the images portrayed by television, magazines, and movies to be exact portrayals of all Americans. This misperception dictates how many Indonesians respond to American women and men. Due to the conservative culture of many Indonesian cities, the images found in American media cause Indonesians to believe all Americans to be promiscuous, among other things. The friendly wave and smile that I learned to give people as a child from the South would now be considered an invitation for more than just a conversation. It did not take long for me to realize that if I wanted to stay clear of any type of harassment, it was best to look at my feet and ignore the comments made by men. Looking down at my feet became a part of everyday life until I would see a friendly face that knew me, and I knew it was safe to talk with her or him.

The harassment that I experienced is common to many Indonesian women. Women in Indonesia often may be dressed from head to toe, but that does not mean they will be protected against the verbal, physical, or sexual abuse. Women are often taught that if any form of abuse occurs it is their fault. Harassment and abuses are commonly swept under the rug to prevent further embarrassment, shame, or punishment. For some Indonesians, punishment entails being disowned by their families or beaten for bringing shame to the family. I would be wrong to say this happens to all women in Indonesia, because that is incorrect. There are many men in Indonesia that I worked alongside who took pride in taking care of the women in their lives. However, I believe that many women in

Indonesia suffer from these abuses. I cannot speak for every woman of Indonesia, but I can speak from my own experiences as a woman in Indonesia and what I witnessed.

The first phrases I learned from my language teacher besides *hello* or *how are you* were *don't touch me* and *that's not polite.* My learning of these phrases transpired from the frustrations I had while walking down the streets of my new home in Indonesia. I learned to use these words and many others during my two-year experience. When men would grab me or say something inappropriate, I would often look them in the eyes and ask if they would like it if someone said or did that to their mother, sister, or daughter. I wouldn't back down because I wanted to make sure they knew what they were doing was inappropriate. Often, while I was among a group of female friends, something might be said from a group of men. The women I was with might try to brush it off like nothing ever happened, but I was never able to let it go. Once relationships were built, I spent much of my time counseling many educated women, who blamed themselves for the abuse or believed they deserved the abuse. Speaking out against such things would only bring more shame to themselves than the shame incurred from the abuse itself.

These experiences have deeply affected my role in higher education. Verbal, physical, and sexual abuse is not unique to Indonesia but experienced by women all over the world. As an educator and student affairs professional, these experiences have made me more aware of how often abuse occurs. However, I also have to be sure not to assume that every international student has experienced such abuses. My own encounters with harassment have given me the courage to speak out and empower other women with similar life experiences and to consider the complexities of intercultural communication and context. It is important to educate women that they no longer have to be victims of abuse and that they have the right to say no. Regardless of culture, women need to understand they have the right to be treated decently and with respect. Women who have suffered abuses can empower other women to stop the cycle of abuse by sharing their stories, being supportive, and being there to listen. Hopefully, through my story, women will find courage and be empowered to speak out against abuse.

Inconsistency as Constant: One's Story of Reclaiming Gender

Robbie

My story of gender has been one of migration, change, evolution, and inconsistency . . . and now, only now, have I learned that this is actually a constant. Young in life, I'd always felt claustrophobic by the closed nature of binary gender boxes. I was comfortable, however, with not having to challenge or question my gender, because it was always assumed for me anyway. College was this awakening—ignorance is not bliss, but rather confinement.

Shaun was his name—the first transgender person I'd met, the first person I'd met who challenged gender construction at all, really. It was my sophomore year of college, and I did not know then how thankful I would be that he came into my life. It was the repetition of his story, his confidence in self, and his mere inner strength that had such a latent impact on me and is what stands out in my memory today.

I met Shaun at a time in my life when I could remember back to

- ◆ years of being the only female-bodied individual at a particular lunchroom table or playing kickball at recess
- ◆ years of not feeling authentic in skirts or dresses, make-up or jewelry
- ◆ years of changing nicknames—from Teddy, to Rob, to Robbie (all traditionally men's names)

My lived story was one of never fitting into the expectations of gender but never consciously questioning this fit. Shaun's story caused me to question if I was supposed to fit—for the first time.

Now, I write to you with a longer hirstory to share.[1] With seven additional years of reflection since meeting Shaun, I've come to realize that sometimes I do feel like I fit the mold and expectations of womanhood. And sometimes, I feel very much like I fit the mold and expectations of manhood. More often, I feel like I'm somewhere in between and outside of these two binary constructs, operating from a postgender self-identity in a gendered society and at a gendered university.

Where do these molds and expectations come from, anyway? What has shaped them and therefore had this influence on me and my perception of self? The only answers I can come up with are stereotypes, society, and generalizations, for what does it mean to feel like a woman or man, anyway, but to fit into these generalized societal understandings of womanhood and manhood? Trying to step away from these limiting conceptions, I find myself at a loss of how to imagine myself.

For some time, I tried to step out of a gendered world and was expectedly met with challenges. I claimed no gender identity but was referred to as woman. I claimed a preference of being pronounless but was referred to as she/her. At times, I was laughed at, people not realizing that this was not a phase and that this was indeed a valid way of considering oneself.

I was frustrated.

Frustration led me to reconsider (for better or for worse), wanting language to articulate to myself and others how I was feeling and who I was, both inside and out. Searching and seeking, I discovered gender-neutral pronouns: ze/hir. Searching and seeking, I created terms such as *pangender,* articulating a spectrum and changeable nature of gender. Language, for me, was key, as it gave me the confidence and self-assuredness that I'd always respected and admired in Shaun. It is important to name that language does not serve this purpose for everyone, of course, and for many it may have an opposite impact. For me, however, it was the piece I was missing in order to embrace the fact that my gender is not static or boxable. Ironically, I realized that it is somewhat boxable: I'd created a new box for myself. This box seemed to have enough room for me though and was more organic and four-dimensional (including the element of time and variance). Through a journey of migration, change, evolution, and inconsistency, I now realized that it was this fluid gender identity that was indeed constant . . . and this was reassuring.

To match this pangender, changing conception of self, I desired pronouns to match. Not loving the fixedness of grammar rules either, I found comfort in a combination of various pronouns. My preference is for people to jumble and interchange any/all pronouns and even dream up new ones. To me, this postmodern approach helps broaden and stretch the gender box in which I've placed myself and helps broaden and stretch the conceptualization of gender as a whole.

What is my future . . . the hirstory yet lived? I have no way of knowing. Regarding gender, I imagine that I'll remain fairly constant for a while: I like the pangender world I've created. Regarding sex, some days I imagine changes from my female body; other days I'm quite content. Gender and sex are not as interlocked

for me as they are for many others, and I'm comfortable with this disconnect. One thing I still struggle with is finding community. Because of my rejection of typical gender expectations and identity, I technically think of myself as part of the transgender community. However, I've often felt pressure from this community to want to transition. Therefore, I often feel "not trans enough." This can be isolating and disempowering at times. I know that my future will involve finding more individuals to connect with and the creation of a larger community of pangender family.

"You learn more quickly under the guidance of experienced teachers. You waste a lot of time going down blind alleys if you have no one to lead you" (Maugham, 1944). On this journey, I constantly think back to those who have shaped me along the way. I have a deep appreciation for individuals like Shaun, and many others. Working at a gendered university within a gendered society can be hard; self-love and these wonderful individuals have meant the world to me.

NOTE

1. Hirstory: In the late 1960s, feminists coined the term *herstory* to capture the past in a way that includes and sometimes emphasizes the role of women. I use the word *hirstory* to articulate a past inclusive of gender beyond a binary construct. In this instance, I'm using it to capture my own lived hirstory; the term could be used to describe a societal hirstory, as well.

REFERENCE

Maugham, S. (1944). *The razor's edge.* London, England: Heinemann.

Section Three

EXPLORING IDENTITY CONTEXTS

The Intersections of Class, Gender, Race, and Sexual Orientation for Faculty, Administrators, and Students

Interest in understanding multiple identities emerges from a growing awareness of the non singular nature in which individual identities are constructed and self-perceived. . . . Student affairs educators must not presume what is most central to individuals, but must instead listen for how a person sees herself.

Susan R. Jones and Marylu K. McEwen

Jones, S., & McEwen, M. K. (2000). A conceptual model of multiple dimensions of identity. *Journal of College Student Development, 41*(4), 405–413 (quote from pages 410–412).

9

How Race Matters

Race as an Instrument for Institutional Transformation: A Study of Tenured Black Female Faculty

Venice Thandi Sulé

Abstract: *Through the employment of Black Feminist Thought and Political Race concepts, this study examines how race matters in the lives of tenured Black female faculty members at predominately White research institutions. The findings indicate that the participants encountered subtle and blatant forms of racism. However, race consciousness served as a catalyst for insurgency and institutional transformation. In all, the study shows that colleges and universities can be a site of collective action on behalf of social equity.*

WE ARE ALIVE DURING AN ERA when race is viewed as a distraction. According to the proponents of the colorblind ideology, race, as a social category, is divisive because it breeds conflict about the distribution of resources. Furthermore, colorblind advocates argue that racism, rather than being a structural constraint, emanates from individual flaws and is mostly a relic of a painful past (Gotanda, 2000; Guinier & Torres, 2002; Marable, 2002; Peller, 1995). In essence, colorblind supporters believe that if people focused on intergroup commonalties then the nasty business of racism would be eradicated. In an essay on race consciousness, Peller (1995) observed that

A commitment to a type of universalism . . . forms the infrastructure of American integrationist con-

sciousness. Within this frame for organizing social perception, controversy revolves around how to categorize particular social practices—as rational and neutral, or as irrational and biased . . . to both liberals and conservatives, racism consists of a form of distortion that could be superseded by an aracial [*sic*] arena of social understanding. Once we remove prejudice, reason will take its place; once we remove discrimination, neutrality will take its place. (p. 130)

Thus, a dominant narrative about the state of race in America is that racial equality requires racial neutrality. For example, the rhetoric that spurred recent anti-affirmative-action victories in higher education was steeped in the notion that individuals are devoid of historical context or group identity. More specifically, in recent years, affirmative action programs in higher education have been abolished in several states, most notably in California, Washington, Michigan, and Nebraska. The American Civil Rights Institute, the organization spearheading constitutional bans on affirmative action, has targeted several more states for ballot initiatives to overturn affirmative action in higher education. Thus, it was argued that individuals should be judged solely by quantitative forms of merit such as test scores. However, what these race-neutral advocates inadvertently demonstrate is that race does matter because what inspire efforts to retrench race-based practices are attempts to uphold White racial privilege rather than promote equity. Essentially, the more privileged classes can avail themselves of resources that allow them to be competitive, and because race has traditionally determined who is most likely to be privileged, certain groups are systemically disadvantaged (Katznelson, 2005; Oliver & Shapiro, 1997). Therefore, the competition for resources will be tipped in favor of privileged groups like White Americans. See Jennifer Sader's chapter (chapter 8) on gender construction and women in computer science for a discussion of gender blindness or gender neutrality.

Despite the mounting support for dismantling race-based programs under the guise of race neutrality, race, as a social category, matters in the United States. One needs only to compare the life outcomes of various racialized groups with Whites to see how much race matters in access to wealth, housing, employment, healthcare, and education (Conley, 1999; Oliver & Shapiro, 1997). Most poignantly, Marable (2002) contended that

> The central difficulty in uprooting racism in America's consciousness . . . is that racism predates national identity. Decades before the American Revolution, enslaved African Americans and American Indians were specifically excluded from the social contract that linked individuals and classes to the state through sets of rights and responsibilities. (p. 29)

Therefore, whether we decide to disregard or rationalize racialized social inequities and historical antecedents, the fact remains that race has always been a key determinant in access to power. With this understanding, a study of how race operates within social institutions can provide invaluable information about how racially marginalized groups negotiate hierarchal power structures. More importantly, a critical analysis of racialized experiences can act as an impetus—collective action that fosters institutional equity.

Based on the premise that race can act as a transformative resource, this chapter looks at how tenured Black female faculty members experience and interrogate race in predominately White research institutions (PWIs).[1] The study of Black women in PWIs is compelling because like their male peers, they were systematically excluded from the professoriate. It was only through social unrest and subsequent government intervention that they gained access to these schools (Bell, 2004; Witt & Shin, 2003). However, their representation and status within these institutions still remains tenuous because of disparities in promotion, mentoring, and job satisfaction (Myers, 2002; Thomas & Hollenshead, 2001; Thompson & Dey, 1998). Nevertheless, Black female faculty members have managed to succeed within PWIs in spite of systemic roadblocks to achievement. This chapter, then, explores how race functions in their lives and how race serves as a mobilizing resource.

THE CONTEXT

Black Women and Opposition

As a collective, Black female engagement with the dominant social structure is characterized by a history of economic exploitation and sexual violence (Collins, 2000; Davis, 1981; Giddings, 1984; Hine, 1994; Hine, Brown, Patterson, & Williams, 1990). As the ultimate antithesis of what was considered true womanhood, African American women had to employ a multiplicity of survival skills. Popularized in the nineteenth century, True Womanhood was an attempt by White males to maintain the religious values of their forebears. The attributes of True Womanhood were whiteness, piety, purity, submissiveness, and domesticity (Giddings, 1984; Perkins, 1997; Welter, 1976). As such, there is a legacy of Black women maintaining an "oppositional position," an awareness of being a member of a socially marginalized group combined with behavioral and attitudinal resistance to individual and collective marginalization (Sulé, 2008).

Simply stated, there is a legacy of Black female opposition to behaviors designed to (1) limit employment, education, and housing opportunities; (2) mar and control Black female sexuality; and (3) restrict physical movement (Harley & The Black Women and Work Collective, 2002; Hine, 1994; Hunter, 1997; Springer, 1999). In this struggle for self-reclamation, formally educated Black women often served as the mouthpiece for the Black female collective.

Education as a Vehicle for Opposition

After being systemically denied access to literacy during slavery, Blacks understood the relationship between education and one's ability to engage society and secure an improved standard of living (Anderson, 1988; Hine & Thompson, 1998; Perkins, 1990). Upon the emancipation of slavery, a small but determined group of educated Black women led a vociferous challenge against social inequities. They fought against social injustice by expanding educational opportunities and by facilitating social services such as housing, job training, and childcare (Giddings, 1984; Hine, 1994; Hine et al., 1990; Hine & Thompson, 1998). These women used their status to dispute the race and gender caste system. This is no more evident than with the establishment of the National Association of Colored Women (NACW) in 1896. Led by such luminaries as Mary Church

Terrill and Mary McLeod Bethune, NACW is the first Black national organization that dealt with the needs of African Americans.

In addition to founding schools, NACW engaged in community development by sponsoring college scholarships, resettlement programs, day care programs, and health-care facilities among other activities. In addition, educated women actively defended the morality of Black women, advocated for suffrage, and publicly challenged sexual violence (Cooper, 1998; Giddings, 1984; Hine, 1994). In essence, these women expressed their dissatisfaction with institutionalized discrimination by engaging in capacity building within the Black community. They were pivotal in defending the worthiness of Black womanhood because they had more resources and a broader platform than the average Black women who struggled to survive as domestics or agricultural laborers. Although, during most of the twentieth century, an educated Black woman was an anomaly and belied the image of Black woman as a breeder, whore, nurturer, emasculator, and workhorse, many educated Black women challenged racism and sexism.

Black Female Faculty at Predominately White Institutions

Given that educated Black women played a pivotal role in both challenging dominant discourses and engineering Black community development, Black female academics are an important topic of study. Although Black women have been involved in higher education since the 1860s and the first Black woman from the United States received a PhD in 1921, Black female academics were not employed at predominately White institutions until the 1960s (Evans, 2007; Giddings, 1984). Within these institutions, Black women's rank, tenure, retention, and compensation is among the lowest (Gregory, 1999; Moses, 1997). Narratives from these women are replete with accounts of systemic marginalization (Benjamin, 1997; Gregory, 1999; Moses, 1997;

Myers, 2002). Specifically, Black women feel isolated from key social networks, undervalued by peers, unduly attacked by students, and used as representatives of diversity (Moses, 1997; Myers, 2002; Turner et al., 2002). These structural constraints are vestiges of a longstanding system designed to impede the mobility of people belonging to targeted groups. In the case of Black women, their intersected raced and gendered experiences have historically marked them as objectionable.

THEORETICAL FRAMEWORK

This study is informed by Black Feminist Thought (BFT) and Political Race (PR) theories. In concert, they explain how social identity influences access to resources. The first theory, BFT, argues that the intersection of race and gender gives Black women a distinct and subordinate social location (Collins, 2000). This distinct location fosters common experiences and responses to the social structure creating a Black female standpoint—a form of knowledge that challenges dominant narratives about social identity and privilege. By emphasizing intersected identities, BFT addresses the limitations of ideologies that focus solely on gender or race. King (1995) elaborated,

> A Black feminist ideology, first and foremost, thus declares the visibility of Black women. It acknowledges the fact that two innate and inerasable traits, Black and female, constitute our special status in American society. Second, Black feminism asserts self-determination as essential. Black women are empowered with the right to interpret our reality and define our objectives. While drawing on a rich tradition of struggle as Blacks and as women, we continually establish and reestablish our own priorities. (p. 312)

Therefore, as a standpoint theory, BFT recognizes groups as a unit of analysis in order to analyze privileges and disadvantages accumulated through collective experiences. It provides an interpretive tool that draws upon marginalized identities as a means to understand hierarchal power structures. Furthermore, it elucidates themes that may have particular salience for the Black female experience. Ultimately, BFT is a means to move subjugated knowledge from the margins to the center of ontological discourse as a way to promote social justice.

The second theory, PR, postulates that race is politically constructed because racial assignments are associated with unjust systems of power. Fundamentally, PR asserts that racial categories are designed to rationalize and normalize power hierarchies (Guinier & Torres, 2002). The concept of PR is most useful to this study because it embodies the idea that racialized groups function as barometers of social injustice. In other words, because oppressed groups are most vulnerable to structural constraints, they warn us of toxins in the social environment. Guinier and Torres (2002) elaborated,

> Those who are racially marginalized are like the miner's canary: their distress is the first sign of a danger that threatens us all. It is easy enough to think that when we sacrifice this canary, the only harm is to communities of color. Yet others ignore problems that converge around racial minorities at their own peril, for these problems are symptoms warning us that we are all at risk. (p. 11)

In addition to sensitizing society about structural perils, PR contends that racially subjugated groups act as catalysts for social action. As catalysts, racialized groups are in the best position to direct transformative action. Therefore, PR moves beyond diagnosis of racialized distribution of power to showing how race consciousness can promote structural transformation.

BFT and PR tell us that raced and gendered experiences warn us of dysfunctional facets of PWIs. These frameworks claim that the inequities faced by one marginalized group can lead to awareness of inequities that affect other groups. With this knowledge, this study has implications for how higher education institutions can promote access to diverse communities and alter the climate within PWIs to support Black women.

RESEARCH METHODS

Interviews were the primary form of data collection because they allowed me to collect in-depth information about how participants interpreted their experiences (Creswell, 1998; Patton, 2001). Using open-ended questions, participants were interviewed in person for approximately two hours about various aspects of their professional socialization. After the interview, I recorded my thoughts and observations of the participants. All of the interviews were audio-recorded and transcribed verbatim.

In alignment with criterion sampling, participants were selected based on the purpose of the study. Hence, I sought tenured Black female professors working at predominately White Carnegie Classified doctorate-granting institutions. I recruited associate professors because I wanted participants who could reflect upon how their graduate school and junior faculty experiences influenced their career trajectory. In addition, I targeted faculty in social sciences and humanities because I am interested in disciplines that have a relatively longer history of race and gender representation when compared to science, technology, engineering, and mathematics (STEM). In effect, focusing on social sciences and humanities allowed for insight into the experiences of underrepresented groups in disciplines that have been historically, albeit limited, more accessible.

To analyze transcripts, I began with local integration—summarizing interviews by focusing on the meaning of what was discussed (Weiss,

1994). Then, using Atlas TI, a software program that allows code-based theory building, I created open codes focusing on description and interpretation of what was expressed. To generate meaning, I compared and contrasted codes across cases to bring forth more inclusive categories. I used matrices and a schematic display to help me see patterns and develop thematic groups. All of these methods support the analysis of qualitative data (Miles & Huberman, 1994).

FINDINGS

Participants

The participants included 14 women from four predominately White research universities, and pseudonyms are used to identify participants. Women ranged in age from 35 to 56 years and the median age was 41 years. All of the women self-identified as Black or African American. However, three participants also described themselves as biracial or bicultural. In regard to educational attainment, they received their doctorate degrees between 1986 and 2001, but most of the participants (11 out of 14) received their doctorates between 1990 and 1998. As discussed, the study targeted tenured women, and among the participants, 5.5 years was the median number of years tenured. Lastly, the disciplinary specialties of the participants were predominately in social science. Only 3 participants were from the humanities (see Appendix A for participant demographic table that describes a portion of the lives of participants).[2]

One of the most prominent features of the narratives is that the women expressed that race, as well as gender, mattered in academe. When naming their identity, Black and female were common identifiers, and their identity influenced how they approached their institutions. For instance, their identity factored into what they chose to research, with whom they collaborated, the courses they taught, their commitment to students, and the service they provided. Here, Halima's narrative encapsulates the sentiments expressed by the women:

> It [my social identity] just means... somebody who's connected to their racial identity and that has been critical in informing how I see myself, how I see the world, how I interact and the fact that my understanding of being Black is predicated... on being a woman... so part of my identity is based on my experiences of how other people treat me as a Black woman in this world and that obviously has to do with discrimination. But another piece of my identity has to do with the pride and connections with people... who I see as very similar to myself, and so it's not just based on an identity of oppression, it's also based on an identity connection and pride, and shared vision.

For the participants, self-definition means more than phenotype. It is rooted in a critical understanding of the spectrum of Black female experiences from deep-seated wounds to the causes for exaltation. Furthermore, their race consciousness made them aware of how they are culturally and politically connected to others. The connection between positive self-definition and racial identity is reflective of the women of color in Vaccaro's chapter on adult women learners (chapter 7). Using her employment of Hardiman and Jackson's racial identity development scale, the participants in this study would fall in the Redefinition (creating a self-affirming identity) or Internalization stage (fusing of self-affirming identity and advocacy).

As will be demonstrated in this chapter, participants' articulated connection with the Black female experience prompted them to advance social equity issues. Further, while advancing their agenda for social justice, they were often reminded that the race consciousness of some of their White peers reinforced entitlement and privilege. This dialectic of racial bullying and oppositional positions characterizes their racialized experiences in the academy.

Racism: Academic Interlopers

A dominant theme within racialized experiences is the perception that Blacks are less worthy than their White counterparts. Therefore, Black bodies within academe are viewed with suspicion and are deemed incursive. To illustrate how Blackness is not equated with intellectualism, Sekai described how she was congratulated by her graduate school dean for academic achievement. His nonverbal communication revealed underlying racial apprehension:

> I had never met him until I was just about ready to graduate. And there was some reception or something, for outstanding graduate students and so I was calling to RSVP. The secretary ... said, I think [Dr. Ben] ... wants to speak with you. He got on the phone, he says, Sekai, I've been meaning to meet with you all these years, outstanding work ... would you be able to meet with me beforehand ... I said, sure. He didn't know who I was. I showed up in the office ... and I, maybe you've had this experience. The expression on this man's face was like ... why are you? He says Sekai? I mean, it was just this ... Sekai? And I said, yes, I'm Sekai. And he said, oh, so nice to ... I mean ... it was one of those moments where, again, I spent my time thinking about how do I respond to this white man who has clearly not even put it in his imagination anywhere that I could possibly be the person that he thought I was.

Similarly, Jaha indicated that people are often surprised by the pairing of her racial identity and her professional position.

> Jaha: As a professor, sometimes people don't know, well, if you've never met me, and you've only read my name, you know, the students walk into the class, oh, (*laughs*) you know, because the name is just neutral. You sense it.
>
> Venice: There's a visible reaction?
>
> Jaha: Yeah, yeah, sometimes there is. I've had verbal reactions at presentations and conferences, which are different, though. Like, oh, you are... taller than I thought (*laughs*), or something, [but] you know what they're thinking.

The narratives illustrate the subtleties of racial bias. One respondent, Tracee, labeled the astonished reaction of Whites to Black achievement as an *insulting surprise*, a disingenuous compliment or exaggerated gesture used to mask disbelief about the ability of Blacks to succeed in spaces dominated by Whites. Thus, many racialized experiences are not overt nor are they enacted to debilitate targeted groups. They are mere reflections of deep-seated stereotypes and images of Black people. However, the cumulative effect of these faint forms of racism can be stressful for targeted groups. For instance, Nia believes that being educated and working on campuses with a history of exclusion has made her hypersensitive about race.

> In terms of being Black, this is the metaphor I came up with when I was there. And it still feels like the best one (*sighs*). It was like I had a huge, horrible, scar on my face that I walked around with that everybody could see. And yet, it was polite. Nobody would mention it. We wouldn't talk about the scar on my face. Though, it was disfiguring.

Though covert and subtle forms of racial experiences were predominant, sometimes acts of racial resistance were less subtle. As an example, Carmen explained that students at her first institution did not even have the courtesy to lie about why they were dropping her as an advisor. Many were bold enough to say that it was because of her race. Inadvertently, the experience taught her a lesson about the authorization of racial intolerance.

> I would have never recognized the power that institutions have to respond to racist situations if I hadn't been there. Because if a student will bring you a form to change advisors, and on the bottom of it write, "because I don't want a Black advisor," and the dean and the director of the department have signed off on it before the student brings it to you, that's institutional racism.

Also, when several students complained to the dean about having to take a required course taught by a Black woman, the dean created a new class section and blamed her for the disruption. "He said to me, you're the one that's different, and I understand, but you've got to figure out how to make the students feel comfortable with you."

Other accounts were more directly about the perceived incongruence between Blackness and scholarly pursuits. The participants talked about how Black people were perceived as cognitively deficient and unable to succeed in competitive institutions. For instance, as a graduate student, Chimwala felt ignored or belittled in the classroom.

> I did notice that there were times in a classroom where some of my ... pretty typical male domestic classmates didn't always value what I had to say, and it would only be valued if the male instructor then came behind and said what I said.... It was infuriating, but at the same time I guess I expected it. You know, I wanted it to be different, but it was what it was ... so I think some of that was some subtle racism going on in there. Some subtle gender issues were going on in there.

Later, as a junior faculty person, she felt that her research was not valued because of her social identity and the issues she chose to address.

> The ... department here ... had a really big push towards ... certain types of journals that no matter what ... those aren't where my work would go. It's just not the community that I talk to and I felt a hostile environment around gender and race issues. And it was not the place for me. I found hostility around my research. I felt like my research wasn't respected. I felt, as a woman of color, I felt isolated.

In the similar way, Nia described an encounter she had with graduate students while visiting an Ivy League school as a prospective student, "I thought ... we'd go out to coffee or something. They were all too busy to go to coffee. We sat around the seminar room and they just grilled me.... And, it was horrible. Then she decided to tell me, oh, well they only admitted you because you're Black." Again, what underlies resistance to Black women is that they challenge notions of White intellectual authenticity. For example, as a faculty member, Tracee encountered faculty resistance to underrepresented students.

> In admissions every year... I always have to gear myself up to get ready for the fight because I have to be the one who deals with the test scores discussion that will come up. People who have never heard of an HBCU, are saying, oh that's not a good institution, that person coming from that school, that's not a good school. Well, you don't know about the school, so this person has done research with this person who is a good scholar. You just don't know that scholar because they don't do work in your area. The way that we talk, that diversity is dealt with in that way; we're admitting students kind of out of the goodness of our hearts versus like they're actually bringing in something unique.

These experiences were essentially about meritocracy and legitimacy. Diversity, rather than being a facet of merit, was viewed as a force that subverts merit. Blackness was viewed with suspicion and participants experienced situations where they had to take a defensive position. In addition, in anticipation of attack, the participants also talked about taking an offensive position by working diligently to thwart resistance. In regard to contributing to her department, Jaha said,

> I feel that where you almost feel the spotlights on you. You know, you do your job, but you don't just do it. I have to do it well because you're in the spotlight. You know, I'm of that generation well, you do it exceptionally well. So that people know that you're doing it well.

Jaha's narrative is indicative of the belief that Black people have to work twice as hard to get the same recognition as Whites, even if the Blacks have exceptional qualifications. For instance, in a national survey of female administrators, it

was found that Black women felt "they were held to [a] higher standard because they were always fighting the stereotype of being incompetent, despite having the right education and experience credentials... when they display competence, their colleagues often express surprise" (Bell & Nkomo, 2001, p. 145). Rashida shared a story that exemplifies the work ethic believed to be required of Blacks. What distinguishes her story is the realization that hard work does not guarantee career success.

> A recent tenure case... that I was on... there was a file from a woman of color, and a file from a white man. And her file's unbelievable. It is absolutely unbelievable. Um, four books... she did everything. She killed herself. I mean, I think she really is suffering, sort of health wise, and in her family, to try to do this, to get tenure. And he, it's okay, it's what people expect, if they say, "Well, you should have a book and about six articles, he has a book and six articles." I think the difference with her, and it's interesting, is that she actually didn't get tenure right away. They said, "Well you worked so hard that we really didn't get to know you as a colleague. And we're going to ask you to wait another year, and we're going to see how you get along with students, and how you interact with us." Have you ever heard such a thing at a research institution? He, on the other hand, not a problem, they both deserved it. They both did, and she did the super woman thing, and it still was sometimes never enough.

The claim of meritocracy that predominates in these women's institutions is often in opposition to representations of Blackness in scholarship and in human form. Therefore, having the proper pedigree (e.g., credentials, respected advisor) is not enough to secure approval from those invested in maintaining the current model of merit. McKay (2002) argued that even when tenure is granted, Black women are not welcome into the inner sanctum of legitimacy, "We soon realized that although our status vis-à-vis such things as job security had altered appreciably, we were still excluded from the centers of power vested in the premises of White maleness"

(p. 16). This breeds an environment in which White supremacy reigns and having a Black identity undermines perceptions of achievement. The participants provided accounts of their feelings and experiences as they moved through spaces tinged with racial hostility.

Earlier, Nia equated racial isolation and subtle racialized insults with being physically scarred. Here, she elaborated on how racism complicated her experience as a junior professor. An encounter with a White male colleague in the stairwell left an impression on her.

I was asking him about teaching . . . or something like that. . . . And he said that he loved teaching minstrelsy. And he was sort of leaning over me, you know, like from the top stairs . . . I hardly knew this guy at all, just trying to have friendly conversation. And he said what he likes to do is . . . take a cork and to get a flame and to burn it. And then he was pantomiming as he said how he puts it on his face in class. And I was terrified. I was absolutely shocked. I'm thinking, you can't do this, and you certainly can't do this in class, and you can't do it to me, but I'm like, who are, like, who are you, you big racist, terrible man? And he was pantomiming it, and there was this sort of glee in his face, and it was so horrifying, and I just was looking at him with big eyes. And I said, well, I bet that really has an effect on your students, or something, and he says, yeah, it really does. And it was almost as though there was an assault because I didn't tell anyone about it, thinking nobody would believe me, and maybe these are the norms here. Maybe you can Black up in class as a white man, and nobody thinks anything of it. And oh, my God, what does this say about me and my position here?

Nia then stated that she believed he was one of the people who did not support her tenure application. "I think there was just some blatant racism there," she asserted. Mesi, too, attributed some of her colleagues' behaviors and attitudes to racism. She is sickened by paternalistic approach and underlying racism of her peers.

The deep, deep racism (laughs). . . . You know, uh, it's true. I mean the kind of liberal . . . that we have . . . great white mothers and fathers who are going to save us as individuals and our fields as professionals and . . . I find [it] nauseating . . . I have watched my colleagues take the first train to no more affirmative action.

Mesi's disappointment in her peers also stems from their lack of commitment to hiring diverse faculty members, particularly women of color. She said that Black women were especially treated disrespectfully because they were not afforded the standard courtesies appropriate for job candidates. She bemoaned, "I just don't think people care."

Quintessentially, the narratives explain how race is politicized in the academy.

The ubiquity of racialized experiences is a testament to the role that race plays in determining access to resources and authority. Sekai's recollection of how she dealt with race in graduate school captures the way that the participants were able to work through its limitations yet use what they learned from it to challenge social inequity. She said that living in a White community,

was to remind us that we were not something else, but we were who we were . . . we spent most of that time trying to understand, what does it mean to be Black in the world, and to do something with that? How does it mean to be in these bodies, and actually use them as tools for social progress or for moving an agenda forward? That's what we spent our time thinking about. . . . But I know that every step I took, race mattered. Every moment I was there, race mattered. What I was concerned about was . . . my way of responding to how it mattered.

Although the issue of race predominates, the women also recognized gendered experiences. However, their gender awareness was frequently cloaked within a discussion of race. One reason why gender may not be as salient as race is because race alters the meaning of womanhood in ways that make it a key determinant in how many Black women interpret their experiences. Race is such a powerful concept that it changes the meaning of the mundane and obscures other identities.

> By continually expressing overt and covert analogic relationships, race impregnates the simplest meanings we take for granted. It makes hair "good" or "bad," speech patterns "correct" or "incorrect." It is in fact, the apparent overdeterminacy of race in Western culture, and particularly in the United States, that has permitted it to function as a metalanguage in its discursive representation and construction of social relations. (Higginbotham, 1992, p. 255)

Therefore, the entrenched system of racial hierarchies in the United States precludes the consideration of gender without a discussion of race. Thus, Black women may focus on race because it determines how gender is experienced. For this reason, the narratives of Black women should be viewed through the lens of race and gender. For instance, Nia's experience with the male colleague in the stairwell is about the intermingling of race, gender, and power. Contextualizing this encounter by reflecting upon the long tradition of White male assault on Black female bodies (Davis, 1981; Hine, 1995; Jewell, 1993; Roberts, 1997; White, 1999), one can interpret the engagement as an exercise in White male privilege and Black female subordination. The stereotypes that legitimated the sexual and labor exploitation of Black females during slavery justified their continued mistreatment upon emancipation (for more on stereotypes see Collins, 2000; Jewell, 1993; White, 1999). Hence, whether explicitly discussed or not, gender is never divorced from race because there are distinct ways that Black women experience their racialized and gendered selves.

Furthermore, minimal articulation of gendered experiences among Black women does not mean that gender awareness is not present because awareness can be indicated by their actions. For instance, among the 14 participants, 10 were involved in research or service that explicitly focused on women, particularly women

of color. Like their Black female predecessors, the participants reflect a tradition of using their concern for race-based injustice to address a diversity of humanist concerns such as educational equity, poverty, and sexual violence. The Combahee River Collective's Black feminist statement is indicative of the way that Black female activism reflects their multiple social locations.[3]

> The most general statement of our politics at the present time would be that we are actively committed to struggling against racial, sexual, heterosexual and class oppression and see as our particular task the development of integrated analysis and practice based upon the fact that the major systems of oppression are interlocking. The synthesis of these oppressions creates the conditions of our lives. (The Combahee River Collective, 1984, p. 13)

Race Consciousness as a Catalyst for Innovation

Race as a political construct is both constraining and enabling for Black female faculty. It constrains because it hinders access to spaces of legitimacy. Conversely, those constraints motivate the women to serve and advocate for marginalized groups. Thus, race consciousness advances institutional transformation by illuminating systemic dysfunctions. As such, the race consciousness of the participants acted as a catalytic force toward institutional transformation. For instance, Layla believes that her identity comes with an obligation to service Black people.

> As far as being a professional woman . . . maybe I attribute this to [attending a historically Black college] and maybe to some extent my parents. I just feel like there was a huge emphasis that I don't see here on giving back. You have these opportunities so you have an obligation to give back. In particular one of my professors, before a lecture he was just saying that he really felt . . . he wasn't the kind the person who when the revolution came, he wasn't going to be on the front lines with the machine gun or doing a hunger strike. . . . He felt like his ability to give back was through the kind of research that he did . . . he felt that policy was shaped by

research.... That made a huge impact on me.... So it was a way to frame the type of work you do as an academic with the social responsibility that they kind of kept hammering at you.

Jamila explained how her self-knowledge influences her social interests and engagement with colleagues.

I'm definitely a descendent of one of those Africans on the west coast of Africa that was picked up, swapped around, put in a few slave dungeons for a few months at a time, dragged over the Atlantic Ocean and finally dropped off here in North America... I'm still mad *(laughs)* ... ask my colleagues how they'd describe me. The first thing they'll probably say is very assertive, very confident, and opinionated. And it's probably true. And ... they'd say that I would probably bring up the issue about race and injustice and racism probably pretty often.

Similarly, Rashida views the world through a lens of race or Blackness. She said that she is "really Black." When asked to elaborate, she explained,

The things that hurt me most ... is injustice directed toward Black [people] ... I don't play that. I think that my colleagues know that I will get along and go along in just about anything, but I think that they always have to be careful about those kinds of things, because that sets me off ... everything that I write about is about Black people ... mostly about ... systemic racism and discrimination that are directed toward Black people.

Dziko's comments about Black people encapsulate the sentiments shared by the participants on race. I interpret her narrative to be about survival. She believes that Black people must know their history because it teaches them about how they survived in the midst of atrocities.

I definitely don't want the younger generation to lose track of the idea that there's much to be learned from this particular identity, especially when you think about our survival ... I want them to understand that there's a foundation, it can be [a] source ... to different kinds ... of success. Even though we know this idea of humanness is what

is the bottom line, I think particular social constructs, the way that men have established it, race does have particular value, race does have meaning, and until we get to ... the utopia, 'cause we're not there, until we get there, we have to acknowledge that there's certain kinds of confines, but there's also certain kinds of traditions, values, practices that we can relish in as Black people. I don't know, to maintain who we are and, so that we can see this connectiveness, so that we can understand our place, so that we can understand the origins of people, of human, in the beginning, and to understand our contributions, and to understand who we are, bottom line. I think that it will help again to promulgate these different levels of success for Black students if they understand this identity of Blackness.

Though these narratives demonstrate that race consciousness can advance social equity, they also indicate that race awareness may be a survival strategy because it forces the women to deal with the reality of identity-based structural constraints. In acknowledging this reality, they are able to respond strategically; they are able to maneuver in ways that encourage their longevity. A fundamental component of this negotiation is self-affirmation. This positive sense of self has been called self-investment or the belief that want deserves personal enrichment (see Annemarie Vaccaro, chapter 7). Thus, race consciousness, as discussed in this article, extends beyond mere awareness of racial differences and rejection of disaffirming racial stereotypes to a belief that one has the right to engage in public culture and benefit from its resources.

Advocacy

As noted in the previous section, race consciousness promotes action to institute social equity. The participants viewed their service within the academy as a way to support their libratory agenda. Therefore, it was an act of resistance against racialized constraints. The participants engendered advocacy through research and committee work. For instance, they acted as catalysts for change by challenging prevailing epistemological frameworks. Tracee stated,

> I'm studying things with integrity, so that I'm true to myself in the way that I negotiate academia in terms of what I study and the approaches that I take—whether I take stands. So, in the area that I work in, the predominate paradigm about African-Americans is deficits, you know, which is probably the case in a lot of different areas, and so I could probably be a lot more successful at getting into certain venues if I wrote from that perspective. I often write and criticize that perspective. But that's the thing that helps me look in the mirror, at night, or when I go home . . . I didn't take the easy way . . . I actively take a stand around those issues in my professional writing and scholarly work but also at the level of the institution too, and seeing things that could be or calling out things.

In addition, the women used their research to critique the normalization of racialized power hierarchies. For instance, Halima has a keen interest in developing a theory of race awareness. Here, she spoke about her interest in race.

> I've always been interested in racism and in different times looking at racial identity. . . . And now I've been focused much more on this notion of racial color blind ideology and how people deny, distort, and minimize the existence of structural racism. . . . And what does it mean for Blacks, and other people of color . . .

Although the participants encountered resistance from their colleagues and students, their presence in the academy gave them an opportunity to broaden the discourse on issues pertaining to recruitment and persistence of underrepresented groups. While serving on committees, they were prepared to advocate on behalf of the Black students and faculty members. Layla described an incident of racial resistance:

> Actually it [race] came up when I was chairing the search committee and I was going to hire this Black woman who does research on Black people. Ooh imagine that, and . . . I got several comments . . . in

a faculty meeting. One was "isn't it limiting that she doesn't do comparative." Can you believe that that is coming up in 2007? . . . I said some people find that thinking quite racist, there is so much heterogeneity within groups. There were like three or four comments that come up . . . I just shouted back my response and didn't let it grow into one of these academic things where everyone starts to blah, blah, blah and the next thing you know, your candidate is shot down.

Moreover, Dziko argued that traditional criteria for student and faculty recruitment discriminate against marginalized groups.

> I was on a graduate committee, and there were three of us . . . I had to fight for GRE scores as not indicative of a person's capabilities. And it's something else that I was resistant to giving in to, particularly searches, you know documenting your information for persons and speaking out and standing up for those particular individuals . . . I think that there are just different struggles . . . ideologies that I'm not willing to give up that I want to continue to represent . . . [the] stance of Black people.

For the participants, committee work provides an opportunity to introduce perspectives that may advance racial diversity. For instance, Nia does not want her committee membership to be in vain. She was unapologetic about her intention to change student and faculty retention.

> I try not just to sit there, but to try to articulate something, a viewpoint that other people might not see, or other people aren't talking about and to say, you know, this is really a dire issue, when we have people of color at [the University] who are getting weeded out of the university, whether it's at the third year review, the tenure review, or whether they're unhappy here . . . they feel their research . . . isn't being taken seriously, or there are problems with the people in their department . . .

The confluence of research and committee service with race consciousness alters the academic landscape by both naming structural inequalities and encouraging policy change. The women's efforts may seem minuscule in the face of long-standing racist practices and beliefs, but they are chipping away traditions that belie the missions of these institutions. In essence, their work has a cumulative effect whereupon individual antiracist pronouncements force institutions to be accountable to their small yet vocal Black constituency.

SUMMARY

Upon entering historically and predominately White research institutions, the participants were in spaces where Black female bodies were marginalized, if considered at all. Anderson (2002) remarked, "the transformation of American higher education from a private, elite system to a more public, democratic one paralleled the triumph of white supremacy in the southern states and the emergence of institutionalized racism in the northern states" (p. 5). It was not until the advent of the civil rights movement that more than a handful of Blacks were given some, albeit minimal, opportunities to pursue higher education at highly resourced institutions. Having entered graduate school in the late 1980s and the early 1990s, the participants were still among an embryonic post-civil-rights generation of Blacks pursuing doctorates. Thus, the participants had to negotiate institutions and departments that were unused to difference. Their entrance into bastions of White male hegemony meant that they crossed into a cultural terrain imbued with attitudes, values, and practices that, at best, did not reflect their experiences and, at worst, rejected them.

The testimonials show that the participants aspire to use their positions to make their institutions more reflective of the experiences and contributions of silenced groups, namely Black people. Their concern for Black people is based on their engagement with injustice. It is also rooted in their fascination with in-group complexity. For them, Black communities are sites of homogeneity and heterogeneity. Therefore, the women reject the notion that Black people are only worth studying in relation to White people. They also reject the belief that Black people are devoid of a history that should be celebrated. This brew of historical and sociological awareness fostered a sense of social responsibility that the women actualized through research and committee work. It also reflects the PR perspective in the sense that participants worked toward transformative action.

Concern about social inequities was also fostered by the racialized experiences that participants encountered throughout their career trajectory—from graduate school to associate professor. Most of their experiences with racism were subtle or covert. However, subtle racist behaviors can be equally, if not more, harmful than the more overt forms of racism because they are often premised on concepts of fairness, merit, and hard work. This modern form of racism fails to recognize that life outcomes are greatly influenced by social structure (Dovidio, 1997; Dovidio & Gaertner, 1998; Eberhardt & Fiske, 1998). When structural constraints are ignored, those on the receiving end of racism are labeled the problem, thereby further normalizing racialized access to power. Further, as Black Feminist Thought and PR perspectives tell us, this marginalization also has implications for inequities across other marginalized groups.

Although participants were disturbed by racism, they were not surprised by its appearance within their institutions. They viewed it as just another feature of being Black and female in America. If anything, racism was an occupational hazard that they dealt with by using the tools (e.g., research, institutional service) of the academy. Although it may be true that "the master's tools will never dismantle the master's house" (Lorde, 1984, p. 112), the participants demonstrated that you can reconfigure those tools to make institutions more accessible for groups on the periphery. Race, as employed by the participants, served as a reminder of exclusionary practices and a vector for transformative work.

CONCLUSION

Although the participants operate in contested spaces, they have shown that academe can serve as a site of mobilization on behalf of social equity. Armed with race consciousness, they were able to identify inequities and advocate for systemic change. Most importantly, they used their knowledge of racialized experiences to advocate for changes that can literally be extended to other forms of social marginalization. In accordance with the PR theory, it is fathomable that other social identity groups will join Black women in their campaign for social justice when they realize that they can benefit from an academic environment that promotes inclusion. In other words, the constraints that hinder Black women also hamper other groups to varying degrees. Thus, race consciousness is important because it supports social justice agendas within a framework of race and power. This approach, along with other forms of critical analysis, is needed to help institutions identify ways to optimally recruit and engage a diverse campus community.

NOTES

1. Black and African American will be used interchangeably to designate women who are descendents of enslaved Africans of the Atlantic Slave Trade who arrived in the Americas.

2. The emphasis of the intersectional focus for this study was race and gender (Black and female). Hence, other aspects of social identity such as class, religion, and sexual orientation were not within the scope of this endeavor. However, I recognize that social identities beyond race and gender influence how one operates within various contexts.

3. The Combahee River Collective is a group of Black feminists founded in 1974. Their full statement can be found in the seminal text, *But Some of Us Are Brave*, edited by Gloria T. Hull, Patricia Bell Scott, and Barbara Smith (1982).

REFERENCES

Anderson, E. (2002). *The new professoriate: Characteristics, contributions, and compensation*. Washington, DC: American Council on Education.

Anderson, J. (1988). *The education of Blacks in the south, 1860–1935*. Chapel Hill, NC: The University of North Carolina Press.

Bell, D. (2004). *Silent covenants*. Oxford, England: Oxford University Press.

Bell, E. E., & Nkomo, S. (2001). *Our separate ways: Black and White women and the struggle for professional identity*. Boston, MA: Harvard Business School Press.

Benjamin, L. (Ed.). (1997). *Black women in the academy*. Gainesville, FL: University Press of Florida.

Collins, P. H. (2000). *Black feminist thought*. New York: Routledge.

Combahee River Collective. (1984). A Black feminist statement. In G. T. Hull, B. Smith, & P. B. Scott (Eds.), *But some of us are brave* (pp. 13–22). New York: The Feminist Press.

Conley, D. (1999). *Being Black, living in the red*. Berkeley, CA: University of California Press.

Cooper, A. J. (1998). The intellectual progress of colored women in the United States since the Emancipation Proclamation: A response to Fannie Barrier Williams. In C. Lemert & E. Bhan (Eds.), *The voice of Anna Julia Cooper* (pp. 201–205). New York: Rowman and Littlefield. (Original work produced in 1893)

Creswell, J. (1998). *Qualitative inquiry and research design*. Thousand Oaks, CA: Sage.

Davis, A. (1981). *Women, race and class*. New York: Vintage Books.

Dovidio, J. (1997). "Aversive" racism and the need for affirmative action. *The Chronicle of Higher Education, 43*(46), A60.

Dovidio, J., & Gaertner, S. L. (1998). Affirmative action, unintentional racial biases, and intergroup relations. *The Journal of Social Issues, 52*(4), 51.

Eberhardt, J. L., & Fiske, S. T. (Eds.). (1998). *Confronting racism*. Thousand Oaks, CA: Sage Publications.

Evans, S. Y. (2007). *Black women in the ivory tower, 1850–1954*. Gainesville, FL: University Press of Florida.

Giddings, P. (1984). *When and where I enter*. New York: William Morrow and Company, Inc.

Gotanda, N. (2000). A critique of "our constitution is color-blind." In R. Delgado & J. Stefancic (Eds.), *Critical race theory: The cutting edge* (pp. 35–38). Philadelphia, PA: Temple University Press.

Gregory, S. T. (1999). *Black women in the academy: The secrets to success and achievement*. Lanham, MD: University Press of America.

Guinier, L., & Torres, G. (2002). *The miner's canary*. Cambridge, MA: Harvard University Press.

Harley, S., & The Black Women and Work Collective. (Eds.). (2002). *Sister circle*. New Brunswick, NJ: Rutgers University Press.

Higginbotham, E. B. (1992). African American women's history and the metalanguage of race. *Signs, 17*(2), 251–274.

Hine, D. C. (1994). *Hine sight: Black women and the reconstruction of American history*. Bloomington, IN: Indiana University Press.

Hine, D. C. (1995). Race and the inner lives of Black women in the west: Preliminary thoughts on the culture of dissemblance. In B. Guy-Sheftall (Ed.), *Words of fire: An anthology of African-American feminist thought* (pp. 380–387). New York: The New Press.

Hine, D. C., Brown, E. B., Patterson, T., & Williams, L. (Eds.). (1990). *Black women in United States history: From colonial times to the present*. New York: Carlson Publishing.

Hine, D. C., Brown, E. B., & Teaborg-Penn, R. (Eds.). (1993). *Black women in America: An historical encyclopedia*. Bloomington, IN: Indiana University Press.

Hine, D. C., & Thompson, K. (1998). *A shining thread of hope*. New York: Broadway Books.

Hull, G. T., Scott, P. B., & Smith, B. (Eds.). (1982). *But some of us are brave*. New York: The Feminist Press.

Hunter, T. M. (1997). *To 'joy my freedom*. Cambridge, MA: Harvard University Press.

Jewell, K. S. (1993). *From mammy to Miss America and beyond*. New York: Routledge.

Katznelson, I. (2005). *When affirmative action was White*. New York: W. W. Norton & Company.

King, D. (1995). Multiple jeopardy, multiple consciousness: The context of Black feminist ideology. In B. Guy-Sheftall (Ed.), *Words of fire* (pp. 294–318). New York: The New Press.

Lorde, A. (1984). *Sister outsider*. Berkeley, CA: The Crossing Press.

Marable, M. (2002). *The great wells of democracy*. New York: BasicCivitas Books.

McKay, N. (2002). A troubled peace: Black women in the halls of the White Academy. In *Black women in the academy: Promises and perils* (pp. 11–22). Gainesville, FL: University Press of Florida.

Miles, M. B., & Huberman, A. M. (1994). *Qualitative data analysis*. Thousand Oaks, CA: Sage.

Moses, Y. T. (1997). Black women in academe. In L. Benjamin (Ed.), *Black women in the academy* (pp. 23–38). Gainesville, FL: University of Florida Press.

Myers, L. W. (2002). *A broken silence: Voices of African American women in the academy*. Westport, CT: Bergin & Garvey.

Oliver, M., & Shapiro, T. (1997). *Black wealth/White wealth*. New York: Routledge.

Patton, M. Q. (2001). *Qualitative research and evaluation methods*. Thousand Oaks, CA: Sage.

Peller, G. (1995). Race-consciousness. In K. Crenshaw, N. Gotanda, G. Peller, & K. Thomas (Eds.), *Critical Race Theory*. New York: The New Press.

Perkins, L. (1997). The impact of the "cult of true womanhood" on the education of Black women. In L. Goodchild & H. S. Wechsler (Eds.), *The history of higher education* (pp. 183–190). Boston, MA: Pearson Publishing Company.

Perkins, L. M. (1990). The National Association of College Women: Vanguard of Black Women's Leadership in Education, 1923–1954. *Journal of Education, 172*(3), 65–75.

Roberts, D. (1997). *Killing the Black body*. New York: Vintage Books.

Springer, K. (Ed.). (1999). *Still lifting, still climbing*. New York: New York University Press.

Sulé, V. T. (2008). *Black female faculty and professional socialization: Constraints, enablements and enactments*. Unpublished Doctoral Dissertation. University of Michigan, Ann Arbor.

Thomas, G., & Hollenshead, C. (2001). Resisting from the margins: The coping strategies of Black women and other women of color faculty members at a research university. *Journal of Negro Education, 70*(3), 166–175.

Thompson, C., & Dey, E. (1998). Pushed to the margins. *The Journal of Higher Education, 69*(3), 324–245.

Turner, C. S., Antonio, A. L., Garcia, M., Laden, B., Nora, A., & Presley, C. (Eds.). (2002). *Racial and ethnic diversity in higher education*. Boston, MA: Pearson Custom Publishing.

Weiss, R. (1994). *Learning from strangers: The art and method of qualitative interview studies*. New York: Free Press.

Welter, B. (1976). *Dimity convictions*. Athens, OH: Ohio University Press.

White, D. G. (1999). *Ar'n't I a woman?* New York: W. W. Norton & Company, Inc.

Witt, D., & Shin, C. (2003). Historical summary of Affirmative Action. In M. J. Chang, D. Witt, J. Jones, & K. Hakuta (Eds.), *Compelling interest* (pp. 185–202). Stanford, CA: Stanford University Press.

APPENDIX A. PARTICIPANT DEMOGRAPHIC TABLE

Participants	Children	Partner Status	Doc Degree	Tenure Period	SS or Hum
Layla	Yes	Partnered	Mid-1990s	1–5 Years	SS
Tameka	Yes	Partnered	Mid-1990s		Hum
Halima	Yes	Partnered	Early 1990s	6–10 Years	SS
Tracee	No	Partnered	Mid-1990s	1–5 Years	SS
Nia	No	Divorced; single	Mid-1990s	1–5 Years	Hum
Mesi	No	Partnered	Early 2000s	1–5 Years	SS
Carmen	No	Partnered	Mid-1990s	1–5 Years	SS
Jaha	Yes	Partnered	Early 1990s	6–10 Years	SS
Chimwala	Yes	Partnered	Early 1990s	1–5 Years	SS
Jamila	Yes	Partnered	Mid-1990s	1–5 years	SS
Rashida	No	Partnered	Mid-1990s	1–5 Years	SS
Dziko	Yes	Divorced	Mid-1980s	6–10 Years	Hum
Sekai	No	Partnered	Early 1990s	6–10 Years	SS
Ayo	Yes	Partnered	Mid-1980s	12 Years	SS

Note. Doc Degree: mid-1980s = 1986–1989; early 1990s = 1990–1994; mid-1990s = 1995–1999; early 2000s = 2000–2004. SS = Social Sciences; Hum = Humanities.

10

Life Stories of the Daughter of First-Generation Italian Immigrants

Gender, Ethnicity, Culture, and Class Intertwine to Form an Italian American Feminist

Florence M. Guido

WHEN I WAS ABOUT NINE, I was asked to be a bridesmaid in my mother's first cousin's wedding. My first cousin and I were chosen because our mothers were too old for such a role, a female tradition passed down from "the Italian old country," where first cousins are the bride's chosen attendants. The reception was held at a local Country Club in east central Texas, a first-class affair. I remember feeling awkward because I believed my taller, thinner cousin looked so much better than I did. It is hard to know whether being Italian, Southern, female, or my feeling of a lower social class most influenced my impossible vanity, but I was taught it was my role to look good and I didn't feel that way. My knobby knees poked out between the triangular points scattered evenly on the hem of the white eyelet dress I wore with a wide satin sash tied in a bow in the back. My shoes hurt my feet and felt too narrow. My long dark hair was pulled back and my "baby fat," from my round face to wide hips, seemed to trump any self-regard I might have had.

The shame I felt at looking less than perfect subsided long before my fifth decade, but the women in my family looking rich in their gold jewelry, propped on high heels, and wrapped in tight silk dresses put me in awe of a standard I was unsure I could attain. In the end, I concluded that the time I spent trying to look like my well-coiffed mother, aunts, and cousins could be better spent doing something else. Though I tried to reach this Italian upper-class standard for women, in the end, I traded high heels for casual suede boots. In other words, I gave up seeking the Italian standard of female perfection (i.e., trophy wife and caregiver of family and home) for sustainable (in my case, tenured), respectable (in my eyes, noble) employment in higher education.

I am Italian on both sides of my family as far back as we can trace—about 125 years. I grew up in 1950s San Antonio suburbia with my parents and two brothers in a house my grandfather, a contractor, built. My little sister arrived unexpectedly when I was nine. As the only girl in the family during my formative years, I had plenty to envy in my older brothers. They shared a room, were granted many privileges that extended beyond my reach, and eventually graduating from MIT and Princeton, were considered the family's intellectual promise. Being in constant comparison, my brothers were the first to teach me that females are treated differently from males in an Italian family. The Italian tradition of men with authority and women deferring to men tipped the scales in our family, as with many upwardly mobile Italian families of the time. My experience suggests that my circumstances were at the opposite end of the violence continuum depicted in *The Godfather*, yet men made the important decisions in our family and no one questioned this patriarchal social system.

In our young family's dining room, impressionistic-like, soft-toned wallpaper depicted a boat coming into what looked like a quaint European town harbor, and we would laugh and talk about what we would do when our ship finally docked. My boat landed in higher education teaching me about development and difference in social identity and helping me understand who I am in the world. When I retire from university life, I am confident my boat will find its way to another pier by pointing my compass in the direction of fiction writer and photographer.

The purpose of this chapter is to convey the intersections of gender, ethnicity, and class in the life of a female, Italian American, mixed social class faculty member in a higher education and student affairs leadership doctoral-only program. Through storytelling (Clandinin & Connelly, 2000; Ellis, 2004), I illustrate how these intertwined social identities (Jones, 2009) shaped my developmental journey and led me to seek an unpopular path in my chosen profession, down a feminist road (Fried, 1994; Gilligan, 1993). Woven throughout these stories is analysis informed by relevant social identity theories, models, and concepts related to gender (Gilligan, 1993; Josselson, 1996), ethnicity (Chávez &

Guido-DiBrito, 1999; Phinney, 1990), and class (Ostrander, 1984; Schwartz, Donovan, & Guido-DiBrito, 2009), and those that inform their intersectionality (Abes, Jones, & McEwen, 2007). Ultimately, shaped by my early experiences, some described below, the combination of my social identities (e.g., female, Italian American, mixed social class, heterosexual, and so on) spawned a feminist who now resides in the competitive academic world seeking equality in a 400-year-old U.S. patriarchal system.

SOCIAL IDENTITY AND HISTORICAL CONTEXT

Recent literature exemplifies the complexity involved for an individual to create an integrated multiple social identity (Abes, Jones, & McEwen, 2007). No longer seen as isolated and independent constructs (i.e., racial category or sexual orientation), social identity is now framed within multiple (i.e., ethnicity, gender, religion, race, sexual orientation, geography, ability, class, and so on) integrated and interconnected concepts (Evans, Forney, Guido, Patton & Renn, 2009). Within each identity category, individuals may act as advantaged or privileged, oppressor or disadvantaged oppressed. As a result, an individual may find some identity patterns and contexts linked to privilege and others linked to oppression. As an example, at one time or another, I have felt disadvantaged as a female, Italian American, with mixed social class roots. Though I am honored by these monikers now, this was not always so. Yet, the privilege I have experienced translates to my being the first in my family to receive a PhD and the first to hold a university professorship. As a professor raised in a highly ethnic, gendered, mixed social class family (i.e., both working class and upper-middle/lower-upper-class parental socioeconomic backgrounds), privilege also brings disadvantage—in this case, manifest through the burden of sibling rivalry tied to degree of perceived parental generosity and its perceived connection to parental love.

The historical context of the time set the backdrop for my family's arrival in the United States. In the late nineteenth century and the early 1920s, Southern and Eastern Europeans arrived in the United States as "new immigrants" (Barrett & Roediger, 2008, p. 35). My great grandparents and grandparents were among those who came with this tide as contract labor and helped restructure the U.S. working class. Within this historical context, "political debate turned on whether new immigrants were fit to join the American nation and 'American race' " (Barrett & Roedinger, p. 36). Society's elite and those born in the United States labeled these immigrants as inferior, and as the immigrants also saw themselves this way, a racial hierarchy evolved. In fact, at the 1898 Louisiana state constitutional convention, convened to disenfranchise Blacks and understand which Whites might lose the vote, some legislators declared Italians possess white skin but still insisted on their disenfranchisement. Other legislators from the bayou claimed that "according to our spirit of meaning when we speak of 'white man's government,' [the Italians] are as black as the blackest negro in existence" (Cunningham, 1965, p. 34). Well over a century later, Blacks are still disenfranchised, whereas in the not so distant past, Italians evolved in the eyes of the dominant culture as White and American.

Immigrants flocking to U.S. shores during the late 1800s and early 1900s swirled in a racialized sea of nationality that privileged Whites. For the most part, within the racial social order, Italians were viewed as "in between," or "not yet white" ethnic people, with Whites at the top of the hierarchy, and African and Asian Americans at the bottom (Barrett & Roediger, 2008). The language used to describe race was based on power and conspicuous wealth. For example, at different times in U.S. history, *guinea* referred to Greeks, Jews, Portuguese, Puerto Ricans, and all new immigrant groups. The term first referred to African slaves, but at the end of the nineteenth century, Sicilians and southern Italians faced this indignity and others with negative connotations such as *dago* and *wop*. However, the racialized status of African Americans and the racial in-between status of new immigrants were different in that "the latter *eventually* 'became ethnic' and that their trajectory was predictable" (Barrett & Roediger, 2008, p. 36) and upward. The new immigrant longed for societal status as White and American, which they linked. Not just ethnic but racial oppression too was long felt by non-White immigrants from Italy and Greece (Mormino & Pozzetta, 1987), although in time most became Americanized, either through assimilation or acculturation. My family's ancestors gave up many centuries-old traditions for the unknown and, unbeknownst to them, upcoming discrimination they would face in their chosen home. These familial ancestors faced harsh social and socioeconomic conditions in their newfound country, but eventually, their determined efforts meant success by dominant cultural standards.

STORYTELLING: NARRATIVE UNDERSTANDING

Stories written by and about students (e.g., Borrego & Manning, 2007; Rochlin, 1997), staff (e.g., Marshall, 2006), and faculty (e.g., Neumann & Peterson, 1997) frequently reflect the narrative lives of individuals facing oppression (e.g., Tokarczyk & Fay, 1993). The stories revealed in this chapter may deviate from this norm in that some are stories of privilege, though others are not. By nature, we are storytellers moving forward over time (McAdams, 1993) viewing the developmental rhythm of life:

When we comprehend our actions over time, we see what we do in terms of story. We see obstacles confronted, and intentions realized and frustrated over time. As we move forward from yesterday to today to tomorrow, we move through tensions building to climaxes, climaxes giving way to denouncements, and tensions building again as we continue to move and change. Human time is a storied affair. (McAdams, 1993, p. 30)

Though I consider myself privileged or advantaged by some self-proclaimed identities and disadvantaged by others, depending mostly on context, my story centers on a life primarily of White privilege and social mobility, built by the labor of my immigrant grandparents and first-generation parents. The stories told in this chapter emanate from personal experience and reveal a slender autobiographical (Neumann & Peterson, 1997) sketch at how the identity of the daughter of first-generation Italians has been shaped by gender, ethnicity and culture, and social class. Some of the stories of my childhood are told from "autobiographical memory" defined as "memory for the people, places, objects, events, and feelings that go into the story of [my] life" (Kotre, 1996, p. 5). It is my hope that these stories represent the truth as it happened; yet, I understand that their telling may resemble more of an innovative depiction of what actually occurred (Freeman, 2007).

In *Hunger for Memory,* Rodriguez (1982) detailed the pain his family experienced when their "family secrets" were revealed in autobiographical writing about his formal and informal education. In contrast, Chávez (2009) clearly affirms she will not reveal the private, personal stories or details of her family's life, telling her own deep stories while referring in more general ways to lessons learned from family. I desire to bring no suffering to my family, knowingly or unknowingly. Yet, my family stories reveal the life of a young girl with intersecting identities in a strong ethnic family with plenty of social rules, gender restrictions, and cultural and class habits. Unique in most literature, my story represents immigrant upward social mobility or fulfillment of the twentieth-century immigrant's "American Dream." In addi-

tion to my trusted writing partner's and talented doctoral advisee's review, my 82-year-old mother had the freedom to censor what she felt might bring shame, embarrassment, or social exclusion to family members.

FAMILY STORIES OF INTERTWINED MULTIPLE SOCIAL IDENTITIES: GENDER, ETHNICITY, AND CLASS

My Ancestors: Italian Peasants

To know me, you must know my lineage. My family hails from Calabria, at the southern end of the Italian boot, and Sicily, an island plagued with poverty, violence, and corruption for hundreds of years. For many southern Italians, escaping the hopelessness of raunchy circumstances and returning one day to flaunt the spoils of success was a dream. One family member fulfilled this vision with panache. On several occasions when my grandfather's brother, Uncle Frank, returned to Italy to visit family who stayed behind during the exodus, he sent his big Cadillac to the Mediterranean by boat and drove this ostentatious American vehicle through the narrow Calabrian mountain roads to show proof of his monetary success. A flamboyant gesture, many of my relatives seek praise and affirmation for their financial triumph. Hearing this story as a teenager, I felt embarrassed that a family member would flaunt such material wealth and concluded that, for me, humility is a more appropriate response to success. (Recently, I thought that it might have been my uncle's reaction to leaving such extreme poverty.) Professionally, not allowing success to overpower my relationships with others sets the stage for productive collaboration with students and peers without my ego protruding, while personally, it helps me attain the goal of treating others equally. As I face the daily arrogance embedded in the academy, I find myself wanting to escape it and genuinely live in, naturally observe, and change what I can to create a more equitable social world.

Paternal Grandparents: Looking for Sustenance in America

My paternal grandfather, Louis L. Guido Sr., came to the United States with my great grandfather to apply their carpentry skills in the mines near Morenci, Arizona. My paternal grandmother, Florence Sirianni Guido, lived with her family in the town, above the saloon owned by her father. She told me once, "Momma thought Papa was bringing her to the ends of the world when she moved from Italy to eastern Arizona." Given the impoverished conditions in Italy at the beginning of the twentieth century (Gambino, 1997; Mangione & Morraele, 1992), it must have been scary to leave the only home they had ever known to come to a place they had never seen, across an ocean that took days to traverse, in conditions far less than accommodating.

My paternal grandmother, my namesake, Florence Guido, was born in Arizona, one of nine children. Given the ties that bind in Italian families, she retained the culture of Italian life through the language (her mother lived with the family but did not speak English), food, the Catholic Church, and other customs from Italy. I still cook her 100-year-old recipe for homemade lasagna, which among other ingredients includes hard-boiled eggs and labor-intensive, garlic-saturated tiny meatballs. Recently, I served this dish to someone who said he had been eating lasagna all his life but had never eaten anything this good. It made me proud to represent Grandma and keep alive a tradition she practiced everyday of her life, in one large room of the house, where she was more often than not cooking the next meal.

When I was growing up, my paternal grandparents lived one block south on the next street—in other words, a skip down the alley. I saw them often and never left their home without Grandma's garden vegetables stuffed in a brown paper bag. Grandpa would grab a Hershey's kiss and hand me one from the stash he hid on the top shelf in his closet as a symbol of his love. My grandparents' home was a gathering spot for our large extended family (eight of my grandmother's siblings and their offspring also lived in town), who stopped by often for good food and family gossip. At 95 years, Grandma was still making deer sausage in her garage with her children and grandchildren and giving it to her large extended family. She lived until she was 98 years. I can still smell the garlic in her kitchen and be inspired by her indomitable determination to get what she wanted, her family nearby. As a professional, I find the same resolve when making policy change reflecting social justice for graduate students and supporting colleagues treated unfairly—indomitable determination for social justice. Grandma also taught me the power of a collaborative family, which transfers to my working with groups in many higher education contexts.

My Dad, Cosmo Frank Guido: Works Hard and Loves His Family

My father, much like his mother just described, is the hardest working person I will ever know. At 86 years, he still drives to work daily, and with a dry sense of humor, his body shelters a much younger spirit than his age implies. When he was 85 years, he told me that in his mind, he was still 35. Like wind blowing on a mountaintop, he never seems to stop. In addition to Dad's successful roles as a self-made contractor and lumber executive, winemaker, hunter, gardener, short-order cook, fix-it guy, and gourmet chef are other roles in which he excels. Through my father, I come from working-class people who believe unending hard work (with periodic equally hard play), discipline, and love of God and family are the sources of a good life. I try to emulate many of these values as I live my life. For example, most of my "free" time in the last two years has been spent meeting a book's deadlines and flying or driving to Texas from Colorado to visit my parents. This takes discipline and family often trumps work, even though most of the year my ethnic Italian family is 1,000 miles away and I am expected to be there often (Guido-DiBrito & Chávez, 2003).

Dad's stories of life and growing up were filled with relatives' affirmation and one of others' discrimination against him. The most poignant story he tells is one that occurred around 1930 in San Antonio when he was with several Mexican American boys who were prohibited from entering the roller skating rink in town. He told me how the imprint of this exclusionary experience motivated him to work especially hard to demonstrate his worthiness of inclusion in the dominant culture he so wanted to emulate. When he was a teenager, he changed his birth name from Cosimaio Guido to his new name Cosmo Guido. I think it made him feel more assimilated and not so ethnic, although the majority of his friends were Italian male relatives. Although he spoke three languages—English, Spanish, and Italian—only English was spoken in our home. Though he has never said it, the road to success for his children and grandchildren depends on us assimilating into the dominant culture with the supreme caveat that loyalty to family comes first. In effect, my father, and mother too, want the next generation of Guidos to function fully both within this tight-knit Italian clan and the social and economic world beyond it. Although some of their behaviors indicate a desire to assimilate their children into U.S. society, my parents chose acculturation, encouraging us to keep the values and traditions they passed down from their Italian ancestors, while also succeeding in the dominant culture.

When I was a child, my father, with his father, built the foundation for Guido Brothers Construction and Lumber companies, while mom stayed home to raise the three children she had in five years. In my youth, we were working class, my father's family, and upper-middle/lower-upper class, my mother's family, by dominant culture economic, though not necessarily social, standards. My father's money messages were strong such as "save for a rainy day," "waste not want not," and "spend your money wisely," while seek-

ing affirmation and respect from the more privileged. Social class differences between my parents are highlighted in an interaction with my grandfather. A few years after Mom and Dad were married, Dad insisted Mom give her father back the car he gave her; however, my charismatic grandfather convinced my father he had no reason to work if Grandpa could not give what he wanted to his children. Perhaps evidence of class distinctions, my father wanted nothing for his family he had not earned.

The Guido family's dinner conversation ritual played out in ways that showed my father's ability to move easily among people of different ethnic and social class groups. I remember small talk about "how was your day?" details among all of us, but mostly, I recall the endless stories my father told about the wide range of people with whom he had daily contact from bankers, archbishops, and attorneys to carpenters, plumbers, and laborers. His willingness to share the detailed "he said, I said" aspects of their conversations left me mesmerized by what I perceived as his connection to the vast range of both the powerful and the not so powerful. Often, stories of these men involved my father offering food or wine; he is still generous with his blessings, bringing barbeque he prepared to a laborer's wake and homemade Guido wine when he visits the Chief Executive Officer of a bank. Dad was my first model for treating others equally and affirming diversity.

One of the most memorable moments of my life was the day my father left office as president of the National Lumber Dealers in the fall of 1970, during my first year in college. I have never been so proud to be Italian and my father's daughter. The national conference was held in Toronto and the entire family gathered to watch Dad celebrate his success. As we walked from the hotel to the conference center, Dad grabbed my hand and with a tear in his eye said, "Who could believe that the son of an Italian immigrant would become president of a national organization?" His dedication paid off many times over as he continues today to oversee the family businesses, operated by a third generation of Guidos. From Dad, I take the lessons that discipline can bring quality work and praise, love of family is unending, and relating to many different people brings a rich life. In one generation, Italian immigrants in the United States could be upwardly mobile.

Maternal Grandparents: Escaping Poverty in Italy

My maternal grandparents (Variscos and Scardinos) immigrated to the United States from Sicily and found their way to Houston via New Orleans in the early 1900s. My maternal great grandmother, a woman the family called "Momma Dora," who I knew as a teenager, told me that her husband, my great grandfather, "Papa Tony," whom I never knew, "loved the land." My ancestors found their way to the Brazos River's black bottom from a Houston macaroni factory and began to grow cotton in a familiar hot climate. My grandfather willingly helped his father work the flat, white-puffed fields but was pulled out of school permanently after sixth grade to lend a hand on the farm. Grandpa's lack of education did not keep him from success, though it appears to have influenced the premium he placed on this commodity, even for his two daughters. In fact, my grandfather may have perpetrated one of the first feminist acts in our family. Even though he had no sons, Italian male heirs to carry his name, he was determined his daughters would receive the best possible education, so he sent them to Vassar. Not without his Achilles' heel, my grandfather and his attitudes about people of color reflected a double standard and were oddly dichotomous. For example, he treated the Blacks who picked cotton on his farm with ultimate respect and gratitude, yet he told me that I could not date a Mexican American boy when I was in high school. When I inquired why, Grandpa told me "Mexicans beat their wives." This seemed odd to me because I knew Italians beat their wives too.

I knew Grandpa was doing what he thought was right for me. He taught me he was molded by his time, as am I, but judging people by their skin color alone does not confirm my experience of others. In fact, I have sought out different others all my life, acting consistently with my belief in the rich learning that occurs from difference.

My maternal grandmother, Lucille Scardino, met my grandfather, Brazos Varisco, in Bryan, Texas, where she was born and lived 80 of her 84 years. Born in the Victorian era, she held values congruent with righteousness, vanity, and surrendering all power to her husband. In fact, when Grandpa died, Grandma could not do simple tasks such as change the blade in a razor to shave her legs or write a check. I had the privilege of living two doors down from her for about eight years when I was a doctoral student at Texas A&M. She depended on me for groceries and shopping, and I often drove her to church and family events. She loved good food, laughed easily, and derived great pleasure seeing her grandchildren happy. We teased each other often and got along well. Her number one priority was her family, and she provided food and shelter for us whenever we needed it. For over 25 years, my parents drove to Bryan weekly and then monthly to manage my grandfather's estate. Grandma welcomed them for their overnight stay with her Italian recipes and other tasty edible morsels cooking on the stove. These same smells resonate from my mother's kitchen, particularly at Christmas time, with Grandma's favorite, pinalates, a honey dripping, sticky, square, carbohydrate rock. Even now I can smell the onions cooking on Grandma's stove whenever I think of walking in her backdoor.

My Mom, Antoinette Varisco Guido: Victorian Values and Generous Spirit

My mother was, and still is, an insatiable reader. She graduated from high school when she was 15 years and from Vassar when she was 18 years. Accepted to Tulane Medical School in 1946, she decided not to attend but marry Cosmo Guido and begin our family. She told me once that my generation of peers had too many choices, and she felt her choices were limited. Mom was 19 years, a mere child herself, when her first child, my oldest brother, was born and 24 years when I came into this world.

As a full-time Mom, she supplied all the daily needs for our family of five including meals and laundry, vegetable and flower gardening, and those magical touches on all family gatherings. She was the machine that ran our home. She arranged for me to learn outside school with ballet, swimming, and piano lessons, Catholic Youth Organization softball, Brownies and Girl Scouts, and with charm school in my early teens and ballroom dancing in high school. Throughout our K–12 years, she did not allow the television to be switched on during the week, so my brothers and I could do our homework and practice the piano. I remember her words of wisdom when I was a child such as "do your work first, and then play," or she might tell me to go "read a good book" when I complained I was bored. She spent her youth in a tree on a cotton farm near the Brazos River devouring whatever books were available and still belongs to a book discussion group. Mom also taught me that every Italian kitchen has a big can of olive oil in the pantry, even when financial resources are scarce. She was my first teacher, and her love of reading and the consistency with which she read to her children and read quietly by herself gave me my first model for lifelong learning and the gifts it brings.

My mother is a Southern woman, with an independent Texan spirit, but prior to college, she rarely peeked beyond her family tree. In her 80s now, Mom is a proud woman who gives her energy and support to her children and grandchildren and when she is not reading or playing bridge, finds time to support her favorite philanthropic causes (e.g., the San Antonio Symphony, Southwest Texas Research Center, and so on). Her love of education and her grandchildren have merged to create one of the greatest higher edu-

cation philanthropists I will ever know. By 2023, Mom will have sent all 12 of her grandchildren to the undergraduate institution of their choice including four-years' tuition, room, and board. My siblings and their offspring are recipients of my mother's Herculean generosity, likely comparable only to a few elite. As a child she would tell me, "no one can ever take away your education."

DAUGHTER OF FIRST-GENERATION, MIXED-CLASS ITALIAN IMMIGRANTS

My mother has always called me her happy child. As the third child and first girl, I wanted to please Mom and the three other men in our lives—my father and two older brothers. Though I did not understand it at the time, I was in a daily competition with all of them to shine the brightest. My demeanor was more get along, go along—keep the peace, help out, scream loudly, and maybe when our work is done, we can have some fun (my parents' motto). Had I been a boy, I would have talked Dad into tearing down the wall between my brothers' room and mine to make one big kid playground. Instead, my room, although large, was in the front of the house facing the street. For nine years, I was the only one of the five of us who slept in a room alone and it made me feel different. Even now, in this familial group of engineers and accountants, I often feel misplaced as an educator, as if maybe I was switched with someone else at birth.

I learned early that being a girl in this Italian family had perks and drawbacks. Some of the perks came later, but sleeping alone as a child with four other family members in the same house, being on call for dish and clothesline duty, rarely ever leaving anyone's sight, and helping my mother were female expectations and duties in which my brothers rarely, if at all, participated. Not much to my liking, traditional ethnic and dominant culture gender roles that were commonplace in the 1950s middle-class suburbia (for a taste of 1950s culture, see the TV series *Mad-men*) were adhered to in the Guido household.

Flo's Childhood: Early Experiences Shaping My Feminist Perspective (1950s–1960s)

As the first daughter in an Italian family, I led a childhood unhindered by devastating loss or tragedy. Although I did not escape emotional pain, I have led a "blessed life," reflecting the sentiment my mother expressed when she wanted me to be thankful and told me to "count my blessings." Capable of experiencing a broad range of emotions, I can remember a happy childhood playing tag, baseball, hide and seek, hop scotch, jacks, and basketball in the driveway with my brothers and their friends, gardening with my parents to reap the unending vegetable supply, and attending a small parochial school within rock-kicking distance from home. With a dry sense of humor like my Dad and a different kind of intelligence than my engineer brothers', I often felt like a misplaced modifier. Little about me seemed "normal" in the way I thought others around me defined it. Though I wanted to please, somehow I never seemed to measure up and, at some point, allowed myself the physical and emotional break from the clan in order to find my own path (Josselson, 1973; Phinney, 1990).

Based on my parents' treatment of me in line with certain Italian cultural practices ascribed to their daughters, I saw my role as my mother's daughter first. Often, I would help in the kitchen and then wander to the garden or BBQ pit. I remember complaining that my brothers had all the fun helping Dad outside. At Christmas, I made Italian cookies and homemade lasagna and was in the kitchen for days, responsible for setting the table, clearing it and helping wash the dishes, and usually the next day, putting everything back in its place. My brothers sat idly after dinner or watched football on TV with the other men of the family and were rarely involved in what seemed like endless chores on holidays and family occasions. This gendered, ethnic behavior continues today and, as I grow older, I find solace in thinking of this different treatment as part of my expected role as the first daughter in an acculturated ethnic (Evans, et al., 2009) Italian American family.

Growing up in San Antonio, my world evolved primarily around the Blessed Sacrament, the local parochial school I attended for eight years, and St. Francis of Padua, the Italian Church my grandfather built in downtown San Antonio in 1926. Other than two different family vacation car trips to Yellowstone and Big Bend National Parks and another drive from Texas to Boston for my brothers to look at colleges, the Guido family traveled several times a year to visit my mother's extended Italian family 150 miles away. These adventures stood out for their rarity as most of my life revolved around school, family, and the Catholic Church.

Gender played a role in my differentiation while growing up, but ethnicity and class were also woven into my identity. Freedoms given to my brothers to explore the outside world were far greater than anything I experienced as an adolescent. In fact, I was rarely permitted to spend the night away from home. One dynamic exception was a month-long stay at camp in Tennessee. On a moment's notice and with my grandfather's generous resources, I flew alone at age 11 to Nashville, stayed overnight with people no one in my family knew, and hopped a bus to camp the next day, where my cousin was waiting for me. The freedom was exhilarating and scary simultaneously. Raised in a traditional Italian enclave, I still cannot believe my parents let their daughter travel alone at such a young age, because it was in stark contrast to their overprotective behavior. Being a girl in this Guido family made me different.

As a group, the family socialized in San Antonio with other middle- and upper-middle-class neighborhood families, such as the Johnson's, Bohmfalk's, Molak's, and Rippstein's—but no Italians. All of these families, including ours, had a stay-at-home mother and a working father, the epitome of traditional 1950s suburban life. Yet, in my youth, I learned early that life existed both inside the family and outside it. Inside the family, life was safe and protected. The glimpses of life I was permitted outside the security of family and church made me crave the treasures lying beyond. I was 17 years when vistas I could not imagine found my view. However, later, it was the tie to my Italian family that sustained me in difficult times, always cementing our family loyalty.

The summer of 1969, between my junior and senior high school years, I traveled to Europe from New York on a ship filled with 1,500 college students and a family friend, a junior at the University of Oklahoma. We spent the summer touring Europe by bus and were sailing on a small ship through the Strait of Corinth in Greece the night the U.S. astronauts landed on the moon. I met people from all over Europe, learned some of their history, and saw castles, museums, cathedrals, aqueducts, art, sculptures, and paintings in every country from England and Holland south to Yugoslavia, Italy, Spain, and France. I was enchanted by the diversity and beauty to behold. The inspiration stayed with me and, after trying several "practical" majors in my first semester in college, I finally decided on art history as the culmination of this impressionable journey.

The privilege involved in touring Europe all summer as a teenager and the decision to attend a private college and choose a life-giving, but impractical, academic major has not escaped me. Even the privilege of exposure to individuals from many cultural backgrounds in and outside the United States and in my hometown at an early age, while staying intricately tied to my family and heritage, is a gift, which I hope did not leave others disadvantaged in its wake.

Flo's 20s and 30s: Identity Shift in Gender and Class (1970s and 1980s)

My mother is an avid supporter of her alma mater, Vassar, the first women's college to offer a curriculum similar to that taught at Ivy League institutions (Guido-DiBrito, 2002). Yet, neither her two daughters nor four granddaughters have attended Vassar, though her eldest granddaughter graduated from Yale. When I was not accepted at Vassar, my mother wanted to "pull some strings" to enroll me. I told her I did not want to spend my college career in the library. When she tried to use her San Antonio Wellesley alumnae admissions contacts, she was told several Hispanic women from South San Antonio were accepted over me in order to diversify Wellesley's student composition. Occurring the same spring as Kent State and in the midst of the civil rights movement, it seemed reasonable to me that institutions would scramble to enroll from a limited diverse pool of potential applicants. At the time, I was dating a Mexican American boy and intuitively knew it was valuable at all levels of society for females from all races to be represented at elite U.S. women's colleges. I knew I would find a college home somewhere else and I did, down the Hudson River from Vassar and closer (only 50 minutes by train) to New York City, an endless playground.

My days at Briarcliff College, a tiny (i.e., 750 students) all-women's institution located in Briarcliff Manor, New York, were filled with opportunity to excel and adventure in the "Big Apple." My classmates who lived down the hall included a Rockefeller descendant and heirs to Hasbro Toys and Busch Beer. My roommates and college friends came from places such as Bucks County, Pennsylvania; Swampscott, Massachusetts; and Shaker Heights, Ohio. I slowly learned the social class meanings of these places and the difference in status between "old" and "new" money. Most of my college friends and roommates drove small, often old, foreign cars, while I drove a new Oldsmobile Cutlass Supreme, one of the biggest cars in the college parking lot. My father, a protector and patriot, wanted me to drive a big American car and be safe on the 1,500-mile drive from South Texas to New York. I never thought of my family as having money, but because of the high social status of many of my college peers, I attended college feeling at the bottom of the financial hierarchy and teetering clumsily on the social ladder. I was a passionate, sometimes loud, crazy Italian willing to be involved in good harmless pranks, while most of my college peers from the east coast and upper social strata came from quiet, demure, and prosperous families, where conspicuous consumption was not considered good taste, and in some circles among the extremely rich, not socially acceptable.

Long after college graduation, I learned these rules were socially constructed and my opinions about myself may not have been clear. I neglected to consider that the people with whom I compared myself fostered long-held wealth passed down from generation to generation. My maternal grandfather, whom some might consider a self-made man, amassed sizeable wealth in his lifetime as did my father, but both came from working-class roots. Thus, in some circles on Briarcliff's campus, I was considered "beneath" those with decades of accumulated wealth. My mixed social breeding was often confusing, and my pride and shame were volatile depending on whether I was at college or at home. Genetics counted heavily for social status privilege at college and my breeding excluded me on some occasions.

I took advantage of every opportunity I could at college. Little kept me from catching the bus from campus to the Metropolitan Museum almost every Friday to look firsthand at the artwork I studied. I qualified for a job on campus and also spent several hours each week refiling my art history professor's class slides. Opportunities to examine the works again and review for exams also put spending money in my pocket. In my first true teaching opportunity as a docent at a small museum in Yonkers, New York, I had the honor of bringing art to underprivileged elementary children who had no exposure to great works of art. When asking a class of second graders why they thought Monet might have painted a picture the way he did, one enthusiastic Black child

in the back of the room responded, "to please my eyes." I agreed with his claim and at that moment held heightened awareness of my privilege as the child of first-generation immigrants to travel in the United States and abroad to discover primarily Western art and its superstars firsthand.

Exposure to the dynamic tension between conservatism and liberalism by attendance at a small women's college punctuated the experiences that shaped my views on being a woman in a changing society. Many of my college peers came from longstanding, high-profile, conservative families (e.g., a Presidential Cabinet Secretary under Nixon) and yet some of these women were politically and socially liberal (e.g., newly legalized abortion was not unheard of among my peers), a reflection of the early women's rights movement. As the first generation to have easy access to birth control, I remember sitting in a Human Sexuality class discussing the pill when two classmates announced they were going back to their dormitory room to take the birth control pills they had forgotten that morning. Mary Cheever, author in her own right and wife of author John Cheever, taught my freshman rhetoric class and exposed me to new ideas, which stretched me to become a good writer through the awareness and importance of language in making my ideas known. In hindsight, Cheever's tutelage, as one of five students, was a highlight of my academic career. Though my writing was as naive as I was and filled with hyperbole, Mary gave useful feedback and unwittingly launched my love/hate relationship with writing.

The privilege to study in this tiny, unique women's college offered experiences I could not imagine (e.g., studying art in the Museum of Modern Art, learning about Wall Street from the perch of the Federal Reserve and the Stock Exchange), yet being a woman was a condition most of us had to survive. The majority of professors at Briarcliff were men and some shined light on women's contributions in the subject matter they taught from political science to sociology to biology. One of my only female art history professors, a Roman Art scholar who did not receive tenure, often pointed out that the classic text we used in the introductory Art History survey course lacked acknowledgment of women's contributions in art and architecture. On the other hand, one of the tenured male professors who abused his power in a small classroom of women encouraged students to give him sexual favors in exchange for an A letter grade. Sometimes, my friends and I saw him leaving the dormitory in the middle of the night. (I am pleased to announce I earned a C in his course.) Woodstock was over, and the sexual revolution was expanding sexual boundaries, but today this behavior is considered blatant sexual harassment. Although the advantages of attending an all-women's college outweighed the disadvantages, my potential was impeded through this male professor's lack of respect for women students.

I graduated from college in 1974. When my folks showed up at Briarcliff from Texas for graduation and to take me back home, I had not begun to pack. I had become mesmerized by New York City, but gainful employment was limited for someone with a degree in art history. One employment agency in New York City told me they might be able to find me a job washing dishes, an irony not lost on me. When we returned to Texas, my mother encouraged me to get a business degree, not a Master of Business Administration, but skills to help me get a job as a secretary. Although she meant to be helpful, I had no intention of becoming a slave to a male boss. As an expectation of women from the Italian upper class, my mother believed that a woman should receive a college degree in order to be a helpful wife to her professional husband and a competent mother to her multiple children. My brothers, on the other hand, were expected to be competent engineers who could run a multimillion-dollar family business and support their families.

Different treatment for women and men has been a prominent theme throughout my life and I have come to expect it. In one of my first student affairs positions at a small Church of the Brethren College, I had the freedom to create whatever programs I wanted, and some of the traditions that I began still continue. When I left this position voluntarily after two years, my supervisor, the dean of students, proclaimed I had "renewed his faith in young professionals" in the way I executed my job. Interestingly, I later learned that a White male with a family was hired in this position and paid thousands more than was offered me to stay. I was told he needed more money because he had a family to support. In the midst of a divorce myself, this would not be the only time I would feel the sting of gender inequality in a higher education workplace.

Wanting to become a dean of students someday, I believed I could learn most from living with students and became director of an all-women's residence hall at the University of Wisconsin–Stevens Point. Here, I observed firsthand difficult decisions women students make such as those related to eating, dating, marriage, career, and family and how much power women surrender to men (Holland & Eisenhart, 1990; hooks, 2000). At the same time, I began to facilitate weekend campus leadership workshops and realized the scarcity of literature available to distinguish the leadership of women and men. Later, as I pursued doctoral studies, I was inspired by leadership scholars (e.g., Astin & Leland, 1991) who articulated differences between women and men and found an outlet for my early research on gender and leadership (see Guido-DiBrito, DiBrito, & Carpenter, 1986; Guido-DiBrito, Nathan, Noteboom, & Fenty, 1997), which among its findings revealed leadership is not gender specific, but gender related.

INTERSECTING GENDER, ETHNICITY AND CULTURE, AND CLASS: THE MAKING OF A FEMINIST

For over 30 years of my professional career, administration, teaching, and scholarship have consumed the majority of my life. Indeed, I am one of a handful of faculty I know who have earned tenure twice (i.e., Universities of Northern Colorado and Northern Iowa), which says much about my desire to move West and what I was willing to give up to live here. In my career, I have experienced privilege and oppression as a result of my gender, ethnicity, and class. These stories will have to wait for another time, but as I embrace my differences and demonstrate my competence, I recognize the role of my intersecting identities in my journey to professional success.

As a philosopher, historian, writer, and photographer, among other professional identities, I found the rational, linear, practical, concrete world of engineers, contractors, bankers, and the like to be laborious, with uninteresting technical aspects. With good intentions and mostly unspoken, I was taught that going to college was to meet a man or at least to learn to communicate intelligently to meet a man, who would ultimately marry and support me. These values reflect my parents' Victorian upbringing and had I not been exposed to a wealth of people and ideas, perhaps I would hold these values too, as Josselson (1973) suggested about women who foreclose before questioning. I followed the Victorian marriage path congruent with my parent's values but found a rewarding career in teaching and research, which was not congruent with the expectations of upper-class Italian women at the time I came of age.

As a self-described curious contrarian, I was forever examining the world around me and questioning the social world through my intuition and feelings. As a second-generation immigrant who came of age in the late 1960s, it is no wonder I questioned the previous generations' values and rules and, unbeknownst to me at the time, desired a world with less patriarchy and more women leaders. During my first three decades, experiences related to my gender, ethnicity, culture, and social class created a "perfect storm" of integration for me to form attitudes congruent with White feminist beliefs—gender

equity and its implications, particularly in higher education. As the first in my family to obtain a PhD and hold a tenured professorship, I am still navigating territory, but I believe I am making a difference in the lives of a broad range of students and colleagues.

CONCLUSION

In *The Lost Ravioli Recipes of Hoboken: A Search for Family and Food*, Schenone (2008) artfully describes how her search for a family ravioli recipe led her to finding her family's lost Italian heritage. In contrast, my life unfolded in a different way that reveals an acculturated Italian American family, making a search for our roots unnecessary, as we lived both in Italian culture and American culture. As first-generation immigrants, my parents assumed their children, at some level, would acculturate and not fully assimilate into the dominant culture. My mother told me once I could go to college in the East, but I was expected to return home to San Antonio, another sign of family wanting family nearby.

The story I tell at the beginning of this chapter is one of me as a frightened little girl looking for a way out of the high beauty and traditional life expectations of the women in her Italian family. I have heard my father's stories about the discrimination he faced as a child and how these injustices motivated him to work toward the same high esteem as dominant culture individuals. As a privileged individual wanting to give back, my stories and Dad's spur me to research and write about social identity and make transparent some of the injustices placed on those in higher education not from the dominant culture. The aisles I walk down now are not for weddings but for graduation exercises and hooding my doctoral advisees. I bypassed spiked heels, expensive jewelry, and designer dresses for mid-calf suede boots, colorful scarves, and native jewelry. My gown and robe for graduation is usually hot but not as uncomfortable as the white eyelet dress I wore all those years ago. At December graduation each year, my suede boots are highly visible under my gown, reminding me of my difference as a mixed class Italian American woman in a centuries-old institution and the route my family and I took, so I can help others down the graduation aisle.

REFERENCES

Abes, E. S., Jones, S. R., & McEwen, M. K. (2007). Reconceptualizing the model of multiple dimensions of identity: The role of meaning-making capacity in the construction of multiple identities. *Journal of College Student Development, 48*, 1–22.

Astin, H. S., & Leland, C. (1991). *Women of influence, women of vision: A cross-generational study of leaders and social change.* San Francisco, CA: Jossey-Bass.

Barrett, J. E., & Roediger, D. (2008). How white people became white. In P. S. Rothenberg (Ed.), *White privilege: Essential readings on the other side of racism* (3rd ed., pp. 35–40). New York: Worth Publishers.

Borrego, S. E., & Manning, K. M. (2007). *Where I am from: Student affairs practice from the whole of students' lives.* Washington, DC: NASPA.

Chávez, A. F. (2009). Leading in the borderlands: Negotiating ethnic patriarchy for the benefit of students. *Journal About Women in Higher Education, 2*, 39–65.

Chávez, A. F., & Guido-DiBrito, F. (1999). Race and ethnicity in development. In C. Clark & R. Caffarella (Eds.), *An update on adult development theory* (pp. 39–47). New Directions in Adult and Continuing Education, No. 84. San Francisco, CA: Jossey-Bass.

Clandinin, D. J., & Connelly, F. M. (2000). *Narrative inquiry: Experience and story in qualitative research.* San Francisco, CA: Jossey-Bass.

Cunningham, G. (1965). The Italian: A hindrance to white solidarity in Louisiana, 1890–1898. *Journal of Negro History, 50*, 22–36.

Ellis, C. (2004). *The ethnographic I: A methodological novel about autoethnography.* Walnut Creek, CA: Alta Mira Press.

Evans, N. J., Forney, D. S., Guido, F. M., Patton, L. & Renn, K. A. (2009). *Student development in college: Theory, research, and practice*, 2nd ed. San Francisco, CA: Jossey-Bass.

Freeman, M. (2007). Autobiographical understanding and narrative inquiry. In D. J. Clandinin (Ed.), *Handbook of narrative inquiry: Mapping a methodology* (pp. 120–145). Thousand Oaks, CA: Sage.

Fried, J. (Ed.). (1994). *Different voices: Gender and perspective in student affairs administration.* Washington, DC: NASPA.

Gambino, R. (1997). *Blood of my blood: The dilemma of the Italian-Americans* (2nd ed.). Toronto, ON: Guernica. (First published 1974)

Gilligan, C. (1993). *In a different voice: Psychological theory and women's development.* Cambridge, MA: Harvard University Press. (First published 1982)

Guido-DiBrito, F. (2002). Women students: An overview. In A. M. Martínez Alemán & K. A. Renn (Eds.), *Women in higher education: An encyclopedia* (pp. 249–262). Santa Barbara, CA: ABC-CLIO.

Guido-DiBrito, F., Carpenter, D. S., & DiBrito, W. F. (1986). Women in management and leadership: Review of the literature, 1985 update. *National Association of Student Personnel Administrators Journal, 23*(3), 22–31.

Guido-DiBrito, F., & Chávez, A. F. (2003). Understanding the ethnic self: Learning and teaching in a multicultural world. *Journal of Student Affairs, 7*, 11–21.

Guido-DiBrito, F., Nathan, L. E., Noteboom, P. A., & Fenty, J. E. (1997). Traditional and new paradigm leadership: The gender link. *Initiatives, 58*(1), 27–38.

Holland, D. C., & Eisenhart, M. A. (1990). *Educated in romance: Women, achievement, and college culture.* Chicago, IL: University of Chicago Press.

hooks, b. (2000). *Feminism is for everybody: Passionate politics.* Cambridge, MA: South End Press.

Jones, S. R. (2009). Constructing identities at the intersections: An autoethnographic exploration of multiple dimensions of identity. *Journal of College Student Development, 50*(2), 287–304.

Josselson, R. (1973). Psychodynamic aspects of identity formation in college women. *Journal of Youth and Adolescents, 2*, 3–52.

Josselson, R. (1996). *Revising herself: the story of women's identity from college to midlife.* New York: Oxford University Press.

Kotre, J. (1996). *White gloves: How we create ourselves through memory.* New York: W. W. Norton.

Mangione, J., & Morreale, B. (1992). *La storia: Five centuries of the Italian American experience.* New York: Harper Perennial.

Marshall, S. M. (Ed.). (2006). *Stories of inspiration: Lessons and laughter in student affairs.* Washington, DC: NASPA.

McAdams, D. P. (1993). *The stories we live by: Personal myths and the making of the self.* New York: Guilford.

Mormino, G. R., & Pozzetta, G. F. (1987). *The immigrant world of Ybor city: Italians and their Latin neighbors in Tampa, 1885–1985*. Urbana, IL: University of Illinois press.

Neumann, A., & Peterson, P. L. (1997). *Learning from our lives: Women, research and autobiography in education*. New York: Teacher's College Press.

Ostrander, S. A. (1984). *Women of the upper class*. Philadelphia, PA: Temple University Press.

Phinney, J. S. (1990). Ethnic identity in adolescents and adults: Review of research. *Psychological Bulletin, 108*, 499–514.

Rochlin, J. M. (1997). *Race and class on campus: Conversations with Ricardo's daughter*. Tucson, AZ: University of Arizona Press.

Rodriguez, R. (1982). *Hunger of memory: The education of Richard Rodriguez*. New York: Bantam Books.

Schenone, L. (2008). *The lost ravioli recipes of Hoboken: A search for food and family*. New York: Norton & Co.

Schwartz, J. L., Donovan, J., & Guido-DiBrito, F. (2009). Stories of social class: Self-identified Mexican male students crack the silence. *Journal of College Student Development, 50*, 50–66.

Tokarczyk, M. M., & Fay, E. A. (Eds). (1993). *Working-class women in the academy: Laborers in the knowledge factory*. Amherst, MA: The University of Massachusetts Press.

11

Economically Disadvantaged Women in Higher Education

Hearing Their Stories and Striving for Social Justice

Penny J. Rice

Abstract: *Higher education opens doors to opportunities that change lives. Single mothers surviving on the reformed welfare system no longer have the freedom of choice to enroll in college. Mandated Work First programs have shut the doors on this pathway out of poverty. The public discourse is silent on this crisis and we cannot afford to ignore their lived experiences any longer. A brief overview on current welfare statistics is introduced. The stories of three single mothers, and the author, are shared to demonstrate the struggles that come when you are forgotten. A call to action is presented for higher education and the government to acknowledge their needs and the opportunity education brings to all of our futures.*

ECONOMIC STATUS CROSSES OTHER socially constructed lines of difference: race/ethnicity, gender, ability, age, sexuality, religion, and others (Mantsios, 2004). Understanding the power and privilege dynamics within economic statuses presents a strong foundation for understanding other systems of power, privilege, oppression, and social injustice.

Higher education provides a window of opportunity to enter the middle class for the low class/working class/working poor. In 1996 the Personal Responsibility and Work Opportunity Reconciliation Act (PRWOR) mandated that recipients of assistance work in ex-change for their benefits (Phillips-Fein, 2002). Low-income single parents are working in greater percentages following this alleged reform; however, 78% are employed in four typically low-wage occupations with single mothers working more hours and earning less than single fathers (Jones-DeWeever, Peterson, & Song, 2003).

The impact of this legislation on the lives of women and their families has been ignored other than to report the reduced numbers of families receiving welfare assistance. At the same time, communities around the country state, "Our food banks are reporting a 15 to 20% increase on average in the number of people turning to them for help now compared to one year ago" (America's Second Harvest, 2008). What is happening to women who are economically disadvantaged? What is happening to their children and family members? Where are the stories of this population of U.S. citizens?

This chapter shares the stories of a much forgotten population of students—economically disadvantaged women with children. This group of female students has been arriving on college campuses for a number of years, yet they continue to receive inadequate financial support from the federal or state government to achieve their academic goals or the campus support systems to navigate through higher education bureaucracy successfully. The challenges and invisibility of this group of women and children has become even more prevalent since the passage of the PRWOR in 1996. Three years after the passage of this legislation, "welfare recipients are less likely to be in college, less likely to have access to health insurance and more likely to be concentrated in urban areas" (Jones-DeWeever et al., 2003, p. ix). Their stories, along with mine, are embedded throughout this chapter and include a call to action for colleges and universities to increase services and financial support to not just the women but their children and families, because when you educate a woman, you educate all who touch her life.

In addition to sharing these stories, this chapter will provide a literature review so as to inform the reader of past research into issues of economic disparity and to provide a societal context in which to place these stories. Finally, this chapter will examine the study done at Iowa State University, "The Missing Story of Ourselves: Poverty and the Promise of Higher Education," a project coordinated by The ACCESS Project at Hamilton College in Clinton, New York (Adair, n.d.). While at Iowa State University, this research project allowed me the opportunity to inquire into what was happening in my community.

MY STORY

My plan was to graduate from college, four years after finishing high school, with a degree in nursing, work three to four years, return to college and earn a master's degree in nursing, and begin teaching. After these goals were attained, I planned to get married and have at least two children. Several factors played into messing up my plan: surviving a sexual assault during my first quarter in college, not being able to understand or name that I was being sexually harassed by two different professors during this same quarter, and the unexpected death of my 21-year-old brother (17 months older). The trauma I was experiencing was displayed in my failing grades and increased reliance on alcohol and drugs to take me away from my life. My plan altered; in fact, it was completely abandoned. I failed out of college in three short quarters.

Ten years after my first enrollment in college, I found myself with a technical degree of occupational proficiency in cosmetology, the mother of two children, and divorced. I returned to the town in which I grew up and struggled to provide basic needs for my children and myself. The day I lined up in Department of Human Services (DHS) was not the last day I asked myself, "What happened to me?"

For my first meeting with a caseworker, I needed to bring my children (my daughter was 4 years old and my son was 15 months old). The caseworker looked at my file and looked up at us and said, "Penny, you're young and pretty. Why don't you just go find yourself a sugar daddy to take care of you? You don't want to put your kids and yourself through this system." After pausing a few minutes my response to her was, "I don't understand. It was men who put me in a position of needing to stand in this line. Why would I go back to that?" I had to tell her about the psychological abuse, sexual abuse, the running away in the middle of the night to friends and family to be safe. I had to share with her that I didn't think I could manage on my own, so I moved in with a man who was more abusive than my husband, that I sustained five beatings by him, which still cause me pain today. "I ran away from the men in my life that said they loved me," I told her. "I need to find a way to take care of myself in order to care for my children." She processed my paperwork.

After one year of working full time as a hairdresser making less than $6,000, I managed to pay 12 monthly installments on my defaulted student loans, and I enrolled in a course called Expanded Career Choices (ECC) offered by the local Job Training Partnership Act (JTPA) Office. I learned a great deal about myself, established short- and long-term goals, and identified areas where I needed to develop skills in order to be successful personally, academically, and professionally. The class was made up of men and women of different ages who had a variety of experiences that brought them to this 15-week class.

After completing Expanded Career Choices, I enrolled in classes at a local community college. My daughter attended kindergarten in the morning and would join her brother at an in-home family day care across the street from her school. This arrangement ended when my daughter shared her fears about going to the day care because the woman and her husband were mean and yelled at the kids all day. We were fortunate to find another in-home day care provider that was loving, kind, and not scary to my children.

Each day, I walked my daughter to school, my son to day care, and myself to the community college. During the warmer months, we used our red wagon to move about, and during the winter we used the red sled to get to our destinations. Each night, we shared dinner, and between eight and nine o'clock, the house was quiet and I began my studies until around three o'clock in the morning.

I was terrified each day of so many things: Would Human Services find something wrong with my application? Did I forget to tell them something about my finances? Would the man who beat me break into our home again and threaten me? What if I am stupid, like my husband repeatedly told me, and fail out of college again? What if I don't know how to best parent my children; will I lose custody of them? Some of our biggest challenges were getting through each month with adequate food. Most months ended with 7–10 days of grilled cheese sandwiches, scrambled eggs, or boxed macaroni and cheese. I frequently found myself managing this terror and fear by jamming a hand towel into my mouth and screaming and crying until my voice was hoarse and I was exhausted.

I graduated with honors from the community college with my associate of arts degree and developed a plan to transfer to a four-year bachelor/master's degree–granting university 90 minutes away from where we currently lived. I purchased a used car for $250, making sure that it was not worth too much to violate DHS standards, and began searching for a new residence that would accept a Title 8 Housing Voucher. My daughter enrolled in her second elementary school in first grade and her fourth day care provider, and my son began preschool.

The next two years my studies focused on a major in psychology and women's studies. I became active with a student organization called Feminist Single Moms and volunteered at a county crisis intervention hotline. Life was good and we were happy, even with a steady supply of grilled cheese and inadequate food supplies. I distinctly remember the dilemmas of living on a fixed income and the challenges this reality presents: I have $5 and need both milk and tampons; I have $20 for the next 2 weeks and need gas and a birthday present for my daughter; and I have a penny to my name for the next 10 days and need to pay our phone bill today. We frequently experienced the power or phone being shut off and never enjoyed things such as extra toilet paper in the closet or cable television. We would have never survived these times if I had not developed friendships with other single moms who were also enrolled in college and on welfare. We shared each other's burdens, joys, and fears. When a friend needed a bill paid fast, one of us would take care of it for her, and the next month, she would do the same of another woman. I learned that if I ever needed anything the person most likely to give me the help I needed was not the wealthy, middle- or upper-class individual, it was the working-class or working-poor person who was ready to do what needed to be done to help others currently in a tougher place than they were.

When the clothes dryer stopped heating in the trailer we rented, it was my responsibility to fix it. Time spent in class, studying, and caring for the kids, and limited financial resources delayed this repair and for many weeks our clothes dried on the line I constructed down our long hallway in the trailer. One day at the library, I found a book on the mechanics of a clothes dryer and learned that this motor was one of the simplest types to understand and repair. I determined through a trouble shooting section of the book that the heating coil was not working. I took the dryer apart, removed the heating coil, took it to a parts supplier, and asked for a replacement. The part cost less than $12. After I repaired the dryer, I felt a sense of empowerment I had never known. I was ready to fix anything—even my current life situation.

The second year of college was nearly over when our trailer was burglarized. Whoever invaded our home spent a significant amount of time in the living room and on my bed as measured by the number of cigarette butts scattered about the trailer. Our clothes and personal belongings were dispersed throughout the trailer. We no longer felt safe in our home. The university I attended had a credit union available for students, staff, and faculty. In order to move, I needed to obtain a loan for a security deposit and first and last month's rent. I applied for the loan through the credit union and was immediately denied. A staff member of the university whom I had become friends with intervened on my behalf. She very effectively inquired why I was denied, what was the purpose of the union if

not to assist students just like me, and eventually convinced the banker that the loan would be an investment that the university would reap many benefits from. We relocated to a secure apartment building farther from campus and the children's day care, and it resulted in a transfer of both the children to another new school. We all felt safer and slept much better.

I graduated with my Bachelor of Science degree in 1994 and was accepted into a master's degree program that year at the same university. The income from my graduate assistantship was $121 greater than our Aid to Families with Dependent Children (AFDC) monthly check and I was dropped from the program. Title 8 Housing assistance and Medical Assistance continued, but my portion of the rent increased in proportion to the increase in my income. Food Stamps decreased by half and we started visiting the local food shelf each month to survive. Three years later, in 1997, I earned my Master of Science in Counseling and College Student Personnel.

President Clinton signed the PRWORA in 1996. My opportunity to attain the kind of educational training in the area of my choice was not dictated by this legislation. However, on one of my last days on campus, I crossed paths with a young woman who was looking for the Admissions and Financial Aid Offices. She explained to me with great enthusiasm that she had recently divorced her abusive husband and was eager to enroll in college in order to take care of her five children and herself. I escorted her to each office and listened to her dreams and desires, her pain and suffering, and wondered to myself, "How would she ever accomplish her goals as the federal government had abandoned the needs of economically disadvantaged women and children?" I did not have the heart to tell her of the challenges before her.

My first year completely free from government assistance was shocking. I no longer qualified for the Earned Income Credit on my federal income taxes, even though my annual salary was $26,000 and I was living in an area where the average three-bedroom home or apartment rented for $900 per month. My children and I were financially strained every month. However, I had earned both a bachelor's and master's degree and within the next 13 months relocated to a job where my annual salary increased by 39% and to a community where the cost of living was much lower. Within the next 10 years, my salary increased over 135% from that first job out of graduate school. The educational investment not only benefited my children and myself, it also benefited the local, state, and national government by providing an increased salary that results in increased taxes paid, increased purchases, and financial stability in the lives of three U.S. citizens.

My life story and the experiences my children and I had, being assisted by the state and federal government for six years, frames my perspective and position of this chapter. Our European American ethnicity affected how we were treated in every line we waited in from DHS to Financial Aid. I have been terrified of the outcomes of "welfare reform" for women and children since I left assistance. Higher education saved my life and made a life for my children and me.

Today, I recognize the privilege of identifying as European American in every experience I have described: my treatment by DHS, grocery store clerks, community agencies offering assistance, faculty, other students, my academic advisors, and admissions personnel. Reflecting back on my life experiences, I did not have to question or consider if my race played a role in the experience. During my women's studies coursework, I began to develop an awareness and understanding of race and racism; however, I was lacking in theoretical underpinnings to identify, name, and address these actions. The opportunity to continue my education into a master's degree was not hindered, questioned, or blocked. My coursework was steeped in White hegemonic theory and practice. It was not until I was enrolled in my doctoral degree and had a number of professional/career opportunities to engage in

experiential learning focused on race, social justice, and ally development that I began to see the systemic barriers within higher education. As with increased awareness in many areas, I can no longer ignore these realities and I am a better person, educator, and ally because I can see them.

REVIEW OF THE LITERATURE

Welfare Statistics

In 1990, 14.1% or $18.5 million of the $131 billion spent to assist families with children was spent on cash welfare payments; this figure was 26.6% in 1975 (Currie, 2006). AFDC reached a "historic high of 5.1 million families" (Currie, 2006, p. 1) in 1994 and was cut in half by the late 1990s when the economy was strong.

AFDC was allegedly reformed in 1996 with the passage of the PRWOR, which made securing of any employment a mandatory program requirement for the recipients. The caseload fell from 12,645,000 in 1996 to 5,146,000 in 2002 recipients (Currie, 2006). Employment data for single mothers followed the caseload reductions with 52.5% working in 1996 and 67.5% in 2002 (Currie, 2006). The increase in income felt by these single working mothers amounts to roughly $100 each month and a decrease in access to employment-based health insurance. Seventy-eight percent of the employees are concentrated in four low-wage occupations: service, administrative support or clerical, operators/fabricators/laborers, and sales (Jones et al., 2003).

Effects of Reform

The short- and long-term effects of this reform have been that welfare recipients, especially single mothers, are less likely to be in college, have access to health insurance, and are persistently employed in low-paying jobs (Jones-DeWeever et al., 2003). The percentage of children receiving welfare assistance changed between 1996 and 2002 from 12.5% to 5.3% (Currie, 2006). The Work First mandate of PRWOR has resulted in severe restrictions and barriers to higher education (Jones-DeWeever & Gault, 2006). These restrictions have resulted in more low-achieving, high-income students attending college at higher rates than high-achieving, low-income students (Moreno, Smith, Parker, Clayton-Pedersen, & Teraguchi, 2006). Today, "one in every three children is living with a single parent and more than a third of single mothers live in poverty" (Hays, 2003, p. 232).

Barriers to Success

Higher education provides opportunities for those with low-income status to possibly access the benefits and privileges of the middle class. The reform of AFDC by the passage of PRWOR has created a serious barrier for low-income students interested in higher education. This new policy conflicts with the original mission of land-grant institutions to open up higher education opportunities for working-class citizens (Altbach, Gumport, & Johnstone, 2001) and the mission of the U.S. Department of Education, "to ensure equal access to education" (U.S. Department of Education, 1980, p. 1). The Administration for Children and Families, within the U.S. Department of Health and Human Services, has the administrative oversight of AFDC (renamed nationally as Temporary Aid to Needy Families or TANF) and PRWOR. The policy also appears to be in conflict with the realities of the lives of women and children in the programs. The mission of the Administration for Children and Families states their responsibility "for federal programs that promote the economic and social well-being of families, children, individuals and communities" (U.S. Department of Education, n.d.). As a result of PRWOR, higher education has once again become an opportunity offered to a select few members of privileged groups and excludes those with economic disadvantage.

President Clinton signed the PRWOR Act of 1996 and changed millions of women and children's lives. Working and searching for work became a primary mandate of this legislation, without regard to the wage earned from the job; available, affordable, and quality childcare; or healthcare benefits. The option to choose training, education, and studying for a livable wage career was no longer defined as "work" under this new program. In New York City, 21,000 students were forced out of the City University of New York system (Applied Research Center, 2001) as a result of this reform. Welfare data analysis shows that three years following this reform, women with children who were previously receiving welfare assistance were no longer enrolled in college and did not have access to health care (Jones-DeWeever et al., 2003). The economic well-being of a majority of the single mothers on welfare has diminished three years after reform, with 3.1 million families living in dire poverty (income below the 50% poverty line) with limited access to health care, food stamps, and childcare assistance (Jones-DeWeever, 2003; Jones-DeWeever et al., 2003). Women of color experience both institutionalized and individual sexism and racism, as caseworkers restrict the kinds of information shared, which results in segregating women into the lowest paying jobs across the nation (Hartman, Allen, & Owens, 1999; Henrici, 2006; Jones-DeWeever et al., 2003).

Educational opportunities are vital for all women in the United States today as the wages earned by women leaving welfare remain lower than those earned by men ($8.03 vs. $9.42) (Jones-DeWeever et al., 2003). The newly imposed restriction to higher education has occurred as federal and state funding to higher education has been diminished (Institute for Higher Education Policy, 2002), and a predicted two-thirds of the most rapidly expanding careers for the twenty-first century will require a postsecondary education with 57% requiring at minimum a bachelor's degree (U.S. Department of Labor, Bureau of Labor Statistics, 2004).

Generational Effects

The personal crisis of millions of women with children becomes a national crisis quickly when the long-term negative impact of the revised PRWOR legislation is considered. Women in low-paying jobs cannot afford to save or grow a college fund for their children or a retirement fund for themselves and their family. What will the educational opportunities for their children be? How will these women survive in their senior years? Welfare will not be an option with the lifetime caps currently being mandated. Without health care for themselves and their children, what will the long-term effects be for women, their families, and society? Where will the children of these economically disadvantaged single mothers be in 25 years?

The investment in higher education has a proven, positive, long-term impact on the lives of women and their children: higher median hourly earnings ($13.14 vs. $7.50), expanded dreams and possibilities, increased self-esteem and sense of empowerment, improved grades and study habits of children, increased enrollment in college by children, and increased participation in community activities (Jones-DeWeever & Gault, 2006). Understanding the positive impacts of education is something that may be lacking in our communities, colleges, and legislatures. "The Missing Story of Ourselves," the Iowa State University (ISU) project, provides low-income women the opportunity to share their stories and educate our community and country on the importance of access to higher education for the individual, institutional, and global family.

Misdiagnosed Situation

The unchallenged prejudice projected toward women and their children receiving governmental assistance has not improved with the signing of the PRWOR Act. The issue has moved further from the daily consciousness of the U.S. citizens as reports highlight the lower numbers of recipients of welfare benefits each year. This, however, does not represent that the problem has been eliminated.

The real issue without media or public attention is the long-term negative impact of the PRWOR Act on single women and their children. PRWOR includes a work mandate and prevents recipients from entry into or the option to remain in higher education until degree attainment (Jones-DeWeever et al., 2003). The positive economic gains received by college graduates has been documented (Dodson, Manuel, & Bravo, 2002); however, this alleged improved management of the welfare program has created a much ignored inequity to who can and cannot attend college. Further, this academic elitism does not stop at the current generation. The children of the women receiving welfare benefits will not have financial support from their family to enroll in college (Jones-DeWeever et al., 2003). This dynamic will continue with each future generation unless something shifts and social justice is achieved for economically disadvantaged women and children.

METHODS OF THE STUDY

"The Missing Story of Ourselves: Poverty and the Promise of Higher Education," a project coordinated by The ACCESS Project at Hamilton College in Clinton, New York (Adair, n.d.), was a project instituted at Iowa State University, which provides a wealth of information about students from low socioeconomic homes. This project shares the stories and courage of single parents in higher education during the postwelfare reform period. The stories are important in naming and putting a face to the experiences of this much ignored population of students, and the stories also assist in the reflective learning for each student to acknowledge their growth, strength, and perseverance.

"The Missing Story of Ourselves" is a collection of 50 framed portraits and first-person narratives describing the individuals' struggles, joys, challenges, and growth as single parents receiving welfare benefits while earning a college degree. The exhibit was brought to the ISU community during September 2007 to provide a learning and empowering opportunity for the community and campus. The current study is part of a larger national project, "The Missing Story of Ourselves." A schedule of events during the four-week exhibition was coordinated and included an opening reception and on-campus guest lecture by Dr. Vivian Adair, Curator and Director of "The Missing Story of Ourselves: Poverty and the Promise of Higher Education." Requests for participants from the community were solicited during fall semester 2006 to be included in the local project. Participants were recruited by placement of flyers throughout campus and within the Ames community, e-mail solicitations, word of mouth, and in collaboration with agencies serving the needs of low-income families (food shelves, child-care centers, laundries, grocery stores, etc.). A photograph of each participant was taken; it included any member of the women's family or support network that the individual women felt should be included. A narrative of her experiences in higher education was created based on each interview with the participants, who approved the final version to be shared publicly.

The national exhibit was connected to the local community of Ames, Iowa, with the inclusion of portraits and first-person narratives from single mothers enrolled at or who have recently earned their degree from a two- or four-year higher education institution. All participants in the local project received some form of federal or state assistance before or during their time in undergraduate school. The local participants were interviewed and photographed during fall 2006 and spring 2007 semesters. Following their interview, a narrative was developed by the author and approved by the participants. Each participant received a copy of her photographs and narrative. A copy of all participants is available for public viewing at the Margaret Sloss Women's Center at ISU. As additional participants in the local project are identified and agree to participate, the photo and narrative album will expand.

The project highlighted several ethical considerations that needed to be managed. When strangers, faculty, family, or friends learn that someone they know is or has been on government assistance, there is always the possibility that they will begin to treat this person differently. Because of this possibility, the care and respect of the participants in this project was mandatory. This project asked low-income single parents to "out themselves" to an undetermined audience. This action could result in negative treatment of the women by community members or, conversely, provide background that may educate the community to better understand and support this population of students. It was a risk that the participants must be willing to take while considering the possible benefits to the participant and the community hearing individuals' stories. Each participant was fully informed about the project and how it will be utilized at ISU prior to each interview. As the principal researcher, I provided support, referrals, and resources as needed based upon the information shared by the participants. In addition, the interviews could provide insight concerning new programs and support systems that could be developed.

Definition of Terms

The debate on public assistance programs continues and the survival strategies of low-income families are still not well understood by policymakers and the general public (Hartman, Splater-Roth, Sills, & Yi, 2003). This lack of understanding continues to perpetuate stereotypes and inaccurate judgments about recipients of public assistance. One of the barriers to hearing and understanding the stories of women and children's lived reality is the lack of vocabulary to discuss the issue. The following definitions are included to assist in the understanding of this issue.

Personal Responsibility and Work Opportunity Reconciliation (PRWOR) Act. Congress passed the PRWOR Act in 1996 and in so doing ended the guarantee that federal support could be available to parents and children meeting low-income guidelines (Heymann, Boynton-Jarrett, Carter, Bond, & Galinsky, 2002). The act replaced federal assistance with block grants to each state, with the latitude at the state level to interpret and enact guidelines as determined within specific governments (Jones-DeWeever et al., 2003). In addition, the PRWOR Act included new lifetime limits for receiving welfare benefits and mandatory work requirements for anyone receiving food stamps or income assistance (Heymann et al., 2002). The work requirement in the former federal income support program provided the recipient the option of working, enrollment in vocational training programs, or enrolling in higher education to fulfill work requirements (Heymann et al., 2002; Jones-DeWeever et al., 2003). PRWOR allows for vocations education for only one year (Negrey, Golin, Lee, Mead, & Gault, 2001). President Clinton and many of the more moderate Democrats supported the principal aspects of PRWORA. Clinton initially supported the inclusion of "new training and job creation programs and improvements in healthcare and child care to facilitate employment, but the cost of these measures contradicted his top advisors' deficit reduction agenda" (Reese, 2005, p. 175).

Poverty. The U.S. Social Security Administration developed the official definition of poverty in the early 1960s. This definition established a *poverty threshold* that is based on the cost of a minimally adequate diet (as defined by the Department of Agriculture in 1961) multiplied by three to allow for shelter, clothing, and other basic needs (at the time, it was thought that low-income families spent about one-third of their income on food). A family's cash income before taxes is then compared with the poverty threshold to determine their poverty status (Hartman

et al., 2003). In general, poverty is the inability to establish income that provides the basics needs (food, housing, clothing, and transportation) for individuals and families (Gentle, n.d.). The current measure of poverty compares incomes that vary by family size and composition to established thresholds or lines (Commission on Behavioral and Social Sciences and Education, 1995) and poses several challenges when applying these measures to people's lives: no distinction between working and nonworking households, ignorance of the status of health and insurance coverage, thresholds uniform across the United States even though cost of living fluctuates, and ignorance of changing demographics and cultural differences within families (Commission on Behavioral and Social Sciences and Education, 1995; Hartman et al., 2003).

Temporary Assistance for Needy Families (TANF). In 1996, when PRWORA was signed into legislation, the TANF Program replaced AFDC in the distribution of cash benefits to qualified recipients (Hart, 2002). This program shifted welfare from an entitlement to "stiff, new work requirements . . . enforced by time limits—states must require recipients to work after a maximum of 24 months on aid or less and there was a cumulative lifetime limit of five years on receipt of aid" (Handler & Hasenfeld, 2007, p. 1).

Participants

Several women contacted me (telephone, e-mail, and in person) regarding the ISU project. After hearing or reading more about the requirements for involvement, many decided to not participate. When I inquired as to what was preventing them from being involved in the project, many talked about not wanting to become more public with their own stories and wanting to keep themselves and their children away from any potential public criticism. I understood their perspective and chose to honor their decisions rather than attempt to assure them that this would not be an outcome, because I certainly could not guarantee it would not be. Three women agreed to participate and their stories and life experiences touched my heart and spoke of many challenges and joys. The description of the women and their lives come from interviews. During these interviews, the focus was primarily on the impact of their socioeconomic status on their success in higher education; however, all three shared the complexities and multilayered aspects of their lives—some more than others. The words used to describe each woman were taken from how she self-described her own experience.

Both Annemarie Vaccaro's and Venice Thandi Sulé's chapters (chapter 7 and 9, respectively) address the intersections of identities, specifically Vacarro's chapter, as she has examined racial identities, motivations, self-esteem, and sense of empowerment as they intersected in the formation of identity development. This has a direct correlation to the intersection of all gender identities including those of socioeconomic level and gender.

The intersection of gender and race is important to recognize in order to address inequalities. Taken together, the richness of these three chapters (the current chapter, plus chapters 7 and 9) considered collectively provides a platform for acknowledging, understanding, and addressing social justice. More specifically, social justice includes addressing issues of power relations, equity, and systemic or institutionalized oppression (Goodman, 2001) in addition to promoting, understanding, accepting, and appreciating cultural differences. Social justice strives to achieve a society where resources are distributed in an equitable way; members are self-determining to achieve their fullest abilities; and all are safe, secure, interdependent, and possess a self-awareness that leads to a sense of social responsibility to all (Bell, 1997). Further, I utilize the Racial Identity Development stages (Hardiman & Jackson, 1992) moving from naive through to internalization. For the entire table see Annemarie Vaccaro's chapter in this text.

HER STORIES

Kim

Kim began her college career in 1994 at age 17 at a predominately White and male institution. Women from different racial backgrounds can experience a campus environment differently, as noted in Annemarie Vaccaro's chapter in this text. In particular, this campus being predominately White and male, Kim's experiences were frequently overlooked or disregarded as a woman being overly sensitive. In addition, the space to connect race and gender was not offered, frequently leaving an experience unnamed.

When Kim discovered she was pregnant when she was 19 years old, she never doubted that she would continue to attend college, "I realized I was going to be responsible for another human and planned to move forward and earn my degree with my baby." Kim, like the other women in this project, began to foster self-investment, defined as the valuing of oneself enough to believe that personal growth, learning, and development are not merely needed but deserved. It includes an investment of time, energy, and funding to oneself as a person, not merely toward a degree (Vaccaro, 2005). Kim recognized she would need financial and medical assistance, and she qualified for the U.S. Department of Agriculture Special Supplemental Nutrition Program of Women, Infants, and Children, Food Stamps Program, Title 19 (Medicaid), Family Investment Program, and the State Childcare Block Grant and was put on a waiting list for subsidized housing. Kim wondered if people were judging the young, pregnant, unwed Black girl taking advantage of their tax dollars:

> No one ever said anything overtly to make me feel this way, but it was always there in the way the checker looked at me in the grocery store when I pulled out my WIC coupons, or when the receptionist at the dentist's office needed to verify my medical coverage and put the call on the speaker phone for everyone in the office to hear that I was a DHS case.

As with the other women, including myself, Kim's academic advisor was crucial to her success in college. "He helped me understand how to return and what I needed to do in order to make it work." Kim shared her college experience as a parent and a student with two other friends who had children around the same time, "We hung out while our kids hung out, we traded babysitting when we needed breaks and we shared babysitters when we wanted to go out together." She graduated in 1999 with her degree in elementary education and started working on her master's degree. Medical assistance continued along with food stamps, but by this time, this assistance was contingent upon Kim working with Workforce Development and completing at least 10 job applications a week. "I jumped through the hoops to get what I needed, but it was very obvious that they were not interested in supporting me in the ways I needed support." Kim moved off assistance when she got a full-time job and shortly afterwards, in 2007, married the father of her daughter. Today, she continues to work full-time, has had another baby, and has started working toward her doctoral degree.

> Through this whole time I eventually learned that I had nothing to be ashamed of. I had every right to take advantage of the assistance available to me while I was working to become a productive citizen. I now know that the assistance I received will pale in comparison to the contribution I will make to this world. Those programs were designed to help people reach their goals and that is what it did for me. I could not have gotten through school if I had not gotten the help I needed at the time.

Applying racial identity development theory to Kim's story, one can see that her stage of racial identity development and motivation to continue to enroll in higher education supports the finding of Annemarie Vaccaro (chapter 7). Kim appears to have entered higher education already at the redefinition stage of racial identity, and at the time of the interview, she appears to be in the internalization stage. Kim benefited from a close

support network with other women experiencing similar potential challenges to their academic success. She shared that they understood the importance of attaining an education because they were Black and women. (See Thandi Sulé's chapter 9 for additional information.) Kim, like Mary Church Terrill, increased her capacity building within the Black community and supported her success along with the success of others during her undergraduate education. I had the privilege of being a teaching assistant in one of the courses Kim was enrolled in, Social Justice: Theory, Research, and Practice, and this gave me insight into her experience outside of the one-to-one interviews. Kim is an outstanding advocate of social justice (self and other) and a strong ally to individuals marginalized and oppressed by individual and systemic oppression.

LaShai

LaShai is a 28-year-old, African American, single mother of three daughters. Her story includes a history of family violence and economic disadvantage. During our time together, I recognized that it was my responsibility to provide LaShai with an environment where she felt safer and could trust me. We initially talked about my life experiences and why I was interested in the research project. The longer we talked, the more at ease LaShai appeared; however, I am not certain I was able to capture the depth and breadth of her story. LaShai provided the following words of advice to other single mothers:

> Don't give up on the dream. Keep striving. Read daily affirmations to lift your spirits. Find a support system. Make daily goals if you have to and if you accomplish these, then make them bigger. I keep three different journals. After I re-read them, I feel refreshed and encouraged to meet my goals.

LaShai earned her General Educational Development degree in 2003 and started her college career at a local community college and had recently transferred to a four-year school. "I'm doing it for my kids. I wanted to show my kids the opportunity to see a better side of life, so they could see a real college and they will know what they could do." LaShai was incarcerated for 12 months prior to completing her General Educational Development; at that time, her daughters were 7, 4, and 2 years old. She received Family Investment Program in 2003. "I got off FIP in 2005 because I wanted to go back to school and they said there weren't going to pay for my childcare unless I was working." LaShai was denied Section 8 Housing because of her prior criminal history, and she and her daughters stayed with a relative until it was necessary to relocate to the Family Violence Center for personal safety reasons. It was through this center that she was able to obtain housing outside of the shelter that was based on her income and furnished utilities for two years. "It was a blessing. At the end of two years, I applied for housing with the Central Iowa Regional Housing Authority and we got accepted." LaShai worked full time as she attended classes (full time some semesters and part time other semesters) and continued to role model healthy choices for her children. She had a strong role model at her community college that dramatically and positively affected her focus and determination to earn her college degree. "He is someone who cared enough for and about me to do what he loves to do and that is instilling positivism within one's mind, spirit, and body." He gave the most fulfilling affirmation,

> When you have come to the edge of all the light you know, and are about to step off into the darkness of the unknown, faith in knowing one of two things will happen; there will be something solid to stand on, or you will be taught to fly.

LaShai transferred 46 credits from two different community colleges to a four-year, predominately White and male university. She talked about this transition as a time of many challenges—food, shelter, transportation, school, health care, time, energy, safety, respect, and

keeping clothes and shoes on the girls. After two semesters at this four-year university, she withdrew from college.

She talked at great length about the White folks in the prison where she was held (I never asked nor did she provide the exact time or cause of her incarceration), and it was very apparent to me that she was beyond the Acceptance stage or Racial Identity Development, and perhaps situated in resistance. LaShai understood, firsthand, the impact of individual and institutional racism; however, from our short conversations, it was not apparent that she had come to a place where she identified with others and felt safe enough to become a part of a network of support people who are like-minded and like-experienced, as is also reflected in Annemarie Vaccaro's chapter (chapter 7). After a short two semesters or one academic year, LaShai returned to her hometown and family. At the time of writing this chapter, this is all I know about her decision to leave the university. I was not able to gain a close enough understanding of LaShai, her life experiences, or her current situation to conclude what happened. However, LaShai was very much self-invested and self-motivated through her community college experiences. It is highly likely that the four-year, predominately White male institution failed to meet the needs of her and her three daughters. The subtleties of racial bias, as noted in Thandi Sulé's chapter, are present both covertly and overtly in the predominately White, male institution LaShai left.

Melissa

Melissa grew up in a middle-class, White family as an only child. She always knew that going to college was expected of her. She enrolled in a four-year college directly out of high school knowing not only what she wanted to major in but also that she was not ready for college yet. She attended two years earning "a really crappy grade point average." Melissa got married at age 19 and was a mother and divorced before she turned 24 years of age. "That's when it hit me—I knew I needed to do something different, I knew I needed to provide for my daughter." While attending college, Melissa worked a variety of different jobs both full and part time, and depending upon her finances, she attended college full time or part time. She received a variety of different types of government assistance and had many minimum wage jobs that did not cover her monthly expenses. "I struggled through most of my 20s with dead-end jobs that weren't going very far or paying me enough." She enrolled in college full time in a paralegal program, "That is what I've always wanted to do. Since the 6th grade I knew I wanted to work in the legal system." Similar to Kim, LaShai, and myself, Melissa had an important support person on her campus that guided her around or through challenges, told her she could be successful, and if she fell behind, was right there to push her and get her going again. Melissa's mentor would say, "OK, you worked your tail off getting this far, I'm not going to let you screw it up again! So, you're not going to like me by the end of the term, but this is what we're going to do!" If Melissa had not had this mentor doing what she did to help her, she said, "I may very well have said, 'You know what, I can't do this.'" Education can change people, their perspectives of themselves, their world, and their place in the world. Melissa explained,

> It is something that until you've lived it, you have no clue—you can't even fathom what it's like to go through life struggling so much. I don't regret any of it, though, because it helped make me who I am now, but oh my, if I could go back and do things just a little bit different, I may! Part of it was just the circumstances of life and sometimes things happen to you that you never see coming.

Melissa provided additional advice for a single mother going to college:

> Don't give up. Don't ever give up. Even though you may feel like you can't ever do this or that, you'll never get it done—stick with it. The resources are out there and sometimes you have to dig a little

bit deeper to find them, but you can do it. The more times you say that to somebody, especially somebody that has been down on their luck, the more they hear it and the more they start to believe it. And eventually, it becomes their mantra and they can pass it on to the next person.

Melissa graduated with her bachelor's degree in paralegal studies at the end of fall semester 2008 and is now working full-time as a paralegal.

Annmarie Vaccaro stated in her chapter (chapter 7), "Racial identity development happens for all people, yet the process is experienced differently by people of color and White people, as they have differing access to power and privilege." Melissa did not mention any life experiences with people of color or discuss her own racial identity beyond my question on how she identified. According to the Hardiman and Jackson (1992) table in Vaccaro's chapter, Melissa would be at the naive stage of racial identity development.

CONCLUSION

Society must become aware of and understand the hidden impact welfare reform has had on the lives of women and children. In addition, the long-term negative impacts of ignoring and not caring for economically disadvantaged women and children on the individuals and the society as a whole must be understood. Economic instability is a reality of today's marketplace and, at any moment, there is the possibility that any member of society could find himself or herself needing some form of welfare assistance. It is time to shatter the myths regarding women on welfare, critically examine the PRWOR Act and its intentions, and collectively demand improved care of our community members.

Poverty, as with financial stability and success, has mistakenly come to be viewed as the product of an individual's abilities, or lack of abilities, rather than the result of an economic and political system steeped in maintaining positions of privilege and power to those who currently hold these positions or to whom these will soon be given. In order to provide the opportunity to achieve a livable wage and health-care benefits for women and their children, we must begin to provide the option for an extensive education and training that will make women eligible for the kinds of jobs that will sustain them and their families over the long run (Henrici, 2006).

As a society, it is currently accepted that millions of women and children can fend for themselves. This is certainly not the case. The level of educational attainment of a child is directly correlated to the level of educational attainment of the mother (Pascarella & Terenzini, 2005). We perpetuate the oppression of a working-poor class of people with the current PRWORA policy.

Perhaps the objective President Clinton and the federal government had when passing PRWORA was to reduce the number of people receiving welfare assistance, and in analyzing just the number of cases, this goal was achieved. However, we must look beyond the numbers, which we must remember are people—mainly women and children—whose lives have been forgotten, who must work two and three jobs to maintain a low-income standard of life, who must utilize child-care services that are sometimes unsafe or a high risk, and who have lost their dreams, hopes, and desires. Of the families who have left welfare, the families our government and many of our citizens consider the success story, "one-half are sometimes without enough money to buy food. One-third have to cut the size of meals. Almost half find themselves unable to pay their rent or utility bills" (Hays, 2003, p. 227).

The outcome of welfare reform has been the forced labor of women in low-paying jobs, primarily in four areas of work (service, administrative support, laborers, and sales industries) that lack health-care benefits. Ultimately corporations, service industries, and their owners have benefited the most from the welfare reforms (Hays, 2003). "Unfortunately, discussion of poverty and inequality has nearly disappeared as well—even though significant poverty remains, especially child poverty, and inequality has been increasing over the past decades" (Handler & Hasenfeld, 2007, p. 1). Rather than recognize the source of the inequity and strive for social injustice, what has been created is a target for all that is wrong with this country—single mothers and the choices they make. "The problem is that there are significant economic and cultural inadequacies in the choices available to them" (Hays, 2003, p. 231).

My plan was never to raise two children on my own for a significant number of years of their lives. If we did not have the safety net of federal assistance when we needed it, I cannot imagine where our lives would be today. I anticipate completing my doctoral degree in educational leadership and policy studies in the next year. My daughter is in her final year of college studying criminal justice, and my son is in his third year of college studying dance. My son recalls the days we walked everywhere and at one time told me he missed those days because I was much happier. My daughter thanked me for teaching her how to get through tough times by purchasing a bag of used clothes at the Goodwill and a box of hair color. They remember the moments of terror as well as the moments of joy.

Higher education changed my life and the lives of my children. It simultaneously gave us another chance at life. No one imagines that surviving on welfare will be a part of their life, but without this support, what happens to the women and children? What is the long-term cost of denying short-term support?

REFERENCES

Adair, V. C. (n.d.). *The missing stories of ourselves: Poverty and the promise of higher education.* Retrieved July 2, 2006, from http://my.hamilton.edu/college/emerson_gallery/MissingStory.html

Altbach, P. G., Gumport, P. J., & Johnstone, D. B. (Eds.). (2001). *In defense of American higher education.* Baltimore, MD: Johns Hopkins University Press.

America's Second Harvest: The Nation's Food Bank Network. (2008). *Local impact survey.* Retrieved June 29, 2008, from http://www.secondharvest.org/news_room/local_impact/

Applied Research Center. (2001). *Worthwhile welfare reforms.* Oakland, CA: Applied Research Center. Retrieved July 16, 2006, from http://www.arc.org

Bell, L. A. (1997). Theoretical foundations for social justice education. In M. Adams, L. A. Bell, & P. Griffin (Eds.), *Teaching for diversity and social justice* (pp. 3–15). New York: Routledge.

Commission on Behavioral and Social Sciences and Education. (1995). *Measuring poverty: A new approach.* Retrieved July 8, 2006, from http://newton.nap.edu/catalog/4759.html#orgs

Currie, J. M. (2006). *The invisible safety net: Protecting the nation's poor children and families.* Princeton, NJ: Princeton University Press.

Dodson, L., Manuel, T., & Bravo, E. (2002). *Keeping jobs and raising families in low-income America: It just doesn't work.* Retrieved September 2, 2002, from http://www.radcliffe.edu/research/pubpol/boundaries.pdf

Gentle, T. (n.d.). *Official government poverty lines shows signs of old age.* Retrieved July 8, 2006, from http://eesc.orst.edu/agcomwebfile/edmat/html/em/em8743/part1/officialgovt.html

Goodman, D. J. (2001). *Promoting diversity and social justice: Educating people from privileged groups.* Thousand Oaks, CA: Sage.

Handler, J. F., & Hasenfeld, Y. (2007). *Blame welfare, ignore poverty and inequality.* New York: Cambridge University Press.

Hardiman, R., & Jackson, B. (1992). Racial identity development: Understanding racial dynamics in college classrooms and on campus. In M. Adams (Ed.), *Promoting diversity in college classrooms: Innovative responses for the curriculum, faculty, and institutions* (pp. 21–37). New Directions for Teaching and Learning: Vol. 115. San Francisco, CA: Jossey-Bass.

Hart, M. U. (2002). *The poverty of life-affirming work: Motherhood, education, and social change.* Westport, CT: Greenwood Press.

Hartman, H., Allen, K., & Owens, C. (1999). Equal pay for working families: National and State data on the pay gap and its costs. In *A joint research project of the AFL-CIO and the Institute for Women's Policy Research.* Retrieved July 13, 2003, from http://www.iwpr.org/pdf/C343.pdf

Hartman, H., Spalter-Roth, R., Sills, M., & Yi, H. (2003). *Survival at the bottom: In income package of low-income families with children.* (Institute for Women's Policy Research Rep. No. D453). Retrieved July 13, 2006, from http://www.iwpr.org/D453.pdf

Hays, S. (2003). *Flat broke with children: Women in age of welfare reform.* New York: Oxford University Press.

Henrici, J. (Ed.). (2006). *Doing without: Women and work after welfare reform.* Tucson, AZ: The University of Arizona Press.

Heymann, J., Boynton-Jarrett, R. Carter, P., Bond, J. T., & Galinksy, E. (2002). *Work-family issues and low-income families.* Retrieved July 2, 2006, from http://www.economythatworks.org/PDFs/ford_analysisfinal.pdf

Institute for Higher Education Policy. (2002). *The policy of choice: Expanding student options in higher education.* Retrieved September 23, 2002, from http://www.iwpr.org/pdf/D453.pdf

Jones-DeWeever, A. (2003). *The children left behind: Deeper poverty, fewer supports.* (Institute for Women's Policy Research Rep. No. D548). Retrieved July 2, 2006, from http://www.iwpr.org/pdf/D457a.pdf

Jones-DeWeever, A., & Gault, B. (2006). *Resilient and reaching for more: Challenges and benefits of higher education for welfare participants and their children.* (Institute for Women's Policy Research Rep. No. D466). Retrieved July 2, 2006, from http://www.iwpr.org/pdf/D466

Jones-DeWeever, A., Peterson, J., & Song, X. (2003). *Before and after welfare reform: The work and well-being of low-income single parent families.* (Institute for Women's Policy Research Rep. No. D454). Retrieved July 1, 2006, from http://www.iwpr.org/pdf/D454.pdf

Mantsios, G. (2004). Class in America—2003. In P. S. Rothenberg (Ed.), *Race, class, and gender in the United States* (6th ed., pp. 193–206). New York: Worth Publications.

Moreno, J. F., Smith, D. G., Parker, S., Clayton-Pedersen, & Teraguchi, D. H. (2006). *Using multiple lenses: An examination of the economic and racial/ethnic diversity of college students: An analysis from the campus diversity initiative.* San Francisco, CA: The James Irvine Foundation. Retrieved July 1, 2006, from http://www.irvine.org/assets/pdf/pubs/education/insight_Multiple_Lenses.pdf

Negrey, C., Golin, S., Lee, S., Mead, H., & Gault, B. (2001). *Working first but working poor: The need for education and training following welfare reform.* Retrieved July 3, 2006, from http://www.iwpr.org/pdf/7states-exec.pdf

Pascarella, E. T., & Terenzini, P. T. (2005). *How college affects students: Findings and insights from twenty years of research, Vol 2*. San Francisco, CA: Jossey-Bass.

Phillips-Fein, K. (2002). The education of Jessica Rivera. *The Nation*, 20–23. Retrieved January 29, 2010, from http://www.thenation.com/doc/20021125/phillips-fein

Reese, E. (2005). *Backlash against welfare mothers: Past and present*. Berkeley, CA: University of California Press.

United States Department of Education. (1980). *Department of Education Mission*. Retrieved January 29, 2010, from http://www2.ed.gov/about/overview/mission/mission.html

United States Department of Labor, Bureau of Labor Statistics. (2004). *Occupational outlook handbook: 2004–2005 Edition*. Washington, DC: U.S. Government Printing Office. Retrieved July 10, 2006, from http://permanent.access.gpo.gov/lps4235/2004–05/2004–2005/home.htm

Vaccaro, A. (2005). Self-investment and engagement of older women students: Uncovering connections to racial identity, gender, support, and motivation. Unpublished doctoral dissertation, University of Denver, Colorado.

12

Sister Circles

A Dialogue on the Intersections of Gender, Race, and Student Affairs

Amanda Suniti Niskodé-Dossett, Mariama Boney, Linda Contreras Bullock, Cynthia Cochran, and Irene Kao

INTRODUCTION

In this dialogic chapter, we hope to share with the readers the depth of the discussion that has transpired over the years at the Sister Circle roundtable discussions at the annual convention of the American College Personnel Association (ACPA). Sister Circles are roundtables sponsored by the Standing Committee for Women (SCW) and an opportunity for women graduate students, administrators, and faculty members of color who work in the field of student affairs to come together to discuss contemporary topics relevant to their personal and professional lives.

We want this chapter to reflect the kind of intimate and professional dialogue found in these roundtables in order to relay the complexities of multiple identities in the field and, in particular, the intersections of gender, race, and ethnicity. In order to mirror the depth of the Sister Circle dialogues, this chapter is itself a dialogue between African American, Asian American, Latina, and multiracial women, and facilitated by Mariama Boney, Director of Member Initiatives and Con-

stituent Relations at ACPA and former SCW directorate member. It is important to note that not all women of color are represented in this dialogue (e.g., we are missing Native American and Middle Eastern women) and that there are multiple identities within groups that are also not represented (e.g., Asian American can include people who are Laotian American, Japanese American, Korean American, etc.).

As five strong, dynamic women who took part in this dialogue, we share much in common, including friendships, professional connections, and shared experiences. Each of us also brings our unique perspectives, wisdom, and individual identities to the discussion. Notably, we recognize that we are privileged to contribute to this chapter representing women of color and want to acknowledge that we by no means believe we are speaking "for" our respective groups, or "for" women of color as a whole. We know that each woman has her own story to share and each of our individual journeys is one of many. In addition, while the particular focus of our chapter is on gender, race, and ethnicity, we recognize that our multiple identities make each of us special, such as socioeconomic status, age, sexual orientation, ability, national origin (among many others); it is impossible to think about aspects of our identity in silos. Nevertheless, we believe that by focusing this dialogue on women of color, we will contribute to the understanding of women in higher education and student affairs as we dive into the different aspects of our identities and explore how multiple identities influence our work as professionals. We hope our conversation inspires dialogues on your own campuses and at gatherings of associations across the country.

We perceive this chapter as only the beginning of a much deeper, longer conversation regarding women of color in the field but hope it sheds some light on the intersections of social identities. From here, we encourage you to read about each of the authors in the Contributors section of this book, where we share a short description about ourselves to provide context to this discussion. Below, we provide the dialogue itself as it transpired, conclude with reflections on the themes that were interwoven throughout the dialogue, and explore the implications of these themes for our work in higher education. As you read the dialogue, we invite you to consider additional themes from our discussion, juxtapose the stories provided here with other chapters in this book, and identify topics that have yet to be discussed.

A "SISTER CIRCLE" DIALOGUE

MARIAMA: Is everyone here? Okay, good. Welcome everyone. Amanda did you want to say any words of welcome before we get started?

AMANDA SUNITI: Oh! I just wanted to say, *thank you*. I know everyone is extremely busy and so I personally appreciate this, and also know our editors, Penny and Shelley, also appreciate your contribution. I think that this conversation is really exciting and that, in addition to this being part of the book, it's great that we just have this chance to talk.

MARIAMA: Okay, I too just wanted to extend my thanks to everyone. SCW, and many of you, continue to be near and dear to my heart, my journey with ACPA, and my journey as a woman in higher education. I think that all of this is awesome and that you are fabulous for agreeing to do this Sister Circle. This is an opportunity for us to have some real talk and real discussion and see where it leads us. So, if we could just go ahead and start briefly with that; does anyone have any thoughts or reflections that they want to share?

LINDA: Well I'm just excited to be able to include this piece in the book. Clearly as the Standing Committee for Women—and I know Mariama, you and I have been involved with it [SCW] for a really long time—has always strived to have a very diverse group and I think this just kind of lends itself to our idea in the very beginning of really reaching out to everybody and I think our conversation today falls right in place.

MARIAMA: Thanks for that. Okay, for the first couple minutes—so that we can all kind of get a sense of where we're coming from—I want to ask you—I know that this is probably the most challenging thing that you have to do all week maybe—to really think about how it is that you became connected to work with students and student affairs. And, if you could do that in the most brief way, if possible, 250 words or less; what is your "I" story? How did you end up working in student affairs as a woman of color?

IRENE: I guess it started when I was in college and I was really involved in co-curriculars. I actually thought that I was going to go to law school, which is ironic because that's where I am now. But at the time I realized that law school wasn't for me. And so, when I thought about what was going to be my life path I went and talked to some mentors who had suggested student affairs. I was really very encouraged by them to go into the field, but not without first asking me to consider whether I really wanted to be an advocate for students or if I just wanted to continue being a student leader.

I had been so involved so I wondered if I needed to be in the limelight or if I could do a job that would nurture students' development and not necessarily get the credit. I decided to go into student affairs. I grew a lot as a person when I was at University of Maryland for my grad program.

MARIAMA: That's great. Thank you, Irene, for sharing that. Okay, and, who's next?

AMANDA SUNITI: I'll go next. Irene and I actually went to graduate school together at the University of Maryland; that's how I met her. I went into the field of student affairs probably because I just loved the college experience so much, and I felt that was my place. That's what I wanted to do; I knew that was my passion. But as I went through my master's program, my first job, and now my doctoral work, I've really gained a sense of what drives me: the advocacy role. This influences how I try to enhance students' experiences within higher education as well as within my sphere of influence as a woman of color.

MARIAMA: Great, thank you.

LINDA: Pretty much the same story, advocacy. I came to this work not as my first career. This is probably my fourth or fifth career! [Chuckles] I came later for grad school at a predominately White university and found that there weren't many people here who looked like me. I got involved in a scholarship program that a professor and I started, scholarships for students who wrote about African American and Hispanic elders. I began working in the community, fundraising, and that kind of work. I tied it in to this university and as

we expanded these programs, the diversity here started to increase. Stepping into that leadership and advocacy role as a student leader, at a nontraditional university, was very easy for me as a Latina woman, which hadn't happened very much here. And so from there, I ended up in student affairs—straight from my student leadership experiences into student affairs and as director of this office.

CIE (CYNTHIA): I became involved in student affairs because of my supervisor when I was a work-study student. She eventually became a mentor to me. I think that it was her example as a woman, a woman of color, and a good student affairs professional that really inspired me and showed me how you can help students grow and develop. I saw by her example how I could use my talents to "make a difference" on my campus as a professional. I think that I was most impressed because she worked really hard, was great at her job, but also maintained a healthy work/life balance. Her family was always her top priority and her relationship never suffered as a result. As someone who always knew that I wanted a family it was important to see this role modeled. I saw enough of the opposite end to know that I wanted and needed something more. I would say another contributing factor was that I grew up on college campuses as well. My mother and father have spent all my life working with college or high school students. They and my brother have also always been advocates for change on college campuses and I heard every night around the dinner table how they created change, sometimes in small ways and sometimes in big ways, and that really inspired me (even though I will admit I didn't recognize this until I was much older—but isn't that always the case).

MARIAMA: Awesome, wonderful, thank you. And myself. I always tell folks that

I was raised on a college campus as well. My father was a senior student affairs officer at Syracuse University for 25 years so I was forced, I guess you might say, in a good way, to participate in all the summer programs and all the summer initiatives that he would do for students and particularly with students of color and college entry programs. And my mom is also an educator at the K–12 level. So, with that, and having him as a role model, and all the individuals around him, when it was time for me to declare my major I decided to go the social work route. After I finished, I did a couple of different internships and then worked. I started working on a college campus in academic advising, in the college of nursing, and just really enjoyed it. That's where I also fell in love with diversity work and women's issues. I was an active student leader on campus for a women's organization and so I just continued to really love working with students of color and students from underrepresented or disadvantaged backgrounds, economically disadvantaged backgrounds. I continued on that path and came to work on a couple of different campuses. Then, with ACPA and SCW, I developed a connection to Linda and Cie, and then Amanda through the Multiracial and Multiple Identities institute, so that's kind of how I ended up here. When I decided to leave higher education, I still had this longing to want to make a difference in a broad sense. So, I worked for a national nonprofit, AAUW [American Association for University Women], which is a women's organization focused on education equity for women and girls, and then the job opportunity became available here at ACPA. So, it's my way of continuing to give back.

Anyone else? No? Okay. Now for the real meat! So, how would you say the intersection of race and gender influences your work in student affairs? How does that inform the lens that you practice through or that you look through?

AMANDA SUNITI: It kind of struck me that not only has the intersection of my gender and race influenced my work in student affairs, but my work in student affairs has also influenced my identity development in a way that I don't think would have happened or would continue to happen if I was in any other field. I don't know if I've really reflected on that before, but I think that's pretty exciting. I am glad that I am in the field, in a profession that gives me the opportunity to explore my identity and help others explore theirs as well. So whether I'm working in residence life or writing my dissertation, there are always themes I'm looking for—sometimes consciously, sometimes unconsciously—in relation to my race and gender. I also think that who I am each day develops because I am pushing and being pushed by others to really think critically about these aspects of identity for myself and other students in higher education.

IRENE: I agree. I feel really fortunate that I have been offered different opportunities during grad school and working in multicultural affairs to really understand the intersection of being a woman and a person of color. I faced challenges with this unique intersection as I moved up in student affairs. I don't think that the challenges are new. I don't think that by any means, but I think it is surprising given a field that is so open at the outset, wanting to be so encouraging. We encourage our students as well as our colleagues to think about those intersections and how they apply in the professional context; however, I am then confronted with the fact that things haven't changed. At least it isn't like other fields, where they maybe want a person of color in a particular position, but they don't offer mentorship or the system doesn't change in any way to accommodate for that person. I mean, I don't want that to sound like everything has to change for the person, but it is set up in a way that is historically very White and very male. Some of those issues led me to the place I am now where I want to have a strong foundation to address issues of injustice in a more systematic way.

My journey has definitely been interesting. Even though it has been a hard journey, I've developed some wonderful friendships along the way, and largely with women of color. It was nice to have other women of color as friends to be reassured that I wasn't totally off in perceiving a situation or interaction with others. I needed this reassurance because my White, male colleagues weren't supportive when I named something as sexist or racist. Instead, they would give me all sorts of excuses. It was my support group, which was largely women of color, who would say "you're not imagining things; it is what it is."

LINDA: First, I need to explain something as a Latina woman. I never call myself a person of color. For me that is a term that is designed somewhere to identify a group of people. I already have a lot of labels. I'm Mexican American, Latina, Chicana, Tejana, Americana, and then I have one more and I just refuse to accept it for myself. I understand that it's an easy term to use and so I go along with it when necessary, like in this venue where we're having to use it for the Sister Circles. But for me, I identify as a Latina woman in the organizations that I belong to and serve. So for me, when I'm operating at this university, I'm always conscious that the system is set up for White males, has been for a very long time, and it is changing slowly, and that is good, but we're still chipping away at it. When I go to a meeting as a Latina woman,

I know that I have to have all the answers, I have to speak smarter, I have to be smarter, I have to have the most information in order to be able to go into that meeting and have my information accepted along with everyone else's. There are not many women administrators on this campus. My boss is one and she's great and has been a great mentor. But, there's always something to remind me that I'm Latina. I'm not always totally comfortable approaching any meeting or policy making without being really conscious of who I am and what I must contribute to be able to be accepted.

AMANDA SUNITI: If I could add to that, I think Linda brought up a really interesting point and this kind of lends itself to the next question in how we work with students and, for me, with colleagues using the label of women of color. It was really interesting because that [the label] is not necessarily something I would just identify with on a daily basis. But in my own racial identity development as a biracial person, what I call myself sometimes changes depending on who I'm with, how comfortable I am, and my goal. For example, in my ethnographic dissertation research, I've joined numerous student organizations in an effort to become part of the campus community; one of these groups is the Women of Color student organization. Given my phenotype, I do not necessarily look to many people like a woman of color. So I felt that I should disclose my racial background so that might be something that helps these particular women relate to me.

In general, it's sometimes a challenge when I'm trying to address issues of race, whether it's in ACPA or within other groups, because I don't always feel like I'm recognized as being a woman of color. My main point is that the labels are sometimes troubling because they do have certain connotations that make us uncomfortable, but other times I feel like we kind of need some kind of larger group language to have some solidarity with each other, for strength. But it is important to do that in a way that we don't also lose the individuality of the aspects of our identity that are most important to us personally and professionally.

MARIAMA: Right. Amanda and Linda, as you talk about that, it makes me wonder if we can also think about how the intersection of our multiple identities, our perspective of being a woman, and the varying backgrounds that we come from, kind of play out on different types of campuses with different types of students and colleagues. Can anybody speak to that?

I'll just start off. For me, as an African American, as a woman, and as a lesbian woman, the layers have just continued to change my perspective at different points in my career. I can also look back at my career in terms of where I am now and think about how, for example, when I worked on a predominately White campus doing diversity work, what that meant for me as an African American woman working with students of color and how my relationships were different with students of color than they may have been to a certain degree with my White colleagues or even with my African American colleagues. When I think about when I transitioned to JMU [James Madison University], which is still a predominately White campus, I think about the challenges, struggles, and/or opportunities that I had there, both as a woman and then also, identifying as a lesbian woman at that particular time; I think about what Amanda talked about, just in terms of the identification and where you identify, and how you identify, and what situations you're expected to identify; depending on what situation

you go into, a different level of leadership may be needed based on the cultural orientation that you are bringing at that particular moment.

LINDA: I still have a hard time, I think, understanding what exactly women of color means. We don't use that term as much in Texas. Latinos in Texas don't identify as people of color as much as they do in other parts of the United States and I think that's where it originates for me. So that's a little bit different and I think eventually it will be accepted across the United States pretty easily, as Amanda said, as a form of identification. But I don't believe we're there yet in Texas. And it's interesting for us, we're pretty out there about "we're Latina" or "we're Mexican American," or "we're Horandana or Salvadoran," or whatever. And we identify more that way. I think the African American community may identify that way a little bit more than Latinas do. I don't think they're quite there yet. And I know some Vietnamese people do not label themselves people of color. Or, or most of them do not. So, it's very different down here. I think we're still getting used to the term.

IRENE: I think that's a great point. I'm an Asian American woman in Minnesota. There just aren't very many of us. I do use "of color" more because there aren't very many people of color. When you're looking for solidarity, and there are not very many people who are ethnically or racially like you, you expand whom you look to for solidarity. There are some exceptions. There are various immigrant or refugee communities and, for those communities, I think it is more similar to what Linda was talking about. They don't necessarily identify as people of color and that makes a lot of sense for all sorts of reasons.

It's still a struggle to find a community like that in Minnesota because it doesn't take very long before you walk outside and see that it is largely predominately White. I still wanted to add a piece about the question that was asked. I'm a single mother and I get all sorts of questions when it comes to my multiple identities. It is enough to deal with just being a single mother. Why are you a single mother? How did that happen? Where is the dad? How can you raise a son without a father figure? On top of that, I am also Chinese American, which just is an additional layer. I get even more criticism that being a single mother is unacceptable and it's just hard. And so I try to be on the offensive by saying, "I'm a proud single mother" and not deal with the questions from my colleagues, focus on how wonderful my son is, and not talk too much about the difficulties. I can do without the criticism. Even though it was a hard choice to bring a child into the world whose father was not ready to be a parent, I would never change it. I am in a unique situation. For example, there was this student at the last campus I was at who got pregnant her junior year. And she was fortunate that the man was going to stay in her life and so they were going to raise the child together. And, I had a unique perspective and could be there to say "You know what, no matter what choice you make, one parent, two-parent home, you're going to be fine." At the same time, being a single mother is not something I'm going to share with everybody—like when I was going to ACPA. I didn't walk into any of those large meetings and say "Hi, I'm a single mom" because I don't know where people are at with their opinions regarding single parents and it can hamper relationship building in a community. I know that some people hold prejudices. Does that make sense?

CIE: I think that I am always aware that people see me as a woman and a person of color. As a result, I try and understand the multiple identities that are represented by the students. I work and help them in their journey of understanding their multiple identities and what that means for them as they explore career and other opportunities. I would add that I was blessed with parents who reminded me every day that I am strong person and I have an obligation to be a good and productive member of the human race and, in a way, I think that helped me understand that even though I have multiple identities and that some may be more pronounced at different times in my life, my main identity is that of a member of the human race.

I don't think you can be a minority in this country and not have your race and at times your gender impact what you do. I am mindful that my work and my appearance have to be 110% at all times. I feel that I am looked at with one set of expectations and it is not until people interact with me that they shift those expectations to what is more in line with other members of the community. I recognize that I may be the only person of color in an administrative position that some folks have interacted with and so I am constantly an educator. Sometimes that education comes from setting an example and other times it is helping students understand where their prejudices come from.

MARIAMA: Talk about some of the accomplishments you feel have been made regarding women of color—or AALNA women is what we used when I was at New York State, which includes African, Asian, Latina, Native American women in higher education or student affairs. What accomplishments do you feel have been made over the years?

CIE: I think part of it is that even though there are not as many as we would like, I do feel like I see, or I'm starting to see more women in senior student affairs positions in higher education and not just at historically Black institutions, which I think is positive and will continue. I think the role modeling and the mentoring, even since I was an undergraduate, has greatly improved. I know that I've had opportunity to speak with lots of different women in student affairs, partly through the pre-conference that ACPA always has for African American women in student affairs, different titles each year, has basically brought together women to talk about some of those things, such as what do you do when it comes to raising a family, or when do you start thinking about those decisions, and how do you balance that with going back to get a Ph.D.?

AMANDA SUNITI: I think that another area that is becoming increasingly better is research about women, women of color, and women and their multiple identities. It's really something that people are much more aware of and embracing this topic. Scholars are doing a lot of excellent research in this area; as people are going into doctoral programs it is encouraged and acceptable to do research about something that is personal to you, such as something related to your own identity. I think these types of research are now seen as important contributions to the field. And it's important to make sure that the work of these scholars and their work are represented, embraced, and celebrated.

LINDA: I see quite a bit of research done about women of color and yet I'm not seeing a lot of research done on specific groups. If I was to go out today and look for research on Latina women, very few people are doing that. I always go back to Vasti Torres, former ACPA president, because she's done some great work with Latinas in general. If I went to look for research for my Vietnamese students on my campus, particularly females, and their

identity and development in higher education, I'm not finding a whole lot. I think we've done great work in research generally and I see the trend needs to be more intentional with certain groups. And I applaud what has been done and what's beginning to be done. I think we're really moving in the right direction, in that perspective. I really admire everyone who's involved in those types of research because we do need those pieces to help us—to help us help our students in their development. And, speaking as a Latina woman, I know that we come with different cultural pieces that are unlike some other groups. It's important to have that information available as well.

MARIAMA: Good point.

IRENE: The only thing that I would add regarding accomplishments—because I agree with everything everyone's said—is the ability to have outward and public support for women of color, like Cie was talking about with the pre-conference for African American women. It is an accomplishment just to have venues like that, with less stigma than I can see right now in the legal field about "well why would you need that?" Allowing for spaces like that in such public ways at our national conventions is really great and demonstrates support from the field as a whole.

MARIAMA: Can you think of challenges that still exist regarding African, Latina, Asian, Native American women, in higher education or in student affairs?

AMANDA SUNITI: And multiracial.

MARIAMA: And multiracial, yes.

LINDA: I agree with what Irene just said. One of the challenges is that when we do want to sponsor a program or have a pre-conference for African American women or Latina women and/or any other groups, sometimes people question the purpose. They may not say it out loud, but there is that underlying question of "why do they need that?" There may not be an understanding that there are additional needs and mentoring that need to take place. While we are accepted more broadly across higher education, we're not that accepted broadly in the corporate world. Women have made some strides, but not to the same degree as the CEOs that are out there right now. So, in student affairs, we should be able to do that mentoring and assist students into moving into positions of power. It has to start somewhere and it has to start with us.

AMANDA SUNITI: Again advocating from my perspective, personally and professionally, we need to think about how we can stretch the paradigm for talking about women of color—or whichever term that you feel might be most appropriate—to make sure that our language, and how we talk about diversity and inclusiveness, is addressing multiracial and biracial identities. And I realize that it has been, and continues to be, such a struggle just to get to the point where issues of diversity and services for people of color are addressed. So, it is a bit of a challenge to shift that paradigm to make sure we're being as inclusive as possible, to bring in those who identify as mixed-race, including myself. That's something that I've been thinking about a lot. For example, there are usually student services for many of the different racial groups, but rarely if ever do you see one for people who identify as multi-racial and bi-racial.

But at the same time, it is important to think about not only advocating for our own group, but also how are we advocating for other groups who may not have someone to advocate for them? I believe that is a challenge, but I also see that as an opportunity to achieve the next step. The other challenge that I would say exists within

ACPA, and within higher education institutions, is this inherent structure of how we function. Sometimes for organizational reasons, there are different campus offices or, for example, in ACPA there are different committees and networks [for different identity groups] because that's the way they've emerged and that's the structure that makes sense. But I think that sometimes this structure doesn't necessarily account for our multiple identities as women, as women of color, and these other parts of who we are. So how to do that, I'm not sure, but I think it is the next place that we need to go.

IRENE: I just want to emphasize some of what Amanda has said because I think that it's not just incorporating multiracial and biracial students into our programs and services, but we also need to do the personal work to understand our beliefs and understanding of multiracial people. We need to do more than just *say* that multiracial people are important; we need to examine how we interact and think in our personal lives. I know that I need to do that work. When I went to the Social Justice Training Institute, there was someone there that I hold near and dear to my heart, who was a mentor of mine, who is multiracial herself. At the time, when I looked at her, I didn't see that she was also Asian. I would do things or say things that would exclude her. While what I was doing and saying was not conscious, I realized that I had lots of work to do in order to really believe that I am doing this work for *everyone*. I had to think about where my own prejudices were, and how I was unconsciously excluding people, not just putting on the programs and putting on a good face, but doing my personal work and at the same time still trying to address some of the issues we were talking about, like showing up the most professional as you can. You can't just be prepared, like Linda was saying, you have to be the most prepared to even appear competent. Doing all of those things at the same time can be very tiring. In addition, sometimes I think that there is competition among women of color. There is sometimes criticism for showing up as "enough" or "not enough," whatever that means within your own respective community. I think the field sometimes doesn't honor that struggle for women of color.

CIE: I would agree with you. That sometimes when women of color get to wherever it is that they want to be, they need to look back and see how they are helping other young women of color and multiracial women to do the same or similar things. I thought of the HNIC complex and I won't say what the "N" is, but the "head person in charge" complex, and sometimes it seems like there's this fear that these professionals, who worked so hard to get where they are, believe there should be this requirement that everyone else should have to pay their dues, and so on. These seasoned professionals could engage in mentoring and support roles that are important for new and mid-level professionals.

MARIAMA: Okay. Going back to Linda's point, I think the women that we see are not necessarily in these key roles within higher education or within student affairs. This occurs because (A) there are not enough women, and (B) they may or may not have the opportunities to reach out because the critical mass is not there. Options are limited and then this is also compounded by—I believe, Irene, as you were talking about and I think Amanda also discussed—a need to connect across multiple identities; the need to connect with our own groups and folks needing other folks similar to themselves. I think some other ethnicities and races needed to be okay with that. So I think one of the challenges

is some underlying or inherent stereotype that having an opportunity for us to get together and connect is somehow not okay anymore. There is this whole concept of segregation and reverse segregation, which I don't ascribe to; it's a challenge because then I feel like if you walk into a room and your first orientation might be to connect with people who look like you regardless of what commonalities you might share in background. But sometimes you have to consciously think "okay, I need to then make my way around to connect with everyone else" because the perception might be that we're being not inclusive, when really the environment should be such that we can connect and share with whomever we would like. So that's one of the challenges that I think still exists.

And so along with that, has there been a critical incident or significant experience that you can draw upon or that stands out in your minds, you don't necessarily have to go into all the details, but something that's impacted your growth or development as a women of color, professionally in the field of student affairs? Something that maybe changed your perspective and how you see things, or how you started to, to work as a woman of color, or whatever term you would like to use?

IRENE: There are two things that really build upon each other, that formed how I was going to be as a professional woman of color. When I was in grad school there was a Latina in the program who would talk about this White man who was really cool. She told him that she really looked up to him, how cool it was that he would show up to work in jeans, how he's really well respected as this great researcher and how she wanted to be just like him. The White man had told her, "you know that you can't do that, right? You can't show up to work in your jeans. Even though it may not be right, you have to do more because the world won't accept your awesome work if you show up to work in jeans." This story made me ponder about what kind of professional I was going to be. The second part happened when I was a professional. There was an instance where I was in this meeting largely with the administration, who were mostly White men, and one other woman of color who identified as African American. I can't even remember what the meeting was about, but I do remember that as the meeting was progressing, I was getting really upset. I started to tear up and although I wasn't balling or crying in the meeting, it was evident that I was having an emotional reaction. After the meeting she pulled me aside and said that you need to be careful because you can't let yourself show. You have to keep that passion aside. You have to know how to play the game when you're in meetings like that. I think that conversation was jarring for me, to be told to check my passion at the door. I'm still figuring that out what that means and how I want to incorporate or not incorporate passion in my professional life. I struggle with the contradiction of telling students that they should be who they are and how they should not be ashamed of who they are. Then, I feel like I'm being a little hypocritical because I am going into these meetings not showing up truly as me. It's still with me when I think about how I want to be as a professional.

LINDA: Irene, you touched something in my memory. It doesn't just happen as a new professional, it happened to me just recently. Someone on this campus told me I'm too passionate about Latinos. [Small chuckle] And, that came from the fact we sometimes we get labeled and become "the" diversity person because there not a lot of us in any positions. And so, we serve on all these committees as the "diversity" person.

From my perspective, the largest underrepresented group of students on my campus is Hispanic; yet, we have the lowest percentages of Latino faculty and professional staff. We do have many Latino employees, but the majority are support staff. When I bring this up, it hasn't always been appreciated. Thus, I'm told "you're just too passionate about Latinos." I said, "Yes I am and I will continue to be." And so I have to operate—I don't know how exactly to put it—but I temper myself only to a small degree because I just can't change who I am to please other people. As a social change agent, it's a fine line. So I know where you're coming from.

AMANDA SUNITI: The two stories you've just shared really kind of struck a chord with me, an emotional chord, in this conversation. I know that for each it's different, but kind of a feeling of things welling up. I can think of things that very much relate to how much of yourself do you share and how much of yourself needs to be the person who is educating others; in what ways does that help you as a person and in what ways does that really sometimes hurt you? Sometimes it's hard just trying to explain myself—and it happens not only in student affairs, but in general. I think that I often feel like I'm in a position where I'm having to justify who I am, especially in terms of my racial identity. And there are times when I am glad to have discussions with students, faculty, or colleagues about my racial identity if it is going to help other people think about things in different ways and help me think about things in different ways. But I also come home at night and sometimes I'm emotionally exhausted. It hurts sometimes to have to go through that again and again . . . so, I don't know if there's much more to say. It just hurts. So I'm glad to hopefully help the dialogue and advocate for things I believe in, but it's tough. It's tough and that's why I think it's so important that we all advocate for each other when possible. And also work with people, for whom race is not their major issue, but help them understand that they should also be advocating for racial issues as well, just as we should be advocating for the different parts of their identity. We all are trying to be understood and help people understand others and be inclusive. That's an honor and a privilege, but it's an emotional fight.

MARIAMA: I think one of the pivotal moments in higher education and student affairs was related to my identity as a woman; this particular instance occurred at an institution that I was working for at the time. I was very close to the EEOC process and definitely had to negotiate some things out of that. And that whole sense of advocacy and fight, and having to do that alone—really informed the perspective and the manner in which sometimes I move forward with things, especially when it's of my own key issues, involving women—and just some of the disparities and inequities that still exist within higher education and student affairs. And how you continue to break, or tap on, the glass ceiling, or work through it; having some great relationships with men, but also having some not so great relationships with men and then how race and gender also intersect with that. So, I think that that was, for me, probably the most pivotal, or one of the most pivotal moments, that I had in my career in terms of having to really self-advocate.

CIE: I think my example is similar to that of the stories that Irene and Linda shared. I remember, distinctly, several conversations surrounding one new professional woman who was working on campus. I think that others would describe her dress as less than professional but not items that would warrant her being sent home for dressing in-

appropriately. I would also say that much of her style was derived both from her culture and more specifically the way she felt that culture was expressed by woman in her previous geographic region. I remember that a seasoned professional who had great style and was often looked to to help others with appropriate dress pulled her aside and told her "You're too flashy, you know, you call unnecessary attention to yourself, but not in the right ways." And, of course I wasn't there for the conversation, but after hearing that I really had mixed emotions. On the one hand, I can appreciate where the more experienced woman was trying to help her navigate in a new environment. But at the same time I kind of wondered "well, should she have been maybe then advocating the other way by telling those who might be raising comments about this other woman that this is okay." And so I think that has really stuck with me. Even when I speak with students about what they want to do later, I always remind them to really be observant about the culture of a place when they go for an interview or internship, to make sure that it matches what they want and how they want to express themselves in their own identities.

MARIAMA: Okay, good. Thank you. So then, as we focus toward the future, what do you envision as some of the opportunities that are out there regarding women of color in higher education and student affairs? Where are the areas that perhaps we haven't really capitalized on?

CIE: I think tapping into undergraduates; I know both ACPA and NASPA [National Association for Student Personnel Administrators] have different programs that are geared toward attracting undergrads to the field but I think this is a particularly good opportunity for women of color in student affairs to reach out to undergraduate students who are still not sure about how they can utilize their talents. Expose them to this field as an opportunity.

LINDA: Yes, there are great opportunities out there to tap into our young women, from all different groups. I remember, Amanda, this is directed to you, I remember when the multiracial group first started out of CMA [Standing Committee for Multicultural Affairs in ACPA]. I was so excited because I had not seen that before. And your e-mails kept flying through and I thought, "Wow! This young woman is going to really go places." I was so proud of you, and you didn't even know that! [Chuckles] So tapping into all of our young women is the key; I think we're so much more savvy; our young women are so much more savvy than I was certainly at that age. And, it's exciting. I'm looking forward to seeing what comes next.

AMANDA: *Thank you*, Linda.

MARIAMA: Although we don't necessarily look to them, it would also be awesome to look to our seasoned professionals. I think sometimes we think "Oh, they're too busy or too tired." [Chuckles] Women that have really laid the foundation for us should be looked to; we need to really incorporate more women who have walked the path before us into some of the activities that we are currently trying to initiate. Doing so would provide an opportunity to talk about the journey or share insights and words of wisdom. I think doing so could be another great opportunity and should be documented. We all, I think, come from a variety of cultures that really value oral history, so it would be great to see some of that oral history documented as well.

The only other thing is in regards to something that was spurred by what Cie said in terms of understanding where people are developmentally. How do I want to say this? The woman that Cie was talking about earlier [about the appropriateness of her attire] perceived her interaction as not so positive, right? Am I correct?

CIE: Yes.

IRENE: I would resonate with that when I was younger, and I probably still do a little bit, regarding how I'd receive that type of feedback. Having programs that kind of address some of those things could bridge those gaps and help people come to mentoring more easily. But when you're giving feedback like that, it is important to be explicit: "I'm not trying to tell you what to do; I'm just trying to tell you in my experience this is what has worked."

MARIAMA: So, when you think about what you want people to know most about being a woman of color in student affairs, are there things that come to mind? And this question arose for me because I think a lot of times we don't have an opportunity to share with folks, either what we appreciate or the things that we would appreciate that they stopped doing, or just things that we want folks to keep at the forefront. So, does anyone have any thoughts on that?

IRENE: Some words of advice, or things that I would share, is that it's really been helpful to love myself and get to know myself better. I think that, in some environments, depending on where you are and how supportive your office or your environment is, it can be difficult because you can feel that the work is tearing away at who you are, whether or not it's purposeful on the part of the institution or with whom you are talking. So just remember to love yourself and, as I said earlier, to surround yourself with people who truly support you. Whoever that may be for you—be it partner, friends, people who are like you, people who are different. Surround yourself with people who will help you love yourself, so you don't feel so stripped away and forget who you are.

MARIAMA: I would want people to know that although women are very strong and we're great multi-taskers, the superwoman complex is a little overrated. We do need support too. We need assistance and help and guidance. We're not always superwomen. I think that when we're put on a pedestal, sometimes we get ignored as if we don't need care and attention or some dusting off as well. And so, the overall recognition is something we want folks to know.

LINDA: I feel that we don't necessarily need to have all mentors that look like us. And so I struggle with that because I'm constantly wanting more faculty [of color] on this campus, more staff [of color] in higher-level positions so that our students see people and interact with people who look like them. I think that's extremely important but, on the other hand, I've also learned, through my own personal experience, that we can have great mentors from all different groups and walks of life and functional areas. I feel very supported on my campus to do the work that I do, and I'm really grateful for that. I've worked hard for it; it hasn't come easy, but I do feel like I have been supported in student affairs on this campus.

AMANDA SUNITI: Following up on what Linda said, I was thinking about a professor of mine—professor of Irene's and mine, Dr. Marylu McEwen, who's now retired. She has been a mentor to many different people, in many different ways. But one of the things that is so touching to me was that she seems to recognize and just appreciate who we are and the work we do to make a difference. And I think that if all of us try to show appreciation, not so much in the form of an award, but just saying "I value you and what you're doing," it demonstrates that you recognize where a person is coming from, and I think that can go a long way. Whether it's someone you designate as a mentor or somebody who just may be a colleague of yours, I think that mentoring makes a huge difference. It can help us to keep going.

CIE: I would agree. This may sound cliché but it is the truth. My family has always been my biggest mentors; they encourage, challenge, and support me in all the ways that we have talked about. There have also been those folks who have provided encouragement along the way without necessarily filling the role of mentor and one was a senior student affairs professional who is a White woman and the other is a Black male.

MARIAMA: I would concur, as well, that your mentors don't always have to look like you. And I've had several throughout my career. And then I've also had great mentors that have looked like me as well. I feel like it's important for folks to give us the room to grow, give us the room to make mistakes, give us the room to ask the questions about why, and give us the room to challenge in a safe environment certain thinking, policies, procedures, and then figure out how to bundle all of that and put that in a form that others can hear. I also think that balance, or creating that sense of work/life balance, is also really important for women, and women of color, and wish that higher education and student affairs could do that more. I think that that is really, really, really critical, because, I know just myself; I've personally been afflicted and my stress-related incidents at least two times in my career. I think that individual drive, in addition to that perceptual drive, and the reality of certain positions also has an impact on our health and well-being—and so that is critically important as well.

IRENE: I need to have direct feedback. I think particularly from my supervisor. I have had experiences where people are scared to give me feedback, either because I'm a woman or because I am a person of color; they don't want it to be perceived as sexist or racist. The result is that I'm stuck where I'm at; I don't advance professionally. I think that a lot of us really want to strive to be the best we can be and without honest feedback, that is difficult. The other thing would be the importance of discussing things that happen. I think about, with men in my life, both white men and men of color, when sexist things have happened that I've been able to discuss the issues with them. They're open to it and they don't just hear it; they really take in and take it as important. They really do their own work around it. It makes me feel validated that I can make a difference, that I can address these issues, that things can change, and that it can be a part of how I have helped myself and hopefully will have helped other women of color who come after me. Hopefully after having these conversations with these men, they won't have to go through some of the same things.

MARIAMA: Absolutely. I'd also like to add that some of the things that mentors do, and some of the things that my mentors have done really well, is to help us think about opportunities and how to think about the next level. I think sometimes as women and as women of color, because there may not necessarily be a critical mass of us on a particular campus or you might be really, really valued for your position that you hold, folks don't want to let go of you and they don't want you to leave; but then I don't think that it's a purposeful kind of thing. However, I think sometimes there can be a tendency to get stifled in a particular position because folks value us so much that we don't necessarily move on, or we don't necessarily go to the next step if that's what we desire to do. So, opening up some of those opportuni-

ties in new and different ways is one of the things that I'd like to see folks do for women of color in terms of fostering that support.

Does anyone have anything that they wanted to share about role models or mentors that have hindered them? Or supervisors that have hindered them? And what was not helpful?

CIE: I am aware of supervisors who have maybe been exposed to only male leadership styles or have adopted them as their leadership style (even if they do not necessarily recognize that they have adopted this style), and have a hard time relating to women they supervise. I don't know if "threat" is the right word, but maybe they aren't comfortable working with other women who are adept in leadership positions or are confident taking responsibility for making things happen. This can be detrimental, especially because there's sometimes a false misconception that "Oh, I work for a woman and so she's going to be a mentor or a potential role model." I think that is not necessarily the case. And it can be hard for someone looking for a role model or mentor or even good feedback to move past that.

MARIAMA: Okay. Anyone else?

IRENE: I have talked with my past supervisors about how they can be more supportive and a better ally for me in meetings. One supervisor, in particular, acknowledged that he could do a better job of having my back, but then would end up leaving me alone to defend whatever issue was going on. If you are going to call yourself an ally, if you're going to call yourself my advocate, you really need to show up. Because the truth is that I don't have the energy to continually address that issue. I don't have the energy to engage in the same conversation. "Okay you said you were going to be right and you were not an ally in that situation . . . again." It's important to have a better understanding of what it means when you say that you're going to "be there." You can't just say that you'll be there. If you are not going to "be there" because you don't have the energy or don't support my ideas, then just tell me. I won't expect it.

MARIAMA: As we come to some of our final moments of our Sister Circle, are there any primary guiding principles or words of wisdom that you would share for women of color who are currently graduate students, entry level professionals?

LINDA: Words of wisdom? I guess what came to my mind is for new professionals who graduate with their degrees and then go into their first professional job, first professional position: to be open to learn more. It's a very different story to go from graduate school into an actual position and there's still a lot of learning to do; to be receptive, particularly with constructive criticism, guidelines, or just assistance. It saves a lot of hurt feelings and, sometimes if you're not willing to accept assistance from other folks who have already been in the field, you set yourself up for hurt or for self-doubt. It's a continual learning process, so when you go from the classroom into your work environment, there's still a lot to learn.

MARIAMA: What comes to mind for me is that piece about taking care of yourself. And I believe that, when you feel good, you look good. You can have a positive attitude about yourself and that can also help you through some of those challenging times. Also, get clear about your journey and your destiny. Although sometimes that is undetermined and we're not sure what twists in the road will be presented, just having that sense of vision about yourself, your life, and your career can hopefully instill some of that confidence.

AMANDA SUNITI: I would just say basically that it takes time, or at least for me it took some time, to find my voice—and I'm still finding it. Everybody has something to contribute. I strongly agree with what Linda was saying—that you need to listen, you're always learning, that each person and each woman of color has something to bring to the table and she should not doubt that; figuring out the best way to express yourself is invaluable.

CIE: Mine falls in line with one of my favorite quotes by Thoreau, "Go confidently in the direction of your dreams, live the life you've imagined." So if what you're doing all of the sudden doesn't look like the life you've imagined, don't be afraid to reexamine. Maybe that means a new institution, a new functional area, and a new career— but do not be afraid to look at that and to always do what it is that you think you should be doing.

MARIAMA: As we close up, I'd like to ask you to reflect upon how your involvement in ACPA has impacted your professional growth as a woman of color and what hopes you might have for the future.

AMANDA SUNITI: I am excited about this question because ACPA has [been], and continues to be, a significant part of my professional growth; it's the people I've met and the relationships I've built. Even with SCW I can already see that that is going to be a meaningful kind of experience. It is amazing to connect with people who foster in me the things that I really care about, whether its women, or people of color, or mixed-race folks. It's so nice to have this community, even though it often feels like we are virtual. I know that those people are there for me, who really understand you and who, even if you do disagree, can share a passion. This helps me keep going. I think there are things that can be improved, for sure, but so far, it's been a definite learning journey that I've appreciated.

LINDA: For me, ACPA, wow, has impacted my life, not only as a woman, but as a Latina woman, as well as a professional. I've been with SCW for a really long time. I looked around. I kept looking for my niche, I kept looking for the group that I could connect with and it turned out to be SCW. It has been a very positive experience for me as you can tell, because by the time I rotate off it will be seven years. So, I just couldn't leave it. I've seen young women come and go and I've learned a lot, and I think that's one of the most important pieces that I haven't addressed today: that I have learned a lot from the younger professionals coming up. They are full of new ideas, full of new ways of thinking and operating, and that has all been so positive for me. I respect all of these young women who are in student affairs. They just really add a lot to my life. I have good friends. I'm an assistant dean and director of my office and at times I have had some very traumatic experiences. This is the group that I've gone to, and have always been supported. So, I love SCW and ACPA!

[Chuckles from the group]

LINDA: And Mariama, we met at the ACPA mid-level managers institute didn't we? With Donna Bourassa?

MARIAMA: Absolutely.

LINDA: A long, long time ago. So that was my beginning.

MARIAMA: It's just been the connections and the sense of community that I've been able to foster within ACPA, all the wonderfully awesome and talented professionals, and just the wealth of scholarship is amazing. And folks being so giving of themselves and of their knowledge, and are willing to share and support me in ways that

I had never really offered or imagined. So, just to have that second family is great. I don't have a real large family personally, and so the climate of ACPA has been very much like my family with the folks that I've had an opportunity to interact with.

CIE: I would agree about the space for personal connections and your "go-to" set of people. I think that it's been really nice to have, particularly at SCW, a place where everyone is on the same page. We might not all do everything the same way, but to have a group of women who all agree that supporting women in higher education and student affairs is important and then being able to get together and that's what we focus on—it's really refreshing. I know that when I'm with SCW that I, that we, are going to make it happen. So that's always really exciting and motivating for me.

IRENE: I think the thing that I appreciate is the desire to improve and address these issues. A lot of props for you all for doing this [Sister Circle dialogue]. I think this is great and it's extremely exciting to have this book and chapter, and have it be taken seriously in the first place.

MARIAMA: So as we get ready to close are there any things that you would suggest are included in the chapter of the dialogue that we hadn't mentioned or that you wanted to emphasize?

LINDA: I don't think any of us really talked about motherhood and women and young professionals and student affairs, and how the need for the rest of us who are not in that phase of our lives to be supportive of young families. I don't think we addressed that at all and particularly our young women of color who have such a strong familial attachment.

AMANDA SUNITI: Yes, and it's almost impossible to cover all of our multiple identities or to do all of them justice. There is always so much more to say and do.

LINDA: Right.

MARIAMA: It has been a pleasure to talk with you all. Thank you so much for sharing in this Sister Circle.

CONCLUSION

We hope that reading this dialogue was meaningful for you and that it resonated with one or more of your various social identities or personal experiences. Having the opportunity to discuss being women of color in higher education and student affairs was amazing for each of us; being able to reflect with each other in this way was more significant than any of us could have imagined when we agreed to take part in this project. After reviewing our own words, we identified some topics that emerged from the discussion and want to share what we believe they mean for advancing our field.

Without a doubt, the complexity of multiple identities surfaced in the Sister Circle dialogue. Being not only women of color, but also mothers, daughters, partners, friends, colleagues, and allies influence how we carry out our personal and professional lives. We learned that not only do our racial and gender identities influence our work in student affairs, but our careers and educational experiences have also influenced our identity development. This reciprocal relationship is extremely important to note.

While many of us expressed the emotional/physical/professional exhaustion that often comes with our work, we also saw that we have the opportunity, privilege, and responsibility to serve as advocates for not only women of color but also any group that is marginalized in higher education. We are aware of the potential impact such advocacy can have on one's health and balance; it is challenging to do both. This challenge can be addressed through the support that women of color provide each other and the support that people can provide to each other in general. The connections and relationships that can be formed are immeasurable sources of strength, whether it is with someone local in the community or 2,000 miles away.

The notion of labels was also an important theme that emerged from the dialogue. While some of us were comfortable with the concept of *women of color*, others felt that it did not reflect who we were and how we lived our lives. The significance of language cannot be underestimated. In addition, we talked about the importance of doing our own "personal work," learning to be more inclusive not just from a professional perspective but expanding our own worldview. We also discussed the notion of trying to reach beyond the "choir." For example, how do we educate and empower those who do not normally think about these issues to consider the importance of multiple identities? And in particular, how do we build support for women of color?

Toward the end of the formal dialogue, we continued to talk about what—or who—was not addressed in our discussion. The notion of motherhood and caretaking was not fully explored. That is an important part of many women's lives that needs to be nurtured by employers, colleagues, and ACPA, and is addressed in other chapters in this book.

We acknowledge that while the five of us represented various racial/ethnic groups, there is tremendous, wonderful diversity within those groups that should be further celebrated and explored. In addition, there were so many other integral aspects of ourselves that were not really touched upon, such as our sexual orientation, socioeconomic status, and ability, among many others.

What do all of these themes mean for higher education and student affairs? The questions that arose regarding the complexity of multiple identities of students, staff, and faculty beg for an answer. However, to provide a solution in our concluding remarks suggests that the intersections of our identities are "problems" and that there is one answer to "fix" the situation. Instead, we argue that the complexities of multiple identities do not need one solution but a genuine commitment to understanding and respect for what each person brings to the table. On the basis of our dialogue, we propose the following overarching ideas as a starting point for communication and action:

- Promote balance and health for yourself and those you supervise.
- Be an advocate with your language and your actions.
- Provide respectful feedback.
- Be receptive to feedback, particularly with constructive criticism, guidelines, or assistance.
- Shift from a monoracial to a multiracial paradigm.
- Recognize and show appreciation for those who make a difference "behind the curtain."
- Take time to pay it forward and thank those who do.
- Be aware of the power (positive and negative) of labels.
- Recognize and respect the research regarding women of color and multiple identities.
- Do your own "personal work" on identity and inclusivity; do not just go through the motions as a professional.
- Remember that it is not enough to just bring women of color into the system; we need to challenge the system to incorporate support mechanisms for various aspects of a person's identity.
- Not only advocate for issues related to your own identity, but also be a voice for others who may not have one.
- Keep in mind that a person's outward appearance does not necessarily reflect the entire being of a person.
- Make the time to mentor. Mentoring can happen not only between women of color but also between people with different identities. Mentoring can be bidirectional—senior to junior and junior to senior.

Thank you for taking the time to share in our Sister Circle dialogue. We invite you to join in the dialogue at the annual ACPA convention. In addition, we hope that the conversation about the intersections of multiple identities continues for you and enhances your work in higher education and student affairs.

NOTE

1. Every person played an important role in the development and editorial revision of this chapter. Amanda Suniti Niskodé-Dossett served as the coordinator of the chapter, taking the lead on organizing the group conversations, revising the transcript into chapter form, and preparing the additional pieces to support the dialogue. Mariama Boney facilitated the dialogue itself.

REFERENCE

Thoreau, H. D. (1817–1862). *Quotations by author*. Retrieved on June 12, 2009, from http://www .quotationspage.com/quotes/Henry_David_ Thoreau/

13

Using Queer Theory to Explore Lesbian College Students' Multiple Dimensions of Identity

Elisa S. Abes and David Kasch

Abstract: *By introducing queer theory to Abes and Jones's (2004) constructivist narrative inquiry of lesbian college students' perceptions of their multiple identities, we retell the developmental narrative of one participant's negotiation of her sexuality, religion, gender, and social class. This queer retelling of a developmental story shows how identities are constantly forming and reforming and challenges heteronormative assumptions underlying student development theory, including the construct of self-authorship. We propose a fluid perspective on student development that accounts for lesbian college students' resistance of heteronormative structures. We also encourage student affairs practice that centers lesbian college students' agency and resistance.*

STUDENT DEVELOPMENT THEORY literature must include more attention to the ways in which social power structures, such as racism, classism, and heterosexism, mediate student development. In the context of heterosexism, D'Augelli (1994), Rhoads (1997), Talburt (2004), and Renn and Bilodeau (2005) argued that gay, lesbian, and bisexual identity development theories do not account for heterosexism reify heterosexual privilege. This research explores the relationship between heterosexism and student development theory by using queer theory to study the nature of lesbian college students' intersections of sexual orientation identity with other identity dimensions, such as religion, social class, and gender. What new insights about

college students' negotiation of multiple identities are gained through the use of queer theory? What new insights into student development theory might queer theory uncover? To explore these questions, we focus on two tellings of the identity story of KT, one of the participants in a longitudinal study of lesbian college students' perceptions of their multiple dimensions of identity (Abes & Jones, 2004). Elisa tells a story of KT's perceptions of her multiple identities using constructivist-developmental theory as the theoretical framework (Baxter Magolda, 2001; Kegan, 1994). Dave then applies a queer theoretical framework to KT's developmental story and retells her narrative through this perspective. Together, we hope to offer new understandings

213

of how lesbian students negotiate their multiple identities and how educators can support students in these identity negotiations.

LITERATURE REVIEW

We review the two theoretical frameworks that we use to tell and then retell a narrative about the relationships among KT's sexual orientation identity and other dimensions of her identity: constructivist-developmental theory and queer theory.

Constructivist-Developmental Theory

Constructivist-developmental theorists suggest that people develop through a relatively linear trajectory of increasingly complex meaning-making structures, which are sets of assumptions that determine how an individual perceives and organizes life experiences (Kegan, 1994). Building on Kegan's constructivist-developmental theory of self-evolution, Baxter Magolda (2001) described a framework for understanding young adult development. Specifically, Baxter Magolda described a process in which young adults move from external to internal ways of making meaning of knowledge (cognitive domain), relationships with others (interpersonal domain), and who they are as individuals (intrapersonal domain).

Cognitive development theory describes how people perceive the nature of knowledge. Complex cognitive capacity enables a person to internally generate knowledge and beliefs rather than uncritically accepting knowledge claims from external authorities (e.g., Perry, 1970). Interpersonal development describes how people construct relationships. Mature relationships are characterized by mutuality (Jordan, 1997). Mutuality involves respect for both self and others' identities, and the integration of multiple perspectives and needs. Intrapersonal development describes how people construct their identities.

Complex identity construction requires the ability to reflect on and choose enduring values and beliefs that allow a person to internally develop a sense of self rather than relying on external influences to define identity (Baxter Magolda, 2001). These three domains are integrated; development in one domain typically fosters development in another. Complex meaning making in all three domains is necessary for a person to reach self-authorship, which is the internal capacity to construct one's beliefs, sense of self, and relationships with others (Baxter Magolda, 2001; Kegan, 1994). Kegan also described postmodern development beyond self-authorship, the fifth order of consciousness, in which individuals demonstrate an ability through relationships to recognize their incompleteness and simultaneously author multiple forms of self-authorship. Kegan suggested that achieving the fifth order is rare and the earliest an individual does so is typically in his or her forties.

Writing about the first phase of the longitudinal study that provides the data for this analysis, Abes and Jones (2004) explored the relationship between constructivist-developmental theory and lesbian college students' perceptions of their sexual orientation identity and its relationships with other identity dimensions. They found how context-influenced participants' perceptions of their identity was related to the complexity of their meaning-making capacity. Participants with complex meaning-making capacity were able, more so than those with less developed capacity, to filter contextual influences, such as family background, peer culture, and social norms, and determine how context influenced their identity. Also based on the results of the first phase of that study, Abes, Jones, and McEwen (2007) focused in more depth on the role of meaning-making capacity in students' understanding of the salience of and relationships among their multiple identities. They found that meaning-making capacity mediated participants' perceptions of relationships among multiple identities, and the ease with which sexual orientation was integrated or peacefully coexisted with other dimensions.

Queer Theory

Unlike constructivist-developmental theory, which explains development toward complex ways of understanding identity, queer theory critically analyzes the meaning of identity, focusing on intersections of identities and resisting oppressive social constructions of sexual orientation and gender. Queer theory is built from the poststructural theories of Foucault (1978), Derrida (1978), and Lyotard (1984). Sullivan (2003) stated, "Poststructural theorists such as Foucault argue that there are no objective and universal truths, but that particular forms of knowledge, and the ways of being that they engender, become 'naturalised,' in culturally and historically specific ways" (p. 39). Queer theorists apply these ideas to gender and sexuality to suggest that they are socially constructed (Butler, 1990). Genders and sexualities reflect the time and place in which they exist and the individuals who enact them. The expression of gender and sexuality is unstable, changing as the individual affects society and as society affects the individual. To narrow our focus within queer theory, we isolated three concepts that resonated with the development of multiple identities: heteronormativity, performativity, and liminality.

Heteronormativity is the use of heterosexuality as the norm for understanding gender and sexuality (Warner, 1991). Queer theory offers a threefold critique of this dominant social construction of gender and sexuality. First, heteronormativity creates a binary between identification as heterosexual and nonheterosexual, in which nonheterosexuality is abnormal and measured in its difference from heterosexuality. This binary suggests that individuals separate into two distinct groups with identifiable differences. Second, heteronormativity consolidates nonheterosexuality into one essentialized group (Muñoz, 1999). The use of the label "LGBTQ" to rep-

resent students who identify as lesbian, gay, bisexual, transgender, or queer as one group is an example of consolidating nonheterosexual identities. Essentializing this diverse group of students reinforces the binary. Third, by privileging heterosexuality, society does not acknowledge gender and sexual orientation as reflections of social power structures (Foucault, 1978). Heterosexuality's hegemony creates the perception (or lack thereof) that heterosexuality defines what is natural or acceptable (Britzman, 1997). Queer theory provides a framework for resisting heteronormativity.

The second concept that informs this analysis, performativity, uses heteronormativity as a point of tension. Performativity describes how individuals create genders and sexual identities through everyday behaviors or performatives (Butler, 1990). As performatives, actions do not represent identity; instead, actions create identity (Butler, 1990). As such, an individual's gender and sexuality do not exist before she or he performs them; they are not predetermined by physiological sex or attraction to a specific gender. Instead, the individual learns how to perform gender and sexual identity and socially constructs them into being through her or his behavior. Because individuals enact genders and sexualities that do not exist prior to their enactment, performatives provide the potential for resisting dominant social constructions of gender and sexuality. This process depends on creating an identity through repeating actions; however, an individual never repeats actions precisely the same. Thus, identity is always changing.

The third concept supporting this analysis is the idea of liminality, a transitional period of indeterminacy (van Gennep, 1909/1960). Liminality represents a state of flux between two distinct and stable stages of being. This idea is critical to understanding how heteronormativity and performativity play out in students' lives. For example, heteronormativity creates a binary of two fixed sexualities: heterosexuality and nonheterosexuality. Liminality is a resistance strategy in which elements of heterosexuality and nonheterosexuality are incorporated into one identity that rejects normalized definitions of either heterosexuality or nonheterosexuality. Liminality, as resistance, is a state of becoming (Grosz, 2004). It facilitates flexible genders and sexualities and reflects how an individual may perform a seemingly contradictory performative in ever-changing ways. As such, liminality provides a framework for understanding the complex ways in which an individual performs sexuality in resistance to and as part of heteronormativity. The "becoming" quality of liminality emphasizes the unstable meaning of gender and sexuality (Halberstram, 2005), reflecting queer theory's resistance to stable identities.

A key connection among these three ideas is the use of resistance as a primary force behind queer theory. Foucault noted, "where there is power, there is resistance . . . and this resistance is never in a position of exteriority in relation to power" (Foucault, 1978, p. 95). Queer theory creates complex intersections of identities through multiple strategies of resistance.

STUDY DESIGN

The data upon which the two tellings of KT's identity story are based came from the first two phases of Elisa's longitudinal study of lesbian identity development. That study was guided by a constructivist theoretical perspective (Denzin & Lincoln, 2000) and a narrative inquiry methodology (Lieblich, Tuval-Mashiach, & Zilber, 1998). There were 10 participants, identified through purposeful sampling (Patton, 1990) in the first phase, and 8 participants in the second, all of whom were ages 18–25 over the span of the two study phases. These women, who were identified as lesbian or queer, attended the same large public research university in the Midwest at the time of the first phase of the study. Data were collected through open-ended interviews

that lasted between one and three hours. Interview questions elicited stories about how participants experienced their multiple identity dimensions. Examples of the questions included: "tell me what it means to you to be a lesbian," or "tell me about a time that you were aware of your gender."

For this project, we chose to feature one participant, KT. By focusing on only one participant, we are able to richly analyze her identity stories. Focusing on only one participant is also a way to honor the unique story of one student typically considered on the margins, thus subverting the essentializing to which lesbian students are often subjected, which is one of the aims of queer theory (Muñoz, 1999). We chose to feature KT for several reasons. We identified a participant whose experiences might resonate with other lesbian or queer students. KT was not actively involved in queer student organizations, but instead explored her identity through her family, work, and social life. She did not take courses that provided her the language to analyze her identity from an academic perspective; instead, she explored her identity and developed her own language through her lived experiences. KT earnestly, even if sometimes without realizing she was doing so, tried to integrate her multiple identity dimensions. She wanted an integrated identity so that she could be honest with herself and others and reach her personal and professional goals. Although KT was initially tentative about participating in this study, explaining she had not thought about these issues, she deeply considered each question and thoughtfully articulated each response. Clearly, she had done more prior identity work than she realized. We now believe that queer theory provides insights into why KT was unknowingly working so hard to understand her identity: she was living within the ambiguous liminality of her multiple identities.

For data analysis, we reanalyzed the data collected in both study phases. To create the constructivist-developmental narrative, we analyzed KT's interview transcripts using a categorical content approach to narrative analysis, which utilizes constant comparative analysis (Lieblich et al., 1998). We first reviewed each line of the transcript, focusing on KT's words, and then grouped these words into concepts representing the same phenomena. We grouped these concepts into more abstract categories. We then considered these abstract categories in relationship to cognitive, interpersonal, and intrapersonal development.

To create the queer narrative, we reanalyzed KT's interview transcripts using queer theory. For purposes of this paper, we introduced queer theory as a new theoretical perspective only for data analysis to "queer" the constructivist narratives. We realize that it is not typical practice to analyze the same data using different theoretical perspectives. However, rereading an existing text to analyze how queer notions undergird and drive the text is a common queer theory methodological approach (Plummer, 2005). To conduct the queer analysis, a process that does not have a fixed approach (Plummer, 2005), we reread KT's transcripts to understand how the queer notions of heteronormativity, performativity, and liminality were present in KT's stories.

Peer debriefing and member checking ensured trustworthiness (Patton, 1990). As part of peer debriefing, we conducted individual analyses of the data and then discussed our interpretations. We discussed how queer theory did and did not apply, challenging our notions of what is queer, while making sure that we were consistent with both bodies of literature and the language of KT's interviews. For member checking, KT read both the constructivist and queer narratives. She commented that she readily saw herself in the constructivist narrative and was interested in the use of the three domains of development to explain her experiences. Not surprisingly, she found the queer theory analysis harder to get her head around, but the more she thought about it, the more she could see it as an intriguing way to describe her experiences.

KT's Constructivist-Developmental Narrative

Thoughtful and mature, KT is a goal-oriented person, proud of her educational and professional accomplishments. She received her undergraduate degree in physical education at the age of 22 years during the first phase of the study and then completed a master's degree in physical education in the time between the two phases. During the second phase, KT was in her first year as a physical education teacher. A White woman raised as a devout Catholic, KT realized that she was a lesbian near the end of high school. Her mother conveyed immense disapproval, telling KT that as a lesbian she could no longer practice Catholicism, be professionally successful, or be feminine, each of which was important to KT. In the face of this critique, KT was proud of her decision to come out as a lesbian, a decision from which she has derived significant strength.

At the time of the first study phase, four years after that initial conversation, KT had not again discussed her sexual orientation with her parents, an avoidance that distressed her because she believed they deserved to know the truth. As KT was tentatively coming out to friends about her sexual orientation, everything she knew about what it meant to be a lesbian was based on negative stereotypes she heard from other people, especially her mother. During college, it became important to KT to be her own person as a lesbian rather than a stereotype. Before she could consider that possibility, however, she had to figure out whether or not the stereotypes were true, especially those related to the relationship between her sexual orientation and her religion, social class, and gender.

The first study phase was marked by KT experiencing dissonance between her mother's perspectives and the new perspectives she was exploring. This dissonance spurred cognitive, interpersonal, and intrapersonal development. Although KT was encouraged by glimmers of possible perspectives different from those of her mother, she was not ready to develop her own perspective on what it meant to be lesbian and how that related to her religion, gender, and social class. Over the next 18 months, KT experienced much development. Continuing to investigate multiple perspectives on what it meant to be a lesbian, KT was tentatively developing her own perspectives and starting to understand that her multiple identities were not mutually exclusive. KT's development in how she made meaning of some of these identity dimensions is described below. By writing about only sexuality, religion, social class, and gender, we are omitting identity dimensions that shape KT's perceptions of each of the other dimensions, in particular, her identity as a White person. In telling KT's story, we decided, despite the limitations of doing so, to describe development only for dimensions of identity most salient to KT.

Sexual orientation and religion. KT was raised as a Catholic and had a deep faith in God; reconciling her religion and sexual orientation was among KT's most significant challenges. During the first study phase, KT reflected on a time when she believed others' perspectives that identifying as a lesbian precluded her from being religious. She explained: "My mother told me I can't be a lesbian [and Catholic]. I still want to be in touch with God. I want to go to church.... I felt that because of my mother I couldn't do that." KT sought out reading material to help her understand that her mother's interpretation of the Bible is not the only correct one. She cast her desire for religion as a future goal though still uncertain whether or not she could adopt a perspective different from what others taught her. Cognitively, she experienced some dissonance as she learned about multiple perspectives but was not yet prepared to adopt her own perspective.

KT's interpersonal development also interacted with her understanding of the relationship between her sexual orientation and religious identities. Because of her friends' attitudes toward religion, KT described herself as a "religious

closet case": "None of my friends go to church. Knowing that I want to go to church, I really keep that a secret because everything that they say about religion is bad. I'm in the closet about religion." Although KT tentatively believed that she could be religious and a lesbian (demonstrating her intrapersonal development), she had not yet developed agency in her relationships with her friends and thus hid her religious beliefs.

During the second study phase, and a result of continuing to seek out multiple perspectives, KT developed in how she understood her identity as a lesbian for whom religion is important. She more confidently believed that there were multiple ways to be lesbian and religious and started creating her own perspectives on this relationship. She explained:

> I know I can have God in my life and be gay and be everything I want to be. I can still put God first. I don't have to be in the church to pray.... I consider myself Catholic... but I go to a church where I'm welcome because of who I am.

For KT, a new, supportive relationship mediated her intrapersonal and interpersonal development because her girlfriend respected her religious beliefs. This support allowed KT to reflect on prior relationships and see how she had allowed others to define her identity. KT explained that if her current girlfriend did not support her faith, "I would have issues with that.... It would be an issue with me right now if I just didn't see any kind of religious beliefs in [my girlfriend]." KT demonstrated development in all three domains. She was coming to understand multiple perspectives on the relationship between religion and sexual orientation (cognitive development); gaining a stronger sense of how she wanted to reconcile these two aspects of her identity (intrapersonal development); and hoping to maintain her religious beliefs in a relationship (interpersonal development).

Sexual orientation and social class. KT also sought out concrete examples to help her learn that the stereotype that lesbians typically inhabit a lower social class was not necessarily true. Again, she was exposing herself to and seeing validity in multiple perspectives (cognitive development). Based on comments from her mother and exposure only to lesbians who were college students, KT believed for many years that identifying as a lesbian and as an upper-class professional were mutually exclusive. Through a relationship at the time of the first study phase with a "professional" woman, KT attended parties at nice homes owned by lesbians. Seeing these professional women allowed KT to consider, albeit tentatively, the possibility that identifying as a lesbian might not preclude her from achieving her professional and financial goals (intrapersonal development).

During the second phase, KT was more confident that her sexual orientation need not dictate her social class. KT attributed her new perspective that "you can be gay and successful" to her growing confidence that resulted from graduating from college and becoming a successful teacher. By accomplishing her educational goals, which her mother told her she could not do as a lesbian, KT gained the confidence to accept perspectives different from what her mother taught her and to believe in her own thinking (interpersonal development). KT's evolution in how she perceived the relationship between her sexual orientation and social class demonstrates development in all three domains as she is integrating into her sense of self (intrapersonal), her own perspectives on the relationship between her sexual orientation and social class (cognitive), rather than defining these possibilities through her mother (interpersonal).

Sexual orientation and gender. One of KT's obstacles in her journey toward reconciling her social class ambitions with her sexual orientation was her assumption that other people perceived lesbians to be masculine women. It was important to KT to always be professional in all aspects of her life, and she associated being professional with being feminine. From her perspective, especially during the first study phase, "masculine women" were not perceived as professional women. Even though she considered herself "a feminine woman who can be a little butch sometimes," KT assumed many people would think that because she was a lesbian she was also masculine and therefore unprofessional, which would hurt her career. This perception, again based on what others told her, was especially troubling as a physical education teacher because of the stereotypes about lesbians associated with this position. KT spoke to the pressure she felt teaching: "You almost have to be perfect in the schools as a teacher. So I don't want to be portrayed as a lesbian because I don't know where they stand, and I'm scared to death I'm going to get fired." However, by meeting other lesbians she considered to be professional and feminine, in particular one of her professors, she was coming to realize, again tentatively, the possibility of being perceived by others as feminine. Although KT still held onto gender stereotypes, she was starting to juggle multiple perspectives and entertain new possibilities for her identity.

KT did not give as much thought to her gender at the time of the second phase of the study. Still, she related gender and social class. When asked to describe her gender, KT, who was confident wearing short hair and stylish, athletic clothes, responded by saying "professional." Although she continued to equate professional with feminine, she was starting to define her own meaning of feminine rather than defining it through stereotypes. She explained: "When I am professional I try to be feminine. But feminine to me is more on the plain side. Just, you know, clean, nice clothes, sophisticated if you have to dress up, feminine in that way." Although she worried about being fired from teaching if others knew she was gay, she grew more comfortable portraying her gender in a way that makes her comfortable and in which she feels professional, rather than according to other people's standards. As with religion and social class, KT was not only entertaining the possibility of multiple perspectives but was also starting to develop her own perspectives (cognitive development) and defining her own identity (intrapersonal development), rather than losing herself in others' perceptions of her (interpersonal development).

At the end of the first phase, KT explained that she wanted her sexual orientation, gender, and social class to "come together" so she could be the person she aspires to be. Between the two study phases, KT's development toward self-authorship contributed to her multiple identities in fact coming closer together. Closer to self-authorship than before, KT reflected at the end of the second study phase that by gaining the ability to define her identities for herself and in less conflict with one another, she was "allowing [her] true self to evolve."

Queering KT's Constructivist-Developmental Narrative

Retelling KT's story from a queer theory perspective recasts it to reflect KT's resistance to stereotypes, as well as queer resistance to the linearity and heteronormativity of constructivist student development theory. KT's queer narrative is complex. Her life forms a text of resistance to heteronormative social constructions that exclude or oppress her sense of self (e.g., her mother's statements about how lesbians cannot be Catholics). It is a story of her enacting an identity performative in which she fluctuates between heteronormative constructions of self and constructions of self that resist heteronormativity. Initially, these fluctuations may appear to be a type of identity negotiation between heteronormative and nonheteronormative, but KT's struggle is different from a simple negotiation. Instead, as detailed in the following narrative, KT is redefining the meaning of heteronormative and nonheteronormative identities.

Before identifying as a lesbian, KT was identified as a Catholic from a working-class family, and as a woman who conducts herself in a professional manner. Once identifying as a lesbian, the meaning of these prior identities became problematic for KT and caused her to question her sense of self. She formed her earlier identities based on a heteronormative understanding of the world (e.g., Catholics are straight, hard work can change a person's class status, and professional women must be feminine) and struggled to understand her conflicting experiences of these identities. KT's new primary identity as a lesbian created resistance to the stereotypes of lesbians her mother promoted because KT continued to engage each of these identities and be a lesbian, which her mother suggested was not possible. Still, she feared some of her own resistance, explaining: "I was like one foot in the closet and one foot out of the closet . . . I would tell certain people that I trusted. And I would not tell other people that I didn't trust because I felt that they would use it against me." Heteronormativity, performativity, and liminality provide a framework for understanding how KT queered religion, gender, and social class.

Queering Catholicism. KT understood Catholicism to be exclusive of lesbians and to be a lesbian meant that she could no longer be a Catholic. This understanding was problematic because KT's faith was a pillar of how she understood herself. Her faith in God offered KT a cohesive sense of self, a sense of self built on the idea of only heterosexual partnerships. When KT was first identified as a lesbian, she necessarily excluded herself from the opportunity to have a relationship with God under this framework. This pushed KT into a liminal state, where she knew she believed in God but could not live her faith as she knew it. Instead, she needed to create a new performative that resisted the idea of faith and God only supporting heterosexual relationships.

The constructivist narrative discussed KT's process of seeking support for a new understanding of religion that included her as a lesbian. KT sought out people, churches, and readings that resisted her mother's messages about the church's limited acceptance of lesbians, and the gay community's limited acceptance of organized religion. These actions demonstrated KT's new performative of religion. Through this dual resistance she enacted the performative of "religious closet case." KT struggled to find acceptance in either community because she wanted to be part of both communities. KT explained: "There were bad moments in my life, and it was when I didn't have religion, I didn't believe in it. When I think about it, I need it. So, I feel that's very important to who I am as a lesbian." This quote reflects KT's complex construction of religion and sexuality: She believes in God as a lesbian. Her understanding of God depends on her understanding of her sexuality, and her understanding of her sexuality depends on her understanding of God; the two identities are interwoven. This interwoven quality emphasizes an important queer feature of KT's new understanding of faith—her performative of faith changes as her understanding of her sexuality changes and vice versa. This conflation of religion and sexuality creates a unique identity in which KT is constantly redefining what it means to be a lesbian and what it means to be Catholic. She is performing a strategy of liminality in which these identities share the same identity material. Her faith in God is intelligible to her only as a lesbian because, for KT, the two are based on the same threads of identity.

Queering social class with gender. One of the most complex identity constructions that KT describes is that of her gender. In the first study phase, KT defined gender as "professional." When pushed further about what professional means to her, KT connected hard work and social class. Professionalism, then, was the performative reflection of her work ethic based on a feminine gender: "I think gender and social class kind of go together for me because I always want to be portrayed as a woman and professional and lesbian." Gender for KT, then, is part of social class and sexual orientation. Through a physical performative, KT linked representations of

woman, professional, and lesbian into one complex expression of identity. In doing so, KT is resisting the stereotypes that lesbians are masculine, and masculine women are not professionally successful.

KT's understanding of sexuality and professionalism is another example of infused identities. No longer financially dependent on her family because of her postcollege salary, KT explained: "I pay everything. I even pay a loan that my mom took out for me . . . . So, I'm taking more ownership of my sexuality now." For KT, professionalism and sexuality help to define her sense of self. Being a professional (gender/social class) and having income (social class) allow KT to "own," or create the meaning of, her sexuality. KT's sense of professionalism and gender influences how she understands the relationship between sexual orientation and social class and vice versa. The two groups are mutually influencing.

The meaning of KT's gender and sexuality are not preexistent. KT brings them into being through the process of enacting them described in the idea of performatives. What is significant about this gender/social class performative is that it resists multiple constructions of heteronormative and nonheteronormative genders and sexualities at the same time. By defining her gender through social class, KT has subverted conventional understandings of gender. KT noted, "I guess when I am looked at as a lesbian, I want to know that my job is something that I'm very happy with, I have a good living, I can make it on my own or with a partner." To KT, being a lesbian is now more than just a sexual orientation; it has an impact on work, happiness, and relationships. In subtle ways, KT's performative of social class and gender is defining work, happiness, and relationships through and with her sexuality.

Queering identity intersections. KT transformed the meaning of social class by combining social class with gender to create "professionalism." This performative of professionalism also depends on KT's construction of what it means to be a lesbian because this construction informs how she understands her gender. Given this relationship, KT's social class/gender is also a reflection of her Catholicism because her religion is important to who she is, as a lesbian. As a result, the intersection of social class and gender in professionalism is also an intersection of religion and sexuality. Through professionalism, KT is enacting a time and place, a unique reality of identity, specific to her. By enacting an identity that combines all of these identity dimensions, she is performing an infused identity.

From one perspective, KT's infused identity appears to be a negotiation of identities (e.g., a balancing of lesbian and Catholic, lesbian and professional) rather than interconnected identities; however, it is not that simple. This "negotiation of identities" perspective considers all of these identities as distinct but connected. KT's infusement, on the other hand, makes these elements of identity inseparable in her sense of self. KT's infusing of identities is a departure from simple intersections of identities. It reflects something more like "intrasections," where identities do not simply connect with each other, but rather they share the same identity material. In other words, each of these threads of identity (i.e., Catholic, professional, lesbian) are all the same identity. KT's infused identity is not evidence of progressively complex development, as constructivist-development theory suggests; it is a performative of inseparable identities.

KT's creation of infused, intrasected identities is a complex example of her resistance to heteronormativity through the performative of a liminal identity. For example, in her developmental narrative, KT's understanding of heteronormativity is inseparable from her understanding of her mother. To resist her mother's stereotypes of lesbians is to resist heteronormativity. KT created intrasections of identity that incorporate, build from, and refuse definitions of identities from her mother. KT used the definitions of lesbian, Catholicism, and professionalism she

learned from her mother and changed them to create her own unique identity that reflected KT's enactment of Catholicism and professionalism as a lesbian. KT redefined the meaning of each of these labels into one coherent intrasected identity by creating a singular identity that neither confirmed her mother's definitions nor created a counter definition.

Queering the relationship between KT and her external environment. So far, this queer narrative has resisted the traditional structuralist framework of a binary between KT and society in which KT has the ability to affect society, society has the ability to affect KT, or the two influence each other. This structuralist binary is common in constructivist-developmental narratives (e.g., internal/external sources of authority). From a queer (poststructuralist) perspective, this binary is an artificial construction imposed upon KT and society. The binary does not exist until a third party chooses to locate KT and society as distinct and opposing entities. In using this KT/society binary, the subtle complexities of KT's performative, or the intrasections of KT's multiple dimensions of identity, are obscured and create a false stability to the meaning of identities. Using a constructivist lens, KT's construction of identity initially appears to be a negotiation between heteronormative and nonheteronormative. It denies KT's queer development and the insight queer theory has into KT's ongoing resistance to definitions of identity that obscure her "evolving" sense of "true self."

KT's queer narrative demonstrates the ongoing performative of one woman creating an intrasected identity that resists engagement in traditional binaries. Using a queer perspective, both KT and the social constructions of identity become liminal, unstable, and constant in states of becoming. These "becomings" resist binary frameworks in which the individual is abnormal in relation to her heterosexual environment. From the perspective of queer theory, KT's story is one of resistance to heteronormativity.

By identifying as a lesbian, KT unknowingly began a process of resisting the heteronormativity of her mother and society. As KT's identification as a lesbian intensified, and her perception of the intersections between other identity dimensions and being a lesbian increased, her resistance to heteronormativity also intensified. KT also became increasingly aware of her resistance to heteronormativity and used that sense of awareness to develop her personal sense of agency. Rather than a story of developmental arrival, KT's queer narrative is a story of continued resistance and an ever-changing network of complex intrasections within dimensions of identity.

DISCUSSION

Implications for Student Development Theory

Queer-authorship: Identity construction as social change. From a constructivist-developmental perspective, KT is developing an increased capacity to construct the meaning of and relationships among her multiple identities through internally defined perceptions rather than defining herself through external expectations. From a queer perspective, KT was reconstructing external authority by resisting heteronormativity and destabilizing structures it created. KT was enacting an identity that redefined her own identity perceptions in relationship to external influences (i.e., developing toward self-authorship), as she simultaneously redefined the *meaning* of those same external influences (i.e., deconstructing and reconstructing power structures). KT's performatives were creating a sexual orientation identity that no longer precluded her religious, social class, and gender identities because she changed the meaning of religious, social class, and gender identities to include her lesbian identity.

A queer theoretical perspective on development thus illuminates that for students who do not identify as heterosexual, identity development as part of the journey toward self-authorship requires resisting power structures that define one as abnormal. Whereas self-authorship focuses on how students construct internal frameworks to navigate external influences, queer resistance focuses on how students deconstruct and reconstruct external influences. Rather than challenging heteronormativity, self-authorship describes the developmental capacities students need to make meaning of their lives within a heteronormative society. When students necessarily deconstruct the heteronormative framework in order to reconstruct their identities, they offer a resistance that is development toward a form of self-authorship as social change, a type of development we call *queer authorship*.

Queer authorship is the necessary deconstruction of heteronormativity that enables lesbian students to change the dominant social order in order to redefine the meaning of their multiple identities and the contexts in which their lives are situated. Queer authorship suggests that self-authorship alone is an incomplete theoretical framework to describe the experiences of lesbian college students. It suggests that the developmental process looks different for lesbian college students, an observation suggesting that the nature of the developmental process might also be reexamined for other dimensions of identity, such as social class, race, and ethnicity.

To understand the social change aspect of queer authorship, it helps to distinguish queer authorship from the findings of other literature that explores how dissonance associated with marginalized identities fosters development toward self-authorship. Pizzolato (2003) described how high-risk college students who encountered challenges to their abilities developed self-authoring ways of knowing earlier than many participants in Baxter Magolda's (2001) longitudinal study. She found that students' encounters with provocative experiences, such as choosing to attend college despite a lack of community or family support, often prompted the disequilibrium needed to construct their own self-perceptions. Using a similar framework, it could be argued that the external influence of heteronormativity fostered complex development in KT, allowing her to develop toward self-authorship. Although likely true, this describes only part of KT's story. It describes only how KT positively defined herself in relationship to heteronormativity, accommodating this power structure rather than changing it. The queer view shifts the gaze from how KT is changing her self-perceptions within a heterosexist society to how KT is changing the heterosexist society and thus her identity. Using a constructivist perspective, Pizzolato focused on the individual's development in response to marginalization, not how her participants changed the meaning of high risk, race, and class; however, her work suggests that a similar process may be taking place for high-risk students.

Further, it is insufficient to argue that only marginalization is an external factor that fosters development toward self-authorship because the theoretical framework of self-authorship does not wholly describe KT's development. Indeed, our research began with our mutual sense that student development theory was missing part of the developmental story of lesbian students. We encountered this concern when initially analyzing KT's interview transcripts using a constructivist-developmental framework. Our analysis resulted in thinking that heterosexism was contributing to KT's complex cognitive capacity but stalling her interpersonal development given her tendencies to define herself through her mother, peers, and girlfriends. It felt wrong to describe KT's experiences as stalled interpersonal development, even though at first glance the way she defined herself in relationship to others was reminiscent of Kegan's (1994) third order or Baxter Magolda's (2001) early crossroads. It was evident that KT was trying to push back against dominant social structures, engaging in sophisticated interpersonal pursuits, and slowly defining herself in

relation to others who tried to define her identity for her. Stepping outside of the self-authorship framework allowed us to incorporate KT's efforts at deconstructing heteronormativity into her development. Doing so led us to understand her development as more complex than what the language of self-authorship allows.

Queer authorship as fluid, nonlinear development. The queer authorship of KT serves as an example of how she must first form a resistance to heteronormative structures in her life before she exhibits development typically understood as self-authorship. Although we critique the heteronormativity of development toward self-authorship, Kegan's (1994) fifth order of consciousness, which he describes as a postmodern view of the world, explains some aspects of queer authorship. He described the fifth order as

> [Moving] form or system from subject to object, and brings into being a new "trans-system" or "cross-form" way of organizing reality . . . . the good working of the self and its recognition by the other begins with a refusal to see oneself or the other as a single system or form. The relationship is a context for sharing and an interacting in which both are helped to experience their "multipleness," in which the *many* forms or systems that *each self is* are helped to emerge. (p. 313, emphasis in original)

In the fifth order, people recognize that the relationship itself creates the individual elements, rather than the individual elements creating the relationship. Differences among individuals are necessary for the relationship, and through the relationship, people recognize these differences within themselves. As described in KT's queer narrative, KT and the contexts in which she lives are a mutually influencing relationship; they are part of a "trans-system," with each bringing out "multipleness" of the other. As a social change agent, KT is changing the meaning of the context that influences the meaning of her multiple identities, while that changing context changes the meaning of her identity. The relationship between the two creates multiple and changing meanings.

KT is exhibiting aspects of the fifth order, at the same time that she has not yet reached the fourth order, or self-authorship. The concept of queer authorship therefore suggests that the linear developmental trajectory associated with Kegan's orders, and upon which the concept of self-authorship is based, is insufficient to describe the experiences of all students. Rather than a linear developmental trajectory, queer authorship suggests that people simultaneously exhibit qualities from multiple orders. This argument differs from the constructivist-developmental perspective that people don't always exhibit their most complex ways of making meaning. Although linear trajectories allow students to enact elements of previous stages of development, there remains a general notion that once a student achieves self-authorship she or he will be able to maintain or return to that higher level of development. This assumption suggests that student development is finite and measurable and that changes in students' expression of their identity reflect development along a trajectory. Using the notions of liminality and performativity, queer theorists argue that identities are always in flux and development does not accommodate "arriving" at a stage of development (Butler, 1990; Halberstram, 2005; Sedgwick, 1990). Sullivan (2003) offered a similar observation about identity multiplicity:

> One's being in the world is always marked, molded, formed, and transformed in and through encounters with others and with a world .... [I]dentity is never simply a question of self-authorship .... [I]dentity categories are ... continuously fracturing, multiplying, and metamorphosing. Identity, one could argue, is already always haunted by the other, by that which is not "I." (p. 149)

We recognize that according to Kegan (1994) most people do not reach the fifth order, and doing so is extremely unlikely for a traditional-aged college student. We are not suggesting that KT

arrived at the fifth order. Instead, we are suggesting that this linear trajectory does not describe KT's development because her queer resistance causes her to interact with society in a manner similar to the fifth order, even though she has might not have reached the fourth order. KT's development is more fluid than the process described by Kegan and Baxter Magolda (2001). Our argument is consistent with Talburt's (2006) proposed "queering of our ideas of development" in which "development does not occur in a straight line, so to speak," but is about "multiple practices, complex relations, and dynamic positionings across contexts" (p. 90).

Kegan (1994) acknowledged that his theory would not survive a deconstructive postmodern critique because it, like most theories, is not universally applicable. Citing Burbules and Rice (1991), Kegan distinguished between what he calls deconstructive and reconstructive postmodernism. Unlike deconstructive postmodernism, reconstructive postmodernism uses the products of deconstruction to create better theory that is constantly reforming. He argues that subject-object theory supports the reconstructive postmodern perspective because it avoids ideological absolutism, and meaning-making complexity allows for supporting others' positions on their own terms. Nonetheless, KT's queer narrative demonstrates that development toward self-authorship does not encompass the resistance and social change necessary for queer authorship, thus resulting in an incomplete understanding of how lesbian college students experience their multiple identities.

The fusion of multiple identities: Rethinking the model of multiple dimensions of identity. Queer theory also challenges the portrayal of multiple identities offered in the Model of Multiple Dimensions of Identity (Jones & McEwen, 2000), a conceptual depiction of students' perceptions of their identity. The model portrays how students' perceptions of the saliency of each of their multiple identity dimensions, portrayed as dots on ellipses surrounding a core sense of self, changes depending on contextual influences. Recently reconceptualized, the model includes meaning-making capacity, explained through constructivist-developmental theory, as a filter between contextual factors and students' perceptions of their multiple identities (Abes et al., 2007). Through the model's depiction of identity, Jones and McEwen (2000) remind educators of the importance of "seeing students as they see themselves" (p. 412). In part, as a result of meaning-making capacity, students often see themselves as a combination of distinct and sometimes conflicting dimensions of identity (Abes et al., 2007).

Queer theory, however, starts from the perspective that multiple identity dimensions are always fused (Fuss, 1989) intrasections rather than intersections. Although students might perform certain aspects of their identities more prominently than others at different times, depending on context, identities cannot be separated. By starting from this fused perspective, queer theory prompts an exploration as to why when lesbian students "see themselves," they often see identity dimensions as distinct. Starting from the perspective that students' identities are fused prompts a focus on how heteronormativity contributes to students' perceptions of identity dimensions as distinct. Connecting queer theory with the model draws attention to social power structures with which students must contend in developing their multiple identities.

Furthermore, when queer theory informs the model, the result portrays students as changing, through resistance, the meaning of the contextual factors that shape their identity. Thus, the interaction between context and identity dimensions is mutually influencing, which is not portrayed in the current model. Still further, viewing the model through a queer lens, the identity "dots" surrounding the core no longer could be portrayed as distinct, currently a possibility in the model, but merge together and change in meaning, depending on the meaning of each of the other changing identities. Because KT and society are simultaneously changing and mutually influencing, not only are KT's self-perceptions changing but also the meaning of each of her multiple identities, each of which is in constant motion. This queer perspective opens up new possibilities for depicting the relationship between students' multiple identities and contextual influences. The queer perspective also challenges the heteronormative meaning-making filter recently incorporated into the reconceptualized model that filters external influences depending on development toward self-authorship (Abes et al., 2007).

The fusion of identities brings to light one of the limitations of this paper. By choosing to focus on only the four identities most salient to KT, sexuality, religion, social class, and gender, this paper does not address how the meaning of each of those identities depends on the meaning of each of her other social identities less salient to her, in particular her identity as a White woman. Not addressing KT's whiteness could contribute to one of the critiques of queer theory, namely that it has been blind when it comes to race (Sullivan, 2003).

IMPLICATIONS OF QUEER THEORY FOR STUDENT AFFAIRS PRACTICE

By describing how lesbian college students resist heteronormativity to construct their identities, this research raises the question as to how educators can support students' resistance, helping them identify and deconstruct heteronormative obstacles within and between identities. At the same time, it challenges educators to identify and deconstruct these same obstacles.

One of the challenges in KT's queer narrative is a call to reexamine how educators see and interact with students. Educators act as viewers and interpreters of students' life experiences. Aspects of KT's queer narrative are about the viewer, not the viewed. It is the viewer's perception of KT's identities that constructs distinctions and unities among KT's dimensions of identity. The identity dimensions themselves do not change, but the viewer's perception of the relationships among the dimensions changes. One of the implications for practice, then, is the need to reconsider how educators frame students. Do educators align students along a trajectory and measure their development through a process of stages, or do educators move outside of linear models to consider the influence that students are having on their environment to reshape their contexts? KT's developmental and queer narratives are examples of how one student met situations in which she was on the subordinate side of power and what she did to resist larger heteronormative structures. KT's experiences can help sensitize educators to issues that students may face and offer insight into how educators can challenge their own understanding of student development theory and the heteronormative assumptions upon which it is built.

Perhaps one of the most subtle implications of queer theory for work with students is the commentary on power in the relationship between students and educators. How student affairs educators see students' development reflects how they position themselves in relation to the students. This is not a simple matter of trying to do no harm but moving beyond that to carefully consider how they establish, maintain, and share power in relationships with students. One measure of how student affairs professionals build power relationships with students can be seen in how students cooperate or offer resistance to those relationships. This is a call to check and challenge the ways in which cultural power is expressed with students. As KT's narratives reflect, how "normal" is constructed can create tremendous obstacles and difficulties for students. Abes (2008) demonstrated the transformations that occurred for one college student in how she thought about relationships among her sexuality, ethnicity, and gender when educators intentionally challenged heteronormativ-

ity and the meaning of normal through classes and cocurricular experiences. One approach to helping students deconstruct heteronormativity is supporting and perceiving student organizations and experiences as sites of resistance rather than only means to help students (Blackburn, 2004; Renn & Bilodeau, 2005; Talburt, 2004). Examples of this approach include, allowing students' increased levels of freedom to define the purpose and mission of student groups, challenging school policy structures that expect all students to behave in similar ways (e.g., clothing, social attitudes, interests, and cocurriculars), and assuming that the pedagogical relationship between student and advisor moves from advisor down to student.

Where student affairs professionals have to exert caution is in making sure that the support offered to students does not create resistance groups that are reflections of the professionals' power rather than that of the students. This is not to say that students are always victims of power relationships. Talburt (2006) offered the challenge to move beyond the use of queer theory to reify a victimology of queer students; we take that challenge seriously. KT's queer narrative offers an alternative view of victimization. It offers a hopeful relationship in which educators help students define themselves in positive terms of what they value, rather than as survivors or victims of power structures they cannot control. It is a fundamental shift from being an onlooker with students to being an ally with students on their terms. When educators view students from a distance, imposing their own perspectives on how students are negotiating their multiple identities, they are too far removed to develop the caring relationships that nurture students. This reflects an "educator knows best" mentality in which students are passive receptors of knowledge or development. It is only where educators share a closer space with students, allowing students' invested control of the relationship, that the real transformative work of helping students resist and influence heteronormativity occurs. Consistent with Noddings's (1984) ethic of care, in which care is demonstrated through "feeling with" (p. 30) another by receiving another into oneself rather than projecting oneself onto the other, it is important that educators work with students to identify and deconstruct the social constructions of their multiple identities rather than imposing their own power and perceptions onto the students. For instance, does the school define expectations of students based solely on administrators' interests? Do students have a participatory role in defining what is expected of them? Without empowering students within the culture of a school, the focus on administrators' interests eliminates significant potential for student development because it rewards identities that conform to administrators' definitions of students and punishes expressions of identity (performatives) that challenge how the school's culture defines what a "student" is. As in the case of KT, such a restrictive definition of identity would miss the critical intrasections of resistance that make KT's narratives such a compelling example.

IMPLICATIONS FOR RESEARCH

We encourage more research that uses critical perspectives, queer or otherwise, to study college student development. Critical approaches, such as critical race theory, lend themselves to telling resistance narratives (e.g., Delgado & Stefancic, 2001) that address power structures. Critical perspectives should be applied to the study of dimensions of identity beyond sexual orientation, such as social class, race, and ethnicity to explore how other dominant structures, such as classism and racism, might be embedded within student development theories. We also encourage research that further explores possibilities for partnering queer theory and student development theory. We urge the design of student development research that utilizes queer theory as the theoretical perspective guiding all phases of the research. No doubt that the process will bring with it methodological challenges that will be fruitful in uncovering more of the nuances of juxtaposing a poststructural perspective with the lived experiences of college students. Such challenges might spur educators to think differently about student development.

SUMMARY

By exploring the intersection of queer theory and constructivist-developmental theory, we are responding to calls within student development literature for attention to the relationship between power structures and student development. Just as gay, lesbian, and bisexual identity development theories that do not account for heterosexism reify heterosexual privilege (D'Augelli, 1994; Renn & Bilodeau, 2005; Rhoads, 1997; Talburt, 2004), KT's queer narrative shows that student development theory does not yet adequately account for how heteronormativity contributes to lesbian students' negotiation of their multiple identities. Constructivist-developmental theory suggests that students are less developmentally complex if they are unable to overcome the heteronormativity that defines and separates their multiple identities. We do not intend to undermine the constructivist approach to development, which provides a rich understanding of the development of college students, but only to challenge its normative assumptions so that educators can more effectively work with the intrasections of students' identities.

REFERENCES

Abes, E. S. (2008). Applying queer theory in practice with college students: Transformation of a researcher's and participant's perspectives on identity, a case study. *Journal of LGBT Youth, 5*(1), 57–77.

Abes, E. S., & Jones, S. R. (2004). Meaning-making capacity and the dynamics of lesbian college students' multiple dimensions of identity. *Journal of College Student Development, 45,* 612–632.

Abes, E. S., Jones, S. R., & McEwen, M. K. (2007). Reconceptualizing the Model of Multiple Dimensions of Identity: The role of meaning-making capacity in the construction of multiple identities. *Journal of College Student Development, 48,* 1–22.

Baxter Magolda, M. B. (2001). *Making their own way: Narratives for transforming higher education to promote self-development.* Sterling, VA: Stylus.

Blackburn, M. (2004). Understanding agency beyond school-sanctioned activities. *Theory Into Practice, 43*(2), 102–110.

Britzman, D. P. (1997). What is this thing called love?: New discourses for understanding gay and lesbian youth. In S. de Castell & M. Bryson (Eds.), *Radical in(ter)ventions: Identity, politics, and difference/s on educational praxis* (pp. 183–207). Albany, NY: State University of New York Press.

Burbules, N. C., & Rice, S. (1991). Dialogue across differences: Continuing the conversation. *Harvard Educational Review, 61,* 393–416.

Butler, J. (1990). *Gender trouble: Feminism and the subversion of identity.* New York: Routledge.

D'Augelli, A. R. (1994). Identity development and sexual orientation: Toward a model of lesbian, gay, and bisexual development. In E. J. Trickett, R. J. Watts, & D. Birman (Eds.), *Human diversity: Perspectives on people in context* (pp. 312–333). San Francisco, CA: Jossey-Bass.

Delgado, R., & Stefancic, J. (2001). *Critical race theory: An introduction.* New York: New York University Press.

Denzin, N. K., & Lincoln, Y. S. (2000). The discipline and practice of qualitative research. In N. K. Denzin & Y. S. Lincoln (Eds.), *Handbook of qualitative research* (2nd ed., pp. 1–28). Thousand Oaks, CA: Sage.

Derrida, J. (1978). *Writing and difference* (A. Bass, Trans.). Chicago, IL: The University of Chicago Press. (Original work published 1967)

Foucault, M. (1978). *The history of sexuality: Volume 1, an introduction.* (R. Hurley, Trans.). New York: Vantage Books. (Original work published 1976)

Fuss, D. (1989). *Essentially speaking: Feminism, nature, and difference.* New York: Routledge.

Grosz, E. A. (2004). *The nick of time: Politics, evolution, and the untimely.* Durham, NC: Duke University Press.

Halberstram, J. (2005). *In a queer time and place: Transgender bodies and subcultural lives.* New York: New York University Press.

Jones, S. R., & McEwen, M. K. (2000). A conceptual model of multiple dimensions of identity. *Journal of College Student Development, 41,* 405–414.

Jordan, J. V. (Ed.). (1997). *Women's growth in diversity: More writings from the stone center.* New York: Guilford.

Kegan, R. (1994). *In over our heads: The mental demands of modern life.* Cambridge, MA: Harvard University Press.

Lieblich, A., Tuval-Mashiach, R., & Zilber, T. (1998). *Narrative research: Readings, analysis, interpretation.* Thousand Oaks, CA: Sage.

Lyotard, J. F. (1984). *The postmodern condition: A report on knowledge (theory and history of literature, volume 10).* Manchester, United Kingdom: Manchester University Press.

Muñoz, J. E. (1999). *Disidentifications: Queers of color and the performance of politics.* Minneapolis, MN: University of Minnesota Press.

Noddings, N. (1984). *Caring: A feminine approach to ethics and moral education.* Berkeley, CA: University of California Press.

Patton, M. (1990). *Qualitative evaluation and research methods* (2nd ed.). Newbury Park, CA: Sage.

Perry, W. (1970). *Forms of intellectual and ethical development in the college years: A scheme.* Troy, MO: Holt, Rinehart, & Winston.

Pizzolato, J. E. (2003). Developing self-authorship: Exploring the experiences of high-risk college students. *Journal of College Student Development, 44*(6), 797–812.

Plummer, K. (2005). Critical humanism and queer theory: Living with the tensions. In N. K. Denzin & Y. S. Lincoln (Eds.), *The SAGE handbook of qualitative research* (pp. 357–386). Thousand Oaks, CA: SAGE Publications.

Renn, K. A., & Bilodeau, B. (2005). Queer student leaders: An exploratory case study of identity development and LGBT student involvement at a midwestern research university. *Journal of Gay & Lesbian Issues in Education, 2*(4), 49–71.

Rhoads, R. A. (1997). A subcultural study of gay and bisexual males: Resisting developmental inclinations. *Journal of Higher Education, 68*(4), 460–482.

Sedgwick, E. K. (1990). *Epistemology of the closet.* Berkeley, CA: University of California Press.

Sullivan, N. (2003). *A critical introduction to queer theory.* New York: New York University Press.

Talburt, S. (2004).Constructions of LGBT youth: Opening up subject positions. *Theory into Practice, 43*(2), 116–121.

Talburt, S. (2006).Queer research and queer youth. *Journal of Gay & Lesbian Issues in Education, 3*(2/3), 87–93.

van Gennep, A. (1960).*The rites of passage.* (M. B. Vizedom & G. L. Caffe, Trans.). Chicago, IL: University of Chicago Press. (Original work published 1909)

Warner, M. (1991). Introduction: Fear of a queer planet. *Social Text, 29*, 3–17.

14

Identity Development in College Women

Amy Stalzer Sengupta and Yvette Loury Upton

Abstract: College is a time of substantial identity development for the traditional-aged student. Typically, college students work on developing autonomy, building competence, and forging mature relationships. Women students and students of color face additional identity challenges during this time layered upon that basic developmental work, as they struggle to create their unique and relational identities based on gender and race. This chapter discusses the theoretical models of identity development specific to college women. Through the use of the women's own voices from two separate studies, examples of identity challenges in action on college campuses will be detailed. Educators are offered recommendations on ways to positively affect the experiences of women students.

"NO FINISH LINE." This clock with sayings on it reminds me of the fact that no matter how much you wish that everything was truly equal in this world (like most people think it already is), I'll always have to work harder than those around to get the same amount of respect and responsibilities from my peers and instructors. You'll never know how many times (day and night) I prayed about this issue, but praying just made me realize that it was strength I need to get through this school, not a change of heart from my peers because that probably won't happen and work to my advantage while I'm in school.

While the women's movement has afforded women both education and careers in (debatably) equal measure to men, the alluring promise that one can "have it all" is offset by the challenging and often painful process of deciding who one is and what one wants. Adolescence is full of pitfalls: an emotional roller coaster of puberty and interpersonal dramas; an intellectual minefield of personal desire to excel versus peer-dictated "status quo" to fit in; and a navigational explosion of peer culture, disparate treatment in schools, parental expectations, and other-imposed rules of what being a young woman should entail. What a young woman thinks, acts, or attributes to herself is constantly questioned and evaluated (Brown & Gilligan, 1992; Brumberg, 1997; Orenstein, 1994; Piper, 1994).

By the time a traditional-aged student has reached the university gates, she has often navigated the adolescent development to a point that she can self-attribute unique characteristics, attitudes, and values. Yet, now she must leave at home the self-reinforcing community and start self-evaluation again in a broader and more diverse context. Traditional authorities of guardians and teachers are left behind, along with close friends and romantic partners. New terrain must be navigated, such as sharing space with roommates, facing more difficult curriculum with less built-in support, and starting new, more mature relationships. College is a time of questioning what one thought she already knew and reestablishing new answers for a more authentic self.

This chapter details the challenges young college women face in developing identity, as young adults and as women in particular. Theories that focus on college identity development, female identity development, and identity development for women of color will be deconstructed and intertwined to achieve a more comprehensive understanding of the unique experiences of young women. Throughout the discussion, the reader will encounter voices of young women who participated in two local studies of college women's experiences on a southeastern public university campus. Both studies sought to better understand the everyday lived experiences of undergraduate women on university campuses and the daily mundane interactions that became prominent in identity formation. One study captured voices of 19 women students through a journal-and-photographic depiction project, whereas the other utilized a fixed interview technique with a different group of young women. These voices are poignant examples of the theoretical discussion of this developmentally critical time. Further, this chapter details the challenges women experience and areas where student affairs practitioners, faculty members, and administrators may intervene.

IDENTITIES AS YOUNG ADULTS

College has made me do things I never have done at home. (Referring to a photograph of a pile of laundry)

First-year students arrive on campus, perhaps never having shared a room or even a bathroom. They eat at the dining hall for every meal and study more than they ever have before. They are learning to adjust to a whole new world, and though students' guardians may live nearby, many may be on their own with only their cell phone for a safety net. These women soften some of the conformity of their living spaces with their own bright comforters and photographs of friends and family. They complain of dining hall food and shaving in narrow shower stalls, "We're supposed to shave our legs in that?" They also begin to develop competence by learning new living skills, such as navigating transportation or being responsible for their own nutrition. Later in their first year, the struggle to adjust continues, but the problems turn more introspective, focused on their academics and relationships with their roommates and new friends. The women are struggling with how to cope with the challenges they are facing at the university, issues that may be purely academic, psychosocial, gender-related, or connected to the "irreducibly complex intersections" of gender, race, ethnicity, class, and sexual identities (Moraga & Anzaldua, 1981, as cited in Martin, 1993, p. 277).

College is noted as a time of rapid and significant identity development: behavioral and psychological changes that are affected by the people and situations surrounding the students (Chickering & Reisser, 1993). In order to understand the female student, one must deconstruct all of the related messages and psychological processes. In this section, we explore several theories of identity development. Many of the components of identity formation overlap and all components help us begin to understand the changes and challenges women face during college.

Identity development for college students has been documented and largely explored by the work of Chickering (1969) and then updated by Chickering and Reisser (1993). Their collaborative research has a college-specific focus developed from the general identity developmental work of Erikson. The authors detailed seven vectors that students will be challenged by as they develop; however, three are of particular note for most of students' college careers. Chickering and Reisser explored the developmental tasks or "vectors" that a student encounters, including the development of competence, the movement through autonomy toward independence, and the development of mature interpersonal relationships.

In *developing competence*, a student must achieve mastery in three general areas: intellectual competence, physical and manual competence, and interpersonal competence (Chickering & Reisser, 1993). Each area is challenging for a college student, including women. For example, facing a difficult curriculum and being asked to think theoretically challenges students who previously prided themselves on intellectual capabilities in high school. Students must navigate the university on their own, rather than being handheld by guardians or high school guidance counselors as in past experiences. They are put into situations where they must interact with others by listening, self-disclosing, and giving feedback to new acquaintances and friends.

Also challenging to students is the need to *establish independent autonomy* from others, particularly guardians and authorities such as professors, academic advisors, or religious ministers. Here students are challenged to develop emotional independence and self-sufficiency (Chickering & Reisser, 1993). It may be a very stressful and frustrating venture to first trust their own instincts and then navigate processes (such as college administrative forms) on their own.

A final key area of identity growth for students, particularly women students, is the development of *mature interpersonal relationships*, which involves "tolerance and appreciation of differences" and "capacity for intimacy" (Chickering & Reisser, 1993, p. 48). Most notably during the first year of college, the greatest challenge comes from exposure to unfamiliar lifestyles and personalities, compounded by the close living quarters in which they find themselves in the residence halls. Throughout college, navigating more mature romantic relationships and developing new relationships are areas to which women students in particular devote much time and reflection. These three vectors of Chickering and Reisser's seven-stage model are most relevant for all students, and create many self-related struggles: Will I be able to do what is expected? What do I expect for my experience? How will I survive the transitions? Who will help me?

IDENTITIES AS WOMEN

College life means sharing your life with so many people every day. You gain a huge new family as a result.

Starting the first weeks of their first year, these young women are actively creating community and, in turn, helping to define themselves. From bonding in the residence hall bathrooms to socializing at the senior send-off picnic, women college students continue to demonstrate relational behavior and value it highly. In carrying out these relationships, women are learning more about themselves, their own values, attitudes, and priorities (Gilligan, 1982). They find courage to act autonomously through their relationships and find competence in their own self as validated by and in relation to others. For the woman college student, identity is achieved in relation "to" something or someone.

Helms has created a Womanist identity model that focuses on the "premise that women's healthy gender identity development involves movement from an external- and societal-based definition of womanhood to an internal definition in which the woman's own values, beliefs, and abilities determine the quality of her womanhood" (Ossana, Helms, & Leonard, 1990, p. 402). Ossana et al. found that increased self-esteem was related to the positive development of a Womanist identity. They also found that perception of gender bias was negatively correlated to self-esteem. More specifically, women are less likely to have confidence in their abilities, beliefs, and values when these very attributes are being challenged during their attempts to develop competence, autonomy, and relationships.

Two identity development theories are most relevant in examining the challenges faced by women students: Carol Gilligan's work and the work of Mary Belenky, Blythe Clinchy, Nancy Goldberger, and Jill Tarule. Gilligan's (1982) work *In a Different Voice* is an exemplary study that highlights the limitations of many other developmental models of identity that were based on men alone; her research shows that classic developmental models ignore the critical component for women—self in relation to other. Within this relationship, women are giving and receiving knowledge, support, direction, advice, and exchange. But within these roles, much conflict, stress, and anxiety can arise that could potentially leave a woman feeling overwhelmed. Voice is a critical component of Gilligan's and later Brown and Gilligan's (1992) research: the connection, affirmation, and relationships by which women define themselves are based on having a voice. "Women's voices, in articulating a connected sense of self and approaches to conflict that centered on strengthening or maintaining relationship, were different voices within a male voiced world" (Brown & Gilligan, 1992, p. 20). Women's ability to understand themselves grows through connection, yet the voices they offer are sometimes silenced by encounters they experience daily. One student in the study stated,

> Do It Right. Sometimes I get the feeling that guys don't think of you like they do their male counterparts. It's like in a group setting females are viewed as weak links. I feel like I'm constantly having to work 10 times as hard just to get the respect a guy gets right from the start.

The work of Belenky, Clinchy, Goldberger, and Tarule (1986, 1997) focused on ways women come to know and develop as authorities of their own identity. In their research, detailed in five different perspectives of knowledge and role of authority, self-identity was developed as the women

began to know themselves as capable of learning and knowledge. "They needed to know that they already knew something . . . that there was something good inside them. They worried there was not" (Belenky et al., 1986, p. 195). Self-worth comes from owning "knowing," moving from absolute obedience to extreme authorities to the sense of authority as part of self-identity and, in this, a development of self-concept as being a person with knowledge. While our universities are focused on dispensing or creating knowledge, our students are in the passive receiver role— being instructed by authorities in the field as to what they should know and learn, often foreign and complex content compared with high school work. Women in nontraditional majors have the dual role of receiving knowledge from the authority (the faculty) and also having to prove themselves as capable learners in male-dominated fields—a concept that can be truly overwhelming. This is clearly displayed in Jennifer Sader's chapter (chapter 8) that uncovers the challenges of women doctoral students in computer science.

Women of color often have a compounded challenge in developing identity during the college experience. While working on definition of self as an autonomous being and as a woman, a woman of color is also navigating the development of racial identity and the unique messages received from culture and community.

IDENTITIES AS WOMEN OF COLOR

For women of color, developing their identities as women involves far more than the gender identity theories described in the previous section; they must negotiate both their own culture's views of gender identity and the dominant culture's views of gender identity, and this negatively affects their self-perception (Watt, 2006, p. 329). As early as Sojourner Truth, Black women were aware of the disparities among women based on the roles assigned to their ethnicity. When Sojourner Truth gave her now famous "Ain't I a Woman" speech in 1851, she put into words what women of color still deal with in today's culture—the differences of gender expectations among privileged and oppressed groups.

Many women of color also have described the expectation they face to choose their race over their gender, but this choice cannot be made: "Black women must struggle for black liberation *and* gender equality simultaneously," wrote Guy-Sheftall (1995) in *Words of Fire: An Anthology of African–American Feminist Thought,* an anthology that illustrates African American women's long history of feminism (p. 2). In *Making Waves: An Anthology of Writing by and about Asian American Women,* Mazumdar (as cited in Lim, 1993) made a similar point, "For women of color, concerns arising out of racial identity are an integral aspect of their overall identity" (p. 813). She described the varied—but also universal—cultural view of the superiority of men in Asian cultures: "The impact of gender on Asian women in America varies enormously within the same class and ethnic group while the idea that female children are of less value than male children permeates all Asian cultures" (p. 183).

Feminist and Womanist scholars continue to push the boundaries of gender-centric analysis to focus more on intersections of gender, race, ethnicity, class, sexuality, age, ability, and other "significant social identities (Dill, 1983; Hull, Scott, & Smith, 1982; Moraga & Anzaldúa, 1981)" (Shields, 2008, p. 302). Similarly, broader racial identity models were being developed, including those by Cross in 1971, Phinney in 1990, and Hardiman and Jackson in 1992 and Helms' Womanist theory (1992) as detailed in an earlier section.

Although gender is a major component of identity development, these equally important facets of identity intertwine so powerfully that they are "irreducibly complex intersections" (Moraga & Anzaldua, 1981, as cited in Martin, 1993, p. 277). As researchers and practitioners, we work with students with multidimensional identities and we, too, must continue to think beyond students or women students as a collective entity. A woman's identity, her life story, and experiences are based on many factors that cannot be overshadowed by her gender: ethnicity, class, sexuality, geographic location, family, and individual experiences.

Throughout their lives, girls from diverse cultural, racial, and class backgrounds and with different sexual identities encounter and negotiate the voices, stories, fantasies, and explanations that regulate and maintain the dominant culture's polarized discourse of gender. They hear about and witness what is deemed appropriate behavior; they learn how girls should look and sound if they are to be acceptable. Girls are either initiated into or, with the support of their families and communities, encouraged to actively resist this dominant social construction of reality (Brown, 1998, p. 18).

On a related point, Anzaldua (1990) wrote of the coping strategies women of color have created to survive in the dominant culture. She wrote, in particular, about Latina women.

> To become less vulnerable to all these oppressors, we have had to change faces, *hemos tenido que cambiar caras como el cambio de color en el camaleòn—cuando los peligros son muchos y las opciones son pocas*... Some of us who already wear many changes/inside our skin (Audre Lorde) have been forced to adopt a face that would pass. (p. xv)

Women of color have tried to find a "face that would pass" in the dominant culture, in this case, our predominantly White colleges and universities. While women of color on our campuses are experiencing all the identity challenges of the typical college student—transitioning from high school, being in less contact with their families, dealing with their academic expectations of themselves—they are also navigating their identity development as women and women of a particular (or multiple) racial and ethnic background. In addition, they may be very close to their families and expected to go to college close to home, spend the weekends at home, or even live at home while attending college. This arrangement could dramatically impact students' opportunities to build relationships with their peers if they are not on campus during the late-night study sessions or social times but can also provide much-needed support from family to cope.

While women of color may enter college understanding the challenges they may encounter due to the intersections of their gender and ethnicity, this awareness does not exempt students from challenging experiences as they struggle to form their own identities in these environments. Greer and Chwalisz (2007) found that African American students at historically Black colleges and universities have greater chances of excelling academically than those at predominantly White colleges and universities (PWCUs) because of "minority-related stress." They note that African American students at PWCUs develop coping skills to deal with the stress from "racial tension and conflict within their campus environment" (Greer & Chwalisz, 2007, p. 389). These students are most likely, however, to cope by avoiding tensions instead of addressing them. A study by Watt (2006) indicates that African American women from historically black colleges and universities are more likely to pursue graduate degrees and become leaders in their fields than women at PWCUs. These studies reinforce the importance for women of color at PWCUs to have strong support systems and role models to encourage them to succeed.

Women of color who participated in the photo study conducted by one of the authors illustrated the need for interaction with other students of their ethnicity. The women illustrated this by photographing events of student groups or friendship circles, highlighting the importance of the interaction. More specifically, one student described that she needed fewer "superficial friendships" and emphasized how much her relationship with another woman of the same ethnicity had helped. She explained, "It's nice to

have someone going through the same things you are in terms of your classes and your relationships between teachers and fellow classmates." The women recognized their need for community and attempted to find community within their spheres on campus.

A BRIEF NOTE ON METHODS

Upton (2001) conducted a "participant photography" study with 19 first-year and senior women students. The students, selected electronically at random and contacted via e-mail, agreed to document their experiences as women students at the predominantly male university through use of a questionnaire, disposable camera, and journal. The author also participated by documenting her experience as a professional in the predominantly male setting.

Stalzer's (2003) study was a two-part interview with seven women who reported feeling "frequently overwhelmed" with all they had to do in a 2001 first-year survey. The interviews were conducted with these women two years after their initial response to explore reflections on past feelings along with current experiences. The following scholarly discussion melds the two studies into one comprehensive look at the experiences of women on this particular campus while utilizing the theoretical framework described earlier. Recommendations for practitioners based on this discussion are provided in the "Conclusion" section and are believed to be generalizable for other campuses.

IDENTITY CHALLENGES IN ACTION

This review of the literature has detailed five main identity challenges at the forefront for women students during their college careers: competence, autonomy, connection, voice, and authority. Some of these challenges overlap among several theorists. It is useful for educators to identify the milestones in the common, everyday experiences of college students. In this section, examples will be explored through the use of related theory and examples from studies conducted on one college campus (Stalzer, 2003; Upton, 2001). Specifically, we discuss disconnection from others, lack of positive affirmation from others, doubting ability or ability to give and receive knowledge, frustration with authorities, and hindrances in developing relationships.

Disconnection From Others

> I guess socially it sometimes is overwhelming too . . . ha, don't know how to explain it . . . like a lot of my friends went to hang out with fraternities that I've never been to and they drag me along and that's kind of overwhelming to have to meet all these new people. So yeah, I'm, there's a lot. . . . You want to be comfortable and it's hard to meet ten new people in one night and feel you've got anywhere. I mean, you don't make new friends in one night.

The first main college challenge is connection, or in the case of the participant's words, disconnection from others. Others may be defined as faculty, classmates, family, or friends. The work of Carol Gilligan (1982) details the great need of women to have connection with others. Women learn about themselves, literally their *selves*, through the intimacy and relationship that comes with connection. They often define themselves using terms that others have given them—a good listener, a smart student, a kind friend. This constant source of feedback solicited from connections is key to women being able to understand the self, or the self in relation to others.

Chickering and Reisser (1993) also pointed to the importance of relationships. A forward progression in identity development for them includes moving from dependence on others to interdependence with others. Further, women rely on social support and their social ties with others to find their own voice and identity

(Gilligan, 1982). The importance of social support is even more critical because the relationship between balance and well-being directly relates to the amount and type of support being given (Jung, 1997). Jung found that those women who received less informational and tangible support than they provided for others were more depressed and that well-being relates to receiving the amount of support that is expected. When women cannot see themselves as part of a collective experience, this low social connectedness has implications for the individual's health and wellness. It also impacts their ability to see themselves as having commonalities with others in the community.

Along with social support, a large body of research details the importance of a sense of belonging and/or social connectedness as critical to the success of women in their environment. Lee, Keough, and Sexton (2002) found in their study that social connectedness, enduring and ubiquitous sense of interpersonal closeness with the social world, was a strong indicator of emotional well-being. In contrast, low social connectedness led to feelings of chronic loneliness, low self-esteem, higher anxiety, and greater social mistrust. Hagerty, Williams, Coyne, and Early (1996) confirmed that a sense of belonging is also strongly related to social and psychological functioning; they also found it to be more important for women than for men. Fitting in and feeling valued, they continue, are "important components of self" (p. 243).

But finding a group where she fits and feels valued, and relying on them for assistance, is not a given. Connecting with others takes a certain amount of vulnerability. Once the tie is made, however, it can be life changing, inside and outside the classroom. Consider the following statements made by students in the study: "I guess pride gets in the way, but the idea of having to go ask for help in multiple subjects was unbearable. That is, until you know that you've been beat and it's the only way. Then office hours take on a whole new and blessed meaning."

"At [my university], the work can sometimes be overwhelming so study groups are critical to helping share the load." "A lot of weeks during the past 2 years, I've seen these people [in my major] more than I've seen my roommate much less my social circle. . . . These people have defined my classes. We've studied together, stressed about test and toiled over projects and have laughed forever." "Some people find their school support groups in fraternities or sororities. I find mine in religious organizations and in my roommates."

As is reflected in these words, there are many barriers on college campuses that may hinder women's ability to conquer this identity challenge: unavailability of faculty for personal relationships, roommate conflicts, and distorted perceptions of other women on campus. Each of these concerns relates to instances where a student finds herself outside of a relationship or connection.

Women of color and women in nontraditional majors often have even more pronounced experiences in this regard. Gender and race are both critical parts of identity and, as such, often influence the people from whom they seek connection. In seeking out relationships in the same classroom, the participants are faced with men who receive offers of friendship mistakenly as offers of romantic interest, or men who don't offer friendship at all, seeing the women as less intelligent (Stalzer, 2003). That rebuff of connection is more significant in an institution where there are limited alternatives to find others of the same gender to fill the gap.

Financial Concerns

The saddest part in college life, so many things to do, so little money (accompanies a photo of people on line at the ATM).

Women students with financial concerns or from low-income families also have additional challenges of disconnection, as is revealed in the previous quote from a participant. Sax's (2008) study of entering college students showed that low-income women are the fastest growing group in education. These students may need to work more hours than their peers, potentially affecting their academic and social experiences, and certainly adding to their stress levels. In addition, as the student quoted above implied throughout her journal, these students are usually well aware of the socioeconomic differences between their classmates and themselves.

Sowinska (1993), hooks (1993), and other working-class women in academe have explored these compounded differences. Sowinska wrote that she found "passing" as middle-class to be a "valuable tool" at the time during college.

> My own passing included, among its other manifestations, altering my speech, changing the way I dressed, remaining silent during conversations about family, pretending to have enough money when I didn't, claiming I wasn't hungry when I was. . . . At that time in my life, these parts of me that I was giving up seemed unimportant, and I felt them as necessary sacrifices in order for me to be seen as legitimate. (Sowinska, p.152)

Time and financial resources might prohibit making connections with others because students are busy with jobs, unable to afford to join a club that has membership dues, or even feel as if they "don't belong." hooks (1993) wrote about being "materially underprivileged at a university where most folks (with the exceptions of workers) are materially privileged":

> Class differences were boundaries no one wanted to face or talk about. It was easier to downplay them, to act as though we were all from privileged backgrounds, to work around them, to confront them privately in the solitude of one's room, or to pretend that just being chosen to study at such an institution meant that those of us who did not come from privilege were already in transition toward privilege. . . . It was a kind of treason not to believe that it was better to be identified with the world of material privilege than with the world of the working class, the poor. (hooks, p. 101)

Why is this important? What we observe here is a situation of extreme isolation. Not only is the individual participant left on her own to develop some sense of self but is in an environment where there are few role models or people like herself to emulate. While being a minority on the campus and in a discipline sets women up to be trailblazers, without the support structure behind them to reinforce their successful progress they are forced down a very hard road. A sense of belonging is a significant and powerful element of coping. To go without a sense of belonging is to go a difficult road alone, leading to loneliness and decreasing resiliency (Hagerty et al., 1996). High levels of anxiety and negative affectivity (which for women are associated with isolation) have been shown to be associated with increased numbers of health symptoms and lower levels of life satisfaction (Zirkel, 1992). Dangerous and detrimental behaviors, including psychosomatic illness, suicide, and substance abuse, could potentially follow (Jones, 1992). Recognizing the importance of connections with others and creating that support network is critical to the success of these women as is mentioned in a number of chapters in this book including the one by Lee Hawthorne Calizo in chapter 18.

Lack of Positive Affirmation From Others

One student in the study stated, "Can't think of much I could be proud of my first year."

Positive affirmation is the key to successful movement through identity development for women in terms of developing a sense of competence, a feeling of authority, and a voice. Whether from other women or men, esteemed authorities or younger friends, women define themselves by what others see them do successfully. For the "good girl" always seeking to please, as Brown and Gilligan (1992) found in their study of adolescent girls, affirmation from teachers is key. Girls, particularly White girls, are taught to behave according to rules and are rewarded when their behavior is appropriate. In adolescence, girls incorporate this into sense of self, and their

actions and thoughts are focused on that which will get validation and affirmation for doing the correct behavior. Belenky and her colleagues (1986, 1997) focused on college-aged and adult women, and their research followed suit. The presence of an "authority" was what women gauged their knowledge on—in early stages of identity development there is an authority that dictates action, and in later stages the woman is able to find some areas where she is authority and capable of knowledge. The key to movement from not knowing to knowing is affirmation of an authority that confirms the woman can, indeed, be capable of having knowledge. At the stage a first-year student enters college she is still being guided by the external authorities.

The unavailability of faculty for personal relationships with their students is a huge blow to the affirmed self that women are used to in high school. Hegarty, Williams, Coyne, and Early (1992) cited lower levels of institutional support, absence of positive feedback, and absence of encouragement from faculty as three characteristics that may form barriers to women's education, no matter their race (and to male students of color). Harder coursework leads to lower grades. These blows replace what was past affirmation on written work in high school. Add to this the inability to connect with faculty for conversations or assistance, and you'll find students who doubt themselves in every way. Such is the case for this student:

> I wish there were those teachers, you know, that were my friend. And that they actually understand. That was the big thing. That way I, it wasn't about my grades so much, it was that I could show them that I was intelligent and smart by knowing them and having conversations with them. I mean, the teachers that I actually do know and talk to, they know I'm very intelligent. But the other ones think I'm an average student, the ones that don't talk to me, and you know, I think I'm decently average but you know, I mean, I can't just do that on a test. I have to be able to talk to people and relay what I know.

The source of this student's main affirmation has been removed from what she was previously exposed to in high school. The role of faculty in the successful identity development of women is clear and forthright. Hackett et al.'s (1992) study of women and academics revealed that higher levels of verbal encouragement and lower levels of discouragement were correlated to student achievement. Higher levels of self-efficacy in careers and academics were present in situations where faculty played a positive, encouraging role with the women students, which fosters the development of competence, autonomy, and voice. Not surprising, this connects to Brown and Gilligan's (1992) research when they found authority to play a large role in girls' self-esteem.

Doubting Ability or Ability to Give and Receive Knowledge

One student expressed, "I have enjoyed being at (my university), but I'm not sure I've enjoyed this experience enough to stay. . . . No matter how hard I work, I cannot make the grades I want to make, which is very frustrating." It is important for women to see themselves as knowers, capable of authority on certain subjects. While positive affirmation is necessary to seeing one's self as a knower, the fundamental knowledge one has is also relevant. For one group of high-achieving women, their high school careers were characterized by being the "smart" girls, by succeeding in coursework with very little effort. When asked to describe themselves as they were in high school, all but one started their description with some reference to studies such as "smart, the valedictorian," "I didn't study much, didn't have to," "top of my class, I fit in, that was my place." Academic achievement clearly was their niche, and was reflected by their performance on exams and in class rankings. In high school, they self-defined and were defined by others as intelligent and bright, and they received awards and recognitions (such as class valedictorian or acceptance to gifted programs).

Sometimes I really enjoy being here, but my mood changes depending on the grades I get.

Yet overwhelmingly these women responded that academic struggles in college created extremely stressful situations, affecting their health and resiliency. The burden of not having a strong self-concept in relation to academics is significant, the equivalent of having a carpet swept out from beneath them. Academics were once their source of pride and their niche within school, but their struggles with college material, compounded by the lack of affirmation from faculty or others, is extremely detrimental to their identification of themselves as capable knowers. In college, these women feel acutely how difficult the academics are, how radical the change in their study and work habits eventually had to become, and how disappointing it was not to do well.

Capability as a knower is reflected in the current literature. Helms's Womanist identity model includes shifting from an externalized definition of womanhood to the internalized knowledge of one's abilities (Ossana et al., 1992). In this model, a woman advances in her identity development when she can know her abilities without the external nod from societal structures, such as grades or awards. For Chickering and Reisser (1993), developing competence in one's abilities—be they intellectual abilities, physical/motor abilities, or emotional competence to have a handle on emotions—is a key factor in the progression of identity development. For Brown and Gilligan (1992), the ability to give and receive knowledge—both to understand what is being shared and to initiate the sharing on certain topics—was key to the confidence and identity progress of the high-achieving adolescent women with whom they worked.

Consider the following two related quotes from participants: "Sometimes I don't fit in well because I just don't know the same things everyone else does." "In many ways, it is about struggling to get by rather than struggling to really learn." Many women self-impose feelings of failure, feeling that they do not have the base of knowledge expected by either classmates or faculty. They characterize the college experience as "sink or swim," and many feel they are sinking. Women sometimes see themselves at a disadvantage in ability or knowledge that they assume others have. Why is this important? This is the cornerstone of societal gender differences. At an institution, which is led in the instructional methods that best address male styles of learning (due to academic tradition, authoritarian teaching styles of lecturing that connote "imparting wisdom," and the predominantly male faculty that lead most American universities), it is clear that organizations such as this do not foster positive development of women as owners of knowledge (Belenky et al., 1986; Davis, 1999; Rosser, 1995). Women don't assert themselves and what they know. They express and internalize self-doubt. They state fact as opinions, or with qualifiers, when they volunteer information at all. hooks (1996) commented on the roles of race and culture in communication to further compound the issue:

> Many feminist thinkers writing and talking about girlhood right now like to suggest that black girls have a better self-esteem than their white counterparts. The measurements of this difference is often that black girls are more assertive, speak more, appear more confident. Yet in traditional southern-based black life, it was and it is expected of girls to be articulate, to hold ourselves with dignity. Our parents and teachers were always urging us to stand up right and speak clearly. These traits were meant to uplift the race. They were not necessarily traits associated with building female self-esteem. An outspoken girl might still feel like she was worthless because her skin was not light enough or her hair the right texture . . . White girls of all classes are often encouraged to be silent. But to see the opposite in different ethnic groups as a sign of female empowerment is to miss the reality that the cultural codes of that group may dictate a quite different standard by which female self-esteem is measured. (p. xii)

Frustration With Authorities

> Seems like they are out to get you, they make things much more difficult than they need to be.

Many students in this study expressed frustration with various authorities around campus, be it administrative offices or faculty. Some disenchantment with authorities is expected in the growth of identity, as the identity struggles to emerge from what has been confining it prior, be it rules, cultural norms, or expectations from others. Indeed, frustration with these entities shows positive identity development. Belenky et al. (1986) acknowledged that those in later stages of identity are taking on more authorship of their opinions and are more confident in seeing themselves as authorities of what they know. For less developed stages of identity development, and for some students who encounter the need to handle student business on their own for the first time, these struggles with authority are internalized as personal reflections of self. For example, one participant stated, "I couldn't complete the process, I don't know what to do." More developed identities can adjust that frame of reference, placing blame on inefficient processes at the university or individuals external to themselves.

Women students in the two studies struggled to voice similar frustrations with faculty, where the women assumed responsibility for their unmet needs. In these situations, the approach is often that they themselves should adjust to "the way it is" rather than having the situation be remedied. Adapting their own behaviors, learning styles, or self-concept to make up for the teaching style or unavailability of the faculty shows limits to the authority the women are willing to challenge. It stops short of criticizing the authority of the teachers who have always been the ones who set the rules. The participants were not yet at a place in their development where they saw that it was possible to confront the behavior of those authorities.

This is significant. A healthy dissatisfaction with systems they participate in is empowering.

It shows independent thinking, a sense of self in relation to others while knowing one's own values and beliefs. It owns knowledge and the thought of a better way of doing things. It relays a sense of competence and autonomy, that the individual can disagree with a current system and believe he or she can do better. However, unquestioned submission to faculty authority is detrimental. In higher education especially, it is imperative that we are creating independent minds who own original thought, including critique of the authority of faculty.

This unquestioned acceptance of authority from faculty suggests that women are continuing the "good girl" experience of adolescence. Even in adolescence it was distressing to have a voice of disagreement and not be able to share it for fear of societal disapproval. As women become more knowledgeable and begin to see themselves as autonomous individuals, the continued unchecked power that they give to authorities, in this case faculty, can be a source of frustration, stress, and anxiety. Yet the participants in this study seemed indifferent or unable to identify that they might have the ability to question the authority of faculty.

Hindrances in Developing Relationships

One student in the study stated,

> I don't go out and meet people and I didn't really see that as my own fault. I just thought that it just should happen and I should just make new friends and I wasn't making new friends. And I thought that maybe if I were somewhere else that would have been easier. But I don't think that's true . . . I should have gone out and been, uhm, open to meeting new people and that sort of thing.

Brown and Gilligan's (1992) work with adolescent girls noted very clearly the struggle girls have in developing authentic relationships with others. The girls must resolve the disparity between cultural norms, what they are told is true

with their actual experiences and observations of what is true; they must then decide how to proceed in a way that is authentic. For relationships, that often means examining the implications for self and for others, and being able to actively make decisions that are either selfish or selfless (where selfless means absence of self in a negative light and selfish means focused on self in a beneficial way). Circumstantial decisions must be made, and for the adolescents of Brown and Gilligan's (1992) studies, the level of risk was equivalent to the level of risk that our college-age students are facing: both ages faced decisions about whom to be friends with and whom to let go, how to confront others in relationships if needed, and resolving the sometimes contradictory experiences one has within herself (e.g., my friend has angered me).

> There are the select few that are very cute and very popular—it's annoying to me that they can party and still do well. There are sorority women. There are those who study a lot. Those in my major, a lot in my major.

Women in college often experience similar relational struggles. They can find themselves resorting to learned stereotypes of women as a way to explain themselves, highlight differences with other women, or justify a position in a relational dispute. In working on addressing their own self-understanding, women in earlier stages of development may find themselves creating descriptions of what they are not. For example, a woman who is not in a sorority might define a type as "sorority women" with mostly negative connotations. It is both a normal developmental process and a potentially detrimental one to define self through what one observes of others. Categorization of "other" or "others not like me" indicates a group that defines itself by what it is not.

Annemarie Vaccaro's study (chapter 7) of racial identity in nontraditional women students in an all-women's college speaks to this identity challenge as well. Women of color in later stages of racial identity development were likely to see themselves as alienated from those around them, experiencing the "others not like me" in a similarly isolating manner.

For some women, a full immersion into a student organization will give them a temporary role to try on, complete with set uniform, identifiers, values, and characteristics. Some organizations offer more explicit descriptors that the student may apply to herself. For example, sororities often provide guidance on behaviors and values for younger members by older members or through handbooks and policies. Other clubs might be less explicit, and students will learn roles through the students they spend time with during organization functions. Students who take on leadership roles often fully embrace the culture and its identity as their own. As one student states, "When you're the head of an organization, you eat, sleep, live and breathe that organization. We have a couch in the office so I don't have to go back to my room to sleep." Another student reports, "Getting involved is the best way to meet people."

But is this a positive or negative phenomenon? Universities often encourage involvement for its positive effects on retention to the institution. The benefits to student development are important as well; organizations often provide a nonthreatening ground where students can be exposed to differences and try on roles in a supportive environment. Later in their development, women are able to start identifying purpose; both unique attributes of self and commonalities to a group of women and the comparisons with other women can be healthier and more positive. Yet, as noted in chapter 7, Vaccaro's (2008) study found that White women in earlier stages of racial identity development were more likely to place assumptions on others based on their own views and experiences, and that women of color in earlier stages were more likely to adopt the majority culture and attempt to assimilate. Neither situation encourages women to grow in unique ways. It is the role of higher education administrators

to challenge broad assumptions and encourage reflective analysis to help women grow both in connection and in unique ways.

How can such women then create relationships in which they will grow and develop their identity? The ability to see positive generalizations and individual characteristics of other women on campus is critical to the formation of relationships. It provides a way for women to clearly identify one thing they, as women, have in common and create some sense of unity and strength. But it also publicly refutes many negative and alienating stereotypes considered cultural norms that the women then internalize and incorporate into self. If the women participants are exposed to relationships that create doubts about women's abilities, they will then internalize these same doubts. However, if women are introduced to affirming relationships, they will provide an opportunity to move into interpersonal and balanced relationships.

CONCLUSION

As one student in the study stated, "I took another picture of the door of her apartment. I've been coming to that apartment for the last four years. It's sad to think that I'll probably never go back into it again." It would seem that there are almost too many possible challenges for women to face as they transition through their college experience. The way that women anticipate these challenges, cope with stress, and see their own efficacy are all important variables. The connection to those around them may assist women with the transition and/or may create additional barriers or stressors that compound the transition. The messages women receive from the institution and the fulfillment they get from their chosen major are both factors in their success and retention.

Educators have a responsibility to positively facilitate the developmental process. Although the domain of educators varies with specific roles, some common guidelines are appropriate to consider. First, represent gender in a positive and equitable way in course materials, workshops, and displays. The detailed representation of strong women allows college women to envision possibilities and own the ability to create knowledge for themselves (American Association of University Women, 1992; Broughton & Fairbanks, 2003). Second, create opportunities for reflective self-expression and validate the expressions presented in a personal manner. In the hustle and bustle of college life, students rarely take time to deeply reflect on experience and its meaning, much less growth and change. Educators can create opportunities for students to force such reflection. Use those opportunities to give positive affirmation and praise, offer a mentoring or advising relationship, and normalize the experiences of women for a group that often sees themselves as "other."

Third, affect relationship building in both macro and micro levels. Classes, programs, services, and organizations all offer opportunities to build connections among women students. Educators should deliberately seek out ways to connect women students to each other and the campus. Both faculty–student relationships and student–student relationships offer women students the opportunity to grow and develop identity through interaction with another. Educators should intentionally facilitate such interaction to the extent they are able. Next, recognize that in today's multicultural world, there are still women who will have few role models like themselves to emulate. As Watt (2006) noted, practitioners need to be aware that students of color are utilizing coping strategies to survive and urges educators not to underestimate what might be going on under the surface. Personal outreach and encouragement could support these women to continue to pursue their dreams; they may become a trailblazer for others to follow. Furthermore, educators should work with their institutions to ensure qualified women of different ethnicities are represented in recruitment pools and new hires to provide more role models on campus for female students.

Finally, intervene on an individual basis. Some women will need more formal support to address identity challenges as they occur and develop coping skills to deal with the challenges successfully. An educator's offer of concern for students could encourage them to go to a support program for assistance and salvage their academic pursuits.

Incorporating these common guidelines is a positive step toward helping college women develop and gain confidence in their abilities. As one of the students in these studies quoted, from the bathroom stall of a local bar, "Hey you. Get this. You are beautiful. LOVE yourself & others will too!"

REFERENCES

American Association of University Women. (1992). *How schools shortchange girls—The AAUW report: A study of major findings on girls and education*. New York: Marlowe & Co.

Anzaldua, G. (Ed.). (1990). *Making face, making soul: Haciendo caras: Creative and critical perspectives by feminists of color*. San Francisco, CA: Aunt Lute Books.

Belenky, M. F., Clinchy, B. M., Goldberger, N. R., & Tarule, J. M. (1986). *Women's ways of knowing: The development of self, voice and mind*. New York: Basic Books.

Belenky, M. F., Clinchy, B. M., Goldberger, N. R., & Tarule, J. M. (1997). *Women's ways of knowing: The development of self, voice and mind. Tenth anniversary edition*. New York: Basic Books.

Broughton, M., & Fairbanks, C. (2003). In the middle of the middle: Seventh-grade girls' literacy and identity development. *Journal of Adolescent and Adult Literacy, 46*(5), 426–435.

Brown, L. M. (1998). *Raising their voices: The politics of girls' anger*. Cambridge, MA: Harvard University Press.

Brown, L., & Gilligan, C. (1992). *Meeting at the crossroads: Women's psychology and girls' development*. New York: Ballantine Books.

Brumberg, J. J. (1997). *The body project: An intimate history of American girls*. New York: Vintage Books.

Chickering, A. (1969). *Education and identity*. San Francisco, CA: Jossey-Bass.

Chickering, A., & Reisser, L. (1993). *Education and identity* (2nd ed.). San Francisco, CA: Jossey-Bass.

Cross, W. E., Jr. (1971). The negro-to-black conversion experience: Toward a psychology of black liberation. *Black World, 20*(9), 13–27.

Davis, S. (1999). Creating a collaborative classroom. In S. Davis, M. Crawford, & J. Sebrechts (Eds.), *Coming into her own: Educational success in girls and women* (pp. 123–139). San Francisco, CA: Jossey-Bass.

Dill, B. T. (1983). Race, class, and gender: Prospects for an all-inclusive sisterhood. *Feminist Studies, 9*(1), 131–150.

Gilligan, C. (1982). *In a different voice*. Cambridge, MA: Harvard University Press.

Greer, T. M., & Chwalisz, K. (2007). Minority-related stressors and coping processes among African American college students. *Journal of College Student Development, 48*(4), 388–404.

Guy-Sheftall, B. (Ed.). (1995). *Words of fire: An anthology of African-American feminist thought*. New York: The New Press.

Hackett, G., Betz, N., Casas, J., & Rocha-Singh, I. (1992). Gender, ethnicity, and social cognitive factors predicting the academic achievement of students in engineering. *Journal of Counseling Psychology, 39*(4), 527–538.

Hagerty, B., Williams, R., Coyne, J., & Early, M. (1996). Sense of belonging indicators of social and psychological functioning. *Archives of Psychiatric Nursing, 10*(4), 235–244.

Hardiman, R., & Jackson, B. (1992). Racial identity development: Understanding racial dynamics in college classrooms and on campus. In M. Adams (Ed.), *Promoting diversity in college classrooms: Innovative responses for the curriculum, faculty, and institutions* (pp. 21–37). New Directions for Teaching and Learning, No. 115. San Francisco, CA: Jossey-Bass.

hooks, b. (1993). Keeping close to home: Class and education. In M. M. Tokarczyk & E. A. Fay (Eds.), *Working-class women in the academy: Laborers in the knowledge factory* (pp. 99–111). Amherst, MA: The University of Massachusetts Press.

hooks, b. (1996). *Bone black: Memories of girlhood*. New York: Henry Holt and Company.

Hull, G. T., Scott, P. B., & Smith, B. (Eds.). (1982). *All the women are White, all the Blacks are men, but some of us are brave: Black women's studies*. Old Westbury, NY: Feminist Press.

Jones, R. (1992). Gender specific differences in the perceived antecedents of academic stress. (Report No. R189002001). (ERIC Document Reproduction Services No. ED364492).

Jung, J. (1997). Balance and source of social support in relation to well-being. *The Journal of General Psychology, 124*(1), 77–90.

Lee, R., Keough, K., & Sexton, J. (2002). Social connectedness, social appraisal, and perceived stress in college women and men. *Journal of Counseling and Development, 80*, 355–361.

Lim, S. G. (1993). Feminist and ethnic literary theories in Asian American literature. In R. R. Warhol & D. P. Herndl (Eds.), *Feminisms: An anthology of literary theory and criticism* (pp. 807–826). New Jersey: Rutgers University Press.

Martin, B. (1993). Lesbian identity and autobiographical difference[s]. In H. Abelove, M. A. Barale, & D. M. Halperin (Eds.), *The lesbian and gay studies reader* (pp. 274–293). New York: Routledge.

Moraga, C., & Anzaldua, G. (Eds.). (1981). *This bridge called my back: Writings by radical women of color*. Watertown, MA: Persephone Press.

Orenstein, P. (1994). *Schoolgirls: Young women, self esteem and the confidence gap*. New York: Doubleday.

Ossana, S., Helms, J., & Leonard, M. (1992). Do "Womanist" identity attitudes influence college women's self-esteem and perceptions of environmental bias? *Journal of Counseling and Development, 70*, 402–408.

Phinney, J. S., & Alipuria, L. L. (1990). Ethnic identity in college students from four ethnic groups. *Journal of Adolescence, 13*(2), 171–183.

Piper, M. (1994). *Reviving Ophelia: Saving the selves of adolescent girls*. New York: Ballantine Books.

Rosser, S. (Ed.). (1995). *Teaching the majority: Breaking the gender barrier in science, mathematics and engineering*. New York: Teachers College Press.

Sax, L. (2008). *The gender gap in college: Maximizing the developmental potential of women and men*. San Francisco, CA: Jossey Bass.

Shields, S. A. (2008). Gender: An intersectionality perspective. *Sex Roles, 59*, 301–311.

Sowinska, S. (1993). Yer own motha wouldna reckanized ya: Surviving an apprenticeship in the "Knowledge Factory." In M. M. Tokarczyk & E. A. Fay (Eds.), *Working-class women in the academy: Laborers in the knowledge factory* (pp. 148–161). Amherst, MA: The University of Massachusetts Press.

Stalzer, A. (2003). *Too much: Understanding how fresh-men women's feelings of being overwhelmed affect identity development.* Unpublished master's thesis, Georgia State University, Atlanta, Georgia, USA.

Upton, Y. L. (2001). *Lasting impressions: Viewing the Georgia Institute of Technology experience through the lenses of first-year and senior women.* Unpublished master's thesis, Georgia State University, Atlanta, Georgia, USA.

Watt, S. K. (2006). Racial identity attitudes, woman-ist identity attitudes, and self-esteem in African American college women attending historically Black single-sex and coeducational institutions. *Journal of College Student Development, 47*(3), 319–334.

Zirkel, S. (1992). Developing independence in a life transition: Investing the self in the concerns of the day. *Journal of Personality and Social Psychology, 62*(3), 506–521.

NARRATIVES ON GENDER AND FEMINISM

The Story of Maya

Xyanthe Neider

I'm not sure that I was ever conscious of gender, my gender, until some point during my midthirties while working on my master's degree in higher education administration. Honestly, issues of class, capital, and power seemed much more salient to me in understanding my own experiences. After all, I was of the generation—GenX—that had been told that we could be anything we wanted to be but lacked examples of how to get there. For those like me, first-generation college students, nontraditionally aged, single parents, and those living meagerly, we hoped that the magic of a bachelor's degree would grant us access to a world we'd only seen on television shows of the 1970s. Instead of finding the magic of a bachelor's degree, I was trying to figure out how to leverage the degree in a way that would get me out of stereotypical professional women's work as a secretary.

My return to school was about me finding and claiming my own power again, and once again I was searching for the magic of educational credentials. Dysfunctional abusive relationships with my supervisor and husband kept me feeling pretty powerless. Now the mother of two, fear prevented me from ending either of these relationships for quite some time. One year into working on my master's degree part time, I transitioned from my full-time job to a half-time graduate assistantship, soon realized that I was a married single parent, and ended my marriage as well. Both of these relationships had invaded my psyche and left me feeling incompetent and incapable. Burying myself into academics has always been a way for me to imagine escaping my past and rising above my public assistance upbringing.

Nearing the end of my master's program, my world still in upheaval due to a particularly contentious divorce and inadequate custody arrangements, I found myself in disequilibrium again, becoming the power of attorney for my grandmother, my best friend. My life at that time consisted of dropping children off at school and driving 75 miles one way tending to my grandmother's medical, legal, and physical needs. Some days, I made that trip twice a day, putting over 14,000 miles on the road in less than three months. My children alone, the teenager caring for the younger one, me caring for my grandmother, the stress of an inadequate parenting plan for the youngest child, a master's thesis to write, and driving 150–300 miles every day left me weary. These burdens should have crushed me; instead, I applied to the Ph.D. program. It was at this point that I became aware of gender, my gender, and the role it was playing in my life. Few men will accept responsibility of caring for and raising children while caring and being responsible for an elderly family member. And certainly fewer men would assume these responsibilities while beginning a Ph.D. program. The reality of my life circumstances has driven me and motivated me in ways I am only now beginning to unearth.

To understand the story of Maya, I have had to reflect upon the legacies from which I grew. I was raised by my mom, a single parent, and my grandma, also a single parent while she was raising her children. Both of these women struggled to carve their own place in the world while trying to help me find mine. They both believed in the promise of education and impressed that upon me. Although I was not yet born during Kennedy's and Johnson's presidencies or the height of the civil rights movement, the history of hope permeated my upbringing as a biracial daughter in a White family of a single mother. My grandma perhaps understood best that language was power and in order to be competitive in the man's world I must read extensively—primarily modern classics. She believed I would learn to speak properly through reading. Speaking properly was also a core factor in my upbringing. I did not realize the gift at the time that she and my mom bestowed upon me nor the contradictory nature of that gift. For to buy into this status quo was also to support the hegemony of what is labeled classical and proper and in some ways removed me all the more further from my gendered and raced self. I now understand the import of learning the language of the educated while also recognizing how that language has developed my European

American identity and atrophied my African American identity. This language has also contributed to masculinized thinking, cognitive development, and epistemological ways of being while stunting my feminine growth. This language has served me well by fostering within me some drive, motivation, and good old-fashioned "pull yourself up by your bootstraps" ways of approaching life's challenges.

Scholars, such as Foucault, have long held that language forms the basis for thinking in terms of what can be thought, who can think "it," and how to think about whatever "it" is; therefore, I employ a postcolonial theoretical lens to develop my research questions, methodologies, and to analyze my data. Because postcolonial theory centers on asking about what constitutes knowledge and authority, I am able to utilize feminist methods and methodologies that honor me as a researcher and woman while also honoring my participants as authentic knowers. As for race, a critical race theory perspective provides for the understanding that racism and categorizing people based upon the socially constructed notion of race is normal. For example, I conduct my work in the Middle Eastern student populations; critical race theory helps me to notice and illuminate how members of this mythically broad group are being racialized in ways that legitimate some hegemonies to coexist side by side with particular forms of capital. In this, I am better able to recognize that it is both a liability as well as an asset—economically, educationally, socially, etc.—for members of Middle Eastern groups because critical race theory assumes racism is normal, which also speaks to my biracial experience in ways that standard European American understandings cannot.

I understand my fair olive complexion, the nature of my European American language development, and the culmination of my experiences to be an asset, a legitimation of sorts, while my curly black hair, my gender, and my always tan skin to be a liability in ways that I can only understand through theoretical frameworks. In retrospect, my academic life has been as much about finding answers to questions and theoretical explorations as it has been about me finding and nurturing my racial and gender identities. Although my work does not explore my race or gender at the moment, many of the theoretical tools I have used open the spaces for these reflective explorations to take place.

Intersection of Identities: One Woman's Journey

Kimberley Fernandes

These are the experiences of a woman whose story is not unlike many that you may have previously heard. In fact the connection to her story is the very reason she is compelled to share hers, for often, she hears her own experience reflected in the voice of others. And although initially that recognition of voice justified her silence, the learning of how to break out and take pride in that which is uniquely hers and hers alone is where this story begins.

The she, the her, is me.

We often answer the question posed "Where are you from?" and for many of us that question is unobtrusive, and a simple "I'm from New Jersey" would suffice. For me that question only perpetuated the fear that I was from "somewhere else" and did not belong; and while no one explicitly had to tell me "go back where you came from" as is the experience for many others, what I heard was enough to cause me to want to be like everyone else. The trouble with doing that, however, is that at some point, you get so good at being someone else, you forget exactly who you started out as being in the first place.

I don't know how to tell my story anymore, without referring to where I am now, for I am so blessed to now have a space where I have the language and support to reflect on my own journey, both where I have been and where I hope to go. And so please excuse me when my references or verbage seem too esoteric; I certainly did not understand then what I struggle to understand now.

The color of my skin is undoubtedly one of the first aspects of my identity a person encounters. Perhaps the second is gender, or maybe for some it is reversed. Irrespective of the order, you may make some assumptions regarding my ethnicity or gender or both. For a long time, I took pride in only one of those identities. I was proud to be a woman, a girl, because fortunately I came from a progressive household where both my parents would be considered contemporary feminists even if they didn't self-identify as such. I understand now, what I didn't then, that their quiet acceptance of feminism rather than a large declaration of the fact was only one of the many cultural nuances I would question and fight, and only much more recently, come to love and respect. I felt powerful when I was in the presence of women, for I bonded easily with girls; I enjoyed playing with Barbie dolls and saw no contradictions between playing dress up at home and standing first in my classes. I was always the first student to raise my hand and was competitive in the classroom with anyone, especially boys because they were more often than not my competitors.

I remember vividly the first time a teacher called me aggressive. I was nine years old. I remember the first time a teacher called me aggressive and meant it positively, I was 16. I remember the first time I began substituting assertive for aggressive because I thought it made me seem less masculine, less threatening. I remember the first time I used aggressive to describe myself and meant it positively; it was only a year ago.

My race/ethnicity has been the harder identity to take pride in outside of my home. I did not have positive role models who had navigated the U.S. racial context and who could help me understand that my desire to assimilate, my confusion around who I was, and my need for community were a part of a larger fabric of human experience that was just awaiting my discovery. For me this liberating feeling came at my undergraduate institution, where I was one of the few brown faces in the crowd. It was there that I found a community among my peers, students of color who came from all walks of life. They all welcomed me with a shared understanding that we were all lost but could be found together. I took up the cause as though I had been waiting to take center stage my entire life; I majored in sociology and fell in love with scholarship around race and identity. I became the quintessential student leader and subsequently became the "successful student of color"; all of a sudden it was my picture that was displayed on all of the campus recruitment literature and fundraises/endowment events. I was honored by this tokenist expression for I believed that I was the face of change, not just the symbolic expression of it. And so upon graduation, I believed my "identity work" was finished and the exhausting question of "who are you" was answered.

Funny thing was that my gender and my race/ethnicity had, in large part, remained relatively separated. I knew that I was an Indian person (from South Asia) and that I was a woman, but I rarely put the words together let alone the complexities of that intersection. It has only been recently in my adulthood and in relationships with those currently in my life that I have adopted the term "woman of color." Although I studied the conceptual nature of this identity, I never embodied the lived reality of that identity. I separated those identities to such a large degree that I would constantly make choices regarding which identity group I wanted to affiliate with depending on the context, the individuals, and how comfortable I would or wouldn't be. I didn't know that there were spaces created by others in which the intersection of these two identities was celebrated and that as an Indian woman, I could be whole in all my complexities.

Alice Walker (1983) coined the phrase "A womanist is to feminist as purple is to lavender," and its relevance is one I live every day. As women, we all bring a complex set of identities with us, and our gender is only a piece of that puzzle. And even though the adoption of the term "woman of color" still leaves me confused at times as to how to bridge my Indian identity with other women who come from all corners of the globe and where perhaps our greatest commonality is the oppression we have experienced in White dominant culture, I know there is a power in our collective voice. In my own process of self-reflection, I have sought opportunities and spaces where it is safe enough to encounter those multiple identities at once, to create friendships where the richness of your own story is treasured, and where you can in turn validate someone else's identities. As for me, and my story, well the rest is still unwritten, but thankfully, I get to author my own story, one chapter at a time.

REFERENCES

Walker, A. (1983). *In search of our mothers' gardens: Womanist prose.* Orlando, FL: Harcourt Books.

Is Your Profundity a Trammel or a Treasure?
Lessons in Ability and Identity

Rachel Wagner

Profound sensorineural hearing loss was the medical terminology. That's what the doctors called it. They said I caught a virus, and this was the result. I didn't know that I was sick; paying attention to my body wasn't a part of my childhood programming.

I had been tired, and maybe a bit achy, but it was the last few days of exams during my first year of college, and sleep hadn't been much of a priority. I had to keep my scholarship, and a solid C+ performance my first semester was putting that in some serious jeopardy. I was heartsick at the thought of not coming back to school; this journey wasn't just about me, and my goals, but what it meant for my family, the cousins behind me for whom college was like winning the lottery—a commonplace dream uncommonly realized. Besides, this was how I contributed. School was always easy for me, teachers liked me, bubble tests always affirmed my particular brand of intelligence. Did I feel a bit off? Perhaps, but in my recollection it would not have diminished my attention from the task at hand; my health was secondary to what I knew to be at stake.

I assured myself that the lack of sleep was the real source of my difficulties. I resembled a drunk walking up the auditorium steps to my biology exam. Like Uncle Spank emerging from the mangle of his iron pony motorcycle to challenge taunting, whiskey-fleshed demons. I found out later that this feeling was from the disequilibrium from the inner ear infection. By the time the steroids began working, the virus had devastated the interpretive function in my right ear. My left ear was unaffected. I remember thinking, how can one part of my body be under siege while the other half either idled or cowered? I wondered if it was a terrible blessing, that in saving some portion of my hearing, my head split in half, turned its back on itself.

That was the extent of my ruminations. The damned ringing didn't give me the opportunity to construct a thought. The first three weeks I was irritable and a bit unhinged from the sleep deprivation. The constant static was annoying enough during the day, but nighttime offered unparalleled misery. Unchecked ringing eroded the precarious grip I exercised upon my sanity. Sixteen years later I learned that the ringing didn't go away, it just took a bit of time for my brain to create new pathways to circumvent it.

I found out about my ear a few months ago because of an absurd combination of unthinkable coincidences that temporarily robbed me of the left ear, too. The procedures, visits, and consultations that ensued were informative. I learned that our brains are alive and able to adapt in a way that I never really thought about before. Given enough time, the circuitry in my brain literally rerouted itself around the ringing. For the first time I saw the actual numbers from the hearing tests, providing confirmation that the condition of my right ear is every bit as bad as I've come to understand through my daily life. Yet, those numbers were precious to me as perhaps they couldn't be at 18. I have a different relationship with my doctors now, less dictatorial, more collaborative. My experiences as a scholar have prepared me to change the orthodoxy of our relationship. No longer reliant upon their authority for a definitive interpretation of what the results mean, I have come to trust my own interpretation.

Such an exercise of agency has been transcendent. The satisfaction I've enjoyed in making meaning of the doctor's insights, the test results, and my direct personal experience is difficult to capture. In the tidal wave of insights that have flooded my consciousness recently, my sensorineural loss has demonstrated itself to be more profound than a head and neck specialist could have possibly predicted.

For instance, I'm beginning to understand that the accommodations I employ have a price. The frustration and fatigue engendered by overcrowded rooms and poor acoustics needn't be a reminder of my limitations. Rather, they can provide an invitation to foreground my physical and emotional health. Headaches and exhaustion are not the inevitable conclusion of my day but a choice I make. Occasionally, I knowingly invite such symptoms, because some things really are important enough. Not everything, however. Hearing is a conscious decision, and the cost is too dear to swindle upon a cacophony of surface interactions and shallow-minded people.

The profundity I've reaped from this "loss" transcends the complexities of sensorineural function or learning to prioritize my health. I've learned in a material, visceral way that the purpose of my past accommodations has been to ensure comprehensive access to everyday conversation. I've literally embodied the modern preoccupation with mastering the "text," and applied it to every conversation I entered. I was so certain that if I missed something, that if I didn't hear every single thing that someone else said, I was at an unacceptable disadvantage, that I would be losing something or might appear confused or judged ignorant. Mostly, I wished to hear everything, so that I could understand others, not necessarily in the interest of encountering something new, but in order to confirm the boxes and categories I already believed to exist. I have been forgoing the magic that occupies the in-between spaces, and the significance that lurks about in the imperfect, idiosyncratic, imprecise terrain of discourse, meaning, and identity in order to dwell in the safe climes of certainty.

Not anymore, however. I refuse to be seduced by the surety embedded in the familiar and normalized ways of doing and being. My disability, a linguistic depiction that criminally undermines and underimagines the vast landscape of my capacities, has ushered in new freedoms from old narratives, new opportunities to elevate my awareness, and new commitments to myself and my place in the world. I'm confident that it is part of what the creator intended for me to learn. Profound is such a small, inadequate representation of the impact of my hearing "loss." In a delightfully trickster-like turn of events, my body's "frailty" has liberated my consciousness. With new knowledge and cautious conviction I face the uncertainties, open to the possibilities, ready to embrace the lessons, and the delights as they come.

Section Four

ADVANCING THE FUTURE
Strategies for Changing Dominant Paradigms

A new awareness of the role paradigms play in shaping perceptions should give courage to all those who function from nondominant paradigms and have been silenced by old paradigm positivism. Instead of looking through our paradigmatic filters, we have begun to look at the filters, the assumptions upon which our paradigms are organized.

Jane Fried

Fried, J. (1994). In groups, out groups, paradigms, and perceptions. In J. Fried (Ed.), *different voices: Gender and perspective in student affairs administration* (pp. 30–45). Washington DC: National Association of Student Personnel Administrators. (quote from page 40).

15

The Campus Women's Center as Classroom
A Model for Thinking and Action

Jennifer R. Wies

Abstract: *Grounded in women's movements focusing on political activism, Women's Centers located within colleges and universities simultaneously seek to educate and further actions seeking gender equity. However, the body of literature focusing on the work of Women's Centers often overemphasizes the activist component of Women's Centers, thereby overshadowing their commitment to education and learning. The Campus Women's Center as Classroom is a model for advancing the work of these units by fully articulating their mission to simultaneously and dialectically inspire education and activism. Using the example of the Xavier University Women's Center, the Women's Center as Classroom model is described, as well as the development of a program evaluation instrument designed to capture outcomes according to resource provision, learning, and research.*

THE CAMPUS WOMEN'S CENTER was born of women's movements around the globe seeking gender equity in the private and public spheres. In the effort to advance women and create a gender equitable world, Women's Centers simultaneously seek to educate and further action toward those goals. This chapter investigates how Women's Centers have been addressed in the peer-reviewed literature and the ways scholars and practitioners have theorized Women's Centers' work as both educational and action-oriented. A review of the scholarship illustrates that the Women's Center scholarship often overemphasizes the activist component of

Women's Centers, thereby overshadowing their commitment to education and learning. Thus, the challenge for Women's Centers is to substantiate their work in a model that simultaneously and dialectically inspires education and activism, a model posited here as the "Campus Women's Center as Classroom."

WOMEN'S MOVEMENTS

Beginning in the 1920s and continuing through the 1960s, a number of demographic and social trends emerged that contributed to the transformation of life for American women. During this period, women increasingly participated in work outside the home, gradually increased attendance in higher education, experienced an era of sexual freedom, increased control over their bodies' fertility, and won the right to vote (Ferree & Hess, 1995). However, these "advancements" did not alleviate gender inequality. Women worked in the public domain but still earned a lower wage, participated in higher education but were unable to equally pursue the same career goals as men, and were voted in to office but struggled with significantly influencing government. Women's experiences during this era provided the framework and living examples of inequality and unfairness based on gender. At the same time, they opened the door for a segment of social movement actors to demand change and new opportunities.

Feminist social movements have followed different trajectories from other social movements by asserting models focused on "organizing community" that embrace heterogeneous actors in both the private and public spheres (Lamphere, 1997; Stall & Stoecker, 1998). Women's movements, in their diversity, have confronted numerous issues worldwide, including civic participation among underrepresented racial populations (Goode, 2001; Goode & Schneider, 1994), activism among people in middle-class and working-class socioeconomic statuses (Hall, 2004; Nash, 2001; Weinbaum, 2001), welfare rights and/or welfare reform (Povinelli, 1991), environmental rights (O'Neil, Elias, & Yassi, 1998), access to health care and health care rights (Anglin, 1997; Kaufert, 1998; Susser, 2005), and reproductive control (Ginsburg, 1989; Glenn, Chang, & Forcey, 1994; Inhorn, 2003; Kanaaneh, 2002; Lopez, 1998; Luttrell, 2003; Rapp, 1999). Special attention has been paid to the unique struggles, needs, and activism among immigrant women (Nash, 2001), Asian American women (Abraham, 1995; Benson, 1994), Latina women (Zavella, 1991), and women of various sexualities (Jenness & Broad,

1994; Taylor & Rupp, 1998). Within these movements, campus Women's Centers emerged at colleges and universities in the United States in response to the coeducational movement.

CAMPUS WOMEN'S CENTERS

The first documented campus Women's Center was established at the University of Minnesota in 1948. Women's Centers now exist at more than 400 higher education institutions in the United States (Davie, 2002). Women's Centers are seemingly infinitely diverse; however, "Despite their diversity, women's centers share many commonalities; they generally advocate institutional and individual change to improve women's position, status, and training in academia" (Kunkel, 1994, pp. 21–22).

The history of campus Women's Centers is formally and informally documented in the personal oral histories of those women who organized to open Women's Centers, in plays and poems about the experiences of women in higher education, through the creation of websites, and multiple other venues. Interestingly, Women's Centers are noticeably absent in peer-reviewed literature across disciplines, as only a handful of journal articles and texts focus on Women's Centers as the center of investigation. However, one can broadly categorize the pieces that do exist as attending to the following themes: the structure of Women's Centers challenges and struggles Women's Centers face, and Women's Centers action/activist practices .

The literature concerning campus Women's Centers begins amid the bodies of knowledge describing the challenges women in the academy face and the parallel challenges in opening and establishing a place/space to center on women. For the past three decades, the literature has described the processes of establishing Women's Centers in the early 1970s and the struggles surrounding their emergence (Farley, 2005; Girard, 1978; TenElshof & Searle, 1974). More recent pieces describe contemporary strategies for opening Women's Centers, amid the closure of decades-old Women's Centers (Guy-Sheftall & Wallace-Sanders, 2002; Kunkel, 2002). Furthermore, a great deal of the Women's Centers literature addresses the topic of organizational structures and functions (Bertelson, 1975; Borland, 1976; Buckley & Heatherington, 1988; Clevenger, 1988; Kasper, 2004a, 2004b; Kowalski-Braun & Underwood, 2005; Kunkel, 1994; Lonnquist & Reesor, 1987; Sweeney, 1978; TenElshof & Searle, 1974). These pieces illustrate the vast heterogeneity among Women's Centers, including reporting lines, previous experiences of staff and leaders, and missions and objectives. In addition, structural nuances reflect the dedication of Women's Centers leaders' commitment to ascertaining the needs of their constituents when developing their missions and programming by conducting needs assessments of their campuses (Kunkel, 1994) and the needs of Women's Centers nationwide (Sweeney, 1978).

The struggles and challenges that Women's Centers face is another predominant theme in the available literature. For example, the struggle to maintain adequate levels of funding and/or sponsorship for campus Women's Centers is a significant area of emphasis for scholars and practitioners (Kasper, 2004b), as are the challenges associated with reliance on soft monies, that is, state/federal/private granting agencies (Lockwood, 2005). In addition to inadequate resources, a challenge often discussed is Women's Centers having to overcome stereotypical perceptions of militant, unfriendly activists to establish credibility. This includes negotiating the millennium generation's negative or apathetic attitudes toward feminism (Kasper, 2004b), which may in turn explain reports of poor attendance trends at Women's Center events (Kasper, 2004b). Stereotypical imaginings of Women's Centers, their staff, and their purpose also contribute to the increased likelihood that Women's Centers face unsupportive administrative structures (Kasper, 2004b), an issue discussed in the literature describing strategies for opening Women's Centers.

Interestingly, the third predominant theme in the body of literature addressing Women's Centers emphasizes action and activism conducted at, and through, campus Women's Centers (see Susan Marine's chapter 2 of this book). Women's Centers have often led the proactive and reactive efforts to reach gender equity on college campuses by responding to any number of issues that disproportionately affect women in American society. Significantly, Women's Centers have led campus cultures to recognize and address the persistence of sexual harassment and intimate partner violence among the women in a campus community (Childers, 2002; Firestein, 2002a; Lisker, 2002b; also see Lindsay Orchowski et al. in chapter 17). Programming initiatives also include an emphasis on overcoming societal discriminations within the academy and society at large by targeting outreach efforts to vulnerable and/or underrepresented populations, such as Black and Latina students (Buford, 1988; DiLapi & Gay, 2002), lesbian and bisexual women (Firestein, 2002c), nontraditional students (Firestein, 2002b), female institutional administrators (Mellow, 1988), and women in mathematics and computer science (Miller, 2002).

Grounding their action in a model of collaboration with various constituents has long been a significant aim of Women's Centers. These collaborations often include partnerships with women's studies departments (Brooks, Chapman, & McMartin, 2002; Girard, 1977; Kowalski-Braun & Underwood, 2005). In addition, many Women's Centers have sought innovative partnerships to expand their program offerings, such as outdoor recreation departments (Upton, 2005) and seemingly unlikely departments such as athletics (Lisker, 2002a), to expand their sphere of influence. Other collaborations have sought to engage communities beyond the university by offering resource and referral provision through the service of Women's Center volunteers (Lockwood, 2005), writing collectives comprising diverse women (Valenzuela, 2005), and creative entertainment, such as theater performances (Parker, 2005).

THINKING AND ACTION: THE CAMPUS WOMEN'S CENTER AS CLASSROOM

Women's Centers continue to emerge on college and university campuses both because of, but also in spite of, the numerous measures the academy has instituted to achieve gender equity for students, faculty members, and employees in higher education. However, as this literature review suggests, the educational foundation that Women's Centers rest upon is all too often overshadowed by the successes and failures with the "action" portion of their missions. Decades of history have emphasized the actions taken by and supported by Women's Centers, such as organizing students against intimate partner violence (Orchowski et al. chapter 17), creating women-centered or women only programming, and lobbying for pay equity for faculty and employees.

Despite the creation of Standards and Guidelines for Women Student Programs and Services endorsed by the Council for the Advancement of Standards in Higher Education (Bethman, Plummer, & Rietveld, 2006), literature articulating the *learning* outcomes of Women's Centers is noticeably absent. As demonstrated by the literature review, Women's Centers seemingly focus solely on programs and actions, not on education and learning. Women's Centers that do emphasize education and/or research are silent in the literature concerning these unique departments on college and university campuses.

Scholars and practitioners have, thus, positioned Women's Centers within an educational model or an activist model, and rarely have successes been demonstrated in accomplishing a merged model that combines the two. One

could hypothesize that the overemphasis on activism is a reaction to underfunded and underresourced Women's Centers seeking to substantiate the quantity of activities in an effort to argue additional resources. However, as witnessed by the contemporary pieces that indicate resource shortages are a significant barrier to success for many Women's Centers (Kasper, 2004a, 2004b), this strategy has yielded limited success of combining the two models in one center.

Furthermore, by constructing Women's Centers as oppositional within a binary system of either educational or activist orientation, there is a potential to fail in implementing the fullest extent of the overarching goal: uniting education and activism to advance women and thereby all people. Thus, this chapter proposes a model wherein Women's Centers as Classrooms are conceptualized as successfully functioning as both centers of education and activism.

A brief piece in NWSAction from the Fall of 2005 situates this model. In her piece "Witness/Praise for Campus Women's Centers," Arcana (2005) considered the relationship between education and activism in Women's Centers,

> Campus women's centers are among the few deliberately constructed connections between thinking and action inside the academy. They remind us that women's . . . scholarship can live in the university only because of women's ongoing struggle for liberation—because of women's actions. (p. 4)

The key words to highlight in Arcana's manifesto are "thinking and action." Women's Centers exist within institutions of higher education because they are first and foremost sites of knowledge acquisition, exploration, and experimentation. The "thinking" component translates into education, which integrates campus Women's Centers into the fabric of the institution. The action component speaks to the activism and activities of Women's Centers further on campuses. To operationalize the "deliberately constructed connections between thinking and action," Women's Centers must not only create initiatives that specifically advance education and further action but also collect data demonstrating their effectiveness.

Thus, the challenge for Women's Centers seeking to advance women professionally and personally, through higher education, is establishing a Women's Center that is both educational and action-oriented. In addition to implementing this model, Women's Centers are also compelled to adequately measure the outcomes of the model to engage in a constant process of evaluation and dissemination of results to the university and/or larger community. To illustrate the operationalization of the Women's Center as Classroom model that the Xavier University Women's Center utilizes, this chapter turns to examples of initiatives implemented that align with an educational mission. In addition, the strategies the Xavier University Women's Center used to conduct a comprehensive program evaluation that captures information pertaining to resource provision and learning outcomes of the initiatives are presented.

XAVIER UNIVERSITY WOMEN'S CENTER: A MODEL FOR THINKING AND ACTION

In 1969, Xavier University, a Jesuit Catholic university in Cincinnati, Ohio, welcomed women students into the full-time, day student population. Women had been present on campus for many years as part-time students and students in the evening and weekend schools. Subsequent to the arrival of women at Xavier, an organization was founded to support women students and seek avenues to promote gender equality. Breen Lodge, Xavier University's first Educational Resource and Women's Center, was opened in 1970 to serve the needs of women students by providing support, programming, and, according to archival material, to serve as a badly needed and identifiable resource center for

women's activities at Xavier. The center's activities included a weekly radio show, speakers program, student–faculty discussion series, courses, a reentry program, a library, drop-in center, symposia, and workshops. In 1980, Breen Lodge was closed to accommodate the growing need for faculty offices. The administrative decision was made despite protests from students, faculty, staff, alumnae, and community members.

Petitions for its return ensued for decades, reaching a zenith in the spring of 2005, when the provost/academic vice president was presented with a proposal for a new women's center. It was accompanied by letters of support from faculty members, staff members, and student organizational leaders, as well as the signatures of more than 500 students. The efforts to invigorate the campus with a new Women's Center were truly a collaborative effort on behalf of Xavier University students, faculty, staff, alumnae, and friends in the community.

However, opening a Women's Center in the new millennium begs the question, "Is there a need for a Women's Center and what will its purpose be?" As the numbers of women students and employees have multiplied, Xavier University has made noteworthy strides in seeking to ensure their equal educational and employment opportunity. Nevertheless, according to a report issued by the Xavier University Women's Center Committee (2006), many barriers to equity remain. Women comprise 47% of the full-time faculty, but only 26% of full-time professors. While they represent 57% of full-time nonfaculty employees, they hold only 25% of the top administrative positions and remain vastly overrepresented in several of the lowest paying and hourly job groups. Furthermore, women students are disproportionately concentrated in the fields of nursing, education, and social work.

While the Xavier University Women's Center confronts many, if not all, of the challenges mentioned in the Women's Centers literature, the emphasis on education and advancing learning opportunities for all members of the university community has proven successful. Contrary to Kasper's (2004a) conclusion that the "most difficult struggles for campus-based women's centers . . . involve the apathy of students, the notion that special attention to women's issues isn't 'necessary' anymore" (p. 197), the Xavier University Women's Center begins with the idea that learning and education is an ongoing, lifelong process, and thus the Women's Center is useful, necessary, and legitimized because the Women's Center plays a vital role in furthering knowledge acquisition and critical thinking among the members of the campus community and beyond (Kasper, 2004a). The development of three mission areas (resources, learning, and research) deliberately aligns with the educational missions of institutions of higher education. The following examples illustrate this commitment and establish the mechanisms for measuring outcomes.

Providing Resources

The Xavier University Women's Center follows the tradition of campus Women's Centers by providing resources and advocacy for a seemingly limitless array of issues, questions, and needs for the campus community. The Women's Center provides information and access to vital resources that enhance and advance the success of the Xavier University community. The Women's Center staff provides resources directly to individuals and groups, as well as providing referrals to other campus and community departments and agencies to support individual needs. Primarily, two areas of resource provision are emphasized. The first is broadly conceptualized as personal wellness assistance and advocacy. To this end, the Xavier University Women's Center provides information, support, and referrals related to intimate partner violence; assistance and referrals for life/work issues; referrals to campus and community-based mental and physical health professionals; and other need-based services.

The second area of resource provision is defined as academic advocacy. This area is unique to the campus setting in that the majority population consists of full- and part-time students. Services provided range from assisting students and employees with resume writing and review (in collaboration with the campus career center); discussions, groups, and retreats focusing on future goals for vocations and/or graduate schools; and advancing people professionally by examining degree and nondegree education options to further educational attainment (particularly among nonexempt university workers). These individual-level services are, in addition to providing cocurricular opportunities, to expand classroom learning into the community.

Advancing Learning

The Xavier University Women's Center emphasizes education and advancing learning opportunities for all members of the university community. Beginning with the belief that learning and education is an ongoing, lifelong process, the Women's Center plays a vital role in furthering knowledge acquisition and critical thinking among the members of the campus community and beyond. Immediately upon opening, a brown bag lunch series was initiated, called *(thinking) outside the (lunch) BOX*. The play on words is consistent with the mission to challenge people to critically examine their assumptions about inequities locally and globally. The gatherings bring together a diverse audience in an informal atmosphere to investigate a wide range of topics, including gendered political participation in Norway, research on scales to measure transphobia, and stories of breast cancer survivorship. The goal is to expose individuals to new bodies of research, programs, practices, and policies in the United States and beyond that center on the situations of women, girls, and/or gender.

In addition to this initiative, the Women's Center developed a highly selective internship program for students. Through the Women's Center Internship Program, undergraduate and graduate students from the campus community have the opportunity to explore four "tracks" simultaneously, as well as the option to focus on one of the following areas in depth. The Community Leadership and Administration track offers students the opportunity to learn the many facets of creating and maintaining a women-centered organization within a university setting by observing and assisting in the day-to-day operations of the organization and participating in strategic planning, funding issues, relationship building, and a broad array of responsibilities. In the Research track, students explore the center's research agendas, other scholars' research agendas, and participate actively as research assistants with the Women's Center and its partners. As Program Development interns, students take active roles in developing the program themes, recruiting presenters, researching background information, and participating in the program. Furthermore, interns focusing on programming are challenged to provide evidence-based research to support program proposals. The fourth track is Advocacy, where students learn about the theories and methods of advocating for people seeking support, resources, and referrals. Students become familiar with the resources the Women's Center relies upon to provide the services and support to individuals in the Xavier University community and learn about the university, local, state, and federal laws and policies related to advocacy.

The internship program is designed to foster an independent research or practice agenda for students to pursue throughout their time with the Women's Center. Each student completes the internship program with a "deliverable," which may include a manuscript suitable for publication submission, a technical report, a creative contribution (such as a photography exhibit), or a portfolio of accomplishments. Requirements include the completion of a learning agreement, a minimum number of hours at the Women's Center, and active participation in a weekly internship team meeting. Team meetings provide an opportunity for dialogue around each person's projects and allow the team to trou-

bleshoot any issues that arise at the Women's Center. These meetings have proven to be an amazingly valuable component of the Internship Program, as the team gathers together over snacks to engage in collaborative learning and critical thinking.

Promoting Research

The third primary function area is that of furthering research centering on women, girls, and gender. This area exemplifies a deliberate commitment to supporting and advancing learning in the institution. This area includes consultations with professors to enhance course content with regard to women, girls, and gender. Furthermore, the Women's Center supports student research explorations of topics that center on women, girls, and/or gender through mentorship and the availability of grants to support student research presentations at national, regional, and local conferences. In addition, the Women's Center pursues research that focuses on women, girls, and gender to establish the unit and the staff as equal partners in the academic community of scholars. This initiative has been essential to garnering faculty partners in the pursuit of university, local, state, and national research and practice grants.

MEASURING OUTCOMES, ESTABLISHING SUCCESSES

Evaluating the work of Women's Centers has long been a challenge and one that is unique and specific to each campus as a result of the variety of missions, charges, and institutional positionalities of Women's Centers (Goldsmith, 2002). However, theorizing Women's Centers, that is, "thinking" of them, their mission, and the subsequent actions taken must be translated into instruments designed to measure outcomes. To that end, instrument development is a unique process for every Women's Center as the instrument should specifically query a community based on the mission, vision, and philosophy of the Women's Center. Building upon the example presented here, the goal of the Xavier University Women's Center instrument was creating a program evaluation instrument that assessed the unit's role as a resource unit, an educational site, and a research station at the institution. The instrument was designed to be simultaneously a data collection instrument and an instrument to educate the campus community and beyond about the broad visions a Women's Center can posit. Thus, the instrument itself was an avenue for distributing information about the Women's Center and its goals. A female employee respondent nicely summarized this point:

> Looking at the questions above it seems like they offer a lot more services than I thought. I kind of thought it was only a support center for women who have been raped or sexually assaulted or something.

The process of developing a program evaluation instrument is translating thinking into action and ensuring measurement of both the educational outcomes and actions supported by the Women's Center. Furthermore, the development of a program evaluation instrument is political in that a body of leaders selects best practices, guidelines, and/or standards to draw upon for their data collection. The presence or absence of some guidelines and not others, for example, may reflect larger philosophical positionalities at a Women's Center.

The Xavier University Women's Center Program Evaluation (XUWCPE) is a mixed qualitative and quantitative instrument that utilizes Women Student Programs and Services from the Council for the Advancement of Standards in Higher Education Standards and Guidelines, nonprofit organization, program evaluation questions, and teaching evaluations. By combining these guidelines that transcend discipline allegiance and focus on education and learning

through action, the Women's Center demonstrated to the campus community a commitment to the Women's Center as Classroom model.

The XUWCPE includes questions created from the learning outcomes identified by the Council for the Advancement of Standards in Higher Education (CAS) (Bethman et al., 2006). The council has identified areas of learning specifically for students who interact with Women Student Programs and Services. In the introduction to the standards descriptions, the purpose of Women Student Programs and Services is articulated as promoting a "supportive, equitable, and safe environment for women" and that Women Student Programs "must enhance the overall educational experiences" while focusing primarily on the education of students (Bethman et al., 2006, p. 340). The Xavier University Women's Center demonstrates that Women Student Programs can be an educational experience that overlaps with classroom curricula in a model of integrated and holistic learning. This philosophy is noticeable in the questions selected from the outcomes identified in the CAS Standards and Guidelines, as questions pertaining to learning and development were offered to faculty, staff, and community members in addition to students.

Thus, questions were developed that ascertained self-assessment from diverse constituents in the following areas: intellectual growth, effective communication, enhanced self-esteem, realistic self-appraisal, clarified values, career choices, leadership development, healthy behaviors, meaningful interpersonal relationships, independence, collaboration, social responsibility, satisfying and productive lifestyles, appreciating diversity, spiritual awareness, and personal and educational goals.

The second set of instruments selected to evaluate the educational outcomes at the Xavier University Women's Center were standard classroom and professor course evaluations. The goals of this strategy are twofold. First, it situates the activities, programs, and events operated by the Women's Center as designed to advance learning. Specifically posing questions about how the content is delivered and rating intellectual stimulation are expected on course evaluations. Including these questions in the XUWCPE challenged the assumptions that Women's Centers are solely sites of service and resource distribution or units devoted to collecting data. Querying the community about their learning outcomes using these questions challenged the community's assumptions about what to expect from a Women's Center and compelled them to situate the work of the Xavier University Women's Center within a system of integrated, seamless learning for multiple populations.

The third area of program evaluation explored in the development of the XUWCPE was nonprofit organization evaluations, particularly with regard to service provision. Questions were asked about the atmosphere of the Women's Center, the responsiveness of the staff, the appropriateness of services provided, and the expertise with which services were delivered.

METHODS

The XUWCPE was developed to assess the learning outcomes of four primary populations: Xavier University students, Xavier University faculty members, Xavier University employees (including administrators, support staff, managers, etc.), and a broad category of "community members" that includes Xavier University alumnae, members of advisory groups to the university's administration, and local community members. The program evaluation was initially distributed to 1,935 faculty and employees, 6,447 students, and an additional 40 community partners and targeted alumnae, bringing the total number distributed to 8,442. A total of 654 responses were collected for a response rate of 7.7%. The percentage of respondents according to population are as follows: full-time students, 51.4%; part-time students, 15.4%; faculty, 9%; employees,

23%; and other (alumnae and community members), 1.2%.

Outcomes Data

The case descriptions of mechanisms to unite an educational model and activist model of Women's Centers are supported by quantitative and qualitative data collected in the course of a comprehensive program evaluation. The results of the XUWCPE demonstrate (with both quantitative and qualitative effectiveness) that Women's Centers can not only be centers for both thinking and action but also substantiate their outcomes according to a body of literature used in the academy.

Types of Support and Resources

The data illustrate that the campus community was satisfied with the types, delivery, and follow-up of resources the Women's Center provides. Overall, the results indicate that 9.3% of respondents sought services, support, and/or resources during the 2007–2008 academic year. The largest percentage of respondents indicated that they sought "Other" academic assistance, including "help with reentry after studying abroad," "course-related event support," "partnership to provide an academic and vocational retreat for honors students," and "assistance and advice for a student organization." The second largest area of resources sought fell under the "Leadership advancement mentorship and advising" category (18%), followed by "Career mentorship/advising" (11.5%).

Not surprisingly, the largest percentage of respondents indicated that they sought resources for sexual assault and/or rape under Personal Wellness Assistance and Advocacy at 19.7%. Sexual harassment was the next highest self-reported issue (16.4%), followed by physical assault and/or domestic violence (13.1%), workplace equity issues (13.1%), and mental/emotional health (13.1%).

Evaluation of Services, Support, and Resources

The data illustrate the effectiveness of the Women's Center in encouraging individuals to seek resources. In the data pertaining to the Evaluation of Services, Support, and Resources, respondents were asked to react to several statements and measure their satisfaction using a Likert Scale, with 1 equaling *strong disagreement* and 5 corresponding to *strong agreement* with the statement. All evaluation measures were averaged and the range of average responses fell between 4.2 and 4.6. The highest average response rating was in response to asking a respondent's agreement with the statement, "The Services, Support, and Resources provided through the Women's Center were delivered by knowledgeable individuals." The strength of the positive evaluation of services, support, and resources is validated by the increase in the quantity of resource provision encounters from the fall semester to the spring semester, where the number of people seeking support more than doubled.

Combined, both sets of data demonstrate the effectiveness of the resource provision area of the Xavier University Women's Center. By broadly defining resource provision, the instrument was able to ascertain not only the percentage of respondents who sought the Women's Center for victimization resources but also pertinent work/life issues such as breastfeeding and/or academic-related support such as mentoring students considering graduate school education. Furthermore, evaluating satisfaction using questions from commonly found nonprofit and social service organizations allows the Women's Center to describe the story of the strength and power of providing resources to women and men across the campus community and beyond. For example, a rating of 4.3 for "included adequate follow-up" could imply that there was effectiveness regarding the number of hours on the phone and in meetings to ensure that a person was cared for

long after the initial contact or request with the Women's Center.

The qualitative data yield corresponding results. One full-time student (female) responded to the question asking respondents to indicate the least useful resource or service of the Women's Center by stating,

> I really feel like all of the services are important. It is very situational, and I applaud your efforts to serve a variety of needs. In fact, I wish I had known more about this and taken advantage of it while I had the chance.

This quote captures respondents' feelings of the value of a women's center and its services. Respondents were particularly appreciative of the varying needs of the campus community as this quote illustrates. Qualitative responses regarding resource provision were fewer than those pertaining to education; however, a female employee summarized her reaction to the types and quality of resources provided by saying, "I especially like the mission as a centering place for women—a place where women and men can come together to support and empower women."

Educational Initiatives

Presenting information pertaining to resource provision must also be paired with outcomes data related to learning. Linking the Women's Center's activities to learning outcomes substantiates its role in an academic institution. This set of data began by showing the average percent of participants at the Women's Center signature initiatives and additional one-time or recurring initiatives. The most attended initiatives include (1) *thinking outside the (lunch)BOX*, referred to as a Brown Bag Lunch Session (34.7%), participation in the city's annual Take Back the Night March and Rally (29.7%), and a presentation delivered by the director entitled "Gender and Leadership" (16.1%). The quantitative data are supported by qualitative responses such as,

"The most important educational initiatives the Women's Center offers are one-on-one mentoring, followed-up with fitting events, such as an invitation to a brown-bag that fits students' interests." Internally collected data at the Women's Center indicate that a total number of 1,004 people attended educational initiatives sponsored by the Women's Center during the 2007 and 2008 academic year.

But what did the participants learn? How were learning outcomes measured? The CAS Standards and Guidelines for Women Student Programs (Bethman et al., 2006) and course/professor evaluations provided guidance. The measurement of learning outcomes is very similar to the scale used to understand satisfaction with resource provision. Thus, the instrument itself conveys an emphasis on both resource provision and learning, uniting the activist model and the education model.

Evaluation of Educational Initiatives

Data measuring the learning outcomes from educational initiatives were also telling. Average responses range from 3.2 for "developed a deeper awareness of my spirituality" to 4.5 for "created an opportunity for people's voices to be heard." The majority of average responses hold ratings above 4.0, meaning respondents generally "agreed" that the prompt described their learning outcomes as a result of participating in a Women's Center educational initiative. Prompts that earned less than a 4.0 rating are thus areas for improvement and additional collaboration.

The qualitative data yield rich reflections about the educational initiatives offered by the Women's Center. Many people commented on the brown bag lunch series offered. A full-time male student offered this statement: "The brown bags occasioned a rarely seen interaction of students (across gender), faculty, staff (across classification levels) and community members." In a similar fashion, a female student said the lunch series offered "the chance for people across the

University (staff, faculty, students, etc.) to come together in one space and exchange ideas, hopes, concerns, etc." In addition, an employee recognized the goal of constantly creating educational opportunities in all aspects of the initiatives by saying, "The Women's Center's best work is in pulling people into these initiatives, not only through participation, but also through actively helping plan them."

The richness of the educational initiatives evaluation substantiates the Women's Center's role within the overall educational institution. A key indicator, prompted as "stimulated my intellectual growth," earned a rating of 4.3. By linking the Women's Center's activities to these measures, the Xavier University Women's Center is able to transcend stereotypical assumptions that Women's Centers are solely sites of activism. Using these data the Women's Center can articulate that its actions are a result of a deepened understanding of gender and diversity theories, and that furthering the community's understanding of issues related to gender and diversity inspires action. Thus, the data demonstrate the dialectical nature of thinking and action and successfully unite activism and educational models.

Research Assistance

However, an additional area of emphasis is that of promoting research on women, girls, and gender. This area is more difficult to measure in a program evaluation; however, data were collected to understand how many respondents sought assistance related to research. The majority of respondents sought "information regarding conference opportunities." This might include assistance in identifying an appropriate conference to present a research paper; assistance in locating funds to attend a local, regional, or national conference; or mentorship during abstract preparation and submission.

Qualitative responses also provide evidence to substantiate the emphasis on research. A full-time student who had sought research assistance at the Women's Center said, "The staff are incredibly knowledgeable and can help you find the resources or information that you are looking for, especially when you have no idea where to begin. It is a great place to begin any project." Often, assistance seekers indicate that they were referred to the Women's Center by another student who had a positive experience. Thus, these endorsements provide the voices and stories of the Women's Center's constituents, which can then share with a broader public. As a female full-time student concluded in her assessment of the Women's Center, its strengths lie in its "ability to collaborate with constituencies across the university [and] provide information about relevant research and advisement about research projects about women, girls, and gender."

Identifying research as a key emphasis area also expands the Women's Center as Classroom model that merges education and action. Conducting and exploring research requires both thinking and action, the creation of a research protocol and the subsequent actions to implement the project. Engaging students in research agendas is a particularly powerful mechanism for demonstrating the relationship between education and activism, particularly when grounded in participatory research methods that require active collaboration with local communities.

Thus, the Women's Center as Classroom model is completed with the inclusion of a research emphasis and data, demonstrating that people use the Women's Center for that purpose. In addition, a female student respondent indicated her satisfaction with the combined education and action mission, stating, "I appreciate that it combines academic support, personal support and educational programming." Similarly, a female employee shared the following reflection about the positive effect of a campus Women's Center,

> It spreads knowledge, which empowers. Sometimes people just don't know what opportunities are out there, and no one steps up to tell them, even if

they ask. The staff at the Women's Center not only answers your questions, but they follow-up with you and make sure you have found what you are looking for—and more.

The female employee who succinctly summarized the power of a Women's Center does so by spreading knowledge. Women's Centers must honor the desires of their constituents to model and mentor them by weaving learning and activism into a seamless framework that furthers social justice.

CONCLUSION

Women's Centers continue to be challenged by various obstacles, from stereotypical biases to resource shortages. Decades of literature outlining the seemingly insurmountable barriers to daily operations have yielded rich historical accounts of the women's movement on campus, focusing primarily on activism. However, the shortage of literature discussing learning or placing Women's Centers within an educational framework poses a new challenge for Women's Centers, that is, centering the work as vital to the campus learning environment while providing the necessary support services that distinguish Women's Centers from other campus units.

The Women's Center as Classroom model places the campus Women's Center at the nexus of education and activism, of thinking and action. The model requires Women's Centers to consider the possible learning outcomes when providing resources and developing initiatives. Furthermore, the model compels individuals and communities to take action as a result of their knowledge acquisition. Action may be translated in various ways, including the creation of a new programming initiative, organizing a campus or community rally or awareness event, the pursuit of a volunteer opportunity, or the development of a research agenda.

Amid a society that continues to perpetuate gender inequities in numerous spheres, the campus Women's Center continues to be of value to the college or university and beyond. However, translating the value into measures that are commonly used to evaluate campus units has been a struggle for Women's Centers. Developing deliberate instruments designed to capture the intersection of education and action provides a mechanism for articulating the multiple positive outcomes constituents experience as a result of Women's Centers. The results of such an instrument can liberate Women's Center leaders from focusing on challenges and barriers to a focus on the necessity of Women's Centers for all members of a community: an important step for the future of Women's Centers.

Thus, the Women's Center as Classroom model is also a call to reinvigorate the body of scholarship focusing on Women's Centers to accurately portray the variety of work conducted through Women's Centers paired with evaluative data demonstrating positive outcomes. By committing to this call to action, Women's Center leaders acquire the leverage they need to garner additional resources by focusing on the successes. A body of scholarship testifying to the resource provision outcomes, learning outcomes, and research outcomes is possibly the missing piece of an argument to advance the work of Women's Centers in an era of increased scrutiny of nonacademic student programs. When advancing the Women's Center agenda, the data illustrate that with additional resources, stronger and more robust resource provision and learning outcomes may be attainable.

The detailed example presented in this piece stimulates the movement to situate Women's Centers as essential to campus culture now and in the future. Using qualitative responses such as "[The Women's Center has] made it clear that everyone can come to it, men and women, those who need support and those giving support" presents the narrative of the work of one Women's Center that, when combined with quantitative data, situates the campus Women's Center within an integrated learning community. By connect-ing the Women's Center's initiatives to the academic and learning goals of the institution, the mission directly connects to the overall objectives of the university and the pursuit of social justice.

REFERENCES

Abraham, M. (1995). Ethnicity, gender, and marital violence: South Asian women's organizations in the United States. *Gender & Society, 9*(4), 450–468.

Anglin, M. (1997). Working from the inside out: Implications of breast cancer activism for biomedical policies and practices. *Social Science and Medicine, 44*(9), 1403–1415.

Arcana, J. (2005). Witness/Praise for Campus Women's Centers. *NWS Action*, Vol. 17. No 1. (pp. 14). http://www.iiav.nl/ezines/email/NWSAction/2005/No1.pdf

Benson, J. E. (1994). The effects of packinghouse work on southeast Asian refugee families. In L. Lamphere, G. Grenier, & A. Stepick (Eds.), *Newcomers in the workplace: Immigrants and the restructuring of the U. S. economy* (pp. 99–128). Philadelphia, PA: Temple University Press.

Bertelson, J. (1975). *Women's centers: Where are they?* Washington, DC: Project on the Status and Education of Women.

Bethman, B., Plummer, E., & Rietveld, B. (2006). Women student programs and services. In L. Dean (Ed.), *CAS professional standards for higher education* (6th ed.). Washington, DC: Council for the Advancement of Standards in Higher Education.

Borland, D. T. (1976, April 13). *Organizational development and goals: A consultant's view of women's centers.* Paper presented at the American Personnel and Guidance Association/American College Personnel Association, Chicago, IL.

Brooks, K. H., Chapman, S. C., & McMartin, F. (2002). Women's centers and women's studies: The case for coexistence and beyond. In S. L. Davie (Ed.), *University and college women's centers: A journey toward equity* (pp. 365–370). Westport, CT: Greenwood Press.

Buckley, S., & Heatherington, C. (1988). Diversity and success: The University of Iowa women's resource and action center. *Initiatives, 51,* 23–30.

Buford, C. (1988). Multicultural programming in a university women's center. *Initiatives, 51,* 31–35.

Childers, M. (2002). The response to sexual harassment claims in one women's resource center. In

S. L. Davie (Ed.), *University and college women's centers: A journey toward equity* (pp. 317–331). Westport, CT: Greenwood Press.

Clevenger, B. M. (1988). Women's centers on campus: A profile. *Initiatives, 51,* 3–9.

Davie, S. L. (2002). How women's centers shape our journey: Transformation, education, leadership. In S. L. Davie (Ed.), *University and college women's centers: A journey toward equity* (pp. 19–46). Westport, CT: Greenwood Press.

DiLapi, E. M., & Gay, G. M. (2002). Women's centers responding to racism. In S. L. Davie (Ed.), *University and college women's centers: A journey toward equity* (pp. 203–226). Westport, CT: Greenwood Press.

Farley, P. T. (2005). Establishing a women's center in the mid-1970s. *NWSAction, 12*(1), 50–51.

Ferree, M. M., & Hess, B. B. (1995). *Controversy and coalition: The new feminist movement across three decades of change.* New York: Twayne Publishers.

Firestein, B. A. (2002a). Empowering ourselves and each other: Counseling services for women at the college and university women's center. In S. L. Davie (Ed.), *University and college women's centers: A journey toward equity* (pp. 259–303). Westport, CT: Greenwood Press.

Firestein, B. A. (2002b). The new face of the academy: Women's centers and the nontraditional woman student. In S. L. Davie (Ed.), *University and college women's centers: A journey toward equity* (pp. 333–362). Westport, CT: Greenwood Press.

Firestein, B. A. (2002c). Out of the closet and into the center: Women's centers serve lesbians and bisexual women. In S. L. Davie (Ed.), *University and college women's centers: A journey toward equity* (pp. 227–255). Westport, CT: Greenwood Press.

Ginsburg, F. (1989). *Contested lives: The abortion debate in an American community.* Berkeley, CA: University of California Press.

Girard, K. (1977, January). *Campus based women's centers.* (ERIC Document Reproduction Service No. ED171170).

Girard, K. L. (1978). *Developing women's program.* (ERIC Document Reproduction Service No. ED172444).

Glenn, E. N., Chang, G., & Forcey, L. R. (Eds.). (1994). *Mothering: Ideology, experience, and agency.* New York: Routledge.

Goldsmith, D. J. (2002). How do we know how well we're doing? Evaluating women's centers. In S. L. Davie (Ed.), *University and college women's centers: A journey toward equity* (pp. 113–129). Westport, CT: Greenwood Press.

Goode, J. (2001). Let's get our act together: How racial discourses disrupt neighborhood activism. In J. Goode & J. Maskovsky (Eds.), *The new poverty studies: The ethnography of power, politics, and impoverished people in the United States* (pp. 364–398). New York: New York University Press.

Goode, J., & Schneider, J. A. (1994). *Reshaping ethnic and racial relations in Philadelphia: Immigrants in a divided city.* Philadelphia, PA: Temple University Press.

Guy-Sheftall, B., & Wallace-Sanders, K. (2002). Building a women's center at Spelman College. In S. L. Davie (Ed.), *University and college women's centers: A journey toward equity* (pp. 79–89). Westport, CT: Greenwood Press.

Hall, J. (2004). It hurts to be a girl: Growing up poor, white, and female. In L. D. Baker (Ed.), *Life in America: Identity and everyday experience* (pp. 329–338). Malden, MA: Blackwell Publishers.

Inhorn, M. C. (2003). *Local babies, global science: Gender, religion, and in vitro fertilization in Egypt.* New York: Routledge.

Jenness, V., & Broad, K. (1994). Antiviolence activism and the (in)visibility of gender in the gay/lesbian and women's movements. *Gender & Society, 8*(3), 402–423.

Kanaaneh, R. A. (2002). *Birthing the nation: Strategies of Palestinian women in Israel.* Berkeley, CA: University of California Press.

Kasper, B. (2004a). Campus-based women's centers: A review of problems and practices. *Affilia, 19*(2), 185–198.

Kasper, B. (2004b). Campus-based women's centers: Administration, structure, and resources. *NASPA Journal, 41*(3), 487–499.

Kaufert, P. (1998). Women, resistance, and the breast cancer movement. In M. Lock & P. Kaufert (Eds.), *Pragmatic women and body politics* (pp. 287–309). Cambridge, MA: Cambridge University Press.

Kowalski-Braun, M., & Underwood, K. (2005). Supporting the whole student: A model for women's center-women's/gender studies collaboration. *NWSAction, 12*(1), 16–17.

Kunkel, C. A. (1994). Women's needs on campus: How universities meet them. *Initiatives, 56,* 15–28.

Kunkel, C. A. (2002). Starting a women's center: Key issues. In S. L. Davie (Ed.), *University and college women's centers: A journey toward equity* (pp. 65–78). Westport, CT: Greenwood Press.

Lamphere, L. (Ed.). (1997). *Situated lives.* New York: Routledge.

Lisker, D. (2002a). Forging unlikely alliances—the women's center and the locker room: A case study. In S. L. Davie (Ed.), *University and college women's centers: A journey toward equity* (pp. 365–370). Westport, CT: Greenwood Press.

Lisker, D. (2002b). Uneasy juxtapositions within Virginia Tech culture: The women's center's role in enforcing the new sexual harassment policy. In S. L. Davie (Ed.), *University and college women's centers: A journey toward equity* (pp. 305–315). Westport, CT: Greenwood Press.

Lockwood, B. (2005). Transforming community through volunteer service at the everywoman's center. *NWSAction, 12*(1), 24–26.

Lonnquist, M. P., & Reesor, L. M. (1987). The Margaret Sloss women's center at Iowa State University: A model. *NASPA Journal, 25*(2), 137–140.

Lopez, I. (1998). An ethnography of the medicalization of Puerto Rican women's reproduction. In M. Lock & P. Kaufert (Eds.), *Pragmatic women and body politics* (pp. 240–259). Cambridge, MA: Cambridge University Press.

Luttrell, W. (2003). *Pregnant bodies, fertile minds.* New York: Routledge.

Mellow, G. O. (1988). Women's centers and women administrators: Breaking the glass slipper together. *Initiatives, 51,* 53–58.

Miller, A. (2002). Barbie can't do math, and it's OK because she's a girl: Women's centers and gender equity in mathematics and the sciences. In S. L. Davie (Ed.), *University and college women's centers: A journey toward equity* (pp. 133–147). Westport, CT: Greenwood Press.

Nash, J. (2001). Labor struggles: Gender, ethnicity, and the new migration. In I. Susser & T. C. Patterson (Eds.), *Cultural diversity in the United States* (pp. 206–228). Oxford, England: Blackwell.

O'Neil, J. D., Elias, B. D., & Yassi, A. (1998). Situating resistance in fields of resistance: Aboriginal women and environmentalism. In M. Lock & P. Kaufert (Eds.), *Pragmatic women and body politics* (pp. 260–286). Cambridge, MA: Cambridge University Press.

Parker, J. (2005). Women's funny shorts: Comedy and praxis. *NWSAction, 12*(1), 26–27.

Povinelli, E. A. (1991). Organizing women: Rhetoric, economy, and politics in process among Australian Aborigines. In M. di Leonardo (Ed.), *Gender at the crossroads of knowledge: Feminits anthropology in the postmodern era* (pp. 235–256). Berkeley, CA: University of California Press.

Rapp, R. (1999). *Testing women, testing the fetus: The social impact of amniocentesis in America.* New York: Routledge.

Stall, S., & Stoecker, R. (1998). Community organizing or organizing community? Gender and the crafts of empowerment. *Gender & Society, 12*(6), 729–756.

Susser, I. (2005). From the cosmopolitan to the personal: Women's mobilization to combat HIV/AIDS. In J. Nash (Ed.), *Social movements: An anthropological reader* (pp. 272–284). Malden, MA: Blackwell Publishing.

Sweeney, J. L. (1978). *Women's centers: Organizational and institutional constraints on meeting educational needs.* Paper presented at the Annual Meeting of the American Educational Research Association, Toronto, Canada.

Taylor, V., & Rupp, L. J. (1998). Women's culture and lesbian feminist activism: A reconsideration of cultural feminism. In N. A. Naples (Ed.), *Community activism and feminist politics: Organizing across race, class, and gender* (pp. 57–80). New York: Routledge.

TenElshof, A., & Searle, S. E. (1974). Developing a women's center. *Journal of National Association for Women Deans, Administrators, and Counselors, 37*(4), 173–178.

Upton, Y. (2005). Women in the wilderness: Georgia Tech women's resource center goes wild. *NWSAction, 12*(1), 20–21.

Valenzuela, V. (2005). Encuentro De Mujeres: Women's collective cultural memory in San Antonio, Texas. *NWSAction, 12*(1), 20–21.

Weinbaum, E. S. (2001). From plant closing to political movement: Challenging the logic of economic destruction in Tennessee. In J. Goode & J. Maskovsky (Eds.), *The new poverty studies: The ethnography of power, politics, and impoverished people in the United States* (pp. 399–434). New York: New York University Press.

Xavier University Women's Center Committee. (2006). *Xavier University's Women's Center proposal.* Cincinnati, OH: Xavier University.

Zavella, P. (1991). Mujeres in factories: Race and class perspectives on women, work, and family. In M. di Leonardo (Ed.), *Gender at the crossroads of knowledge: Feminist anthropology in the postmodern era* (pp. 312–338). Berkeley, CA: University of California Press.

16

In (Re)Search of Women in Student Affairs Administration

Tamara Yakaboski and Saran Donahoo

Abstract: *This chapter assesses the current state of research on women student affairs administrators. To that end, this chapter provides a review of the existing literature, which we argue has shifted from women to a broader definition of gender issues in student affairs that has moved attention away from the experiences and needs of women. Recognizing this shift, the chapter also discusses the role and influence that gender continues to have on higher education organizations and the nature of work especially within student affairs administration. The chapter concludes with recommendations for future research and scholarship that will refocus attention on women student affairs administrators.*

JONES AND KOMIVES (2001) observed that research focusing on women in student affairs administration changed between the 1980s and 1990s. Specifically, frameworks and agendas shifted away from a documentation of women's experiences to a more gender-neutral approach. The authors suggested this evolution reflects a backlash against women and has resulted in diverting "Focus away from gender and its relation to the career pathways and contemporary issues of women student affairs officers" (p. 231).

The shift away from researching the unique experiences of women in student affairs is visible through a general examination of the research and literature. Where it does exist, there is a heavier focus on historical research as well as anecdotal narratives combined with dissertations that look at the population of women in student affairs administration. This trend reverses a post–Title IX pattern that recognized profound, institutionalized gender differences. Our beliefs are that organizations are not gender neutral (Acker, 1990) and this chapter will help to advocate for more gender-specific research.

While historical and narrative research and studies are important contributions to the field, we argue that the role and presence women have on college and university campuses should be an area of scholarly research that can have policy applications and create a climate for culture changes. The significant presence of women on campus is recognizable most among mid-level administrators who comprise the largest administrative group within higher education organizations and "can significantly affect the tone, manner and style of the entire institution" (Johnsrud & Rosser, 1999, p. 121). We argue that the lack of a research focus on women in student affairs administration is one way that this population continues to be marginalized and pushed to the periphery within the higher education community.

CHAPTER FRAMEWORK

There are four main areas within higher education administration (student services, academic support, business services, and external affairs). This chapter focuses on student affairs/student services as a highly feminized field within higher education (Hamrick & Carlisle, 1990; Hughes, 1989; McEwen, Williams, & Engstrom, 1991). Our approach is to examine gender within student affairs/student services area as influenced by organizational and societal structures rather than biological or psychological aspects of women (for more information on women's identity development, see Amy Stalzer Sengupta & Yvette Loury Upton, chapter 14).

We begin by reviewing the main areas of research on women in student affairs via searches through published books, dissertations, journals, including those of the American College Personnel Association (ACPA) and the National Association for Student Personnel Administrators (NASPA), and other scholarly higher education publications. While this review is not comprehensive, we compiled and categorized the broad, general areas of research in order to demonstrate what literature exists so that we may offer suggestions and recommendations for further study.

We also acknowledge that our focus is primarily on four-year higher education institutions rather than examining in detail the community college institutions. In addition, we have not included, even though we do refer to it occasionally, the works on women college presidents and Chief

Executive Officers or Chief Information Officers because presumably, higher level academic administration positions have a faculty or academic track and much research already focuses on women in faculty ranks. Thus, we advocate a focus on the nonfaculty administrative track and the experiences of the women in those student affairs lines.

We categorized the literature into five overarching areas: historical, leadership, career process and shifting strategies, race and ethnicity, and perceptions. The first two areas consist of extensive research and scholarship, which we acknowledge but do not review in this chapter as they are thoroughly discussed elsewhere and are not the specific focus of our analysis. Historical research often begins with examining the history of deans of women and the shift away from women to men in these positions, as is found in Thalia Mulvihill's chapter in this book (chapter 4). The leadership literature covers a wide range and often includes presidency of four-year and community college viewpoints, leadership characteristics, and other high-level academic administration positions. Literature reviews on leadership may be found throughout this book including chapters by Monica Marcelis Fochtman (chapter 6) and Lee Hawthorne Calizo (chapter 18).

This chapter offers a more in-depth review and analysis of the other three pertinent areas. The primary categories that we use to identify and discuss the remaining literature are career process and shifting strategies, race and ethnicity, and perceptions, as each of these areas not only influence the work life and experiences of women in student affairs but are also driven or influenced by the organizational and societal structures within higher education organizations.

In addition to the review of literature, this chapter also provides an examination of the direct impact that gender has on both the work lives of women and the practice of student affairs. This section uses both historical and theoretical analysis of gender and student affairs to help explain the dissatisfaction, discontent, and disparities presented within the existing literature. Finally, the chapter ends with conclusions about the state of research on women in student affairs and recommendations for further scholarship as we change dominant paradigms in the field.

REVIEW OF LITERATURE

Career Process and Shifting Strategies

Compared to history, leadership, and mentoring, career process is a less-developed topic area within scholarship on women in student affairs. Even so, the literature on career process, career shifts, and other related issues has significantly expanded since the 1990s. We categorize the umbrella of career process and strategies to include career paths (Anderson, 1993; Donohue, 1981, Herbrand, 2001; Scott, 2003; Slack, 1993; Warner & DeFleur, 1994), mobility and advancement (Finlay, 1986, Holloway, 1986); family and children (Jones, 1994; Nobbe & Manning, 1997; Padulo, 2001), attrition (Lorden, 1998; Robbins, 1996; Tull, 2006), and organizational barriers and obstacles (Johnsrud, 1991; LeBlanc, 1994; Sagaria, 1988; Zuschin, 2003).

Career paths. Important works on the career paths of women in student affairs include Renn and Hughes's (2004) edited collection, *Roads Taken: Women in Student Affair at Mid-Career.* This anthology examined career development within student services from pursuing a doctorate to issues surrounding dual-career administrative couples. Taking a more direct research approach to the topic, Warner and DeFleur (1994) conducted a survey of 394 senior-level women administrators across the United States to study what their career paths were within higher education administration. They found that there is occupational segregation between men and women in this field and that the career paths are different for women and men. Their findings suggested that women are disproportionately in lower

levels of administration and in nontenured track positions. To address this disparity, they posited that women need to learn more skills and possibly attend leadership workshops put up by the American Council on Education or Bryn Mawr's Summer Institute for Women in Higher Education Administration.

Family and children. The ability of women in student affairs to negotiate education and career progression depends on their ability to develop strategies that provide some personal balance between education, work, the role of motherhood, and the impact of having children. In chapter 5 of this book, Rachael Stimpson and Kim Filer examined female graduate students and their "difficulty in balancing her academic workload and personal life responsibilities." They recognized the scant literature on female graduate student life–work balance and questioned why student affairs focuses most of its attention on the undergraduate student population and not the graduate student.

Monica Marcelis Fochtman, in chapter 6, recognized the continuing absence of literature on work–life balancing for women administrators and conducted a qualitative study to find how high-achieving women balance work and family. Jones (1994) took a different approach to this issue and discussed the need to redesign higher education so that women's multiple roles are integrated into the work environment rather than having "the campus and the home...be mutually exclusive" (p. 68). In addition, an entire section of *Roads Taken: Women in Student Affair at Mid-Career* is devoted to this "skillful art of managing work and family" (Jones, 1993).

Importantly, Marshall and Jones (1990) found that rank, salary, and title were not affected for female student affairs professionals by the timing of children (before, during, or after career initiation). However, they did cite that the women believed that childbirth negatively impacted their careers. Studies on student affairs women who are mothers found that there are women who are met with consequences and challenges as they try to find a balance between work and family (Nobbe & Manning, 1997; Padulo, 2001). This combination requires women to create strategies for establishing balance, including becoming more efficient and effective and developing support systems. The responsibilities of child rearing can be at odds with a career that often demands working nights and weekends, as well as lower compensation, when considering the educational level required for employment.

Attrition versus advancement in student affairs. Working nights and weekends, beyond the traditional 8:00 a.m. to 5:00 p.m. workdays, may be one reason why there is relatively high attrition within student affairs. Literature shows that life needs and organizational socialization and requirements do not always match up (Lorden, 1998; Robbins, 1996; Tull, 2006). Lorden (1998) reviewed the attrition literature and statistics within student affairs and found some inconsistent data and an inability to compare this information across other fields. While there were no specific attrition numbers available, Lorden (1998) cited some main reasons found in the literature for attrition, one being a general dissatisfaction, which she acknowledges might be the result of a larger societal pattern of career changing. Additional reasons include burnout due to odd work hours and conditions, unclear expectations related to the hours, socialization to dominant perspectives in the field, and lower pay or compensation (Lorden, 1998). Another frequently cited reason for the lack of career advancement opportunities or promotion is women's limited or lack of ability to relocate. When women administrators are promoted, they most often come from within the institution, whereas men are more likely to be recruited from both outside and within (Sagaria, 1988). Sagaria stated that this was not caused by women's disinterest or inability to relocate; rather, she suggested that the lack of outside hiring and promotion of women is due more to organizational practices.

A barrier in hiring comes from the role of trust and homogenous hiring practices where individuals hire people that are like themselves (Acker & Van Houten, 1974; Baron, Davis-Blake, & Bielby, 1986). This is prevalent in hiring individuals for student affairs leadership positions. Employing all White males as administrators who often operate as hiring authorities has an influence on the organization. If White males hire individuals that mirror their values and experiences, women will continue to be left out of the ranks of administration. The consequence of this is that administration will lack the ability to respond to the diversifying student body and lower level professional staff who are increasingly women. Part of the barrier to promotion that often leads to attrition receives further attention in the perceptions literature outlined later in this chapter.

LeBlanc (1994) found that barriers to advancement persist because of two sets of norms that coexist within higher education administration. There is the "social and political commitments to individual equality, openness of opportunity, and equal responsibility for men and women" (LeBlanc, 1994, p. 43) and then opposite that is the "old beliefs in the fact and rightness of inequality—in the fact and rightness of a distinction between men and women in their capacities and proper roles" (p. 43). She outlined barriers as negative self-esteem and need for self-improvement; limited external interactions, the balancing of motherhood, family and the academic environment; and the notion of being lonely at the top. Other barriers included the choice to go from academia to administration; the need to develop a career plan, mentoring, and external and internal support systems; and finally the need to know the "big picture" of the organization. An issue is that much literature and scholarship written on women in higher education continues to focus primarily on women that come from a faculty line rather than those who come out of student affairs, and the research on both faculty members and administrators could continue to be unpacked in more detail.

Dale (2007) conducted a qualitative dissertation to understand the experiences of success for the women administrators who did make it into senior leadership positions. She found that survival within these ranks was based on (1) the establishment of collaborative relationships; (2) ensuring that individual values are mirrored by the office culture; (3) acknowledging and accepting the existence of gender issues; (4) being self-reflective; and (5) utilizing constructive knowing. This information is useful as we consider the future of women in student affairs, and will be discussed further in this chapter.

Race and Ethnicity

In addition to process and strategies, race and ethnicity also influence the careers of women in student affairs. While race and ethnicity receive much attention in the literature, most of the available scholarship focuses on the experiences of minority faculty members, as is discussed in Thandi Sulé's chapter 9 in this book (also see Berry & Mizelle, 2006; Mabokela & Green, 2001; Seifert & Umbach, 2008). Even so, a small segment of the literature has explored race and ethnicity as these factors affect the experiences of female student affairs administrators.

Utilizing data obtained from a biannual salary survey conducted by NASPA, Reason, Walker, and Robinson (2002) analyzed the impact that gender, ethnicity, and level of education have on the salaries earned by senior student affairs officers (SSAOs) at public, four-year institutions. Within this data, 79.8% of the respondents identified as Caucasian/non-Hispanic, while the remainder included 14% African American, 3.6% Latino/Hispanic, 1.6% Asian American, and 5% Native American respondents. Controlling for institutional size, the authors focused their analysis on 155 out of the 419 completed surveys yielded from the study. In doing so, these authors found that gender, by itself, did not have a negative impact on the salary of female SSAOs because the mean salary of $106,905 for the 60 women

surveyed was slightly higher than the mean salary of $105,679 for the male respondents. Likewise, the data also failed to illustrate a negative impact related to ethnicity, because the SSAOs of color (all non-Whites; $N = 29$) actually had a higher mean salary of $123,126 than the SSAOs who identified as Caucasian/non-Hispanic ($N = 126$) who had a mean salary of $102,140 (Reason et al., 2002).

When ethnicity, gender, and highest degree earned are taken together, Caucasian women actually earned higher mean salaries than their male colleagues regardless of the degree earned. Conversely, women of color with master's degree had the lowest mean salary within the sample, earning just over $14,000 less than Caucasian males, more than $21,000 less than Caucasian women, and over $57,000 less than men of color (Reason et al., 2002). Although mediated by the level of education, the combination of race and gender continue to influence the inequitable compensation received by women of color working in student affairs.

Women of color. Moving away from compensation concerns, various scholars look at the lives and experiences of women of color in higher education. *Women in Higher Education: An Encyclopedia* (Martinez & Renn, 2002) provides a range of entries on topics such as history and culture, feminism, curriculum, policy, faculty, and administration. Authored by various higher education scholars, the entries provide an overview on specified issues. The section on women administrators includes entries on African American, American Indian, Asian American, and Latina women (Grady, 2002a, 2002b; Ideta, 2002; Tyson, 2002). While these entries provide a glimpse of the racial, gender, and professional issues affecting these women, these texts generally reiterate the obstacles that women of color have and continue to face as they work in higher education. Moreover, these entries focus on women of color in academic administration generally, thus ignoring the specific issues these professional women experience in practicing student affairs.

Renn and Hughes's (2004) work features a variety of reflective and experiential chapters authored by women in student affairs. Among these, Ortiz (2004) described the impact of racial concerns from both her students and herself on her way to achieving tenure as a faculty member preparing others to work as administrators in student affairs. In her chapter, Keeton (2004) described the experiences of working as a student affairs professional in the face of race, class, and gender stereotypes and discriminations as she discussed issues women administrators need to consider in deciding whether or not to pursue a doctoral degree. Similarly, Wong (2004) shared her life as an Asian American woman administrator in student affairs as influenced by her divorce. The stories detailed by these and the other authors in *Roads Taken* offer a blend of the personal and the professional, illustrating the fact that women often choose not to or simply cannot easily separate the two.

African American women. Beyond the attention to women of color generally, much of the existing literature offers a specific focus on African American women administrators. Jackson's (1985) mixed methods dissertation on members of the New England Minority Women Administrators organization provides information on perceptions of group members as raced and gendered professionals at predominantly White institutions (PWIs) but does not offer specific insights on those working in student affairs. Rusher's (1996) survey and quantitative analysis offered information on the "recruitment, retention, and promotion of 154 African American women administrators" (p. vii). Yet, the fact that she did not specifically identify institutional areas (student affairs vs. academic affairs) and all of her participants were at the dean level or higher suggests that most of Rusher's (1996) participants were not working in student affairs units. Although Hirt, Strayhorn, Amelink, and Bennett

(2006) examined the work life of student affairs professionals at historically Black colleges and universities (HBCUs), their work does not provide any assessment of the impact gender has on these experiences. Moreover, their examination of race generally focuses on the racial uplift mission of their participants, not the influence race had on their career experiences (Hirt et al., 2006).

Conversely, Harvey's *Grass Roots and Glass Ceilings* (1999) provides a collection of chapters that consider the experiences of African American administrators at PWIs. Chapters in this edited book addressing African American women administrators include personal accounts by Farris (1999), King (1999), and McDemmond (1999) of their rise to and terms as presidents of PWIs, deGraft-Johnson's (1999) time as vice president for academic affairs at a PWI, and Solomon's (1999) tenure as an administrator in minority affairs and dean of a graduate school. Although these texts offer insights into the collision between race and gender, all of these women followed traditional faculty career paths into administration, not student affairs.

Essentially, only a small segment of the literature specifically examines the intersection between race and gender among women in student affairs administration. Inspired by her own experiences as an African American administrator in student affairs, Hinton's (2001) dissertation examines the experiences of similar colleagues working at PWIs. From her interviews with five African American women administrators (four from student affairs and one from academic affairs), Hinton (2001; Patitu & Hinton, 2003) found that issues of race and gender continue to influence the work and personal lives of women. Within their institutions, these women often lacked support for their efforts to assist students, felt that their race prevented them from ascending in their careers, and illustrated that "racism and sexism are not always distinguishable" (Hinton, 2001; Patitu & Hinton, 2003, p. 81). For one participant in the study, sexuality and homophobia added an additional layer of discrimination, isolation, and oppression by working in concert with her race and gender to further marginalize her within her institution. While the women in her work relied upon their faith and inner strength to cope with their situations, Hinton (2001; Patitu & Hinton, 2003) recommends the establishment of on- and off-campus support systems to address the isolation experienced by African American women administrators. Despite the high representation of women administrators in student affairs within Hinton's (2001; Patitu & Hinton, 2003) work, her analysis does not specifically distinguish the needs of student affairs administrators from African American women serving in other capacities in higher education.

Comparing the careers of African American women administrators at both HBCUs and PWIs, Scott's (2003) dissertation directly focused attention on individuals who work in student affairs. Through interviews and case studies of 10 African American female senior student affairs administrators (5 from HBCUs and 5 from PWIs), Scott (2003) found that race and gender influenced the careers and work experiences of these women both independently and concurrently. Similar to the data discussed by Hinton (2001; Patitu & Hinton, 2003), Scott (2003) found that the participants in her study repeatedly encountered race, gender, and color discrimination. Drawing upon images from slavery and plantation life, Scott (2003) used colorism to refer to the perceived privileges or disadvantages directed at women based on their complexion, hair texture, and physical features. Even with the addition of colorism from one participant, the stories provided by these women echo the experiences of other women in higher education of having their leadership and contributions questioned, devalued, and ignored. While they acknowledged the existence of barriers, a common theme expressed by her participants was their desire to overcome all of the barriers placed before them including issues grounded in racism and sexism. However, Scott (2003) determined that the senior women administrators in her study generally ignored or overlooked the impact of sexism and gender on their careers and work life.

While some of the narratives provided by these women suggested the existence of gender-based discrimination and bias, these women did not give much credence to their influence. Growing up under *de jure* segregation and the civil rights movement may have influenced these women to take greater notice of racial issues without always clearly recognizing its intersections with gender. Overall, Scott's (2003) study expands the literature on African American women administrators in student affairs. At the same time, her research also suggests the need for research on female student affairs administrators of varying age groups because they appear to consider the influence of race on their careers differently.

Asian and Asian American women. Of the research on women administrators, only one specifically examines the lives and careers of Asian women. Centered on individual narratives related to race, gender, and discrimination, Ideta and Cooper (1997/2000) revealed the stories of four Asian women administrators in higher education. Of the four, two served in academic affairs and two in student affairs positions with one of each coming from the community college and university sectors. Although the authors did not generalize the experiences of these women, the narratives provided by these female administrators revealed some common elements.

Similar to the research on African American women, the Asian women encountered discrimination and difficulties in the workplace resulting from a combination of both their race and their gender. Indeed, the Asian women administrators in this study reported enduring more discrimination from other women in the workplace than men (Ideta & Cooper, 1997/2000). Regardless of the source, the women utilized these negative experiences as opportunities to strengthen their resolve and invest more of their personal and professional efforts into working against discrimination within higher education (Ideta & Cooper, 1997/2000).

Perceptions

Within the literature on women administrators, various works examine the perceptions these professionals have of their careers and work environments. In two quantitative studies, Sue Street and Ellen Kimmel examine gender roles and perceptions among men and women. The earliest study drew data from students, faculty members, and administrators finding that university professionals expressed a stronger preference for perceived male personality traits (intellect, power, and sexuality) (Street, Kimmel, & Kromery, 1996). Focusing more specifically on university administrators, Street and Kimmel (1999) found that both female and male administrators tended to favor the proscribed male characteristics. However, they also found the female-associated characteristic of compassion to be a favorable trait (Street & Kimmel, 1999). Although the authors attributed the fact that 51% of their sample were women to the overrepresentation of student affairs professionals within the sample (Street & Kimmel, 1999), the text does not offer any particular discussion of gender roles and perceptions on administrators working in that area.

Acker (1990) examined how perceptions are the construction of symbols and images that reinforce or oppose these gender divisions. She stated that processes that examine the interactions between men and women see men as "the actors, [and] women the emotional support" (p. 117 citing Hochschild, 1983). With organizations emphasizing hegemonic masculinity, or "the image of the strong, technically competent, authoritative leader who is sexually potent and attractive, has a family, and has his emotions under control" (Acker, 1990, p. 153), women within higher education are expected to acculturate to this model of performance if they want to ascend to higher positional levels.

One common reference made to student affairs is this idea that it involves more emotional characteristics and thereby more feminine ones get assigned to the field. It is the "softer" area of higher education, which corresponds to a Western traditional view of femininity. Street and Kimmel (1999) discussed how there has been a "feminization of student affairs" (Hamrick & Carlisle, 1990; Hughes, 1989; McEwen et al., 1991), which points to the correlation of femininity and student services. How does this "softer" side of administration fit with the masculine behaviors of what might be seen as "management material"? Perhaps it does not.

One example of this incongruence surfaces in *Shattering the Myths* (2001) when Judith Rodin became the first woman president of University of Pennsylvania and the *New York Times* described her as having a "cover-girl smile and designer clothes" with a "pert manner and bouncy determination" and saw her as a more "serious country club tennis player" than "board-room predator" (Glazer-Raymo, 2001, p. 147). The article did eventually get around to acknowledging her two decades at Yale as provost and "intellectual achievements included 20 grants totally nearly $30 million, 203 academic articles, 64 book chapters, and 10 academic books" (Glazer-Raymo, 2001, p. 147). This focus on symbolic femininity rather than acknowledging and giving support to her more "masculine" characteristics of intellectual superiority and administrative and academic expertise is not only a societal focus but also an organizational feature of marginalizing efforts and achievements of women who serve as competitors with male power and positions.

Other literature on perceptions focuses on work life and career satisfaction. Kuk's (1981) quantitative study explored the career aspirations and professional climate encountered by women in student affairs administration. Many of her respondents aspired to middle management positions because the duties of various upper level positions did not appeal to them. Kuk (1981) suggested that this limited aspiration may be a result of the fact that women are not socialized to make work the sole purpose of their lives and that the need to balance work with family and other personal considerations may have discouraged these women from seeking some advanced administrative roles. The feeling that their institutions did not support their work also contributed to these women's career decisions (Kuk, 1981).

Similar to Kuk (1981), Holliday (1992) and Blackhurst (2000) also studied the perceptions of women administrators. In her work, Blackhurst (2000) surveyed female professionals who were NASPA members. On the basis of her interview data, Holliday (1992) suggested that four of the five frameworks that influence the career life of women revolve around the structure and nature of their organizations. While personal issues such as race, gender, and family life also affect career choices, elements of organizational culture and structure seem to have a greater impact on those decisions (Holliday, 1992). Likewise, Blackhurst (2000) also found that work life had a significant impact on careers because many of the women in her survey expressed dissatisfaction stemming from sex discrimination and racial issues experienced in the workplace. Survey results showed that women of color (Blackhurst, 2000) and older female administrators (Blackhurst, 2000; Rosser & Janivar, 2003)[1] experienced higher rates of dissatisfaction at work. In turn, women of color and lower level professionals communicated a greater desire to leave their positions (Blackhurst, 2000).

Collectively, the works on the perceptions of women student affairs administrators reveal common themes of dissatisfaction: low salaries, the continuing presence of varying forms of discrimination, and a desire for organizational change. At the same time, research also indicates that assumptions about gender roles and gender identity continue to restrict the career trajectory and routine work lives of women in student affairs. While women are obtaining more positions in student affairs, just being there is simply not enough.

GENDER-BASED ASSUMPTIONS AND NARRATIVES IN STUDENT AFFAIRS ADMINISTRATION

The literature on women in student affairs illustrates the need for more scholarship as existing texts merely scratch the surface of various issues affecting these professionals. At the same time, current research and scholarship also demonstrate the continued impact that social assumptions about gender continue to have on the careers and personal lives of women in student affairs. For that reason, this section discusses social assumptions about gender and the influence these assumptions have on the nature and practice of student affairs.

Gender affects the research of women in student affairs administration in three key ways. First, issues related to and stemming from gender shape the assumptions, stereotypes, and social norms ascribed to women within both public and private context. In turn, the social structures of gender, femininity, and womanhood impose additional and unique limitations and implications specifically in and around the workplace. Finally, the structure and nature of student affairs as an area of higher education practice places gendered value on the role that these functions, offices, and professionals have within the institution. This information is helpful as we consider strategies for changing dominant paradigms in the field.

Social Assumptions of Gender

Although repeatedly challenged and repudiated by scholars in a variety of disciplines (e.g., Jones, 1985; Kerber, 1988; Novkov, 1996; Risman, 2004; Ropers-Huilman, 1998; Strom, 1989; Zorn, 2007), U.S. culture continues to grapple with the assumption that women and men are inherently different. To be more specific, the idea that biological differences between the sexes mandate different sets of opportunities, expectations, and treatment continues to influence the social, economic, and political lives of women. Historically, reserving the public sphere and its benefits (personal autonomy, higher education, a range of wage-earning opportunities, etc.) for men, U.S. culture relegated women to the home physically, economically, and intellectually (Jones, 1985; Kerber, 1988). Even when mediated by race and class, the idea that "a woman's place is in the home" affected all women by preventing wealthy White women from accessing male-dominated spaces while also penalizing poor and non-White women with low-wage employment centered around female-ascribed activities related to children, nurturing, and other elements of domesticity (Hewitt, 2002; Jones, 1985; Kerber, 1988; Martin, 1990; Risman, 2004). Upon gaining access to higher education, the home limitation continued to affect women of all races because the curricula offered to them focused on activities designed to improve their domestic skills such as cooking, sewing, and cleaning (Brazzell, 1992; Graham, 1978; Kerber, 1988; Rohan, 2006). As such, women's entrée into public life relied on the needs and nature of home to legitimize both their presence and their activities.

Gender in the Workplace

The nature of home and domesticity has indeed proven to be a double-edged sword for women seeking access to the workplace. On the one hand, the characterization and expectation that women serve as caring nurturers helped them to gain work as cashiers, librarians, nurses, secretaries, social workers, teachers, waitresses, and other positions considered part of the *pink-collar ghetto*[2] (Anderson, 2000; Kennelly, 2006; Kerber, 1988; Stauffer, 2005; Strober & Tyack, 1980; Strom, 1989). Yet, on the other hand, the belief that women could best serve in professions that rely on emotions and nurturing hindered their ability to make a complete transition into public life because they were only welcome in places and in ways where society was willing to accept connections and elements of home (Acker,

1990; Kerber, 1988). At the same time, while men traditionally experienced wage earning as a private benefit and responsibility, the way that women expend both their labor and income faces the scrutiny and limitations from public policies interested in controlling their reproduction and family structures, which relegated women's labor and the fruits thereof as household property generally controlled by men (Kerber, 1988; Novkov, 1996). Essentially, the use of the home and domesticity as the doorway into the public sphere helped to bring direct attention to the influence of gender on the workplace.

Although women now have a greater variety of employment options, gender continues to influence the workplace. In spite of increased access to historically male-dominated careers and fields of education, the notion of separate spheres continues to structure life at work (Acker, 1990; Martin, 1990; Zorn, 2007). As discussed by Acker (1990), gender segregation and limitations in the workplace persist because organizations present themselves as equitable arenas focused on qualifications and performance, when the experiences of their employees do not reflect the existence or practice of such equity. She stated,

> The concept "a job" is thus implicitly a gendered concept, even though organizational logic presents it as gender neutral. "A job" already contains the gender-based division of labor and the separation between the public and the private sphere. The concept of "a job" assumes a particular gendered organization of domestic life and social production. (p. 149)

The fact that the workplace and work life continue to draw upon the notion of separate public and private spaces for women and men prevents organizations from moving toward becoming gender neutral. In practice, the structure of work devalues the contributions of women through low wages, limited mobility often blamed on childbirth and child rearing, and the expectation that women will continue to fulfill their domestic functions within the household regardless of the demands placed on them by their external employment, without compensation for their labors at home (Acker, 1990; Cohen & Huffman, 2003; Kerber, 1988; Stallard, Ehrenreich, & Sklar, 1983). In the context of higher education, women have similar experiences in the work life of the organization as they do in other industries. Even though women make up more than 55% of the college student population, the woman in the president's office at a four-year institution is still five times more likely to be an administrative assistant than a chief executive officer (Wilson, 2008; Zorn, 2007).

Gender and Student Affairs

The position occupied by student affairs and student service departments within higher education exemplifies both the assumptions about separate spheres and the gendered structure of the workplace. Similar to nursing, teaching, and social work, nurturing is part of the foundation of student affairs practice. Built on and developed under the prime directive of *in loco parentis*, student affairs began with the intent of monitoring, guiding, and controlling the out-of-class time and activities of college students who simply could not be trusted to behave morally or responsibly on their own (Hamrick, Evans, & Schuh, 2002; Rentz, 2004). Even now when *in loco parentis* no longer dominates campus life, student affairs offices and programs continue to serve more of a familial role in the lives of college students by investing time, staff, and material resources into assisting with identity development, self-discovery, and other emotional concerns. Indeed, it is this connection to home, nurturing, and emotion that leads some to disregard the contributions that student affairs offices make to the higher education landscape because these initiatives do not always have a clear, direct impact on either the academic growth of students or the financial growth of institutions (Hamrick et al., 2002; Magolda, 2003). As a result, higher education genders the work of student affairs by

regarding their efforts as less important than the activities of academic and business affairs units, thereby pushing student affairs to the periphery of the hierarchy of the institution. As evidenced by the limited number of ascensions from student affairs into the college presidency, student affairs units and their well-educated, experienced, highly capable, often female administrators do not have the same opportunities for career mobility available to their colleagues assigned to other areas of the campus (Jacobson, 2002).

Despite the marginalized status generally accorded to student affairs within higher education organizations, both these offices and the professionals who staff them provide key and lasting service to the their institutions. As described by Ortiz (1999), "the components of student life central to student affairs units (for example, athletics, Greek social organizations, student organizations, residential living) are what contribute to an individual's sense of identification with a college" (p. 47). Documented and depicted in numerous movies and television shows, the services provided by student affairs are not only an integral part of the college experience; rather, student affairs *is* college. In recognition of this perception, women working in student affairs administration merit greater mobility within higher education and more attention from researchers examining issues related to gender, organizations, and higher education.

RECOMMENDATIONS

The reviewed literature in this chapter reflects a significant number of dissertations written about women student affairs administrators, presumably by women student affairs administrators (25 dissertations are cited in this chapter alone, and this is not a comprehensive listing). As researchers, scholars, and researching practitioners, we need to focus more of our research on this population. The transformation of dissertation into scholarly articles, thereby making them more accessible, is one suggestion. Developing a deeper understanding of this research will help to break the status quo of assuming a nurturing, undervalued component to student affairs and the women who work in this field. As previously stated, more of a research presence regarding student affairs administration will help to decrease the marginalization of this population and of this higher education area. We advocate for a return to post–Title IX's focus on women's issues, while combining a feminist framework to examine not only women's experiences but also organizations, including higher education, as gendered.

In order to decrease marginalization within the research community, there is a need to promote the anecdotal or narrative style research as scholarly research. An overall recommendation is the need to encourage researchers to conduct their research on women in student affairs that the mainstream (man-stream) community will view and recognize as scholarly, while not denying the agency and voice of the women at the center of such studies. This can be done for both qualitative and quantitative research. Although at the onset it may seem more of a challenge in regard to quantitative research, this may be done by designing larger quantitative studies that utilize a feminist mindset and framework (see Ramazanoğlu & Holland, 2002, and Sprague, 2005, for more information).

To address why institutions are gendered, future research can utilize Acker's (1990) theoretical framework of gendered organizations and hierarchies to start to unravel the marginalization of women in student affairs and, perhaps, the marginalization of student affairs as a whole within the larger higher education organization. Acker noted that organizational hierarchies are male dominated and inherent within them is the pressure to conform to the hierarchy regardless of predispositions because gender is implicit to the everyday functions and activities of the organizational and social structures. Because of this implicitness, change occurs not by requiring women to assimilate or acculturate to the

masculine nature of higher education but rather "transformation" occurs when the organizational culture values equally the contribution of women and their multiple identities and roles within personal and work life. The "radical transformation" that Acker called for would require higher education to acknowledge the value of student affairs and the role that this largely feminized field plays within the organization. Through her framework, we in student affairs may start to understand the depth of the marginalization and start to move out of the periphery.

To strive toward this deeper understanding, the following are suggestions for future researchers, on the basis of the literature reviewed. First, research questions should avoid frameworks that focus on how women do not fit into the organization or deficiency models (i.e., skills that women need to "learn" in order to be "successful" in administration). Instead, researchers might reframe questions so that we look critically at how the organization or culture is following one main model and what needs to be done overall so that it is not women who are the ones that continue to be forced to assimilate to the mainstream masculine environment, but that it is the environment that changes.

Second, because of the nontraditional work hours in the field of student affairs, more research needs to center on answering some important questions, including the following:

- ◆ Are the nontraditional work hours experienced differently by men and women?
- ◆ Can the expectations shift or is this a necessary component to the field?
- ◆ How much does this tie into attrition in the profession and, if it does, what adjustments can be made within the field and culture?
- ◆ Do the nontraditional work hours change once women get into upper management and, if so, is this a greater reason why women should try to get into these ranks— because of family/personal life demands

and the need to balance those with work demands?

Next, given the nontraditional work hours and the impact of children/family on professionals in this field, what can be done within the work environment or culture to allow the crossing over of these multiple identities? Do more women in management positions adequately shift the environment to be more "family friendly"? Do "family friendly" policies have a positive effect on satisfaction? Or perhaps do they not matter as much as the unwritten norm or culture of an institution/department? Are some student affairs departments/areas more "tolerable" of families such as residence life where there are live-in positions?

In addition, we need to more closely examine attrition rates and causes within student affairs. How are they different between men and women? How do race, ethnicity, and sexual orientation interact with other identities? Perhaps a longitudinal study should be conducted that followed graduate assistants in a master's program into their first full-time entry-level position for five years to determine attrition rates as well as the experiences of those who stayed and those who left. Are there higher attrition rates within certain areas of student affairs over others (i.e., perhaps residence life with its more 24/7 live-in schedule has higher attrition over other functional areas of student affairs)?

Another field of study is management performance. Within student affairs do women administrators and men administrators perform management similarly or differently? How do staffs respond to this? How does upper management receive it? Is there a masculine and a feminine way of being a student affairs administrator? Or do all assimilate toward one style with the assumption that having a more masculine management style is desired, particularly if promotion or advancement is a career goal? Moreover, do the management styles of lower level administration, where there are more women, reflect more feminine behaviors than that of upper level administration, where there are more men and where increased

assimilation of masculine management behaviors might be necessary? If we view the women who have masculine behaviors as "strong," how are these women perceived by those around them? And how much in conflict is this with the "nurturing" nature of student affairs? Can a woman administrator have masculine management behaviors in a "motherly" field?

Finally, there is also a lack of research on minority women in student affairs, specifically the experiences of Asian, Hispanic, and Latina women. Future research in this area should do more than simply consider the racial issues. Instead, research should focus specifically on where gender and race intersect in the lives of these women and how this influences their professional experiences and overall careers.

CONCLUSION

Research on women faculty members and women students abounds, and we understand the importance of researching these populations to increase our understanding of their experiences as well as to improve retention rates. So why has there not been as much attention paid to the one area where the majority of women professionals reside on campus?

In order to improve women's experiences in student affairs administration, we must dig deeper in terms of our understanding of the cross sections of their experiences and consider if such experiences are a result of organizational structures and barriers. We must do this by continuing research on a wider scale leading to policy implementation and culture shifts in order to retain and include more women in all the levels of student affairs administration. Specifically, more research on women will help to better inform the higher education community as a whole as to the importance and presence of this area of administration in order to lessen the marginalization of student affairs on college and university campuses.

NOTES

1. Although Rosser and Javinar (2003) did not focus exclusively on women administrators, 54% of their respondents were female.

2. Coined by Stallard, Ehrenreich, and Sklar (1983), the *pink-collar ghetto* refers to the occupational segregation that women experience when they work outside of the home. The low wages and poor mobility that accompanies these positions often lead many women, especially those with children, to experience poverty in spite of their employment status.

REFERENCES

Acker, J. (1990). Hierarchies, jobs, bodies: A theory of gendered organizations. *Gender & Society, 4*(2), 139–158.

Acker, J., & Van Houten, D. R. (1974). Differential recruitment and control: The sex structuring of organizations. *Administrative Science Quarterly, 19,* 152–163.

Anderson, C. M. (1993). *A case study of the career acquisition and professional experiences of female chief student affairs officers.* Unpublished doctoral dissertation, Northern Arizona University.

Anderson, C. M. (2000). Catholic nuns and the invention of social work: The sisters of Santa Maria Institute of Cincinnati, Ohio, 1897 through the 1920s. *Journal of Women's History, 12*(1), 60–88.

Baron, J. N., Davis-Blake, A., & Bielby, W. T. (1986). The structure of opportunity: How promotion ladders vary within and among organizations. *Administrative Science Quarterly, 31,* 248–273.

Berry, T. R., & Mizelle, N. D. (Ed.). (2006). *From Oppression to Grace; Women of Color and Their Dilemmas within the Academy.* Sterling, VA: Stylus Publishing.

Blackhurst, A. E. (2000). Career satisfaction and perceptions of sex discrimination among women student affairs professionals. *NASPA Journal, 37*(2), 399–413.

Brazzell, J. C. (1992). Bricks without straws: Missionary-sponsored black higher education in the post-emancipation era. *The Journal of Higher Education, 63*(1), 26–49.

Cohen, P. N., & Huffman, M. L. (2003, March). Occupational segregation and the devaluation of women's work across U.S. labor markets. *Social Forces, 81*(3), 881–908.

Dale, D. C. (2007). *Women student affairs leaders advancing and succeeding in higher education senior leadership teams.* Unpublished doctoral dissertation, Drexel University.

DeGraft-Johnson, A. (1999). A dream turned into reality. In W. Harvey (Ed.), *Grass roots and glass ceilings: African American administrators in predominantly White colleges and universities* (pp. 113–127). Albany, NY: State University of New York Press.

Donohue, W. G. (1981). *The life cycles and career strategies of senior-level administrative women in higher education.* Unpublished doctoral dissertation, Memphis State University.

Farris, V. (1999). Succeeding as a female African American president at a predominantly White college. In W. Harvey (Ed.), *Grass roots and glass ceilings: African American administrators in predominantly White colleges and universities* (pp. 57–69). Albany, NY: State University of New York Press.

Finlay, C. S. (1986). *Perceptions of chief administrative officers at Pennsylvania colleges and universities concerning the career advancement potential of women administrator within higher education.* Unpublished doctoral dissertation, University of Pittsburgh.

Glazer-Raymo, J. (2001). *Shattering the myths: Women in academe.* Baltimore, MA: The Johns Hopkins University Press.

Grady, M. L. (2002a). American Indian administrators. In A. M. M. Alemán & K. A. Renn (Eds.), *Women in higher education: An encyclopedia* (pp. 469–472). Santa Barbara, CA: ABC-CLIO, Inc.

Grady, M. L. (2002b). Latina administrators. In A. M. M. Alemán & K. A. Renn (Eds.), *Women in higher education: An encyclopedia* (pp. 478–482). Santa Barbara, CA: ABC-CLIO, Inc.

Graham, P. A. (1978). Expansion and exclusion: A history of women in American higher education. *Signs, 3*(4), 759–773.

Hamrick, F., & Carlisle, W. (1990). Gender diversity in student affairs: Administrative perceptions and recommendations. *NASPA Journal, 27,* 306–311.

Hamrick, F. A., Evans, N. J., & Schuh, J. H. (2002). *Foundations of student affairs practice: How philosophy, theory, and research strengthen educational outcomes.* San Francisco, CA: Jossey-Bass.

Harvey, W. (Ed.). (1999). *Grass roots and glass ceilings: African American administrators in predominantly White colleges and universities.* Albany, NY: State University of New York Press.

Herbrand, L. (2001). *Career paths of female senior student affairs officers in American four-year institutions of higher education.* Unpublished doctoral dissertation, Ball State University.

Hewitt, N. J. (2002). Taking the true woman hostage. *Journal of Women's History, 14*(1), 156–162.

Hinton, K. G. (2001). *The experiences of African American women administrators at predominantly White institutions of higher education.* Unpublished doctoral dissertation, Indiana University.

Hirt, J. B., Strayhorn, T. L., Amelink, C. T., & Bennett, B. R. (2006). The nature of student affairs work at historically black colleges and universities. *Journal of College Student Development, 47*(6), 661–676.

Hochschild, A. R. (1983). *The managed heart: Commercialization of human feeling.* Berkeley, CA: University of California Press.

Holliday, G. (1992). *The concept of organizational opportunity: The perceptions of women mid-level administrators in higher education.* Unpublished doctoral dissertation, University of Massachusetts, Amherst.

Holloway, E. (1986). *Upward mobility in higher education: A study of female administrators in selected southern states.* Unpublished doctoral dissertation, The University of Southern Mississippi.

Hughes, M. (1989). Feminization and student affairs. *NASPA Journal, 27,* 18–27.

Ideta, L. M. (2002). Asian American administrators. In A. M. M. Alemán & K. A. Renn (Eds.), *Women in higher education: An encyclopedia* (pp. 472–475). Santa Barbara, CA: ABC-CLIO, Inc.

Ideta, L. M., & Cooper, J. E. (1997/2000). Asian women leaders of higher education. In J. Glazer-Raymo, B. K. Townsend, & B. Ropers-Huilman (Eds.), *Women in higher education: A feminist perspective* (pp. 259–268). Boston: Pearson Custom Publishing.

Jackson, N. (1985). *The roles and perceptions of Black female administrators in predominantly White institutions of higher education in the New England area.* Unpublished doctoral dissertation, University of Massachusetts.

Jacobson, J. (2002). Moving up from student affairs, or staying put. *The Chronicle of Higher Education.* Retrieved May 20, 2008, from http//chronicle.com/article/Moving-Up-from-Student-Affa/45970/

Johnsrud, L. K., & Rosser, V. J. (1999). College and university midlevel administrators: Explaining and improving their morale. *Review of Higher Education, 22,* 121–141.

Johnsrud, L. K. (1991). Administration promotion: The power of gender. *The Journal of Higher Education, 62*(2), 119–149.

Jones, B. (1994). Redesigning the ivory tower: Opening the drawbridge to women with multiple roles. In P. T. Mitchell (Ed.), *Cracking the wall: Women in higher education administration.* Washington, DC: College & University Personnel Association.

Jones, J. (1985). *Labor of love, labor of sorrow: Black women, work, and the family from slavery to the present.* New York: Vintage.

Jones, S. R., & Komives, S. R. (2001). Contemporary issues of women as senior student affairs officers. In J. Nidiffer & C. T. Bashaw (Eds.), *Women administrators in higher education: Historical and contemporary perspectives* (pp. 231–248). Albany, NY: State University of New York Press.

Keeton, R. G. (2004). "Sueños y valor" (dreams and courage). In K. A. Renn & C. Hughes (Eds.), *Roads taken: Women in student affairs at mid-career* (pp. 23–33). Sterling, VA: Stylus.

Kennelly, I. (2006, Summer). Secretarial work, nurturing, and the ethic of service. *NWSA Journal, 18*(2), 170–192.

Kerber, L. K. (1988, Jun.). Separate spheres, female worlds, woman's place: The rhetoric of women's history. *The Journal of American History, 75*(1), 9–39.

King, R. C. (1999). Succeeding against the odds in higher education: Advancing society by overcoming obstacles due to race and gender. In W. Harvey (Ed.), *Grass roots and glass ceilings: African American administrators in predominantly White colleges and universities* (pp. 9–37). Albany, NY: State University of New York Press.

Kuk, L. S. (1981). *Perceptions of work climate and their relationship to the career aspiration of women student affairs administrators.* Unpublished doctoral dissertation, Iowa State University.

LeBlanc, D. S. (1994). Barriers to women's advancement into higher education administration. In P. T. Mitchell (Ed.), *Cracking the wall: Women in higher education administration.* Washington, DC: College & University Personnel Association.

Lorden, L. P. (1998). Attrition in the student affairs profession. *NASPA Journal, 35,* 207–16.

Mabokela, R., & Green, A. L. (Eds.). (2001). *Sisters of the academy: Emergent Black women scholars in higher education.* Sterling, VA: Stylus Publishing.

Magolda, M. B. (2003). Identity and learning: Student affairs' role in transforming higher education. *Journal of College Student Development, 44*(2), 231–247.

Marshall, M. R., & Jones, C. H. (1990). Childbearing sequence and the career development of women administrators in higher education. *Journal of College Student Development, 31,* 531–537.

Martin, J. (1990). Deconstructing organizational taboos: The suppressing of gender conflict in organizations. *Organization Science, 1*(4), 339–359.

Martínez Alemán, A. M., & Renn, K. (2002). Women in higher education: An encyclopedia. Santa Barbara, CA: ABC-CLIO Press.

McDemmond, M. (1999). "On the outside looking in." In W. Harvey (Ed.), *Grass roots and glass ceilings: African American administrators in predominantly White colleges and universities* (pp. 71–81). Albany, NY: State University of New York Press.

McEwen, M. K., Williams, T. E., & Engstrom, C. M. (1991). Feminization in student affairs: A qualitative investigation. *Journal of College Student Development, 32,* 440–446.

Nobbe, J., & Manning, S. (1997). Issues for women in student affairs with children. *NASPA Journal, 34,* 101–11.

Novkov, J. (1996, Autumn). Liberty, protection, and women's work: Investigating the boundaries between public and private. *Law & Social Inquiry, 21*(4), 857–899.

Ortiz, A. M. (1999). The student affairs establishment and the institutionalization of the collegiate ideal. *New Directions for Higher Education, 105,* 47–57.

Ortiz, A. M. (2004). Arriving at tenure. In K. A. Renn & C. Hughes (Eds.), *Roads taken: Women in student affairs at mid-career* (pp. 161–170). Sterling, VA: Stylus.

Padulo, M. K. B. (2001). The balancing act: Work environment issues for women with children in Student Affairs. (Ed.D. dissertation, University of San Diego, 2001) Retrieved June 5, 2008, from Dissertations & Theses: A&I database. (Publication No. AAT 3007296).

Patitu, C. L., & Hinton, K. G. (2003). In C. L. Patitu & K. G. Hinton (Eds.), *The experience of African American women faculty and administrators in higher education: Has anything changed?* (pp. 79–93). New Directions for Student Services, No. 104. San Francisco, CA: Jossey-Bass.

Ramazanoğlu, C., & Holland, J. (2002). *Feminist methodology: Challenges and choices.* Thousand Oaks, CA: Sage Publications Ltd.

Reason, R. D., Walker, D. A., & Robinson, D. C. (2002, Spr.). Gender, ethnicity, and highest degree earned as salary determinants for senior student affairs officers at public institutions. *NASPA Journal, 39*(3), 251–265.

Renn, K. A., & Hughes, C. (2004). *Roads taken: Women in student affairs at mid-career.* Sterling, VA: Stylus.

Rentz, A. L. (2004). Student affairs: An historical perspective. In F. J. D. MacKinnon, & Associates (Eds.), *Rentz's student affairs practice in higher education* (3rd ed., pp. 27–57). Springfield, IL: Charles C. Thomas Publisher, Ltd.

Risman, B. J. (2004). Gender as a social structure: Theory wrestling with activism. *Gender and Society, 18*(4), 429–450.

Robbins, D. V. (1996). *An exploratory study of expectations versus realities in the socialization of women into entry-level positions in higher education administration.* Unpublished doctoral dissertation, Boston College.

Rohan, L. (2006). A material pedagogy: Lessons from early-twentieth-century domestic arts curricula. *Pedagogy, 6*(1), 79–101.

Ropers-Huilman, B. (1998). *Feminist leaders in higher education: A textual analysis of power and resistance.* Paper presentation at the 1998 Annual Meeting of the American Educational Research Association, San Diego, CA. (ERIC Document Reproduction Service No. ED423729)

Rosser, V. J., & Javinar, J. M. (2003). Mid-level student affairs leaders' intentions to leave: Improving the quality of their professional and institutional work life. *Journal of College Student Development, 44*(6), 813–830.

Rusher, A. W. (1996). *African American women administrators.* Lanham, MD: University Press of America, Inc.

Sagaria, M. A. D. (1988). Administrative mobility and gender: Patterns and process in higher education. *The Journal of Higher Education, 59*(3), 305–326.

Scott, F. J. (2003). *African American female senior student affairs officers: A case study of ten career pathways at both historically Black institutions and predominantly White institutions.* Unpublished doctoral dissertation, Texas A&M University.

Seifert, T., & Umbach, P. (2008, Jun.). The effects of faculty demographic characteristics and disciplinary context on dimensions of job satisfaction. *Research in Higher Education, 49*(4), 357–381.

Slack, V. L. (1993). *Gender differences in positions, career influences, and career paths of senior student affairs administrators.* Unpublished doctoral dissertation, University of Florida.

Solomon, B. (1999). Out of the mainstream: An unorthodox pathway to the office of graduate dean. In W. Harvey (Ed.), *Grass roots and glass ceilings: African American administrators in predominantly White colleges and universities* (pp. 135–149). Albany, NY: State University of New York Press.

Sprague, J. (2005). *Feminist methodologies for cultural researchers: Bridging differences*. Lanham, MD: AltaMira Press.

Stallard, K., Ehrenreich, B., & Sklar, H. (1983). *Poverty in the American dream: Women & children first*. Cambridge, MA: South End Press.

Stauffer, S. M. (2005). "She speaks as one having authority": Mary E. Downey's use of libraries as a means to public power. *Libraries & Culture, 40*(1), 38–62.

Street, S., & Kimmel, E. (1999.). Gender role preferences and perceptions of university administrators. *NASPA Journal, 36*(3), 222–239.

Street, S., Kimmel, E., & Kromrey, J. D. (1996). Gender role preferences and perceptions of university students, faculty, and administrators. *Research in Higher Education, 37*(5), 615–632.

Strober, M. H., & Tyack, D. (1980). Why do women teach and men manage? A report on research on schools. *Signs, 5*(3), 494–503.

Strom, S. H. (1989). "Light manufacturing": The feminization of American office work, 1900–1930. *Industrial and Labor Relations Review, 43*(1), 53–71.

Tull, A. (2006). Synergistic supervision, job satisfaction, and intention to turnover in new professionals in student affairs. *Journal of College Student Development, 47*(4), 465–480.

Tyson, V. K. (2002). Asian American administrators. In A. M. M. Alemán & K. A. Renn (Eds.), *Women in higher education: An encyclopedia* (pp. 466–469). Santa Barbara, CA: ABC-CLIO, Inc.

Warner, R., & DeFleur, L. B. (1994). Career paths of women in higher education administration. In P. T. Mitchell (Ed.), *Cracking the wall: Women in higher education administration*. College & University Personnel Association.

Wilson, R. (2008, February 22). 2 colleges, 2 presidents, one marriage. *The Chronicle of Higher Education, 54*(24), A1.

Wong, J. M. (2004). My life a. d. (after divorce). In K. A. Renn & C. Hughes (Eds.), *Roads taken: Women in student affairs at mid-career* (pp. 35–40). Sterling, VA: Stylus.

Zorn, J. (2007). It's women's work. *Yearbook of the Association of Pacific Coast Geographers, 69*, 14–30.

Zuschin, A. P. (2003). *Alienation among female senior student affairs officers: Correlation between gender traits, organizational culture, and alienation*. Unpublished doctoral dissertation, Kent State University.

17

Campus-Based Sexual Assault Prevention
Perspectives and Recommendations From Program Facilitators

*Lindsay M. Orchowski, Eric Zimak, Troy Robison, Justin Reeder,
Ryan Rhoades, Christine A. Gidycz, and Alan Berkowitz*

Abstract: *Despite years of feminist work and change toward raising awareness of the prevalence of sexual victimization, girls and women continue to disproportionately struggle for safety and justice. Sexual assault occurs at particularly high rates on college campuses. The purpose of this chapter is unique in that in addition to providing syntheses of literature and reflections regarding sexual assault prevention, we provide an "insider's view" of the step-by-step procedures for implementing and facilitating campus-based sexual assault prevention programming. More broadly, the overarching goal of this chapter is to assist educators, health professionals, and student affairs personnel in gaining an understanding of the fundamental components, as well as the personal and procedural challenges, of campus-based sexual assault prevention.*

THE EXPERIENCES DESCRIBED in this chapter reflect the experiences of facilitators and supervisors administering the *Community Program Initiative*, a large scale, dual-pronged sexual assault prevention and risk-reduction program, administered and evaluated within the residence halls at a medium-sized Midwestern university (Gidycz, 2006). Explanations of the various approaches in sexual assault prevention and risk reduction are provided, as well as a detailed description of the procedural aspects of program administration. It is our hope that the material assists campus personnel in further developing and administering comprehensive,

collaborative, and evidence-based approaches to combat the endemic problem of campus-based violence against women.

Rates of sexual victimization on college campuses have shown little decline since Koss, Gidycz, and Wisniewski's (1987) landmark prevalence study. Studies conducted over the last 10 years at one Midwestern university document that 16%–32% of college women report experiencing some form of sexual victimization over a two- to three-month period (Gidycz, Coble, Latham, & Layman, 1993; Gidycz, Rich, Orchowski, King, & Miller, 2006; Orchowski, Gidycz, & Raffle, 2008). Alarmingly, college women are three times more likely to experience sexual victimization compared with women the same age in the general population (Corbin, Bernat, Calhoun, McNair, & Seals, 2001). Notably, all educational institutes of higher learning that receive federal funding are mandated by U.S. federal law to implement some form of violence prevention program on campus (National Association of Student Personnel Administrators, 1994). The overarching goal of sexual assault prevention programming is to reduce rates of violence by engendering attitude and behavior change (see Bachar & Koss, 2000; Gidycz, Rich, & Marioni, 2002, for reviews). Sexual violence prevention efforts with men are often referred to as "prevention programs," whereas programming efforts with women are referred to as "risk reduction programs." Use of this terminology highlights the belief that *only potential perpetrators of violence against women can truly prevent its occurrence*.

Because of high rates of sexual violence, we agree with fellow researchers (e.g., Breitenbecher, 2000; Gidycz et al., 2002; Yeater & O'Donohue, 1999) who proposed that it is of vital importance to develop sexual assault prevention and risk reduction programs demonstrating *efficacy* not only in changing attitudes and behaviors that perpetuate sexual violence but also in reducing rates of sexual violence. Establishing methods for assessing participants' attitudes, behaviors, and experiences of sexual aggression and victimization necessitates that program administrators establish methods for surveying attitudes and behaviors prior to program participation and at multiple points following program participation. These assessments should utilize surveys, which have already been shown to be reliable and valid measures of program objectives. The program itself must also be administered consistently.

With the exception of research conducted by Lonsway and colleagues (1998), documenting a semester-long training course for sexual assault peer educators, there are very few descriptions of the *process* of facilitating, training, and super-

vising the administration of campus-based violence prevention programs that include an evaluation component. This chapter addresses this gap in the literature by documenting the "behind-the-scenes" perspectives and recommendations from facilitators of a nationally funded evaluation of campus-based violence prevention programming, the Community Programming Initiative, in which sexual assault prevention and risk reduction programs were concurrently administered to single-sex audiences of men and women living within the same residence halls (Gidycz, 2006). To assist future professional and peer health educators in administering large-scale, empirically evaluated, violence prevention programs, this chapter explores the following questions:

1. What are the training needs of men and women facilitators of sexual assault prevention and risk reduction programs?
2. What are the common personal and procedural challenges faced when working to facilitate sexual assault prevention and risk reduction programs with groups of men and groups of women?
3. Do the personal and procedural challenges of program facilitation differ between men and women program facilitators?
4. What recommendations do current program facilitators have for other peer educators engaging in efforts to prevent violence against women?

These research questions were chosen deliberately, with the hope that this chapter could be distributed to current undergraduate health-educators and sexual assault prevention program facilitators in order to normalize some of the personal challenges faced when working with college students in the context of violence prevention programs. With this goal in mind, personal stories from 10 male and female program facilitators are the foundation for a series of recommendations for future program facilitators. We also list strategies for coping with emotional reactions, handling challenging group dynamics, and addressing sensitive issues and statements in violence prevention programming. These recommendations highlight not only the different *approaches* to working with male and female college students in the context of violence prevention work but also how the *process, dynamics, and impact* of violence prevention programs differed between male and female facilitators.

We have developed this chapter with supervisors of sexual assault prevention program efforts in mind as well. Because secondary victimization—including reactions of burnout, anger, and disillusionment—is common among individuals working to prevent violence against women, it is important for supervisors to be aware of the challenges faced by needs of male and female peer educators. Thus, it is our hope that material on the selection, training, and supervision of program facilitators assists supervisors in supporting the individuals working to administer prevention efforts.

APPROACHES TO SEXUAL ASSAULT PREVENTION PROGRAMS FOR COLLEGE MEN

Various educational programs exist to bring awareness to men of the prevalence of sexual assault and rape on college campuses. Various theoretical approaches and methods are used in these programs. According to Berkowitz (1994), most programs describe facts and statistics, without attending to the theoretical and research literature on male sexual assault. Berkowitz (2004) posited that scholars in the field generally agree that the following components are integral to successful programs. First, men should be approached as partners who need to assume responsibility for their actions. Second, programs should include intimate discussions in small, peer-based groups. Third, men should have a forum to discuss their understanding of masculinity and perceptions of typical male behavior. Fourth, descriptions of

ways to intervene must be included in programs, to help males feel efficacious in preventing sexual assault. Finally, programs for males should be run in conjunction with female programs to create a collaborative, nonthreatening, and healthy campus environment.

Engaging men in ending violence against women is often approached as encouraging men to—more broadly—become allies in social justice efforts. This stance emphasizes that men must be the agents of social change if they are serious about bringing an end to sexual assault (Berkowitz, 2005). To accomplish this, Berkowitz (2005) asserted that men must challenge notions of traditional masculine gender role and sexist beliefs, which are fostered via peer- and society-based socialization processes. As social justice allies, men should recognize that traditional notions of masculinity harm everyone by sustaining a culture that tolerates violence against women, as well as sustaining harmful notions of how men think, emote, and behave (e.g., "real men don't cry"). By becoming social justice allies, men encourage other men to notice, challenge, and change harmful and limiting misperceptions regarding masculine gender roles.

Further, Janis (1972) defined groupthink as a mode of thinking in cohesive groups where unanimity is valued over realistic appraisal. Perception of realism and moral judgment become subservient to pressures of the group, and groups are unable to engage in critical thinking and make informed/correct decisions (Janis & Mann, 1977). Consequences of groupthink include generation of few alternative behaviors/actions, selective information gathering, and hindered development of alternative courses of action. Conditions that contribute to the occurrence of groupthink include the use of directive leadership, similar demographics, and beliefs of group members, and group isolation from information sources outside of the group (McCauley, 1989). Given that groupthink underlies peer group interactions, it is likely that it plays a key role in maintaining ascription to hypermasculine norms.

Since many sexual assaults occur because men believe that they have consent when indeed they do not, the consent model may be one of the most important components of sexual assault prevention (Berkowitz, 1994). Consent includes four conditions: both parties are equally free to act, are fully conscious, have clearly communicated their intent (either verbally or nonverbally), and are positive and sincere in their desires. An emphasis on the consent model encourages students to define positive and respectable behavior, rather than focusing on discussions of legality (Berkowitz, 1994).

APPROACHES TO SEXUAL ASSAULT RISK REDUCTION PROGRAMS FOR COLLEGE WOMEN

Sexual assault risk reduction programs operate under the belief that although true prevention of sexual assault is achieved by working with potential perpetrators of sexual aggression, some experiences of sexual assault are unavoidable and, thus, women must be provided with strategies to fight back against potential perpetrators. According to Rozee and Koss (2001), women can be more effective in resisting the perpetrators when they are aware of characteristics of potential perpetrators, situational risk cues, and the signs that a social or dating experience is moving toward a potentially coercive or threatening situation. Rozee and Koss (2001) delineated the "AAA" strategy for reducing risk for victimization, which includes (1) assessing whether a social or dating experience is potentially dangerous, (2) acknowledging and labeling that a situation is potentially threatening when it is so, and (3) assertively and forcefully taking action via immediate verbal or physical resistance. Following detection of threat, women are encouraged to increasingly use more assertive verbal and physical resistance strategies (Rozee & Koss, 2001). This model serves as the general framework for many risk reduction efforts (e.g., Gidycz et al., 2006; Orchowski et al.,

2008). Some recent risk reduction programs also include a self-defense component focused on engaging women in intensive practice of resistance tactics, such as forms of immediate verbal and physical self-defense (see Gidycz et al., 2006; Orchowski et al., 2008).

Risk reduction programs educate women on risk factors for sexual victimization so that they can notice when a dating situation may be becoming dangerous and respond assertively. The literature documents a range of characteristics relating to the perpetrator (see Abbey, Zawicki, Buck, Clinton, & McAuslan, 2004), as well as certain social and dating situations (Gross, Winslett, Roberts, & Gohm, 2006), which may increase a women's likelihood of sexual victimization. Substances used by the victim and/or the perpetrator are commonly discussed in programs as a risk factor for sexual victimization (Abbey et al., 2004; Gross et al., 2006). Videos that model and encourage discussion of risk factors for victimization may be used to enhance women's ability to identify risk factors and also brainstorm resistance strategies. When developing self-protective strategies, women are informed that there is no "right or wrong" way to respond to a potential threat. Rather, women are encouraged to identify the resistance strategy that *works best for them* (Gidycz et al., 2006; Orchowski et al., 2008).

Dating situations are rarely clear-cut. When in a social scenario, women face a number of competing demands, such as wanting to be liked, while also wanting to remain safe (Nurius, 2000). Fear of rejection, or fear of feeling embarrassed if the threat is unfounded, make it likely that women dismiss the cues to respond protectively when they feel uncomfortable in a dating situation (Norris, Nurius, & Dimeff, 1996; Nurius & Norris, 1995). Further, cultural dating norms increase the likelihood that women focus on the social cues within a dating situation, as opposed to "safety cues" that indicate a situation is unsafe (Nurius, 2000). As a result, cues that indicate to a woman that she may be in a risky dating situation may be normalized or even ignored as a result of competing social demands (Norris et al., 1996; Norris, Nurius, & Graham, 1999; Nurius, 2000; Nurius & Norris, 1995), particularly when substance use is involved.

In addition, risk reduction programs aim to enhance women's effectiveness in responding to potential threats by helping women to identify their personal "psychological barriers to resistance" (Breitenbecher & Scarce, 2001; Norris et al., 1996, 1999; Nurius, 2000; Nurius & Norris, 1995). Orchowski and her colleagues (2008) presented risk reduction strategies as a lifestyle and note that women should make a plan for how they may respond when they feel uncomfortable. Women may also be informed that it is natural to feel hesitant to engage in self-protective behavior, and that it can be difficult to make choices in social situations that prioritize personal safety over perceived social demands (Orchowski et al., 2008).

RECRUITING, SELECTING, AND TRAINING PROGRAM FACILITATORS

Community Programming Initiative

The sexual violence prevention program discussed here is the Community Programming Initiative, a campus-based sexual assault prevention program evaluation study funded by the Centers for Disease Control and Prevention from 2006 to 2008 (Gidycz, 2006). First-year college students from a single Midwestern university were recruited from six campus residence halls each year to participate. Over 1,300 students agreed to participate in the research, which was advertised via posters in the residence halls and personal contact from resident advisors. Residence halls were randomly assigned to either a program or control group so that the research team could compare how the attitudes and behaviors of those who received the programs changed over

time in comparison to those who did not receive the program. Male and female undergraduate students in both groups completed a pretest, four-month, and seven-month follow-up assessment, where they reported on dating behaviors, attitudes, beliefs, and experiences of sexual aggression/victimization they experienced since the last assessment session.

The format of the sexual assault prevention and risk reduction program in the Community Programming Initiative is strategic, in that single-sex programs are tailored to meet the needs of women and men in gaining skills to prevent violence or reduce risk for experiencing violence. The program is also synergistic, in that it targets first-year women and men living together in the *same* campus residence halls, in order to encourage dialogue between students and create a community-based change in the norms that perpetuate violence against women. The program also highlights service provision by coordinating with a campus-based *Counselor-in-Residence Program*, which is available to assist program and control group participants who wish to discuss concerns regarding violence (see Orchowski, Castelino, Ng, & Cosio, 2007). The specific program protocols administered in the Community Programming Initiative are described in detail now.

Program Protocols

The Men's Workshop (Berkowitz, 2006, in press) consists of two sessions. The first session lasts approximately two hours and aims to inform men of social norms and to facilitate the expression of discomfort with the coercive and opportunistic sexual behavior of some men. The program also encourages men to take responsibility for decreasing their peers' inappropriate coercive behaviors. During the program warm-up, the purposes of the group are outlined and open, honest communication is fostered. Following the introduction, definitions and statistics regarding the prevalence of sexual assault and sexual harassment are provided. To increase the saliency of program material, incidence rates of sexual assault from the local university are provided. Next, scenarios highlighting the definition of consent and the difficulties that are encountered in social situations when alcohol is being consumed are discussed. Following this, participants complete a small group norms activity in which they generate data to correct misperceptions about men's sexual activity on campus. Additional scenarios are presented and the session concludes with small-group practice of bystander intervention strategies. The second session is a one and a half hours booster session of program material and is held approximately four months following session one. Facilitators reviewed social norms information as well as condition for consent. Next, in both small-group and large-group formats, men discuss how they have utilized program information over the interim, as well as what they found most useful about the program.

Risk Reduction Program

The Ohio University Sexual Assault Risk Reduction Program (Gidycz et al., 2006) consists of three sessions and is designed to increase women's awareness of risky dating situations and encourage women to respond assertively when faced with a potential threat. The program also aims to increase women's awareness of common reactions to sexual victimization and encourages women to seek support if they experience a sexual assault. The first session is two and a half hours in length and begins by introducing the conceptual framework of the program as well as definitions and statistics regarding sexual assault. Statistics regarding the frequency of sexual assault at the local university are provided to increase the saliency of program material. Women next view a video titled "I Thought It Would Never Happen to Me," in which survivors of sexual assault discuss the "warning signs" that the situation was potentially risky as well as their own process of recovery (Gidycz, Dowdall, Lynn, Marioni, &

Loh, 1997). Following the video, women discuss the risk factors for sexual assault, including characteristics of the perpetrators, as well as the situation involved. Next, the facilitators present information regarding the role of date rape drugs and alcohol in sexual assault as well as common postassault reactions. To encourage women to brainstorm reactions to risky dating scenarios, a video titled "Keep Your Options Open: Alternative Solutions for Stressful Social Situations" is shown (Gidycz, 2000). The benefits to responding assertively to the situation are discussed, as well as potential barriers to resistance (e.g., embarrassment), and women are provided with a handout listing strategies for responding to risky situations and campus resources. The program concludes by encouraging women to trust their intuition and to find the best way to integrate self-protective strategies into their lifestyle.

The second part of the program is a two and a half hours self-defense program, taught by Cheryl Cesta, a national expert in self-defense for women and girls. The workshop emphasizes the self-protective strategies introduced in the workshop and aims to further develop women's awareness of risky dating scenarios and potential responses to threat. Goals of the workshop include (1) increasing awareness of body language, (2) increasing awareness of risk factors, (3) enhancing women's ability to trust their intuition, (4) learning and practicing verbal and immediate resistance tactics, and (5) learning and practicing physical resistance strategies to disable an attacker and escape. The workshop reminds women that there is no single way to respond to a risky dating situation and emphasizes the importance of responding assertively when a threat is detected.

The third part of the program is a booster session review of program material, which is one and a half hours in length and occurs approximately four months following initial program participation. Facilitators review risk factors for sexual victimization, including characteristics of the perpetrator, characteristics of the situation, as well as the role of alcohol in risky dating situations. In small-group and large-group discussion, participants share how they have utilized program information over the interim, as well as what was most useful about the program.

RECRUITING PROGRAM FACILITATORS

Prior to the onset of the Community Programming Initiative, the principal investigator and project coordinator collaborated with the Department of Residence Life and the Department of Health Education and Wellness at the university to recruit potential program facilitators. The goal was to recruit five men and five women to serve as program facilitators and assistant program facilitators. Given the excellent leadership abilities of residential advisors and students trained in health promotion, these students were targeted via e-mails and letters to apply. This process was repeated during both years of program administration. Following the first year of program administration, program facilitators who were still attending the university were invited to return to the project. Because it might be uncomfortable for a man or woman to participate in a sexual assault risk reduction or prevention program led by their own resident advisor, it was made clear to participants and the staff that no resident advisor would facilitate a program within his or her own residence hall.

Facilitators were selected on the basis of their ability to clearly communicate ideas, their enthusiasm for the project and for issues of violence prevention, level of maturity, skills in managing groups and addressing difficult questions, and level of critical thinking. In the first year of program facilitation, two undergraduate men were invited to join the research team. Given difficulties recruiting male facilitators, two male graduate students were invited to join the project team as well. Since none of the men graduated following the first year of the project, all facilitators were invited to join the research team again during the

second year of program administration. One new male undergraduate joined the facilitation team during the second year of the project. In the first year of program facilitation, four women were invited to join the project. Since only one women's program facilitator remained on campus following the first year of the project, four new facilitators were recruited to facilitate the project during the second year of program administration. Over the course of the project, none of the facilitators left the research team, were asked to leave the project, or declined to continue facilitating.

Training

Individuals who facilitate scripted health-intervention programs must conduct each program in a reliable fashion and must be skilled in addressing the unique questions posed by group members in a consistent manner. Reliable and consistent program facilitation is essential to evaluating the effectiveness of a program protocol. Training for the Community Programming Initiative contained several components designed to assist facilitators in gaining a background on the theory of the programs, strategies for managing group dynamics and difficult questions, and tips for reliably and consistently administering the programs. All program facilitators received training binders that included (1) program scripts, (2) background information on the theory of sexual assault prevention and risk reduction programming on college campuses, (3) empirical articles documenting current findings on risk factors for sexual victimization, (4) empirical articles documenting prevalence and incidence of sexual assault on college campuses and the local university, (5) empirical articles documenting prior evaluation of the program protocol, and (6) pamphlets on local resources.

Over the course of an intensive weekend of training, men and women program facilitators attended a mock presentation of their respective program protocol. Next, facilitators of the men's sexual assault prevention program attended a series of presentations by Dr. Alan Berkowitz, which included discussion on social norms, engaging men as social justice allies, the role of groupthink in program administration, and strategies for responding to difficult audience members. Facilitators of the risk reduction program attended presentations on rape myths, debunking myths surrounding sexual assault, responding to disclosure of sexual victimization, aftereffects of sexual victimization, resources for survivors, and how to respond to audience members who blame victims of sexual assault for the experience. These sessions were designed to address some of the unique issues addressed in prevention programming for men and risk reduction programming for women, as well as the differing group dynamics that often occur within groups of college men and college women.

Men's and women's program facilitators practiced the programs for small audiences, including members of the Department of Residence Life, as well as small groups of undergraduates in Introductory Psychology courses. Program facilitators observed their peers' program administration, and audience members provided written and verbal feedback. Next, the project supervisors met with program facilitators to process the experience, provide feedback, and further discuss how to respond to difficult questions and comments from audience members. In order to increase reliability and fluidity of group discussions, facilitators and supervisors worked together to generate lists of key points to cover during group discussions and phrases to use to generate group discussion.

Throughout training, facilitators practiced responding to challenging, incorrect, and/or inappropriate (e.g., victim-blaming, ascription to rape myth ideology) responses from participants by encouraging group members to generate alternative responses or differing opinions rather than directly challenging incorrect or inappropriate statements. Supervisors emphasized that the role of the program facilitators was not to take an "expert" stance, to tell participants "what to do or what not to do," but rather to help group members develop their own strategies for creating a safer community for themselves and their peers.

Supervision

Health professionals, student affairs professionals, researchers, and health advocates who supervise the administration of sexual assault prevention and risk reduction efforts have an ethical obligation to ensure that prevention programs are conducted in a sensitive manner. Above all, practitioners must "do no harm" when engaging in preventative practice. However, while program supervisors are often acutely attuned to protecting the participants in a prevention or risk reduction program, program supervisors may overlook the need to support the emotional and professional growth of the individuals who facilitate the program (see Bernard & Goodyear, 2004). Multiple supervision strategies are likely to be most effective in ensuring that programs are administered in a sensitive, reliable, and consistent manner. Opportunities for group discussion as well as personal reflection are also important strategies for encouraging self-reflection and ensuring that facilitators' reactions are normalized and processed. Supervision is also an important component to ensuring that interventions are administered reliably over time.

Facilitators met with the on-site and off-site project supervisors on a weekly and biweekly basis. At the onset of the program evaluation study, supervision sessions were held directly after program facilitation in order to share information regarding specific questions from audience members, troubleshoot any technological difficulties, and process their emotional reaction to especially challenging group dynamics (e.g., cliques, jokes, demeaning statements, disinterest, disbelief, blame). Facilitators fill out and submit process evaluation forms, program evaluation forms, and journal entries.

WOMEN'S AND MEN'S REACTIONS TO PROGRAM FACILITATION

Almost universally, the men felt unprepared to facilitate the program at the outset of training and program facilitation. They described feeling hesitant to lead a program for undergraduates, when they did not feel like experts themselves. However, the training offered support granted through cofacilitation, which helped the facilitators grow and feel skilled and proficient by the end of the study. Conversely, facilitators of the women's risk reduction program often noted professional reasons for being interested in the program—such as wanting to gain leadership skills or being personally committed to violence prevention. As Sax (2008) noted, college women generally demonstrate a strong commitment to improving the lives of others. Nonetheless, female facilitators tended to underestimate the personal impact that the program would have on their own lives. Generally, supervisors observed that male and female program facilitators started the process of program facilitation with different levels of intellectual and emotional awareness regarding violence against women, which also may have accounted for some of the differences in the process of personal growth experienced between male and female program facilitators.

Uniquely, recognizing personal contributions to the program was particularly important in men's process of overcoming feelings of "being an imposter" as a social justice advocate. For example, several male facilitators noted that learning to view their personal experiences and personalities as strengths in program facilitation was a unique growth experience. Personal assets helped male facilitators effectively disseminate knowledge and promote active learning and discussion. Men suggested that their personality also played a role in facilitation. For example, some male facilitators promoted a healthy atmosphere during the program by using humor and levity, whereas others used great interpersonal skills to relate to the participants. Differences between male and

female program facilitators' initial interest in the study and personal challenges faced over time also raises the question of how the process of *self-selection* among students who apply for positions as rape education facilitators influences their experience. Many of the men reported being alerted to the option of participating in the project by a friend or supervisor who believed that they would be a good fit for the job. For female program facilitators, interest in the project stemmed from personal experiences involving unwanted sexual contact, supporting friends who experienced sexual assault, or having an interest in women's studies or feminist issues.

Feminist Identity Development

The process of raising consciousness among the current group of program facilitators was similar to the emotional growth and development documented by Klaw and colleagues (2005). They describe the feminist identity development of a group of college students participating in a semester-long course designed to train peer educators in sexual assault awareness. Feminist identity development is outlined as a series of stages, including (1) passive acceptance (e.g., denying or accepting sexism); (2) revelation of gender discrimination and altering of worldview—which is often accompanied by anger; (3) embeddedness-emanation (e.g., integrating gender oppression with sense of individuality); and (4) active commitment to a feminist identity by engaging in activism (see Nassi & Abramowitz, 1978). Of note, Amy Stalzer Sengupta and Yvette Loury Upton's chapter (chapter 14) in this book, titled "Identity Development in College Women," provides a thought-provoking description of the complex process by which gender influences the process of social and psychological development among college women. Further, an extensive examination of the process of identity development among college students is provided by Elisa Abes and David Kasch's (chapter 13) work, titled "Using Queer Theory to Explore Lesbian College

Students' Multiple Dimensions of Identity," in this book.

Indeed, the process of developing a feminist identity as a result of program participation was self-evident to some program facilitators, especially those facilitating the risk reduction program. For example, one risk reduction program facilitator noted, "I've become more of a feminist. I'm more aware of control issues in society between men and women." Women reported beginning the program already with a sense of commitment to advocating to end gender-based violence, which may account for some of the differences in emotional and professional growth experienced by male and female facilitators over the course of the project. Program training and facilitation further strengthened the women's resolve to act as a social advocate. The onset of a feminist identity and development of an interest in social justice was also commonly reported by male facilitators. Although only a minority of the men reported personal interest in violence prevention prior to commencement of the study, over time, it appeared that men's interest in social justice and advocacy began to develop, despite their initial hesitancy of engaging in such work, identifying as an advocate, and feeling like an imposter.

For both male and female facilitators, this process was gradual and often involved a significant amount of anger in response to derogatory jokes, sexist comments, or remarks that blamed victims for the experience of sexual victimization. For example, most facilitators documented intense feelings of disillusionment at their peers' often blatant expressions of victim blame during the sessions. This anger was often so marked that facilitators reported feelings of burnout. Processing the anger associated with hearing peers discuss sexist or victim-blaming attitudes within supervision sessions, with graduate student supervisors, and with cofacilitators was described as a key component of facilitators' ability to continue engagement in activism. After several weeks

of program facilitation, many of the female facilitators expressed feeling a renewed sense of confidence in women's ability to support each other, noting that "women can and do empower other women."

Vicarious Traumatization

Vicarious traumatization refers to the process by which individuals who work with trauma survivors incorporate painful experiences of their patients into their own memory systems (Figley, 2002; Jenmorri, 2006; Pearlman & Mac Ian, 1995; Rager, 2005; Salson & Figley, 2003). Over time individuals who work with trauma victims often experience intrusive thoughts, images, and emotional reactions that can be related to symptoms of posttraumatic stress disorder (McCann & Pearlman, 1990). Individuals who have personally experienced a traumatic event have a significantly harder time coping with disclosure of trauma (Pearlman & Mac Ian, 1995; Salson & Figley, 2003). Several female facilitators reported that listening to female participants' stories of interpersonal and sexual violence triggered intense personal feelings, ranging from helplessness to the urge to control, rage to numbness, and detachment to overidentification among the facilitation team. Several of the facilitators of the risk reduction program reported feeling *personally engaged* with the participants in the session, noting that they often "took work home with them" following difficult sessions. Importantly, overidentification with survivors of sexual victimization may impede a facilitator's ability to process participants' reactions to program material (Figley, 2002), especially if they disclose victim blame or ascription with rape myth ideology. In some cases, facilitators may seek to meet their own needs by giving advice to the participants' disclosing their own experiences, or becoming instructive within the session, as opposed to generating group discussion (Figley, 2002).

Dealing With Difficult Comments and Victim Blame

Difficulties coping with some of the participant's disrespectful comments were another frequent problem for both men's and women's program facilitators. Female program facilitators commonly reported feelings of frustration when participants blamed women for sexual assault, expressed disbelief in the rates of violence, or noted, "it could never happen to them." Men's program facilitators often became frustrated when participants failed to take the material seriously, noted that "their friends would never do that" (i.e., be aggressive), or became engrossed in discussing rates of false accusations of sexual assault. We believe these are important distinctions between the group dynamics of men's and women's programming.

Men's program facilitators were generally less frustrated by the demeaning or joking comments of the participants. However, such comments became more difficult for female program facilitators to manage as they became more invested in the program and identified more strongly as an advocate for ending violence. It is possible that as the female facilitators' investment in the program increased, it became more distressing that their peers did not share the same level of concern for violence against women. It was common for supervisors to help female program facilitators to process their anger and frustration following particularly difficult sessions, and to reframe participants' disbelief and disregard of program material. Discussing the developmental level of the freshman program participants or reasons why women audience members may distance themselves from the material were particularly helpful in decreasing female facilitators' frustration.

Personal Growth

The reactions of men's and women's program facilitators mirror those documented by Lonsway et al. (1998), who suggested that undergraduate program facilitators became more willing to engage in assertive sexual communication within their own intimate relationships after participating in the training course to facilitate rape education programming. All facilitators in this project also discussed tremendous personal growth. The program challenged the facilitators' personal beliefs and made them contemplate their worldviews, behaviors, and decisions. For female facilitators, this shift mirrors Stalzer Sengupta and Upton's (chapter 14) description of Helms's Womanist identity model, whereby identity development is characterized by altering one's worldviews regarding womanhood from an externalized conceptualization to an internalized understanding of self.

Some differences were noted between male and female facilitators as well. Male program facilitators realized that some biases and stereotypes they held about sexual assault assailants (e.g., "you can pick them out of a crowd," "they are always 'big' guys") had little merit. Conversely, female program facilitators reported a sense of empowerment following program facilitation, noting that being asked to model assertive behavior within the group sessions encouraged them to take a more confident, self-protective, and assertive stance in their own social, family, and interpersonal relationships. It is important to note that the women's reactions to program facilitation suggested that although they were now more confident in asserting themselves to take protective action within dating situations, they also recognized that they were also at risk to experience unwanted sexual experiences. Such an understanding is important, in that there is a concern that peer educators may wrongly assume that as an advocate and leader in rape awareness programming, they can "handle" any risky dating situation, or that they would be able to prevent sexual assault from occurring. More broadly, this shift in the female facilitators' sense of self-concept reflects the discussion of Belenky, Clinchy, Goldberger, and Tarule's (1986) research in this book in chapter 14, documenting the process by which women come to understand themselves as self-confident, knowledgeable, and capable of learning.

RECOMMENDATIONS FOR PROGRAM FACILITATORS

Program facilitators and supervisors compiled a number of recommendations for facilitating sexual assault prevention and risk reduction programs. These recommendations are targeted for both male and female groups; however, when appropriate, distinctions are made when recommendations are specific to either all-female or all-male program groups.

Create an Open, Safe Environment for Discussion

It is important that program facilitators for both men's and women's programs create a safe environment in which participants can openly discuss their reactions to program material. Given that women face a number of psychological barriers in responding to uncomfortable dating situations, it is important that program facilitators create an environment where women can openly discuss their reservations to using self-protective strategies. It is often the case that women and men can identify the "correct" way to respond to a risky dating situation; however, when given the opportunity to discuss whether they "truly" engage in such behavior, they identify a range of reasons why they refrain from behaving assertively when actually in the social situation. For example, college men may report fears that they would experience physical injury if they take steps to intervene when they notice a male peer behaving in a coercive way. Further, many college women indicate that they refrain from responding assertively in a dating situation, for fear that they will look "mean" or "rude." Thus, it is helpful that facilitators are skilled in creating a safe, nonthreatening environment where participants can

discuss the conflicting social demands often experienced when in social and dating situations. Processing the benefits and drawbacks of engaging in bystander intervention and assertive sexual communication can be a useful way to encourage participants to reflect on what might hold them back from engaging in appropriate or self-protective behavior while in a dating situation.

Take a Collaborative, as Opposed to Expert, Stance

The way in which program material is conveyed to the participant audience varies between programs. It is our belief, however, that students are more engaged in programming in which the facilitators take a collaborative, as opposed to an expert, stance. Within the Community Programming Initiative, facilitators of the men's prevention program allowed the male participants to discover how male socialization patterns can lead to internalized misconceptions through guided group discussions. This dialogue included covering the different aspects of consent, discussing how men may sometimes jump to conclusions and engage in sex play without consent, understanding the reasons behind these communication breakdowns, and talking about the role that alcohol and other drugs play in exacerbating these breakdowns. In this format, audience members were encouraged to be active participants in the program, as opposed to passive recipients of information. Program facilitators have compared this collaborative approach to the adage, "Give a man a fish and he can eat for a night; teach a man to fish and he can feed himself for a lifetime."

Group Size

Small or large groups may also require creative strategies to elicit discussion or manage side conversations within the group. One risk reduction facilitator noted that "the biggest obstacle was having a large group. They would get offtrack and it was hard to keep them focused. And some people getting up to use the bathroom or using their phones during the videos was distracting." A prevention program facilitator agreed with the difficulty of presenting to large groups of men, noting that

> larger groups tend to require facilitators to exert more effort to get everyone involved and to keep the peace. Looking back, however, although it felt difficult to handle, I do not think that this obstacle has substantially affected the presentation in a detrimental way. We've learned to just go with the flow.

Accommodating the Research Protocol

Staying "on script" in order to adhere to the research protocol was also a challenge, especially when attempting to address difficult questions, distracting group members, or high levels of disbelief or victim blame. A facilitator described that "although we cover the necessary information on the script, it is sometimes difficult to do it in the order that is laid out for us." Encouraging facilitators to stay on the script, while also being flexible in addressing problematic group dynamics, personal disclosures, and questions, was a critical component of supervision. Often, supervisors normalized the nervousness that program facilitators felt when "going off script," reminding facilitators that variation among topics of discussion was a normal part of the program protocol.

Managing Cliques

Facilitating programs within peer groups, while likely the most effective strategy for changing group norms, is also likely to foster potentially distracting conversations within groups. For example, one men's program facilitator addressed a difficult group in the following way:

> I separated a particularly difficult group of friends during the survey portion of the program. When separated, they were fine but I made the mistake of allowing to move back. They were disruptive

enough that I considered moving them again, but not enough to give me the final push. I wished I would've followed through, and suggest that you trust your gut and follow through on separating individuals if you have an indication that some cliques might get disruptive.

Strategies for addressing some of these technological concerns, as well as problematic group dynamics, are provided in Table 17.1.

Disclosure of Personal Experiences

It is vital for facilitators to be aware of appropriate response to disclosure of trauma in order to avoid retraumatizing participants who share their experiences. Directly practicing supportive responses to disclosure can decrease the likelihood that facilitators become "caught up" in processing the disclosures of participants, pushing the program participant to recount details of the trauma, past the point of healthy processing or self-directed sharing. This may cause the participant, as well as group members, to feel unduly distressed during the session and overwhelmed. Such experiences may also retraumatize the survivor and dissuade other group members from participating honestly or sharing their own experiences.

On the other hand, some facilitators may be so distressed by participants' personal disclosure of traumatic events that they unconsciously distance themselves from processing the event with the participant, change the subject, provide minimal response, or fail to provide emotional support to the group members. Such reactions may be a result of the facilitator's personal feelings of avoidance, denial, guilt, shame, or helplessness. The detachment from the participant's disclosure may also be interpreted by audience members as victim blame, or disbelief. In such situations, it is vital that facilitators practice reacting to disclosure of traumatic experiences prior to facilitating program sessions. Utilizing two program facilitators, as opposed to one, may also increase the likelihood that the pair of program facilitators

Table 17.1 Strategies for Addressing Difficult Group Dynamics

Type of Concern	Strategies for Intervention
Participants don't want to be there	Let the group members know that they are free to leave at any time.
Technology malfunctions	Problem solved! Get the participants involved in their own discussion (e.g., ask for names) while another facilitator works to address technology problems.
Cofacilitator is absent	If group appears to be difficult, let participants know that you are working shorthanded. At times, participants will "give you a break."
Group is unexpectedly large	Get group members involved by asking questions to all sections of the audience.
Dominant participants	State your awareness of the perspective of the dominant group member and draw out opinions from other group members (e.g., "We know what this group member thinks, do other people agree/disagree? How so?").
Jokes and laughing	If individuals are making jokes or find program material humorous, it is OK to ignore it if it is not interfering with the program. This is a normal reaction to sensitive topics. Address the issue directly once participants become obscene, loud, or detract from others' experience.
Following the script	When a facilitator is drawn off the script of the program, it is OK to address the topic at a later point. Assigning two facilitators to each intervention can help to reduce the likelihood that topics are omitted, as cofacilitators may notice and correct omissions in the protocol.
Quiet participants	Remember that as long as participants are listening, they are most likely processing the material. Some groups are less talkative than others. Since interventions are administered within a community, they may talk about the material with their peers after the program, when they feel more comfortable.
Differences among facilitators	Program facilitators bring a unique personality, background, culture, and style to the facilitation team. There is no "one" personality for a facilitator, since different participants may relate better to different facilitators. Overall, it is important to work together to communicate a cohesive message to the audience.

can work together to effectively respond. Specifically, if one program facilitator fails to provide an appropriate emotional response, the second facilitator may help to provide a response. It is important for facilitators to practice finding the right balance of validating the individual's experience, expressing appreciation for the disclosure, communicating empathy, belief, and support for the survivor—while not making the survivor feel the uncomfortable focus of attention. It is also important for facilitators to be prepared to redirect discussion if those individuals who disclose trauma histories are at risk to be further victimized by questions from other group members, which convey that she is to blame for the experience.

Confronting Disbelief and Victim Blame

Often, individuals distance themselves from thinking that they could experience a traumatic event, such as sexual assault, believing that "it could not happen to me." For example, one risk reduction program facilitator noted,

> I think a lot of the female participants came into the session and were really nervous about the topic. Many women laughed. I was not sure if they just thought some of the words were funny or if they were a little uneasy with this discussion.

Humor is one way that women may downplay the seriousness of sexual assault, or protect themselves from the frightening realization that all women are at risk to experience violence. Women may also blame victims for their assaults by indicating that what they were wearing or their actions "caused" the assault. Such comments allow women to maintain the false "Just World Belief," wherein good things happen to good people and bad things happen to bad people (Janoff-Bulman, 1992)—when in actuality, it is the perpetrator of sexual aggression who is responsible for an assault, regardless of women's actions or behaviors.

Men may also distance themselves from the issue of sexual violence by joking about the experience. One men's program facilitator stressed the importance of preparing for demeaning comments and jokes, noting that

> you just don't want to hear those things, and you want to address them in a professional way, but it's quite difficult when what was said has really angered you. It helped to be prepared for it—we weren't caught off guard.

Within men's programs, victim blame may be portrayed less overtly, often in rejection or disbelief of the rate at which rapes are falsely reported. To handle these objections, facilitators would sometimes cite other sources, which showed slightly higher false accusation rates, and ask men to reflect on these statistics. An alternative strategy may be to ask men to ponder why they believe men tend to doubt a female who accuses a male of sexual assault. Facilitators also may relate to the participants the stigma attached to women who accuse men of assault as well as the heavy burden of proof required to convict the accused.

Confronting comments that place blame on victims of sexual assault is a delicate task within group settings. Facilitators working from a collaborative stance must engage with audience members, as opposed to talk to them, in order to avoid being perceived as an expert. The goal of addressing these difficult interactions is to create attitude change by allowing the group to express differing opinions, which offer alter-

natives to victim blame, derogatory comments, or disbelief of statistics. For specific strategies for addressing victim blame, see Table 17.2.

Groupthink

Expressions of victim blame and disbelief of the severity and prevalence of sexual violence may be linked to social norms and groupthink. Thus, helping men to recognize and focus on the discomfort they feel is a useful starting point in engaging men's feelings of responsibility during sexual assault prevention programs (Berkowitz, 2002). One place to begin is by helping leaders or facilitators of men's groups become aware of their own misconceptions or beliefs (Berkowitz, 2005). Unless this is integrated into training, the leaders' biases might contribute to group relational cohesion or directive leadership. In fact, research has provided many different strategies that can be used to facilitate groups and overcome groupthink. Originally these included educating the group about groupthink and its consequences, using nondirective leadership, allowing and fostering critical thinking, considering unpopular alternatives, and dividing the group up into smaller groups to generate various opinions (Janis & Mann, 1977). Subsequent research in this area has also shown that holding group members accountable for their decisions and reducing the pressure put on them to conform can decrease groupthink (t'Hart, 1998).

Another crucial element is enlisting the aid of members of the group who feel pressured not to voice their opinion or feel ignored. This may be particularly useful for addressing quiet participants. Often group members will experience groupthink and feel that those who do not speak are in agreement with the opinions that are being expressed. Several specific tools can be used as well, including using separate gender groups, presenting ambiguous scenarios to participants, and focusing on the commonality of all people (Berkowitz, 2005). Recommendations for facilitating groups should foster a diversity of

Table 17.2 Strategies for Victim Blame

Strategies for Intervention	Example
Use a metaphor	Use the mugging analogy: no one asks a woman whose purse was stolen, "Why were you carrying a purse?" It's a situation that forces study participants to think about their own misconceptions and double standards.
Discuss the harm involved	Date rape is especially hard for some to understand. The bottom line is a person who cares for you, and is a good person in general, would never do something to hurt you. Why would you want to spend time and energy on a person who doesn't care about you? This is an important lesson for students coming out of their teen years, an age group associated with social aggression.
Ask for consensus	There are some participants who have a hard time accepting that sexual assault victims are never to be blamed. In these situations, it may be best to let the group handle it. Since they all live in the same residence hall, they often have more influence over one another. If there is a dissenter, ask the group if they agree/disagree/have anything to say.
Use different wording	Rephrase the response in a way that takes the blame away from the female; rephrase the question asked, or the way the scenario was presented.
Postprogram processing	Facilitators often report feeling disheartened and frustrated when they felt unsuccessful in diffusing a group's victim-blaming attitudes. Program supervisors may consider using the participants' postprogram evaluations to help facilitators to understand the group dynamic, and recognize the positive components of the program administration as opposed to dwelling on the attitudes of victim blame expressed by some participants. As suggested by one women's program facilitator, "a couple of girls do not ruin the experience for the whole group. If the other group members seem engaged, it may be best to ignore the unresponsive members."

perspectives and encourage the unshared or silent information to be expressed.

Self-Care

Data suggest that therapists who include self-care strategies into their regular routines report lower stress levels than those who do not. These strategies include regular exercise, eating healthy, and having time to recuperate or meditate (Meadors & Lamson, 2008). Participating in group discussions, support groups, and journal writing also help reduce the negative effects of trauma therapy (Rager, 2005). Discussing personal reactions to program facilitation with others who are involved in the project may help to normalize some of the intense emotions stirred by discussing sexual assault. Maintaining involvement in activities outside the project is also essential in continuing to develop personal interests. Some program facilitators may find it useful to share the information they are learning in training with friends and family.

CONCLUSION

The current chapter provided a behind-the-scenes description of the personal challenges, transformative experiences, and process of facilitating dual-pronged sexual assault prevention and risk reduction programming on a college campus. Uniquely, programs were facilitated within residence halls, and programming was evaluated over a four-month and seven-month follow-up period. The experiences of program facilitators provided here document some of the unique challenges for facilitating violence prevention campaigns that contain a program evaluation component. We believe that these recommendations can be utilized by other educators, researchers, health professionals, and student affairs professionals in the development and orchestration of campus-based sexual assault prevention efforts.

Given that rates of sexual assault on college campuses have yet to decline despite over 30 years of preventative efforts, it is the responsibility of individuals working in violence prevention to improve the quality, intensity, and comprehensiveness of intervention programs. Programs must be empirically and theoretically driven, and program administrators must prioritize efforts to evaluate the effectiveness of the program by implementing valid methods of surveying pre- and postprogram attitudes, behaviors, and rates of perpetrating or experiencing sexual violence. Within college campuses, and in communities, efforts are likely to be most effective when campus personnel and offices work systematically to coordinate services and collaborate in programming efforts. It is also the responsibility of those administering violence prevention efforts to ensure that those involved in trauma intervention are prepared, and more important, supported in their efforts.

REFERENCES

Abbey, A., Zawacki, T., Buck, P. O., Clinton, A. M., & McAuslan, P. (2004). Sexual assault and alcohol consumption: What do we know about their relationship and what types of research are still needed? *Aggression and Violent Behavior, 9,* 271–303.

Bachar, K., & Koss, M. P. (2000). From prevalence to prevention: Closing the gap between what we know about rape and what we do. In C. M. Renzetti, J. L. Edleson, & R. K. Bergen (Eds.), *Sourcebook on violence against women* (pp. 117–142). Thousand Oaks, CA: Sage.

Belenky, M. F., Clinchy, B. M., Goldberger, N. R., & Tarule, J. M. (1986). *Women's ways of knowing: The development of self, voice and mind*. New York: Basic Books.

Berkowitz, A. D. (1994). *Men and rape: Theory, research, and prevention programs in higher education*. San Francisco, CA: Jossey-Bass.

Berkowitz, A. D. (2001). Critical elements of sexual-assault prevention and risk-reduction programs for men and women. In C. Kilmartin & A. D. Berkowitz (Eds.), *Sexual assault in context* (pp. 75–96). Mahwah, NJ: Erlbaum.

Berkowitz, A. D. (2002). Fostering men's responsibility for preventing sexual assault. In P. A. Schewe (Ed.), *Preventing violence in relationships: Implementations across the life span* (pp. 163–196). Washington DC: American Psychological Association.

Berkowitz, A. D. (2003). Applications of social norms theory to other health and social justice issues. In W. Perkins (Ed.), *The social norms approach to preventing school and college age substance abuse: A handbook for educators, counselors, and clinicians* (pp. 259–279). San Francisco, CA: Jossey-Bass.

Berkowitz, A. D. (2004). Part II: Working with men to prevent violence against women: Program modalities and formats. *National Electronic Network on Violence Against Women, 1–6.*

Berkowitz, A. D. (2005). An overview of the social norms approach. In L. C. Lederman & L. P. Stewart (Eds.), *Changing the culture of college drinking: A socially situated health communication campaign* (pp. 193–214). Cresskill, NJ: Hampton Press.

Berkowitz, A. D. (2006). *The men's workshop (The Community Programming Initiative program protocol)*. Unpublished program protocol.

Berkowitz, A. D. (in press). Fostering healthy norms to prevent violence and abuse: The social norms approach. In K. Kaufman (Ed), *Preventing sexual violence: A practitioners' sourcebook*. Holyoke, MA: NEARI Press.

Bernard, J. M., & Goodyear, R. K. (2004). *Fundamentals of clinical supervision* (3rd ed.). Boston: Pearson.

Bernthal, P. R., & Insko, C. A. (1993). Cohesiveness without groupthink: The interactive effects of social task cohesion. *Group and Organization Management, 18,* 66–87.

Breitenbecher, K. H. (2000). Sexual assault on college campuses: Is an ounce of prevention enough? *Applied and Preventative Psychology, 9,* 23–52.

Breitenbecher, K. H., & Scarce, M. (1999). A longitudinal evaluation of the effectiveness of a sexual assault education program. *Journal of Interpersonal Violence, 14,* 459–478.

Breitenbecher, K. H., & Scarce, M. (2001). An evaluation of the effectiveness of a sexual assault education program focusing on psychological barriers to resistance. *Journal of Interpersonal Violence, 16*, 387–407.

Burt, M. R. (1980). Cultural myths and supports for rape. *Journal of Personality and Social Psychology, 38*, 217–230.

Corbin, W. R., Bernat, J. A., Calhoun, K. S., McNair, L. D., & Seals, K. L. (2001). The role of alcohol expectancies and alcohol consumption among sexually victimized and nonvictimized college women. *Journal of Interpersonal Violence, 16*(4), 297–311.

Figley, C. R. (2002). Compassion fatigue: Psychotherapists' chronic lack of care. *Journal of Clinical Psychology/In Session: Psychotherapy in Practice, 58*, 1433–1441.

Flippen, A. R. (1999). Understanding group think from a self-regulatory perspective. *Small Group Research, 30*(2), 139–165.

Foubert, J. D., & Newberry, J. T. (2006). Effects of two versions of an empathy-based rape prevention program on fraternity men's survivor empathy, attitudes, and behavioral intent to commit rape or sexual assault. *Journal of College Student Development, 47*, 133–148.

Gidycz, C. A. (Producer and Director). (2000). *Keep your options open: Alternative solutions for stressful social situations* (Film). (Available from Christine A. Gidycz, Department of Psychology, Ohio University, Athens, OH 45701)

Gidycz, C. A. (2006). *Preventing sexual assault on college campuses*. Grant funded by the Centers for Disease Control and Prevention (1 R49 CE000923).

Gidycz, C. A., Coble, C. N., Latham, L., & Layman, M. (1993). Relation of a sexual assault experience in adulthood to prior victimization experiences: A prospective analysis. *Psychology of Women Quarterly, 17*, 151–158.

Gidycz, C. A. (Producer and Director), Dowdall, C. L., Lynn, S. J., Marioni, N. L., & Loh, C. (Assistant Directors). (1997). *I thought it could never happen to me* (Film). (Available from Christine A. Gidycz, Department of Psychology, Ohio University, Athens, OH 45701)

Gidycz, C. A., Lynn, S. J., Rich, C. L., Loh, C., Marioni, N. L., & Orchowski, L. M. (2006). *The Ohio University Sexual Assault Risk Reduction Program (The Community Programming Initiative program protocol)*. Unpublished manuscript.

Gidycz, C. A., Lynn, S. J., Rich, C. L., Marioni, N. L., Loh, C., Blackwell, L. M., et al. (2001). The evaluation of a sexual assault risk reduction program: A multi-site investigation. *Journal of Consulting and Clinical Psychology, 69*, 1073–1078.

Gidycz, C. A., Rich, C. L., & Marioni, N. L. (2002). Interventions to prevent rape and sexual assault. In J. Petrak & B. Hedge (Eds.), *The trauma of adult sexual assault: Treatment, prevention, and policy* (pp. 235–260). New York: John Wiley & Sons.

Gidycz, C. A., Rich, C. L., Orchowski, L., King, C., & Miller, A. (2006). The evaluation of a sexual assault self-defense and risk-reduction program for college women: A prospective study. *Psychology of Women Quarterly, 30*, 173–186.

Gross, A. M., Winslett, A., Roberts, M., & Gohm, C. L. (2006). An examination of sexual violence against college women. *Violence Against Women, 12*, 288–300.

Janis, I. L. (1972). *Victims of groupthink: A psychological study of foreign policy decisions and fiascoes*. Boston, MA: Houghton Mifflin.

Janis, I. L., & Mann, L. (1977). *Decision making: A psychological analysis of conflict, choice, and commitment*. New York: Free Press.

Janoff-Bulman, R. (1992). *Shattered assumptions: Towards a new psychology of trauma*. New York: Free Press.

Jenmorri, K. (2006). Of rainbows and tears: Exploring hope and despair in trauma therapy. *Child & Youth Care Forum, 35*, 41–54.

Klaw, E. L., Lonsway, K. A., Berg, D. R., Waldo, C. R., Kothari, C., Mazurek, C. J., et al. (2005). Challenging rape culture: Awareness, emotion and action through campus acquaintance rape education. *Women & Therapy, 28*, 47–63.

Koss, M. P., Gidycz, C. A., & Wisniewski, N. (1987). The scope of rape: Incidence and prevalence of sexual aggression and victimization in a national sample of higher education students. *Journal of Consulting and Clinical Psychology, 55*, 162–170.

Lonsway, K. A., Klaw, E. L., Berg, D. R., Waldo, C. R., Kothari, C. J., & Hegeman, K. E. (1998). Beyond "No means no": Outcomes of an intensive program to train peer facilitators for campus acquaintance rape education. *Journal of Interpersonal Violence, 13*, 73–92.

Lyon, P. M. A., & Brew, A. (2003). Reflection on learning in the operating theatre. *Reflective Practice, 4*, 53–66.

McCann, L., & Pearlman, L. A. (1990). Vicarious traumatization: A framework for understanding the psychological effects of working with victims. *Journal of Traumatic Stress, 3*, 131–149.

McCauley, C. (1989). The nature of social influence in groupthink: Compliance and internalization. *Journal of Personality and Social Psychology. 57*(2), 250–260.

Meadors, P., & Lamson, A. (2008). Compassion fatigue and secondary traumatization: Provider self care on intensive care units for children. *Journal of Pediatric Health Care, 22*, 24–34.

Nassi, A. J., & Abramowitz, S. I. (1978). Raising consciousness about women's groups: Process and outcome research. *Psychology of Women Quarterly, 3*, 139–156.

National Association of Student Personnel Administrators. (1994). *Complying with the final regulations: The student right to know and campus security act*. Washington, DC: Author.

Norris, J., Nurius, P. S., & Dimeff, L. A. (1996). Through her eyes: Factors affecting women's perception of and resistance to acquaintance sexual aggression threat. *Psychology of Women Quarterly, 20*, 123–145.

Norris, J., Nurius, P. A., & Graham, T. L. (1999). When a date changes from fun to dangerous: Factors affecting women's ability to distinguish. *Violence Against Women, 5*, 230–250.

Nurius, P. S. (2000). Risk perception for acquaintance sexual aggression: A social-cognitive perspective. *Aggression and Violent Behavior, 5*(1), 63–78.

Nurius, P. S., & Norris, J. (1995). A cognitive ecological model of women's responses to male sexual coercion in dating. *Journal of Psychology and Human Sexuality, 8*, 117–139.

Orchowski, L. M. (2009). *Disclosure of unwanted sexual experiences: A prospective study of social reactions and subsequent adjustment*. Unpublished doctoral dissertation.

Orchowski, L. M., Castelino, P., Ng, M., & Cosio, D. (2007, November). *The Ohio University counselor-in-residence program: An innovative approach to psychological care*. Paper presented at the National Association of Student Personnel Administrators Region IV East Regional Conference, Indianapolis, IN.

Orchowski, L. M., Gidycz, C. A., & Raffle, H. (2008). Evaluation of a sexual assault risk reduction and self-defense program: A prospective analysis of a revised protocol. *Psychology of Women Quarterly, 32*, 204–218.

Pearlman, L. A., & Mac Ian, P. S. (1995). Vicarious traumatization: An empirical study of the effects of trauma work on trauma therapists. *Professional Psychology: Research and Practice, 26*, 558–565.

Rager, K. B. (2005). Compassion stress and the qualitative researcher. *Qualitative Health Research, 15*, 423–430.

Rozee, P. D., & Koss, M. P. (2001). Rape: A century of resistance. *Psychology of Women Quarterly, 25*, 295–311.

Salson, M., & Figley, C. R. (2003). Secondary traumatic stress effects of working with survivors of criminal victimization. *Journal of Traumatic Stress, 16*, 167–174.

Sax, L. (2008). *The gender gap in college: Maximizing the developmental potential of women and men*. San Francisco, CA: Jossey-Bass.

t'Hart, P. (1998). Preventing groupthink revisited: Evaluating and reforming groups in government. *Organizational Behavior and Human Decision Making Processes, 73*, 306–326.

Van Minnen, A., & Keijsers, G. P. (2000). A controlled study into the (cognitive) effects of exposure treatment on trauma therapists. *Journal of Behavior Therapy and Experimental Psychiatry, 31*, 189–200.

Yeater, E. A., & O'Donohue, W. (1999). Sexual assault prevention programs: Current issues, future directions and the potential efficacy of interventions with women. *Clinical Psychology Review, 19*, 739–771.

18

Learning and Leading Together

A Cohort-Based Model for Women's Advancement

Lee S. Hawthorne Calizo

Abstract: This chapter tells the story of six women administrators from the University of Maryland Baltimore County who created a women's leadership group focused on issues of leadership, advancement, and power. As an intern working with the women's leadership group, the author spent one semester learning about the experiences of these women and the significant potential of women-only cohort groups as one model for leadership development. The chapter highlights the formation of the group, the "work" of the group, important learning the women gained from participation in the group, and recommendations for starting similar groups. While there are many obstacles that hinder women from advancing into leadership positions in higher education, this may be one option to provide support and encouragement to women seeking to persevere despite the obstacles.

The group [functioned like] a collective. It's odd, I don't feel I'm best friends with anybody in this group. . . . However, as a group, I would trust them with anything. I would defend them. I would believe them. When I go about my work here on the campus, I remember them. I mention them. I know what they are doing. It's a strange kind of bond for me . . . I know this is the group that will make a difference. I know I have to always have them in mind, whatever I am doing, wherever I am going.

THIS NARRATIVE DESCRIBES the women's leadership cohort, a group of six senior and mid-level women administra-

tors at the University of Maryland Baltimore County (UMBC). Two years after the inception of the group, the women reflected on their experiences as sojourners on a transformative, consciousness raising, intentional leadership exploration. They have granted their permission to share their thoughts and experiences in this chapter. What the women learned from this group experience will have lasting impact on their own professional careers, as well as on other women who may choose to engage in peer-assisted group experiences related to advancement. If there is any question about the value of all-female group experiences, let the stories of these women serve as proof that there can be significant power and learning in women-only groups.

Dr. Lynn Zimmerman, vice provost for academic initiatives, introduced the idea of the women's leadership cohort and served as a key facilitator in the group's work. In addition to being vice provost, Lynn was the coprincipal investigator of the National Science Foundation ADVANCE grant designed to help advance women in the STEM (science, technology, engineering, and math) areas. Before the group was conceived, Lynn was frequently thinking about her own career path and what she wanted next. She earnestly began looking at her portfolio and examining the experiences and credentials she needed if she wanted to advance in her field. Through informal conversations with other women administrators on campus, she knew that she was not alone in the quest for advancement and in feeling constrained by "the system." Dr. Zimmerman invited five women to join her on a journey of clarifying values, setting goals, exploring leadership and power, and, ultimately, building a remarkable cohort of women colleagues, confidants, challengers, and champions.

The cohort began its group experience getting to know each other over dinner and sharing what led each to accept Dr. Zimmerman's invitation to join the group. They quickly realized the conversation that night was only the beginning of many affirming discussions to come. Dr. Zimmerman reflected on that first gathering:

> We were all so energized and so excited to be taking off on this journey together . . . I vividly remember a visual: I was standing on the edge of a cliff, looking out over this incredible vista and really feeling like I was ready to spread my wings. It was such a strong visual image for me. We found out later that several of us were overflowing with excitement, optimism and energy. It was a remarkable evening.

The members of the UMBC Women's Leadership Group, as they are called, are proud of what they have learned and accomplished over the last two years. They believe in the concept of a women-only cohort as one model for improving and supporting women's opportunities for advancement in any field. This chapter describes what we know about advancement of women in higher education, the focus and intent of this specific women's group (including the barriers identified), expectations of the group, how the group spent its time, the role of women's cohort groups, and the significant learning that took place in the group. The chapter concludes with an update of the group and a short biography of the members of the group.

WHAT WE KNOW ABOUT ADVANCEMENT OF WOMEN IN HIGHER EDUCATION

Women have made significant strides in advancing to leadership roles in the academy in the United States over the years. However, statistics show that women are not advancing at the same rate as men and are noticeably still underrepresented in leadership positions in American higher educational institutions (American Association for University Women, 2003; Babcock & Laschever, 2003; National Center for Education Statistics [NCES], 2004). Although leadership theory has made a dramatic shift from the more masculine *industrial model* (where qualities of individualism, change, competition, power, data, and action often characterize effective leadership) to the more relational *postindustrial* model of leadership (where relationships, consensus, influence, and democratic practices characterize effective leadership), the systems and structures of institutions of higher education have not shifted to accommodate these changing models (Badaracco, 2002; Beer, 1999; Komives, Lucas, & McMahon, 2007). In a study conducted in 2005 by the American Council on Education (ACE), data showed that only 17.8% of college presidents and chancellors were female. Dramatic differences also exist in the numbers of women and men holding ranks of professor, associate professor, and assistant professor compared with those holding ranks of instructor and lecturer (Babcock & Laschever, 2003; Warner & De-Fleur, 1993). As one might expect on the basis of gender inequities in society, men hold a much higher percentage of the top-tier faculty positions, whereas females dominate the less prestigious, nontenured faculty positions. Data from the NCES suggest that over the last decade, the percentage of men earning doctorate degrees has remained consistent, whereas the percentage of women earning doctorate degrees has increased 46%, and for the last seven years, men and women have been earning doctorates at about the same rate (NCES, 2004). Degree attainment is not the primary reason women are not advancing at the same rate as men. If women have the degrees, why are they not advancing to higher ranking faculty positions and into senior level administrative positions like their male counterparts?

The literature related to women and higher education leadership suggests the "glass ceiling" and the "chilly climate" are concepts that still exist and are widely experienced (Eliasson, Berggren, & Bondestam, 2000; Hall & Sandler, 1982; McCormick, Tanguma, & Lopez-Forment, 2003; Sandler & Hall, 1986; Scanlon, 1997); however, research also points to the important role mentoring and networking play in the advancement process (Brown, 2005; Chovwen, 2004; Eliasson et al., 2000; O'Brien & Janssen, 2005). While men have created and benefited greatly from such professional relationships, women continue to walk down lonely paths in search of female mentors (Bower, 1993; Chovwen, 2004; Rhode, 2003). Despite the fact that most of the literature on mentoring in education and the business sector describes the traditional model of a more senior person guiding and serving as a resource for the less seasoned professional regardless of gender, the low number of women in top leadership positions in higher education institutions suggests that it may be part of the problem (Kram, 1985). Finding female role models and mentors is not easy to do.

Peer education is not a new concept for higher education. We know that students are often very effective at assisting other students with learning. However, the research on peer education and peer-assisted learning has primarily focused on students helping students (Badura, Millard, Peluso, & Ortman, 2000; Ender & Newton, 2000; Mavrinac, 2005). Very little has been written about peer groups as a form of mentoring for administrators (Kram, 1988). Despite the limited research on peer mentoring for administrators, women have been working in groups for many years now, and there is some indication that this collaborative process can result in enhanced leadership skills and efficacy (Astin & Leland, 1991; Freeman, 1995). Similarly, it is evident from the UMBC group's experience that it is a model that can make a significant impact on participants.

Clearly, structural and societal barriers have a significant influence on women's advancement (LeBlanc, 1993; Meyerson & Ely, 2003; Mitchell, 1993), but another concept also plays a role in the rate at which women advance to leadership positions: self-efficacy. The concept of self-efficacy, which refers to an individual's belief in her or his ability to accomplish a particular task or set of tasks, is closely related to goal-setting, achievement, motivation, and job performance (Bandura, 1993). Much research about leadership self-efficacy suggests that men are more likely to have higher self-confidence about their skills and abilities than do women, even when their actual leadership skills and abilities may be less advanced or effective (Hoyt, 2005; McCormick et al., 2003). The notion of confidence strongly surfaced for the women in the UMBC leadership group, and they found this cohort experience to have a particularly positive impact on their self-perceptions.

THE ORIGINAL FOCUS AND INTENT OF THE GROUP—ADVANCEMENT

From the beginning, the focus of this group was on the advancement of women in higher education. As Annemarie Vaccaro (chapter 7) called it, these women were "self-investing" in their own futures. They believed that their personal growth, learning, and development was needed and deserved, and they took it upon themselves to explore their own potential and opportunity for advancement. Over the course of the two years, the women talked about barriers and obstacles that often stifle women in the process of advancement, and they also explored experiences that are supportive of advancement for women. Each woman in the group identified both structural and systemic obstacles, as well as self-imposed or learned barriers. Most acknowledged that each had "bought into" these dated structures but now felt empowered to take a different path. Others in the group reflected on the established pathway to leadership in academic affairs, commenting that many of the college and university women presidents they knew had not followed a "typical path." One woman said, "the model for advancement, the path, the social relationships that are required, and the specific types of activities productivity requires, came out of nineteenth-century masculine participation in the public sphere with the full-time worker in the home." Another said, "We can become our own barriers to our path because we believe in those [typical] pathways, but they are not always true." As a result of this leadership group, the women were exposed to different paths to leadership and they created the opportunity to explore what was really important.

Other significant barriers that the women identified related to the lack of access to information about how to advance and the general lack of emphasis on preparing others for leadership. One woman, who had thought about advancement prior to this group's formation, said, "the biggest obstacle was the lack of information, and there did not seem to be anyone to ask. There was not any conversation around being deliberate about advancing people to a higher level within the administration." In other words, she was not aware of any efforts being made to bring emerging leaders into the leadership circle of the institution, and while she believed her path was leading her to higher administrative leadership, there was nothing in the current structure or environment supporting her along the way.

Several women in the cohort said they previously thought women leaders, presidents, and other top administrators had to have some sort of magical qualities that propelled them into successful leadership. "I had a belief that those who are a step ahead may have something that I don't have," commented one. Another said,

> The one area where women do have a big obstacle is in their confidence. Where that comes from is a whole topic in and of itself, but it's not necessarily even confidence about being able to do the job ultimately. It's confidence that they are ready, confidence that others will see them as qualified.

What the women came to realize through their personal exploration and in meetings with various women college and university presidents is that these "magical" leaders are "smart, capable, thoughtful, analytical, personable women." But, as one group member commented, "So am I." The women reflected positively on the conversations they scheduled with women university presidents and commented that speaking directly with senior-level women helped to demystify their success.

It is important to note that while the women's leadership group identified obstacles and barriers to advancement, the group did not get stuck in a place of feeling like victims. Instead, they put their energy into thinking about how to overcome or circumvent such obstacles. This course of action was important to the group. Several women negatively recalled being in other women's groups that spent much of their time complaining about the barriers rather than creating solutions and moving forward. The structural and systemic barriers indeed exist; however, these women felt empowered to forge new paths and to push through previously closed doors.

When thinking about experiences that are supportive to women and advancement, group members cited some of the nationally known experiences for women including Higher Education Resources (HERS), the Bryn Mawr Summer Institute for Women in Higher Education program, and the ACE Fellows program. It is particularly striking that the specific institutional barriers noted by the women in this leadership group would likely be similar to obstacles identified on any campus, yet the supportive experiences were formal programs outside of any one university designed to train women in leadership and to improve the status of women in higher education. One woman said that from being a part of women's groups over the years, she had learned that the utility of networking is significant. She said,

> Knowing and being able to trust other persons, other persons perhaps with influence, other persons with connections that could be meaningful, that could be part of a partnership or consortium to make a difference . . . you cannot close your eyes to that.

EXPECTATIONS WHEN JOINING THE GROUP

The women in the leadership group determined their own agenda and activities, and how they would go about their work together. They created this experience for themselves, without any previously determined course. In many ways, this serendipitous creativity allowed each woman to find what she wanted and needed from the group although most did not have specific expectations of the group when it started. One woman even felt,

> I wasn't sure what this group could do for me other than provide companionship, but I liked them [the other women] so well . . . I recognized it was an opportunity to create something that even though I might not benefit much from it, it would provide a new structure at UMBC that would help.

Another stated,

> My expectations really focused more on me and what I wanted to get out of the group. The fact that I was going to have other people along on my journey was a bonus. I certainly didn't anticipate the richness of the experience as it did happen.

Despite the rather uncertain expectations going into the experience, each woman in the group exclaimed emphatically that she had benefited greatly from the experience and that she would most definitely create something like this wherever she may go in the future.

HOW THE GROUP SPENT ITS TIME

The group members met several times a month, sometimes by themselves and at other times with invited guests. The group members met for breakfasts, lunches, and dinners depending on what their schedules allowed. Because of their very busy schedules, these women set meeting dates well in advance to ensure that they could all be present, and most reflected humorously on the benefit of having a diligent organizer among the group. However, many commented that the group would not have been successful without this organizer. The meetings had a cyclical pattern or rhythm to them. Some of the meetings would involve "check ins" with each other, a time when they provided emotional support for each other. Through these conversations, different issues emerged. As the group members became clearer on the issues, they would identify readings, writing assignments, or other "homework" to engage deeper in the topic. The next meeting would be a little more formal as they discussed their learning from the homework. During this meeting, the group would then decide if further action needed to be taken on the issue or topic. This was typically when they would identify the leaders with whom they wanted to meet or some other follow-up activity to close the loop on their initial questions.

Meetings With Invited Guests

Over the course of two years, the UMBC women's leadership group met with a number of top administrators at UMBC, several women college presidents, a career coach, and an executive search firm consultant. All of the women expressed enthusiasm and great anticipation for their meeting times and for the safe respite the meetings provided during busy days filled with numerous meetings and appointments. The small group meetings were described by one woman as "Our time as a group is just so precious and so incredibly powerful," but another experience also held much value for the women: they especially valued meeting with women college presidents from around the country. In some cases, a president would visit UMBC's campus, and in other instances the women's leadership group visited other campuses. In these gatherings, as well as in the meetings with various UMBC campus leaders, the women used a common set of questions to launch their conversations: "What is power? How do you get it? How do you use it? How do you keep it?" The development of these questions originated from early conversations about institutional values and individual values. Following the cyclical pattern that became common to their meetings, the women identified a "problem topic" related to values, and then identified a "tool" or exercise in which to engage to further explore their own values and the university's values. They came together again to discuss their responses and through a guided conversation with a facilitator, the questions about power emerged. They decided to use these "power questions" to engage in conversations with invited guests.

Power Questions

Responses to the "power questions" and others that naturally followed provided much information and avenues of exploration for the group. One member reflected, "To be honest, I can't really say I thought a whole lot about power before. I've always known that I am powerful. I really believe power is not defined by position, it's defined by our ability to influence.... There are some real gender differences from my perspective as it related to power." Another commented,

> I came in with the assumption that leadership for the individual woman and the power that comes with it was probably dangerous and had to be carefully handled. At the end of this group, I realized I had a very narrow definition of power and that it foreclosed lots of possibilities.

Career Mapping

The career mapping exercises also proved to be among the most meaningful activities for the women in the group. While they did significant work on their own, they benefited from the ADVANCE grant funding when setting up time with a career coach. In addition, each woman had her resume critiqued by an executive search consultant. The career coach asked each woman to write about where she wanted to be in five years and how she wanted to get there. For some in the group, this "was the single most profound exercise" in which they participated. Similarly, most of the women commented on the significant impact of identifying and articulating their personal values, the espoused values of the institution employing them, and the institution's enacted values. This process of values clarification revealed a lack of congruence that had been stirring in some of the women, even though they had not been able to identify this conflict prior to the exercise. One woman explained,

> The group had an interesting conversation about the ways in which UMBC's explicit mission and

values match us so well, yet we had to recognize that there are tacit values that don't always match as well . . . . At first we thought this [could be] the time we all [might need] to leave UMBC because [these values] didn't always match, but then we realized that we were actually agents who could make the tacit and the explicit values and their intended practices match.

REFLECTING ON THE ROLE OF WOMEN-ONLY PEER GROUPS

The six women in the leadership cohort were radiant as they spoke about the value of a women-only peer group. Importantly, one woman who did not believe there was value in women-only groups about five years ago came to believe that there is nothing more important for the achievement of women after the cohort experience. The women's descriptions of the group included transformative, refreshing, sanity check, freeing, deep, positive, tight-knit, intentional, personal and professional, connection, support, and trust. One member explained what is not so obvious to many: "More often than not, women are collaborative learners. In some ways we put ourselves as learners in one of the best learning environments for us, which is a collaborative, supportive learning environment." Several women spoke about intentionally incorporating cross-functional, collaborative leading and learning into their own styles of leadership. Most of the women agreed that being in an all-women's group created a space where they did not always have to explain or give background because there was a shared experience. This common foundation allowed the group to go deeper in each conversation. As one woman relayed,

There is a candidness. There is an honesty. There is a shared experience. I love the fact that I can say things and women will nod their heads, women will understand, and I know that is not just a politeness code or a social code of "I'm paying attention." It's a real "yes, I know exactly what you are saying." And they do. That is both affirming and confirming.

The women also viewed their group experience as a form of mentoring. Support came from each other and "expertise" came from the individuals they identified and invited to meet with the group. The women in the group controlled the power imbalance found in typical mentor-protégé relationships as they determined their own process, who would be invited guests and under what terms and conditions. The women in this group defined and directed their interactions with more senior mentors and created a more comfortable mentoring structure for themselves.

SIGNIFICANT LEARNING RESULTED FROM THE EXPERIENCE

There were many tangible benefits the women gained from participating in the women's leadership group. Not only did they create a cadre of colleagues with whom to learn and grow professionally, they also found their experience at UMBC became more complete. Several women commented, "I've been able to put pieces of the puzzle together. I have a more complete picture [of issues and dynamics on campus] and that is empowering." One woman also said her supervisor noticed that she is "walking around with more confidence" and he now asks her questions because he thinks she knows more about what is going on around campus. Another said, "We were able to create a more authentic gestalt. In the past we would each have disparate parts, and we created the whole together, which really did help my work and, I think, all of our work at UMBC."

Many of the women in the group, when reflecting on what they had learned from this experience, talked about the value of having women colleagues across campus, the value of others with a shared experience. As one woman noted, you cannot underestimate the impact one individual can have.

It can seem kind of daunting if you think about taking on the university to effect change [alone], but we didn't do that. With just the work of a few individuals, it didn't take very long to become so much stronger and bigger than that.

Another said, "If you take five, six, or seven women on a campus, and one or two of you then go into meetings together, you become allies. Strong women-bonds, colleagues, and friends, who support each other." All of these women carried themselves with a stronger sense of self, of confidence, and of empowerment as a result of this small group experience and of knowing that a few others shared and supported their experiences.

Another significant result of this group's work was finding more clarity in terms of professional goals and the scope of possibilities for future positions. For example, one woman commented, "My ability and capacity as a leader has been fully realized or validated . . . I have thought about senior leadership positions in ways that I have not thought about before." Another talked about moving to a higher level position and stated, "Prior to the group, I thought that it would be way off [in the future]. I would have to prepare a lot, and I realize now that I could do it tomorrow." Still another said,

> I did get clearer on where I might want to be in five years, what kind of institution I'd want to be in, and what I'd want my life to look like in terms of balance of professional and personal endeavors.

A third woman explained, "One of the things I have come to realize, not in an ego-centered way, just in a truthful way, is that I have leadership capacity . . . . It comes naturally to me." Each of the women in the group aspires to continue in leadership positions in higher education and to continue doing "transformative work." While each had been thinking quietly and independently about the possibilities for the next steps, they found much greater potential and more answers by exploring possibilities with others. Sev-eral of the women also credited the women presidents with whom they met for confirming that these six women have what it takes to achieve whatever they aspire.

SHARING THEIR WISDOM

The women in the cohort believe that the self-created leadership experience has enhanced their personal and professional lives in ways they could not have imagined when they first started meeting. Not only do they all plan to stay involved in groups like this one, they also want to encourage other women to start their own groups. To borrow a phrase from Monica Marcelis Fochtman's study (chapter 6) and to support her findings with my own, these women felt it was very important to "pay it forward" and share what they learned with other women on campus. In fact, at UMBC, there are already a couple of new cohorts that began meeting and charting their own path. Several of the women in the original group commented that they feel they have an obligation to pass on what they have learned and to encourage other women to create this same type of experience for themselves.

Why Women Only?

Peer mentoring groups do not have to consist of only women or focus on advancement and leadership. However, the women in the UMBC cohort believe strongly in the value of women-only groups.

> [They] are not the only pathway, but a very important pathway . . . . There is value in shared experience. In that shared experience there are unspoken realities, unspoken truths, shared experiences that just are understood, that don't need to be defended or validated. You start with a similar basis. Clearly we are individual women with different experiences, but the experience of being a woman, particularly in this country . . . . There are some shared experiences that are undeniable.

One of the women in Annemarie Vaccaro's study (chapter 7) even called the all-female environment a "sanctuary" where women could find their identity. This sentiment indeed resonated with the women I interviewed. Women have much to learn from each other, and establishing peer relationships or groups may serve the more basic function of expanding one's familiarity with a particular campus and campus culture, while creating networks within an institution that provides a safe support mechanism for employees. Peer-mentoring groups can also serve as a springboard for women to navigate the various career paths within higher education.

Creating Your Own Group

The women in the initial cohort believe that the organic nature of the group is what has made it a great success. Having the endorsement and support of the campus leadership helps in forming a group; however, it is not necessary or a prerequisite. Women seeking to advance in their careers can find colleagues from across campus with whom to create a group for themselves, and anyone who appreciates or understands the value of this type of peer mentoring can easily encourage women on any campus to establish a group.

Selection of group members is also very significant to the success of the experience, so attention to objectives and options is needed in the beginning. The women in the UMBC group were from different offices and divisions on campus and were able to become more informed, knowledgeable, and confident practitioners as a result. In addition, instead of getting mired in the specific challenges of one department or office, the women were able to find similarities in their varied situations and then to find solutions or options for responding to such challenges. Creating a group representing diverse areas on campus is a worthwhile approach that can add more depth and breadth to the experience. Given what we know about the value of diverse groups in enhancing and enriching learning, selecting

women who represent racial, ethnic, religious, sexual orientation, and other aspects of diversity will only add to the group's experience (Gurin, Dey, Gurin, & Hurtado, 2003; Hurtado, Milem, Clayton-Pedersen, & Allen, 1999). Obviously, women should look to include other women in the group whom they respect, whose company they enjoy, and who may be in similar stages of their careers. Although knowing each other well and being friends was a valued outcome of the UMBC women's leadership group, it was not something the women expected or felt was a necessary component to their experience. The size of the group is also important as the larger the group, the more difficulty in scheduling meetings and the less "air time" each woman has when they get together. Women seeking to start a peer mentoring group should think about the group configuration and determine through informal conversations with other women who may best fit together.

Types of Activities to Consider

The UMBC women's leadership group identified the following activities as particularly powerful and poignant: meeting with campus leaders, meeting with leaders from other campuses, career mapping, and finding time for just the group members to come together. This group met with college presidents from other campuses, but other peer groups may choose to meet with a different tier of campus leaders. The specifics of which individuals with whom a group meets should be defined by the group based upon the goals and outcomes group members identify. Each group needs to define its own goals and then create its path, which can of course be altered or revised as the group matures.

UPDATE ON THE UMBC WOMEN'S LEADERSHIP GROUP

The individuals in the UMBC women's leadership group continue to support each other's advancement, but they do so in a different way. Two of the women have advanced to new opportunities within higher education leadership at different institutions and two of the women have advanced within the UMBC administration. This group has, however, continued to meet once a year to further this exploration. This particular cohort's dynamics have shifted now as two of the six have left UMBC, but the impact of this experience will stay with them forever. These women strongly believe that their collective work toward understanding leadership and defining their own styles was accomplished through a group process that can enhance and propel the personal and professional lives of women on any campus. Our hope is that you feel empowered to begin your own group and that supervisors at all levels will encourage, empower, and support the formation of such groups.

WOMEN IN THE GROUP

Dr. J. Lynn Zimmerman was the Vice Provost for Academic Initiatives and Professor of Biology at UMBC. She oversaw several initiatives focused on improving access and diversity in science, technology, engineering, and mathematics and served as leader of the university's efforts in advancing the careers of women faculty in STEM supported by the NSF's ADVANCE program. Dr. Zimmerman is now the Senior Vice Provost for Academic Programs at Emory University in Atlanta.

Dr. Janet C. Rutledge has been promoted to Senior Associate Dean of the Graduate School and Affiliate Associate Professor of Computer Science and Electrical Engineering. She has played a key role in the growth of graduate student enrollment, the increase in the number of graduate programs, and improvement in graduate student retention. She serves as a leader in several externally supported projects such as NSF's Alliances for Graduate Education and the Professoriate (AGEP) program and the

Council of Graduate Schools' PhD Completion Project.

Dr. Diane M. Lee is Vice Provost and the Dean of Undergraduate Education. She leads campuswide efforts to foster student success and to extend an honors experience to all UMBC undergraduates. Dr. Lee also serves as Special Assistant to the President for K–16 Initiatives. She brings a strong background in the field of education, many years of experience as a faculty member and graduate level mentor, and a passion for the work to be done in advancing students at all levels.

Dr. Patty Perillo was the Assistant Vice President for Student Affairs/Director of Student Life. Having served the UMBC community for seven years, Dr. Perillo has advanced to Davidson College as the Associate Dean of Students. Patty also served as the President for the American College Personnel Association (ACPA).

Dr. Kathy O'Dell is Associate Dean of Arts, Humanities, and Social Sciences and Associate Professor of Visual Arts. An art historian and critic, she is working on her second book and will pursue the rank of full professor within the next two years and a position as a dean where she can share her administrative and scholarly expertise in and passion for the arts.

Dr. Patrice McDermott is Chair of the American Studies and the ADVANCE Program at UMBC. Dr. McDermott has served as special assistant to two deans for gender and diversity initiatives. She has led multiple efforts at UMBC designed to support the advancement of women and underrepresented minority faculty and promote social change strategies to eliminate gender and racial inequality.

REFERENCES

American Association of University Women. (2003). *Women at work*. Retrieved December 3, 2008, from http://www.aauw.org/research/womenatwork.cfm

Astin, H. S., & Leland, C. (1991). *Women of influence, women of vision: A cross-generational study of leaders and social change.* San Francisco, CA: Jossey-Bass.

Babcock, L., & Laschever, S. (2003). *Women don't ask: Negotiation and the gender divide.* Princeton, NJ: Princeton University Press.

Badaracco, J. (2002). *Leading quietly.* Cambridge, MA: Harvard Business School Press.

Badura, A. S., Millard, M., Peluso, E. A., & Ortman, N. (2000). Effects of peer education training on peer educators: Leadership, self-esteem, health knowledge, and health behaviors. *Journal of College Student Development, 41,* 471–478.

Bandura, A. (1993). Perceived self-efficacy in cognitive development and functioning. *Educational Psychologist, 28,* 117–148.

Beer, M. (1999). Leading learning and learning to lead. In J. Conger, G. Spreitzer, & E. Lawler (Eds.), *The leader's change handbook* (pp. 127–161). San Francisco, CA: Jossey-Bass.

Bower, F. L. (1993). Women and mentoring in higher education administration. In P. T. Mitchell (Ed.), *Cracking the wall: Women in higher education administration* (pp. 90–97). Washington, DC: College and University Personnel Association.

Brown, T. M. (2005). Mentorship and the female college president. *Sex Roles, 52*(9/10), 659–666.

Chovwen, C. O. (2004). Mentoring and women's perceived professional growth. *Ife PsychologIA, 12*(1), 126–132.

Eliasson, M., Berggren, H., & Bondestam, F. (2000). Mentor programmes—A shortcut for women's academic careers? *Higher Education in Europe, 25*(2), 173.

Ender, S. C., & Newton, F. B. (2000). *Students helping students: A guide for peer educators on college campuses.* San Francisco, CA: Jossey-Bass.

Freeman, J. S. (1995). From suffrage to women's liberation: Feminism in twentieth-century America. In J. Freeman (Ed.), *Women: A feminist perspective* (5th ed., pp. 509–528). Mountain View, CA: Mayfield Publishing Company.

Gurin, P. Y., Dey, E. L., Gurin, G., & Hurtado, S. (2003). How does racial/ethnic diversity promote education? *Western Journal of Black Studies, 27*(1), 20.

Hall, R. M., & Sandler, B. R. (1982). *The classroom climate: A chilly one for women?* Washington, DC: Association of American Colleges.

Hoyt, C. L. (2005). The role of leadership efficacy and stereotype activation in women's identification with leadership. *Journal of Leadership and Organizational Studies, 11*(4), 2–14.

Hurtado, S., Milem, J., Clayton-Pedersen, A., & Allen, W. (1999). Enacting diverse learning environments: Improving the climate for racial/ethnic diversity in higher education. *ASHE-ERIC Higher Education Report, 26*(8), 1–116.

Komives, S. R., Lucas, N., & McMahon, T. R. (2007). *Exploring leadership: For college students who want to make a difference* (2nd ed.). San Francisco, CA: Jossey-Bass.

Kram, K. E. (1985). Improving the mentoring process. *Training & Development Journal, 39*(4), 40–43.

Kram, K. E. (1988). *Mentoring at work: Developmental relationships in organizational life.* Lanham, MD: University Press of America, Inc.

LeBlanc, D. S. (1993). Barriers to women's advancement into higher education administration. In P. T. Mitchell (Ed.), *Cracking the wall: Women in higher education administration* (pp. 40–49). Washington, DC: College and University Personnel Administration.

Mavrinac, M. A. (2005). Transformational leadership: Peer mentoring as a values-based learning process. *Libraries and the Academy, 5*(3), 391.

McCormick, M., Tanguma, J., & Lopez-Forment, A. S. (2003). *Gender differences in beliefs about leadership capabilities: Exploring the glass ceiling phenomenon with self-efficacy theory, Leadership Review.* Claremont, CA: Claremont McKenna College, Kravis Leadership Institute.

Meyerson, D. E., & Ely, R. J. (2003). Using difference to make a difference. In D. L. Rhode (Ed.), *The difference "difference" makes: Women and leadership* (pp. 129–143). Stanford, CA: Stanford University Press.

Mitchell, P. T. (Ed.). (1993). *Cracking the wall: Women in higher education administration.* Washington, DC: College and University Personnel Association.

National Center for Education Statistics. (2004). *Digest of Education Statistics (chap. 3).* Retrieved December 3, 2008, from http://nces.ed.gov/programs/digest/d04/ch_3.asp

O'Brien, S. P., & Janssen, K. N. (2005). Internships for women in higher education administration: Springboards for success? *Work: Journal of Prevention, Assessment & Rehabilitation, 24*(4), 353–359.

Rhode, D. L. (Ed.). (2003). *The difference "difference" makes: Women and leadership.* Stanford, CA: Stanford University Press.

Sandler, B. R., & Hall, R. M. (1986). *The campus climate revisited: Chilly for women faculty, administrators, and graduate students.* Washington, DC: Association of American Colleges.

Scanlon, K. (1997). Mentoring women administrators: Breaking through the glass ceiling. *Initiatives, 58,* 39–59.

Warner, R., & DeFleur, L. B. (1993). Career paths of women in higher education administration. In P. T. Mitchell (Ed.), *Cracking the wall: Women in higher education administration* (pp. 1–18). Washington, DC: College and University Personnel Association.

NARRATIVES ON GENDER AND FEMINISM

Testimonial and Future Thinking

Kelly E. Maxwell

I came out as a feminist and a lesbian when I was 22 years old. I was just starting my master's degree in student affairs and had recently moved far away from both my undergraduate institution and the town where I grew up. No one knew me and it was finally safe to come out. Like many in their initial identity development stages, I was "out and proud." For me, that meant a rainbow flag on my car and the Indigo Girls playing on my CD player. While I may have struggled with whom to publicly and openly tell about this revelation, those who knew the symbols would have known immediately that I was a lesbian. That was the early 1990s. Yet one symbol of that time remains with me to this day: a woman's symbolic gold earring. I have worn it nearly every day since that time in my life. It was the purist symbol for me to remember what it means to be a woman, a feminist, and a lesbian.

Today it reminds me that still, despite the cliché, the personal is political. My life is at the center of a cultural struggle about some of the most centrally defining institutions in our lives: about what it means to be a family, to be married, to be me. The dominant narrative that heterosexuality is the norm and should be codified in state institutions, such as marriage and adoption law, fundamentally affects my family. So when I think about my earring in the midst of this seemingly intolerable institutional oppression, I sometimes chuckle at how I even got the one extra hole in my left ear. It was a radical act of empowerment at age 15 when I went to the mall and came home with one extra piercing. It took my mom less than a day to notice it. Her reaction was muted and I realized that this "radical" act was much more a work of empowering self, not changing the world. It was my way of defining life for myself. It was neither earth-shattering nor "radical" in the true sense of the word—but that's been true about most of my life.

So when I think about my earring today, my radical act of empowerment is more about me—living life on my own terms—than on any restructuring of basic institutions. Yet, my personal action of living "out" in the world, raising a son, and living with my partner is so problematic that constitutional amendments abound to restrict our lives. On the other hand, it is so regular that no one would take notice except that a multiracial lesbian family can't help but raise eyebrows. We're the type of family that gets talked about by the conservative right. We're wrecking family values and ruining traditional marriage. The dominant heteronormativity of society then makes my act of personal empowerment a very public, very political action. The two cannot be separated, which makes it vital that I address inequality (on all fronts, not just sexual orientation) so critical to my life and my work.

I cannot pinpoint when the two, life and work, became so intertwined. My career in student affairs certainly nurtured my desire to learn all about my own identities and their relationship to structures of societal inequality. Somewhere along my trajectory, I decided my professional focus had to shift away from the broader residence education, new student orientation, and student leadership programming agenda of my early career. I realized that intergroup relations and helping others recognize and address privilege and power in the academy and in society had to be central to my work. Yet it was within the traditional student affairs career path that my identity exploration truly began. My identity as a lesbian helped me first to recognize heterosexism and homophobia. My identity as a woman helped me to question my experiences and wonder why similar things happened to women and not men. I was able to examine sexism. My targeted identities also helped shape my understanding of privileged ones. I would think, "Oh, if I can understand how heterosexuals express their privilege in the context of sexual orientation issues, I can also see how Whites do the same in relation to race." Even as my positionality was different (I am privileged in terms of race) my sexual orientation allowed me a lens to explore whiteness and White privilege. Because my career in student affairs nurtured my identity exploration, it allowed me to test my learning in professional settings. I still have to cringe when I think about those "diversity workshops" I facilitated early in my career. I knew so little and yet tried to bang everyone else over the head with what they should understand about other people. No wonder the students were so resistant!

But kindhearted and firm mentors showed me the way. They modeled the balancing act between the personal and the professional. They showed me how to ask good questions and probe deeply and honestly about someone else's experiences. Still, how does one talk about and teach about intergroup relations without one's own experiences entering in? Frankly, I don't and can't separate the two. A positivist framework just won't do. In fact, it

can be both personally liberating and pedagogically important to weave them together appropriately and use oneself as a learning tool for others.

We ask this of our students in intergroup dialogue. I feel I must ask it of myself as well. Intergroup dialogues are one way that we engage students in structured learning environments around these issues. Intergroup dialogues are face-to-face interactions between two social identity groups that are sustained over time (often a full semester). In the dialogue process, students from different backgrounds (lesbian, gay, bisexual, and heterosexual students in a sexual orientation dialogue, for example) share their personal testimonies about their lived experience related to the identity topic of the dialogue. They learn about commonalities and differences in the context of social inequality. They dialogue about hot topics and consider future action or alliance building across groups.

Intergroup dialogues are different from any pedagogical approach I experienced as a student and therefore had few models for how to teach and train facilitators to do it well. Dialogues help us to make sense of our experiences in the context of a dominant narrative that confines us all. We learn about privilege and oppression by listening to lived experiences and sharing our own. There is a balance of sharing content (about social inequality, stereotyping, prejudice, etc.) and process (how we talk together, how we develop as a group, etc.). This is not a traditional classroom nor is it a support group.

As a teacher/facilitator, I am responsible for training undergraduates to co-lead the dialogue efforts. Because self-expression is so critical and experiential learning paramount, my teaching must reflect and model what I hope the students will do as facilitators. That means sharing some of my own story and listening deeply to the stories of others. It means perfecting my craft as a teacher of student-centered learning. That means connecting with them, providing experiential opportunities for growth and development, and listening to their needs (particularly when they are unable to truly articulate what those needs really are). Empathy plays a key role, too.

My "self" as a teacher is tied to my own identity experiences. I can both understand the story of the White student who feels guilty for "not knowing" and empathize with the student of color who is frustrated by it. I have been in both places because of my interconnected identities. I can place myself in their stories and see myself there. That is why I think our own identity work is so critical to moving forward as higher education professionals and faculty. It is important to work to understand my own triggers in relation to someone's comments and try to look through my emotional reaction to the truth they are telling about their experience. "Love the sinner, hate the sin" is admittedly still a trigger for me. But I have heard it so often, I can now respond with questions that might deepen the conversation rather than a reaction that will shut it down.

I used to believe that when I entered "intergroup relations" as a field in higher education, I was in the midst of identity work, almost as if I wasn't doing it before. But, of course, identities matter everywhere. Power and privilege are enacted everywhere. As a residence education professional, when a student came to me complaining about her roommate's choice of music, there was usually a (racial) identity implication there. As an orientation coordinator, how we talked about our religious campus organizations to parents and incoming students represented how we viewed spiritual identity development. When issues of accessibility in our campus facilities arose, it was more than accommodating individuals, but rather about structural (in)equality. Identities and their implication are, in fact, central to the work we do on campuses. We must be aware of their impact not only on the students we serve but also on how those identities play out for each of us, how we are reacted to, and how we are triggered by these discussions.

Doing our own identity work in the context of intergroup dialogue is a powerful way to learn more deeply about our own selves and learn about the experiences of others as well. Are sharing experiences, listening to others, and talking across differences radical acts? They are in the sense that we are rarely intentional about doing them. They are ordinary acts that actually happen infrequently. If speaking to another is so difficult and so uncommon that our Attorney General, Eric Holder, calls us a "nation of cowards" because we don't do it, then dialogue becomes a radical action. Like the act of living "out," dialogue itself is a rather innocuous action. Yet in the context of our lack of conversation, it is powerful and right. Intergroup dialogue: to speak truth to power, to be heard, to struggle with dominant narratives and the ways inequality is lived or enacted in our lives has the ability to deepen relationships across groups and both solidify and change one's own perspectives. Our future as a profession lies in staying committed to a path of understanding ourselves and others. Intergroup dialogue is one way to begin.

On Love, and Its Place in the Academy

Cayden Mak

I had been looking forward to it for years, and suddenly it was real: I was a part of one of the most respected philosophy departments in the country, learning from some of the most brilliant minds in the field, and finally, living on my own. Coming to the University of Michigan as an undergraduate meant an opportunity to take my life in a different direction, personally and academically. I came out as transgender my senior year of high school, and I was ready for a fresh start.

But before I even packed my things, I encountered antitrans bias in the on-campus housing system and in my orientation session.

I was worried I wouldn't be able to find like-minded queer people. College wasn't exactly inviting, but at the very least I was excited to be a part of an intellectual community. I was glad I was living away from home, so I could have more freedom to do as I pleased.

Part of the reason I was worried about finding like-minded friends was that I was done with being a gay activist. I was driven away from activist work after high school because I wanted to immerse myself in my studies. I was also turned off by the posturing and sloganism that was the core of so much of the activism I was a part of in the past. I was attracted to the idea of intellectual rigor and removing myself from the mudslinging to do "serious" academic work. I knew I wanted to study philosophy for exactly these reasons. Although philosophy is a discipline dominated by White men, I wasn't too worried. I thought I could hide in the department from the issues I was most frustrated by; I wanted to find austerity and intellectual fulfillment.

I found it, of course, but not just in philosophy, and not just in the ways I had imagined. I got called back to activism via the Program on Intergroup Relations. My first dialogue was on race, and I went into it worried that I'd hear a lot of the same prattle that had alienated me before. To my surprise, the class was a mix of thoughtful students from different backgrounds and disciplines. It was also incredible to discover that there are people who are concerned about issues of inequality and are sensitive to subtlety, complexity, and theory, without losing the spirit I'd come to expect from the kinds of activists who frustrated me. That semester opened my mind and my heart. My facilitators recommended me to train, to facilitate, and I decided to take up the challenge. For all the intellectual changes I was undergoing, I learned a less cerebral lesson, too. I discovered how important love is to learning.

"Dialogue cannot exist," writes Paulo Friere (2006), "in the absence of a profound love for the world and for people" (p. 89). Nothing could be more true—becoming an effective facilitator meant overcoming my cynicism about other people and their intentions. It also meant overcoming cynicism about activism. Progress in a dialogue setting is impossible without love, humility, and forgiveness. Dialogue was a place where I really grew up—in addition to learning love, patience, and forgiveness, I have gotten in touch with my racial identity and my many levels of hybridity.

For a while I believed that these two halves of my life on campus were irreconcilable. There did not seem to be a place for love in the classroom outside of so-called identity work. I couldn't see how the pedagogical principles I had learned as a dialogue facilitator applied to my broader academic environment. I was frustrated by the blindness of the philosophical traditions I studied to the daily realities of life as a minority student. I was annoyed when I had to hold back my intellectualizing urges in dialogue settings. I hated leaving my identities at the door—especially when they were becoming increasingly salient to my life, as I became higher profile on campus as a gender rights activist.

I was also coming to a personal crisis—in the process of applying to graduate schools, many of which would put me on the path to being a career academic, I was discovering more and more how hard it can be to be a scholar who is also a member of an oppressed group. Bias still exists within the academy, just like in the world generally, but it's hard to confront. Would I be able to succeed as a professional academic who also happens to be a transgender person of color?

During my senior year I met a mentor who has really shaped the way I think about identity and the academy for the future. In the winter semester, I took a course with Jennifer Wenzel on postcolonial critical theory. I had hoped to learn some things about the intellectual underpinnings of the identity work I had been a part of for the past few years. I certainly didn't expect to see an exceptional example of radical pedagogy in action, in a serious academic classroom. The first day of Jennifer's class, she said that we'd be collaborating on the course, because she wanted to make sure what we were reading and talking about was engaging. Over the course of the semester, anyone in the class was invited to steer the discussion toward something that interested them about the texts we read.

The second thing that set Jennifer's class apart was that we were encouraged to bring our self-understandings and personal identities into the classroom with us. Our discussion of Jamaica Kincaid's *A Small Place* was not just about its literary merit, it was also about our political relationship with it as students in the United States. We didn't just talk about oil exploitation, human rights abuses, and the movement to reclaim natural resources by the people in Nigeria, but also what ordinary consumers, stuck inside the capitalist system, can reasonably do to stand behind movements for justice.

While I learned a lot in Jennifer's class, the real revelation I walked away with was that love does have a place in the academy. I originally thought that the only place for dialogue was in identity work. Jennifer proved that you can live your values in *how* you teach, not just *what* you teach. I wasn't just interested in the material for its own sake—but also because she encouraged making the connections to my life and experience. Her willingness to confront the pain and confusion that surfaced and because of the topics we addressed, she was courageous. Although there were days when we left the class frustrated and confused, Jennifer was clearly invested in all of us making sense for ourselves, the material we covered, and the conversations we had.

That's where love brought it together: not all the topics were easy, intellectually or emotionally. Jennifer's willingness to go the extra mile in encouraging us to confront those difficulties, her support for us when we were confused or upset, and her leadership by example made a huge difference in the way I engaged the class and the things I took away from it. She clearly enjoyed learning *with* us,

entertaining our ideas and our worries, encouraging us to answer each others' questions rather than feed us the answers she had already formulated. She was always excited to hear what we had to say. Our discussions never fell apart into shouting matches or tears, but when they were deeply affective, they were heavy with emotional importance. I remember feeling deep sadness, anger, excitement, optimism, hope, and fellowship with the other students in the class, and I always felt like I could say so. My experience as a minority student was never pushed out of the room. We, as individuals, were important to the course.

I'm beginning to believe that an academic community more committed to love—of knowledge, of each other, of challenges—as a guiding principle of its pedagogical practice is one where everyone can belong, without having to check their identities at the door. It is possible to teach and to learn in an environment that is supportive, challenging, and intellectually rigorous. That kind of academic community is not so far away, but it isn't necessarily easy to get there. It requires dedication on the part of educators, support on the part of departments and administrators, and the spark of curiosity and passion on the part of students.

I'm no optimist, but I think we have reason to be hopeful: I've met many brilliant people at Michigan who believe in inclusive higher education and are willing to be creative in their commitment to that ideal. As for myself, I'll be staying the course. In the future, I want to share with my students the love for my subject, for people and for the world that made my years at Michigan so fruitful.

REFERENCE

Freire, P. (2006). *Pedagogy of the oppressed* (30th anniversary edition). New York: Continuum.

Change a Life

Vanidy Bailey

I am getting married. This seems like every woman's dream. Every woman's moment. A chaotic moment, but a moment that seems a part of the traditional American dream. I looked in the mirror, holding my engagement ring. What am I going to tell my parents? Thoughts of rejection and disgust haunted me. My marriage would taint the sanctity of their apostolic-coated reality; their lesbian daughter is getting married.

When I first graduated college, I figured my parents, or rather my mother, wouldn't be as hard on me. Perhaps, it would finally be okay to wear a tie and a faded haircut. Perhaps, my weight and "masculine" appearance wouldn't make my mother roll her eyes in shame and pray that maybe one day, I'd be *normal*. I guess perhaps I am "sister outsider." I am a woman who isn't feminine enough for their Bible-thumping reality. Or just too smart for her own good.

My coming out experience wasn't my own. I was pushed out of the closet, and I was made to answer questions that I had never considered. What about children? What would my grandmother think? The list of questions goes on and on. However, none of these questions had anything to do with me. I wanted to be asked, "Are you happy?" Instead, I was supposed to be concerned with everyone but myself. So, my life became a cage. I resorted to escaping through my writings. It seemed like I was my only refuge. One of my first pieces was about my first love.

I remember her red lipstick.
Her perfume was sweet.
She held all knowledge.
She wore pearls.

My first love was my kindergarten teacher. But love means nothing on a Monday morning after recess. I felt with each love I gained a new perspective. I learned about pain from my family and I learned about love from strangers.

I figured that my first day of college would be different. I was no stranger to isolation. So, I withdrew myself and hid behind the shell of leadership. I was a theater student my freshman year, so it was easy to perform. Leadership at the time was a performance. I could be whoever the student body needed me to be. But, behind every mask lies scars. The first person I allowed to see my scars was an administrator. He seemed so genuine and vulnerable, something I never experienced firsthand, especially from someone in a leadership position. He became my muse and I was his pupil. He encouraged me to find support in the Women's Center. I chuckled but entertained the thought. Next thing you know I was in a support group for women of color. So, for the first time I sat there: vulnerable. I was clay. Cold and malleable. But, easily shaped.

It only takes one person to change a life. It only takes one moment to destroy a dream. I am thankful for genuine people in my life. For that support, I say "Thank You."

Higher education is full of vulnerability. We have the power to shape tomorrow. Let's be good stewards of this power.

Section Five

ENVISIONING AND ACTING ON A FEMINIST FUTURE

"Understanding and eliminating oppression and inequality oblige us to examine our relative privilege, to move out of our internalized positions as victims, to take control over our own lives, and to take responsibility for change. Such an undertaking is by definition risky and therefore requires commitment to a different vision of society than that which we now take for granted."

Roxana Ng

Ng. R. (2000). *A woman out of control: Deconstructing sexism and racism in the university.* In J. Glazer-Raymo, B. K. Townsend, & B. Ropers-Huilman (Eds.) *Women in higher education: A feminist perspective* (pp. 360–370). Boston: Pearson (quote from page 368).

19

Envisioning a New Future With Feminist Voices

Research and Practice From Feminist Perspectives

Amanda Suniti Niskodé-Dossett, Penny A. Pasque,
and Shelley Errington Nicholson

EMINISM IS ONE OF THE MOST POWERFUL concepts in higher education and student affairs today. It has the potential to serve as a tremendous basis of empowerment and inclusion; yet, it also has the means to alienate and infuriate. Through different feminist lenses, the authors within this book have examined various areas of higher education and student affairs, and the implications of their findings have the capability to affect future research and practice in our field. We hope this book has enabled readers to think about feminism in new ways and to perhaps reframe how we approach our work while grounding it in a more thorough understanding of the complexities of women.

This concluding chapter makes a deliberate call for women, men, and transgender scholars and educators to work toward centering feminist perspectives (and other marginalized perspectives) in research and practice as the complexities of college and university life continue to evolve. We issue this call for the next decade in order to further the interconnections between research and practice, highlight feminist perspectives often missed in the literature, and make change for women on college campuses across the United States and the globe. We feel a sense of urgency for a paradigm shift in the field because, as these chapters and narratives have shown, deep-seated problems for women students, administrators, and faculty remain.

As we issue this call for continued change in research and practice, we focus on three main points that emerged from across the chapters in this book: (1) feminist inquiry: uncovering lenses and assumptions; (2) feminist inquiry: influencing research and scholarship; and (3) questions and implications for future feminist research and practice.

We fully recognize that these three themes are not exhaustive and thus want readers to know that the feminist approaches available across fields and disciplines reach far beyond what we provide here. However, we hope this analysis provides readers with an additional understanding of how feminism may enhance research, scholarship, and practice in different ways.

As we review each theme, we turn to a discussion of how we may enhance our work to better serve women in higher education and student affairs. Doing so will highlight ways in which to implement feminism in our daily work, with the ultimate goal of promoting a leadership approach that "bring[s] about change in an organization, an institution, or the social system—in other words, an action to make a positive difference in people's lives" (Astin & Leland, 1991, p. 116).

FEMINIST INQUIRY: UNCOVERING LENSES AND ASSUMPTIONS

Raising Consciousness

Some feminist researchers, such as Catharine MacKinnon, believe that "consciousness raising *is* feminist method" (as cited in Harding, 1987, p. 135). We began this project to attain this very goal—to offer the latest insights about women in higher education and student affairs. We hoped to raise consciousness about feminist perspectives and feminist research throughout the field, including within ourselves. Reflecting back on the process, we believe that consciousness was also raised for the authors through the specific research process that accompanied this book. For example, during the revision phase, each author received copies of additional chapters in the book and was asked to take the original chapter to a deeper level of understanding through the process of "talking" to one another within the chapters. In this way, the writing and revision process became more iterative—where many of the authors informed the analysis process or observations of other authors.

In *On Method and Hope*, Tierney (1994) mentioned that research should be a "struggle to investigate how individuals and groups might be better able to change their situations" (p. 99). In fact, it appears that through their research and practice, many of the authors actually helped to raise the consciousness of their participants (and themselves) with regard to their own identities and the myriad of issues that women face today (Guerrero, 1999; Olsexn, 2000; Thompson, 1992, as cited in Patton, 2002). For example,

in Lee Hawthorne Calizo's chapter about the cohort-based model for women's advancement (chapter 18), members discussed how empowering the experience was for them, both personally and professionally. One woman articulated, "It can seem kind of daunting if you think about taking on the university to effect change [alone] but we didn't do that. With just the work of a few individuals, it didn't take very long to become so much stronger and bigger than that." As the women in this chapter describe, a cohort-based model that brings women together to discuss the complexities of the campus culture (practice), accompanied by reflection on that model (research process), helped to effect strong change on this particular campus.

Placing Women's Perspectives at the Forefront

Standpoint research (one type of feminist approach) is built on notions that women have been marginalized from research and, consequently, places women's knowledge, emerging from their situated experiences, at the forefront (Harding, 1987). Those with this approach also asserted that

> all knowledge claims are socially located and that some social locations, especially those at the bottom of social and economic hierarchies, are better than others as starting points for seeking knowledge not only about those particular women but others as well. (Olesen, 2003, p. 343)

For example, many scholars focus on women's worldview and put women's daily lives at the center of their research studies (Harding, 1987; Hart, 2006; Lather, 1992; Ropers-Huilman, 1998; Smith, 1987; Wolf, 1992). This is mirrored eloquently in Penny Rice's chapter (chapter 11) on economically disadvantaged women in higher education, epitomizing the need to examine how a patriarchal society causes distress to women whose stories are often unheard. The stories in this chapter represent a missing voice—women who are single parents and students. Penny explains that the "unchallenged prejudice toward women and their kids receiving assistance has not improved with the signing of the PRWOR Act"; thus, even though fewer people are on welfare each year, the problem of poverty has not been eradicated. Penny's approach to this chapter—highlighting the stories of these student parents who struggled to work through the system—"foregrounds women's knowledge as emergent from women's situated experiences" (Harding, 1987, p. 184).

Similarly, many of the chapters reflect the importance of listening to how women construct their experiences instead of how they fit into (or are excluded from) existing models. For instance, Thandi Sulé's chapter (chapter 9) on "how race matters" for Black female faculty is a strong example of centering voices not often centered, while utilizing Black feminist thought and political race concepts. In addition, Flo Guido (chapter 10) centers her perspective as a daughter of Italian immigrants through her narrative feminist approach. Moreover, in this book, we placed great value on women's narratives—women's own stories. Many of the chapters include direct quotes and each section of this book includes short narratives from various women and transgender people across colleges and universities, social identities, and roles. Specifically, Rachel Wagner, Xyanthe Neider, Cindy Clark, and Dorothy Nkhata share their own experiences in relation to various aspects of their identity including ability, race, life as a stay-at-home mom, and nationality, respectively. The inclusion of such narratives would not necessarily be found in traditional models of scholarship, yet this approach adds perspectives that enrich our understanding of many different feminist experiences and holds lived experiences at the core of this book. The authors display great courage as they offer some of the most private parts of their lives in the hopes that they would connect with readers and enhance our work as faculty and administrators. We encourage the centering of women's perspectives as we step into the future of higher education and student affairs.

Resisting Dominant Paradigms

Within many of the chapters and narratives throughout this book, we detect an underlying assumption about the resiliency of women who have been oppressed by dominant paradigms. Recognizing the explicit and implicit ways in which women have been oppressed, survived, and advanced is imperative in how we think about women and how we address women's issues in higher education and student affairs. While women have undoubtedly been oppressed, they have also found their own ways to fight and bring about positive change. This is evident in Monica Marcelis Fochtman's chapter (chapter 6) about high-achieving women balancing multiple roles. Her participants shared stories of health scares, loss, and divorce that could have been paralyzing, but the women actually emerged from the experiences even stronger.

Likewise, some of the authors show that it is only through struggle against an exploitative system, such as male domination, that a woman can come to understand her own strength and resilience. Concurrently, women need men and transgendered persons as allies and the vital role of allies cannot be understated (Reason, Broido, Davis, & Evans, 2005). Furthermore, as Bensimon and Marshall (2003) also pointed out, we have no interest in inverting the old logic of the academic hierarchy and excluding White men. We do have an interest, however, in highlighting cultural exclusions and developing inclusive spaces for emancipatory change in higher education and student affairs.

As scholars and practitioners, it is imperative that we recognize how women have been (and continue to be) oppressed and also address the ways in which women have the ability to ignite change. With women now constituting over half of the undergraduate students in higher education (National Center for Educational Statistics, 2007), the media, college and university leaders, and even some researchers have claimed that women have achieved equity and the time to focus on the special needs of women is over. However, as Sax (2008) explained,

> The popular messages are oversimplified: Gender equity has been achieved, women are an academic success story, and men are experiencing an educational crisis. Each of those messages has some truth, but they tend to convey the status of women and men as a zero-sum game: If one gender is succeeding, the other must be failing. The reality is that both genders face obstacles and challenges in their pursuit of higher education, and we need a deeper understanding of the nuances and implications of the gender gap in college. (pp. 1–2)

Thus, faculty and staff in higher education must continue to highlight the issues that women (and men and transgender persons) face, so that the obstacles and challenges are not lost. Examples of historical and contemporary male dominance must be coupled with examples of women's self-empowerment and viable solutions for women to make a difference within their own sphere of influence.

FEMINIST INQUIRY: INFLUENCING RESEARCH AND SCHOLARSHIP

Foundations of Feminist Methodology

So, is there a feminist method of inquiry? Harding (1987) posed this question, arguing that there is *not* a distinctive feminist method of research. Some of her reasoning stems from the fact that discussions of method, methodology, and epistemology are often intertwined in feminist and nonfeminist research, which makes identifying what constitutes research as *feminist* very challenging. More specifically, is it the data collections techniques, analysis, or theoretical assumptions of what is considered "knowledge" that determine feminist research?

Feminist researchers, themselves, have different interpretations of what it means to practice feminist research, as is reflected in the numerous approaches in this book. Olesen (2003) agreed, explaining that "Feminisms partake of different theoretical and pragmatic orientations and reflect national contexts among which feminist agendas differ widely" (p. 333). However, we should be clear that this diversity within the tradition of feminist research is not necessarily a negative thing; disagreements within research traditions may provide important opportunities for scholars to challenge each other, hopefully uncovering greater complexities and understandings. Again, we resist dualistic paradigms of men versus women and good versus bad feminist research paradigms and argue instead for congruence in research (Jones, Torres, & Arminio, 2006).

Even without claiming the notion of a singular feminist methodology or method, Olesen (2003) argued that feminist research in its numerous manifestations

> centers and makes problematic women's diverse situations as well as the institutions that frame those situations. It can refer the examination of that problematic to theoretical, policy, or action frameworks to realize social justice for women in specific contexts (Eichler, 1986, p. 68; 1997, pp. 12–13), or it can present new ideas generated in the research for destabilizing knowledges about oppressive situations for women, or for action or further research (Olesen & Clark, 1999). (Olesen, 2003, p. 333)

According to Millman and Kanter (1987), "once one begins to see the world through women's eyes, radically new sociological assumptions are called for" (p. 29). We believe that this is a particularly important element of a feminist approach to research and practice. Although seeing the world through women's eyes might sound easy enough, all too often women are "studied" as objects and still viewed through the eyes of a dominant worldview (even by some female researchers). Harding (1987) captured this idea by critiquing what she calls the "adding women" approach. Although this occurs less now than in the past, oftentimes researchers claim that they are addressing women's needs by examining how they fare in the same arenas as men. By centering men as the standard by which women are judged, researchers are not critically examining sources of social power that continue to reinforce an unjust system of power. Harding argued that

> this focus still leaves some powerfully androcentric standards firmly in place, thereby insuring only partial and distorted analyses of gender and women's social activities. It falsely suggests that only those activities that men have found it important to study are the ones which constitute and shape social life. (p. 4)

Thus, other critical issues are often ignored, such as reproduction, parenting/caregiving, and sexuality, or if examined, the research is intended to help institutions address the "women problem," as opposed to conducting studies that help participants themselves, as is found, we argue, in the research and scholarship provided in this book.

Power and Discourse

Raising consciousness in research and practice is another important issue; conceptualizations and enactments of power that are implicit need to be made explicit. In particular, within our research, personal, and professional lives, we have a choice to purposefully use inclusive language and address instances where exclusive language is perpetuated. For example, the term *freshmen* (as opposed to first-year students) is frequently used in institutions of higher education that clearly reflect old models of education that prohibited women's matriculation. In another example, women in college are often referred to as *girls*—supposedly as a term of endearment or affection—but in actuality, it equates grown women with children. Language implicitly carries meaning (Cameron, 2001), and the choice

of words in research and practice carries tangible implications for people's daily lives. The use of terms such as *those people* or *others* automatically puts further distance between people who are marginalized and people who have privilege; although the use of such words may not be the intent of any researcher, the impact is still the same.

The need to address educational inequities through feminist inquiry, particularly around issues of gender, may be intuitive for some; however, many higher education leaders do not talk often about the topic and it has been shown that leaders silence the important voices of women in the national discourse (Pasque, 2010). The practice of silencing women is a detriment to inclusive research. We argue that including all perspectives provides researchers with vital options needed to address educational inequities and serve the needs of all people; the absence of particular perspectives or voices reduces our ability to consider additional options and frameworks. Stated a different way, it is critical that marginalized groups are brought into the conversation; otherwise, we exclude important perspectives and ideas. For example, when initiating a research study, it is imperative that people who are "researched" are provided with an opportunity to be a part of the process. This could happen through providing participants with the chance to offer input into the data collection and analysis or by collaborating on the research design, as is found in participant action research.

In research and practice, it becomes imperative that the responsibility of addressing issues of "diversity" is not siphoned off onto one person who is expected to represent all minority groups. While inclusion is beneficial, it makes it easy to put all of the responsibility on one person (or one office or one participant) to represent a plurality of opinions and life experiences. Similarly, we should not look only at one aspect of a person's identity when addressing issues of diversity; women are not a monolithic notion (Olesen, 2003). As evidenced throughout this book, the multiple identities of women (and men and transgender persons) are important to consider in our research and practice. In Amanda's dissertation, for example (an ethnography of a women's college), she often heard faculty and staff discuss the idea of what it means to provide education that is "uniquely suited to women," while also honoring the multiple identities that each student brings to the institution. It is important to note that these multiple identities are as, or in some cases more, salient as gender for some women.

Power in Feminist Inquiry

A primary consideration for feminist scholars is the relationship between researcher and the participants. Developing a strong relationship "is a way to gain greater engagement and understanding into the phenomenon of interest" (Reinharz, 1992, as cited in Jones et al., 2006, p. 95). Beyond a trustworthy means of gathering data, this relationship speaks to the foundation of the feminist researcher's value orientation; collaboration between the researcher and the participant necessitates sharing of power (Patton, 2002).

The focus on power—and efforts to dismantle it—is a common theme throughout feminist inquiry. Wolf (1992) drew an interesting parallel for this concept: "Just as the reality of male privilege affects the lives of every woman, whether she is conscious of it or not, the concept of power is by definition a face in every feminist's research" (p. 133). This concept applies to the topic of study, methods, analysis, and, of course, the researcher–participant relationship, which is always at the foreground of the research process (Jones et al., 2006).

One specific way in which feminist researchers try to address issues of power is through researcher reflexivity (Guerrero, 1999; Jones et al., 2006; Thompson, 1992, as cited in Patton, 2002). Van Manen (1990) reminded us that reflection is at once both an easy and difficult proposition. Theoretically, it is easy to rationalize the need for reflection and understand how it informs our research. Practically, reflection is a much more nuanced and complex endeavor. Consequently, it is in the complexities—or grey area—between theory and practice where a problem originates for researchers; simple clarity does not often exist (Carducci, Contreras-McGavin, Kuntz, & Pasque, 2006). To combat this problem, Jones et al. (2006) described that before, during, and after the research project, the researcher should address the following questions:

♦ Why is it that I am engaged in the present study? What is it about me and my personal experiences that lead me to this study?
♦ What personal biases and assumptions do I bring with me to this study?
♦ What is my relationship with those in the study? (p. 125).

These questions may be answered through self-reflection, reflection with other researchers and/or participants, and reflection on what is known from existing research and literature. Engaging in reflexivity enables feminist researchers to ask questions regarding who is in power and who is powerless (Wolf, 1992). Doing so helps researchers consider (and change if necessary) the processes by which we may purposefully or inadvertently use power to manipulate a situation throughout the study.

While many scholars who embrace a feminist approach conduct research about women or gender, many of these aforementioned concepts can also be applied to various social identities and research topics. In addition, while some of the ideas presented are not necessarily unique to feminist research, they are considered to be hallmarks of many feminist approaches.

QUESTIONS AND IMPLICATIONS

We have addressed lenses and assumptions of feminism and concepts related to feminist inquiry. In summary, we pose some questions to ourselves and the readers in order to incite a call to action, a call for more research and practice that centers on women and feminist perspectives and discusses the myriad implications of these important approaches.

The nature of feminist research and practice is often grounded in challenging traditional frameworks and paradigms that have marginalized people, including, but not limited to, women. For example, the NASPA *Journal about Women in Higher Education* has worked toward shifting this paradigm by intentionally centering women and feminist perspectives. By way of another example, we have put *feminist* in the call for chapters and title of this book, something that rarely happens in the higher education and student affairs literature. Many of the chapters in this book also pose questions that have not been asked before and/or seek answers in a distinct way. For instance, in her chapter "Reflections From Professional Feminists' in Higher Education: Women's and Gender Centers at the Start of the Twenty-First Century," Susan Marine (chapter 2) notes that while "activist stances are essential for transforming the contemporary university (Ng, 1999), doing so can make it hard to get things done in a hierarchical institution that expects you to 'play nice.'"

This begs the question—how does one balance competing forces that reinforce traditional conceptualizations of the academy with a commitment to centering feminist perspectives? As Tamara Yakaboski and Saran Donahoo explain (chapter 16), this can be a particular challenge for scholars who try to "maintain the integrity and voice of feminist work, while still being accepted into the mainstream masculine scholarly literature." It is up to higher education leaders to assess the current sociopolitical and cultural climates at their institutions and consider the ways in which we may push the boundaries on the cycle of socialization and work toward change. For some leaders, this could mean "playing nice" and, for others, it could mean challenging the establishment in more direct ways. In this manner, we encourage multiple and idiosyncratic approaches toward change in the academy; we encourage scholars and practitioners to simultaneously employ multiple strategies in order to enact change.

In addition, many chapters in this book raise important questions regarding women's multiple identities and roles. For example, Elisa Abes and David Kasch (chapter 13) raise questions about identity and student development such as the following: What new insights about college students' negotiation of multiple identities are gained through the use of queer theory? What new insights into student development theory might queer theory uncover? We encourage the next generation of student affairs scholars to expand on the various identity and student development questions raised in this book and dive even deeper into the experiences of women in order to advance our knowledge and, in turn, our practice about the complexities of multiple social identities and roles. Women are not cookie cutters nor should we be treated as such in developmental theories. By way of another example, the dialogue between Amanda Suniti Niskodé-Dossett, Mariama Boney, Linda Contreras Bullock, Cynthia Cochran, and Irene Kao (chapter 12) highlights the nuanced ways in which race and gender intertwine along with our other aspects, such as motherhood, career paths, and sexual orientation. While the authors explain that their multiple identities bring richness to their lives, they also note how it can cause conflicts in their work as student affairs professionals and researchers. Yet, finding their way through the conflicts has helped them become stronger.

Moreover, many of the chapters also question "Who does the culture silence?" and search for ways to bring light to certain populations, based on gender, race, ethnicity, nationality, class, ability, position, and role, to name a few. The individual narratives at the end of each section also speak to this dynamic dialogue in our field. The research on the topics and populations presented in this book demonstrate that women continue to be marginalized in one way, shape, or form throughout the academy. Producing women-centered research challenges traditional frameworks in scholarship as well as practice. For example, in the chapter about sexual assault, Lindsay M. Orchowski and colleagues (chapter 17) challenge the notion that only women can prevent sexual assault and argue for men to also take responsibility to effect change in a culture that tends to hold women responsible for their own assaults. Similarly, in her narrative, Kristie Atkinson demonstrates how commonplace verbal, physical, and sexual abuse is pervasive around the world and calls for women in the academy to speak out against abuse and empower women to not blame themselves for the situation. In addition, some of the authors throughout the book focus on the personal experiences of women that may not have been heard or valued in other arenas.

We also suggest that researchers and practitioners embrace opportunities to collaborate with women at different stages of their personal and professional lives. This intergenerational approach, as is modeled in the Standing Committee for Women (SCW) editorial board for this book, has the opportunity to create fresh perspectives and empower emerging faculty and staff to contribute to the dialogue about women in higher education and student affairs. This process may also build a strong network among scholars and practitioners who embrace feminism. In this way, we hope each new generation of scholars and practitioners pushes beyond the current instantiations of feminist practice and advances the field beyond current expectations.

In sum, feminist research may be distinguished from traditional frameworks in that its primary goal is to examine what women's contributions in various realms of their life means for their lives as women (Harding, 1987). This may seem obvious, but consider how such research might differ from research that has been designed for the establishment or existing dominant power structures. We perceive that one of

the next challenges for women and allies in the field is to examine how we can continue to challenge traditional frameworks, understand and respect multiple identities, ask "Who continues to be silenced?", discuss the implications of the perpetuation of the status quo, and advance substantive change in theory and practice. We encourage reflexive processes during research, policy development, and administrative processes that may help foster the next generation of critical questions around feminist scholarship and practice in the field of higher education and student affairs.

REFERENCES

Astin, H. S., & Leland, C. (1991). *Women of influence, women of vision: A cross-generational study of leaders and social change.* San Francisco: Jossey-Bass.

Bensimon, E. M., & Marshall, C. (2003). Like it or not: Feminist critical policy matters. *Journal of Higher Education, 74*(3), 337–349.

Cameron, D. (2001). *Working with spoken discourse.* Thousand Oaks, CA: Sage.

Carducci, R., Contreras-McGavin, M., Kuntz, A., & Pasque, P. A. (2006, November). *Methodological borderlines: A dialogue on the intersection of positionality and quality in critical qualitative inquiry.* Symposium presented at the Association for the Study of Higher Education, Anaheim, CA.

Guerrero, S. H. (Ed.). (1999). *Gender-sensitive & feminist methodologies: A handbook for health and social researchers.* Quezon City: University of the Philippines Center for Women's Studies.

Harding, S. (Ed.). (1987). *Feminism and methodology.* Bloomington, IN: Indiana University Press.

Hart, J. (2006). Women and feminism in higher education scholarship. *The Journal of Higher Education, 77*(1), 40–61.

Jones, S. R., Torres, V., & Arminio, J. (2006). *Negotiating the complexities of qualitative research in higher education: Fundamental elements and issues.* New York: Routledge.

Lather, P. (1992) Theory into practice. *Qualitative Issues in Educational Research, 31*(2), 87–99.

Millman, M., & Kanter, R. M. (1987). Introduction to another voice: Feminist perspective on social life and social science. In S. Harding (Ed.), *Feminism and methodology* (pp. 29–36). Bloomington, IN: Indiana University Press.

National Center for Educational Statistics. (2007). *Enrollment: Fast facts.* Retrieved August 5, 2009, from http://nces.ed.gov/fastfacts/display.asp?id=98

Ng, R. (2000). A woman out of control: Deconstructing sexism and racism in the university. In J. Glazer-Raymo, B. K. Townsend, & B. Ropers-Huilman (Eds.), *Women in higher education: A feminist perspective* (2nd ed., pp. 360–370). Boston, MA: Pearson publishing.

Olesen, V. L. (2003). Feminism and qualitative research at and into the new millennium. In N. K. Denzin & Y. S. Lincoln (Eds.), *The landscape of qualitative research: Theories and issues* (2nd ed., pp. 332–397). Thousand Oaks, CA: Sage.

Pasque, P. A. (2010). *American higher education, leadership and policy: Critical issues and the public good.* New York: Palgrave Macmillan.

Patton, M. Q. (2002). *Qualitative research & evaluation methods* (3rd ed.). Thousand Oaks, CA: Sage.

Reason, R., Broido, E., Davis, T., & Evans, N. (Eds.). (2005). *Developing social justice allies.* San Francisco, CA: Jossey-Bass.

Ropers-Huilman, B. (1998). *Feminist teaching in theory and practice: Situating power and knowledge in poststructural classrooms.* New York: Teachers College Press.

Sax, L. J. (2008, Sept. 26). Her experience is not his. Accessed at http://chronicle.com. Section: Commentary. Volume 55, Issue 5, Page A32.

Smith, D. E. (1987). *The everyday world as problematic.* Boston, MA: Northeastern University Press.

Thompson, L. (1992). "Feminist methodology for family studies." *Journal of Marriage and the Family, 54*(1), 3–18.

Tierney, W. G. (1994). On method and hope. In A. Gitlin (Ed.), *Power and method: Political activism and educational research* (pp. 97–115). New York: Routledge.

Van Manen, M. (1990). *Researching lived experience: Human science for an action sensitive pedagogy.* Albany, NY: SUNY Press.

Wolf, M. (1992). *A thrice told tale: Feminism, postmodernism, & ethnographic responsibility.* Stanford, CA: Stanford University Press.

About the Contributors

Elisa S. Abes is an assistant professor in the Student Affairs in Higher Education program at Miami University in Oxford, Ohio. She earned her BA and PhD at The Ohio State University and her JD at Harvard Law School. Prior to teaching at Miami University, she was an assistant professor at the University of South Florida and a litigation attorney at Frost and Jacobs LLP. Dr. Abes was named an Association for College Student Personnel Emerging Scholar and also received the American College Personnel Association (ACPA) Annuit Coeptis award for an emerging professional. She has published in the areas of lesbian identity development, development of multiple identities, queer theory and student development, and service-learning. She is on the editorial board for the *Journal of College Student Development*.

Kristie Atkinson graduated from the University of Southern Mississippi in 2004 with a degree in International Studies. Throughout her collegiate experience, Kristie was exposed to different cultures. This experience broadened her worldview and gave her a passion to learn culture and language. Upon graduating, she moved to Southeast Asia to work as a teacher, where she had the opportunity to help college students get involved in reaching out to their communities. Returning to the States, she enrolled in graduate school at the University of Oklahoma (OU). She is currently at OU working on her degree in Adult and Higher Education. Once finished with her degree, she would like to eventually move back overseas and work in a collegiate setting.

Vanidy Bailey is a Senior Community Director at California State University, Northridge. She is the daughter of LaRon and Denise Bailey. Vanidy was raised in various parts of the United States, but she considers New York and North Carolina home. Vanidy graduated from Denison University in 2005 with a BA in English and Black Studies. In addition, she attained her MA from The Ohio State University in Higher Education and Student Affairs with a concentration in student development. Vanidy's first love was writing but her undergraduate experience created a passion for student affairs and university leadership.

Alan Berkowitz completed his PhD in Psychology at Cornell University in 1981 and is a New York state licensed psychologist and an independent consultant who helps colleges, universities, public health agencies, and communities design programs that address health and social justice issues. He is well-known for scholarship and innovative programs that address issues of substance abuse, sexual assault, gender, and diversity. He has received five national awards for his work in these areas.

Mariama Boney works at the ACPA International Office and helps association leaders to develop ongoing communication, programs, and services for ACPA state and international divisions, standing committees, and commissions. For over a decade, Mariama has specialized in diversity and social justice education, student leadership, and program development. Previously,

Mariama worked as the Associate Director of Programs and Partnerships for the national office of the American Association of University Women (AAUW). Mariama earned her BS and MS degrees in Social Work at Syracuse University and has served as a diversity trainer/consultant.

Linda Contreras Bullock is a Latina born and raised in Texas. She has served as Director of Intercultural and International Student Services for nine years and Assistant Dean of Student Diversity for three years at the University of Houston-Clear Lake (UHCL), Houston, Texas. Linda has her MA from UHCL. She has served on the Standing Committee for Women in ACPA for seven years. Linda also serves on the Texas Association of Chicanos in Higher Education (TACHE) Board as Gulf Coast Regional Representative and as Vice President of the Houston TACHE Chapter. She is a senior diversity training leader in the internationally known National Coalition Building Institute (NCBI). Linda and her husband share three children and six grandchildren.

Lee S. Hawthorne Calizo is a doctoral student at the University of Maryland studying College Student Personnel, and her research interests involve the role of cohort groups in leadership development of women. Calizo is the Director of Student Life at University of Maryland, Baltimore County (UMBC), and as part of her studies, she did an internship with the UMBC women's leadership group. Inspired by her experience, Lee has started her own women's group with other colleagues at UMBC.

Cindy Clark was born and raised in Central Oklahoma. She earned her Bachelor of Business Administration degree in Management Information Systems, with a minor in Legal Studies, from OU in 1995. She also worked as a staff member for OU for several years and graduated from OU in 2009 with a Master of Education degree in Adult and Higher Education. Her emphasis is on

adult and continuing education, and she is interested in studying the challenges faced by women returning to college.

Cynthia Cochran (Cie) is the coordinator for Student Organizations and Leadership Programs in the Center for Student Involvement at Northwestern University. Cie has been a member of ACPA since the beginning of her professional career. As an African American woman, Cie has been proud to serve on the Directorate of the Standing Committee for Women for the past four years and has enjoyed volunteering with the Commission for Student Involvement and the Latino Network.

Saran Donahoo is an assistant professor in the Department of Educational Administration and Higher Education and Director of the College Student Personnel Program at Southern Illinois University, Carbondale. She earned both her doctorate in Higher Education Administration and her MA in History at the University of Illinois at Urbana-Champaign. She completed her BA in Secondary Education at the University of Arizona. Her research interests include legal issues affecting education, educational policy, international/comparative education, and educational diversity and equity for both K–12 and postsecondary education. Her published works include coediting *Teaching Leaders to Lead Teachers: Educational Administration in the Era of Constant Crisis* and articles in *Teachers College Record, Equity and Excellence in Education, Christian Higher Education, Urban Education*, and *Education and Urban Society*, as well as an array of book chapters.

Jennifer Dudeck-Lenis is a New Jersey native and graduated from Douglass College of Rutgers University summa cum laude in 1999 with a bachelor's degree in English. She obtained her Master of Arts degree in College Student Personnel in 2003 from the University of Maryland, College Park (UMCP). She is a member of Phi Beta Kappa and Omicron Delta Kappa. Jennifer's student affairs experience spans involvement in admissions, career services, residence life and housing, orientation, and student leadership development. Before assuming her current position as Assistant Director of Recruitment and New Student Programs at Douglass Residential College of Rutgers University, Jennifer held positions at Fairleigh Dickinson University, UMCP, and The George Washington University.

Kimberley Fernandes is a Diversity Educator in the field of higher education and currently works in the Multicultural Center at the University of San Diego. She holds a BA in Sociology and Communications from Villanova University with minors in Theatre and Women's Studies. She holds an MA in Higher Education from Teachers College, Columbia University. Her passion lies in identity development as it relates to the individual and the collective; specifically, her research interests lie in the intersection of race and gender and the medium of "voice" as it serves to liberate women of color to define a space within feminism that is reflective of their voices and experiences.

Kimberly L. Filer is a doctoral candidate in the Educational Research and Evaluation program at Virginia Tech. With a background in mathematics and science education, her research interests include social capital theory and its implications for higher level mathematics and science course taking for traditionally underrepresented groups.

Monica Marcelis Fochtman has a Ph.D. from the Higher, Adult, and Lifelong Education (HALE) program at Michigan State University. Her research interests include gender and leadership, high-achieving women leaders, and professional women with children. She has worked as a student affairs professional in residence life, student activities, and academic advising. She is married and the proud mother of two busy and loving children.

Christine A. Gidycz completed her PhD in Clinical Psychology at Kent State University in 1988 and is actively involved with conducting research on sexual assault. She is particularly interested in the evaluation of sexual assault prevention and risk reduction programs and had developed the Ohio University Sexual Assault Risk Reduction Program, a curriculum designed to reduce women's risk for sexual victimization. She is currently a professor of psychology at Ohio University and the Director of Clinical Training.

Florence M. Guido is a writer, photographer, researcher, and associate professor in the Higher Education and Student Affairs Leadership doctoral program at the University of Northern Colorado. She is coauthor of *Student Development in College: Theory, Research and Practice* and has published on women and leadership, women's moral development, history of women in higher education, diversity development, ethnic identity, and Mexican men and social class.

Jennifer Lee Hoffman is currently a research associate with the Intercollegiate Athletic Leadership Graduate Program at the University of Washington. Her research focuses on Title IX policy in intercollegiate athletics, with a specific interest on issues related to gender and ethnicity. Her research has been published in the *Journal for the Study of Sports and Athletes in Education* and presented at the Association for the Study of Higher Education and the American Educational Research Association. She also holds an appointment in the Department of Physical Education at Seattle Pacific University. Her degrees include a PhD from the University of Washington, MA in Student Development Administration from Seattle University, and BS from Washington State University in Physical Education.

Irene Kao is an Asian American woman who has worked five years in student affairs. She has her MA from the University of Maryland, College Park. Irene worked as Multicultural Coordinator at University of New Hampshire in Durham and Assistant Dean of Students at Macalester College in St. Paul, Minnesota. Irene served as cochair for the Asian Pacific American Network in ACPA. She is currently in law school at Hamline University in St. Paul, Minnesota.

David Kasch is a PhD student in the Higher Education and Organizational Change (HEOC) program and a research analyst in the Center for Educational Assessment at UCLA. He earned his BA from Loyola Marymount University and his MS from Miami University. Prior to entering the HEOC program, David worked for several years in student affairs through offices of campus activities, residence life, judicial affairs, and enrollment services. David's research interests concern the influence of sociocultural power dynamics on college students: sexuality as a site of critical resistance, the role of social network sites in identity development, and the commodification of identity and self-concept.

Cayden Mak is a graduate student in the Department of Media Study at the State University of New York at Buffalo. His research and teaching concerns augmented reality and technology for activism in virtual spaces. Cayden blogs about research and theory at thenoiseofthestreet.net.

Susan Marine is the Director of the Harvard College Women's Center at Harvard University. Prior to directing the women's center, she served as founding Director of Harvard's Office of Sexual Assault Prevention and Response. Susan has specific expertise in developing effective initiatives for the support of transgender and other gender-variant college students. She holds a master's degree in Higher Education and Student Affairs from Bowling Green State University and is a recent doctoral graduate in Higher Education at Boston College.

Kelly E. Maxwell is a faculty member in the Psychology Department and Codirector of the Program on Intergroup Relations at the University of Michigan. She codirects a partnership unit between the College of Literature, Science, and the Arts and the Division of Student Affairs. She also teaches courses on intergroup issues including social identity, privilege, oppression, and power. In addition, she trains students to facilitate intergroup dialogue on campus. She is a graduate of the Educational Leadership and Policy Studies program at Arizona State University and worked for three years in its Intergroup Relations Center coordinating Voices of Discovery, the university's intergroup dialogues program. Kelly has a Master of Science degree in Higher Education in Student Affairs from Florida State University and a Bachelor of Arts degree from Baldwin Wallace College in Political Science and Business. Her research interests include dialogue and intergroup relations issues in higher education, particularly related to the critical examination of White privilege and its role in maintaining systems of inequity in education.

Thalia Mulvihill, a tenured Professor of Social Foundations and Higher Education at Ball State University, currently serves as the Assistant Department Chair/Director of Doctoral Programs and the Director of the Certificate Program in College and University Teaching. Dr. Mulvihill holds a PhD in Cultural Foundations of Education and Curriculum (Syracuse University) and an MA in Higher Education Research/Student Affairs Administration (Syracuse University). Her research agenda focuses on the history and sociology of higher education, with a focus on women and gender issues, and innovative teaching practices for higher education. She was the 2009 recipient of the Dr. Robert O. Foster Faculty Award for her work with cultural diversity, the 2004 University Excellence in Teaching Award, and the 2003 Virginia B. Ball Center for Creative Inquiry Fellowship.

Xyanthe Neider is a PhD Candidate at Washington State University in Higher Education

Administration and Cultural Studies and Social Thought in Education who explores how globalization is changing the face of diversity in U.S. higher education. An interest that has emerged from her work is how groups have been constructed as *trouble* in the current sociopolitical climate in the West. Although she comes from a Western standpoint, her hope is to open the spaces where the complicated conversations can occur, and scholars and practitioners can then engage in reflections that will challenge the systems of power and oppression that inherently exist within the institutions in which they work and research.

Shelley Errington Nicholson has worked in higher education and student affairs for over a decade. Her history includes Director of Women's Programs/Assessment Coordinator for Student Affairs at Worcester Polytechnic Institute as well as positions at Rice University in Houston, the University of Edinburgh in Scotland, and the Massachusetts College of Pharmacy and Health Sciences (MCPHS). While at MCPHS, Shelley was awarded the National Association of College Student Personnel 2004 Best Practices in International Education and Learning award. Shelley is the current President of the Massachusetts College Personnel Association and a Directorate board member of the ACPA Standing Committee for Women. Shelley received her BA in Corporate Communications with a minor in Music from Roger Williams University and her MS in Human Development and Family Studies from the University of Rhode Island.

Amanda Suniti Niskodé-Dossett currently serves as the Director of Student Engagement at the University of St. Thomas in St. Paul, Minnesota. She is in the process of completing her PhD in Higher Education and Student Affairs from Indiana University. Her ethnographic dissertation examines the culture of a women's college through the lens of critical and feminist theoretical perspectives. Amanda Suniti earned her

MA from the University of Maryland and has worked at Miami University (Ohio) and at the National Survey of Student Engagement (NSSE) at Indiana University. She is also a directorate member of the Standing Committee for Women and has served as the chair of the ACPA's MultiRacial Network.

Dorothy B. Nkhata is a doctoral student in the Adult and Higher Education Program at OU, where she serves as graduate research assistant. Dorothy Nkhata received her BS in Physics from the University of Malawi, Chancellor College, and her MS in Secondary Science Education from Indiana University Purdue University Indianapolis. Between 1994 and 2006, she served as science teacher and Dean of Medical Sciences in secondary schools in Malawi and at the Malawi College of Health Sciences, respectively. She was a finalist in the Fulbright Junior Staff Development Scholarship competition in 2004 and later (2006) received the American Association of University Women International Fellowship.

Lindsay M. Orchowski received her PhD in Clinical Psychology from Ohio University and is currently a postdoctoral research fellow at the Center for Alcohol and Addiction Studies at Brown University. Her research examines the risk factors and consequences of sexual victimization and campus-based sexual assault prevention.

Penny A. Pasque is Assistant Professor of Adult and Higher Education in the Department of Educational Leadership and Policy Studies and Women's and Gender Studies at OU. Her research includes addressing in/equities in higher education and student affairs, exploring the connections between higher education and society, and uncovering complexities in critical qualitative methodologies. She received a PhD from the Center for the Study of Higher and Postsecondary Education at the University of Michigan and her work has been published in the *Journal of College Student Development, Review of*

Higher Education, and *Multicultural Perspectives*, among others. Penny has presented her research on women leaders in higher education at Oxford University, England, and this research is included in her latest book, *American Higher Education, Leadership, and Policy: Critical Issues and the Public Good* (Palgrave Macmillan, 2010). Penny also serves as faculty committee chair for the Center for Social Justice at OU.

Rosemary J. Perez is a doctoral student at the University of Michigan's Center for the Study of Higher and Postsecondary Education and is currently a research assistant for the Wabash National Study of Liberal Arts Education. Her research interests include identity development, professional socialization, and social movements. Prior to pursuing her terminal degree, Rosie completed her BS in Biological Sciences with an additional major in Psychology at Carnegie Mellon University and her MEd in Higher Education and Student Affairs at the University of Vermont. She also served as a Hall Director at the University of San Francisco and as an Area Director at American University. Rosie has been actively engaged in professional associations throughout her career and is a proud alumna of the ACPA Standing Committee for Women's EmpowHer Fellowship program and Directorate Board.

Justin Reeder completed his undergraduate degree at Ohio University, with a triple major in Education, Math, and Psychology. Justin was also a facilitator of the Men's Sexual Assault Prevention program within the Community Programming Initiative.

Ryan Rhoades completed his undergraduate degree at Ohio University, where he majored in Education. Ryan was a facilitator of the Men's Sexual Assault Prevention program in the Community Programming Initiative and also has experience facilitating an empathy-based sexual assault prevention program for college men.

Penny J. Rice has been the Director of the Margaret Sloss Women's Center at Iowa State University (ISU) since 2000. Prior to this position, she was the Director of Off Campus and Adult Students Services at ISU and Director of Adult and Graduate Student Services at Texas A&M University. She earned her bachelor's degree in Psychology/Women's Studies and her master's in Counseling and Student Personnel from Minnesota State University, Mankato. Penny is currently "all but dissertation" in her doctoral degree in Educational Leadership and Policy Studies from Iowa State University. As a returning adult student to higher education, she acknowledges the privilege and responsibility that come with these opportunities and continues to educate herself and others on issues of social justice and equity.

Robbie graduated with a bachelor of arts from a small public institution in New York, studying Sociology, Psychology, and Cognitive Science. Directly after she completed an undergraduate degree, he continued into a master's program, studying Higher Education Administration. After graduating and now in the field, ze has been coordinating dialogue opportunities to promote intergroup understanding and self-exploration regarding identity and social justice. Robbie enjoys gardening, playing and writing music, and daydreaming in her free time.

Troy Robison completed his MS in Clinical Psychology at Ohio University, and is currently pursuing a PhD. In addition to his interest in sexual assault prevention, Troy researches the media's portrayal of psychotherapy.

Jennifer Sader is an assistant professor in the Master of Organizational Leadership at Lourdes College in Sylvania, Ohio. She graduated in 2007 with her PhD in Higher Education Administration from Bowling Green State University, also in Ohio. Before and during most of her doctoral study, she worked in information technology as a systems administrator and a training and documentation specialist. Jennifer also spent some time in the nonprofit sector with the National Institute for Technology in Liberal Education (NITLE), where she designed, researched, and delivered professional development programs to help faculty and staff members at small colleges use technology to promote student learning.

Linda J. Sax is Associate Professor in the Graduate School of Education and Information Studies at UCLA. Her research focuses on gender differences in college student development, specifically how institutional characteristics, peer and faculty environments, and forms of student involvement differentially affect male and female college students. Dr. Sax is the author of more than 70 publications, including *The Gender Gap in College: Maximizing the Developmental Potential of Women and Men* (Jossey-Bass, 2008), as well as the recipient of the 2005 Scholar-in-Residence Award from the American Association of University Women and the 1999 Early Career Award from the Association for the Study of Higher Education.

Amy Stalzer Sengupta currently works in MBA Admissions for the Goizueta Business School at Emory University. Prior to this post, she served in student affairs for many years at Georgia Institute of Technology, most notably in new student programs where she directed orientation and first-year seminar programs. Amy is completing a PhD in Sociology at Georgia State University and holds master's degrees in Higher Education and Women's Studies. Her research and presentations have focused on social developmental transitions, particularly of college first-year students and young women.

Racheal L. Stimpson is a doctoral candidate in the Higher Education program in the Department of Educational Leadership and Policy Studies at Virginia Tech. Her background is

in student affairs and her research interests include first-generation college students, women in higher education, and college access.

Venice Thandi Sulé holds an MSW and received her doctorate from the Center for the Study of Higher and Postsecondary Education at the University of Michigan. She uses critical theory to analyze how women access and persist within higher education settings. In addition, her work interrogates notions of diversity by exploring how intersecting identities and social practices promote educational equity. Upon completion of her doctorate, Thandi was granted a two-year postdoctoral fellowship at the Center for the Education of Women at the University of Michigan. Her research looks at how low-income women engage in (and disengage from) higher education with a particular emphasis on community college students.

Yvette Loury Upton is currently Director of Outreach and Student Affairs at the Georgia Institute of Technology, Savannah Campus. Prior to this promotion, Yvette served as assistant dean of students and Director of the Women's Resource Center at Georgia Tech. As the first professional staff member of the center, she advised student programming on women's interests and issues, provided support and crisis intervention to women who have experienced sexual violence, and researched and implemented policy recommendations to improve the campus environment for women. Yvette has a bachelor's degree in Journalism and a master's degree in Women's Studies, both from Georgia State University. Her research and presentations have focused on women's leadership as well as the experiences of female students in predominantly male environments.

Annemarie Vaccaro is an assistant Professor of College Student Personnel in the Department of Human Development and Family Studies at the University of Rhode Island. Her PhD is in Higher Education Administration with a cognate in teaching about diversity and social justice from the University of Denver. She has two MA degrees, one in Sociology and another in Student Affairs. She has taught undergraduate and graduate courses that range in scope and include student affairs, social justice, women's studies, and sociology. Her research centers on issues of multiple identities, especially race, gender, sexual orientation, and class in the context of higher education settings. Her most recent research project was a qualitative study of the identity intersections of 49 lesbian, gay, bisexual, transgender, and questioning (LGBTQ) faculty, staff, and students.

Rachel Wagner is currently an Assistant Director in Residence Life at the University of Dayton and is a doctoral student in the Social Justice Education program at the University of Massachusetts Amherst. Her research interests include masculine gender expression and the influence of masculinity performance on diversity related outcomes. She has been the national cochair for the Men and Masculinities Knowledge Community in NASPA and served on the planning committee for the Conference on College Men. Rachel has published on fostering social justice attitudes in male students and developmental considerations of sophomore resident assistants.

Jennifer R. Wies became the founding Director of the Xavier University Women's Center in 2007, dedicating her energies to creating a center that simultaneously provides resources, advances education, and promotes research. She completed her doctoral education in Anthropology at the University of Kentucky, focusing on Applied and Medical Anthropology. Her research efforts center on examining structural inequalities that prevent individuals from establishing and maintaining a high quality of life and well-being, which includes access to education. To date, she has focused on social movement advocates and activists working in nonprofit organizations to understand the grassroots perspectives of

human service care work as they articulate with multiple power structures. Her pedagogical research includes identifying barriers to graduate education among first-generation college women and the politics of service-learning.

Kelly T. Winters is a PhD student in Higher Education at the University of Minnesota, where she is a graduate research assistant in the Postsecondary Education Research Institute (PERI). Her research interests are in narrative inquiry, feminist poststructuralism, and higher education policy analysis. She was most recently employed as a student affairs staff member at the College of St. Catherine where she worked in roles as varied as instructor in the CORE curriculum department, coordinator of the writing center, and first-year student adviser. She holds a BA in English from the College of St. Catherine (St. Paul, Minnesota) and an EdM in Higher Education from Harvard University.

Tamara Yakaboski is an assistant professor in the Department of Educational Administration and Higher Education and an affiliated Women's Studies faculty member at Southern Illinois University Carbondale (SIUC). She earned both her PhD in Higher Education with a minor in Sociology and her MA in College Student Personnel from the University of Arizona (UA). She completed her BA in English from Louisiana Tech University. She teaches qualitative research and higher education. Her current research projects include international women faculty and students, the representation of college women in media, women administrators in higher education institutions, and student affairs administration.

Eric Zimak completed his MS in Clinical Psychology at Ohio University and is currently pursuing a PhD in Clinical Psychology at Ohio University. His research focuses on the neuropsychological correlates of risk-taking behaviors and risky personality traits.

Index

able, ableism, ability
  care, helpfulness, 54, 133
  economic status and ability, 178
  perceptions of ability, 122–123, 134, 141, 331
  physical ability, 62, 250
  racial identity, 108
  social identity, 164, 195, 211, 235, 327
academic advisor, advisor, advising
  administrative roles, xiv, 33, 64
  counseling, career counseling, 54, 134
  faculty role, 74, 131
  gender identity, 130
  mentors, support figures, 61, 91–92, 121, 135, 197, 227, 233
  racial identity, 153–154, 182, 188
ACCESS Project, 179, 184
admissions, xiv, 15, 33, 36, 57, 64, 74, 131, 135, 154, 172, 182
ADVANCE grant, 307, 311
advancement, xx, 13, 27, 29–30, 38, 42, 96, 137, 256, 263, 272–273, 282–283, 285, 306–317, 326
advocacy, advocate, xx, 19, 20, 24, 48, 148–149, 152, 156–158, 160, 196, 202, 204–205, 208, 211–212, 260–261, 263, 296
affirmation, women and girls, 24, 114, 157, 166, 168, 188–189, 234, 237, 23–240, 244
affirmative action, 15, 45, 147–148, 155, 160–161
African, 138, 157, 165
African American
  economic disadvantages, poverty, xvi, 188
  educational experiences, 34, 88, 151, 196, 236
  experiences in administration, xix, 201, 204, 274–276
  feminism, 7, 14, 150, 235
  racial identity, 107, 158, 194, 199, 247
  racism toward, 34, 148–149, 165
  sexual orientation, 199
  work–life balance, 76
age, ageism, xiv, xviii, 21, 87–89, 93, 98, 100, 104–106, 108, 112, 114, 116, 151, 167, 171–172, 175, 194, 206, 216–217, 225

agency, 17, 29, 174, 213, 218, 223, 229, 250, 268, 281
American Intercollegiate Athletics Association for Women (AIAW), 39–42, 45, 58
alcohol , 179, 292, 298, 303, 304
allies, ally, xiii, 16, 18–19, 23–24, 111, 211, 208, 227, 289, 294, 313, 327, 332–333
American Association of University Women (AAUW), xvi, 58, 197, 244, 315
American College Personnel Association (ACPA), 61, 80, 117, 194–195, 197–198, 200–202, 205, 209, 212, 271, 315
Asian American, xix, 60–62, 107, 165, 194, 199–202, 235, 245, 256, 274–276, 284, 286
Asian American feminism, 9
assimilation, 101, 110, 117, 165, 282
attrition, 70–73, 79, 83–84, 272–273, 281–282, 285

biracial, 18, 198, 202
bisexual, 6, 213, 215, 228, 257, 268, 318
Black Feminism, 7, 14, 150
Black Feminist Thought (BFT), 7, 13, 150

career
  career and identity, 61, 65, 71, 104, 111–112, 114–115, 121–122, 125–127, 134, 136, 138, 159, 172, 199–200, 209, 211, 231, 262, 274–276, 278–279, 282, 317–318, 331
  professional development, 28, 73, 76, 81–82, 107, 132–133, 140, 151, 154, 183, 196, 205, 272–273, 275–278, 280, 282, 306–307, 314–315, 318, 320
  career process, 270–272
  feminism and careers, 6, 8, 174–175, 256
  mentoring in careers, role models, xviii, 72, 90, 92–94, 97, 130, 135, 173, 207, 240, 263, 311, 314
  work–life balance in careers, 86–87, 90, 95, 98, 100–101, 123, 128–129, 132–133, 140, 174, 180, 272–273, 278
Chicana, 119, 198

343

Chicana feminism, 9–10

children

childcare, 6, 20, 25, 28, 81, 99, 149, 180, 191

child custody, 9

cultural, ethnic, and/or racial identity, 110, 113, 138, 166–168, 170–171, 173, 187–189, 235, 246–247, 282, 322

gender identity, 8, 62, 235, 329

parental careers, xix, 70–71, 85–86, 88–90, 92, 98–99, 129, 272–273

parental development, 65, 75, 87, 94, 100, 140, 169–170, 179, 200

poverty, economic challenges, 179–192, 283

traditional roles and expectations for children and parents, 34, 99, 138, 142, 168, 174–175, 279, 329

work–life balance for parents, 69–70, 72, 76–80, 95, 101–102, 133, 273, 282

chilly climate, 104, 116, 118, 134, 308

Chinese, 200

class

classism and oppression, 7, 111, 156, 213, 228,

first–class or state of the art, 41, 163,

social class and identity, xiv, xvi, xviii, xix, 3, 5, 7, 10, 12, 23, 30, 96, 108, 145, 148, 160, 163–172, 175–176, 213, 217–222, 224, 226, 228, 232, 235, 238, 246, 275, 279, 331

socioeconomic status, 5–7, 23, 34, 128, 164–165, 167–168, 170–171, 173–175, 178, 181, 183, 189, 191, 219–220, 238, 241, 256

class/year standing (i.e. first year, second year), 50–51, 58, 106, 240

cocurricular, 42, 72–75, 137, 140, 260

coeducation, coeducational, xvii, 6, 16, 29, 32–39, 42–44, 49–51, 56, 59, 66, 104, 246, 256

Committee on Women's Athletics (CWA), 36

community college, xvi, 17, 20, 24, 27, 87, 89, 98, 180, 188–189, 271, 276, 283

Council of the Advancement of Standards (CAS), 262, 265, 267

Critical Race Theory (CRT), viii, 12, 105, 108, 114, 228, 247

crucible, crucible event, 90, 97, 98, 101

Dean of Women, 33, 36, 38, 42–43, 48–50, 52–57

discourse, 12, 84, 149–150, 158, 178, 329, 332–333

diversity

among women, 116, 315

ethnic and racial , 154, 158, 196, 202, 211

ethnic and social class, 168

feminism, 11, 328–329

gender, race, class, sexual orientation, age, and additional social identities, xiv, 75, 88, 154, 197, 262, 265, 314, 315, 329

of experiences and perspectives, 115–118, 172, 301

theories, 265

women of color, 150, 154

work, xv, 197, 199, 204, 315, 318

dominant, ix, xv, xix, 11, 61, 66, 107, 109–110, 147–150, 152–153, 215, 223–224, 228, 234–235, 249, 253, 272–273, 278, 300, 317–319

Eastern Associations of Directors of Physical Education for College Women (EADPECW), 50, 52–54

eco feminism, xvii, 3–4, 10

empowerment, 21–22, 29–30, 104–105, 111–117, 181, 187, 241, 269, 297, 313, 317, 325, 328

equality feminism, 8

ethnicity, xiv, xvi, 9, 34, 110, 121, 163–164, 166, 171, 174–175, 178, 182, 194, 223, 227–228, 232, 234–236, 245, 248–249, 267, 269, 271, 274, 282, 285, 331

existential feminism, 3–4, 9

family

cultural, ethnic, and/or racial identity, 63, 108–109, 163–172, 174–175, 201, 247

economic challenges, 140, 179–180, 184–189, 238, 279

educational experiences, 63, 69, 74, 125–126, 154

familial identity, xix, 62, 89, 93, 112, 144, 163–172, 174–175, 207, 210, 214, 216, 220, 233, 235, 317, 322

family–friendly culture, policies, 8, 86, 99, 282

family relationships, 74, 79, 99, 163–172, 224, 232, 236, 237, 297, 302

family roles and expectations, 4, 86, 90, 114, 123, 126, 129, 133, 141–142, 163–172, 247, 250, 279

work–life balance, career expectations, 28, 48, 61, 69–72, 74, 79, 92, 94–95, 98, 101, 123, 127, 133, 140–141, 196, 201, 221, 272–273, 277–278, 281–282

feminine, femininity, 5–8, 133, 135, 217, 219–221, 247, 277, 282, 322

feminist epistemology 11–12, 88, 328

feminist identity development, xix, 295–296

feminist inquiry, xviii, xx, 17, 325, 326, 328–332

feminist philosophy, 13, 63

feminist research, feminist researcher, xi, xvi, xx, 10–13, 16–17, 87, 106, 114, 325–326, 328, 330–332

Filipina, 60–61
financial aid, 20, 182
first–generation, viii, xix, 8, 35, 39, 43, 49, 163, 166,
     170, 173, 175, 246
focus group, 12, 17–19, 24, 82, 106–108

gender–combined gender equity era, 37
gender construction, xviii, 125–126, 136, 143, 148
gender in/equity
     campus activism, 16, 19, 257
     feminism, xvii, 8, 9, 175
     gender in/equity in higher education, xiii–xiv, xvi,
          33, 37, 41–42, 175
     remaining work, 26, 32, 328
     social dynamics, 9, 34, 43
     Title IX, effects on women leadership, 32–33,
          37–39, 43
     women's centers, 15, 255–258
gender feminism, 8
gender role/s, 8–9, 11, 20, 62, 125–126, 128, 134,
     141, 170, 277–278, 286, 289
GI Bill, 36
global feminism, xvii, 9
group think, 304

harass, harassment, sexual harassment, 4–9, 25, 174,
     179, 257, 267, 269
health
     education, 50, 91, 207, 211–212
     feminism, xiv, 9
     health care, health insurance, 20, 179, 182, 256
     outreach, support, 20, 22, 211–212, 237,
          262–263, 287–288, 293–295, 303
     poverty, economic disadvantage, 183–184, 186,
          189, 191
     race, 148–149, 154, 211
     risks to health, health scares, 73, 89, 97–98,
          239–240, 250–251, 302, 327
     work–life balance, 95, 126, 196
hegemony, 159, 215, 247
heterogeneous/heterogeneity, 158–159, 256–257
heteronormative, heteronormativity, xix, 213,
     215–217, 220–224, 226–228, 317
heterosexism, heterosexist, 7, 13, 111, 213, 224, 228
heterosexual, heterosexuality, heterosexual norms, xx,
     156, 164, 213, 215–216, 220, 222–223
hidden pregnancy phenomenon, 99
hir, hirstory, 143–144, 340
Hispanic, 16, 24, 76, 107, 109, 172, 196, 204, 274,
     282
Historically Black Colleges and Universities
     (HBCU), 34, 154, 275–276
homogeneity/homogeneous, 88, 159, 273

identity, identity development, xiii, ix, xix, 5–11, 82,
     95, 107, 109, 140,143–144, 187–190, 192,
     197, 211, 213–228, 231–251, 268, 271, 280,
     295, 297, 317, 319, 327, 329, 331
immigration, immigrant, viii, 65, 163, 165–166,
     168–170, 173, 175
Indonesia, Indonesian, 141–142
intercultural, viii, xviii, 141–142
internalized racism, 60, 109
international student, international women,
     international education, 19, 76, 99, 141–142
intersectionality, xiv, 23, 30, 164, 245
isolation, 61, 93, 99, 155, 121, 130, 134, 137,
     238–239, 276, 289, 322

Journal About Women in Higher Education, xvi,
     283–284, 331

Latina, 107, 109, 112–113, 235, 256–257, 274,
     282–283, 194, 196, 198–201, 203, 209
leadership, xiv, xv, xvii, 10, 16–17, 22, 29–30,
     32–34, 36, 45, 47–48, 58–59, 64, 67, 72, 81,
     85–86, 88–92, 94, 96–97, 100–101, 140, 164,
     174, 191, 196, 199, 208, 243, 261–264, 268,
     289, 293, 295, 301, 306–316, 318–319,
     321–322, 326
lesbian, lesbianism, ix, xix, 6, 88–89, 199, 213–228,
     245, 257, 268–269, 295, 317–318, 322
lesbian, gay, bisexual, and transgender (LGBT), xiv,
     21, 24–25, 215, 228–230
liberal feminism, xvii, 3–6, 44
liminality, 215–217, 220–221, 225

masculine, masculinity, 6–8, 16, 71–72, 219, 221,
     249, 281–282, 289, 307, 309, 322, 331
marginalize, marginalization, xviii, xx, 13, 22–23,
     148–151, 156, 158–160, 188, 211, 223–224,
     325–326, 329, 331
marriage, 63, 74, 83, 89, 126, 138, 174–175, 286,
     317, 322
Marxist feminism, xvii, 3–4, 7–9
mentoring
     feminism, 27, 61
     identity, 61–62, 74, 85, 96, 116, 135–136, 198,
          201–202, 207, 212, 263, 313, 315, 320
     intergenerational mentoring, 94, 96, 98, 101,
          212
     mentoring in careers, for leadership, xviii, 6, 19,
          27, 72, 81, 90–94, 97, 101, 130, 133, 148, 190,
          196, 203, 207–208, 244, 264–265, 272–273,
          308, 312, 314, 318
     networking, 81, 93–94, 206, 261, 265, 308
     work-life balance, 72, 88, 92–93

methodology, methodologies, feminist methodology, xv, xvii, xviii, xx, 11–13, 16, 87–88, 105, 216–217, 228, 285, 328

Mexican American, 109–110, 168–169, 172, 198–199

Middle Eastern women, Middle Eastern American women, xvi, 194, 247

mission, xx, 16, 19–21, 23–24, 27–28, 40, 47–48, 56, 89, 124, 159, 183, 193, 227, 255, 257–262, 264–267, 275, 311

Model of Multiple Dimensions of Identity, 145, 176, 225, 229

Morrill Act, 34

mother, grandmother
    administrators and faculty, academic motherhood, 85–87, 89, 95, 98, 100–101, 196, 246, 282
    feminism, feminist perspectives, 6, 36, 171
    identity, empowerment, xiv–xv, 62, 87, 97, 101, 113, 126, 155, 211, 222–224, 247, 322, 331
    single mothers, 178, 182–185, 188, 190–191, 200
    students, 19, 23
    traditional motherhood roles, cultural roles, 34, 36, 63, 126, 129, 138, 141–142, 163, 166–172, 174–175, 217–220
    work-life balance, 28, 63, 79, 85–88, 95, 98–101, 129, 210, 272–273

multicultural feminism, 3–4, 9–10

multiracial, 10, 76, 106, 108, 194, 197, 201–203, 206, 212, 317

National Association of Deans of Women (NADW), 8, 33, 36, 42

narrative
    administrative roles, 267, 270, 278, 306
    feminism, feminist perspectives, xiv–xv, xvii, 7, 10, 12, 60, 88, 317–319, 325, 327
    identity, identity development, personal narrative, xiii, xix, 64, 98, 150, 165, 227, 246, 251, 331–332
    personal challenges, 24, 184–185, 222, 281
    race, 10, 60, 108, 138, 147, 149, 151–157, 276
    sexual orientation, 213–214, 216–217, 220, 222–229, 317–319

National Association of Student Personnel Administrators (NASPA), xxi, 45, 70, 83–83, 102, 176, 205, 268–269, 271, 274, 278, 283–286

National Collegiate Athletic Association (NCAA), 33, 40–41, 58

nationality, xix, 3, 73, 165, 327, 331

Native American, American Indian, xvi, 3–4, 9–10, 76, 107, 148, 194, 200–201, 274

Native American feminism, 10

nontraditional student, xviii, xix, 73, 101, 104–106, 114, 138–139, 257

oppression, xvi, 4–8, 10–11, 13, 26, 28, 61–62, 105, 107, 109, 111, 152, 156, 164–165, 175, 178, 187–188, 191, 249, 276, 283, 295, 317–318, 323

paradigm, ix, xv, xix, xx, 16, 61, 66, 110, 122, 158, 202, 212, 253, 272, 278, 325, 327–328, 331

paternal, paternalism, paternalistic, 60, 155, 167

patriarchy, patriarchal, xv, xvi, xix, xx, 28, 30, 90, 105, 164, 175, 326

pedagogy, pedagogies, 52, 64, 227, 285, 320–321

physical education, vii, xiv, xvii, 5, 33,45, 47–60, 89, 217, 219

Political Race (PR) theory, 150, 159–160

postmodern feminism, postmodernism, 3–4, 11, 14, 17, 144, 214, 224–225

poverty, 26, 156, 166, 169, 178–179, 183–186, 190–192, 268–269, 283, 286, 327

power
    access, 148
    cultural, 227
    empower, 142–143
    influence, 72, 130, 311
    intersections of race, gender, and power, 156
    leadership, 306–307
    male/men, 174, 277
    organizational and institutional power, 28, 42, 51, 52, 153
    personality trait, 277
    political, 34
    positions of, 15, 39, 41, 202
    power and knowledge, 12, 174, 227
    power and race, 160, 165
    power distributions, xiii, 22, 28, 64, 113, 116, 135, 154, 169, 178, 187, 190, 212, 216, 227, 242, 246–249, 312, 318–319, 329–330
    power structures, 148, 150, 213, 215, 223–224, 226, 227, 228, 332
    powerful, power, 87, 264, 266, 306–307, 311, 314, 322, 330
    privilege, xx, 60, 107, 187, 190, 228, 246, 318–319
    racialized, 150, 158–159
    relations, 187, 190, 227
    social, 329
    status, 133
    strength, 59, 167, 264
    subordinate, powerless, surrendering, 169, 174, 227, 246
    systems of, 150, 154, 329

prevention programs, 288–289, 294, 301, 303, 305
privilege
    culture, 172–173, 235
    gender, 61–63, 164, 169, 175, 235, 323,
        329–330
    intersecting types, 166
    privilege, general reference, 107–109, 137, 148,
        150, 152, 156, 164–166, 168–169, 172–173,
        175, 178, 182–183, 188, 190–192, 194, 205,
        211, 213, 228, 323, 329–330
    race, ethnicity, 60, 64, 107–109, 148, 150, 152,
        156, 165, 175, 182, 188, 190, 194, 205, 211,
        276, 318
    sexual orientation, 64, 213, 228, 318
    socioeconomic status, 11, 148, 164, 168, 173,
        175, 178, 183, 238, 318
programming, xiv, xviii, 19–20, 75, 91, 136,
    257–259, 261, 266–267, 287–289, 291,
    293–294, 297–298, 303–304, 318
psychoanalytic feminism, 3–4, 8

queer, queer theory, ix, xix, 6, 12, 213–228, 295,
    320, 331

race
    "American race," 165
    consciousness, 147, 150, 152, 156–158, 160
    critical race, xviii, 12, 104, 106, 116
    critical race theory, viii, 12, 105, 108, 114, 228,
        247
    human race, 200
    intersections of, xvi, 30,
    intersections of race and gender, 7–10, 60, 105,
        187, 194, 197, 205, 282, 331
    intersections of race, gender, and ethnicity, 194
    multiple, mixed, 9, 106, 202, 209,
    political, xviii, 147, 150, 155–156, 327
    privilege, 108
    race and class, 224, 279
    race and ethnicity, 110, 203, 248, 271, 274
    race and gender, 34, 60–61, 62, 95, 122, 134,
        149–151, 153, 156, 160, 231, 235, 238–239,
        241, 247–248, 274–276, 278
    race, feminism, and women, 21, 61
    race-neutral advocates, 148
    race, the meaning of, 156
    salience, 110, 155
    social category, vii, viii, ix, xi, xiv, xvi, xviii, xix, 4,
        5, 7–10, 12, 21, 23, 73, 96,106–112, 121, 134,
        145, 147, 153, 155–159, 164–165, 172, 178,
        182, 198, 200, 205, 223, 226, 228, 232, 235,
        241, 247–249, 275–276, 279, 282, 318, 320,
        327, 331

racial in/equity, racial in/equality, 15, 164–165, 172,
    198, 211, 213, 223–224, 226, 228, 315
racial identity development, xviii, 104, 107–110,
    114, 116, 152, 198, 204
racism, 7, 11, 60, 65, 105, 107, 108–109, 110–111,
    115–117, 147–148, 152–153, 155, 157–159,
    182, 213, 228, 247
    anti-racism, 26
    internalized, xviii, 60, 109
    institutional, 26, 111, 153, 159, 189,
    racism and sexism, 105, 116, 149, 183, 275–276,
        323
    reverse racism, 109
    structural, 158
    systemic, 157
radical feminism, xvii, 3–4, 6–9
rape, 23, 25, 262–263, 289, 292, 294–297,
    301–305
recruitment, 9, 17, 135, 137, 140, 158, 244, 249,
    275, 283
religion, xvi, 9–10, 70, 160, 164, 178, 213, 217–222,
    226, 268
residence life, residence hall, residential, residential
    cottage, xiv, 100, 116, 174, 197, 282,
    293–294
resources
    financial resources, material resources, 22–23, 73,
        170–171, 181, 190, 238, 257, 261, 280
    gender, gender in/equity, women's centers, xiii, xvi,
        xvii, 29, 41, 56, 187, 258, 260, 263–264,
        266–267, 292–294, 312
    international resources, 19
    race, 147–150, 155, 157, 159, 321
    resource limitations, resource allocation, 22–23,
        263
    technological resources, research resources, 17, 71,
        136, 185, 260
risk reduction programs, 287–288, 290–296, 298,
    300, 303–305
role model, 72, 81, 101, 113, 116, 126, 130, 133,
    135–136, 140–141, 189, 196–197, 201, 208,
    236, 239, 244, 249, 308

safety, 19, 21–22, 189, 191–192, 232, 287, 290–291
salary, pay
    career decisions, 126, 133, 272
    education status, 181–182
    freedom from financial dependence, 181–182,
        221
    gender, gender inequity, xiii, xvi, 33, 58, 97, 100,
        112, 182–184, 191–192, 258–259, 274
    higher education, 18, 27, 33, 57, 272
    paying forward, 90, 96, 101, 212

self-authorship, 213–228

self-efficacy, 152, 240, 308, 316

self-esteem, 104–117, 140, 184, 187, 240–241, 245–246, 262, 273, 316

sexual assault, sexual abuse, ix, xx, 20, 25–26, 28, 142, 156, 179, 262–263, 287–305, 332

sexual orientation, viii, xiv, xvi, xviii, 3, 10–12, 43, 96, 108, 145, 164, 174, 194, 211, 213–215, 217–228, 282, 314, 317–318, 331

silence, silencing, 12–13, 66, 234–248, 253

Sister Circle, viii, xi, xix, 10, 61, 194–195, 198, 209–212

social assumptions of gender, 278

social justice, xix, xx, 7, 9, 13, 20, 22–23, 26, 107, 150, 152, 160, 167, 202, 178, 184, 187–188, 192, 266–267, 289, 294–296, 303, 328

socialist feminism, 3–4, 7–9

spiritual, spirituality, 48, 53, 55, 65, 262, 265, 319

Standing Committee for Women (SCW), xv, xvi, xix, xx, 61, 194–195, 197, 209–210, 332

standpoint theory, standpoint research, 150, 326

stereotype
    experience in higher education, 64, 242–243
    feminism, feminists, 22, 28
    gender, 143, 219, 275, 278
    race, ethnicity, 109, 111–112, 153–154, 156–157, 203, 275
    recipients of public assistance, 185
    sexual assault, 297
    sexual orientation, 217, 219–222

storytelling, xix, 12, 164–165

Student Personnel Point of View (SPPV), 47–48, 53, 54

support groups, support networks, peer support, xviii, 19, 23, 27, 88, 90, 92, 94, 101, 110, 128, 134, 136–137, 167, 185–188, 198, 203, 210–211, 212, 224

tenure
    equity, 8–9, 15, 25, 174
    personal identity, 62, 163, 175

racial dynamics, xviii, 62, 112, 147–149, 151, 154–155, 158, 162, 275, 285
    work–life balance, 70, 85–86, 89

Title IX, 5, 32–46

training programs, 37–38, 54, 186

transgender, xv, xvi, xx, 3–4, 6, 13, 16, 143–144, 215, 319–320, 325, 327–328, 330

Vietnamese, 199, 201

violence, sexual violence, 9, 15, 17, 19–20, 25, 148–149, 156, 164, 166, 188–189, 257–258, 260, 263, 267, 287–289, 291–293, 295–297, 301, 303–305

wave, first, second and third waves of feminism, 3–5, 7, 10–11, 13, 15–16, 26, 30

womanhood, 121, 143, 149, 155, 233, 240, 278, 297

womanist feminism, xvii, 3–4, 7, 9–10, 14, 233, 235, 240, 245–246, 249, 297

women of color
    consideration in studies, 104, 106, 108, 194–195, 201
    hostility toward, 105, 152, 155, 183, 203, 208, 238
    identity, experiences shaping identity, xix, 18, 21, 108–117, 198, 200–202, 207, 210, 212, 232, 234–235, 238, 242–243
    leadership, leadership positions, xv, 33–34, 88, 211, 274–275, 278
    response to needs, 23, 26, 109, 156, 209
    role in feminism, 5, 7, 235
    support systems, xix, 198, 205, 211, 322

Women's Athletic Association, 35

women's centers, xiv, xvii, xix, 15–31, 102, 185, 255–269, 322

women's rights, Women's Rights Movement/s, 4, 173

work, work–life balance, viii, xiii, xviii, 25, 27–28, 69–86, 88, 90, 92, 94–96, 100–101, 133, 140–141, 196, 207, 212

ze, 340

Women in Academic Leadership
Professional Strategies, Personal Choices
Edited by Diane R. Dean, Susan J. Bracken and Jeanie K. Allen
Foreword by Claire Van Ummersen

Women in Academic Leadership complements its companion volumes in the Women in Academe series, provoking readers to think critically about the gendered nature of academic leadership across the spectrum of institutional types. It argues that leadership, the academy, and the nexus of academic leadership, remain gendered structures steeped in male-oriented norms and mores. Blending research and reflection, it explores the barriers and dilemmas that these structures present and the professional strategies and the personal choices women make in order to successfully surmount them.

Sty/us

22883 Quicksilver Drive
Sterling, VA 20166-2102

Subscribe to our e-mail alerts: www.Styluspub.com

An ACPA title available from Stylus

The First Generation Student Experience
Who They Are, Their Characteristics, and Strategies for Improving Their Persistence and Success
Jeff Davis

"Jeff Davis does an excellent job of defining, deciphering, and discussing the experiences, issues, and successes of first generation college students on both the individual and institutional levels. However, the real richness of this resource comes from the voices of students themselves. Hearing their stories through personal narratives illustrates both the diversity of background yet the commonality of challenge that first generation college students experience in their transitions into and through higher education. The content of this book has the power to inspire higher educators to examine their commitment to the success of first generation college students, provides concrete recommendations for practice in service to this growing population of undergraduates, and, thus, brings us several steps closer to an answer." —*Jennifer R. Keup*, *Director, National Resource Center for The First-Year Experience and Students in Transition*

The Balancing Act
Gendered Perspectives in Faculty Roles and Work Lives
Edited by Susan J. Bracken, Jeanie K. Allen and Diane R. Dean
Foreword by Ann E. Austin

This book brings together new and original research–representing a broad range of institutional types–that reveals the pressures women face to postpone childbirth and limit the size of their families; that exposes the often the inequitable treatment of their scholarship when women are part of a dual-career couples; and that identifies other tacit and structural barriers to women's advancement.

This book challenges assumptions about how men and women manage the boundaries between their personal and professional lives and suggests new ways to creatively and collaboratively combine productive work lives and satisfying personal lives. It shows how women have agency in structuring their careers and describes a multiplicity of solutions that they and institutions can adopt to create new couple- and family-friendly structures and practices that will encourage women to stay in the pipeline.

Most College Students Are Women
Implications for Teaching, Learning, and Policy
Edited by Jeanie K. Allen, Susan J. Bracken and Diane R. Dean
Foreword by David Sadker

"*Most College Students Are Women* [is] filled with thought provoking perspectives on how we can do better for women students and, by extension, for all students with their diverse needs and learning styles. [It] offers a collection of essays by a variety of women, each bringing a different angle and voice. They invite readers to join a scintillating conversation among a dozen leading experts on student development and feminist pedagogy. For centuries higher education was designed around men, even when women are added. These chapters suggest that today, models of teaching and guidance designed around women can best serve the varied needs of all our students." —*Women in Higher Education*